Entrepreneurship Marketing

Small- and medium-sized enterprises (SMEs) dominate the market in terms of sheer number of organizations. Their role in the business world is difficult to overstate. Despite this, there is a high failure rate among smaller organizations, which can be explained to a significant degree by a lack of marketing understanding in this sector.

Introducing the importance of marketing to entrepreneurial firms, this book guides the student through the fundamentals of marketing within the SME context, providing a more value-added learning experience than your standard marketing run-through. The authors deal directly with 'people issues' (i.e. everyday entrepreneurship marketing interactions) to prepare students for the 'dragons' den' of entrepreneurialism.

This new and lively textbook provides a fresh and unfettered approach for marketing students who require a more real-world understanding of the impact of their discipline on entrepreneurial firms. The growing student body studying entrepreneurship will also benefit from the customer insight offered by this approach.

Sonny Nwankwo is Professor of Marketing and Director of the Petchey Centre for Entrepreneurship at the University of East London, UK. He was the inaugural Editor of the *International Journal of Applied Management* and has authored numerous books including *Cross-Cultural Marketing* for Cengage Learning.

Ayantunji Gbadamosi is Senior Lecturer of Marketing at the Royal Docks Business School of the University of East London, UK. His research interests are SME marketing, marketing communications, consumer involvement and children and marketing activities.

Entrepreneurship Marketing

Principles and practice of SME marketing

Edited by Sonny Nwankwo and Ayantunji Gbadamosi

Routledge
Taylor & Francis Group

LONDON AND NEW YORK

First published 2011
by Routledge
2 Park Square, Milton Park, Abingdon, Oxon, OX14 4RN

Simultaneously published in the USA and Canada
by Routledge
270 Madison Avenue, New York, NY 10016

Routledge is an imprint of the Taylor & Francis Group, an Informa business

Typeset in Goudy by Pindar NZ, Auckland, New Zealand
Printed and bound in Great Britain by CPI Antony Rowe, Chippenham, Wiltshire

British Library Cataloguing in Publication Data
A catalogue record for this book is available from the British Library

Library of Congress Cataloging-in-Publication Data
Entrepreneurship marketing: principles and practice of SME marketing / [edited by] Sonny Nwankwo & Ayantunji Gbadamosi.
    p. cm.
  1. Marketing—Management. 2. Entrepreneurship. 3. Small business—Management. 4. New business enterprises—Management. I. Nwankwo, Sonny. II. Gbadamosi, Ayantunji.
  HF5415.13.E58 2010
    658.8—dc22   2010020897

ISBN: 978-0-415-57375-7 (hbk)
ISBN: 978-0-415-57376-4 (pbk)
ISBN: 978-0-203-83864-8 (ebk)

Contents

Illustrations

FIGURES

TABLES

BOXES

Case studies

Contributors

Jaya Akunuri is a Senior Lecturer in Marketing at the University of East London (UEL). She lectures and manages various marketing modules on the BA (Hons) Marketing, MSc International Marketing and MBA programmes. Jaya also manages a cluster of four undergraduate programmes at UEL. She has a keen research interest in areas like SME and entrepreneurship marketing with specific focus on ethnic minority entrepreneurship and understanding entrepreneurial behaviour through qualitative methodologies.

Mathew Analogbei is a PhD researcher in the Department of Marketing, University of Strathclyde, Glasgow. He received his Bachelors and MBA degrees in Marketing from the University of Nigeria, Enugu, and MSc in Marketing from the University of Glamorgan, Wales. Prior to commencing his doctoral studies in the UK, Mathew taught for some years in a number of Nigerian universities. His doctoral research focuses on retail internationalization.

David Bamber, PhD, FCoT, is Research Coordinator at Liverpool Hope University Business School, UK. He is Visiting Research Fellow at Christ University, Bangalore, in India. He has managed SMEs in the UK. He is course director for the MSc in Marketing Management at Liverpool Hope University. David has presented at many international conferences of the UK Academy of Marketing and the Academy of Marketing Science, and is the Organizational Studies track co-chair at the British Academy of Management. He supervises PhDs in qualitative and quantitative studies of international marketing and values in organizations.

Ian K. Bathgate is a Principal Lecturer and Academic Field Leader in Strategy, Operations, Marketing and Management in the Royal Docks Business School (RDBS) at the University of East London. His key research areas are e-commerce and buyer behaviour and marketing/strategic planning issues encountered by SMEs. He has many years experience working in the media industry and running his own SME and consultancy business. He is currently a lead consultant for RDBS working in conjunction with Knowledge Dock, the university's industry-facing facility. In this capacity Ian has worked on many European Union-funded initiatives for a variety of SMEs in London and the Thames Gateway Development Region.

Kofi Dadzie, PhD, is Associate Professor of Marketing at the Mack Robinson College of Business at Georgia State University (GSU) and immediate past editor of the *Journal of African Business*. His research interests are in international marketing with an emphasis on Third World countries, the design of distribution systems and minority business marketing. Prior to joining the GSU faculty, Dadzie was a visiting assistant professor of marketing at Duke University and the University of North Carolina. His research has been published in several journals, including *Journal of Global Marketing, Journal of the Academy of Marketing Science, Journal of Small Business Management* and *Journal of Business Logistics Management*.

Isobel Doole, PhD, is Professor of International Marketing and Assistant Dean at Sheffield Business School, Sheffield Hallam University. She is an experienced marketing professional and senior academic in international marketing and the international competitiveness of small firms. With her co-author Robin Lowe she has built an international reputation through the highly successful textbooks *Strategic Marketing Decisions* and *International Marketing Strategy*. The latter is in its fifth edition (2008) and has sold over 70,000 copies across the globe. She is a senior examiner for the Chartered Institute of Marketing and has acted as an expert adviser on a number of governmental committees.

Frances Ekwulugo is Senior Lecturer in Marketing, with instructional expertise in marketing management and marketing communications. Her research interests and consulting activities comprise studies in small business marketing, cross-cultural branding and international marketing. She has published several papers in reputable peer-reviewed journals and contributed to book chapters. She is a member of the Chartered Institute of Marketing, Trainers of Financial Services and the Higher Education Academy.

Teck-Yong Eng, PhD, is Professor of Marketing and Director of Centre for Research in Management at the Business School of Bournemouth University. He is on the advisory board of ORT Israel for a large grant (in excess of €6 million) funded by the European Commission Framework 7. He has consulted for various corporations and non-profit organizations, including Business Monitor London, BPP Business School, William Jackson Food Group and UNICO Industries Inc., Hong Kong and Mainland China. His work has been published in journals such as *Industrial Marketing Management, Journal of World Business, Journal of Marketing Management* and *Technovation*.

Peter Fraser, PhD, is in the Department of Marketing and Enterprise in the Business School of the University of Hertfordshire, Hatfield. Dr Fraser has several years of teaching experience at both undergraduate and graduate levels. He has supervised many doctoral students in the topical areas of small business management. Dr Fraser's research interests are in small business development and arts marketing.

Ayantunji Gbadamosi, PhD, is a Senior Lecturer in Marketing at the Royal Docks Business School of the University of East London. Prior to joining academia, he has worked as an assistant executive officer in charge of sales of pharmaceutical and electrical products in a group of companies in Lagos, Nigeria. He has taught marketing courses at various institutions including University of Lagos (Nigeria) University of Salford (UK), Manchester Metropolitan University (UK), and Liverpool Hope University (UK). His papers have been published in journals such as the *International Journal of Retail and Distribution Management, Marketing Intelligence and Planning, Social Marketing Quarterly, Nutrition and Food Science* and *Young Consumers*. He is the author of the book titled *Low-Income Consumer Behaviour*, and has contributed chapters to edited books. His research interests are in the areas of SME marketing, marketing communications, consumer behaviour and marketing to children.

Sue Halliday, PhD, is Marketing Subject Group Leader and Senior Lecturer, University of Surrey. She teaches and researches relational marketing, focusing on trust, shared values, branding and innovation/entrepreneurship. She advises on a KTP project transforming a small social enterprise into a market-facing sustainable business. Before joining academia she held management posts in several services firms, ultimately as the Director of Marketing for a city law firm. She is a chartered marketer. She has published widely in journals such as the *European Journal of Marketing*, *Journal of Marketing Management* and the *Journal of Services Marketing*.

Robert Hinson is Senior Lecturer and Head of the Department of Marketing at the University of Ghana Business School. He sits on the board of the International Society of Markets and Development and the Advisory Council of Global Marketing Network in Ghana. Robert is published in the *Journal of Research in Marketing and Entrepreneurship*, *Journal of Place Branding and Public Diplomacy*, *Journal of Research in Interactive Marketing*, *Journal of Business and Industrial Marketing*, *Telematics and Informatics*, *Internet Research*, *Management Decision*, *Online Information Review*, *Corporate Governance* and the *Journal of Internet Commerce*. Robert holds postgraduate degrees in marketing and is a professional marketer.

Kevin Ibeh, PhD, is Professor of Marketing and International Business at the Department of Marketing, University of Strathclyde, Glasgow, where he also serves as Director of Research. His recent work, mainly on firm internationalization and international entrepreneurship, has appeared, or is due to appear, in highly rated outlets such as the *British Journal of Management*, *Journal of World Business*, *Management International Review*, *Industrial Marketing Management*, *European Journal of Marketing*, *Journal of Business Ethics*, *Small Business Economics* and the *International Small Business Journal*. A highly regarded scholar, Professor Ibeh has had recent consulting roles with the World Bank and the OECD. His book *Contemporary Challenges to International Business* was published by Macmillan in 2009.

Hina Khan, PhD, is a Senior Lecturer in Marketing and a Programme Leader for Business Creation at Newcastle Business School, Northumbria University, Newcastle upon Tyne. She has vast practical experience in marketing and research. She has worked as a marketing consultant and project leader for national and international companies. She has also published research articles in refereed journals and presented papers at international conferences. Her current research interests lie in SMEs and entrepreneur development and consumer buying behaviour. She was nominated and shortlisted for the Lloyds TSB Jewel Award in 2007.

Paul Sergius Koku, PhD, JD, is Professor of Business Administration at the College/Graduate School of Business Administration at Florida Atlantic University. He earned a BA (summa cum laude) with a concentration on finance from the University of the Virgin Islands. He holds an MBA (Marketing) from Oregon State University, an MA (Applied Economics) from Rutgers University, an MBA (Finance) from Rutgers University and a PhD in Finance and Marketing from Rutgers University. He also holds a Juris Doctor degree from the University of Miami, School of Law. Professor Koku has taught as a visiting professor to universities in Australia, South Korea and Spain. He conducts interdisciplinary research and has published in several peer-reviewed journals.

Michael Lewrick received his PhD from Napier University, Edinburgh, and holds an MBA from Bristol Business School. His research interests centre on the management issues related to the development and commercialization of technological and business model innovation. Specific areas of focus include developing capabilities for innovativeness and business success.

Andrew Lindridge, PhD, is a Senior Lecturer in Marketing at The Open University, UK. His research is focused on the examination of the tensions which arise from acculturation, culture, ethnicity and consumption. Andrew's work has appeared in a variety of refereed journals and his research has been presented to global audiences at a variety of European and North American conferences. Besides being a reviewer for a number of conferences and journals, he is also a member of the editorial board of the journal *Doing Business Across Borders*. His research work in culture, ethnicity and consumption has also led him into a variety of consultancy projects and he is a founding member of a consultancy called Culture Doctors.

Robin Lowe is the Director of the Centre for Individual and Organisational Development at Sheffield Business School, Sheffield Hallam University. Through his research, consultancy and policy development work in international trade, innovation and entrepreneurship, Robin has made a major contribution to government policy and business support. He also has considerable experience of consulting and training with multinationals around the world, including IBM, Microsoft, Astra Zeneca, Renault Nissan, Huawei and Batelco, as well as being an examiner and course director for the Chartered Institute of Marketing. He is the joint author of several best-selling texts on international marketing, innovation and entrepreneurship.

Nnamdi O. Madichie, PhD, is Assistant Professor of Marketing at the University of Sharjah, UAE. Prior to this he was Programme Leader in Marketing and Business Studies at the University of East London. His research interests are in the fields of consumer behaviour, small business and entrepreneurship. His work has appeared in *Marketing Intelligence and Planning*, *International Journal of Entrepreneurship and Small Business*, *Journal of Enterprising Communities: People and Places in the Global Economy* (JEC), *Journal of African Business* and *Management Decision* (where he is also Book Review Editor). He received the 2009 Emerald Highly Commended Paper Award for a paper entitled 'Cultural determinants of entrepreneurial emergence in a typical sub-Sahara African context', published in the *JEC*.

Felix Mavondo, PhD, is Professor of Marketing and Director of Higher Degrees by Research in the Department of Marketing, Monash University, Australia. A certified management consultant (Australia), his specialist research interests are in marketing strategy, market orientation, relationship marketing, retailing and agribusiness.

Felicity Mendoza is a Research Associate at Sheffield Business School, Sheffield Hallam University, where she obtained a Masters degree in Communication Studies. She manages The Alchemy Exchange, a unique initiative which allows external organizations to access university expertise. The projects that she has worked on with external clients include market analyses for international expansion, feasibility studies to assess the potential for a new product or service, and benchmarking performance against competitors. Prior to joining Sheffield Business School, Felicity's previous experience included working within facilities management, recruitment and tourism in both the UK and Latin America.

Anayo D. Nkamnebe, PhD, is Associate Professor of Marketing, former Head of Department of Marketing, and current Sub Dean, Faculty of Management Sciences at Nnamdi Azikiwe University, Awka, Nigeria. He has presented research papers in several countries and sits on the editorial boards of the *International Journal of Social Entrepreneurship*, *African Journal of Business and Economic Research*, *Journal of Marketing and Management* and other Nigerian journals. He is representing Africa on the Board of International Society of Marketing and Development and is also an ordained priest.

Sonny Nwankwo, PhD, is Professor of Marketing and Director of the Petchey Centre for Entrepreneurship at the University of East London. He is a visiting professor at universities across Africa, Australia, Europe and North America. Prior to joining academia, he was a customer services manager in the telecommunications industry.

Maktoba Omar, PhD, is a graduate of Leeds University Business School. Currently she is a reader in Marketing and International Marketing Strategy at Napier University Business School, Edinburgh, Scotland, and a member of the research committee. Her current research interests focus on globalization, international strategy and marketing policy. She has published in a number of national and international peer-reviewed academic journals, as well as conferences and workshops.

Ogenyi Omar, PhD, is in the Department of Maketing and Enterprise in the Business School of the University of Hertfordshire, Hatfield. Dr Omar is the editor of the *Journal of Retail Marketing Management Research*. His papers have been published in the *Journal of Business Research*, *International Journal of Retail and Distribution Management*, *Journal of Strategic Marketing*, *International Journal of Public Sector Management*, *Service Industries Journal*, *Journal of Food Product Marketing*, *Thunderbird International Business Review* and others. He is the author of one of the best-selling textbooks on retailing, *Retail Marketing*, which is currently in its second edition and is published by Financial Times/Pitman Publishing. He is also the author of *International Marketing*, published by Palgrave Macmillan. He has contributed chapters to several textbooks. Dr Omar is a retail marketing specialist and his current research interests are in retail marketing management, food branding and technology, disribution and supply chain management, multicultural marketing and global retailing.

Jo Padmore is Subject Group Leader for Quantitative Methods and Statistics at the University of Sheffield Management School. She holds a first-class degree in Mathematics, an MSc in Statistics (Distinction), an ME and a PhD in Probability and Statistics (Sheffield). She has performed consultancy work for a number of organizations. Her current research focuses on a variety of management issues within SMEs. She is particularly interested in issues of performance measurement in SMEs and the role of quantitative methods within this context.

Kaushik V. Pandya, PhD, has been researching and teaching in higher education since 1986. He has supervised research students at various levels. He has over 50 publications to his name at national and international levels. His research areas include operations management, knowledge management, e-business, management of sustainable sources and related areas. He has worked as an academic at various higher education institutions in the UK. Dr Pandya has been a visiting lecturer at Royal Docks Business School (University of East London).

Hosein Piranfar, PhD, is a Senior Lecturer and Programme Leader of MSc Risk Management at the Royal Docks Business School, University of East London (UEL). Prior to UEL he worked as a researcher on complexity and organizational learning in Kingston Business School. He has published widely in the fields of foreign direct investment, finance, operations management, logistics, social capital (networking), corporate reputation and organizational learning. Currently he is working on banking risk, construction risk and the biotech-pharmaceutical collaboration for innovation.

Darlington Richards, PhD, is Associate Professor of International Business and Marketing, Earl Graves School of Business and Management at Morgan State University, Baltimore, USA. His research interests include privatization and market deregulation, market reforms, change management and business ethics.

Robert Rugimbana, PhD, is an NRF-rated Professor of Marketing in the Business School, Tshwane University of Technology. His main research focus is in the areas of consumer psychology, diffusion of innovations, microfinance institutions and marketing education and management. Dr Rugimbana has published extensively by way of refereed journal articles and conference papers, books and book chapters. In addition he has consulted and continues to consult for several large organizations as well as federal and state government departments. He is also a senior associate of several international marketing professional bodies.

Maria Shambare is a freelance business consultant based in Canada. She is also a doctoral candidate of the Henley Business School at the University of Reading. Her interests are in the area of SMEs, entrepreneurship and marketing.

Richard Shambare is a research associate and doctoral candidate at the TUT Business School. His research interest is in the areas of bottom-of-the-pyramid marketing, microfinance, diffusion of innovations, poverty and entrepreneurship.

Mike Simpson, PhD, is a Senior Lecturer in Management at the University of Sheffield Management School and teaches Operations Management and Marketing at postgraduate level. Mike's early career was in the semi-conductor and electronics industry, working at Plessey Research (Caswell) and Marconi Electronic Devices Limited, Lincoln. He has worked in a number of high-technology companies and is a consultant for SMEs. Until quite recently he was the Subject Group Leader for both Operations Management and Marketing. Mike has published widely on marketing and operations management in SMEs

Graham Spickett-Jones, PhD (Management), has management experience in promotional marketing and lectures in Communication Theory and Marketing at the University of Hull. His first degree was in Communication Studies, and he has a Masters in Marketing, as well as professional marketing qualifications. He has published in areas that range from neuroscience to campaign research. His research interests cover the way media shapes the social environment and integrated campaign practice within the professional marketing communications industry.

Nick Taylor is the Subject Group Leader for Marketing, Advertising and Public Relations at the University of Lincoln. He has an MBA from the Sheffield Business School and a Diploma in Management Studies, Nottingham Trent University. His associations include senior examiner positions with the University of Sheffield and the Chartered Institute of Marketing, and he is Affiliate Professor at Grenoble Graduate School of Business. He has research publications in a variety of refereed journals on the areas of SMEs, marketing and environmental studies. Journals he has been published in include the *International Journal* *of Entrepreneurial Behaviour and Research, Business Strategy and Environment, Journal of Small Business and Enterprise Development* and *Environment and Planning C: Government and Policy.*

Robert Williams, Jr., is Assistant Professor of Business and Marketing in the School of Business and Leadership at Stevenson University, Maryland. A graduate of Pennsylvania State University, his prior faculty positions include Lycoming College, Susquehanna University and Duquesne University (adjunct). Prior to entering academia he spent over 20 years in various management positions at Fortune 500 companies Tyco International and AMP Inc. Current research interests focus on competitive advantage, branding, innovation, higher education institutions and market entry strategies.

Preface

There is growing evidence that entrepreneurship marketing is becoming an important topic globally. The reasons for this are well founded. In a context of tumultuous global economic upheavals and widespread anticipation of enterprise-led growth, starting up, growing and sustaining small to medium-sized enterprises (SMEs) requires refining and honing specialized skills in order to deliver superior value to customers whose definition of value changes all the time.

The beneficial effects of entrepreneurship and associated marketing operations are well established and are increasingly promoted by governments as a flagship policy. Successful entrepreneurship, in addition to offering business owners the intrinsic satisfaction of owning and running their businesses, contributes significantly to the economy through job creation, widening participation in the economy and economic empowerment. The sheer scale of socio-economic challenges confronting societies and the need to scale up actions to achieve economic stability and growth gives rise to a central role for entrepreneurship. Making progress on these fronts would require carefully studying, analysing, documenting and understanding strategic marketing actions involved in value-defining, value-developing and value-delivering processes for achieving and maintaining the desired level of performance among SMEs.

Marketing and entrepreneurship are philosophically interconnected in the degree to which they are both situated and encapsulated in 'everydayness' of market interactions, and this is increasingly realized. Paradoxically, much of the established marketing knowledge and associated programmes of study largely reflect axioms of large businesses. It is partly for this reason that high business failure rates among SMEs are consistently attributed to a failure on the part of marketing to appreciate the temporal and spatial dimensions of marketing in SMEs or deal with the differences in operating contexts.

Today's entrepreneurs are confronted with opportunities and new challenges. Accordingly, they need to become more dynamic, more innovative and even more skilful in order to successfully navigate through challenges and meet these new opportunities. For this reason, those who are involved in producing and disseminating knowledge on the very important topic of entrepreneurship marketing need to refine their taken-for-granted assumptions about entrepreneurs, their markets and strategies. This has not been the case so far with respect to books designed for teaching and for personal development purposes. More fundamentally, those who teach the subject are frustrated with many of the existing sector-specific textbooks with regard to the apparent lack of depth and sufficient insights in exploring the dynamic interface between marketing and entrepreneurship. Many texts focus primarily on the broad spectrum of large-company-oriented treatments and make only cursory references to SMEs. This can be all too confusing to students, many of whom are left wondering whether the difference between SME marketing and marketing for large-scale enterprises is only super-ficial. This creates the need for SME-focused analyses. Accordingly, this text explores the roles of marketing in shaping SMEs' entrepreneurial identities. It assembles, probably for the first time in a pedagogical manner, original and insightful contributions aimed at illuminating the field and, very importantly, charting new directions for teaching the subject of entre-preneurship marketing.

Accordingly, we present this book as a compendium of teaching and as a learning resource, put together with a clear target user group in mind, and each chapter is contributed by those who themselves are involved in teaching and researching the subject. It is hoped that the book will:

- help students to develop a coherent understanding of marketing processes in SMEs
- provide students with an understanding of marketing strategies adopted by successful SMEs and how lessons learned might be transferred to new situations.

The uniqueness of this book is better appreciated when considered alongside what it delivers. Essentially, we aim to help students to achieve the following:

- Explore the fundamentals of marketing within the context of SMEs in such a way that clearly distinguishes the treatment of SME marketing from the knowledge of marketing associated with managing large organizations. The book explicates the similarities/overlap in principles by using appropriate illustrations to contextually delineate the boundaries.
- Develop an understanding of the nature of the marketing environment within which SMEs operate; consider the causal textures and factors that influence SMEs; examine the techniques and tools of marketing analyses (and planning) and the various means that are available for formulating appropriate marketing.
- Identify, understand and critique the role and function of marketing in SMEs in order to present a detailed and comprehensive discussion of available alternatives by which SMEs can obtain marketing intelligence and other various inputs, and how to make effective use of them.
- Examine the marketing mix elements of SMEs and discuss the peculiarities associated with managing each of these effectively within the constraints of SMEs, while being sensitive to the variability in terms of scope and size of SMEs.
- Present a well-grounded treatment of export market orientation and internationalization of SMEs in the face of pervasive forces of globalization, franchising capabilities and information technology across both product and service offerings.
- Explore the role of the internet in marketing and shaping the frontiers of entrepreneurship, as well as the critical competencies for entrepreneurship marketing (specifically, dealing with risk management, service quality, managing competition, innovation, growth, failure crises and strategic turnarounds), social networks and relationships in SME marketing, issues around the SME marketing challenge of multiculturalism and the impact of dominant socio-cultural values (e.g. religion, sustainable consumption, ethics and social responsibility) on entrepreneurship marketing.

An important feature of this book is that it deals directly with 'people issues' (i.e. the every-day entrepreneurship marketing interactions) and has the underlying objective of preparing students for the realities and complexities of entrepreneurialism. To challenge limited perspectives of the real world of entrepreneurship marketing we have included treatments that focus on developing-country and less-discussed informal economy cases/analyses. The significance of this book is huge and stands to focus our attention and direct our energies while shedding new light on ways in which SME marketing can and does operate – beyond the conventional large-organization treatments. Many of the new roles of marketing in SME contexts and the 'real issues' that matter in unpacking how SMEs engage their markets – as well as valuable suggestions for growing and sustaining entrepreneurship – are captured in this book.

As editors, we are not oblivious to the (sometimes heavy) demands we placed on our contributing authors in the context of the highly pressured environment in which we all work. We are sincerely grateful for their contributions. This book would not have been possible without the commitment to scholarship demonstrated by distinguished academics and researchers whose highly significant contributions have resulted in this unique collection. We would also like to acknowledge the support of Terry Clague and Sharon Golan (Routledge) – great people to work with. We hope that students will find this book as exciting to use as putting it together has been for us.

Sonny Nwankwo
Ayantunji Gbadamosi
University of East London
April 2010

Chapter 1

Marketing in SMEs
An introduction

Mike Simpson, Nick Taylor and Jo Padmore

LEARNING OBJECTIVES

After reading this chapter, you will be able to:
- define what we mean by small- and medium-sized enterprises (SMEs) and why there is a need for theoretical developments in the area of SME marketing
- critically review the extant literature on marketing in SMEs
- consider the relationship between marketing, strategic thinking and small firm survival
- discuss the reasons why big business marketing does not appear to be transferable to SMEs
- discuss how SMEs have adapted marketing to their particular context.

INTRODUCTION

The application of marketing principles is widely accepted as the way in which larger companies generate profits and grow. The supporting marketing literature has been developed over many years and has generally focused on established large organizations. In contrast, the literature surrounding small- and medium-sized enterprises (SMEs) and their marketing efforts is still in the development stage. This chapter explores how the established principles of marketing apply to SMEs. The relationship between marketing and strategic thinking is explored – in particular, the extent to which some SMEs feel that marketing is not relevent to their business needs. There is evidence to suggest that the formal approaches to marketing that have been established for larger organizations do not appear to be easily transferrable to SMEs. However, if these companies are not utilizing these principles to generate success then what are they using, and how does this inform our strategic view of marketing practice in SMEs? Marketing exists to facilitate exchanges – exchanges of value as perceived from both the supplier and the receiver. Core to the understanding of value exchange is the notion that the supplier offers something of less value than they receive in return. Of course, the opposite is also true for the receiver, in that the value of goods and services received is of greater value than the cost of obtaining them. The resultant satisfaction is shared among both parties.

   This chapter examines the nature of SME organizations and how they differ from larger organizations. In addition, the relationship to marketing is explored to reveal how SME organizations manage to create value that promotes profitable exchanges leading to customer satisfaction.

DEFINING SMES IN CONTEXT

Definitions of SMEs vary widely from country to country. Most research defines SMEs by the number of employees. In the UK SMEs are defined as businesses with fewer than 250 employees and in the European Union they are defined as independent businesses with less than 25 per cent owned or controlled by another enterprise(s) and with fewer than 250 employees (EU 2005). The European Union also places stipulations on the turnover and balance sheet figures such that micro businesses (1–9 employees) should not exceed €2 million turnover, small businesses (10–49 employees) should not exceed €10 million turnover and medium-sized businesses (50–249 employees) should not exceed €50 million turnover (EU 2005). In some countries the definition of an SME varies by industry sector as well as number of employees and turnover figures.

SMEs are an important part of all economies, accounting for 99 per cent of businesses in the UK. Worldwide, SMEs account for in excess of 99 per cent of all businesses and are by far the largest contributor to employment and the gross domestic product of nations. Therefore, SMEs are a source of job creation and contribute both innovation and competition to the market. Some, but not all, SMEs grow to be big businesses. Government policies are often aimed at growing SMEs to create employment or to ride out periods of economic crisis, and yet many SMEs either cannot grow or choose not to expand beyond what can be managed and controlled by the owner-manager. Some owner-managers choose lifestyle over growing their business and this view affects the way SMEs behave. Owner-managers also define success in different ways (e.g. being happy rather than wealthy, having a manageable business rather than creating a large business they could not control themselves or simply having enough money and enough freedom to do as they wish). These issues only serve to complicate any theoretical developments in the area of marketing in SMEs.

Research has found that SMEs face the following problems:

- sales and marketing (in 40.2 per cent of SMEs)
- human resource management (15.3 per cent)
- general management (14.3 per cent)
- production/operations management (8.6 per cent) (Huang and Brown, 1999).

Sales and marketing is often the most dominant problem encountered by SME operators and yet it has been acknowledged to be the most important of all business activities and essential for the survival and growth of small businesses (McKenna, 1991; O'Brien, 1998). The areas of marketing with the most frequent problems in SMEs were promotion and market research (Huang and Brown, 1999). The reasons for this were that SMEs lacked the financial resources to employ specialists, that the resource constraints limited the ability of the company to search for information and that a lack of a management information system limited the use of data already held within the organization.

Thus, the typical SME has limited resources, limited cash flows, few customers, is often engaged in management 'firefighting', concentrates on current performance rather than taking a strategic focus, often has a flat organizational structure, has problems with sales and marketing and possibly has high staff turnover (Hudson et al., 2001). The dynamic forces (both internally and externally) affecting SMEs create a very different environment in which marketing activities take place in comparision with larger and often long-established stable businesses that are capable of manipulating the business environment to a degree.

PREVIOUS RESEARCH ON MARKETING IN SMES

It is generally accepted that the basic principles of marketing are universally applicable to large and small businesses (Siu and Kirby, 1998; Reynolds, 2002). The study of marketing in SMEs has been recognized as a problematic area for researchers for over 20 years (Chaston and Mangles, 2002; Siu and Kirby, 1998). SME marketing in practice is thought to be largely done through networking (Gilmore *et al.*, 2001) or a combination of transaction, relationship, interaction and network marketing (Brodie *et al.*, 1997). More recently, the use of internet marketing (Chaffey *et al.*, 2000; Sparkes and Thomas, 2001) or e-commerce (Rayport and Jaworski, 2001) has become popular in all types of businesses, including SMEs. However, academic research appears unable to resolve a number of questions about small businesses and their relationship with, and their use of, marketing. Siu and Kirby (1998) point out that empirical evidence has been generated in an *ad hoc* manner because of a general absence of a systematic approach to the subject. Insufficient knowledge about marketing in small business remains and a small business marketing theory specifically related to the understanding and knowledge of strategic marketing is needed (Siu and Kirby, 1998).

MARKETING MODELS FOR SMES

Research on small businesses and their marketing activities has largely been limited to explanations of certain types of behaviour observed in small businesses (e.g. Hannon and Atherton, 1998; Smith and Whittaker, 1998; Huang and Brown, 1999), or to the search for factors that are missing or present barriers in smaller businesses, thereby accounting for their apparent inability to apply or use marketing ideas and concepts that were often developed for larger businesses (e.g. Barber *et al.*, 1989; O'Brien, 1998; Freel, 2000). Theory development in SME research seems to be somewhat limited in general. The work that has been done is more applied in nature, taking the form of prescriptive or descriptive frameworks and 'models' on how to apply certain business and management theories to the smaller business (e.g. Carson, 1990; Brooksbank, 1996; 1997; Valos and Baker, 1996). Some authors are investigating the applicability of alternative paradigms based on creativity, semiotics and art and employing alternative methodologies such as biography (Fillis, 2002).

Work specifically on marketing models in SMEs has resulted in six interlocking exploratory and qualitative models (Carson, 1990), while Hannon and Atherton (1998) suggested a matrix relating strategic awareness to planning effectiveness. Moller and Anttila (1987) devised a marketing capability framework, which was used to collect data from 36 Finnish and Swedish companies but they described their model as 'a qualitative tool for examining the "state-of-the-art" of marketing in small manufacturing companies' (Moller and Anttila, 1987, p. 185). This model consists of two major components: the external and internal fields of marketing capability (see also Simpson and Taylor, 2002; Simpson *et al.*, 2006).

THEORETICAL APPROACHES TO MARKETING IN SMALL BUSINESSES

According to Romano and Ratnatunga (1995), marketing in small businesses can be categorized as:

■ Marketing as a culture; defined as analysis of consumer needs and wants and assessment of competitiveness of small enterprises.

- Marketing as a strategy; defined as strategy development to enhance actual and potential market position of small enterprises.
- Marketing as tactics; defined as analysis of the 4Ps (i.e. product, price, place and promotion) to influence the performance or growth of small enterprises.

Romano and Ratnatunga (1995) also identified seven methodologies and three study objectives. However, they admit that the categorization of marketing in SMEs is somewhat arbitrary and invite readers to devise their own categories.

Siu and Kirby (1998) identified four theoretical approaches to marketing in small firms:

- Stages/Growth approach
  The stages/growth approach suggests that any model of small firm marketing must take into account the stage of development of the business but does not explain how the changes occur or account for the effects in variability of marketing skills between different owner-managers. The stages/growth approach does not allow for leap-frogging due to technological advances such as the use of the internet.
- Management style approach
  The management style approach acknowledges the limitations and constraints of the small firm (resources and capabilities) and provides a useful explanation for the poor development of marketing in small firms but does not explain the marketing practices actually used by small firms.
- Management function approach
  The management function approach acknowledges that marketing is both an important business function and an essential concept in small firm growth and survival but many owner-managers simplify and misunderstand marketing as the 4Ps or interpret marketing as advertising. The management function approach has been vigorously criticized and few small business researchers have adopted this approach (Siu and Kirby, 1998).
- Contingency approach
  The contingency approach acknowledges that various factors affect the small firm's marketing performance and that there is no universal set of strategic choices that is optimal for all businesses regardless of their resources or business environment in which they operate. The contingency approach is positioned between two extreme views, which state that universal marketing principles exist and are applicable to all firms, or that each small firm is unique and each situation needs to be analysed separately (Siu and Kirby, 1998).

There is no grand unifying theory – the marketing concepts may be the same but the process of implementation is different in each firm. Excellent reviews of the literature in this complex area can be found in Hill (2001a and 2001b) and Siu and Kirby (1998).

MARKETING, STRATEGIC THINKING AND SMALL FIRM SURVIVAL

It is questionable whether small businesses need to practice marketing at all to survive and grow (Hogarth-Scott *et al.*, 1996), although McLarty (1998) has found some evidence of strategic marketing in a growing SME. The study by Hogarth-Scott *et al.* (1996) concluded that small business owner-managers were often generalists, not marketing specialists, and complex marketing theories may not be appropriate for small businesses and probably would not aid in the understanding of their markets. Nevertheless, marketing was practiced to some degree by small businesses. In most cases competitive advantage was based on quality and service, while those competing on price were in the highly competitive markets with little or no product differentiation and low entry barriers (see Campbell-Hunt, 2000, for a discussion on how cost leadership and differentiation strategies can be combined). Product differentiation was a source of competitive advantage in some businesses, while others were looking for niche markets (Hogarth-Scott *et al.*, 1996). It would appear that marketing did contribute positively to small business success and the ability to think strategically. This view is supported to some extent by the much earlier work of Rice (1983), where it was clear that there was a difference between big business strategic rational planning and that carried out in small businesses. This difference was due to the amount of data collected about the external business environment by small companies compared with large companies and how this data was analysed. Small businesses collected considerably less data and in a more *ad hoc* fashion. Yet owner-managers were aware of the strategic nature of their decisions and Rice (1983) suggested that perhaps business persons gather enough information to allow them to make decisions at a 'permissible' level of probable success. It could be argued that today SMEs have access to much larger amounts of information and greater computing power than was available 27 years ago (see Rice, 1983) but this is still considerably less than that available to large organizations. SME owner-managers still have very little time to devote to the analysis of information for strategic decision making and therefore the comments of Rice (1983) still appear valid.

Hannon and Atherton (1998) noted that the level of strategic awareness of owner-managers appears to be strongly influenced by the personal competence of the owner-manager and the type, uncertainty and complexity of the business. In businesses where customer relationships were well defined and relatively stable, strategic awareness was often low. This was due to their perception of the external business environment being narrowly defined and stable. In companies that experienced fast growth and turbulent market conditions the level of strategic awareness was uniformly high and the motivation for a continually better understanding of the external business environment was strong (Hannon and Atherton, 1998).

PLANNING AND PERFORMANCE

The relationship between planning sophistication and financial performance was studied by Rue and Ibrahim (1998). Their results clearly showed that those SMEs with greater planning sophistication also showed greater growth in sales as reported by executives. Yet on objective measures, such as return on investment (ROI) performance, Rue and Ibrahim (1998) reported these were not affected. We note here that ROI (or return on capital employed, ROCE) is a poor performance measure (Frecknall-Hughes *et al.*, 2007). Rue and Ibrahim (1998) suggest that small businesses with a sophisticated planning process may reap the benefits of these efforts in the long term, while Perry (2001) suggests that SMEs using sophisticated planning activities (including written business plans) may enhance their chances of survival and success.

MARKETING ORIENTATION AND PERFORMANCE

There is some debate among academics as to the value of a marketing orientation and how it relates to the success of the firm (Narver and Slater, 1990; Henderson, 1998). Pelham (2000), quoting Levitt (1960), suggests that firms who adopt a marketing philosophy/orientation and convert it into actions should have superior performance. However, Pelham (2000) also points out there are firms that manage to be successful without embracing this concept and that emphasize technical or production capabilities instead. Henderson (1998) claims that there is no such thing as marketing orientation and that adopting those ideas inherent in a marketing orientation can be shown to account for only 10 per cent of business performance. Harris (1998) contends that since market orientation can be viewed as a form of culture, the impediments to market orientation are categorized via a contemporary organizational culture framework. Harris (1996) found that obstacles to market orientation could be classified as assumptions, values, artefacts or symbols. However, the view from the retail shop floor (Harris, 1998) suggests a similar set of obstacles to those found by Harris and Watkins' (1998) study – namely, apathy, instrumentality, limited power, short-termism, compartmentalization, ignorance and weak management support. The solutions proposed involved, *inter alia*, education and empowerment of retail shop floor workers (see also Carson, 1993; Carson *et al.*, 1995).

Denison and McDonald (1995) point out that studies have consistently shown that firms that were marketing-oriented, or competent practitioners of marketing, performed better in terms of ROI and market share. However, ROI can be affected by operational changes and is not a good measure of performance. Rafiq and Pallett (1996) found some limited evidence that marketing-oriented UK engineering firms were more likely to have higher profits. Again, profit is not such a good indicator of performance in SMEs, as companies' choices regarding pay policy on remuneration and the way they run their operations can reduce their profit and, therefore, their tax obligations.

The main inhibitor of marketing effectiveness in UK businesses in the late 1980s and 1990s was poor implementation of basic marketing (Denison and McDonald, 1995). This finding is supported by research carried out by Brooksbank *et al.* (1999). There are many other orientations or approaches that might be adopted by a firm and so a marketing orientation may only be relevant under certain business conditions. The business environment in which SMEs operate is dynamic and may well lend itself to a variety of successful approaches and strategies.

SME MARKETING IN PRACTICE

Marketing in practice in small firms seems to rely on personal contact networks (Hill and Wright, 2001; Gilmore *et al.*, 2001; Brodie *et al.*, 1997; O'Donnell and Cummins, 1999) and is often driven by the particular way in which an owner-manager does business. According to Gilmore *et al.* (2001), marketing in SMEs is likely to be haphazard, informal, loose, unstructured, spontaneous and reactive, and conform to industry norms. Gilmore *et al.* (2001) showed that because of networking there was much more communication between the SME owner-manager and his/her competitors than is usually reported in the literature and that competing firms might be quite supportive of each other. Similarly, networking with customers usually involved building a relationship with one or two important individuals in those companies. Should those individuals leave, the relationship with the company would dissolve (Gilmore *et al.*, 2001; see also Hill *et al.*, 1999; Johnsen and Johnsen, 1999). Hence, SME owner-managers recognized that building relationships was vital to a company's success and they invested considerable time and effort in maintaining good relations with regular clients (Gilmore *et al.*, 2001). The creation and existence of effective networking was concerned with maximizing marketing opportunities and ensuring the enterprise's survival and development (Gilmore *et al.*, 2001).

CONCLUSIONS

There is no clear definition of marketing in SMEs; those definitions of marketing that do exist either relate to larger businesses or are linked to entrepreneurial behaviour in smaller businesses. There are many theoretical and practical approaches to investigating marketing in SMEs and none of these approaches seem to be generally accepted. There is no grand unifying theory of marketing in SMEs. In addition, marketing in SMEs does not appear to evolve or mature, even when the market conditions and business activities change considerably (Brooksbank *et al.*, 1999).

The measurement of the performance of SMEs appears to be problematic. There is very little objective data relating marketing activity to business performance in SMEs yet there are claims by academics and managers that marketing activities do improve business performance. The performance of SMEs is difficult to assess because of normal fluctuations in activities arising from year to year. This is further exacerbated by the potential to manipulate the measures such as ROCE and ROI, which are typically used to measure performance. One of the general problems with accounting ratios is that there is no absolute definition as to what constitutes a 'correct' ratio and many of the ratios used suffer from wide variation year on year because of operational changes within the SME.

Although marketing is an important business function, the relationship between its role within the organization and its relevance with regard to the business environment in which the company operates is complex (Moller and Anttila, 1987). In fact, it is so complex that many other strategies and orientations seem to be equally successful in SMEs (Huang and Brown, 1999; Carter *et al.*, 1994). This makes investigating marketing in SMEs and relating these marketing activities to business performance extremely problematic.

REVIEW QUESTIONS

1. After reading this chapter, what conclusions can be drawn about marketing in SMEs? In your response try to list both positive and negative aspects.

2. An SME owner-manager believes s/he has developed a new in-car audio system that allows drivers to play an iPod through a voice-activated command. S/he believes it is unique and will be a fantastic success. S/he has built a number of samples and the initial tests prove the device is working, but s/he is yet to show it to any potential customers. The manager wants to market the product but has no formal marketing knowledge and comes to you, as a marketing student, to ask for advice. What do you say?

3. Try to construct a formal theoretical model of marketing in SMEs that relates company performance to the various concepts, theories, methods, activities and approaches of marketing. Explain how such a model might be tested.

4. Carry out your own review of the literature on the use of marketing in SMEs. Do we know which concepts, theories, methods, activities and approaches to marketing improve the performance of the company? What recommendations would you give to an SME based on this critical review of the literature?

5. What are the main problems facing researchers investigating the use of marketing in SMEs? How might these problems be overcome?

CASE STUDY 1: ELECTRICAL EQUIPMENT LTD

Introduction

Max Carter stared out across his desk for what was to be the last time. Retirement and a new life in the south of France beckoned. Max had worked for Electrical Equipment Ltd (EEL) for most of the company's existence, rising through the ranks to become marketing director. EEL is a small UK-based company manufacturing and selling alarm, signal, control and communications equipment for use in potentially explosive atmospheres such as the oil, gas and chemical industries. The company has expertise in hazardous area applications and has full in-house manufacturing capability and excellent design and development capabilities. The sales team consider themselves to be sales engineers and have considerable technical expertise when dealing with customers in this market. The barriers to entry into this market are high due to the requirements of formal certification bodies in the UK, Europe and the USA. The company had a turnover of £8.6 million and a gross margin of 50 per cent in 2008.

Corporate plan

In 2005, Max had devised a corporate plan with the managing director, Tim Whitlow, to grow the company turnover to £10 million within five years. Central to Max's strategy was the development of a complementary range of standard (non-explosive atmosphere – hereafter abbreviated to 'non-Ex' – capability) audio equipment. This new range would broaden the portfolio and allow for cross-selling of equipment. Max thought that in every hazardous environment there would be an equally non-hazardous situation that still needed audio communications. This was additional business and would allow the sales turnover to increase while making sales visits and sales account management more efficient. Tim Whitlow agreed to Max's proposal after some considerable discussion. However, the sales engineers were not completely convinced by this approach.

Operations and logistics

The non-Ex audio products contain unsophisticated technology and Max decided it would be more efficient and cost-effective to have these built in Taiwan. However, this introduced a delivery lead time from Taiwan to the UK of up to three months. This type of non-Ex loudspeaker is readily available from other competing companies and so to stay competitive EEL felt next-day delivery was essential. In order to do this EEL keep a full range of these non-Ex loudspeakers at the factory and have £0.5 million of stock.

New markets

In addition, EEL are actively pursuing higher-value market segments for overseas markets by improving their products and gaining higher levels of certification. The company had also designed a range of explosive atmosphere (hereafter abbreviated to 'Ex') compatible process control devices. These process control devices are very popular and have an increasing rate of demand such that they are likely to become the industry standard for this type of Ex compatible process control device.

Competitors

EEL's main competitor is Norloud (a Norwegian company). They have a similar product range and have 20 years of experience in the market. Norloud is very difficult to dislodge from this market and part of the decision to move into the commercial, non-Ex compatible loudspeakers was to try to take some of the market share from Norloud. Other competitors crowd the market offering selected niche products to highly defined markets. However, EEL are able to offer a one-stop shop for industrial audio, and thus save customers time and expense in searching for alternatives. Unfortunately, this strategy came at a cost for EEL. Procurement came under increasing pressure and found some difficulties in dealing with a Taiwanese supplier for the first time. The production team were trying to come to terms with new products and operating systems, resulting in delays in meeting deliveries. The sales engineers reported mixed feelings about having to sell what they considered standard high-street audio equipment, leaving their real competence underutilized. In short, the company was under pressure on a number of fronts. Max consulted the company information detailed in Tables 1.1–1.3 and decided to write to his fellow directors.

December 2009

Max Carter's last memo as marketing director reads as follows:

> The commercial (non-Ex) compatible loudspeakers are a major burden on the sales department and the company as a whole. In order to generate revenue these products are time and resource intensive, hard to differentiate on product characteristics, require sharper pricing and produce lower margins than our other products. I would like to discuss this problem and see what we can do at our next board meeting.

Tables of data were appended to the memo and are shown below.

Table 1.1 Financial information on Electrical Equipment Ltd (EEL) and the contribution from the standard non-Ex atmosphere products from 2005

Item/Year end	2005	2006	2007	2008
Total turnover for EEL (£m)	4.7	6.4	8.0	8.6
Gross margin for EEL (%)	57	50	50	50
Contribution from non-Ex products (£m)	–	0.8	0.97	1.0
Gross margin on non-Ex products (%)	–	35	31	35

Table 1.2 Details of the products for Electrical Equipment Ltd (EEL) (2009)

Product description	Average price (£)	Gross margin on item (%)	Number of competitors on item
Call points (Ex) (EEL)	100	50	1 main comp.
Status lamps (Ex) (EEL)	500–1,000	40–50	2
Beacon/Strobes (Ex) (EEL)	175	60	3

(continued)

Table 1.2 (continued)

Product description	Average price (£)	Gross margin on item (%)	Number of competitors on item
Sounders/Horns (Ex) (EEL)	200	60	3
Loudspeakers (Ex) (EEL)	130	40	2
Commercial loudspeakers (non-Ex)	30	30	10 UK; 50 internationally

Table 1.3 Market information on Electrical Equipment Ltd (EEL) Ex and non-Ex products in 2009

Product	Market growth rate (%)	Market share (£m)	Largest competitor (£m)
Ex products	5.8	7.6	4
Non-Ex products	0.0	1.0	3.0

Note: 'Ex' denotes the product is suitable for use in potentially explosive atmospheres and 'non-Ex' denotes the product is not suitable for use in potentially explosive atmospheres.

CASE QUESTIONS AND TASKS

1. You have just taken over as the new marketing director and your job is to produce an outline strategic marketing plan for Electrical Equipment Ltd (EEL).
2. As a separate report/memorandum to your own department, you should identify any potential problems with the implementation of your strategic marketing plan. Indicate any potential solutions to these problems in your report/memorandum.
3. If you had been Tim Whitlow, the managing director, in 2005, what would have been your response to Max Carter's proposal to grow the company? What alternative course(s) of action were available to the company in 2005? Critically evaluate the options available.
4. Use Porter's Five Forces to analyse the current position of the company and comment on the potential strategies available to EEL.
5. Carry out a Strengths, Weaknesses, Opportunities and Threats (SWOT) analysis on the current position of the company and comment on your answer.
6. Use the Boston Consulting Group Growth-Share Matrix to analyse the data in Tables 1.1–1.3. Comment on the results of your analysis and suggest a way forward for the company.

REFERENCES

Barber, J., Metcalfe, J. and Porteous, M. (1989) 'Barriers to growth: The ACARD study', in Barber, J. and Metcalfe, J. (eds), *Barriers to Growth in Small Firms*, pp. 1–19, London: Routledge.

Brodie, R. J., Coviello, N. E., Brookes, R. W. and Little, V. (1997) 'Towards a paradigm shift in marketing? An examination of current marketing practices', *Journal of Marketing Management*, vol. 13, pp. 383–406.

Brooksbank, R. (1996) 'The BASIC marketing planning process: A practical framework for the smaller business', *Marketing Intelligence and Planning*, vol. 14, no. 4, pp. 16–23.

Brooksbank, R. (1999) 'The theory and practice of marketing planning in the smaller business', *Marketing Intelligence and Planning*, vol. 17, no. 2, pp. 78–90.

Brooksbank, R., Kirby, D. A., Taylor, D. and Jones-Evans, D. (1999) 'Marketing in medium-sized manufacturing firms: The state-of-the-art in Britain, 1987–1992', *European Journal of Marketing*, vol. 33, no. 1/2, pp. 103–120.

Campbell-Hunt, C. (2000) 'What have we learned about generic competitive strategy? A meta-analysis', *Strategic Management Journal*, vol. 21, pp. 127–154.

Carson, D. (1990) 'Some exploratory models for assessing small firms' marketing performance: A qualitative approach', *European Journal of Marketing*, vol. 24, no. 11, pp. 5–49.

Carson, D. (1993) 'A philosophy for marketing education in small firms', *Journal of Marketing Management*, vol. 9, pp. 189–204.

Carson, D., Cromie, S., McGowan, P. and Hill, J. (1995) *Marketing and Entrepreneurship in SMEs: An Innovative Approach*, Harlow, UK: Pearson Education.

Carter, N. M., Stearns, T. M., Reynolds, P. D. and Miller, B. A. (1994) 'New Venture Strategies: Theory development with an empirical base', *Strategic Management Journal*, vol. 15, pp. 21–41.

Chaffey, D., Mayer, R., Johnston, K. and Ellis-Chadwick, F. (2000) *Internet Marketing*, Harlow, UK: Prentice Hall.

Chaston, I. and Mangles, T. (2002) *Small Business Marketing Management*, Basingstoke, UK: Palgrave Publishers.

Denison, T. and McDonald, M. (1995) 'The Role of Marketing: Past, Present and Future', *Journal of Marketing Practice: Applied Marketing Science*, vol. 1, no. 1, pp. 54–76.

European Commission (2005), *The New SME Definition: User Guide and Model Declaration*, Brussels, Enterprise and Industry Publications.

Fillis, I. (2002) 'Small Firm Marketing Theory and Practice: Insights from the Outside', *Journal of Research in Marketing and Entrepreneurship*, vol. 4, no. 2, pp. 134–157.

Frecknall-Hughes, J., Simpson, M. and Padmore, J. (2007) 'Inherent limitations in using financial ratio analysis to assess small and medium sized company performance', Working Paper 2007.01. The Management School, University of Sheffield. Online: <http://www.sheffield.ac.uk/management/research/papers/2007.html>

Freel, M. S. (2000) 'Barriers to product innovation in small manufacturing firms', *International Small Business Journal*, vol. 18, no. 2 (January–March, no. 70), pp. 60–80.

Gilmore, A., Carson, D. and Grant, K. (2001) 'SME marketing in practice', *Marketing Intelligence and Planning*, vol. 19, no. 1, pp. 6–11.

Hannon, P. D. and Atherton, A. (1998) 'Small firm success and the art of orienteering: The value of plans, planning and strategic awareness in the competitive small firm', *Journal of Small Business and Enterprise Development*, vol. 5, no. 2 (Summer), pp. 102–119.

Harris, L. C. (1996) 'Cultural obstacles to market orientation', *Journal of Marketing Practice: Applied Marketing Science*, vol. 4, no. 2, pp. 36–52.

Harris, L. C. (1998) 'Barriers to market orientation: The view from the shop floor', *Marketing Intelligence and Planning*, vol. 16, no. 3, pp. 221–228.

Harris, L. C. and Watkins, P. (1998) 'The impediments to developing a market orientation: An exploratory study of small UK hotels', *International Journal of Contemporary Hospitality Management*, vol. 10, no. 6, pp. 221–226.

Henderson, S. (1998) 'No such thing as marketing orientation – a call for no more papers', *Management Decision*, vol. 36, no. 9, pp. 598–609.

Hill, J. (2001a) 'A multidimensional study of the key determinants of effective SME marketing activity: Part 1', *International Journal of Entrepreneurial Behaviour and Research*, vol. 7, no. 5, pp. 171–204.

Hill, J. (2001b) 'A multidimensional study of the key determinants of effective SME marketing activity: Part 2', *International Journal of Entrepreneurial Behaviour and Research*, vol. 7, no. 6, pp. 211–235.

Hill, J., McGowan, P. and Drummond, P. (1999) 'The development and application of a qualitative approach to researching the marketing networks of small firm entrepreneurs', *Qualitative Market Research: An International Journal*, vol. 2, no. 2, pp. 71–81.

Hill, J. and Wright, L. T. (2001) 'A qualitative research agenda for small to medium-sized enterprises', *Marketing Intelligence and Planning*, vol. 19, no. 6, pp. 432–443.

Hogarth-Scott, S., Watson, K. and Wilson, N. (1996) 'Do small businesses have to practice marketing to survive and grow?', *Marketing Planning and Intelligence*, vol. 14, no. 1, pp. 6–18.

Huang, X. and Brown, A. (1999) 'An analysis and classification of problems in small business', *International Small Business Journal*, vol. 18, no. 1, pp. 73–85.

Hudson, M., Lean, J. and Smart, P. A. (2001) 'Improving control through effective performance measurement in SMEs', *Production Planning and Control*, vol. 12, no. 8, pp. 804–813.

Johnsen, R. E. and Johnsen, T. E. (1999) 'International market development through networks: The case of the Ayrshire knitwear sector', *International Journal of Entrepreneurial Behaviour and Research*, vol. 5, no. 6, pp. 297–312.

Levitt, T. (1960) 'Marketing Myopia', *Harvard Business Review* (July–August), pp. 24–27.

McKenna, P. (1991) 'Marketing is Everything', *Harvard Business Review* (January–February), pp. 65–79.

McLarty, R. (1998) 'Case study: Evidence of a strategic marketing paradigm in a growing SME', *Journal of Marketing Practice: Applied Marketing Science*, vol. 4, no. 4, pp. 105–117.

Moller, K. and Anttila, M. (1987) 'Marketing capability – a key success factor in small business?', *Journal of Marketing Management*, vol. 3, no. 2, pp. 185–203.

Narver, J. C. and Slater, S. F. (1990) 'The effect of market orientation on business profitability', *Journal of Marketing*, vol. 54 (October), pp. 20–35.

O'Brien, E. (1998) 'The DTI marketing initiative: The experience of 35 young Scottish companies', *Journal of Small Business and Enterprise Development*, vol. 5, no. 3 (Autumn), pp. 219–227.

O'Donnell, A. and Cummins, D. (1999) 'The use of qualitative methods to research networking in SMEs', *Qualitative Market Research: An International Journal*, vol. 2, no. 2, pp. 82–91.

Pelham, A. M. (2000) 'Market orientation and other potential influences on performance in small and medium-sized manufacturing firms', *Journal of Small Business Management*, vol. 38, no. 1 (January), pp. 48–67.

Perry, S. C. (2001) 'The relationship between written business plans and the failure of small businesses in the U.S.', *Journal of Small Business Management*, vol. 39, no. 3, pp. 201–208.

Rafiq, M. and Pallett, R. A. (1996) 'Marketing implementation in the UK engineering industry', *Journal of Marketing Practice: Applied Marketing Science*, vol. 2, no. 4, pp. 13–35.

Rayport, J. F. and Jaworski, B. J. (2001) *e-Commerce*, Boston, MA: McGraw-Hill.

Reynolds, P. L. (2002) 'The need for a new paradigm for small business marketing? What was wrong with the old one?', *Journal of Research in Marketing and Entrepreneurship*, vol. 4, no. 3, pp. 191–205.

Rice, G. R. (1983) 'Strategic decision making in small businesses', *Journal of General Management*, vol. 9, no. 1, pp. 58–65.

Romano, C. and Ratnatunga, J. (1995) 'The role of marketing: Its impact on small enterprise research', *European Journal of Marketing*, vol. 29, no. 7, pp. 9–30.

Rue, L. W. and Ibrahim, N. A. (1998) 'The relationship between planning sophistication and performance in small business', *Journal of Small Business Management*, vol. 36, no. 4 (October), pp. 24–32.

Simpson, M., Padmore, J., Taylor, N. and Frecknall-Hughes, J. (2006) 'Marketing in small and medium sized enterprises', *International Journal of Entrepreneurial Behaviour and Research*, vol. 12, no. 6, pp. 361–387.

Simpson, M. and Taylor, N. (2002) 'The role and relevance of marketing in SMEs: Towards a new model', *Journal of Small Business and Enterprise Development*, vol. 9, no. 4, pp. 370–382.

Siu, W. and Kirby, D. A. (1998) 'Approaches to small firm marketing: A critique', *European Journal of Marketing*, vol. 32, no. 1/2, pp. 40–60.

Smith, A. and Whittaker, J. (1998) 'Management development in SMEs: What needs to be done?', *Journal of Small Business and Enterprise Development*, vol. 5, no. 2 (Summer), pp. 176–185.

Sparkes, A. and Thomas, B. (2001) 'The use of the internet as a critical success factor for the marketing of Welsh agri-food SMEs in the twenty-first century', *British Food Journal*, vol. 103, no. 5, pp. 331–347.

Valos, M. and Baker, M. (1996) 'Developing an Australian model of export marketing performance determinants', *Marketing Intelligence and Planning*, vol. 14, no. 3, pp. 11–20.

Chapter 2

Entrepreneurship marketing

Robert Hinson

LEARNING OBJECTIVES

After reading this chapter, you will be able to:
- understand entrepreneurship from the marketing point of view
- explore the use of marketing in small- and medium-sized enterprises (SMEs)
- highlight the benefits of marketing practices to current and prospective entrepreneurs
- find out the extent to which formal and conventional marketing planning processes are practised by entrepreneurs
- understand how SMEs can improve their marketing practices to achieve organizational advantage.

INTRODUCTION

The term 'entrepreneurship marketing' (EM) describes the marketing activities of small- and medium-sized enterprises (SMEs) and has, conceptually, developed within a vibrant and promising fresh field of research. While the analysis of marketing in new and small ventures is an important issue, given the large share of economic activities that can be attributed to these kinds of firms, it is argued that EM describes marketing activities with an entrepreneurial mindset, irrespective of firm size or age. EM research might want to explore the idea that EM can be implemented regardless of firm size or age in order to broaden the scope of the field. In essence, EM defines the role of the entrepreneur as 'fundamental' in marketing and organizational activities, so that flexibility in marketing was important to suitably adapt its principles and practices to the activities of SMEs. In contrast, 'marketing entrepreneurship' emphasizes the importance of marketing and its pivotal role in helping to transform the entrepreneurial activities of SMEs into effective and competitive businesses. In practice there are crossovers between these two emerging fields. Today the key difference is an increased understanding of the importance of carrying out quality research into every aspect of small firms' activities. Given their importance to economic prosperity and the acceptance of the reality that most large firms have their beginnings in small entrepreneurial enterprises, there has been a growing demand for good-quality SME research.

AN OVERVIEW OF ENTREPRENEURSHIP

The early economic literature defined the entrepreneur as an 'arbitrageur'. As the literature on entrepreneurship advanced, entrepreneurs were further described as coordinators in production and distribution, as well as modern leaders and managers (Say, 1971), coordinators and arbitrageurs (Walras, 1954), uncertainty-bearers (Knight, 1921), innovators and creative destructors (Schumpeter, 1934) and alert discoverers of profit opportunities (Kirzner, 1973, 1979). A number of schools of thought have emerged in the history of entrepreneurship. Notable among these are neoclassical (Khilstrom and Laffont, 1979), psychological (Begley and Boyd, 1987) and Austrian economic (Kirzner, 1973; Hayek, 1945) schools. Each offers different assumptions and definitions of entrepreneurship. The more comprehensive perspectives on entrepreneurship stem from the work of two contrasting thinkers in economics: Joseph Schumpeter and Israel M. Kirzner. Given the different ways entrepreneurs fulfil their role in the market, it can be argued that Schumpeterian and Kirznerian entrepreneurs could work simultaneously, as the former engage in arbitrage and the latter in innovation (Styles and Seymour, 2006).

Much of the literature that is concerned with SMEs and small firms is inextricably linked with the entrepreneurship dimensions (Geursen, 1995). In many cases the terms 'small firm owner-manager' and 'entrepreneur' are used interchangeably, but of late there has been some effort among researchers to draw distinctions between the two (Fulop, 1991). It is perhaps appropriate, therefore, to begin with the thorny and contentious issue of actually defining the small firm.

Although there is no accepted generic definition of the term 'entrepreneurship' (Ucbasaran *et al.*, 2001; Watson, 2001), essentially the term refers to individual opportunistic activity that creates value and bears risk, and is strongly associated with innovation: it is a 'process of opportunity recognition and pursuit that leads to growth' (Sexton and Kasarda, 1992, p. xix). Stevenson *et al.* (1989) defined entrepreneurship as the pursuit of an opportunity irrespective of existing resources. Bygrave and Hofer (1991) also defined an entrepreneur as one who perceives an opportunity and creates an organization to pursue it. According to Hoselitz (1960), an entrepreneur is one who buys at a price that is certain and sells at a price that is uncertain. Kirzner (1985) also identified the entrepreneur as one who perceives profit opportunities and initiates action to fill currently unsatisfied needs.

Entrepreneurship, however, has been defined as an attitude towards management that seeks to emphasize innovation, flexibility and responsiveness driven by the perception of opportunity, while providing more sophisticated and efficient management (Guth and Ginsberg, 1990; Naman and Slevin, 1993). Miller (1983) suggests a broader interpretation of the concept which instantly motivates a lot of academic attention – namely, that entrepreneurship represents a characteristic of the firm that goes beyond the efforts of one key manager, especially when the size of the firm increases and its organizational structure becomes more complex. Entrepreneurship has also been defined as the set of behaviours that initiates and manages the reallocation of economic resources and whose purpose is value creation through those means (Herron and Robinson, 1993). Cole (1968) also defined entrepreneurship as a purposeful activity to initiate, maintain and develop a profit-oriented business.

TYPES OF ENTREPRENEURS

A study by Smart and Conant (1994) reveals that business people with higher entrepreneurial orientation report greater possession of distinctive marketing competencies. Thus, it suggests that the personal characteristics of entrepreneurs and the marketing behaviour of small firms are related, to some extent. The misconception of marketing of many owner-managers also makes them take a negative approach to the markets they are serving (Brown, 1984). The marketing behaviour of small firms appears to be related to the motivation, belief, attitude and the objectives of the owner-manager, and also influenced by the limitations and constraints of the small business (Ford and Rowley, 1979).

It has been suggested that the marketing behaviour of small firms is 'pushed' by the owner-managers' personal characteristics (Siu and Kirby, 1998). Smith (1967) identifies two types of entrepreneurs: the craftsman entrepreneur and the opportunistic entrepreneur. The craftsman entrepreneur makes use of personal relationships in marketing while the opportunistic entrepreneur is very much market-oriented, continually seeking new possibilities and new opportunities. The firms founded by opportunistic entrepreneurs tend to experience much higher growth rates than those founded by craftsmen entrepreneurs. Opportunistic and craftsmen entrepreneurs both need some marketing insights to make a success of the entrepreneurial ventures and the importance of the entrepreneur in fostering new-venture success is now well documented in the marketing and management literature (see Vanhonacker *et al.*, 2007; Chakravarthy and Lorange 2007; Anderson and Evangelista 2009).

DEFINITION AND NATURE OF SMES

There is no one universally accepted definition of what SMEs are. As stated by Gore *et al.* (1992), '[l]ike the proverbial elephant the small firm is one of those things that is recognised when seen but difficult to define'. Storey (1994) also notes that there is no single, uniformly acceptable definition of a small firm. He offers an explanation for this, noting, however, that a small firm in an industry like petrochemicals, for example, is likely to have much higher levels of capitalization, sales and possibly employment than a small firm in the car repairs trade (Hill, 2001). What this means is that definitions that relate to 'objective' measures of size, such as number of employees, sales turnover, profitability, net worth, etc., are problematic. In reality, 'in some sectors all firms may be regarded as small, while in other sectors there are possibly no firms which are small' (Storey, 1994, p. 9).

However, the most widely accepted definition is one based on the ideas of the Bolton Committee (Bolton, 1971). They identified three important characteristics that are likely to have a strong effect on management and decision making within a small firm, formulating what they called an 'economic' definition and a 'statistical' definition. The economic definition suggests that small firms meet the following criteria:

- they have a relatively small share of their marketplace
- they are managed by owners or part-owners in a personalized way, and not through the medium of a formalized management structure
- they are independent, in the sense of not forming part of a larger enterprise.

Wynarczyk *et al.* (1993) discuss key aspects that differentiate small and large firms. These are uncertainty, innovation and evolution. There is no doubt, therefore, that uncertainty is a feature of the smaller enterprise that is characterized by limited resources (Hill, 2001).

The abbreviation SME occurs commonly in the European Union (EU) and in international organizations such as the World Bank, the United Nations and the World Trade Organization. The term 'small and medium businesses' or SMBs is predominantly used in the USA. EU member states traditionally have their own definition of what constitutes an

SME; for example, the traditional definition in Germany has a limit of 250 employees, while in Belgium it is 100.

However, the EU has recently started standardizing the concept. Its current definition categorizes companies with fewer than ten employees as 'micro', those with fewer than 50 employees as 'small' and those with fewer than 250 as 'medium'. Small-medium organizations need to have between 20 and 500 employees (European Commission, 2003). In the United States business size is defined by the number of employees: small businesses are those with fewer than 100 employees, while medium-sized businesses are those with fewer than 500 employees.

In the EU, SMEs comprise approximately 99 per cent of all firms and employ among them about 65 million people. In many sectors, SMEs are also responsible for driving innovation and competition. Globally SMEs account for 99 per cent of business numbers and 40–50 per cent of gross domestic product (GDP).

In India, the micro and small enterprise (MSE) sector plays a pivotal role in the overall industrial economy of the country. It is estimated that in terms of value the sector accounts for about 39 per cent of the manufacturing output and about 33 per cent of the total export of the country. Furthermore, in recent years the MSE sector has consistently registered higher growth rates compared with the overall industrial sector. The major advantage of the sector is its employment potential at low capital cost. From the available statistics it can be seen that this sector employs an estimated 31 million persons spread over 12.8 million enterprises and that the labour intensity in the MSE sector is estimated to be almost four times higher than the large enterprise sector (see www.msme.gov.in).

In South Africa the term SMME, for small, medium and micro enterprise, is used. In Ghana and Nigeria the term SME is used to refer to small and medium enterprises and in both countries SMEs are estimated to comprise over 90 per cent of all businesses operating.

Defining SMEs is often considered to be an obstacle for business studies and market research. Definitions in use today define thresholds in terms of employment, turnover and assets. They also incorporate a reasonable amount of flexibility around year-to-year changes in these measures so that a business qualifying as an SME in one year can have a reasonable expectation of remaining an SME in the next. The thresholds themselves, however, vary substantially between countries. As the SME thresholds dictate to some extent the provision of government support, countries in which manufacturing and labour-intensive industries are prioritized politically tend to opt for more relaxed thresholds.

ACTIVITIES OF SMES

Dodge et al. (1994) and Caird (1992) find that the most prevalent problem for SMEs in their bid to incorporate marketing into their management activities was a lack of knowledge about the marketplace and marketing planning. Be that as it may, in a discussion of small firms' marketing activities, Rhys (1989) suggests that a small firm pursues marketing function in a way that insulates it as much as possible from direct competition with larger firms. He points out that, as a consequence, small firms are left with strategic options such as exploiting niches left by larger firms (see also Stasch and Ward, 1989). Though the basic tenets and principles of marketing are universally and equally applicable to both large and small businesses, academic research into such firms has been conducted only in the 1990s (Davis et al., 1985); Reynolds (2002), however, maintains that the conventional marketing approach is not relevant to SMEs.

Cannon (1991) makes the point that research into small businesses has been a little thin on the ground. Davis and Klassen (1991) note that there is currently insufficient knowledge about marketing in small businesses. Hills (1987) has been more precise in his criticism, implying that there is an absence of an appropriate small business marketing theory specifically related to the understanding and knowledge of strategic marketing. Reynolds (2002) notes that SMEs face opportunities and concerns that large corporations do not, and as such they may benefit from marketing theory which considers the particularities of the SME context.

Matthews and Scott (1995) note that minimal empirical attention has been given to the antecedents of strategic or operational planning in small firms. Consequently, the question of why some small firms plan and others do not becomes especially relevant. They state that it is the resource constraints of both small and growth-oriented entrepreneurial firms which will prevent them from maintaining planning activity in the face of increasing uncertainty. It is fair to postulate that generally life in the small firm might be based on day-to-day survival rather than well-thought-out marketing planning and execution. This implies that, when conditions of uncertainty prevail, small firms will focus on doing, instead of engaging in formal strategic planning. Shooting from the hip cowboy-style has also spelled the doom of several SMEs, so some basic knowledge of EM practice could help stem business failure in SMEs.

ENTREPRENEURSHIP MARKETING (EM)
Definition of EM

EM (also known as 'entrepreneurial marketing') describes the marketing activities of small and new ventures. Morris *et al.* (2002) state that 'the term "entrepreneurial marketing" has been used in various ways, and often somewhat loosely' (p. 4). The potential difficulty for this might be that each concept can be interpreted in many different ways. Hence there might be many possible combinations of the conceptualizations of entrepreneurship and marketing, and their interrelations.

Kraus *et al.* (2009) define EM by combining the American Marketing Association (AMA) definition of marketing and the definition of entrepreneurship. In their view,

> [e]ntrepreneurial marketing is an organizational function and a set of processes for creating, communicating and delivering value to customers and for managing customer relationships in ways that benefit the organization and its stakeholders, and that is characterized by innovativeness, risk-taking, proactiveness, and may be performed without resources currently controlled.
>
> (p. 47)

Bäckbrö and Nyström (2006) state:

> Entrepreneurial marketing is the overlapping aspects between entrepreneurship and marketing; therefore it is the behavior shown by any individual and/or organization that attempts to establish and promote market ideas, while developing new ones in order to create value.
>
> (p. 47)

The AMA defines marketing as an

> organizational function and a set of processes for creating, communicating and delivering value to customers and for managing customer relationships in ways that benefit the organization and its stakeholders.
>
> (Keefe, 2004, p. 17)

17 ∎

Because of the heterogeneous interpretations of both domains – entrepreneurship and marketing – it is difficult to come up with a 'standard' definition of EM that is widely agreed upon. The term 'entrepreneurial' might be interpreted as a strategic orientation influencing the organizational function of marketing. Thus 'entrepreneurship' is a noun that describes an approach to marketing that embraces the opportunities of the marketplace in terms of an effective implementation of price, place, promotion and product tactics (the 4Ps) by being risk-taking, innovative and proactive (Kraus *et al.* 2009).

Gungaphul and Boolaky (2009) conducted a study on entrepreneurship and marketing in Mauritius. Findings from the study indicated that entrepreneurs used marketing to a large extent, although some applied it unknowingly. They tended to emphasize product development rather than improving product offering based on customer needs and wants. On the whole, the results of this survey indicate that entrepreneurs view marketing as an important function in achieving their business goals.

Marketing and entrepreneurship interface

Marketing is widely considered as the key to survival, development and success of small or new ventures (Bjerke and Hultman, 2002; Carson *et al.*, 1995; Gumpert, 1997; Teach and Tarpley, 1987). Murray (1981) postulates that marketing is the logical home for the entrepreneurial process in organizations. Similarly, Foxal and Minkes (1996) attribute the locus of entrepreneurship to marketing. However, their analysis pertained to already-established businesses and large firms. To them marketing is inherently entrepreneurship in small firms and start-up businesses (Hills and LaForge, 1992; Carson *et al.*, 1995; Romano and Ratnatunga, 1995; Morris and Lewis, 1996). Marketing nevertheless makes an enormous contribution to these enterprises, and venture capitalists rate its overall importance for the success of new ventures at 6.7 on a scale of 7, above all other functional areas (Hills and LaForge, 1992). Prior to the 1990s, it was widely assumed that small or new ventures required a simplified version of the more 'sophisticated' marketing practices that were developed for larger companies. However, there might be a gap between standard textbook approaches and actual marketing practice in smaller enterprises (Hills, 1995).

The main approach used by many writers is to take the main concepts used by marketing (the process of planning and executing the conception, pricing, promotion and distribution of ideas, goods and services to create exchange that satisfies individual and organizational objectives (AMA)) and compare them with the entrepreneurial process (Kraus *et al.* 2009). This approach led many writers to identify various common points (Hills and LaForge, 1992; Carson *et al.*, 1995). Thus it was found that the marketing culture, i.e. the belief about the central importance of the customer, prevailed in many small firms. Similarly, market segmentation, targeting and positioning, and defining how the firm is going to compete in its chosen market, were also widely used. Finally, elements of the marketing mix – that is, the 4Ps – are adopted by most firms (Hills and LaForge, 1992).

More recently, Hills *et al.* (2008) investigated the evolution and development of this area of scholarship and concluded that marketing among entrepreneurs deviates from mainstream marketing. Reynolds (2002), however, argues that while a conventional marketing approach may still be relevant to SMEs, they face opportunities and concerns that large corporations do not, and as such they may benefit from marketing theory which considers the particularities of the SME context.

Marketing activities by entrepreneurial firms

Marketing competency

There is little in the literature relating to which competencies are most appropriate for marketing (Carson, 1993). Marketing is on the offensive and future-focused in character and very much about initiating as much as reacting to continuous change opportunities. The literature offers some consideration as to which competencies are appropriate for marketing. Middleton and Long (1990, p. 325), for example, in their literature review offer nothing of significance in the area of marketing skills, stating, '[I]t became clear that there was a dearth of well articulated and considered thought on the issues of marketing skills'. Marketing management competencies, arising from an analysis of their research, are: marketing attributes (e.g. communication, creativity, imagination and initiative), management attributes (e.g. analytical, organizational and planning skills) and personality attributes (e.g. motivation, resilience and entrepreneurship).

Hardy (1992) develops an interesting dimension to the competency debate, when he suggests that every manager is a member of the marketing team and needs marketing skills, knowledge and orientation. Hardy also makes the link between competency models, which he describes as descriptions of required abilities in individual managers or groups of managers. He adds that a set of required competencies can be derived from a description of the challenges that are expected to confront these managers in the future. He outlines typical marketing challenges that face organizations and develops a core set of marketing competencies, which he divides into general skills, sub-skills, knowledge, orientation (including values and standards) and fostering vision, creativity and path-finding.

General skills are described as identification and solution of marketing problems, use of problem-solving frameworks (for example, marketing environment analysis) and evaluation of options. Sub-skills include identification of market opportunity, creatively viewing and analysing markets, assessing competitors and markets, predicting market channel behaviour, managing market information, forecasting, financial analysis and organizational analysis.

Middleton and Long (1990) address the marketing skills issue from the perspective of marketing education and training. They conclude that the attributes which have been identified elsewhere in reference to management skills are broadly the same as those which they have identified as desirable marketing skills in their research context. Their extensive review of the literature draws on the work of Thomas (1991), Cowell (1987) and Kotler (1988). It could be argued, however, that such competency spectra are too descriptive and cumbersome for use in describing entrepreneurial or SME marketing management competencies.

Entrepreneurial competency

Martin and Staines (1994) note that, aside the other well-documented shortcomings and restrictions under which small firms operate, managerial experience, skills and personal qualities are often cited in the business press as the main reasons why firms in the small firm sector fail. Ray (1993) makes the important assertion that, in order to understand why some individuals become entrepreneurs and some entrepreneurs are relatively more successful than others, three key elements must be addressed. These are the entrepreneur's personality or attributes, the entrepreneur's background and experience and the entrepreneur's skills, including how they learn. Significantly, he notes that it is perhaps not so easy to identify entrepreneurial skills. The key conclusion from Ray's study is, however, that the entrepreneurial personality is important in shaping a venture, yet there is no ideal type of personality or marginal set of attributes that guarantees success for a new venture.

The entrepreneurial orientation, distinctive marketing competencies and organizational performance are discussed by Smart and Conant (1994). They conclude that an entrepreneurial orientation is positively and significantly related to distinctive marketing competencies and organizational performance. In particular, their study makes a link with the work of Hills and LaForge (1992), where they suggest that the entrepreneurial orientation has six dimensions. These are:

1. The propensity to take risks.
2. A tendency to engage in strategic planning activities.
3. An ability to identify customer needs and wants.
4. A level of innovation.
5. The ability to persevere in making your vision of the business a reality.
6. The ability to identify new opportunities.

Marketing as a functional problem

The early studies of small business growth and development placed emphasis on organizational development (Churchill and Lewis, 1983), strategic operational decisions (Kazanjian, 1984) and corporate culture (Flamholtz, 1986). As such, marketing was seen as only one of the research areas, not the major research thrust. Churchill and Lewis (1983) identify five stages in the development of a firm. These are Existence, Survival, Success, Take-off and Resource Maturity. Marketing is believed to exist as a major issue in the 'Existence' stage only. The owner-manager at this stage takes charge of the marketing and sales activities. A marketing system does not exist in the firm.

As the small firm grows, marketing becomes a major issue. A marketing system develops and becomes systematized and formalized. Professional managers replace the owner-manager and take charge of the immediate marketing and sales functions. With growth, marketing develops from 'modestly irrelevant' to 'critically important'.

A four-stage model is proposed for business development. Marketing, though regarded as an active ingredient for company growth (Levitt, 1983), is given attention only in Stage 3. This includes developing market share and providing product support and customer services. The predominance of sales and marketing in Stage 3 is typified by growth and the attainment of profitability. However, in Stage 4 the marketing task is to develop a second generation of products. Marketing is identified as a derivative of business strategies.

Flamholtz (1986) uses the organizational culture approach to put forward a seven-stage model of organizational growth and development. Only the first four stages are relevant to this discussion as they depict the behaviour of small business. They are New Venture, Expansion, Professionalism and Consolidation. Marketing, the identification and definition of a market niche and product and services development, receives attention in Stage 1, but its importance decreases alongside firm growth. Marketing is not given an important role in the firm's growth management. Market positioning, niche marketing, market segmentation, and marketing surveillance are treated as minor or secondary strategic tactics.

Entrepreneurial approaches to the marketing functions

EM makes use of the 4Ps + C (price, place, promotion and product + customer) model and these are discussed below. The 4Ps + C model is a variation of the 7Ps services marketing model which emphasizes the importance of product, price, place, promotion, physical evidence, processes and people. The major benefit of the 7Ps framework is that is leads to a superior service orientation; in the case of SMEs this service orientation is captured in the C of the 4 Ps + C model, which represents customer management. The elements of the EM mix are therefore product, price, place, promotion and customer management.

Entrepreneurial approaches to promotion

EM use of promotion is based on word-of-mouth communication and recommendation to develop a customer base (Stokes, 2000). This approach may be more cost-efficient than classical advertising. This is because EM aims at target groups that cannot be reached via TV or print advertisement. It is grounded on the exponential diffusion of communication contents. Since the communication is distributed by the customers, not by the company, the customers need to have a high involvement in the product in order to spread the message (Ahuja *et al.*, 2007). Two of the best-known and successful forms of EM communication in terms of an entrepreneurial approach to promotion are *guerrilla marketing* and *viral marketing*. These partially overlap, since they are both based on the concept of word-of-mouth marketing (Ahuja *et al.*, 2007; Creelman, 1992). Guerilla marketing focuses on creating a unique, engaging and thought-provoking concept to generate buzz, which consequently becomes viral. The term was coined and defined by Jay Conrad Levinson in his book *Guerrilla Marketing*. Guerrilla marketing involves unusual approaches such as intercept encounters in public places, street giveaways of products and any unconventional marketing intended to get maximum results from minimal resources.

Entrepreneurial approaches to product, place and price

The examples from the previous section illustrate EM as applied to the field of promotion. However, an entrepreneurial approach to marketing can also cover the elements of product, place and price.

An impressive example of EM focused on *product* development is the young entrepreneur from New Zealand named Jeremy Moon who created a company called Icebreaker. He realized that wool underwear had a negative image (itchy, bad smell, outdated designs). So he decided to draw up a global product line of underwear made of merino wool. He was sure that the long, fine wool which was already being used for high-end suits and ties would be a bestseller. Moon spent half of his seed financing on creating a concept of what his global brand would look like in a few years' time. Starting from this vision, he developed the product in a retrograde manner and started to build a global brand (Birchfield, 2000).

An example of EM which focuses on the element of *place* is the fundraising programme of the non-profit organization Two Wheel View. Based on the insight that young adults distrust the media and traditional advertising, the organization developed a concept that directly reaches the target group by taking them on adventure trips to countries such as Argentina. The participants return with a deep understanding of the problems confronting the organization and become more devoted to the aims of the organization. By bringing the target group to the 'product', a very strong commitment to the aims of the organization is established (Edwards, 2007).

An interesting case of EM that used mainly the *price* as point of leverage was the online distribution of the 2008 Radiohead album *In Rainbows*. Customers could download the album and decide how much to pay for it. Some fans paid up to US$1,000. The band successfully communicated its new distribution policy as a struggle for freedom of idealistic artists against the corrupt music industry (Peitz and Waelbroeck, 2005).

Managing customers as a route to organizational survival

Customer management is seen as one sure way to survive and outperform competitors in today's marketplace. A company's first task is to create customers. However, creating customers and managing them can be a difficult task. Today's customers face a vast array of services and brand choices, prices and suppliers. For companies to succeed in today's fiercely competitive markets, they have to move from a product-and-selling philosophy to a customer-and-marketing philosophy. Customer management (CM) is the marketing concept that aims at meeting, satisfying and delighting customers by applying a variety of tactics to attract and retain them.

Customer management is about:

- finding the right customers (those with an acceptable current and future net value)
- getting to know them (as individuals or groups)
- growing their value (if appropriate)
- retaining their business in the most efficient and effective way.

This is achieved by companies enabling their people, processes, policies, suppliers and customer-facing technologies to manage all customer interactions proactively during each stage of the customer life cycle in a way that enhances each customer's experience of dealing with the company. However, blindly striving to keep all customers is not necessarily sensible for an entrepreneurial firm, as this depends upon their likely future value. Indeed, 'good' customers can become 'bad' and therefore good candidates for dismissal.

SUMMARY

The chapter began with an introduction to the concept of EM as practised by SMEs. It then set the stage for the discussion by offering various definitions of SMEs from various scholars and from different country contexts. We mentioned specifically that definitions of SMEs in use today revolves around certain thresholds in terms of employment, turnover and assets. The definitions were then followed by discussion of the activities undertaken by SMEs with regard to marketing their products or services. The chapter further provided an overview of entrepreneurship definition and practices from various scholars and outlined the two types of entrepreneurs, i.e. the craftsman entrepreneur and the opportunistic entrepreneur. After discussing issues associated with entrepreneurship the chapter delved into its main area of concern, which is EM. Issues discussed under this section included marketing activities of entrepreneurial firms (marketing competency and entrepreneurial competency) and marketing as a functional problem, which revealed a lack of proper utilization of marketing practices by SMEs. Finally, the chapter concluded by discussing issues with regard to the 4Ps + C model as used by entrepreneurial SMEs.

REVIEW QUESTIONS

1. What key issues should SMEs consider in planning their marketing activities?

2. What are the key features of EM?

3. How important are customers to entrepreneurial enterprises?

CASE STUDY 2: ZOOMLION – AN OVERVIEW

Zoomlion Ghana Limited (ZGL) is a waste management company in Ghana. ZGL was incorporated in January 2006 and commenced operations in May 2006. The vision of the company is to champion the cause of clean and environmentally healthy communities in Ghana and throughout Africa by 2013 (see www.zoomlionghana. com). The mission of ZGL is to be at the forefront of the environmental sanitation services industry and it hopes to achieve this by the introduction and utilization of simple but modern technologies and methods of waste management at affordable and competitive rates. ZGL manages its people element of marketing by:

- demanding total responsibility from each other, collectively supporting the responsibilities of others – team is their goal
- committing to the health and safety of its employees
- recognizing excellence by selecting the right expertise to fit the right jobs.

ZGL manages its process element of marketing by:

- ensuring transparency and mutual trust in all relationships
- committing to providing adequate resources for ongoing training and personnel development.

Joseph Siaw Agyepong: entrepreneur and founder

'The waste management industry in Ghana is a difficult terrain; why are you going to waste your resources in such an industry?' This comment was common with people (friends, colleagues and family) who heard that I was treading the dangerous road of setting up a waste management company. Normally there was a follow-up question – 'Do you know the number of companies that have collapsed as a result of non-payment or delayed payment by the government who is the main customer?'

These are the words of Joseph Siaw Agyepong, the unassuming chief executive officer of ZGL.

In 2004 the Ministry of Local Government and Environment listed the following as the challenges confronting the waste management industry in Ghana:

- there are inadequate funds to pay solid waste contractors who are currently doing about 80 per cent of the collection not paid for by residents
- there are inadequate waste collection vehicles
- the revenue generated is not sufficient to meet waste collection
- there is inadequate financial support from the government

Figure 2.1
Zoomlion HQ

- attention has shifted from the curative to the preventive aspect of sanitation
- there is a lack of public awareness of the need to pay for sanitation services
- the public is indifferent towards good sanitary practices
- there is a lack of intense and sustained public education on sanitation
- land acquisition for public waste disposal is problematic
- law enforcement is inadequate
- there is a lack of adequate recycling plants, e.g. for plastic waste
- there is a lack of inter-institutional cooperation and collaboration.

'Clearly, you cannot begrudge anybody who says that this is not an industry worth investing in – there is no doubt that it takes a lionheart like me to do what I did', Joseph emphasizes.

When asked why he went against the seemingly good advice of his friends and family not to set up ZGL, he had this to say:

> I am definitely not a degree holder but I have the experience required to analyse any industry that I want to operate in. And having studied the waste management industry very closely, I came to the conclusion that I can make it big if I am able to build a company that has the capacity – human, equipment and financial – as well as the development of a customer service culture that ensures that all the people in the company work towards satisfying the customer, who is key to our very survival and growth.

This is the industry that Joseph decided to 'invade' in style and make it big in, using marketing as a platform to ward off the challenges enumerated above. Joseph, the first son of a family of five, had to quit his technical education in the second year to support the family in the caring for his other siblings; however, he took up reading novels as a way of developing himself. He also got inspired reading the success stories of businessmen like Richard Branson and Bill Gates, among others.

Joseph notes that, 'without marketing, there was no way ZGL was even going to get to where it had gotten to'. He stressed the fact that ZGL was set up basically with the customer in mind and that to him the customer is the basis for their success. Joseph is a small business owner who knows nothing about the theory of business administration taught by formal educational institutions but he knew what was most important. Compared with so many companies who over-promise and under-deliver, Joseph says, ZGL under-promises and over-delivers at all times.

ZGL's marketing focus

Joseph lists the following as the basis for ZGL's marketing focus:

1. Continual training of all staff to understand the importance of the customer and the services that can retain him/her (marketing orientation of all staff).
2. Establishment of a monitoring unit that constantly gauges the concerns of customers and gives feedback to the sales and marketing department to inform their relationship with customers.
3. Establishment and advertisement of call centres in all ten regions of the country to give customers a ready platform to give feedback on services rendered or to ask for the provision of services.
4. The printing of ZGL's call centre telephone numbers on all company vehicles as a reminder to customers.
5. Distribution of free refuse containers for customers to cultivate them into paying for refuse removal.
6. Employment of public health educators for the education of customers on good environmental practices.
7. Collaboration with musicians, public figures and experts to educate the public on the consequences of poor sanitation.
8. Sponsorship of educational programmes on sanitation.
9. Provision of financial and logistic support for the general cleaning of communities and suburbs of major towns and cities.

ZGL always seeks to satisfy its customers by continually improving upon its operations to make them cost-effective. They ensure the right quality of personnel are recruited by an external human resource agency and continually trained to build their capacity in order to deliver professional service to their customers. ZGL introduced the concept of supplying free refuse bins as a way of supporting customers who were interested in signing up for their services but did not have the means to buy a bin. Furthermore, to ensure that it delivers on its promise to customers, ZGL continually invests in waste management equipment which ensures that refuse is collected regularly on due days.

Figure 2.2
Zoomlion
truck

Figure 2.3
Man on bike

ZGL from the very onset established a research and monitoring department headed by a retired waste management specialist with the mandate to garner customers' views on the organization's service delivery, as well as to identify the specific needs of the organization's customers. The tricycle concept (a tricycle refuse collector) which ensures easy collection of refuse in areas that are inaccessible to the refuse trucks came out of the research findings of the research and monitoring department. This concept gave the company a competitive edge in winning the contract to partner the government in the implementation of the sanitation module of the National Youth Employment Programme (NYEP). Employees in the company are considered as all part of one family and therefore work as a team to deliver corporate goals.

ZGL has opened a customer relations centre in every regional office to provide a platform for customers to give feedback on company operations and the conduct of its employees. In addition to advertising the locations of these customer relations centres, ZGL also provided telephone numbers for customers to call and get feedback on their requests promptly from well-trained call centre officials. Targets are set and measured on a regular basis to ensure that customer service delivery is high quality.

Joseph is a motivator who ensures that workers are motivated to deliver their best at all times. Regular cross-functional assignments mean that employees work closely to deliver set targets. As a way of ensuring that employees work as a team, the end-of-year bonus scheme is tied to the total corporate performance and not to individual departments.

CASE QUESTIONS

1. How relevant is marketing to an entrepreneurial waste management business?
2. Given the industry challenges enumerated by the Ministry of Local Government and Environment, what specific marketing actions must ZGL take to ensure that they continually remain profitable and ahead of their competition?
3. How important is the involvement of an entrepreneur in the marketing success of his/her firm?

REFERENCES

Ahuja, R.D., Michels, T.A., Walker, M.M. and Weissbuch, M. (2007), 'Ten perceptions of disclosure in buzz marketing', *Journal of Consumer Marketing*, Vol. 24, No. 3, pp. 151–159.

Anderson, S. and Evangelista, F. (2009), 'The entrepreneur in the born global firm in Australia and Sweden', *Journal of Small Business and Enterprise Development*, Vol. 13, No. 4, pp. 642–659.

Bäckbrö, J. and Nyström, H. (2006), 'Entrepreneurial marketing: Innovative value creation', unpublished master's thesis, Jönköping, Sweden.

Begley, T.M. and Boyd, P.P. (1987), 'Psychological characteristics associated with performance in entrepreneurial firms and smaller businesses', *Journal of Business Venturing*, Vol. 2, pp. 79–93.

Birchfield, D. (2000), 'Warm reception for Icebreaker', *NZ Business*, Vol. 14, No. 11, pp. 8–10.

Bjerke, B. and Hultman, C.M. (2002), *Entrepreneurial Marketing: The Growth of Small Firms in the New Economic Era*, Edward Elgar Publishing, Gloucestershire.

Bolton, J.E. (1971), 'Report of the Committee of Enquiry on Small Firms (The Bolton Report)', Cmnd 4811, HMSO, London.

Brown, W.S. (1984), 'A proposed mechanism for commercializing university technology', in Hornaday, J.A., Tarpley, F. Jr., Timmons, J.A. and Vesper K.H. (eds), *Frontier of Entrepreneurship Research*, Babson College, Wellesley, MA, pp. 136–148.

Bygrave, W.D. and Hofer, C.W. (1991), 'Theorizing about entrepreneurship', *Entrepreneurship Theory and Practice*, Vol. 16, pp. 13–22.

Caird, S. (1992), 'Problems with the identification of enterprise competencies and the implications for assessment and development', *Management Education and Development*, Vol. 23, No. 1, pp. 6–17.

Cannon, T. (1991), 'Marketing in small business', in Baker, M.J. (ed.), *The Marketing Book*, 2nd edn, Butterworth-Heinemann, London.

Carson, D. (1993), 'A philosophy for marketing education in small firms', *Journal of Marketing Management*, Vol. 9, No. 2, pp. 189–204.

Carson, D., Cromie, S., McGowan, P. and Hill, J. (1995), *Marketing and Entrepreneurship in SMEs*, Prentice Hall, London.

Chakravarthy, B. and Lorange, P. (2007), 'Driving renewal: The entrepreneur-manager', *Journal of Business Strategy*, Vol. 29, No. 2, pp. 14–21.

Churchill, N.C. and Lewis, V.L. (1983), 'The five stages of small firm growth', *Harvard Business Review*, Vol. 53, pp. 43–54.

Cole, A.H. (1968), 'Introductory remarks', *American Economic Review*, Vol. 58, No. 2, pp. 60–63.

Cowell, D.W. (1987), *Some Insights into the Background and Training of Marketing Executives in the UK*, Plymouth Business School, Plymouth.

Creelman, J. (1992), 'Word of mouth', *Managing Service Quality*, Vol. 2, No. 5, pp. 299–301.

Davis, C.D., Hills, G.E. and LaForge, R.W. (1985), 'The marketing/small enterprise paradox', *International Small Business Journal*, Vol. 3, pp. 31–42.

Davis, C.H. and Klassen, M.L. (1991), 'What entrepreneurs need to know: Are we researching it?', in Hills, G.E. and LaForge, R.W. (eds), *Research at the Marketing/Entrepreneurship Interface*, University of Illinois at Chicago, Chicago, pp. 107–118.

Dodge, H., Fullerton, S. and Robbins, J. (1994), 'Stage of the organisational life cycle and competition as mediators of problem perception for small businesses', *Strategic Management Journal*, Vol. 15, pp. 121–134.

Edwards, T. (2007), 'How I spent my summer cycling through Argentina', *Calgary Herald* (6 September).

European Commission (2003), *Recommendation 2003/361/EC: SME Definition*, online: http://ec.europa.eu/enterprise/enterprise_policy/sme_definition/index_en.htm (accessed 4 May 2009).

Flamholtz, E.G. (1986), *How to Make the Transition from an Entrepreneurship to a Professionally Managed Firm*, Jossey-Bass, San Francisco, CA.

Ford, D., and Rowley, T.P. (1979), 'Marketing and the small industrial firm', *Management Decision*, Vol. 17, No. 2, pp. 144–156.

Foxall, G.R. and Minkes, A.L. (1996), 'Beyond marketing: The diffusion of entrepreneurship in the modern corporation', *Journal of Strategic Management*, Vol. 4, pp. 71–93.

Fulop, L. (1991), 'Middle managers: Victims or vanguards of the entrepreneurial movement?', *Journal of Management Studies*, Vol. 28, No. 1, pp. 25–44.

Geursen, G.M. (1995), 'The parental relationship: A suggested theory for conceptualising structures in small business for decisions, relationships and stress avoidance', UIC/AMA Research Symposium on Marketing and Entrepreneurship, Melbourne.

Gore, C., Murray, K. and Richardson, B. (1992), *Strategic Decision-Making*, Cassell, London.

Gumpert, D.E. (1997), 'Creating a successful business plan', in Bygrave, W.D. (ed.), *The portable MBA in Entrepreneurship*, John Wiley & Sons, New York, pp. 120–147.

Gungaphul, M. and Boolaky, M. (2009), 'Entrepreneurship and marketing: An exploratory study in Mauritius', *Journal of Chinese Entrepreneurship*, Vol. 1, No. 3, pp. 209–226.

Guth, W. and Ginsberg, A. (1990), 'Guest editors' introduction: Corporate entrepreneurship', *Strategic Management Journal*, Vol. 11, pp. 297–308.

Hardy, K.G. (1992), 'Marketing competencies for every manager', *Business Quarterly*, Winter, pp. 51–53.

Hayek, F.A. (1945), 'The use of knowledge in society', *American Economic Review*, Vol. 35, No. 4, pp. 519–530.

Herron, L. and Robinson, R. (1993), 'A structural model of the effects of entrepreneurial characteristics on venture performance', *Journal of Business Venturing*, Vol. 8, pp. 281–294.

Hill, J. (2001), 'A multidimensional study of the key determinants of effective SME marketing activity: Part 1', *International Journal of Entrepreneurial Behaviour and Research*, Vol. 7, No. 5, pp. 171–204.

Hills, G.E. (1987), 'Marketing and entrepreneurship research issues: Scholarly justification?', in Hills, G.E (ed.), *Research at the Marketing/Entrepreneurship Interface*, University of Illinois at Chicago, Chicago, pp. 259–269.

Hills, G.E. (1995), Foreword, in Carson, D., Cromie, S., McGowan, P. and Hill, J. (eds), *Marketing and Entrepreneurship in SMEs: An Innovative Approach*, Prentice Hall, London, pp. xiii–xiv.

Hills, G.E. and LaForge, R.W. (1992), 'Research at the marketing interface to advance entrepreneurship theory', *Entrepreneurship: Theory and Practice*, Vol. 16, Spring, pp. 33–60.

Hills, G.E., Hultman, C.M. and Miles, M.P. (2008), 'The evolution and development of entrepreneurial marketing', *Journal of Small Business Management*, Vol. 46, No. 1, pp. 99–113.

Hoselitz, B.F. (1960), 'Theories of stages of economic growth', in Hoselitz, B., Kuznets, S., Lewis, W.A. and Myint, H. (eds), *Theories of Economic Growth*, Free Press, Glencoe, IL.

Kazanjian, R.K. (1984), 'Operationalizing stage of growth: An empirical assessment of dominant problems', in Hornaday, J.A., Tarpley, F., Timmons, J.A. and Vesper, K.H. (eds), *Frontier of Entrepreneurship Research*, Babson College, Centre for Entrepreneurial Studies, Wellesley, MA, pp. 144–158.

Keefe, L. (2004), 'What is the meaning of "marketing"?', *Marketing News, American Marketing Association*, 15 September, pp. 17–18.

Khilstrom, R.E. and Laffont, J.-J. (1979), 'A general equilibrium entrepreneurial theory of firm formation based on risk aversion', *Journal of Political Economy*, Vol. 87, No. 4, pp. 719–748.

Kirzner, I.M. (1973), *Competition and Entrepreneurship*, University of Chicago Press, Chicago, IL.

Kirzner, I.M. (1985), *Discovery and Capitalist Process*, University of Chicago Press, Chicago, IL.

Knight, F.H. (1921), *Risk, Uncertainty and Profit*, University of Chicago Press, Chicago, IL.

Kotler, P. (1988), *Marketing Management: Analysis, Planning, Implementation and Control*, Prentice-Hall International, London.

Kraus, S., Harms, R. and Fink, M. (2009), 'Entrepreneurial marketing: Moving beyond marketing in new ventures', *International Journal of Entrepreneurship and Innovation Management*, Special Issue. Available online: www.unternehmbar.net/fileadmin/UnternehmBAR_und_SG/SQ/sqlit_kraus.pdf

Levitt, T. (1983), *The Marketing Imagination*, Free Press, New York.

Martin, G. and Staines, H. (1994), 'Management competencies in small firms', *International Journal of Management Development*, Vol. 137, pp. 23–34.

Matthews, C.H. and Scott, S.G. (1995), 'Uncertainty and planning in small and entrepreneurial firms: An empirical assessment', *Journal of Small Business Management*, Vol. 33, No. 4, pp. 34–53.

Middleton, B. and Long, G. (1990), 'Marketing skills: critical issues in marketing education and training', *Journal of Marketing Management*, Vol. 5, No. 3, pp. 325–343.

Miller, D. (1983), 'The correlates of entrepreneurship in three types of firms', *Management Science*, Vol. 29, No. 7, pp. 770–779.

Morris, M.H. and Lewis, P. (1996), 'The determinants of entrepreneurial activity implications for marketing', *European Journal of Marketing*, Vol. 29, No. 7, pp. 31–48.

Morris, M.H., Schindehutte, M. and LaForge, R.W. (2002), 'Entrepreneurial marketing: A construct for integrating emerging entrepreneurship and marketing perspectives', *Journal of Marketing Theory and Practice*, Vol. 10, No. 4, pp. 1–19.

Murray, J.A. (1981), 'Marketing is home for the entrepreneurial process', *Industrial Marketing Management*, Vol. 10, pp. 93–99.

Naman, J.L. and Slevin, D.P. (1993), 'Entrepreneurship and the concept of fit: a model and empirical test', *Strategic Management Journal*, Vol. 14, No. 2, pp. 137–153.

Peitz, M. and Waelbroeck, P. (2005), 'An economist's guide to digital music', *CESifo Economic Studies*, Vol. 51, No. 2/3, pp. 359–429.

Ray, D. (1993), 'Understanding the entrepreneur: entrepreneurial attributes, experience and skills', *Entrepreneurship and Regional Development*, Vol. 5, pp. 345–357.

Reynolds P.L. (2002), 'The need for a new paradigm for small business marketing? What is wrong with the old one?', *Journal of Research in Marketing and Entrepreneurship*, Vol. 10, No. 4, pp. 1–19.

Rhys, G. (1989), 'Smaller car firms – will they survive?', *Long Range Planning*, Vol. 22, No. 5, pp. 22–29.

Romano, C. and Ratnatunga, J. (1995), 'The role of marketing: Its impact on small enterprise research', *European Journal of Marketing*, Vol. 29, No. 7, pp. 9–30.

Say, J.B. (1971), *A Treatise on Political Economy or the Production, Distribution and Consumption of Wealth*, A.M. Kelley Publishers, New York.

Schumpeter, J.A. (1934), *Change and the Entrepreneur*, Cambridge, MA: Harvard University Press.

Sexton, D.L. and Kasarda, J.D. (eds) (1992), *State of the Art of Entrepreneurship*, PWS-Kent Publishing, Boston, MA.

Siu, W. and Kirby, D.A. (1998), 'Approaches to small firm marketing: A critique', *European Journal of Marketing*, Vol. 32, No. 1/2, pp. 40–60.

Smart, D.T. and Conant J.S. (1994), 'Entrepreneurial orientation, distinctive marketing competencies and organisational performance', *Journal of Applied Business Research*, Vol. 10, No. 3, pp. 28–38.

Smith, N.R. (1967), *The Entrepreneur and his Firm: The Relationship between Type of Man and Type of Company*, Michigan State University Press, East Lansing.

Stasch, S.F. and Ward, J.L. (1989), 'Evaluating aggressive marketing strategies for smaller-share firms', *Marketing Intelligence and Planning*, Vol. 7, No. 7/8, pp. 4–15.

Stevenson, H.H., Roberts, M.J. and Grousbeck, H.I. (1989), *New Business Ventures and the Entrepreneur*, Irwin, Homewood, IL.

Stokes, D. (2000), 'Entrepreneurial marketing: A conceptualisation from qualitative research', *Qualitative Market Research: An International Journal*, Vol. 3, No. 1, pp. 47–54.

Storey, D.J. (1994), *Understanding the Small Business Sector*, Routledge, London.

Styles, C. and Seymour, R.G. (2006), 'Viewpoint: Opportunities for marketing researchers in international entrepreneurship', *International Marketing Review*, Vol. 23, No. 2, pp. 126–145.

Teach, R.D. and Tarpley, F.A. (1987), 'Entrepreneurial marketing myopia: The software case', in Hills, G.E. (ed.), *Research at the Marketing/Entrepreneurship Interface*, University of Illinois at Chicago, Chicago, pp. 259–269.

Thomas, R.E. (1991), 'Management competencies', in Silver, M. (ed.), *Competent to Manage*, Routledge, London, pp. 221–227.

Ucbasaran, D., Westhead, P.H. and Wright, M. (2001), 'The focus of entrepreneurial research: Contextual and process issues', *Entrepreneurship Theory and Practice*, Summer, pp. 57–80.

Vanhonacker W.R., Zweig, D. and Chung S.F. (2007), 'A descriptive study of the marketing practices of Chinese Private Entrepreneurs', *Asia Pacific Journal of Marketing and Logistics*, Vol. 19, No. 2, pp. 182–198.

Walras, L. (1954), *Elements of Pure Economics, or, The Theory of Social Welfare*, Allen & Unwin for American Economic Association and Royal Economic Society, London.

Walras, L. (1954), *Elements of Pure Economics, or the Theory of Social Welfare*, Jaffe, W. (trans.), R. D Irwin, Homewood, IL.

Watson, C.H. (2001), 'Small business versus entrepreneurship revisited', in Brockhaus, R.H., Hills, G., Klandt, H. and Welsh, H. (eds), *Entrepreneurship Education: A Global View*, Ashgate Publishing, Burlington, VT, pp. 17–54.

Wynarczyk, P., Watson, R., Storey, D.J., Short, H. and Keasey, K. (1993), *The Managerial Labour Market in Small and Medium-Sized Enterprises*, Routledge, London.

Chapter 3

The role and relevance model of marketing in SMEs

Mike Simpson, Nick Taylor and Jo Padmore

LEARNING OBJECTIVES

After reading this chapter, you will be able to:
- discuss the origin of the role and relevance model
- present the role and relevance model of marketing in SMEs
- discuss the strategies within the model
- explain how the model can be used to aid practitioner SMEs
- critically evaluate the likely value of the model for analysing and predicting the behaviour of SMEs
- present the model in application using case study organizations.

INTRODUCTION

This chapter introduces the role and relevance model of marketing in small- and medium-sized enterprises (SMEs). The role and relevance model of marketing aims to explain how and why SMEs approach the action of marketing the way they do. The role of marketing examines the level of marketing activity in an organization. At a basic level, this could be a job title such as marketing officer or as part of a list of duties undertaken by an individual or team such as an account manager or sales force. On a recent site visit to a Lincoln-based agricultural SME, we were taken to the sales office. En route, we passed a door with a sign saying 'Marketing Department'. Does this tell us anything about the nature of the marketing activity in the company? Probably not very much, but it is a start and we can assume that there is some level of marketing activity going on. The role of marketing in SMEs can be hidden; it is quite likely that an SME will not be so formally structured and marketing activities may be employed in a rather more organic fashion. In a second company visit, the finance director of a construction company explained that everyone in the company could handle most of the jobs. It would not be unusual for the production manager to make sales calls to clients. A third example is a transport company, who often say that their best marketing people are their drivers. It is the drivers who sit in the cafés and talk to other drivers and they often discuss which haulage load is going where and who is the end customer. This information is fed back to the office in an unstructured *ad hoc* way, but is in fact a form of market research and does lead to new business being found. Nobody at the company has the job title of 'marketing manager', but it is clear that marketing is a key activity in the company.

This is then compared with the relevance of marketing to the organization. The relevance level indicates the competitiveness of the organization's markets. Markets which are seen to be highly relevant are characterized by their competitive nature. Competitors sharing similar selling propositions striving to compete and establish advantages will often be characterized by the need for market information and the ability to compile and execute marketing actions. Highly relevant markets are seen as demanding for marketing resources, hence the relationship between the role that marketing plays in an organization can be directly compared with the relevance that marketing has to an organization's markets.

Therefore, this chapter explores how the established principles of marketing apply to SMEs. The underpinning work for this chapter was initiated through case studies of organizations allowing the authors to explore the use of marketing principles and practices in SMEs. This study suggested that the achievement of competitiveness for SMEs was reliant on the relationship between the role that marketing plays in an organization and its relevance to market conditions. These findings were then used to conduct a survey involving a large number of SMEs. The findings enabled the authors to understand the way in which SMEs struggle with the use and value of marketing within their daily business activities. Key to this understanding is the relationship between the role and relevance of marketing in SMEs. The chapter presents a model that goes a long way to explaining the behaviour of SMEs with regard to marketing. The model appears to be viable and could be used to analyse and diagnose the situation regarding marketing within SMEs.

THE ROLE AND RELEVANCE MODEL OF MARKETING IN SMES

The role and relevance model of marketing in SMEs has been thoroughly investigated and tested. The research methods adopted included a literature search and the development and administration of a pilot questionnaire to selected SMEs – a large-scale survey of SMEs within a 60-kilometre radius of Sheffield, UK. In total 853 questionnaires were distributed and 143 usable completed questionnaires were returned, giving a response rate of 17 per cent. In addition, interviews with managers of SMEs and local interest groups and associations (Chamber of Commerce and Industry, Engineering Employers Federation, SME owner-managers, Institute of Management, etc.) were employed to further test the findings. The final results have been published in the *International Journal of Entrepreneurial Behaviour and Research* and the *Journal of Small Business and Enterprise Development* (Simpson *et al.*, 2006; Simpson and Taylor, 2002).

The model offers a straightforward way of diagnosing the situation within an SME. The simplicity of the model allows for a clearer understanding of what is often a complex and messy situation within these companies and their business environment. Some findings suggest a positive link between a company's financial performance and its approach to marketing within the model.

THE ORIGINS OF THE MODEL

The origins of the work were formed when investigating government-funded organizations that offer employment to disabled people. Very often these companies were suppliers to the local authority with virtually guaranteed business at set prices. In such a company would marketing have any part to play in the organization's activities? Would there be a role for a marketing function, a marketing officer, a need for market analysis, for planning and for marketing implementations? In fact, would marketing be totally irrelevant in such circumstances?

This initial work was then extended to other SMEs with varying levels of business guarantees. These guarantees are viewed in the context of each company's competitive environment. Does the level of dynamic market conditions in itself affect the resources and activities the company directs towards marketing? The aim of this work was to evaluate how the need for marketing in these organizations varies with different market conditions. Would a company operating in a highly competitive market have a far higher developed marketing activity and would it be recognizable in comparison with theoretical principles? Would we see a comparative weakening of the role of marketing in companies that exhibited less-challenging market conditions? The model put forward in this chapter not only attempts to explain the nature of marketing in SMEs but goes further to offer potential strategies that companies can adopt to change their competitive position and become more market dominant.

SOME BACKGROUND AND HISTORY

Early work on the role and relevance model began with research on supported employment enterprises (SEEs). SEEs are commercial enterprises that provide meaningful, gainful employment, training and development opportunities for people with a disability. They are often owned and operated by local authorities or charitable trusts. Hence, SEEs are run specifically to provide employment. SEEs, with the exception of Remploy (which is a very large and diverse government-funded business employing disabled people), represent a unique sector of SMEs. It was discovered that the conventional use of marketing activities, tactics and strategies were not used, not understood, not known or the organizations were simply prevented from using public money (via the local authority) for marketing purposes. Yet under these conditions these businesses were expected to compete with other businesses (not all of which were SMEs) in an open market in order to continue to employ and (re)train disabled workers (see Case Study 3.1) (Simpson et al., 2001a; Simpson et al., 2001b).

Following a large number of individual case studies and a national survey of these SEEs (Simpson et al., 2001a; Simpson et al., 2001b) it became clear that there were significant differences among the various companies being studied. There were very big differences in the way these businesses were managed and the degree of autonomy and entrepreneurial activity varied immensely among the organizations. Despite SEEs being a relatively specialized selection of SMEs, there was a very wide range of activities being undertaken by these companies and a very large number of industrial sectors were represented. The use of marketing techniques varied from sophisticated marketing planning activities that were translated into detailed implementation plans to almost openly hostile approaches to marketing often precipitated by local authority interventions. Existing models and frameworks proved to be unsatisfactory in explaining this behaviour or they were focused on entrepreneurial marketing approaches (Carson et al., 1995). This led to some early speculative frameworks and models being developed that could explain the behaviour of these companies. One of the speculative models that seemed to have some general applicability to both SEEs and SMEs was the role and relevance model of marketing.

CASE STUDY 3.1: THE CASE OF BARROW INDUSTRIES

Introduction

Barrow Industries is a supported employment enterprise (SEE). They employ people with disabilities who may lack the skills and confidence to gain normal employment. The aim is that the employees gain work-based skills, grow in confidence and are then able to enter open employment. This in turn creates a vacancy at Barrow for a new recruit and the cycle continues. While doing this, Barrow Industries are also expected to be profit-generating. Support from the public sector is provided in the form of grants and funding to help them achieve these aims. In reality, Barrow makes losses and employees feel too comfortable to want to move into the private sector. The current product range now consists of kitchen furniture (sink units) and uPVC windows. The company's turnover is around £1.1m with roughly 60 per cent of income coming from uPVC windows and 40 per cent from kitchen furniture. Some 95 per cent of the work is for the local authority who use the products for council-owned properties. The company pays competitive wage rates for the industry and this would appear to stifle progression of disabled workers into open employment.

Marketing at Barrow Industries

Marketing is not represented at all well in the organization although the assistant manager has been on an organized marketing course in the past. The company does not see much reason or need for marketing at present because of the ties with the local authority. If the constraints placed on the company by the local authority were to be removed, then the managers felt that the company could expand into other markets and possibly find enough work to double in size. Barrow Industries is not an integrated marketing organization. It has no marketing department; therefore, there is little marketing impact on other departments within the company. The consequences of this are that no marketing research is initiated, no one visits customers and no effort is taken to measure the effectiveness of the company activities. The company business plan contains a single side of A4 regarding marketing strategy. The sales and promotion plan involves sending brochures/price lists to large organizations and offering custom-built windows and kitchen units as required. The strategy relies on the fact that the company is the nominated supplier to a major local authority.

Head office: a centralized approach

The local authority has considerable control over the marketing (and demarketing) activities of the company in that taking advantage of marketing opportunities is actively discouraged. The committee cycle for decision making means that quick responses to new developments are almost impossible. The manager of the company has to seek approval for expenditures as small as £150, despite having the responsibilities of running a £1.1 million turnover business!

The company has a great opportunity to sell to the public and businesses and possibly double in size, employ more disabled workers and become profitable. However, this would require greater resources for marketing and sales and an increase in the workforce to meet demand. The huge constraints placed on the business by the local authority means that there is no autonomy for the managers to run the business.

CASE QUESTIONS AND TASKS

1. Would a company with a guaranteed customer have any need for marketing?
2. How would you advise the managing director of Barrow Industries to address the issues of:
   a) the internal market?

b) the external market?
Ensure you discuss the implications of any actions undertaken.
3. Where would you place Barrow Industries on the continuum of the role and relevance model of marketing used in this chapter? Justify your choice.
4. What action could Barrow Industries reasonably take to improve their marketing efforts? Could they aspire to be a marketing-led organization?

THE ROLE AND RELEVANCE OF MARKETING

The model presented in Figure 3.1 was developed to explain and describe the relationship between the concepts of role and relevance of marketing within SEEs and later expanded into other SMEs. The terminology used tries to describe the type of organization that would be placed in each quadrant within the matrix.

THE ROLE DIMENSION

The role of marketing within an organization can be viewed as an internal focus on the use of marketing by the organization. If marketing plays a big role in the organization then marketing would be expected to be included in all business plans and be used as a way of generating strategies and planning the future of the organization. Marketing would be expected to take up a significant amount of the time spent by senior managers both in planning and in implementing marketing activities. It would also be expected that the organization would have a marketing orientation with the trappings of a marketing department with sufficient staff, resources and a reasonable budget. Marketing strategies and plans would be developed, monitored and evaluated in a systematic way by organizations where marketing plays a major role within the organization.

THE RELEVANCE DIMENSION

The relevance of marketing examines the need for marketing by the organization when operating within the company's particular business environment. The focus of attention here is on the external need for marketing so that the company can remain competitive within its business environment. For example, in a highly competitive industry or a very dynamic industry a company would need a major marketing effort in order to compete and maintain market share. A company not doing this would soon lose market share or be overtaken by changes in the market which were not anticipated. However, in a less competitive and stable industry marketing would be less relevant to the future of the organization. This is especially true if the organization has little or no ambition or ability to grow. It may be that these limitations are artificially imposed but so long as the market remains stable then the relevance of marketing may be regarded as minor. Much of this discussion is already well known to marketers (Porter, 1980).

THE CATEGORIES IN THE ROLE AND RELEVANCE MODEL

Given the two types of dimension above, this leads to four logically distinct categories or quadrants in the model (see Figure 3.1).

Figure 3.1
The role and
relevance of
marketing: the
new model

	Marketing-dominated organization (challengers)	Marketing-led organization (leaders)

Major

ROLE OF MARKETING

(Internal focus)

	Marketing-independent organization (nichers)	Marketing-weak organization (followers)

Minor

Minor   Major

RELEVANCE OF MARKETING

(External focus)

Table 3.1 Some of the dimensions of role and relevance of marketing

Dimensions of role	Dimensions of relevance
Time and effort spent on:	**Business environment assessment:**
Producing business plans for the future.	Guaranteed business.
Creating marketing strategies and plans.	Survival against competition.
Developing new products or services.	Important for expansion of the company.
Designing advertising campaigns.	Highly competitive market.
Maintaining the marketing information database.	Could not survive without marketing.
	More help is needed with marketing.
Producing publicity and press releases.	Intense rivalry between competitors.
Analysing competitors' offerings.	Threats from substitute products/services.
Evaluating the performance of marketing strategies and plans.	Threats from potential new entrants.
	Power of suppliers/buyers.
Tracking the performance of the various promotional and advertising activities.	**Ambitions of the business:**
Marketing organization/structure:	Need for growth of the company.
Marketing department.	Need for market penetration.
Number of personnel in marketing.	Need for market share.
Director-level representation.	Need for new products within the market.
Marketing database.	Need to diversify to grow and develop.

Marketing-led organization (major relevance and major role of marketing)

In a marketing-led organization, marketing is very important to the company's success and plays a major role in the strategic direction of the organization. Marketing is regarded as highly relevant in this type of organization because competition is very fierce in the markets the organization serves. Hence, marketing consumes a lot of organizational effort, but the

35

rewards are seen in maintaining and improving the market share of the organization against tough competition. Noting that SMEs, even the larger ones, usually have a small market share or serve niche markets. The organization would be expected to have a strong marketing orientation and whole-heartedly adopt and adhere to the principles and practices of marketing. Such an organization would be expected to have a marketing department with a reasonable budget, representation of the marketing function at director level on the board of directors and the marketing function should have a significant effect on the strategy adopted by the organization. Such an organization might be viewed as having adopted best practice business sense in dealing with its external business environment. Such a company might be viewed as an SME Leader in the industry.

Marketing-dominated organization (minor relevance and major role of marketing)

In a marketing-dominated organization, marketing would be seen as dominating the strategy making process, using a lot of resources and producing a lot of plans, which may not be very useful because of the markets the organization serves. This is an unbalanced or mismatched approach. Markets served by this type of organization would be 'guaranteed business', e.g. a local authority or much larger company that is the major or sole customer of the organization. Hence, marketing may be seen as an unnecessary burden when considered alongside the 'minor relevance and major role' configuration. In the first case, the marketing department may be powerful and be able to resist reductions in resources. In the second case, the marketing department may have been deliberately boosted to achieve greater market share or penetrate new markets and eventually become a marketing-led organization in the model (see Figure 3.1). Such an organization might be viewed as an SME Challenger in the industry. Any particular case would need to be investigated to decide between these two scenarios. Ideally, there should be a fit with the company's aspirations, corporate strategy and the business environment in which they find themselves. Where there is no clear reason for such a large concentration of resources and effort on marketing, then the company could be described as a marketing-dominated organization and the strategic necessity of such an approach would need urgent attention at senior management level.

Marketing-weak organization (major relevance but minor role of marketing)

A marketing-weak organization could be seen as requiring marketing expertise and effort to maintain its market share and grow in the market it serves. Hence, marketing would be highly relevant for the organization to survive in the longer term against existing competitors but the organization spends little time and effort on marketing activities. Such an organization would be termed a marketing-weak organization in the model (see Figure 3.1) and as such mismatched with the needs of its business environment. The idea that these companies might be called SME Followers might be considered. For example, such an organization would have a very poor marketing effort and may, perhaps, have a sales orientation with a fixation on price rather than any other attribute of the product or service offered. The organization would have no marketing department and have few or no staff able to formulate marketing strategy or carry out basic marketing tasks. Again, there are two simple scenarios to deal with. The first scenario is of a truly ignorant and dysfunctional organization which is unaware of the benefits that marketing can offer and is struggling to maintain its position against its competitors – a marketing-weak organization. The second scenario is of an organization that has no intention of growing and is content to remain small within its chosen market or, alternatively, has tried some marketing but has seen little or no reward for these efforts and has abandoned such marketing efforts, again being content to remain small within its chosen market – an SME Follower. The first scenario can be rectified with some training and effort so long as the business environment indicates that the rewards for marketing effort are there to be had, usually verified via market research. The second scenario could also be rectified but it is likely that complacency has set in and the situation is irretrievable in the minds of the senior managers within the organization. Sometimes being small and less proactive can be used as a survival strategy when the managers feel they have no need to grow and that they are comfortable as they are. This would be an SME Follower strategy.

Marketing-independent organization (minor relevance and minor role)

A marketing-independent organization is similar to a marketing-dominated organization except that it has not been burdened with a big commitment to marketing (see Figure 3.1). Using the same example of guaranteed business with, say, a local authority or much larger company that is the major or sole customer of the organization then here we see there is a balance between the organization's effort in marketing and the needs of the business environment. There is a balance because the organization may have few aspirations beyond the present tied circumstances with the large customer and does not need to engage in marketing efforts to ensure survival. Hence, the role played by marketing is minor and the relevance of marketing is minor because competition is effectively absent altogether. Such an approach could be called an SME Nicher.

The weakness of this approach is that the future of the organization is directly linked to the future of its major customer and the organization has no other strategy or resources to rely upon. Such an organization could be termed a marketing-independent organization as it does not rely upon marketing strategies or marketing initiatives to generate sales. This situation may have been safe in the past but the problems facing local authorities and other large organizations are growing and this may well lead to difficulties in the future for an organization adopting this approach.

STRATEGIES WHICH MAY BE ADOPTED WITH THE NEW MODEL

In developing this new model we have attempted to follow the basic idea of strategic portfolio management:

> Regardless of the particular layout chosen for the matrix, the basic idea behind the portfolio concept remains the same: the position (or box) that a business unit occupies within the matrix should determine the strategic mission and the general characteristics of the strategy for the business.
>
> (Bettis and Hall, 1981, pp. 23–24)

Strategy 1: Develop the business in one or both dimensions

This is where a company has determined that it needs to either develop its commitment to marketing by increasing the time and effort spent in that area or it needs to pay greater attention to the changes in the business environment to capitalize on its investment in marketing. That is, the firm is moving up the matrix to increase the role of marketing (e.g. from a marketing-weak organization to a marketing-led organization). Alternatively, the firm is moving across the matrix from left to right as it becomes more aware of external influences and wishes to capitalize upon the existing role that marketing is playing (e.g. from a marketing-dominated organization to a marketing-led organization). An alternative view, which would be less attractive, is in moving from a marketing-independent organization to a marketing-weak organization. Although, this might prove to be a more natural strategy for a growing SME.

Strategy 2: Stay in the same position

This is where a company has determined that it is in the right position in the matrix for the business environment in which it operates and the role that marketing plays within the company. Such a position might be in the 'marketing-led organization' category or the 'marketing-independent organization' category, depending upon circumstances. It is unlikely that companies in the marketing-weak category or marketing-dominated category would adopt this view, as there are clear imbalances in these categories.

Strategy 3: Reduce the commitment of the firm in one or both dimensions

This is where a company has determined that it has invested too heavily in marketing and the business environment suggests that much of this effort is unnecessary. The company may well choose to move from marketing-dominated towards marketing-independent (or even marketing-led towards marketing-independent) where it has obtained a secure future with a large contract guaranteed for a long time with, say, a local authority or other large organization. However, such an approach would also depend upon the ambitions of the company regarding growth and diversification. If ambitions were limited or restricted in some way by limited resources or by the desire of the owner-manager for a simple business strategy then this approach may be valid.

Strategy 4: Eliminate the commitment of the firm in one or both dimensions

This is where a company has determined that it does not require marketing and is very similar to the previous strategy but here the owner-managers have no desire to grow the business. This strategy may also be adopted in the short term where the firm has cash flow problems and a relatively stable and reliable customer base. However, this strategy will, in the longer term, have a negative effect on the performance of the organization.

ASSUMPTIONS

Given the strategic options above it was assumed that SMEs might want to become marketing-led organizations. The rationale for this thinking was that it was suspected from our research that these types of organizations would perform better and, therefore, have stronger financial results over time that could be used to reinforce the company's position in the longer term. It was also noted that SMEs often start from humble beginnings and that for some owner-managers growth of the business is the only way to ensure that the business

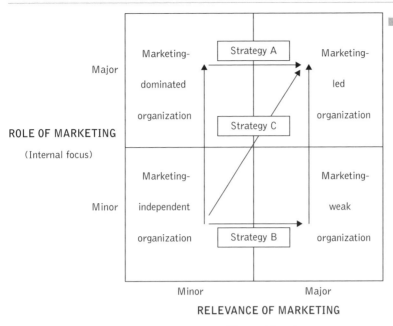

Figure 3.2
Routes or strategies to becoming a marketing-led organization

survives and returns a profit, or at least pays the owner-manager's salary and expenses. While we appreciated that many SMEs were unable to grow and develop and that many owner-managers did not wish to grow their business, the model must provide some guidance according to the principles outlined by Bettis and Hall (1981) on how a company could grow and develop by moving through the matrix in Figure 3.1. Therefore, we suggested that an SME may choose to become a marketing-led organization via three basic routes or strategies through this framework. These three approaches are illustrated in Figure 3.2.

Strategy A (marketing-independent to marketing-dominated to marketing-led) is seen as a proactive approach that would consume a lot of resources initially but would allow the organization to actively search for opportunities within the desired marketplace.

Strategy B (marketing-independent to marketing-weak to marketing-led) is a reactive approach in which the demands of the marketplace in which the company operates/intends to operate require a stronger role for marketing.

Strategy C (marketing-independent to marketing-led) is the normative response where any business environment changes are matched closely with a response from the company by increased marketing effort. Strategy C appears to be rare in SMEs in our experience.

CASE STUDY 3.2: THE CASE OF GRIPPLE LIMITED

Gripple Limited (www.gripple.com), based in Sheffield, UK, was started in 1988 and has grown to a position in 2010 where the company currently employs 230 people and has a turnover of approximately £23 million. The company manufactures a patented device for joining, securing and tensioning wire known as a 'Gripple'. The company has seen excellent growth in turnover with 40 per cent increase in several years during the 1990s and intends to increase turnover to £40 million by 2012. The product has been systematically improved, developed and new patents obtained over the last ten years so that the company now targets four distinct markets. These are the fencing and vineyard trellising market, the construction market, wire-rope connectors and pallet strapping. The Gripple devices were designed to hold a variety of sizes of wires and steel ropes but with the advantage of being fully adjustable for tensioning and positioning.

The company operates in two divisions: an Industrial Division and an Agricultural Division. The company has a marketing department with a marketing director and a marketing assistant; however, everyone in the organization is marketing-oriented. Marketing of the products is sophisticated and the promotional material is of high quality. Target markets are systematically identified and attacked. New product development is seen as vital for the company to grow, with 30 per cent of income expected to come from products developed in the last three years. The strategy is to identify new geographic markets with each new product and systematically attack each market. Margins are kept up by doing much of the work within the company and selling directly to the customer via its own offices abroad rather than via agents and distributors. The company prefers to be close to both its customers and its suppliers and has developed good working relationships. The company uses videos of the products and their applications for both the Gripple and Hang-Fast system. These are useful as product outlines and as training videos. The promotional literature consists of well-designed glossy brochures, quarterly newsletters and press releases on latest developments within the company. The company takes every opportunity to use the media for any new developments. Everything the company does appears to be driven by a marketing orientation. The premises are the very attractively converted Old West Gun Works in Sheffield. The layout of the factory and the offices is very pleasant, open-plan and welcoming to visitors. Products are on display in the reception area. The company uses appropriate high technology to design, manufacture and control the production of Gripples and has highly trained staff on single-status contracts who are also shareholders in the business. The company invites both local university students and industrialists into the company to discuss latest developments. The company sees itself as a leader in the field and an example to other manufacturing companies locally, regionally and nationally, and has won a number of awards for innovation, best new product and best factory. The company uses every opportunity for PR and media coverage of its activities.

The marketplace in which the company operates is extremely competitive, with numerous different types of wire-joining devices. Competitors appear to be ruthless in infringing patents and trademarks. The company has recently successfully defended its rights in the US courts after a company produced a product almost identical to the Gripple called the 'Grabber'. The Gripple Hang-Fast system is seen as a replacement for traditional screw-threaded steel rods and struts. Breaking into this market has been hard but is now being seen as a good method of expansion for the business. Marketing is highly relevant to the future prospects of the company and marketing plays a very strong strategic role within the company. Marketing has a significant impact on the strategic thinking and strategy making process within the company. The overall score using Kotler's (1977) approach to marketing effectiveness is 27 out of 30, which is superior/excellent.

CASE QUESTIONS AND TASKS

1. In your opinion, how does Gripple Limited fit into the role and relevance model of marketing discussed in this chapter? Justify your answer.
2. Given that the company has ambitions to increase turnover to £40 million in 2012, what advice would you give to the managing director of this company? Do you foresee any problems with the company's approach?

CONCLUSIONS

The role and relevance model of marketing remains fairly robust but with a few shortcomings due to the concentration on classical marketing strategy and practices and the omission of postmodern marketing such as networking, internet marketing, e-commerce and e-business. However, there is considerable evidence in the literature that SMEs are also weak in the use of internet methods of marketing (see Sparkes and Thomas, 2001). The omission on network marketing is perhaps a more serious matter (see O'Donnell and Cummins, 1999) that may affect the position of some SMEs in our model and again should be investigated further.

It is worth noting:

> Theories are construed as speculative and tentative conjectures or guesses freely created by the human intellect in an attempt to overcome problems encountered by previous theories and to give an adequate account of the behaviour of some aspects of the world or universe.
>
> (Chalmers, 1982, p. 38)

This is exactly the view we have taken with the model discussed in this chapter. It is not definitive but merely a theoretical development that has been thoroughly tested. It is a step forward that may prove to be a useful development and allow or prompt further discussion of the issues of marketing in SMEs.

Criticism has been received regarding the delineation of the relevance of marketing. The main criticism is that this concept is less well defined and operationalized since it is the result of attempting to define the external business environment and the aspirations of the company with a limited number of questions. These questions may not capture the full impact of the external business environment in which these companies operate. The questions also relied heavily on classical approaches to marketing and business environment issues (e.g. Porter, Ansoff). The position on this axis is also the result of the owner-manager's interpretation of the external business environment and the aspirations for the future of the company. This is dependent upon the owner-manager's own perceptions and strategic awareness, which would be expected to vary considerably across this sample of SMEs (see Hannon and Atherton, 1998). A more carefully selected set of questions may improve the delineation of the concepts plotted on this axis and result in a more robust model.

The model and original data collected also leads to the conclusion that marketing-led organizations perform better and invest more in marketing and this result was expected (Denison and McDonald, 1995). The scatter of data points in the original work could be indicative of SMEs adopting Strategy B, the reactive strategy (see Figure 3.2), through the matrix. Follow-up interviews established that Strategy B is often the most convenient way for SMEs to adopt marketing practices and that often enlightened employees are frustrated by their company's lack of enthusiasm for marketing and the company's confusion of marketing

41

with advertising and selling. Some notable exceptions using the proactive approach of Strategy A were also found but these were often strategically oriented and highly motivated SMEs with a dynamic, well-trained and committed management team. Differentiating between Strategy A, the proactive approach, and Strategy C, the incremental approach, through the matrix was hard to do using the interviews and the telephone interviews in the original research. However, it appeared that few companies were adopting these strategies and that Strategy B was the preferred approach. This result tends to suggest that the stages/growth approach (Siu and Kirby, 1998) may have an effect as many SMEs only felt ready for marketing after reaching a certain size or level of turnover. These SMEs also felt that marketing was only appropriate when the competitive environment required a more carefully considered strategic approach (see McLarty, 1998) and when the company had the resources to implement a marketing programme. Some owner-managers were more hostile towards marketing and thought it expensive and not very effective. Owner-managers with poor experiences of marketing consultants generally took this view.

There is evidence that the role and relevance model of marketing offers some new insights into the behaviour of SMEs regarding marketing. However, there are differences in approach to researching marketing in SMEs and there are different approaches adopted by SMEs towards marketing (Brodie et al., 1997). We recognize that our paradigm may well have left many questions unanswered, particularly where very young companies are involved. However, the role and relevance model does show that SMEs can be categorized to some extent and that these categories do make intrinsic sense of the situation. The categories in the model are good descriptors of the companies studied in our opinion. The original quantitative results are not enough to understand fully what is going on in these companies. Some results appear to partially support other models and ideas such as the stages/growth model (Siu and Kirby, 1998) or the idea that marketing does not evolve in these companies (Brooksbank et al., 1999) and may even regress. This suggests to us that the situation in SMEs regarding their approach to marketing is complex, dynamic and probably influenced by many more factors than we have been able to capture and examine in this work. We conclude that our model is firmly positioned as a contingent model (Siu and Kirby, 1998) but that other factors, which manifest themselves as data in support of other approaches, are probably superimposed on companies in this sample. The sample of SMEs used in our original research may be biased due to the use of mailing lists from local interest groups, whose members may well be more responsive to this type of research. While the role and relevance model may be imperfect, it is self-consistent, adaptable and extendable, and additional questions could be included and scored in a modified questionnaire to cover internet marketing, e-commerce, customer relationship marketing and networking, for example.

We also conclude that some companies have a clear idea of what they are doing about marketing and strategy but many do not know what they are doing and are 'marketing-weak'. The model does offer some new insights into marketing in SMEs and from our results there appear to be certain basic requirements for marketing-led SMEs – that is, a marketing database, an active business plan, marketing representation at board level and a marketing department. This result is not new and is not simply an artefact of the data collection method in our opinion; it does suggest some agreement with the ideas of marketing orientation. The original study did find some limited evidence that marketing-led SMEs had a better financial performance than SMEs in other categories in the model.

Finally, the role and relevance model of marketing in SMEs appears to be a practical and useful theory and has been qualitatively applied over the last few years by undergraduates, postgraduates and a few practitioners when analysing case studies and real companies.

MANAGERIAL AND POLICY IMPLICATIONS

Given the descriptions of the type of SME and the kind of business environment in which they operate, it is possible to qualitatively and also quantitatively determine the quadrant in which a particular SME is positioned. It is then possible to give advice on the strategies, tactics and general marketing approaches that might be used to improve the situation of the SME and develop the SME into a marketing-led company. As a diagnostic tool the role and relevance model is quite useful in this respect. However, we would caution that overly prescriptive approaches to marketing for SMEs would not be beneficial and that careful analysis and interpretation of the particular business situation in which an SME operates should be investigated more thoroughly using many more tools and techniques. That is, the model is a guide that explains only some of the behaviour of SMEs. However, as a starting point for managers and consultants it is a useful approach.

REVIEW QUESTIONS

1. Given the features and dimensions of role and relevance shown in the table in Table 3.1, what other features, activities, concepts, ideas and dimensions of marketing might be used to expand the lists in Table 3.1? How might the (expanded) lists shown in Table 3.1 be operationalized so that reliable data might be collected to populate the model? Justify your answer.

2. Critically review the recent literature concerning marketing in SMEs. Try to examine alternative theoretical approaches and compare and contrast these approaches with the role and relevance model of marketing in SMEs outlined in this chapter.

3. Discuss the way(s) that the performance of SMEs might be determined. Try to establish a methodology that would prove or disprove that marketing-led organizations in the role and relevance model were performing better than those SMEs in other categories in the model.

REFERENCES

Bettis, R.A. and Hall, W.K. (1981) 'Strategic portfolio management in the multi-business firm', *California Management Review*, vol. 24, no.1, pp. 23–38.

Brodie, R.J., Coviello, N.E., Brookes, R.W. and Little, V. (1997) 'Towards a paradigm shift in marketing? An examination of current marketing practices', *Journal of Marketing Management*, vol. 13, pp. 383–406.

Brooksbank, R., Kirby, D.A., Taylor, D. and Jones-Evans, D. (1999) 'Marketing in medium-sized manufacturing firms: The state-of-the-art in Britain, 1987–1992', *European Journal of Marketing*, vol. 33, no. 1/2, pp. 103–120.

Carson, D., Cromie, S., McGowan, P. and Hill, J. (1995) *Marketing and Entrepreneurship in SMEs: An Innovative Approach*, Harlow, UK: Pearson Education.

Chalmers, A.F. (1982) *What Is This Thing Called Science? An Assessment of the Nature and Status of Science and its Methods*, 2nd edn, Milton Keynes: Open University Press.

Denison, T. and McDonald, M. (1995) 'The role of marketing past, present and future', *Journal of Marketing Practice: Applied Marketing Science*, vol. 1, no. 1, pp. 54–76.

Felton, A.P. (1959) 'Making the marketing concept work', *Harvard Business Review*, vol. 37, pp. 55–65.

Hannon, P.D. and Atherton, A. (1998) 'Small firm success and the art of orienteering: The value of plans, planning and strategic awareness in the competitive small firm', *Journal of Small Business and Enterprise Development*, vol. 5, no. 2 (Summer), pp. 102–119.

Kotler, P. (1977) 'From sales obsession to marketing effectiveness', *Harvard Business Review*, November–December, pp. 67–75.

McLarty, R. (1998) 'Case study: Evidence of a strategic marketing paradigm in a growing SME', *Journal of Marketing Practice: Applied Marketing Science*, vol. 4, no. 4, pp. 105–117.

O'Donnell, A. and Cummins, D. (1999) 'The use of qualitative methods to research networking in SMEs', *Qualitative Market Research: An International Journal*, vol. 2, no. 2, pp. 82–91.

Porter, M.E. (1980) *Competitive Strategy: Techniques for Analysing Industries and Competitors*, New York: Free Press.

Simpson, M., Taylor, N. and Padmore, J. (2001a) 'Marketing in supported employment enterprises – Part 1: Case Studies', *Journal of Small Business and Enterprise Development*, vol. 8, no. 3, pp. 233–244.

Simpson, M., Padmore, J. and Taylor, N. (2001b) 'Marketing in supported employment enterprises – Part 2: The national survey results', *Journal of Small Business and Enterprise Development*, vol. 8, no. 4, pp. 301–309.

Simpson, M. and Taylor, N. (2002) 'The role and relevance of marketing in SMEs: Towards a new model', *Journal of Small Business and Enterprise Development*, vol. 9, no. 4, pp. 370–382.

Simpson, M., Padmore, J., Taylor, N. and Frecknall-Hughes, J. (2006) 'Marketing in small and medium sized enterprises', *International Journal of Entrepreneurial Behaviour and Research*, vol. 12, no. 6, pp. 361–387.

Siu, W. and Kirby, D.A. (1998) 'Approaches to small firm marketing: A critique', *European Journal of Marketing*, vol. 32, no. 1/2, pp. 40–60.

Sparkes, A. and Thomas, B. (2001) 'The use of the internet as a critical success factor for the marketing of Welsh agri-food SMEs in the twenty-first century', *British Food Journal*, vol. 103, no. 5, pp. 331–347.

Chapter 4

The marketing concept and market orientation
Evolving definitions of marketing

Felix Mavondo

LEARNING OBJECTIVES

After reading this chapter, you will be able to:
- refresh your understanding of marketing concept and market orientation
- understand why any business, large or small, should be market-oriented
- gain a deeper understanding of the dynamic relationship between market orientation and business growth
- gain a basic knowledge of the issues involved in developing a market orientation, how it might be measured and the complexities that may have to be confronted
- appreciate the barriers that may constrain the development of a market orientation.

INTRODUCTION

It is all too easy to underestimate the role of marketing in small- and medium-sized enterprises (SMEs). But with the growing appreciation of the contribution that SMEs are making in national economic growth there is now a heightened awareness of the importance of marketing – a catalyst for sustaining the growth and sustainability of SMEs. In fact, SMEs are 'raising the bar' in terms of marketing functions, although sometimes they do so unwittingly. They are differentiating their offering to stay in the game, taking some strategic marketing decisions far more regularly. However, the problem is that entrepreneurs often do not fully appreciate the depth of their marketing endeavours.

This chapter, therefore, aims to ferret out the basic principles of growing market strengths through a clearer understanding of two key concepts: marketing concept and market orientation. These are treated with broad generality but the intention is to provide the intellectual base to support further studies.

MARKETING CONCEPT

One of the earliest pieces of codification and definition in the development of the marketing discipline was concerned with the marketing concept. Over 50 years ago Felton (1959) proposed that the marketing concept is:

A corporate state of mind that exists on the integration and co-ordination of all the marketing functions which, in turn, are melded with all other corporate functions, for the basic objective of producing long-range profits.

Kotler *et al.* (1996) suggested that the defining characteristic of the marketing concept is that

[t]he marketing concept holds that achieving organisational goals depends on determining the needs and wants of target markets and delivering the desired satisfaction more effectively and efficiently than competitors do.

At its most fundamental, it is generally understood that the marketing concept holds that, in increasingly dynamic and competitive markets, the companies or organizations most likely to succeed are those that take into account customers' expectations, wants and needs and strive to satisfy these better than their competitors. This is because there is no reason why customers should prefer one organization's offerings unless they are in some way better at serving their wants and needs than those offered by competing organizations.

The American Marketing Association (1985) reviewed more than 25 marketing definitions before arriving at their own definition, which now more or less universally accepted:

Marketing is the process of planning and executing the conception, pricing, planning and distribution of ideas, goods and services to create exchanges that satisfy individual and organizational objectives.

(Ferrell and Lucas, 1987)

This definition places marketing as a process that is performed within an organization. This process may be managed by a dedicated marketing department or by such functions as sales, customer service and IT, among others. This led Webster (1997) to point out that, of all the management functions, marketing has the most difficulty in defining its position in the organization because it is simultaneously culture, strategy and tactics. Webster's argument is that marketing involves the following:

- **Organizational culture** – marketing may be expressed as the 'marketing concept', i.e. a set of values and beliefs that drives the organization towards a fundamental commitment to serving customers' needs as the path to sustained profitability.
- **Strategy** – as strategy, marketing seeks to develop effective responses to changing market environments by defining market segments, and developing and positioning product offerings for those target markets.
- **Tactics** – marketing as tactics is concerned with the day-to-day activities of product management, pricing, distribution and marketing communications such as advertising, personal selling, publicity and sales promotion.

The implementation of the marketing concept presents a big challenge and it is not surprising that many small businesses, including organizations, fall short of these demands. These challenges have given rise to most of the current thinking about market orientation.

MARKET ORIENTATION

Studies by the Market Science Institutes during the 1990s attempted to identify the specific activities that translate the philosophy of marketing into reality (i.e. achieve market orientation). In one of the most widely quoted research streams in modern marketing, Kohli and Jaworski (1990) defined market orientation in the following terms:

> [A] market orientation entails (1) one or more departments engaging in activities geared toward developing an understanding of customers' current and future needs and the factors affecting them, (2) sharing of this understanding across departments, and (3) the various departments engaging in activities designed to meet select customer needs. Thus, a market orientation refers to the organisation-wide generation, dissemination, and responsiveness to market intelligence.

In a parallel study Narver and Slater (1990) defined market orientation as:

> The organizational culture that most effectively and efficiently creates the necessary behaviours for the creation of superior value for buyers and, thus, continuous superior performance for the business.

From this work a number of components of market orientation were developed:

- **customer orientation** – understanding customers well enough continuously to create superior value for them
- **competitor orientation** – awareness of the short- and long-term capabilities of competitors
- **inter-functional coordination** – using all company resources in an integrated way to create value for target customers
- **long-term profit focus** – as the overriding business objective.

Achieving a market orientation involves the following activities:

1. The focus of the business must be the customer for managers and employees.
2. The business must listen to the customer to understand and act on current and latent needs.
3. Assess what the business does best relative to competitors to gain a competitive advantage.
4. Accurately define and target specific customers.
5. Aim for long-term profitability, not sales volume.
6. Seek to deliver superior customer value and hence receive customer loyalty.
7. Continuously measure and manage customer expectations.
8. Build long-term relationships with customers and suppliers.
9. Commit to continuous improvement and innovation.
10. Grow with partners and alliances to meet evolving needs.

There is growing evidence that achieving market orientation is associated with superior financial performance and other internal company benefits, such as employee commitment and *esprit de corps*, human resource management and employee satisfaction, among others.

Market orientation has been studied in many diverse situations including large and small commercial organizations, strategic business units (SBUs), hospitals, universities, services and manufacturing companies, commodity and differentiated product marketing, hotels and lodges, entrepreneurial businesses, the biotechnology industry, retail outlets, banks and other financial services, textile and garment manufacturing, private and publicly owned companies, property developers, food processing, salespeople, daily newspapers, export businesses, foreign affiliates of major corporations, non-profit organizations, international hotels and state-owned enterprises, among many others. For a full review see Gonzalez-Benito and Gonzalez-Benito (2005) and Shoham *et al.* (2006). This makes market orientation one of the most researched marketing concepts and demonstrates it importance and centrality in understanding the role of marketing in organizations and its place in business performance and in developing and implementing business strategies.

Despite these obvious benefits, there are also indications suggesting that there are substantial barriers to achieving market orientation (Harris, 1998; Piercy *et al.*, 2002). These may include the tendency of businesses to focus on internal activities, poor understanding of current and emerging customer needs, lack of commitment to market orientation by senior and middle management, failure to develop an enduring culture to support market-oriented behaviours and inability to see that all the activities of the business are touch points for customer satisfaction.

When thinking about the market orientation of a business, one needs to put it into the broader context of marketing strategy and competitive positioning. The following observations highlight the issues:

- For a business to reach its marketing potential, it must move beyond marketing activities (tactics), to marketing as a company-wide issue of real customer focus (culture) and competitive positioning (strategy). Most research and anecdotal evidence suggests that marketing has generally been highly effective in tactics, but only marginally effective in changing culture, and largely ineffective in the area of strategy. This is because marketing is often not represented in the highest levels of the decision making.
- A central component to successful implementation of market orientation is a deep understanding of the market and the customer throughout the company and building the capabilities for responsiveness to market changes. This assists in building and implementing a marketing strategy.
- The marketing process must be viewed as truly inter-functional and cross-disciplinary. Market orientation is not simply the responsibility of the marketing department. Competitive positioning strategies that provide superior service and value, and innovation to build defensible competitive positions, rely on the coordinated efforts of many functions and people within the organization.
- Businesses need to have a deep understanding of competitors, their strategies and offerings. This should be achieved by adopting the customer's perspective. Viewing the product or service from the customer's viewpoint is often difficult, but without that perspective a marketing strategy is highly vulnerable to attack from unsuspected sources of competition. Competition can come from existing competitors, newcomers to the market and from new technologies meeting the same customer need. Thus an organization needs to have a wide peripheral vision.
- Market orientation should not be viewed as being nice to customers (although this is good). It must always be calibrated to generate long-term financial performance for the organization, not simply short-term results.
- The marketing concept and market orientation must be placed in the context of other drivers of the values and approaches of the organization. A culture that emphasizes customers as key stakeholders in the organization should not be inconsistent with

recognition of the needs and concerns of shareholders, employees, managers and the wider social context in which the organization operates. This is important because meeting the needs of the customer more effectively than competitors is the true source of superior financial performance (meeting the needs of shareholders), a guarantee for employment generation and better pay (for managers and employees) and the true source of reputation and social capital (meeting the needs of society).

■ A market orientation may be less important in certain circumstances than in others. Where the product is essentially a commodity with limited opportunities for value-adding, other approaches to meeting the customer needs may be appropriate, such as low-cost production and distribution. Where the nature of the service is tightly defined by the contract such as in the construction industry market, orientation becomes the ability to meet these contractual requirements. However, in almost all these situations, being market-oriented gives a competitive advantage compared with not being market-oriented.

■ The evolution of market orientation suggests that it had taken hold in the US by the 1940s, in western Europe by the 1950s and in eastern Europe by the 1980s. It has been implemented in developing economies increasingly since the 1990s. These generalized historical periods suggest market orientation becomes increasingly important as competition for customers increases, when customers have choices as to diverse products and suppliers, and when supply exceeds demand and customer consumption becomes more sophisticated. As a result of these observations, researchers in the USA have consistently found a positive relationship between market orientation and financial performance; those in western Europe have found mixed results. In other regions the results have been even more mixed, with some researchers finding positive relationships, others finding no significant relationships and even negative relationships to financial performance and other measures. These observations suggest that there may be issues concerning the measures of market orientation (is it understood the same way in different contexts?), the different conditions under which market orientation is most beneficial (presence of moderators) or the stage of development of the economy.

■ Most research on market orientation has depended on asking managers to evaluate the level of market orientation of their business (on the assumption that they have a broad view of the organization). This may be appropriate for strategy and competitive positioning studies, but the critical issue is the evaluation of market orientation at employee level since employees are at the coalface and are tasked with the actual implementation of market orientation. This may partly explain the inconsistencies in research findings.

■ The best way to evaluate market orientation would appear to be asking customers, suppliers and distributors to evaluate the market orientation of the business. This is the most direct way to evaluate market orientation. After all, it is the customer who pays the bills for the company and their perspective must be considered the most important!

The next section attempts to capture the way marketing orientation has been assessed. The tool for assessing market orientation has been derived from Narver and Slater (1990) and it focuses on the dimension of market orientation discussed in the previous sections. Because of the diverse situations in which the scale has been used, there have been a variety of modifications to fit the context, modifications to accommodate language differences and modifications to suit the level of respondents. The fundamentals of the scale, however, have been largely maintained, allowing studies to be compared and findings interpreted.

MEASURING A FIRM'S MARKET ORIENTATION

A basic outline is presented, dealing with the core components of market orientation.

Table 4.1 *Customer orientation*

	Strongly agree	Agree	Neither	Disagree	Strongly agree	Don't know
Information about customer needs and requirements is collected regularly	5	4	3	2	1	0
Our corporate objective and polices are aimed directly at creating satisfied customers	5	4	3	2	1	0
Levels of customer satisfaction are regularly assessed and action taken to improve matters where necessary	5	4	3	2	1	0
We put major effort into building stronger relationships with key customers and customer groups	5	4	3	2	1	0
We recognize the existence of distinct groups or segments in our markets with different needs and we adapt our offerings accordingly	5	4	3	2	1	0

Total score for customer orientation (out of 25):

Table 4.2 *Competitor orientation*

	Strongly agree	Agree	Neither	Disagree	Strongly agree	Don't know
Information about competitor activities is collected regularly	5	4	3	2	1	0
We conduct regular benchmarkings against major competitor offerings	5	4	3	2	1	0
There is rapid response to major competitor offerings	5	4	3	2	1	0
We put major emphasis on differentiating ourselves from the competition on factors important to customers	5	4	3	2	1	0

Total score for competitor orientation (out of 20):

Table 4.3 Inter-functional coordination

	Strongly agree	Agree	Neither	Disagree	Strongly agree	Don't know
Information about customers is widely circulated and communicated throughout the organization	5	4	3	2	1	0
The different departments in the organization work effectively together to serve customer needs	5	4	3	2	1	0
Tensions and rivalries between departments are not allowed to get in the way of serving customers effectively	5	4	3	2	1	0
Our organization is flexible to enable opportunities to be seized effectively rather than hierarchically constrained	5	4	3	2	1	0

Total score for inter-functional coordination (out of 20):

Table 4.4 Long-term perspectives

	Strongly agree	Agree	Neither	Disagree	Strongly agree	Don't know
We place greater priority on long-term market share gain than short-term profits	5	4	3	2	1	0
We put greater emphasis on improving our market performance than on improving internal efficiencies	5	4	3	2	1	0
Decisions are guided by long-term considerations rather than short-run expediency	5	4	3	2	1	0

Total score for long-term perspectives (out of 15):

Table 4.5 Organizational culture

	Strongly agree	Agree	Neither	Disagree	Strongly agree	Don't know
All employees recognize their role in helping to create satisfied end customers.	5	4	3	2	1	0
Reward structures are closely related to external market performance and customer satisfaction	5	4	3	2	1	0

(continued)

■ *Table 4.5* (continued)

	Strongly agree	Agree	Neither	Disagree	Strongly agree	Don't know
Senior management in all functional areas give top importance to creating satisfied customers	5	4	3	2	1	0
Senior management meetings give high priority to discussing issues that affect customer satisfaction	5	4	3	2	1	0

Total score for organizational culture (out of 20):

Grand total (out of 100):

Interpretation

80–100 indicates a high level of market orientation. Scores below 100 can still, however, be improved.

60–80 indicates moderate market orientation – identify the areas where most improvement is needed.

40–60 shows a long way to go in developing a market orientation. Identify the main gaps and set priorities for action to close them.

20–40 indicates a mountain ahead of you! Start at the beginning and work your way through. Some factors will be more within your control than others. Tackle those first.

These are only guidelines and should be used with care, taking into account many factors identified above that might affect the scores.

POTENTIAL CONCERNS ABOUT MARKET ORIENTATION

A study of market orientation would not be complete without addressing some of the issues it raises:

1. Customers do not always know what they want. The average consumer is concerned with solving today's problem and satisfying the current need. The customer may be unaware of the technological possibilities but the business may be. This has led some researchers to question the value of market orientation, especially in technology products. The business must attempt to anticipate future needs (latent needs) by carefully studying current products and the benefits they deliver. One way to achieve this is to find what customers *do not like* about the current product or service offering or what customers find frustrating when using the current product. This leads to a proactive market orientation and prepares the organization to address the needs as they emerge.
2. Researchers have largely used perceptual measures of performance. For a variety of reasons researchers have not captured the relationship between market orientation and

'hard' financial data. This has made it harder to convince sceptical managers to commit to market orientation. Future work needs to concentrate on addressing this deficiency.

3. Managers often ask, 'By how much should we increase our market orientation and what is the return on that investment?' This is a difficult question to answer given the current stage of development of market orientation. The metrics of marketing orientation are evolving but at the moment it is difficult to say exactly what the benefits of increasing market orientation by one unit would be in terms of return on investment. Part of the problem is that different scales are used to measure the same concept and only limited research links the degree of market orientation to actual dollar performance of organizations.

4. Does the organization need to be highly customer-oriented, competitor-oriented and have high inter-functional coordination? At the conceptual level the answer is 'Yes', but in practice this may be complicated. Where the business for whatever reason has no competitors (e.g. new innovation), there may be no need to worry about competitors but, as noted above, competition can come from unexpected sources so the organization needs to be aware of this. Most of the research on market orientation has been on large organizations, hence the need to understand small businesses where there are no departments or separate marketing functions. This is especially true of very small business where all the marketing activities may be the responsibility of one individual. The point is that all these activities must be performed irrespective of the size of the business or its structure.

REVIEW QUESTIONS

1. What do you understand by market orientation?

2. What is the relationship between the marketing concept and market orientation?

3. Is market orientation appropriate for small businesses? Use appropriate examples to support your answer.

4. What are the barriers that SMEs are likely to encounter in implementing a market orientation?

GROUP ACTIVITY

Choose a company that falls within the conventional categorization of SMEs. Evaluate the company's level of market orientation using the guideline measures provided in this chapter. On the basis of your analysis, suggest strategic choice(s) that the company could make to strengthen its market position. Your report should clearly justify your recommendations.

SELECTED REFERENCES

American Marketing Association (AMA) (2007) Definition of marketing. Available at: www.marketing power.com/aboutmam/pages/defintionofmarketing.aspx (accessed on 26 October 2010)

Gonzalez-Benito, Oscar and Gonzalez-Benito, Javier (2005) Cultural vs operational market orientation and objective vs subjective performance: Perspective of production and operation. *Industrial Marketing Management*, 34, 797–829.

Harris, L. (1996) Cultural obstacles to market orientation. *Journal of Applied Marketing*, 2(4), 36–56.

Kohli, A.K. and Jaworski, B.J. (1990, April) Market orientation: The construct, research propositions and managerial implications. *Journal of Marketing*, 54, 1–18.

Kotler, P., Armstrong, G., Saunders, J. and Wong, V. (2010) Principles of marketing. *Financial Times*. Prentice: Prentice Hall.

Narver, J.C. and Slater, S.F. (1990, October) The effect of market orientation on business profitability. *Journal of Marketing*, 54, 20–35.

Piercy, N.F. and Harris, L.C. (2002), Market orientation and retail operatives experiences. *Journal of Business Research*, 55, 261–273.

Shoham, A., Ruvio, A., Vigoda-Gadot, E. and Schwabsky, N. (2006) Market orientation in the non-profit and voluntary sector: A meta-analysis of their relationship with organisational performance. *Nonprofit and Voluntary Sector Quarterly*, 35, 453–476.

Webster, F.E. (1994) *Market Driven Management*. London: Wiley.

Chapter 5

The entrepreneurship marketing environment

Ayantunji Gbadamosi

LEARNING OBJECTIVES

After reading this chapter, you will be able to:

- understand the meaning of the SME marketing environment
- discuss the nature of the SME marketing environment
- differentiate between the external and internal marketing environments of SMEs
- understand the impact of macro- and micro-environmental factors on the marketing activities of SMEs
- explain environmental scanning and why it is important in SME marketing
- discuss the relevance of SWOT analysis to SME marketing
- understand how SMEs cope with turbulence in the marketing environment.

INTRODUCTION

Irrespective of the size and scale of their operations, business organizations operate within environments which either directly or indirectly influence how they plan, organize and execute their marketing activities. Similarly, regardless of whether they are small or medium-sized enterprises (SMEs) or large corporations, these environments contain certain factors and forces that combine to impinge on how they relate to their customers. Therefore, it is logical to state that having an in-depth understanding of the marketing environment is fundamental to the study of SME marketing. Now, let us first consider a working definition of 'marketing environment' that will guide our discussion in this chapter. We may simply define marketing environment as the totality of factors, actors and their impacts that presently influence or in the future might influence how marketers go about satisfying the needs and wants of their target market.

From this definition we can deduce that organizations interact with the various elements of the environment, and the extent to which they are able to do this effectively is significantly determined by the characteristic of the organization involved. This is where the distinction between the context of SMEs and large corporations can be appreciated. Although there is a clear lack of consensus on what constitutes the definition of SMEs, because they vary across sectors and most importantly across different countries of the world, there is agreement that they are smaller in many areas when compared with their large corporation counterparts. This suggests that the impact of the environmental factors on these organizations and the way they respond to them might be dissimilar, hence our need to look into marketing environment in the context of SMEs.

THE NATURE OF THE SME MARKETING ENVIRONMENT

Although SMEs have limitations that sometimes distinguish them from large corporations, the marketing environment where they operate is *multifaceted* and *dynamic*, as is the case for other organizations. This explains why an SME cannot assume that consumers' taste and needs two years ago will remain the same now, or assume that the laws governing the importation of their productive inputs will remain the same perpetually. The constant interaction of these many dynamic factors comes with some degree of uncertainty; hence, the marketing environment is *complex*. Let us now consider the categories of each of these factors for a better appreciation of how they impact the marketing activities of SMEs.

In its broad sense, marketing environment can be categorized into internal and external environments, and the latter can be categorized further into macro and micro factors. These different categorizations explain the marketing environment from the perspective of the closeness of each of the factors to the SMEs, and also indicate the extent of control that they have in fine-tuning the factors towards satisfying their target markets.

Internal marketing environment

The internal marketing environment of SMEs consists of factors within the organization, including financial resources, human resources, production facilities, and other factors that can be categorized as part of the organization's resources. By their nature, SMEs have a considerable level of control over these factors and can manipulate or combine them in various

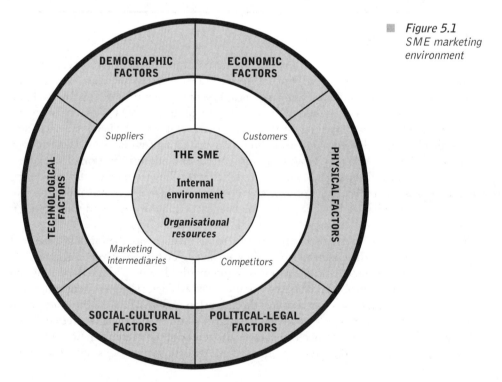

Figure 5.1
SME marketing
environment

forms when responding to threats or opportunities in the external marketing environment that affect their provision of goods and services needed by their target market.

External marketing environment

Some factors are external to business organizations and exert considerable influence on how they function to achieve their objectives. These factors are shown in Figure 5.1. Owing to the nature of the external environment factors, they are uncontrollable for SMEs. These factors can be classified further on the basis of whether their effects relate to all organizations or a particular organization. Those external factors that are quite broad in scope and by nature influence the marketing activities of all business organizations are called *macro-environmental factors*. Basically, they are economic factors, political-legal factors, socio-cultural factors, technological factors, demographical factors and physical environmental factors. The other group of external factors, which are particularly related and very close to the firm, are called *micro-environmental factors* and consist of customers, competitors, suppliers and channel members. Each of these factors is now discussed in turn.

MACRO-ENVIRONMENT OF MARKETING

Economic environment

Significant factors affecting the economic environment include interest rates, inflation rates, unemployment rates, income distribution, savings, credit availability and a host of others. Hence, it is logical to state that this part of the marketing environment embraces the overall health of the economic system in which the organization operates. More specifically, it deals with the management of demand in the economy. Thus, it is crucial for SME marketers to understand the effects of these economic variables because they influence costs, prices and demand for their goods and services. Government often directs the affairs of the economy through the use of interest rate controls, taxation policy and government expenditure. There is hardly any better example to cite here than the prevailing global economic crisis. The effect of this on consumer spending has led to several undesirable changes in business organizations. These include downsizing, rationalizing resources more than ever before and in some cases folding up.

In an economy that is characterized by a high level of inflation, unemployment will pose great challenges to SMEs operating in that environment. From the international marketing perspective, marketing activities like exporting, franchising and direct foreign investment depend greatly on how healthy the economy of the host country is. SMEs operating at this level need to know the level of economic development in prospective target countries. Similarly, at that level, knowing the exchange rates between countries is imperative for the success of SMEs. They also need to gauge relevant indicators such as the gross domestic product (GDP) and the gross national product (GNP) of the economy in order to assess how healthy it is at any point in time. In summary, SMEs must be aware of the standard and cost of living of the society where they operate as this will go a long way towards identifying areas of opportunity.

Political-legal environment

This dimension of the marketing environment has to do with government regulations of businesses of all kinds and the existing relationships between businesses and government.

Imagine a society where there are no regulations: things would go in different directions; people would invest in every and any type of business in such a society. In this situation unscrupulous business operators might produce any product without due care for the safety of consumers. At best, the situation would be chaotic. This illustrates the relevance of the political-legal sector of the marketing environment. Basically, this part of the environment consists of laws, public officials, legislative bodies, courts and political structures and actors that work interactively to regulate business transactions in a particular society. This is a fundamental part of the macro-environment that SMEs cannot afford to ignore as it determines what they can and cannot do in their marketing activities. There are a variety of these legal frameworks. Examples include regulations on business formation, laws on pricing, competition, modes of distribution, methods of marketing communications and employment. One of the key challenges of this environment is that SMEs have to be familiar with the existing laws that guide commercial activities not only at the federal level but also at the state and local levels. In most cases, they will also have to consider international laws guiding business practices, either because they purchase some of their inputs from overseas companies or because they have business commitments abroad. The following are examples of rules and regulations in the UK and European Union (EU) that are relevant to SMEs and could impact on their marketing activities.

Table 5.1 Small Business Act for Europe

10 principles to guide the conception and implementation of policies at both EU and Member state level concerning SMEs
1. Create an environment in which entrepreneurs and family businesses can thrive and entrepreneurship is rewarded
2. Ensure that honest entrepreneurs who have faced bankruptcy quickly get a second chance
3. Design rules according to the "Think Small First" principle
4. Make public administrations responsive to SMEs' needs
5. Adapt public policy tools to SME needs: facilitate SMEs' participation in public procurement and better use State Aid possibilities for SMEs
6. Facilitate SMEs' access to finance and develop a legal and business environment supportive to timely payments in commercial transactions
7. Help SMEs to benefit more from the opportunities offered by the Single Market
8. Promote the upgrading of skills in SMEs and all forms of innovation
9. Enable SMEs to turn environmental challenges into opportunities
10. Encourage and support SMEs to benefit from the growth of markets.

Source: http://eur-lex.europa.eu/LexUriServ/LexUriServ.do?uri=COM:2008:0394:FIN:en:PDF (accessed 10 April 2010). A set of new legislative proposals that are guided by the "Think Small First" principle.

The information in Table 5.1 is from the Small Business Act for Europe which was adopted in June 2008. It indicates the commitment of the EU to promoting the growth of SMEs in the region and that the body recognizes the significant role of the SMEs in the economy. The EU is working towards improving the sector through the partnership approach. The effort is aimed at improving the overall approach to entrepreneurship in the EU and provides more SME-friendly business environments in the form of various packages to encourage SMEs to grow. The onus is on the SMEs to explore the opportunities in the package and similar provisions for the benefit of their entrepreneurial endeavours.

Table 5.2 *Sale of Goods Act 1979 (c.54) – Part II: Formation of the contract*

Contract of sale

1. A contract of sale of goods is a contract by which the seller transfers or agrees to transfer the property in goods to the buyer for a money consideration, called the price.
2. There may be a contract of sale between one part owner and another.
3. A contract of sale may be absolute or conditional.
4. Where under a contract of sale the property in the goods is transferred from the seller to the buyer the contract is called a sale.
5. Where under a contract of sale the transfer of the property in the goods is to take place at a future time or subject to some condition later to be fulfilled the contract is called an agreement to sell.
6. An agreement to sell becomes a sale when the time elapses or the conditions are fulfilled subject to which the property in the goods is to be transferred.

Source: Office of Public Sector Information (2010).

Table 5.2 is an extract of the legislation that relates to sales of goods in the UK. This Act, like many others, is in place to ensure a harmonious market system where parties to commercial transactions will have something to use as a frame of reference for their dealings. Table 5.3 highlights the rights of the consumers in relation to their marketing interactions. It covers their shopping rights, their right to have products fit their intended purposes, the right to get a refund when this is not the case, and directions on how to get help and what to do if things go wrong in their transactions.

Table 5.3 *Consumer rights and where to get help*

Shopping rights

When you go shopping anything you buy is covered by a law called the Sale of Goods Act 1979. This means that when you buy a product it should be:
* as described
* fit for purpose
* of satisfactory quality

As described

This means that the item you buy should be the same as any description of it. A description could be what the seller has said to you about the item or something written in a brochure.

Fit for purpose

What you buy should be able to do the job that it was made for. Also, goods should be fit for any specific purpose you agreed with the seller at the time of sale. For example, if you were looking to buy a printer and asked the seller if it would work with your computer then that advice has to be correct.

Refunds

You can get your money back if an item is:
* faulty (it doesn't work properly)
* incorrectly described
* not fit for purpose

If you find that the item doesn't meet these requirements you can ask for your money back, as long as you do so quickly. Alternatively, you can request a repair or replacement or claim compensation.

You do not have a right to a refund if you:
* change your mind about a product
* decide you do not like it

(continued)

Table 5.3 (continued)

Receipts and proof of purchase
You don't have to have a receipt to get a refund. However a seller can ask you to provide some proof of purchase. This could be a credit card bill or bank statement.

Items bought in a sale
If you buy anything in a sale you are still covered by the Sale of Goods Act. You wouldn't get a refund if:
• you were made aware of a fault before the sale
• the fault should have been obvious when you bought the item

Where to get help if things go wrong
First, ask the company to put things right – put your complaint in writing. If you are still not happy you may have to take the matter to court. Contact your local Citizens Advice Bureau for advice.
    You can also get in touch with the local council's Trading Standards office.

Your rights when you buy a service
If you are using a service such as hiring a builder or using a mechanic then you are covered by the Supply of Goods and Services Act 1982. This means that any goods supplied must be of satisfactory quality and any service you buy must be:
• carried out with reasonable care and skill
• carried out within a reasonable time and at a reasonable charge (if no charge is agreed in advance)
What 'reasonable' means will be different in each case. If you have a problem, you may need to ask the Citizens Advice Bureau what 'reasonable' is for your situation.

What to do if you have a problem
If you have a problem, contact the service supplier straight away to sort out the problem. If you are still not happy, check if they belong to a trade association. An example would be a carpenter belonging to the Federation of Master Builders. You will find trade association details on a company's adverts and bills. The association may be able to help you settle a dispute.
    If you can't sort out the problem, you may have to go to court. Contact your local Citizens Advice Bureau for advice.

Product safety and recalls
If you are worried about the safety of anything you have bought, for example a child's toy, contact your council's trading standards office.
    You can also contact Consumer Direct.

Source: Directgov (2010).

All of these legislations guiding business practices has been put in place for a number of reasons which can be summarized as: (1) to protect companies from each other such as preventing unfair competition, (2) to protect consumers from unfair business practices such as deceptive advertising and (3) to protect the interest of society against unrestrained business behaviour (Kotler *et al.*, 2008). Therefore, SMEs not only need to have a good knowledge of these existing regulations and guidelines but also need to adhere to them.

In the UK, there are many regulatory bodies, some of which are government-instituted, and their impact on how SMEs conduct their marketing activities cannot be overestimated. Examples include the Office of Communications (Ofcom), which is the communication regulator that regulates the TV and radio sectors, fixed-line telecommunication and mobiles, plus the radio frequencies which wireless devices use in the UK. Ofcom works independently of the government and concentrates solely on protecting the interests of citizens and consumers (see www.ofcom.org.uk/what-is-ofcom). Another example is the Office of Fair Trading (OFT) which has the mission of making markets work efficiently and effectively for consumers in the UK by promoting and protecting their interests. It ensures that businesses are fair and competitive (see www.oft.org.uk). Of course there are many more organizations that have no direct linkage to government but equally influence marketing. Trade associations and pressure groups are non-governmental, yet often drive home their points on acceptable standards of conduct by marketers. In some countries, especially developed ones like the United States and the UK, activities of consumer movements are more pronounced. These consumerists strive to make marketers conform to standards that enhance consumers' welfare. The basic rights of consumers often advocated in consumerism are highlighted in Table 5.4.

Table 5.4 Basic rights of consumers

	Consumers' Rights
1	The right to safety
2	The right to be informed
3	The right to choose
4	The right to be heard
5	The right to satisfaction of basic needs
6	The right to redress
7	The right to education
8	The right to a healthy environment

Source: Consumers International (2010).

The first four consumer rights listed in Table 5.4 have their origin in the declarations of the former US president John F. Kennedy, while the last four are new additions originating from consumer movements like Consumer International. SMEs need to be aware of these rights and the implications they have for their transactions as they work towards satisfying their target markets.

Socio-cultural environment

The socio-cultural environment encompasses marketers' relationship with the society and the culture of that society. It is concerned with how people live in relation to their day-to-day activities, which could have a very close link to what they buy, why they buy them, where they buy them, how they buy them, and how often they buy them. This is why it is stated that culture influences our perception of things (Gbadamosi, 2004). In this sense, this segment of marketing environment is undoubtedly important to SMEs and worth thorough investigation. Essentially, factors that make up the socio-cultural environment include religious beliefs, languages spoken, the type of food consumed, the types of dress and family patterns. Since SMEs directly or indirectly produce goods and services for people in the society, such products must be positioned in such a way that conforms to the mores and values of that society, because most consumers are strongly influenced by their socio-cultural environment. In many instances the sale of a product that is forbidden in one society might be culturally acceptable in others. For instance, selling flowers is a very successful venture in the UK as consumers use them to express their emotions such as for love and bereavements. The giving of flowers on Valentine's Day, Mothers' Day and Christmas is on the increase and indicates how successful this business has been in this cultural setting. However, this is unlikely to be the case in most developing countries, where people express their feelings in different ways.

Another major change in socio-cultural environments is brought about by the changing role of women in the society (Lamb *et al.*, 2010). The increased number of women in the labour force has had dramatic effects on societal consumption patterns. It is not that long ago that the belief of most people in the society was that a woman's place was in the home. When compared with men, they had far less employment opportunities. Obviously this trend and belief has changed in recent times. A recent publication of the Office for National Statistics indicates that the percentage of women in employment increased from 56 per cent in 1971 to 70 per cent in 2005 (ONS, 2006), and this marked increase also reflects the number of jobs that women do now compared with the previous decades. The 2008 *Focus on Gender* publication of the Office of National Statistics shows that both men and women filled similar numbers of jobs – estimated at about 13.6 million each – compared with 1985 when men filled 2 million more jobs than women (ONS, 2008a). Family consumption patterns have also changed. Indeed, as SMEs often target relatively small customer groups, tracking these changes will provide directions on how to achieve competitive advantage. Knowledge of this environment will ensure that the product or service they offer to their targeted niche is distributed through the right outlets, priced effectively and promoted in such a way that will reach the target audience effectively. For example, marketing communication messages which used to be targeted only at husbands (as the family breadwinners) today are used to target couples in light of the changes in the family buying roles.

Technological environment

The technological environment embraces the technical skills and equipment that enhance the conversion of inputs into outputs and is pivotal to the success of businesses and society in general. The simple process of how this takes place is demonstrated in Figure 5.2.

Technology supports wealth creation and has a very strong influence on marketing activities. It is, therefore, not surprising that all over the world technology is constantly evolving. We now have inventions that make marketing transactions more efficient and effective compared with the not too distant past. The changes to computing, telecommunication and printing in recent times are just a few examples of how the technological environment changes and influences the marketing of goods and services. While some businesses may not be able to afford newly developed and highly sophisticated equipment that would increase production due to financial constraints, they can nevertheless engage in inter-organizational relationships (IOR) to achieve this. In such arrangements two or more establishments can pool their resources towards buying new technology that will give them the opportunity to satisfy their target markets. The stiff competition in the market means SMEs have to continually update their equipment and processes. They have to be up to date technologically and explore the opportunities towards gaining competitive advantage in the marketplace. Linking this discussion to Figure 5.2, it is apparent that having the right inputs into the transformation process is important and significantly determines the type of outputs. The

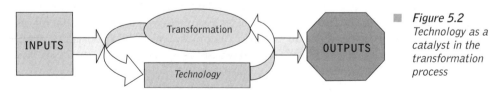

Figure 5.2
Technology as a catalyst in the transformation process

INPUTS Transformation Technology OUTPUTS

BBC programme *Dragons' Den* has featured dozens of inventions and shows how entrepreneurs have used them to improve their production processes, especially in terms of alternative raw materials or more advanced equipment. Such inventions further emphasize the dynamic nature of this environment.

Reflecting on how we have described technology so far and the prevailing changes in this environment, it is clear that the role of research and development (R&D) cannot be trivialized. R&D leads to the introduction of new products and services, and increases productivity in organizations where new, superior processes are adopted. For instance, the advent of the iPhone, iPad and several computer software packages in the information communication technology (ICT) sector has transformed the world of business in recent times and touches our lives every day. Many of these developments offer marketers the opportunity to be more efficient and effective at creating value for their customers. Today, improved technology has widened the scope of online marketing transactions. It allows marketers to communicate more effectively with their target audience, while customers can place orders for products and services in the comfort of their own home. SMEs that are sensitive to developments and inventions in the world of technology will be better able to achieve competitive advantage in their market domain. Overall, this part of the marketing environment contributes towards improving the standard of living of the people in the society.

Despite all the highlighted opportunities in this environment, it is noteworthy to state that changes in it could easily constitute challenges for marketing activities, especially at the SME level. Since the changes in this environment happen independently of the pace that a particular organization embraces them, businesses that are not willing to move with the trend will be left behind, and might lose their competitive edge, market share and profits to the businesses that are making the most of the developments. Interestingly, consumers are not oblivious of these changes and are becoming more demanding and sophisticated accordingly. So, keeping up to date with trends in technological development is not an option but a necessary course of action for businesses that want to survive in this age.

Physical environment

Tackling changes in the physical or natural environment is crucial for businesses. No doubt these changes are beyond the control of SMEs, whether they present opportunities for marketing activities or pose threats to their successful marketing practices. If we consider it from the marketing viewpoint, the relevance of the physical environment could be discussed from numerous perspectives. As noted by Armstrong and Kotler (2009), marketers need to pay particular attention to several trends in the natural environment, which include shortages of raw materials, increased pollution and increased government intervention. Considering these points critically, they offer directions to SME marketers on how to explore opportunities. Monitoring developments in the physical environment will inform marketers of the existing gaps that they could fill with innovations, such as providing alternative raw materials or reducing pollution. There have been unprecedented concerns about managing the environment from government and well-meaning groups in the society in recent times. The clamouring by researchers and environmentalists that countries have to reduce their carbon emissions has been pervasive for some time. Their core message is that if these issues are not addressed early enough the consequences will be undesirable and grave for society in the future. For instance, shortage of raw materials could have enduring effects on many businesses, including SMEs. One of the implications of the shortage of raw materials is that it may lead to substantial increase in the price of goods that require such scarce resources.

This will have a corresponding effect on the competitive advantage of such establishments if they are unable to research and develop cost-effective alternatives. They will most likely lose their market share to others who have cost-effective inputs as the increase in the associated costs may not be easy to pass on to consumers who have access to competitors' offerings. Viewing this from the perspective of opportunity, some businesses have focused on the waste and pollution generated by other businesses and are now exploring the management of such waste as a business opportunity.

Demographic environment

The demographic environment covers issues about market populations based on factors like age, household structure, gender, race and ethnicity, income and location. Like other macro-environmental factors discussed above, this segment of the marketing environment is beyond the control of marketers, yet it has far-reaching implications for their marketing activities. The demographic mix of people varies from one society to another. This is one of the reasons why it is difficult to have one-size-fits-all marketing strategies in some societies, and especially in international marketing. As an example, Table 5.5 relates to the United Kingdom. It presents the population estimates and projections of the country for the period from 1971 to 2026. Looking at the table closely, one can see that the population is ageing. The numbers of the older generations are increasing and the trend is expected to continue for the next few decades. Among the reasons cited for this trend in the population statistics are the decline in death and birth rates (ONS, 2009).

Table 5.5 UK population* by sex and age (thousands)

	Under 16	16–24	25–34	35–44	45–54	55–64	65–74	75+	All ages
Males									
1971	7,318	3,730	3,530	3,271	3,354	3,123	1,999	842	27,165
1981	6,439	4,114	4,036	3,409	3,121	2,967	2,264	1,063	27,412
1991	5,976	3,800	4,432	3,950	3,287	2,835	2,272	1,358	27,909
2001	6,077	3,284	4,215	4,382	3,856	3,090	2,308	1,621	28,832
2007	5,895	3,788	3,936	4,578	3,941	3,546	2,398	1,835	29,916
2011	5,961	3,846	4,235	4,314	4,292	3,592	2,636	2,018	30,893
2016	6,187	3,647	4,707	4,043	4,487	3,642	3,052	2,324	32,088
2021	6,485	3,490	4,784	4,318	4,217	4,045	3,153	2,761	33,253
2026	6,557	3,670	4,553	4,787	3,957	4,238	3,230	3,322	34,313
Females									
1971	6,938	3,626	3,441	3,241	3,482	3,465	2,765	1,802	28,761
1981	6,104	3,966	3,975	3,365	3,148	3,240	2,931	2,218	28,946
1991	5,709	3,691	4,466	3,968	3,296	2,971	2,795	2,634	29,530
2001	5,786	3,220	4,260	4,465	3,920	3,186	2,640	2,805	30,281
2007	5,615	3,580	3,924	4,670	4,039	3,686	2,660	2,887	31,059
2011	5,682	3,613	4,200	4,375	4,413	3,744	2,883	2,958	31,868
2016	5,909	3,420	4,572	4,092	4,620	3,796	3,323	3,156	32,887
2021	6,202	3,272	4,591	4,321	4,323	4,242	3,438	3,549	33,938
2026	6,271	3,453	4,368	4,691	4,048	4,448	3,512	4,155	34,946

Note: *Mid-year estimates for 1971 to 2007; 2006-based projections for 2011 to 2026.

Source: ONS (2009).

From a global perspective, it has been projected that about 60 per cent of the population of less developed countries will be urban in 2025 (Boyd *et al.*, 2002). These projections and speculations are of special relevance for the marketing of goods and services. Trends in a population's age distribution provide useful indicators of demands for products and services. They can also provide better insight into the needs and wants of the target markets, and offer opportunities to design specific marketing programmes to serve those markets. The most populous of the various age categories in the society will likely provide good opportunities for marketers. On the other hand, in light of their limitations, SMEs should also note the trend of specific small groups that could constitute viable niches, so as to be able to design an appropriate marketing mix to satisfy their specific needs and avoid direct competition with large corporations.

Apart from age and geographical settlement, categorization of people on the basis of family structure, social class, income, race and ethnicity and lifestyle could be very rewarding for SMEs when planning their marketing. The shopping patterns of bachelors and newlyweds, for example, are likely to be different from that of large families with children. To a considerable extent, income influences people's purchases. For example, a study of low-income consumers' purchases of grocery products indicates that in some cases their preferences are at variance from people at the other end of the spectrum of income distribution (Gbadamosi, 2009). Some ethnic groups are noted as constituting a good market for certain products, while sometimes people in a particular geographical location might have needs that may be different from those elsewhere. In the UK, leading supermarkets such as ASDA now have product lines with items that appeal to ethnic minority groups in the society. The change in immigration trends has introduced opportunities to the SMEs that can identify and explore them. Obalende Suya, a London-based Nigerian restaurant that was launched in 1987 and became an instant hit among African immigrants (Madichie, 2005), is an example of how SMEs are exploring trends in the demographic environment for marketing purposes. All these are examples of diversity in the demographic environment and have potent implications for marketing activities in the SME context.

GROUP ACTIVITY

Think of a business that you would like to venture into in the future and discuss with two or three other members of your class which marketing opportunities you could get from changes in each of these macro-environmental factors in relation to this business.

MICRO-ENVIRONMENT OF MARKETING

Figure 5.3 shows the interactions among the micro-environmental factors. It shows the SME sourcing its inputs such as raw materials, machineries, human resources and money from the suppliers and using them in the transformation process to yield the needed output, as explained earlier in Figures 5.1 and 5.2. The output that it obtains from this process could be sold either directly to the customers or through intermediaries.

As shown in Figure 5.3, there is a possibility that competitors will have relationships with each of the parties in the micro-environmental system of the business. It is possible that they source their inputs from the same supplier and they could also be using the same intermediaries for the distribution of their offerings to the target customers who have the liberty to buy from any organization that best satisfies their needs, including the competitors. Let us now explore each of these elements in turn to see how they influence marketing activities of SMEs.

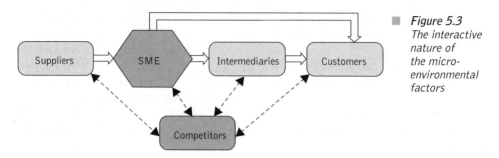

Figure 5.3
The interactive nature of the micro-environmental factors

Customers

Customers constitute a major element of the micro-environmental factors. Essentially, marketing is about satisfying customers whether in the context of SMEs or large corporations. Thus, having the right information about them and pleasing them is crucial for successful marketing practice. Marketers need to be familiar with trends associated with the purchases of their customers and maintain very good relationships with them. Logically, customers are the boss in the marketing system as they dictate which organizations will stay in business and which will have to leave the scene. Fundamentally, one of the constraints of SMEs in comparison with large corporations is finance. However, this cannot be regarded as a tenable excuse for not being able to satisfy their target markets. Hence, most SMEs often target niches with clearly identifiable sets of needs that they would be able to satisfy within their constraints. Otherwise the customers will shift their loyalty to organizations that will give them optimum benefits in their transactions. Hence, SMEs are expected to design their marketing strategies to revolve around satisfying their customers, as shown in Figure 5.4.

Marketing activities are applicable to transactions involving the sale of physical goods and services as in Figure 5.4 which demonstrates the interaction between the customer and the marketing mix elements being managed holistically. This is considered useful as there are many examples of SMEs in the service sector just as there are a good number that offer physical products to their customers. Lawyers, accountants, teachers, musicians, information technology operators and fitness coaches are examples of service-oriented SMEs commonly seen in the British marketing environment. In fact, in most cases when organizations offer physical products to their customers the total package of transaction still includes some elements of services. Nevertheless, the point being made here is that, in all of these marketing transactions, customers must always occupy a pivotal position for the organization to succeed in the marketing environment. The logic in this argument is that satisfied customers are not only likely to make a repeat purchase but also are likely to inform others of their positive experience in the form of positive word-of-mouth communications.

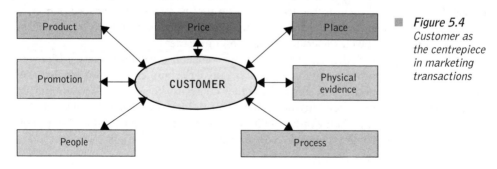

Figure 5.4
Customer as the centrepiece in marketing transactions

On the other hand, dissatisfied customers may not only stop buying from the organization but also are likely to spread negative word-of-mouth communications to friends and neighbours of their dissatisfaction with the transactions. It is evident that organizations exist because there are customers; accordingly, the whole of this book in one form or another is about how SMEs can satisfy their customers more efficiently and effectively than their competitors.

Competitors

One of the dramatic changes that have taken place in the marketing system in recent times is the increasing scale of competition in the marketplace. As consumers have more access to information and are more equipped to select among competing offerings, marketers, including SMEs, are no longer guaranteed patronage unless they are able to outperform their rivals in the business setting. In order to be able to survive and succeed, business organizations compete for virtually all resources needed – manpower, money, materials and machines. In fact, as shown in Figure 5.3, competitors are not only vying to get the money that the customers have to spend but also their activities could permeate the entire marketing system. These include sourcing for their raw materials from suppliers and engaging the services of intermediaries to distribute their products to their target customers. SMEs may face competition from various sources. This may be from organizations of comparable scale or large corporations. Competition may also come from within or outside of the industry, and it could even come from previous employees. In fact, customers of an organization may also be potential competitors (Montgomery and Weinberg, 1979). This is why it is very important for them to identify all current and potential sources of competition for their business. This will give them information on the gaps in the markets and their competitive advantage. Hence, when entering into battle with their direct competitors SMEs should first consider whether it is necessary, as there may be some customers in the market who can be profitably served without venturing into head-on competition (Hill and O'Sullivan, 2004). Nonetheless, this does not necessarily suggest that marketers should always avoid competition. It has been observed that, even when faced with a highly competitive environment, innovative smaller firms can survive and even prosper (Lamb *et al.*, 1999). SMEs could concentrate on niches that have specific needs that could be met by their limited resources. Above all, SMEs should be sensitive to their competitors – their number, their mode of operations, their market share, their marketing mix elements and their strengths and weaknesses. If this is done effectively, they stand a better chance of succeeding, even in a volatile marketing environment.

Suppliers

As businesses engage in exchange to satisfy their customers, they also obtain their inputs from various other organizations, known as *suppliers* (see Figure 5.4). The role of suppliers in the marketing system as a micro-environmental factor is vital and can take several forms. Some supply the raw materials needed by SMEs to produce their final output. Banks and lending agencies provide the needed capital. NatWest, HSBC, Barclays and many other banks in the British marketing environment have various funding schemes for SMEs in the form of loans and overdrafts. Employment agencies that provide the needed human resources as and when needed, consultancy firms that provide business advice, advertising agencies and market research firms are all examples of suppliers that influence how SMEs relate to their customers. Losing a key supplier of raw materials, component parts or critical services can sometimes create extensive disruption to production flow, which would affect how SMEs satisfy their customers. Thus, as these organizations monitor their markets and other environmental factors, they also need to be aware of trends and changes in the activities of their suppliers. Besides, they need to create and maintain very good relationships with them. Similarly, it is important for them to pay particular attention to issues like suppliers' innovations, deals with rivals, supply shortages, delays or quality concerns, strikes or employment difficulties, legal actions or warranty disputes, supply costs and price trends and new entrants into the supply chain (Dibb *et al.*, 2001). Indeed, the quality of the relationships businesses have with their suppliers will influence how well they are able to serve their target markets and how successful they can be in their marketing environment.

Intermediaries

Intermediaries are individuals or other organizations that mediate between SMEs and their customers by engaging in the distribution of their goods and services. Stated differently, they act as the link between production and consumption and bridge the gap between the two ends in the marketing system. Examples include wholesalers, retailers and agents. In a production setting, while producing SMEs provide customers with form utility, intermediaries provide time, place and possession utility. Fundamentally, the ultimate consumers of the products cannot be deemed to have been totally satisfied until they have purchased the product needed at the right time, and able to buy it at the right place. As indicated above, intermediaries occupy a pivotal position in the marketing system for most organizations but they are considered especially relevant for SMEs that need their services to make their products available in areas where they would not ordinarily be able to reach due to their financial limitations. This explains why most SME owner-managers would be very keen to have the support of major intermediaries for wider distribution of their products. Before Levi Roots, the British producer of Reggae Reggae Sauce, pitched his Jamaican sauce on the BBC programme *Dragons' Den* in 2007, the product was practically unknown. However, the opportunity he had through this television appearance and the networks that developed afterwards sparked distribution opportunity for this product in major British supermarkets which has now made the product widely known and successful in the British marketing environment. In most cases, SMEs do not adopt conventional distribution methods, and sometimes combine several methods when applicable to respond to environmental threats. Essentially, it is important to note that intermediaries constitute an important element of the micro-environment and any strategic change to them and their activities could also have strategic implications for the SMEs in their bid to satisfy their customer.

GROUP ACTIVITY

Reflect on your three most recent purchases of products or services from an SME in your locality and discuss with two other members of the class how the customer-oriented approach of the SME has contributed to your satisfaction or how the lack of such a relationship has left you dissatisfied.

ENVIRONMENTAL SCANNING AND ANALYSIS

Having discussed various environmental factors that influence the marketing activities of SMEs, we will now examine environmental scanning and analysis and their relevance to the success of SMEs. Environmental scanning simply involves collecting information about the forces that make up the environment. It is about acquiring relevant information to guide the organization's future course of action (Aguilar, 1967). Thus, SME environmental scanning would involve collecting information related to the economy, taxation, exchange rates, interest rates, legislations, competitors' characteristics, political and legal factors, demographics, socio-cultural factors, customers, suppliers, physical environment and a host of others as highlighted above in the discussion of marketing environmental factors. As noted by Saxby *et al.* (2002), environmental scanning allows managers to become instantly aware of factors in the environment that could significantly influence their activities in the organization, especially in relation to their strategic direction.

While environmental scanning basically deals with obtaining information about the environmental factors, environmental analysis has to do with assessing and interpreting the information gathered in the course of scanning the environment. Scanning and analysis of the environmental factors are interconnected and work interactively. As changes in the marketing environment can lead to opportunities and threats, SMEs would be better positioned in the marketplace if they engaged in environmental analysis after the scanning. Although most of these forces are beyond their control, scanning and analysis together often yield far-reaching benefits.

In order to be able to obtain relevant information, SMEs need to explore various sources including websites, trade publications and newspapers. The rigorousness associated with environmental scanning actually varies from firm to firm. This is an area that has been widely explored in the business literature (Miles and Snow, 1978; McDaniel and Kolari, 1987; Slater and Narver, 1993; Saxby *et al.*, 2002). One of these contributions that has been widely explored and applied differently is that of Miles and Snow (1978), in which the authors developed a typology of strategic behaviour of firms in relation to their environmental scanning. This perspective suggests that firms could be classified as Prospectors, Analysers, Defenders or Reactors. Prospectors are firms that scan the environment proactively and seek to identify and explore opportunities, and tend to be creator of change in their industry, whereas Defenders have narrow product-market domain and tend not to search for opportunities outside their domain of operation (McDaniel and Kolari, 1987). The Analysers exhibit the behaviour of both Prospectors and Defenders, hence they explore new products from a relatively stable customer base (Slater and Narver, 1993). Reactors rank below the other three in their qualities and attitudes towards growth and environmental monitoring (Slater and Narver, 1993). They do not demonstrate consistent strategy; rather, they simply respond to pressures from the environment as they come (McDaniel and Kolari, 1987). This postulation has been widely used, adapted and explored in various forms for many years. But our key interest in this perspective lies in its emphasis on how firms vary in how they approach their strategic choice and environmental scanning activities.

Saxby *et al.* (2002) present a model which incorporates the environmental scanning approach of firms and generic strategy into various organizational culture types. Their work is an improvement on the earlier work of Deshpande *et al.* (1993). In the original model of Deshpande *et al.* (1993), a two-by-two matrix which produces four quadrants, labelled respectively Clan, Advocacy, Market and Hierarchy – was developed. In this study, the Clan describes firms that are internally focused and flexible in how they manage things. Firms in the Market quadrant tend to be market-oriented and their major goal is to get profits through competitive advantage (Saxby *et al.*, 2002). They are the opposite of the Clan firms. Advocacy firms are flexible and market-oriented, whereas Hierarchy firms (the opposite of Advocacy firms) are basically concerned with a stable organizational setting and emphasize orderliness (Saxby *et al.*, 2002).

The core message of Saxby *et al.* (2002), which is summarized in their Enhanced Model of Culture, Strategy and Scanning Modes (see Figure 5.5), is that there is a compelling need to incorporate environmental scanning approaches and generic strategy into the various organizational cultures. Thus, they suggest four environmental scanning approaches to be Informal (for Clan firms), Exploratory (for Advocacy firms), Analytical (for Market firms), and Disciplined and Structured (for Hierarchy firms). Saxby *et al.* (2002) reach an interesting and noteworthy conclusion. They contend that if a manager operates in one quadrant but adopts an inappropriate environmental scanning method the firm will either be missing valuable information or wasting their resources. This postulation also supports the view that firms are not the same and do not approach the scanning of environment in the same way. The implications of these various perspectives on environmental scanning are remarkably relevant to our understanding of SME environmental scanning.

An argument in the same direction but perhaps in a simplified form is presented in this chapter and summarized in Figure 5.6. Some SMEs often ignore environmental scanning, thinking that it amounts to a waste of their time and does not really add anything significant

Organic process/Unanalysable environment

Clan   **Advocacy**

Scanning approach: Scanning approach:
  Informal   Exploratory
Generic strategy: Generic strategy:
  Reactor   Prospector
Dominant attributes: Dominant attributes:
  Cohesiveness, participation,   Entrepreneurship, creativity,
  teamwork, sense of family   adaptability
Leadership style: Leadership style:
  Mentor, facilitator, parent-figure   Entrepreneur, innovator,
Bonding: risk-taker
  Loyalty, tradition   Bonding:
Strategic emphasis: Entrepreneurship, flexibility, risk
  Commitment, morale,   Strategic emphasis:
  development of human   Innovation, growth, new
  resources   resources

Passive methods ←——————————————————————→ **Active methods**

Scanning approach: Scanning approach:
  Disciplined and Structured   Analytical
Generic strategy: Generic strategy:
  Defender   Analyzer
Dominant attributes: Dominant attributes:
  Order, rules, uniformity   Competitiveness, goal
Leadership style: achievement
  Coordinator, administrator   Leadership style:
Bonding: Decisive, achievement-oriented
  Rules, policies, procedure   Bonding:
Strategic emphasis: Goal-oriented, production,
  Stability, smooth operations   competition
                                       Strategic emphasis:
                                         Competitive advantage,
                                         market superiority

Hierarchy   **Market**

Mechanistic process/Analysable environment

Figure 5.5
Enhanced Model of Culture, Strategy and Scanning Modes

Source: Saxby *et al.* (2002, p. 33)

Figure 5.6
Categorization
of SMEs
on their
environmental
scanning
commitment

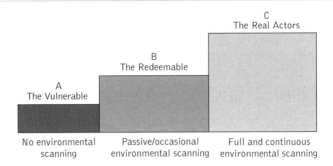

to their marketing transactions. They are shown in Figure 5.6. as Category A and depicted as *The Vulnerable*. Another category of SMEs conduct environmental scanning passively, merely to conform to certain exigencies such as obtaining a bank loan, but often abandon it afterwards and only revisit it when similar needs arise in the future. SMEs in this category are described here as *The Redeemable* (Category B). These SMEs can survive environmental turbulence because the owner-managers may seize opportunities that arise from occasional (not proactively commissioned) environmental scanning. Nonetheless, there are some SMEs that might actively and continuously scan their marketing environment to identify opportunities and threats in it. These SMEs (Category C) are described as *The Real Actors* and stand to benefit in many ways from such an active commitment to environment scanning. They explore the market and engage in innovative marketing within the constraints of a potentially turbulent marketplace.

Since environmental factors are dynamic, multifaceted and complex, a thorough diagnosis of these factors will provide information useful to SMEs. This will serve as input to their marketing decisions and help them to satisfy their customers and gain competitive advantage.

SWOT ANALYSIS: ANALYTICAL TOOL IN ENTREPRENEURSHIP MARKETING

The popularity of the SWOT analysis as an analytical tool used by organizations in their planning activities is not in doubt. The term SWOT is an acronym for Strengths, Weaknesses, Opportunities and Threats.

Essentially, conducting a SWOT analysis involves identifying opportunities for, and threats to, the firm in the marketing environment, and acknowledging its strengths and weaknesses. In other words, SMEs complete the boxes in Figure 5.8 and use the output in their planning process. This should be closely linked to the environmental scanning and analysis of the organization. This is because firms scan their marketing environment for opportunities and threats associated with environmental factors, as shown in Figure 5.7.

As shown in Figure 5.8, opportunities and threats exist in the external marketing environment of SMEs. Changes in this layer of the marketing environment could present excellent opportunities for the firms and, if spotted and explored, such opportunities could make the SME a winner in the marketplace. For example, Ngamkroeckjoti *et al.* (2005) found that SMEs that scan their environment are better able to develop appropriate new products. This is because such firms would have noticed the changes in the environmental factors and be able to match their innovations with the needs of their market.

Unlike opportunities that connote positive developments in the marketing environment, threats connote negative developments (see Figure 5.8). As we experience changes in the

71

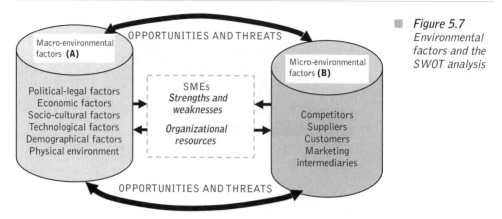

Figure 5.7
Environmental factors and the SWOT analysis

marketing environment, SMEs are confronted with equivalent challenges in relation to these factors. This reiterates the turbulent nature of the marketing environment. Besides the high level of uncertainty confronting SMEs, it is also noteworthy that turbulence varies in degree in relation to various industries in the marketing environment. It is expected that industries experiencing a high level of turbulence will experience unpredictable changes, and an unstable competitive landscape (Gango and Agarwal, 2009). In addition, a change in one factor in the marketing environment can trigger changes in several others. For example, a change in government might affect policy on taxation and SMEs, which could also have an effect on the economy and the socio-cultural factors. However, environmental scanning could help SMEs in this turbulence by enhancing their marketing decision-making activities as doing it implies that they are most unlikely to be caught unawares.

The strengths and weaknesses of an organization are internal and are essentially organizational resources, processes, culture and other similar factors which could be fine-tuned to exploit opportunities and cope with threats in the marketing environment. As popular as SWOT analysis is, some who use it apply it shoddily and realize very little benefit from it. In order to be able to obtain optimal benefits from using SWOT analysis as an analytical tool for achieving success in the marketing environment, Piercy and Giles (1989) provided very useful guidelines: SWOT should be focused, it should be applied with shared vision, it should target enhancing value to the customer (customer orientation), it should incorporate environmental analysis and it should be applied to allow for structured strategy generation.

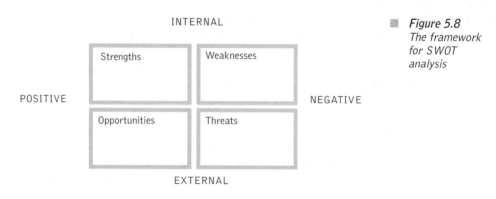

Figure 5.8
The framework for SWOT analysis

SMES' RESPONSE TO THE MARKETING ENVIRONMENT

So far, we have established that SMEs are confronted with environmental turbulence and other associated threats in the external environment. Although the turbulence of the marketing environment often affects all business organizations, the characteristics of SMEs suggest they are more vulnerable than larger enterprises.

The existing literature indicates that SMEs have some noteworthy distinguishing characteristics in comparison with larger enterprises. Wong and Aspinwall (2004) provide a long list of the characteristics of SMEs, classified into clusters of factors: ownership and management; structure, culture and behaviour; system, processes and procedures; human resources and customers; market. Characteristically, SMEs are mostly started, owned and dominated by entrepreneurs, have a simple and less complex structure, have flexible structure and information flow, have a multi-tasking owner-manager, a low degree of specialization and a unified culture. Others characteristics are simple planning and control systems, informal evaluation, flexible and adaptable processes and close information relationships. They are normally dependent on a small customer base which is mostly local and regional rather than international; they have more frequent and close contact with customers, whom they often know personally and socially (Wong and Aspinwall, 2004). Based on a body of literature, Chen et al. (2006) also state that some or all of these features could be used to distinguish SMEs from large firms:

- flexibility and volatility
- skill (or expertise) shortage
- very limited market power
- market behaviour mainly affected by partners, or competitors.

Another view emphasizes that SMEs are small in size, are constrained by a general lack of financial resources (which also suppresses their growth potential) and do not have any control over their external environment (Carson et al., 1995).

Essentially, despite the variations in the characteristics highlighted by these different perspectives, one can still see their point of convergence: SMEs are smaller than large enterprises, which are financially sturdy and more systematic in their marketing approaches, and this reality inhibits the extent to which they are able to explore opportunities in their marketing environment.

Nonetheless, if these characteristics are critically examined, one will note that SMEs also have several characteristics that can help them succeed in the volatile marketing environment. These include their use of a personal contact network (PCN), their flexibility, their informality, their less complex structures and procedures and their closeness to their customers.

To respond to the environment, an SME could obtain and clarify information about the environment from friends, business associates, customers, suppliers and several other contacts. This could provide them with information about the marketing environment that might serve as very useful input to their marketing decisions. Exploring their links to all these individuals or organizations in their network can lead to many opportunities that would not arise without that network. This social network can offer small firms invaluable opportunities for exploring their marketing environment. Laere and Heene (2003) also note that networks have now become critical and are sources from which SMEs could gain competitive success in fast-changing and highly competitive markets.

Moreover, although SMEs are relatively small compared with large enterprises, they have the advantages of being flexible and being close to their customers. As they often target niches, they could explore these as ways of responding to the environment. They can use these advantages to understand the needs and wants of their customers intimately and then design appropriate marketing mix elements to achieve their marketing objectives. Their flexibility also implies that they are more likely to be able to change their internal factors quickly to adapt to the changes in the marketing environment and better meet the needs of their customers. However, not all SMEs are aware of this, as evidenced by the high rate of SME failure. As the turbulence in the marketing environment intensifies, the SMEs that will survive are those who are ready to scan the environment, to be innovative, to explore their characteristics as strengths for gaining competitive advantage and to be customer-focused.

GROUP ACTIVITY

Do you think that non-profit small organizations need to perform environmental scanning and analysis? Share your response with two members of your class and compare your viewpoints.

SUMMARY

All organizations operate within a marketing environment that influences how they are able to serve their customers. However, the extent to which they respond to environmental forces varies with the type of organization. SMEs are known to be smaller in many ramifications than large enterprises and hence are unlikely to respond to environmental changes in the same way. These environmental factors can be classified into internal and external factors. While the former are within the organization and can be fine-tuned by the SMEs to satisfy their customers more effectively, the same cannot be said of the latter. Thus, SMEs should fine-tune their internal factors in such a way that makes them get the best out of the external environment. Essentially, this environment consists of organizational resources, like its personnel and others, that are often used to operate within the environment.

The external environment can also be categorized further into macro- and micro-environmental factors. Macro-environmental factors are broad in scope and affect all organizations. Examples are economic factors, political-legal factors, socio-cultural factors, and technological factors. However, micro factors relate to a particular SME and influence how the business operates to satisfy its target market. The basic micro factors are customers, competitors, intermediaries and suppliers. Given the uncertainties and complexities associated with these environmental factors due to their continuous changes, businesses need to collect information about these factors and analyse it to give them direction for their marketing decisions. This process is known as environmental scanning and analysis.

SMEs should respond to marketing environmental factors by using their marketing advantages, which include flexibility and closeness to their customers. These also give them opportunity to respond quickly to the needs of their customers, who are in most cases niches with specific identifiable characteristics within the larger markets. These advantages also give SMEs the opportunity to enjoy customers' loyalty.

KEY TERMS

- Environmental scanning
- Loyalty/flexibility
- Macro-environment/micro-environment
- Marketing environment
- Opportunities/threats
- Resource constraints
- Strengths/weaknesses
- Uncertainty

REVIEW QUESTIONS

1. Enumerate and discuss three of the macro-environmental factors that you think a small-scale fitness club should be sensitive to. Rationalize your response.

2. What is environment scanning? How is it different from environmental analysis? Use SME examples to support your viewpoint.

3. Identify two areas that technological advancement could benefit an SME that intends to establish its furniture business in one of the European countries and discuss two ways that you think it could suffer setbacks for not matching up with trends in the technological environment.

4. Assume that Rock Parvel, the owner of a local business that sells body lotion in your neighbourhood, has just appointed you as the new marketing manager in his establishment. Your challenge is to highlight the relevance and impact of the socio-cultural environment, demographic environment, intermediaries and suppliers to marketing in that type of business to your subordinates in a forum organized by the chief executive. What are the main highlights that will feature in your presentation?

5. Mrs Favour Duncan is proposing to go into the business of manufacturing and marketing of baby foods. However, Ms Pretty-bay, her confidant, has advised her that she needs to consider very important factors in the environment before pursuing this investment. As the chosen consultant, explain these factors in detail and use appropriate diagrams to support your explanation.

6. Examine the roles of regulatory agencies in the marketing of edible products in your country. Give SME-related examples to justify your standpoint.

7. What in your opinion distinguishes macro-environmental factors from micro-environmental factors? Use one of each type to robustly exemplify your viewpoint.

8. Examine the specific impacts of the economic environment on a small-scale marketing firm based in an urban centre of your country. Illustrate your points with current and relevant examples.

9. Give a conceptual explanation of the relevance of socio-cultural environment to an SME retail business owner in your locality.

CASE STUDY 5: RAMSEY MOORE

Ramsey Moore is a small independent estate agency offering property sales, lettings, management and mortgage advice. It was established in September 2008 by the partners – Mark Harris and Michael O'Brien. Mark has 15 years in estate agency and Michael six years in mortgage advising. According to Mark, 'We opened in Dagenham, Essex, as we became aware there was a need for a professional letting agency and aim to create an agency that is associated with the words: professional, exceptional service, and unrivalled determination to get the job done'.

While there are ten other estate agents in Dagenham, five could be described as being centrally located. Ramsey Moore falls under this latter category as it is on Dagenham Heathway. Estate agents in general, including those in Dagenham, have experienced very profitable years during the last decade. Nonetheless, in August 2007, the market took a turn for the worse as the banks and other lending institutions tightened their lending criteria, and it became more difficult to obtain mortgage finance. As people found it more difficult to obtain finances for their intended mortgage arrangements, fewer houses were sold, which resulted in about a 16 per cent fall in house prices during 2008.

Nevertheless, the prevailing situation seems to have highlighted another associated opportunity in this business. People who have not been able to purchase are looking to rent properties, and this has been seen as a positive development in the letting market. Due to the high-street position of Ramsey Moore, the agency has been able to explore the opportunity of the regular walk-in clients interested in renting properties in the area. They have noticed that this and their 'For Sale' and 'To Let' boards placed outside houses have attracted the majority of their current businesses.

Given that landlords who own properties in these areas could be living anywhere else, the agency finds it difficult to reach this target market effectively. Currently, the marketing communication mix of the organization consists of print ads in local newspapers – the *Newham Recorder*, the *Barking & Dagenham Recorder* and the *Dagenham Post*. The organization also advertises its properties on websites – namely, Rightmove, Property Finder, Homes on View, Globrix and its own website (www. RamseyMoore.co.uk). There are 45,000 residential property addresses in the RM8, RM9 and RM10 postcode areas. The partners designed a leaflet showing what their business is all about, and distributed it over a six-week period to the 45,000 addresses. Although this was good for introducing a new estate agent in town, just how many of them were actually reaching the target landlords still remains a big and strategic question in the minds of the entrepreneurs. Basically, their targets are landlords who own properties in the Dagenham, Barking and Chadwell Heath areas. But the big question now is, *'Will the environmental factors be so favourable as to give Mark and Michael the success they dearly need to transform their company?'*

CASE QUESTIONS AND TASKS
1. Identify points that emphasize the influence of macro-environmental factors in the decisions of these entrepreneurs.
2. Which micro-environmental factors can you identify in the case study? Explain the implications if these entrepreneurs ignore their relevance.

3. What advice would you give the entrepreneurs on how to get the most from their marketing environment towards satisfying their target landlords?
4. Conduct a SWOT analysis for Ramsey Moore and explain how the firm could use your results for competitive advantage.

Source: Used with the kind permission of the management of Ramsey Moore for educational purposes.

BIBLIOGRAPHY

Aguilar, F. J. (1967), *Scanning the Business Environment*, New York: Macmillan, pp. 1–18.

Armstrong, G. and Kotler, P. (2009), *Marketing: An Introduction*, 9th edn, New Jersey: Pearson Education.

Boyd, Jr. H. W. B., Walker, Jr. O. C., Mullins, J. W. and Larréché, J. (2002), *Marketing Management: A Strategic Decision-Making Approach*, 4th edn, New York: McGraw-Hill, pp. 76–77.

Carson, D., Cromie, S., McGowan, P. and Hill J. (1995), 'Marketing and Entrepreneurship in SMEs: An Innovative Approach', Essex: Pearson Education Ltd.

Chen, S., Duan, Y., Edwards, J. S. and Lehaney, B. (2006), 'Toward Understanding Inter-Organizational Knowledge Transfer Needs in SMEs: Insight from a UK Investigation', *Journal of Knowledge Management*, vol. 10, no. 3, pp. 6–23.

Consumers International (2010), 'Basic Rights of Consumers', available online at: http://www.consumersinternational.org/who-we-are/consumer-rights (accessed 12 October 2010).

Department for Business Innovation and Skills (2009), 'SME Statistical Press Release', 14th October, available online at: http://stats.berr.gov.uk/ed/sme/smestats2008-ukspr.pdf (accessed 21 March 2010).

Deshpande, R., Farley, J. U., Webster, F. E. Jr. (1993), 'Corporate Culture, Customer Orientation, and Innovation in Japanese Firms: A Quadrad Analysis', *Journal of Marketing*, January, pp. 23–37.

Dibb, S., Simkin, L., William, M., Pride, W. M. and Ferrell, O. C. (2001), *Marketing: Concepts and Strategies*, Boston: Houghton Mifflin.

Directgov (2010), 'Consumer Rights and Where to Get Help', available online at: http://www.direct.gov.uk/en/Governmentcitizensandrights/Consumerrights/DG_182935 (accessed 13 March 2010).

Gango, M. and Agarwal, R. (2009), 'Performance Differentials Between Diversifying Entrants and Entrepreneurial Start-Ups: A Complexity Approach', *Academy of Management Review*, vol. 34, no. 2, pp. 228–252.

Gbadamosi, A. (2004), 'Cultural Dimension of Comparative Management and Administration', in Ogundele, O. J. K. (ed.) *Comparative Management and Administration: A Book of Readings*. Lagos: Concept Publication, pp. 111–137.

Gbadamosi, A. (2009), 'Cognitive Dissonance: The Implicit Explication in Low-Income Consumers' Shopping Behaviour for "Low-Involvement" Grocery Products', *International Journal of Retail and Distribution Management*, vol. 37, no. 12, pp. 1077–1095.

Hill, L. and O'Sullivan, T. (2004), *Foundation Marketing*, Essex: Pearson Education, pp. 72–73.

Kotler, P. (2004), *Ten Deadly Marketing Sins: Signs and Solutions*, New Jersey: John Wiley & Sons.

Kotler, P., Armstrong, G., Veronica, W. and Saunders, J. (2008), *Principles of Marketing*, 5th edn, Harlow: Pearson Education.

Laere, K. V. and Heene, A. (2003), 'Social Networks as a Source of Competitive Advantage for the Firm', *Journal of Workplace Learning*, vol. 15, no. 6, pp. 248–258.

Lamb, Jr., C. W., Hair, Jr., J. F. and McDaniel, C. (1999), *Essentials of Marketing*, Ohio: South-Western College Publishing.

Lamb, C. W., Hair, J. F. and McDaniel, C. (2010), *MKTG*, 3rd edn, Mason: South-Western Cengage Learning.

McDaniel, S. W. and Kolari, J. W. (1987), 'Marketing Strategy Implications of the Miles and Snow Typology', *Journal of Marketing*, October, pp. 19–30.

Madichie, N. (2005), 'Marketing Assessment of Nigerian Foods in the United Kingdom', paper presented at the Academy of Marketing Conference, Dublin: Dublin Institute of Technology, 4–7 July.

Miles, R. E. and Snow, C. C. (1978), *Organizational Strategy, Structure, and Process*, New York: McGraw-Hill.

Montgomery, D. B. and Weinberg, C. B. (1979), 'Toward Strategic Intelligence Systems', *Journal of Marketing*, vol. 43, Fall, pp. 41–52.

Ngamkroeckjoti, C., Speece, M. and Dimmitt, N. J. (2005), 'Environmental Scanning in Thai Food SMEs', *British Food Journal*, vol. 107, no. 5, pp. 285–305.

Ofcom (2010), 'What is Ofcom?', available online at: http://www.ofcom.org.uk/what-is-ofcom/ (accessed 8 March 2010).

Office of Public Sector Information (2010), 'Sale of Goods Act 1979 (c.54) – Part II: Formation of the contract', available online at: http://www.opsi.gov.uk/RevisedStatutes/Acts/ukpga/1979/cuk-pga_19790054_en_3 (accessed 13 March, 2010).

ONS (Office for National Statistics) (2006), 'News Release: New Report Points to Rise in Women in Work', 23 March, available online at: http://www.statistics.gov.uk/pdfdir/wim0306.pdf (accessed 22 March 2010).

ONS (2008a), *Focus on Gender*, 26 September.

ONS (2008b), 'Working Lives: Employment Rates Higher for Men', *Focus on Gender*, available online at: http://www.statistics.gov.uk/cci/nugget.asp?id=1654 (accessed 22 March, 2010).

ONS (2009), 'Correction Notice: Social Trends', No. 39 – 2009 edition, Harlow: National Statistics, available online at: http://www.statistics.gov.uk/downloads/theme_social/Social_Trends39/Social_Trends_39.pdf (accessed 26 October 2010).

Piercy, N. and Giles, W. (1989), 'Making SWOT Work', *Marketing Intelligence and Planning*, vol.7, no. 5/6, pp. 5–7.

Saxby, C. L., Parker, K. R., Nitse, P. S. and Dishman, P. L. (2002), 'Environmental Scanning and Organizational Culture', *Marketing Intelligence and Planning*, vol. 20, no. 1, pp. 28–34.

Slater, S. F. and Narver, J. C. (1993), 'Product-Market Strategy and Performance: An Analysis of the Miles and Snow Strategy Types', *European Journal of Marketing*, vol. 27, no. 10, pp. 33–51.

Thompson, K. E. and Panayiotopoulos, P. (1999), 'Predicting Behavioural Intention in a Small Business Context', *Journal of Marketing Practice*, vol. 5, no. 3, pp. 89–96.

Wong, K. Y. and Aspinwall, E. (2005), 'An Empirical Study of the Important Factors for Knowledge-Management Adoption in the SME Sector', *Journal of Knowledge Management*, vol. 9, no. 3, pp. 64–82.

Chapter 6

Understanding consumers in entrepreneurship marketing

Nnamdi O. Madichie

LEARNING OBJECTIVES

After reading this chapter, you will be able to:

- understand consumers' level of involvement with product and describe consumer problem-solving processes
- recognize stages of the consumer buying decision process
- explore situational influences of the consumer buying decision process
- understand psychological influences of consumer buying decision process
- examine social influences of consumer buying decision process.

BOX 6.1: WALTER FREDERICK MORRISON—INVENTOR OF THE FRISBEE

How would you get through your youth without learning to throw a Frisbee?

— Kay McIff, lawyer for Walter Frederick Morrison

Frisbee inventor, Walter Frederick Morrison, conceived and developed his aerodynamic plastic disc in the 1950s, and hundreds of millions have been sold worldwide since. Originally called "Pluto Platter," Morrison sold the toy at local fairs. He and his future wife, Lu, got the idea from playing with a metal cake pan on the beach in California. The platter's novel aerodynamic shape allowed it to hover briefly or travel surprisingly long distances, kept aloft by its rotation. In 1957 Morrison sold the rights to the Californian firm Wham-O, which discovered that youngsters were calling the toy a "Frisbie," after the name of a well-known pie. The company changed the spelling to avoid trademark infringement and the Frisbee was born.

In memory of Morrison, who died at home in Monroe, California, on 9 February 2010, Wham-O paid tribute to Morrison (known affectionately as Fred) on its official website: "As Frisbee discs keep flying though the air, bringing smiles to faces, Fred's spirit lives on. Smooth flights, Fred."

So why can't we "get through [our] youth without learning to throw a Frisbee"? Why did Morrison sell the rights to Wham-O if it mattered that much? How does the

Figure 6.1
Dog catching a Frisbee

Frisbee explain, even remotely, consumer behavior? At the end of this chapter you will begin to appreciate how some of these questions might be answered.

Source: BBC News (2010).

INTRODUCTION

The central role of marketing (as both a function and a philosophy of business) is to gain a deep understanding of consumers (no distinction is made between consumer and customers at this level); what makes them buy (or refuse to buy) and what the factors are that influence consumption-related behaviors. It is probably impossible to "satisfy and delight customers" (marketing credos) without sufficiently understanding their behavioral triggers and consequences irrespective of whether the focus is on small to medium-sized enterprises (SMEs) or large businesses. So, in this chapter, we aim to ferret out the key concepts in the field of consumer behavior and see how they apply to entrepreneurship contexts.

Before going into the finer details of consumer behavior in SMEs it is worth identifying the different types of markets. There are two broad types of markets. The first are *Consumer Markets*—which includes purchasers and household members who intend to consume or benefit from the purchased products and do not buy products to make products. The second are *Business Markets* in which buyers buy products for business purposes or for resale.

UNDERSTANDING BUYING BEHAVIOR

Buying Behavior is the decision processes and acts of people involved in buying and using products. **Consumer Buying Behavior** refers to the decision processes and purchasing activities of people who purchase products for personal or household use and not for business purposes.

Very often, how buyers relate to buying situations depends on their level of involvement with the product, service, or idea in question. For example, consumers tend to have a low involvement when buying convenience products like a bottle of Coke or a newspaper. They, however, tend to become more involved (i.e. exihibit high involvement) when it comes to career or university choice. The next section provides some detailed illustrations of this range of levels of involvement.

LEVELS OF INVOLVEMENT

These refer to an individual's intensity of interest in a product and the importance of the product for that person. They can be classified as:

- low
- high
- enduring
- situational.

Low involvement products tend to be less expensive and have less associated social risk, such as many grocery items.

High involvement products tend to be those that are *visible* to others (e.g. clothing, furniture, or automobiles) and *expensive*, as well as issues of *high importance*, such as health care.

Enduring involvement is a person's ongoing and long-term interest in a product or product category.

Situational involvement is a person's temporary and dynamic interest in a product, which usually results from a particular set of circumstances (e.g. the need to buy a new car after being involved in an accident).

Levels of involvement and problem-solving types

Level of involvement, as well as other factors, affects a person's selection of one of three types of consumer problem solving:

- routinized response behavior
- limited problem solving
- extended problem solving.

Routinized response behavior is the consumer problem-solving process used when buying frequently purchased, low-cost items needing very little search-and-decision effort. Examples of these can range from the purchase of convenience products such as a bottle of milk, a newspaper, or a pint of lager at the local pub near the university at lunchtime.

Limited problem solving refers to the consumer problem-solving process employed when buying occasionally or when the consumer needs to obtain information about an unfamiliar brand in a familiar product category. The kinds of products that call for this problem solving include shopping goods such as white goods (e.g. dishwasher, tumble dryer, or fridge-freezer).

Extended problem solving is a consumer problem-solving process employed when purchasing unfamiliar, expensive, or infrequently bought products. Examples here are typically either specialty goods (e.g. golf clubs, camping gear, rare artifacts, or works of art) or unsought goods such as financial services investment choices and decisions (e.g. stocks and shares, premium bonds, or even mortgage advice).

However, it is worth pointing out that buying a product does not always involve a type of problem solving, as the process can also be an unplanned event where consumers buy on impulse. What does this mean? *Impulse buying* is an unplanned buying behavior resulting from a powerful urge to buy something immediately. In other words, it is urgent buying. For example, you might have noticed signs on the front of shops in the high street saying "Closing Down Sale." Particular examples would be the Woolworths closing down sales across the UK at the end of 2009 as the high-street behemoth made its exit.

CONSUMER BUYING DECISION PROCESS

In understanding the buying decision process you may like to take a few minutes to ask the man or woman next to you in class if he or she prefers to shop for fruit and vegetables at farmers' markets (open markets) rather than at supermarkets such as Tesco or Sainsbury's, the key players in the UK. You may also be wondering why there seem to be longer queues at mobile phone kiosks in "China Town" at London's Soho or East London than there are at dedicated mobile phone shops such as T-Mobile, Vodafone, and Carphone Warehouse. Perhaps it may be connected to the fact that there may be more leeway for haggling, little or no hassle of credit checks for mobile phone contracts, options to purchase refurbished handsets, free unlocking as a product bundle, or many other benefits that can be derived from the small-time players. Now let's see what the literature has to say about the factors that affect buying decisions and the prescribed processes involved in reaching such decisions.

The consumer buying decision process is a five-stage purchase decision process (see Figure 6.2) that includes problem recognition, information search, evaluation of alternatives, purchase, and post-purchase evaluation. But some points must be mentioned:

- the actual act of purchase is only one stage that comes late in the process
- not all decision processes, once initiated, lead to an ultimate purchase (the individual may terminate the process at any stage)
- not all consumer buying decisions include all five stages.

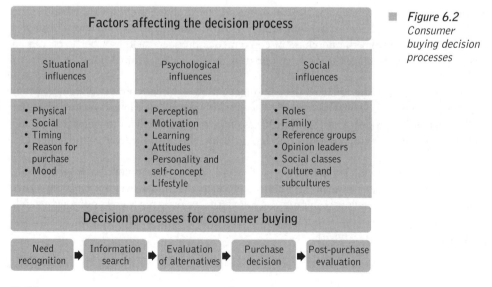

Figure 6.2
Consumer
buying decision
processes

Thompson and Panayiotopoulos (1999) once upheld the premise that small business purchase decisions are frequently taken by a single individual and, therefore, "this raises the possibility that the key predictors of small business decisions may be similar to those of individual consumers."[1] Following this line of reasoning, this chapter, while recognizing that business-to-business (B2B) or organizational buyer behavior may also be relevant here, adopts the business-to-consumer (B2C) approach.

Need recognition (Stage 1): need recognition is simply the difference between a desired state and actual condition (i.e. becoming aware of a need for a particular product). Note that marketers may use sales personnel, advertising, and packaging to trigger recognition of needs or problems. For example, advertisements suggesting that you might have a mouth ulcer can be seen in the marketing of Bonjela! Recognition speed can also be slow or fast. For example, responding to an advertisement about the need for life insurance may take longer than responding to one advocating a new type of shampoo that prevents split ends.

Information search (Stage 2): after the consumer becomes aware of the problem or need, he or she searches for information about products that will help resolve the problem or satisfy the need. There are two broad types of information search—*Internal* and *External*.

- *Internal search*: this is an information search situation in which buyers search their memories for information about their products that might solve their problem. For example, you might want to recall that the last time you went on holiday to the seaside resort of Blackpool you enjoyed the sunscreen that you purchased in an independent health and beauty shop rather than at The Body Shop in London.
- *External search*: this is an information search in which buyers seek information from sources other than memory (friends, relatives, public sources, marketing sources such as advertising, package labeling, and in-store displays).

Evaluation of alternatives (Stage 3): a successful information search yields a *consideration (evoked) set* of products or a group of brands that the buyer views as possible alternatives. At this third stage of the decision process, the consumer establishes a set of *evaluative criteria* against which to compare the characteristics of the products in the consideration set. For example, this could be in terms of price, how natural the sunscreen ingredients may be, the packaging and labeling of the sunscreen, and so on.

The consumer rates and eventually ranks the brands in the consideration set by using the criteria and their relative importance. Marketers can influence consumers' evaluation by *framing* the alternatives—that is, by the manner in which they describe the alternatives and their attributes. A typical example in this case could be your Anadin Extra (an over-the-counter painkiller) which promises to take away that headache even faster than the regular version you may have been used to. Another example could be the '2in1' promise on most shampoo labels—fighting dandruff at the same time as conditioning the hair.

Purchase Decision (Stage 4): at the purchase stage, the consumer selects the product or brand to be purchased. It is also at this stage that the actual purchase is made (unless the process has been terminated earlier). The decision to purchase, however, would depend on a number of factors, including:

- product availability

- seller choice
- terms of sale.

All of these factors may influence the final product selection. Sometimes they may all need to be present for the purchase to occur. For example, a desired product needs to be in stock (or at least easy to order) when needed; purchase might also be tied to the purchase of another product such as soaps with natural extracts or other beach or tanning accessories for the "serial" holidaymaker. Another option would be package deals which provide you with the popular high-street slogan of BOGOF (buy one, get one free)—for example, by throwing in free shuttle bus services, discounts on hotels, cinemas, and car hire all for purchasing an airline ticket at the right time. And if you were traveling to Atlantic City (the East Coast version of Las Vegas) from New York you just might get your first game on the house for getting on the Greyhound (the coach service similar to the National Express in the UK).

Post-purchase evaluation (Stage 5): this is the final stage of the buying decision process, where the buyer begins to evaluate the product after the purchase, based on many of the criteria used in the "evaluation of alternatives" stage. If the buyer is not happy with the product, a *cognitive dissonance* may be experienced. Cognitive dissonance is a buyer's doubts shortly after a purchase about whether it was the right decision or not. It enables the consumer to determine whether he or she is satisfied or otherwise with the purchase. This will ultimately determine any prospects of a repeat purchase or recommendation to friends and family (as we saw in the second stage—"information search"). For example, a nasty experience with a small-time money transfer business in South East London could result in Joe Bloggs' decision to stick with the big players such as Western Union and MoneyGram.

INFLUENCES OF THE BUYING DECISION PROCESS

There are three main types of influence that affect the buying decision process, as already highlighted in Figure 6.2. These are:

- situational influences
- psychological influences
- social influences.

Situational influences

These are factors resulting from circumstances, time, and location that affect the consumer buying decision process. It must be noted, however, that these factors can influence a consumer's actions at any stage of the buying process (i.e. they may serve to shorten, lengthen, or even terminate the buying process). Situational factors typically include physical surroundings, social surroundings, time perspective, reason for purchase, as well as the buyer's mood.

- **Physical surroundings:** these are factors in the physical environment in which the decision process occurs. For example, location, store atmosphere, aromas, sounds, lighting, and even the weather.
- **Social surroundings:** these are the social characteristics and interactions of others who are present during a purchase decision, or when the product is used or consumed, as well

as social conditions in the shopping environment. For example, did the purchase take place during a school trip or at a staff Christmas party?

■ **Time perspective:** the time dimension influences the buying decision process in several ways. For example, the time available to become knowledgeable about a product, to search for it, and to buy/use it, the time of purchase, and the time available to make the decision (i.e. a consumer may make a quick buying decision or delay the decision under time pressure). Typical examples would be last-minute shopping for Christmas, birthdays or Valentine's Day.

■ **Reason for purchase:** the reason for purchase raises the questions of what exactly the product purchase should accomplish and for whom. For example, people who are buying a gift may buy a different product from one they would buy for themselves.

■ **Buyer's mood/condition:** the buyer's momentary mood or momentary condition (e.g. fatigue, illness, feeling happy, being overexcited, or being short of cash) may have a bearing on the consumer buying decision process. However, any of these moods or conditions can affect a person's ability and desire to search for information, receive information, and evaluate alternatives, and can significantly influence a consumer's post-purchase evaluation.

Psychological influences

There are psychological factors that, in part, determine people's general behavior, and thus influence their behavior as consumers. They can be classified into six factors:

1. Perception
2. Motivation
3. Learning
4. Attitudes
5. Personality and self-concept
6. Lifestyle.

1. Perception

This is the process of (i) Selecting, (ii) Organizing, and (iii) Interpreting information inputs in order to produce meaning. This is a three-step process. Information inputs are sensations received, including sight, taste, hearing, smell, and touch. For example, when we hear an advertisement, see a friend, or smell or touch a product, we receive information inputs.

(i) **Selecting:** although we receive numerous pieces of information at once, only a few reach our consciousness. This is usually because of our tendency to be selective—sifting out what really matters to us while blocking out any other inputs that might serve as distractions. For example, Ms Bangers N. Mash from Yorkshire may attend a local event organized by Business Links in central London not because she is keen on sitting through a two-hour flashy presentation of statistics on women businesses and small businesses but because she is seeking out an opportunity for new suppliers or customers. Can you really blame her? Now that's one to debate that could form part of your coursework.

Characteristics of selectivity include:
- *Selective exposure*—an individual selects which inputs will reach awareness.
- *Selective distortion*—an individual changes or twists received information. This occurs when a person receives information inconsistent with personal feelings or beliefs. For

example, when individuals read reports that a glass of wine every day can be good for health then they feel less guilty about what could perhaps become binge drinking.

- *Selective retention*—an individual remembers information inputs that support his/her feelings and beliefs and forgets inputs that do not.

(ii) **Organizing:** mentally organizing and integrating new information with what is already stored in memory in order to produce meaning.

(iii) **Interpreting:** the assignment of meaning to what has been organized. In general, although marketers cannot control buyers' perceptions, they often try to influence them through information.

2. Motivation

Motivation is an internal energizing force that directs a person's behavior toward satisfying needs or achieving goals. A buyer's actions at any time are affected not by just one motive but by a set of motives, with varying degrees of strengths. Motives affect the direction and intensity of behavior.

One of the important theories to explain motivation is Maslow's hierarchy of needs (by psychologist Abraham Maslow). The theory classifies human needs into five levels, from the least important to the most important (see Figure 6.3). Once needs at one level are met, humans try to fulfill needs at the next level. Maslow suggested that our unfulfilled needs motivate us and that our needs are arranged in a hierarchy. The hierarchy of needs includes physiological, safety, social, self-esteem, and self-actualization needs. Maslow suggested that we fill the bottom-level, basic needs first before moving up the hierarchy. Until more basic needs such as safety are fulfilled, an individual has little interest in higher-level needs such as esteem and self-actualization (Kotler and Armstrong, 2010, p. 149).

In Maslow's hierarchy physiological needs are first met before safety, social, esteem, and ultimately self-actualization needs. These are discussed below:

- **Physiological needs:** the most basic level of need, and includes the requirements for survival such as food, water, sex, clothing, and shelter. People try to satisfy these first.
- **Safety needs:** the next level up, which includes security and freedom from physical and emotional pain and suffering.
- **Social needs:** the third level, which includes the human requirements for love and affection, and a sense of belonging.
- **Esteem needs:** the fourth level, in which people require respect and recognition from others as well as self-esteem, a sense of one's own worth.
- **Self-actualization needs:** the highest level of needs, which refers to people's need to grow and develop and to become all they are capable of becoming.

3. Learning

Learning refers to changes in an individual's thought processes and behavior caused by information and experience. The learning process is strongly influenced by the consequences of an individual's behavior. For example, behaviors with satisfying results tend to be repeated, and vice versa. Marketers help customers learn about their products (for example, by helping them gain experience with them, perhaps through free samples or in-store demonstrations). Consumers learn about products indirectly through information from salespeople, friends, relatives, and advertisements.

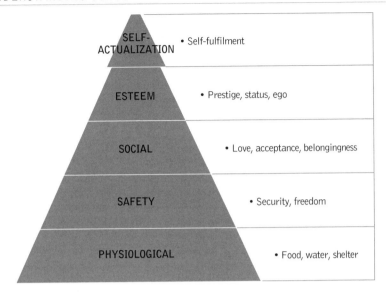

Figure 6.3
Maslow's
hierarchy of
needs

4. Attitudes

Attitudes are an individual's enduring evaluation of feelings about and behavioral tendencies toward an object or idea. It is important to note, however, that (i) attitudes are learned through experience and interaction with others; (ii) attitudes remain generally stable, but they can be changed over a long time; and (iii) attitudes consist of three major components:

1. **Cognitive** (knowledge and information about an object or idea)
2. **Affective** (feelings and emotions toward an object or idea)
3. **Behavioral** (actions regarding an object or idea).

Consumers' attitudes toward a firm and its products strongly influence its success or failure. Although research into buyer behavior in the context of SMEs has been found to be miniscule or scarce (see Morrissey and Pittaway, 2004; Andrews and Rogers, 2005, p. 2), marketers may still use several approaches to measure consumer attitudes: (i) direct questioning of consumers; (ii) projective techniques; and (iii) attitude scales, which are means of measuring consumers' attitudes by gauging the intensity of individuals' reactions to adjectives, phrases, or sentences about an object.

Marketers may also try to change negative attitudes toward an aspect of a marketing mix to make them more favorable. But this is generally a long, expensive, and difficult task and may require promotional efforts.

5. Personality and self-concept (or self-image)

A personality is a set of internal traits and distinct behavioral tendencies that result in consistent patterns of behavior. The uniqueness of one's personality arises from both *hereditary background* and *personal experiences*. When advertisements focus on certain types of personalities, the advertiser uses personality characteristics that are valued positively.

Personality is described in terms of traits such as self-confidence, dominance, sociability, autonomy, defensiveness, adaptability, and aggressiveness. Personality can be useful in analyzing behavior for certain products. Consumers are likely to choose brands with personalities that match their own. For example, someone with a sophisticated personality might be attracted to a more sophisticated product, such as a BMW, while someone with a more rugged personality might be attracted to a more rugged product, such as a Jeep (see Kotler and Armstrong, 2010, p. 148).

Self-concept (or self-image) is a perception or view of oneself. Buyers buy products that reflect or enhance their self-concept. A person's self-concept may influence brand selection.

6. Lifestyle

Lifestyle is an individual's pattern of living expressed through activities, interests, and opinions (i.e. the way people spend time, interact with others, and their general outlook on life and living). A consumer lifestyle influences product needs. People, at least partially, determine their lifestyle. But lifestyles are influenced by other factors (i.e. personality, age, education, income, and social class).

Social influences

Social influences are the forces that other people exert on one's buying behavior. They include the following:

- roles
- family
- reference groups
- opinion leaders
- social classes
- culture and subcultures.

Roles are actions and activities that an individual in a particular position is supposed to perform based on his/her expectations, as well as those of others. Each individual has many roles and each role affects both general behavior and buying behavior.

Family includes an individual's roles within the family that to some extent influences that individual's behavior as a buyer. Within a household, an individual may perform one or more buying-decision roles (see Table 6.1):

- The **gatekeeper** is the household member who collects and controls information, price and quality comparisons, locations of sellers, and assessments of which brand best suits the family's needs.
- The **influencer** is a family member who expresses his or her opinions and tries to influence buying decisions.
- The **decider** is a member who makes the buying choice.
- The **buyer** is a member who actually makes the purchase.
- The **user** is any household member who consumes or uses the product.

Table 6.1 Types of family decision making

Decision-making type	Decision maker	Types of products
Husband-dominant	Male head-of-household	Lawn mowers, hardware and tools, refrigerators, washing machines
Wife-dominant	Female head-of-household	Children's clothing, women's clothing, groceries, toiletries, home décor
Autonomic	Equally likely to be husband or wife, but not both	Men's clothing, luggage, toys and games, cameras and camcorders
Syncratic	Jointly husband and wife	Vacations, TVs, living-room furniture, family cars, financial planning

Reference groups are groups that positively or negatively affect a person's values, attitudes, or behaviors (i.e. family, friends, colleagues, religious groups, sport groups, and professional groups). Another definition describes it as "[a] group that a person identifies with so strongly that he or she adopts the values, attitudes, and behavior of group members" (Pride and Ferrell, 2008, p. 208). In order to appreciate the importance of reference groups, the different types and specific marketing implications need to be provided. First, let us consider the existing types of reference groups.

Types of reference groups include:

- **A membership reference group**—one to which an individual actually belongs; the individual identifies with group members strongly enough to take on the values, attitudes, and behaviors of people in that group.
- **An aspirational reference group**—a group to which a person aspires to belong; the individual desires to be like those group members.
- **A dissociative or negative reference group**—a group that a person does not wish to be associated with; the individual does not want to take on the values, attitudes, and behavior of group members.

Marketing implications of reference groups include:

- A reference group is an individual's point of comparison and a source of information.
- How much a reference group influences a purchasing decision depends on the individual's susceptibility to reference group influence and strength of involvement with the group.
- Reference groups may affect the product decision, the brand decision, or both.
- A marketer sometimes uses reference group influence in advertisements to promote the message that people in a specific group buy such products, and are highly satisfied with them.

An **opinion leader** is member of an informal group (reference group member) who provides information about a specific topic to other group members. An opinion leader is likely to be most influential when:

- consumers have high product involvement with low product knowledge
- they share the opinion leader's values and attitudes
- the product details are numerous or complicated.

Examples of opinion leaders may include a family doctor (medicine); religious leaders and scholars (possibly the Dalai Lama, the Pope, or the Islamic scholar Tariq Ramadan);[2] a well-known computer expert (IT and computing); an automobile expert (e.g. Jeremy Clarkson of *Top Gear*); a well-known journalist (e.g. CNN's Christiane Amanpour or Zeinab Badawi of the BBC); or even a reputable professor, such as the late international business professor John H. Dunning (education). It can be seen that opinion leaders cut across sections of society from medicine right through to education.

Social class refers to society's relatively permanent and ordered divisions whose members share similar values, interests, and behaviors. Unlike nationality or ethnic subculture, social class is determined by a combination of many variables, such as occupation, income, education, and wealth (see Kotler and Armstrong, 2010, p. 140). It has also been defined as an open group of individuals with similar social rank. In other words, social class is the criteria used to group people in their variation from one society to another. In general, occupation, education, income, wealth, and possessions are very important criteria. People can be divided into three to seven categories (e.g. low, middle, high). Individuals within a social class develop common patterns of behavior.

Because social class influences so many aspects of a person's life, it also affects (i) buying decisions; (ii) spending, saving, and credit practices; (iii) type, quality, and quantity of products; and (iv) shopping patterns and stores patronised. In relation to (iv) you could consider why students may favor retail giant Primark over Marks & Spencer when they plan to shop for clothes.

Culture is the accumulation of values, beliefs, knowledge, customs, objects, and concepts of a society. Culture includes three key attributes, made up of both tangible and intangible elements:

1. tangible items such as food, clothing, furniture, buildings, and tools
2. intangible concepts such as education, welfare, and laws
3. values and a broad range of behaviors accepted by a specific society.

Culture is the most basic cause of a person's wants and behavior. Every culture contains smaller subcultures, or groups of people with shared value systems based on common life experiences and situations. A **subculture** is a group of individuals whose characteristic, values, and behavior patterns are similar, but different from those in the surrounding culture. Subcultural boundaries are usually based on geographic designations and demographic factors. Subcultures include nationalities, religions, racial groups, and geographic regions. Many subcultures make up important markets. For example, the West Indian population in Brixton (South London); the Turkish population in Wood Green (North London); the Asian population in Bethnal Green and White Chapel (East London); and the African population in Peckham (South East London) can form the basis for location decision of SMEs targeting these ethnic populations.

The concepts, values, and behavior that make up a culture are learned and passed from one generation to the next. Because culture affects the ways people buy and use products, it influences the development, promotion, distribution, and pricing of products. People from other cultures have different attitudes, values, and needs. A general understanding of culture would enable marketers to adapt to different methods of doing business and develop different types of marketing mixes. It may also partially explain why most SMEs engage in niche marketing activities such as Turkish restaurants and grocery shops in the Wood Green area of London.

SUMMARY

The focus of this chapter has been on buyer behavior in the context of SMEs. While the subject can be looked at from both the B2B and B2C angles, the focus has been through the latter lens. This is due to evidence highlighted in Morrissey and Pittaway (2004) and confirmed by Andrews and Rogers (2005), that small businesses' buyer behavior is very similar to that of individual consumers.

Consequently key consumer behavior elements discussed in this chapter have been divided into two broad levels. The first level is that of involvement. The second concerns the buying decision process and those influences moderating it. The latter is essential to the learning objectives stated at the beginning of the chapter, which include recognizing stages of the consumer buying decision process, as well as understanding the influences impacting on this process. Such influences have been discussed with reference to situational, social, and psychological influences. In the last context, key consumer behavior attributes such as perception, motivation, learning and memory, and attitudes were also discussed. This is primarily because these influences, to a large extent, affect the success or failure of marketers as they seek to tap into the explicit or latent needs of both their existing and their potential customers and consumers.

REVIEW QUESTIONS

1. Explain some of the characteristics affecting consumer behavior and demonstrate how these might apply in entrepreneurship marketing.

2. Using any SME example, identify and discuss the different stages in the buyer decision process.

3. What are the major stages in the consumer buying decision process? To what extent are these applicable to SMEs?

4. What is culture? How does it affect an individual's buying behavior?

5. In what ways do lifestyles affect the consumer buying decision process? Illustrate your answer with relevant examples.

6. How do marketers attempt to shape consumers' learning?

7. Why are marketers concerned about consumer attitudes?

8. What are the categories of situational factors that influence consumer buying behavior? Explain how these may be similar for SMEs.

9. What are reference groups? How do they influence buying behavior?

10. Who are opinion leaders? How can SME marketers effectively use these people?

CASE STUDY 6: DAVIES & SONS—SAVILE ROW TAILORS

Introduction

Davies & Sons is now one of the few bespoke[3] tailors remaining on Savile Row. Savile Row tailoring is one of Britain's most enduring traditions and treasured exports. While the quality of mass-produced, off-the-peg suits has improved while retaining a competitive price-point, this gentlemen's club of enduring tradition, unsurpassed technique, and style lives on. A Savile Row suit is a potent symbol of authority and the global uniform of politics, business, and society. Embedded in its fibres is a history of respectability dating back to suits of armour worn in battle. Each tailoring house was originally associated with a distinct kind of military uniform, such as naval wear from Gieves and Hawkes. The air of respectability, quality, and style that a suit gives its owner has helped seal its enduring appeal. The time-honored tradition contained within a road just a few hundred yards long has acted as the epicentre for men's fashion for over 200 years and remains a dominant force through its continued innovation.

Case background

Thomas Davies inherited the Cork Street tailoring business from his deceased brother and moved to Hanover Street in 1804. Prior to inheriting the business, Thomas Davies worked for Greenwalls, who were procurement agents for the Royal Navy. Davies could boast that he tailored for the most famous sailor of the age, Admiral Lord Nelson, whose victory at Trafalgar led to a buoyant naval officer class keen to order their uniforms and civilian suits at their leader's bespoke tailor. During Thomas Davies's tenure as "guv'nor," Davies & Son claimed to dress "all the crowned heads of Europe."

The last Davies exited the firm in 1935 and it was taken over by its cutters who continued to run the company until 1996. The times were glamorous but turbulent. Davies & Son was swift to capitalize on its Duke of Windsor association and attracted Hollywood royalty like Clark Gable and Tyrone Power. In 1952, another Davies & Son stellar customer, Douglas Fairbanks Jr., was moved to declare "Savile Row has recaptured the tailoring supremacy of the world."

In 1979 the firm left Hanover Street which had had a private room exclusively for the use of George V. It took with it fitting room chairs, fenders, fireplace screens and records rediscovered after a century of neglect. By now 90 per cent of Davies & Sons' turnover was international trade. The firm announced, "our business was built on the clothing requirements of the aristocracy of Europe and Great Britain. Today our business is mainly with the affluent and famous abroad; an ideal commercial profile, we are advised, in times when exports are of prime importance."

Alan Bennett, a keen custodian of Savile Row's history, had trained under Michael Skinner, who had over 40 years' experience in bespoke tailoring. Alan soon had his name above a door on Savile Row in the late 1980s, servicing his own book of "businessmen, stockbrokers, a few Lords, Earls." He then bought Davies & Son in 1997. Davies & Son had already incorporated a number of other tailors including Bostridge and Curties and Watson, Fargerstrom and Hughes (Bunny Roger's tailor) and Alan Bennett went on to add other great bespoke tailoring houses including Johns and Pegg (the nineteenth-century royal, military and Household Cavalry tailor), James and James (who had acquired Scholte when the great man retired), Wells of Mayfair (established on Maddox Street in 1829) and Fallan & Harvey. He gained a reputation as a tailor to the Court of St James's overseas ambassadors and continues to tailor for the High Commissioners in the remaining British colonies. Today, Davies & Son on Savile Row is the only old school bespoke tailoring house left on the west side of the Row and still attracts the great and the good of the British establishment.

Davies & Son's products range from bespoke suits to cufflinks and shoes. The following is taken from their website (www.DaviesandSon.com).

Bespoke suits

Why do our clients come to us for their bespoke clothes? On a practical level, we have over 2,000 cloth samples, we will take 21 direct measurements which we use to draft your individual paper pattern, we build the foundation of the suit by incorporating wool and mohair canvasses and horsehair chest pieces and then we will trim the suit with the addition of the finest linings, interlinings, buttonhole silks and buttons. It is then basted together for your first fitting by the cutter who measured and cut your original pattern. After this fitting your pattern is corrected and your suit re-cut to accommodate all the adjustments we have made.

Our clients come back to us because we're doing what we love and they enjoy wearing probably the finest of Savile Row garments. It's the quality and care with which we construct the suit that sets it apart from most bespoke garments. Each part of the process is undertaken by a skilled tailor who gives the utmost attention and care to every detail of the suit. Simply put, it's our passion and what we love to do! You can order a Savile Row quality made to measure suit online.

Cufflinks

We offer an attractive selection of cufflinks to complement your Davies & Son suit as well as a comprehensive set of accessories such as traditional fob watches, gold or silver tie pins, bridesmaids gift sets, silk top hats and much more.

Shoes

To complement the quality of our suits we stock the complete ranges of Loakes and Trickers shoes. These can be ordered in the Savile Row shop or bought online.

Loakes shoes

Loake 1880 Collection are simply the finest shoes Loakes make. No detail has been compromised in this premium range of luxurious and elegant bench-made footwear produced using the time-honored techniques that can be traced back to when Loakes first started. Only the very best hand-burnished calf leather is used as well as Loakes' own customary leather built heels, leather linings and insoles.

Loakes believe there is no better example the firm's continuing aim to produce the most handsome, comfortable and durable shoes possible. This comprehensive collection of fine, handmade footwear has been carefully designed to provide the very best fit and performance in wear. New variations on traditional designs sit alongside some of their best-selling classics.

In Design Loake Loakes has arguably reinterpreted formal footwear by altering shape, cut and detailing to create shoes with a modern edge and a contemporary feel. The aim is to create the perfect blend of excellence and style by combining traditional manufacturing quality with strong awareness of fashion.

Shoes in the Loakes Comfort range incorporate the following features to provide exceptional comfort in wear:

- cushioned leather insoles for comfort with rubber inserts for extra flexibility and grip
- super soft leathers
- breathable leather linings.

Trickers shoes

These include three main collections—Jermyn Street, 1829, and Country. The Jermyn Street Collection ranges in price from £260 to £285. The 1829 Collection includes Piccadilly, Kensington, Regent, Mayfair, Sloane, and Belgrave—named after London's districts, it is priced between £270 and £275. The Country Collection includes Malton, Henry, Ilkley, Bourton, Stow, Burford and Woodstock and are priced between £270 and £285.

Sources: Boc Ly (7 September 2009) Stitched up on Savile Row. BBC News. Online at: http://news.bbc.co.uk/local/london/hi/people_and_places/newsid_8241000/8241730.stm (accessed 28 February 2010); British Style Genius (n.d.) Tailored: the icon, Savile Row. BBC. Online at: http://www.bbc.co.uk/britishstylegenius/content/21757.shtml (accessed 12 August 2010).

CASE QUESTIONS

1. According to Davies & Sons, "Our clients come back to us because we're doing what we love and they enjoy wearing probably the finest of Savile Row garments." What consumer behavior concept is being alluded to in this remark?
2. In 1952 Douglas Fairbanks Jr., a customer of Davies & Son, was moved to declare that "Savile Row has recaptured the tailoring supremacy of the world." What might this mean for the likes of Davies & Son? Do you agree that customers in the twenty-first century might still hold this view? Why or why not?
3. During Thomas Davies's tenure as "guv'nor," Davies & Son claimed to dress "all the crowned heads of Europe." To what extent do you think this might be an effective marketing strategy?
4. Do you agree with the explanations provided by the management of Davies & Sons under the question, "Why do our clients come to us for their bespoke clothes?"

NOTES

1. See also Morrissey and Pittaway (2004), as well as *Buyer Behaviour in SMEs* by Andrews and Rogers (2005, p. 2).
2. For a profile of Tariq Ramadan see his article in the *Guardian* (29 November 2009), "My compatriots' vote to ban minarets is fuelled by fear." Online at: http://www.guardian.co.uk/commentisfree/belief/2009/nov/29/swiss-vote-ban-minarets-fear (accessed 12 August 2010).
3. The term bespoke has been a source of controversy as Savile Row tries to defend its territory. The definition of "bespoke" is "adj, chiefly Brit (especially of clothing or a website, computer program, etc) made to the customer's specifications" (see *BBC News Magazine* (2008)).

REFERENCES

Andrews, T. and Rogers, B. (2005) *Buyer Behaviour in SMEs*. Research sponsored by DocumentGENie. University of Portsmouth Working Paper Series. 13 September, p. 2.

BBC News (2010) "Frisbee inventor Walter Frederick Morrison dies aged 90." Online at: http://news.bbc.co.uk/2/hi/americas/8512198.stm (accessed 12 February 2010).

BBC News Magazine (19 June 2008) "What does 'bespoke' mean?" Online at: http://news.bbc.co.uk/2/hi/uk_news/magazine/7463790.stm (accessed 12 February 2010).

Boc, Ly (7 September 2009) "Stitched up on Savile Row." BBC News. Online at: http://news.bbc.co.uk/local/london/hi/people_and_places/newsid_8241000/8241730.stm (accessed 28 February 2010).

British Style Genius (n.d.) BBC website. Online at: http://www.bbc.co.uk/britishstylegenius/content/21757.shtml (accessed 12 August 2010).

Davies & Son's official website: http://www.daviesandson.com (accessed 12 August 2010).

Davies & Son's online ordering. https://www.daviesandson.com/daviesandson/neworders/ (accessed 12 August 2010).

Kotler, P. and Armstrong, G. (2010) *Principles of Marketing*. Upper Saddle River, NJ: Pearson Education. Thirteenth Global edition.

Morrissey, B. and Pittaway, L. (2004) "A study of procurement behaviour in small firms." *Journal of Small Business and Enterprise Development*, 11(2), pp. 254–262.

Pride, W. M. and Ferrell, O. C. (2008) *Marketing*. Fourteenth edition. Boston: Houghton Mifflin Company.

Ramadan, T. (2009) "My compatriots' vote to ban minarets is fuelled by fear." *Guardian*, 29 November. Online at: http://www.guardian.co.uk/commentisfree/belief/2009/nov/29/swiss-vote-ban-minarets-fear (accessed 12 August 2010).

Chapter 7

Entrepreneurship marketing research and SMEs

Robert Rugimbana, Richard Shambare and Maria Shambare

LEARNING OBJECTIVES

After reading this chapter, you will be able to:
- understand the essence of entrepreneurship market research (EMR)
- identify key factors affecting EMR in the context of SMEs
- distinguish EMR from traditional marketing research
- appreciate the role of EMR in the context of African countries.

INTRODUCTION

There is increasing interest among marketing researchers and practitioners regarding the important differences in marketing techniques and research strategies employed by small-to-medium and micro enterprises (SMEs) when compared with large corporations. Existing literature reports the use of different marketing approaches adopted by SMEs and large corporations, and that firm size is a key factor in influencing marketing approach (Coviello *et al.*, 2000; Collinson and Shaw, 2001; Gaddefors and Anderson, 2008; Jones and Rowley, 2009).

In addition, there is important recognition that in many transition economies such as the post-Communist countries and Asian and African countries, the growth of private businesses – the vast majority of which are small – is the key to economic prosperity (Rona-Tas and Sagi, 2005; OECD, 1996; Scase, 2003). Much of the market transition literature (e.g. Nee, 1991; Rona-Tas, 1994; Rona-Tas and Sagi, 2005) is built on the important viewpoint that the heart of enterprise development is entrepreneurship. Importantly, SME sector growth is fuelled by entrepreneurial initiative and there is a link between this activity and the size of the economy (Rona-Tas and Sagi, 2005).

Thus, the entrepreneurial paradigm sees economic units in the private sector as being on a continuum from the smallest, single-person business to the largest company. Each size is a stage in the process of entrepreneurial expansion even though not all small business entities will grow into large companies, despite their potential (Rona-Tas and Sagi, 2005). Rona-Tas and Sagi argue that the very expression 'small- and medium-sized enterprises' suggests that all SMEs are similar in principle and there may be a smooth progression from one to the another. In this regard, entrepreneurialism is viewed as being essential in SME or (small private firm) creation, particularly in organizing these entities such that they are innovative, capable, flexible and able to adopt and utilize new ideas and technologies.

Given the notion that the creation of new enterprises depends on environmental pull factors and the ability of entrepreneurs to identify new opportunities, the latter can only be seized through the use of sound research approaches. This has particularly important implications in environments where formal education, literacy rates and infrastructural conditions are not widespread.

Accordingly, this chapter seeks to examine how entrepreneurship marketing research (EMR) as practised by SMEs differs from conventional marketing research as utilized by large corporations. It uses transitional and developing environments such as African countries to contextualize the influence that EMR would have on research approaches that are utilized in these environments.

The structure of the chapter is as follows: first, we present the generic marketing framework as applied by large corporations. Subsequently, we articulate the rationale behind the structured approach and how this fits well within the ethos of larger firms. Next, we outline some characteristics of SMEs that render traditional marketing research approaches inappropriate and inapplicable within SMEs' contexts. We then introduce EMR – a more appropriate marketing tool for small firms – the nexus of entrepreneurship, innovation, creativity and marketing. Finally, we examine the application and implication of EMR in the African context generally.

The application of marketing is critical for the survival of any business, regardless of industry, sector or size. Furthermore, it is widely recognized that marketing is the process that preludes selling (Gaddefors and Anderson, 2008). In other words, it determines which markets present opportunities for selling products, which products to sell, to whom and how to communicate this, through which channels and for how much. To achieve viable marketing practices particular attention must be paid to the research approaches that are selected.

TRADITIONAL MARKETING RESEARCH

Traditional marketing research is understood to represent a systematic process identified through five distinct but interrelated phases: (1) problem definition; (2) research design; (3) research methods; (4) analysis and (5) presentation of findings and implications of these findings (see Figure 7.1). This approach is very similar to the steps followed when conducting academic research. Any (academic) research endeavour almost always begins with the formulation of a research problem. All subsequent activities attempt to resolve the research problem through the selection of an appropriate research design. Naturally, the research is influenced by how the research problem is perceived or how the researcher sees the world (ontological orientation), by what means the research is undertaken to collect data and the choice of data analysis paradigms.

Gaddefors and Anderson (2008) interpret the similarity of academic research to traditional marketing research to be a result of the numerous positivistic research publications that helped lay the foundation for marketing as a discipline in the 1950s. Thus, the resultant complexion of marketing research tilted towards classical positivism that dictates scientific 'measurement' and analyses of variables appears to have been best captured in the axiom 'You can only manage what you can measure.'

Until recently numerous academics in marketing and several other business disciplines conducted research utilizing the well-known positivist paradigm and school of thought. However, within the last two decades or so, there has been a shift towards the use of a constructivist paradigm and its qualitative approaches and methodologies. Essentially, a paradigm is a shared framework of assumptions held within a discipline, sub-discipline or a school of

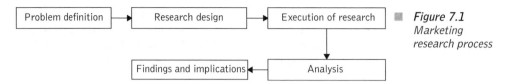

Figure 7.1
Marketing
research process

thought within a discipline (Veal, 2005). Paradigms have also been described as systems of thinking, including basic assumptions, key issues and methods for seeking answers (Neumann, 2006). It is important for the researcher to select the ideal paradigm as it will assist in guiding towards answering the research question. As alluded to above, in conducting research, the two major paradigms (positivism and constructivism) need to be evaluated before choosing a research methodology (Veal, 2005).

Positivism is a research approach that treats 'social facts' as existing independently of the activities of both participants and researchers (Silverman, 2006). In methodological terms, this paradigm is characterized as primarily using quantitative methods that are intervention-ist and de-constructualized (Mertens, 1998). Conversely, the constructivist paradigm is a relatively new school of thought and is characterized by using primarily qualitative methods in a hermeneutical and dialectical manner (Tashakkori and Teddlie, 2003). Constructivism, or the interpretive approach, takes the view that observations cannot be pure in the sense of altogether excluding the interests and values of individuals; investigations must employ empathic understanding of those being studied (Tashakkori and Teddlie, 2003).

Positivism was once regarded by the scientific community as a 'superior and dominant' research paradigm. Thus, marketing researchers pushed for marketing's respectability as a 'researchable' discipline through the use of quantitative methodologies. It is against this background that the emergence and adoption of the structured marketing research approach was adopted and became predominant. Given its routine nature and predictability, such an approach became and still is popular among marketers within large corporations. Above all, the 'classical management' practices of budgeting, measurement and forecasting can be 'wholly' transposed within a top-down marketing framework. Hence, this marketing approach is preferred and more applicable to larger firms because of the following considerations:

- Quantitative research is viewed to be objective, valid and reliable.
- Emphasis on measurement – 'SMART' principles of management that state that 'one can only manage that which can be measured'. Ideally, it must be **S**pecific, **M**easurable, **A**ttainable, **R**elevant and **T**ime-bound. For instance, marketing can be considered to be measurable in that sense (e.g. **x** per cent increase in market share or **y** per cent increase in sales).
- Large firm processes and practices are aligned to traditional marketing theory (such as the 4Ps and top-down attitudes of market segmentation). The positivist approach – the measuring and quantifying of variables such as sales, market share, growth – is aligned to budgeting and planning – processes that large organizations are good at.
- Large firms rely on economies of scale, i.e. selling large quantities to a large enough market. Therefore, quantitative market research is likely to be akin to mass-marketing.

WHAT ARE SMES AND HOW DO THEY CONDUCT MARKETING ACTIVITIES?

When deciding whether a business is an SME or not, there are several factors normally considered. The common ones are number of employees, asset value and annual turnover. As a result, there are multiple definitions and conceptualizations of SMEs. For our purposes we will consider an SME to be any small business that behaves entrepreneurially, i.e. enterprises in which the owners have significant influence on daily operations. These organizations mostly assume the entrepreneur's personality as opposed to policies and systems that govern the larger companies. As discussed above, owner-managed entities, one-person businesses and even family businesses fall within this category. Although important arguments have been presented to suggest that there is an important distinction between entrepreneurship and self-employment on the basis of whether a small private enterprise is an enterprise or household-centred business (Rona-Tas and Sagi, 2005), the need for research is universal, and for smaller private entities one would not expect large differences where research approaches are concerned. This argument is supported by the findings of a review of the literature by Aldrich and Waldinger (1990, p. 112) cited in Malhotra *et al.* (1996, p. 7):

> Many writers have suggested making a distinction between entrepreneurs and owner/managers on the basis of either innovativeness or risk, but few have done a convincing job. Neither economists nor sociologists have been able to operationalize this distinction so that "entrepreneurs" are clearly differentiated from "owners" or even the self-employed.

This is very important in the African context where it could be argued that most small private businesses are in fact self-employment- or household-based entities born of necessity because unemployment levels remain high.

ENTREPRENEURSHIP AND SMES

It has been argued above that the very expression 'small- and medium-sized enterprises' suggests SMEs are similar in principle. In this regard, entrepreneurialism is viewed as being essential in SME or small private firm creation, particularly in organizing these entities so that they are innovative, capable, flexible and able to adopt and utilize new ideas and technologies (Rona-Tas and Sagi, 2005).

Since entrepreneurship is the sum total of social, psychological, commercial and economical interactions, it can best be appreciated as resulting from opportunities in the marketplace. For example, all the dot.com companies, such as Dell, Amazon.com, eBay or Yahoo fall within the category of entrepreneurial SMEs, as these companies' strategies are greatly influenced by founder-owners. Goss (2005) defines entrepreneurship as a social function whose ultimate objective is value creation through opportunity recognition that involves the processes of:

- innovation and creativity
- opportunity creation
- creating a market
- creating an identity.

Bruyat and Julien (2000) contend that entrepreneurship is a process of 'new' value creation in which new products, new identities, new companies and new entrepreneurs are collectively co-created by the entrepreneur and his or her interaction with society (Henry *et al.*, 2005). Figure 7.2. summarizes the entrepreneurial process – beginning with sensing/perception of opportunity and ultimately resulting in a creative process to capitalize on the gap.

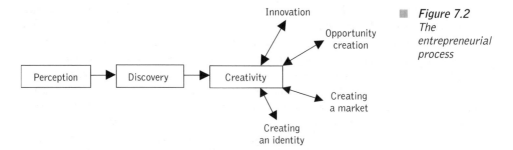

Figure 7.2
The entrepreneurial process

ENTREPRENEURSHIP MARKETING

Unlike traditional marketing management, entrepreneurship is based on a bottom-up marketing approach (Stokes, 2000), which has foundations in the socio-relational aspects of entrepreneurship. But because of the entrepreneurial viewpoint that business is a creative and social process, the traditional five-step marketing approach that requires 'objective measurement' of variables falls out of sync with entrepreneurship.

Table 7.1 SMEs vs corporations

Factor	Large firms	SMEs
Resource base	Usually large.	Limited and often leaner resource base.
Business stability	Stable business that has been in operation for years. Enjoys control over its environment and market due to increased market power.	In its early years, the business is very fluid and still building its resource base. Difficult to control business environment.
Marketing philosophy	Pre-existing market to which the business needs to adjust.	Market can be created. Relatively smaller market share.
Management style	Management. Governed by pre-defined policies and rules.	Leadership, creativity, innovativeness.

Entrepreneurs and entrepreneurship rely on a social lens to view the world; they understand it socially and approach it as such. Hence, entrepreneurship marketing utilizes qualitative methodologies appropriate to their ontological orientation. Furthermore, entrepreneurs view themselves as unorthodox and rarely follow or even understand the traditional ways of business and marketing (Stokes *et al.*, 1997; Gaddefors and Anderson, 2008). Entrepreneurs rely more on constructivist approaches since constructivism, unlike positivism, allows for much wider freedom as well as creativity in choosing methodologies, methods and analysis. In addition, entrepreneurs' own understanding and interpretation of the environment are integral aspects of the marketing research. Moreover, qualitative research is also more suited given the complexity and unpredictability of social relations which small firms operate within. Above all, entrepreneurs find it cumbersome to conduct marketing research using the traditional and systematic five-step approach (Doole and Lowe, 2003).

It should also be noted that the entrepreneurial process (Figure 7.2) is a fluid one. It does not necessarily occur sequentially (from perception to discovery and then creativity) within different markets or for different entrepreneurs. This flexibility, which Stokes (2000) defines as a bottom-up approach, is that which makes qualitative research strategies more appropriate for entrepreneurship marketing. Now let us turn our attention to some SME characteristics that favour the proposed marketing approach indicated above.

SMEs are characterized by a leaner resource base, and such enterprises tend to be vulnerable when young and small. Comparatively, small firms have less market share and less market power, which leads to them operating in less-controllable environments (see Table 7.1 for a comparative analysis of SMEs and large firms).

Revisiting the very essence of entrepreneurship, we see that entrepreneurship was founded on imaginativeness, creativity and resourcefulness, which ultimately results in an entity that processes ideas and dreams into profit, employment and growth. Likewise, such innovative thinking 'outside the box' may be the key in EMR. Much research into entrepreneurship marketing practices has culminated in the entrepreneurship marketing (EM) framework (Jones and Rowley, 2009). Unlike traditional marketing research approaches, this model is an EM technique premised on qualitative research methodologies utilizing key entrepreneurial features. In other words, the EM advocates for value creation through:

- entrepreneurs' social networks and interactions
- innovation and creativity
- technology/social interactions.

Because these attributes are the very essence of entrepreneurship, it makes the EM approach suitable and appropriate for small, micro and medium enterprises. SMEs are different from larger companies in many respects: practices and processes, ownership structure and generally their business ethos and philosophy are also different. In general, SMEs are founded on creativity and innovation; they thrive on creating new ideas or acting 'outside the box'.

Whereas conventional marketing dictates a top-down strategy by which the market is first identified and segmented, following which the business positions itself to fit the market,

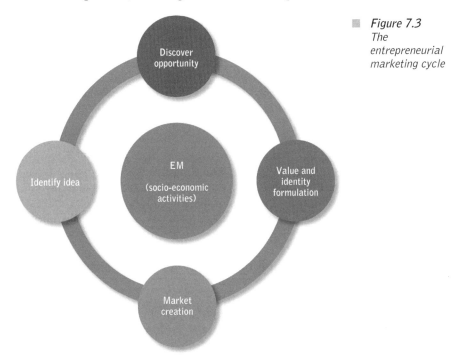

Figure 7.3
The entrepreneurial marketing cycle

smaller firms apply different techniques (Jones and Rowley, 2009). SMEs, for a number of justifiable reasons, use a bottom-up approach in which the entrepreneur has an idea first and then finds (or creates) a market (Stokes, 2000).

SELECTED RESEARCH INTO RESEARCH ISSUES PERTAINING TO SMES

Numerous studies have been conducted on the research issues that affect SMEs. O'Donnell and Cummins (1999a), who examined the graduate labour market, argue that any research conducted on SMEs must abide by a research agenda that grapples with difficult methodological questions. They encourage studies of a broadly ethnographic nature where persons are being studied. Other studies have examined issues for research policy where lifelong learning and SMEs are concerned (Johnson, 2002). Still other studies have examined the use of qualitative research methods in SMEs (O'Donnell and Cummins, 1999b). The last suggest that qualitative methods are more appropriate since network theory is becoming increasingly popular as a means of describing marketing activities in SMEs. This latter finding is significant in so far as EMR is concerned.

The application and implications for EMR in the African context

The applicability of research approaches to developing contexts or transition economies such as exist in Africa is a matter that has been subject to important debate. For the purpose of this chapter we briefly discuss two relevant studies: Malhotra (1998) and Wright *et al.* (2005). Wright *et al.* (2005) reviewed the research that has examined the business research strategies adopted by firms operating in emerging economies (defined as being either rapidly growing developing countries or countries that are in transition from being centrally planned economies).

Wright *et al.* (2005) pose the question as to whether the theories and methodologies which have been used in this kind of research, and which were originally developed for mature developed economies, are suited to the social political and economic contexts found in developing countries. Their study focuses on four conceptual perspectives: transaction cost theory, agency theory, resource-based theory and institutional theory. The authors assess how these theories have been applied to the study of firms in four particular situations – firms from developed countries that are entering emerging economies, domestic companies competing within emerging economies, firms from emerging economies entering other emerging economies and firms from emerging economies entering developed economies. The study found that most of the studies on the above draw on institutional theory in their analysis and that the prediction that the other three conceptual perspectives would become more prominent in research has only been partially realized. Essentially findings are somewhat unequivocal in regard to the application of research methods to developing contexts. Perhaps the most important consideration that arises from many studies that have examined such research strategies relates to the impact on research approaches that such a culturally diverse continent as Africa would have. In any given African country there are important ethnic and cultural differences that influence the entire research process.

According to Malhotra (1998), research that involves developing contexts must of necessity recognize the influence of culture. Therefore, when low-involvement products are focused (a sector where SMEs tend to predominate), the popular measures applied in developed economic settings may be unsuitable for developing economic contexts. He proposes an alternative approach that takes into consideration the need to reduce the data collection demands imposed on the respondents. Malhotra proposes the use of pictorial or visual stimuli and seeks input from respondents using simple binary scales. This obviously has less to do with culture and more to do with literacy and educational levels. In relation to cultural matters, Malhotra *et al.* (1996) suggest a number of important considerations with regard to cross-cultural and cross-national research efforts. Although Malhotra *et al.* (1996) argue that their suggestions apply to businesses working cross-nationally, the African context is so unique as to cast doubt on their proposals being equally applicable to every country in Africa because sometimes national boundaries or nation-states do not coincide with cultural boundaries. Very distinct cultural groups in each African country represent the enormous heterogeneity of the region and these can act as nation-states themselves. Therefore, considerations listed by Malhotra *et al.* (1996) which apply to critical stages of the research process are listed and discussed below and then adapted to the African SME context. Indeed, the following steps may help SME researchers to account for environmental and cultural differences when conducting research in Africa within or between countries and culture groups.

Problem formulation

It is suggested by Malhotra *et al.* (1996) that the research problem needs to be defined in terms of local environmental and cultural factors. This involves the identification of relevant local geographic traits, economics, values, needs or habits. The authors go on to suggest the following steps in the marketing process which are also applicable to SME owner-managers in Africa:

- Define the marketing research problem in terms of local environmental and cultural factors. As far as possible the researcher should make no judgements. Instead the process should involve an identification of the related traits, economics, values, needs or habits in the proposed market culture.
- Isolate the self-reference criterion (SRC) influence on the problem and examine it carefully to see how it complicates the problem. Examine the differences between Steps 1 and 2. If differences are found, they can be attributed to the SRC.
- Redefine the problem without the SRC influence and address it for the target market situation. If the differences in Step 3 are significant, the impact of the SRC should be carefully considered.

Research approach

According to Malhotra *et al.* (1996), the approach developed for the study should address and control alternative explanations for the results. The authors argue that plausible rival hypotheses for the results can be both substantive and methodological. A substantive alternative explanation may be that another cultural variable, not controlled by the researcher, accounts for the differential results obtained. Methodologically, the differences obtained may be attributed to sampling problems, translational inadequacies, interviewing and data collection difficulties and a host of other problems. The authors point out that many stable reference points should be built into the approach so that valid interpretations of the results can be made.

Research design

According to Malhotra *et al.* (1996), in formulating a research design, considerable effort is required to ensure the equivalence and comparability of secondary and primary data obtained from different cultures. In the context of collecting primary data, qualitative research, survey methods, scaling techniques, questionnaire design and sampling considerations are particularly important.

Measurement and scaling

Scientific observation and measurement are theory-laden; rationalism and empiricism interact to produce scientific explanation. Thus, researchers should critically examine the fit between the theoretical concepts they wish to study and the specific measures they employ. Whenever possible, the most direct measures should be used, using indirect measures as a last resort. In addition, several issues pertinent to equivalence, scale construction, reliability and validity should be considered (Malhotra *et al.*, 1996).

Sampling

According to Malhotra *et al.* (1996), in cross-cultural psychology, sampling issues deal with the selection of cultures, individuals, stimuli and responses. First, the cultural unit of analysis should be carefully defined. Indeed, as discussed above, the common practice of using a nation-state as a surrogate for culture may be inappropriate for countries with heterogeneous cultures (e.g. Africa, India, Malaysia). The authors argue that one approach could involve the use of 'cultunit' as the unit of analysis. The cultunit is defined as people who are local speakers of a common distinct language and who belong to either the same country or the same contact group. Thus, the cultunit incorporates three criteria:

- language
- territorial contiguity
- political organization (whenever there is sufficient authoritative political structure).

In addition, Malhotra *et al.* (1996) argue that statistical estimation of sample size may be difficult, as estimates of the population variance may be unavailable or may differ from situation to situation. Hence, the sample size is often determined by such qualitative considerations as:

- the importance of the decision
- the nature of the research
- the number of variables
- the nature of the analysis
- sample sizes used in similar studies
- incidence rates
- completion rates
- resource constraints.

The authors go on to state that it is important to recognize that the sample size may vary across cultures. Homogeneous cultures may require smaller samples while heterogeneous cultures require larger sample sizes.

Level of analysis

In this regard Malhotra *et al.* (1996) correctly point out that the data analysis could be conducted at three levels:

- individual

- within country or cultural unit
- across countries or cultural units.

Methodological fallacies

In conducting cross-cultural research it is important first to consider the use of appropriate measures of culture or dimensions such as is provided by Hofstede (1980) and Triandis (1984). In addition, it is important to avoid what is referred to as an 'ecological fallacy' (Malhotra *et al.*, 1996). This occurs when a researcher uses a culture-level correlation (for example, GNP, epidemiological rates) without conducting individual-level analysis to interpret individual behaviour. Similarly, a reverse ecological fallacy occurs when researchers construct cultural indices based on individual-level measurements (attitudes, values, behaviours) without conducting culture-level analysis (Rugimbana, 2007; Malhotra *et al.*, 1996; Schwartz, 1994).

The above considerations represent important clues for the operationalization of EMR research as adapted to the African context in this chapter. For a more comprehensive discussion please refer to the article 'Methodological issues in cross-cultural marketing research' (Malhotra *et al.*, 1996).

CONCLUDING REMARKS

This chapter set out to provide a general discussion about research and how it relates to SMEs. First, we presented the generic marketing framework as applied by large corporations universally. Subsequent to this, we articulated the rationale behind the structured approach and how this fits nicely within the ethos of larger firms. We then outlined some characteristics of SMEs that render traditional marketing research approaches inappropriate and to some extent inapplicable within SMEs' general contexts. We then introduced the notion of EMR, a more appropriate marketing tool for small firms, which is the nexus of entrepreneurship, innovation, creativity and marketing. Finally, we examined the application and operationalization of, and implications for, EMR in the African context by using a template provided by well-known marketing researchers. In keeping with the theme of the book, this chapter is intended to bring to light issues that pertain to SMEs in the contemporary African context.

REVIEW QUESTIONS

A: Business case scenario

Educational software development SME businesses are steadily growing in the southern African region of Zamunda. In the last few years, however, there has been a mix of SME business performances; some have failed but others have succeeded. Michelle, a software developer and recent college graduate, is interested in starting a software development SME business serving universities in the region, but is unsure as to whether or not she should take the risk.

Based on your knowledge of the research process:

1. How should Michelle go about conducting market research for her business?

2. What information is needed?

3. How could she go about collecting this information?

B: Further review questions

1. Define the following terms:
   a. Entrepreneurship
   b. Marketing research
   c. Entrepreneurship marketing
   d. Methodological fallacy
   e. Ecological fallacy

2. Discuss characteristics that differentiate EMR from traditional marketing research.

3. Using an example of a small business, list and discuss the entrepreneurship marketing research process.

4. Suggest ways of obtaining relevant market and consumer information in an EMR context. Provide examples.

5. Compare and contrast positivism and constructivism, within the context of marketing research.

6. In Africa, national boundaries do not necessarily relate to cultural boundaries. Suggest strategies that marketers could use to collect marketing data in such contexts.

BIBLIOGRAPHY

Bruyat, C. and Julien, P.A. (2000). Defining the field of research in entrepreneurship. *Journal of Business Venturing*, Vol. 16, No. 2, pp. 165–180.

Collinson, E. and Shaw, E. (2001). Entrepreneurial marketing – a historical perspective on development and practice. *Management Decision*, Vol. 39, No. 9, pp. 761–766.

Coviello, N.E., Brodie, R.J. and Munro, H.J. (2000). An investigation of marketing by firm size. *Journal of Business Venturing*, Vol. 15, pp. 523–545.

Doole, I. and Lowe, R. (2003). Cross cultural marketing for SMEs. In Rugimbana, R. and Nwankwo, S. (eds). *Cross Cultural Marketing*, Melbourne: Thomson, Ch. 16.

Gaddefors, J. and Anderson, A.R. (2008). Market creation: the epitome of entrepreneurial marketing practices. *Journal of Research in Marketing and Entrepreneurship*, Vol. 10, No. 1, pp. 19–39.

Goss, D. (2005). Schumpeter's legacy? Interactions and emotions in the society of entrepreneurship. *Entrepreneurship Theory and Practice*, Vol. 29, No. 2, pp. 205–218.

Henry, C., Hill, F. and Leitch, C. (2005). Entrepreneurship education and training: can entrepreneurship be taught? Part 1. *Education + Training*, Vol. 47, No. 2, pp. 98–111.

Hofstede, G. (1980). *Culture's Consequences: International Differences in Work-Related Values*, Beverly Hills, CA: Sage.

Johnson, S. (2002). Lifelong learning and SME: Issues for research and policy. *Journal of Small Business and Enterprise Development*, Vol. 9, No. 3, pp. 285–295.

Jones, R. and Rowley, J. (2009). Presentation of a generic 'EMICO' framework for research exploration of entrepreneurial marketing in SMEs. *Journal of Research in Marketing and Entrepreneurship*, Vol. 11, No. 1, pp. 5–21.

Mai, L. (2003). Cross-cultural marketing research. In Rugimbana, R. and Nwankwo, S. (eds). *Cross Cultural Marketing*, Melbourne: Thomson, Ch. 3.

Malhotra, N.K. (1998). A methodology for measuring consumer preferences in developing countries. *International Marketing Review*, Vol. 5, No. 3, pp. 52–66.

Malhotra, N.K., Agarwal, J. and Petersen, M. (1996). Methodological issues in cross-cultural marketing research. *International Marketing Review*, Vol. 13, No. 5, pp. 7–43.

Mertens, D.M. (1998). *Research Methods in Education and Psychology: Integrating Diversity with Quantitative and Qualitative Approaches*, Thousand Oaks, CA: Sage.

Nee, V. (1991). Social inequalities in reforming state socialism: between re-distribution and markets in China. *American Sociological Review*, Vol. 54, No. 5, pp. 663–681.

Neumann, W.L. (2006). *Social Research Methods: Qualitative and Quantitative Approaches* (6th Edn), Boston, MA: Pearson Education.

O'Donnell, A. and Cummins, D. (1999a). Employing graduates in SMEs: towards a research agenda. *Journal of Small Business and Enterprise Development*, Vol. 9, No. 3, pp. 271–284.

O'Donnell, A. and Cummins, D. (1999b). The use of qualitative methods to research networking in SMEs. *Qualitative Market Research; an International Journal*, Vol. 2, No. 2, pp. 82–91.

OECD (1996). Small business in transition economies. OECD Working Papers No. 4, Paris, p. 7.

Rona-Tas, A. (1994). The first half shall be the last? Entrepreneurship and communist cadres in the transition from socialism. *American Journal of Sociology*, Vol. 100, No. 1, pp. 40–69.

Rona-Tas, A. and Sagi, M. (2005). Entrepreneurship and self employment in transition economies. *Research in the Sociology of Work*, Vol. 15, pp. 279–310.

Rugimbana, R.O. (2007). Youth based segmentation in the Malaysian retail-banking sector: the relationship between values and personal e-banking service preferences. *International Journal of Bank Marketing*, Vol. 25, No. 1, pp. 6–21.

Scase, R. (2003). Entrepreneurship and proprietorship in transition: policy implications for small- and medium-size enterprise sector. In McIntyre, R.J. and Dallago, B. (eds). *Small and Medium Enterprises in Transitional Economies*, New York: Palgrave Macmillan, pp. 64–77.

Schwartz, S.H. (1994). Beyond individualism/collectivism. In Kim, U. *et al.* (eds). *Individualism and Collectivism: Theory, Method and Application*, Newbury Park, CA: Sage.

Silverman, D. (2006). *Doing Qualitative Research* (2nd edn), London, UK: Sage.

Stokes, D. (2000). Putting entrepreneurship into marketing. *Journal of Research in marketing and entrepreneurship*, Vol. 2, No. 1, pp. 1–16.

Stokes, D., Fitchew, S. and Blackburn, R. (1997). *Marketing in Small Firms: A Conceptual Approach*, Kingston upon Thames, UK: Kingston University.

Tashakkori, A. and Teddlie, C. (2003). *Handbook of Mixed Methods in Social and Behavioural Research*, Thousand Oaks, CA: Sage.

Triandis, H.C. (1984). A theoretical framework for the more efficient construction of culture assimilators. *International Journal of Intercultural Relations*, Vol. 8, No.3, pp. 301–30.

Veal, A.J. (2005). *Business Research Methods: A Managerial Approach* (2nd edn), French Forests, NSW: Pearson Education Australia.

Wright, M., Filatotchev, I., Hoskisson, R. and Peng, M. (2005). Strategy research in emerging economies: challenging the conventional wisdom. *Journal of Management Studies*, Vol. 42, No. 1, pp. 1–33.

Chapter 8

Managing products in SMEs
A customer-oriented perspective

Ayantunji Gbadamosi

LEARNING OBJECTIVES

After reading this chapter, you will be able to:
- define a product
- discuss various classifications of products and their relevance to SMEs
- explain how SMEs could use branding and packaging
- explain the stages in the product development and why they may not be strictly applicable in the SME context
- discuss the product life cycle in relation to SMEs
- explain how SMEs could use the diffusion process to achieve competitive advantage.

INTRODUCTION

At any level of marketing transaction – be it at the small- and medium-sized enterprise (SME) level or large corporation context – products are at the heart of marketing activities. This is because they constitute one of the key elements of the marketing system (see Figure 8.1) and are at the centre of the exchange process around which other elements aimed at satisfying the needs of their target markets revolve. It could be described as the bone, the tendon and the ligament of the system without which no marketing process can take place (Gbadamosi, 2000a).

It is important for us to discuss product as an element of the marketing mix in the context of SMEs for two reasons (here our attention will be more concentrated on the first, as the other is explored in Chapter 15):

1. SMEs provide goods and services to their target markets and will need to understand issues and strategies associated with managing them effectively.
2. SMEs also buy goods from other organizations either for resale or for use in producing the offerings with which to satisfy the needs and wants of their customers.

This chapter examines product as a key factor in SME marketing transactions. As the chapter progresses we will constantly use common knowledge about product as the thread to weave and shape our discussion of managing products in SMEs. This is important because marketing activities in large corporations do sometimes contrast with marketing approaches in SMEs

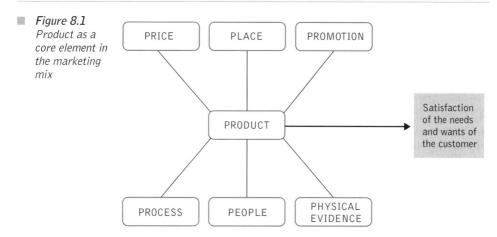

*Figure 8.1
Product as a
core element in
the marketing
mix*

PRICE   PLACE   PROMOTION

PRODUCT

Satisfaction
of the needs
and wants of
the customer

PROCESS   PEOPLE   PHYSICAL
EVIDENCE

(Carson and Cromie, 1990; Gilmore *et al.*, 2001). As a platform for other key issues in the chapter, we now start with the definition of a product.

WHAT IS A PRODUCT?

At the mention of product, what often comes to mind are the tangible products like fast-moving consumer goods such as bread, milk, detergent and salt. Yes! They are products, indeed. However, it will be misleading to limit the definition or explanation of products in a marketing context to these tangible items. This is because people do not buy these products as an end in themselves; rather, they buy them because they are a means to an end. Therefore, a product is defined herein as anything that can be offered to the target market for meeting their various needs. From this definition, product can be tangible materials like books and pens; it can also be in the form of services such as those offered by teachers, lawyers and consultants; it can also be ideas. Hence the local barbers and hairdressers that give their customers better looks, cleaning firms that keep the environment tidy and security firms that safeguard the neighbourhood are, indeed, offering products, though intangible in nature. To buttress this point further, we will now examine various classifications of products that SMEs could be offering to their customers or buying from their suppliers.

PRODUCT CLASSIFICATION AND OPPORTUNITY RECOGNITION IN SMES

It has been well established that entrepreneurship is about recognizing and exploring opportunities (Rae, 2007; Schindehutte *et al.*, 2009; Barringer and Ireland, 2010). Having a good knowledge of product classifications could be one of the steps to achieving opportunities, because it will give entrepreneurs a good indication of the nature and type of the product that could be provided to fill the need identified in the market and how to manage them. Hence, this knowledge will trigger their consciousness of opportunities in the marketing environment when they arise. We will, therefore, explore classifications of products in this segment. From a broader perspective, products could be classified on two bases:

1. on the basis of their attributes, or;
2. on the basis of the type of consumers that use them.

If products are classified on the basis of their attributes, then we can categorize them into durable products, non-durable products and services. *Durable products* are products that provide benefits to the user over a long time as they can survive several uses after their purchase. Examples are cars, PCs, furniture and refrigerators. Conversely, *non-durable products* are those products that can only used once or a few times after which they will need to be replaced. Examples of this category are vegetables and fruits. *Services* are intangible products that consist of activities and benefits offered for sale to satisfy needs and wants. Some examples include transportation services and public relations services. There are many SMEs that offer these and many other services (in-depth discussion of service marketing in the context of SMEs is provided in Chapter 16).

Product classification, when considered from user types, falls into two broad dichotomy; consumer products and organizational products. Consumer products can be classified further into convenience products, shopping products, specialty products and unsought products. Organizational products, on the other hand, can also be classified further into capital products, component parts, accessory products, raw materials and services. These classifications are shown in Figure 8.2

While these classifications are closely related to what we will find in most common textbooks on principles of marketing, our key interest here is to understand how SMEs manage this array of products that they expect will satisfy their customers. Now let us consider each subdivision of the second category – product classification based on the type of customers that use them.

Consumer products: Business-to-consumer marketing offerings in SMEs

In many instances, SMEs offer products or services to buyers whose purpose for purchasing these items is personal gratification. This could be in the form of using them personally or buying for friends, family members or others who will ultimately use such items. In this

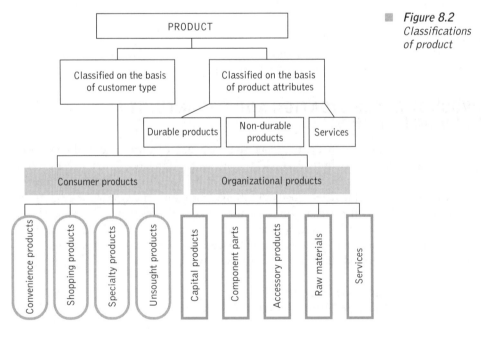

Figure 8.2
Classifications
of product

context, products are usually categorized as *convenience products*, *shopping products*, *specialty products*, and *unsought products*.

Convenience products

These are the products which customers buy on a routine basis with little or no comparison of alternatives. They are usually low in price and are often bought without planning. The convenience of obtaining the product is emphasized more than loyalty to any particular brand. Examples are table salt, sugar and detergents. If we reflect critically on our previous purchases, it will not take a long time to realise that small grocery stores located near our residence, motor parks and train stations are exploring our need for convenience by providing these items at convenient locations and times. These indicate that while SMEs have limitations in relation to their influence in the marketplace, their size and flexibility could stimulate innovation and give them competitive advantage in the marketplace (Hill, 2001; O'Dwyer *et al.*, 2009).

Shopping products

These can be described as products that consumers buy less frequently and make considerable efforts to compare on the basis of quality, price, style and suitability when making the purchase decision. As Brassington and Pettit (2007) explain, this category represents more of a risk and an adventure for consumers. While the purchase of convenience products often involves no planning and little or no comparison of competing brands, the purchase of shopping products is typically a limited problem-solving decision. For purchases in this context, the buyer is willing to shop around to make comparisons with alternatives before the final decision is made. Examples of these products are clothing and computer laptops.

Specialty products

These are consumer products that are bought very infrequently, have unique features sort by buyers, and are very expensive, such that consumers approach their purchase with great care and engage in extensive problem solving. For these products, buyers are willing to pay a premium to get exactly the item needed. Consumers tend to be loyal to specific brands in the purchase of this range of products. Cars, houses, services of legal practitioners, services of civil engineers and services of medical doctors are relevant examples of this category. In this age, the competition faced by SMEs from large businesses intensifies, especially for those offering shopping and specialty products. This underscores the degree of challenge they face to survive in the marketing environment. One of the key strategies for small businesses to survive and succeed when operating in the sectors that provide these products is targeting niches with clear-cut identifiable needs and offering them unique products that are distinctively beneficial to them in relation to specific features covering issues of importance, such as style, quality and suitability. This will not only give small businesses space in the crowded marketplace but also could make them achieve a competitive advantage.

Unsought products

Unsought products are products that the buyers are not aware exist. In some cases, when consumers know that they exist they usually do not have enough zeal to buy them except when such products or services are vigorously promoted to them. Examples are life insurance and some home decoration materials. Since consumers do not usually engage in purposeful search for these products, a lot of marketing communication efforts are required from the marketers to create product awareness. Although SMEs are constrained in terms of how much they could spend on marketing communications, there are some low-cost promotion methods that could be used for this purpose. In-store promotion and personal selling could be very useful in this context. The key aim here is to keep it simple and effective; not doing it at all puts the business at serious risk.

Organizational products: Business-to-business marketing offerings in SMEs

Organisational products are bought by other organisations for resale or for the purpose of using them to produce other goods. They vary in terms of the financial requirements and the degree of risk associated with their purchase. They are shown in Figure 8.2 and are now discussed in turn.

Capital products

These are items bought to aid the production of goods and/or services in the buying organization. They are bought infrequently and involve very substantial financial commitment. Due to the high risk associated with buying the wrong type, and the significance of the purchase, the weight of the inputs of several professionals/experts in the field relevant to the decision is considerable. Therefore, organizations often commit significant time and effort to the purchase because the purchase decision is strategic. Examples of products in this category are machines and buildings. Offering these products would require considerable personal selling efforts on the part of the sellers as the sale requires a close contact relationship between the parties. Besides, buyers will most likely require information and technical support from the seller. With the huge investment in the purchase of these products, acquiring or offering them is arguably one of the major challenges confronting SMEs. Some firms often have to rely on borrowing or funding through various government-initiated programmes to be able to jump the hurdle. In other instances, many SMEs will have to collaborate with one another to be able to supply these items. Whichever form the transaction takes, conforming to buyers' specification remains a major rule in the relationship.

Component parts

These are finished products that are bought to form part of the products the organization offers to its target market. One example is car manufacturing firms, where parts of cars such as tyres and other electrical materials are bought by the car manufacturers in order to construct their finished products. Similarly, to complete a house for a client, construction companies will need items like cement, bricks, wood and many others which will all be skilfully combined to become an inhabitable building post-construction. SMEs supplying these items need to be very conscious of the quality standards of the buyer and adhere to them. Attempts to fiddle with the quality of the component parts will most likely affect the final output of the buying organization. One of the ways to thrive in the marketing environment would be for the firms to gain and maintain the trust of their clients. Breaching the quality standards and the trust of key customers could lead to a severe breakdown of the relationship and severe consequences for enterprises targeting one or a very few niches.

Accessory products

These are organizational products that the buyers use to meet their auxiliary needs. They are also used to facilitate the production of goods and services in the establishment, but not directly as in the case of component parts. Usually the purchase does not involve the scale of risk and financial investment associated with the purchase of capital products. PCs, printers, telephones, bulbs, filing cabinets and shredders are examples of this category of products. Many small and family businesses with very limited funds available may start from this level of marketing. Yet they need to be customer-oriented and be conscious of competition. Issues like prompt delivery and ease of ordering will more likely woo the buyers for this product category.

Raw materials

These are usually in their natural form as inputs that need to go though the transformation process before the buyer can produce the ultimate offerings intended to satisfy the target market. Examples include cocoa, timber, fish and vegetables.

Services

These are intangible offerings bought by organizations to enhance the production of their goods and services. Maintenance and repair of machinery, cleaning of the premises, security services for the organization's property and consultancy services are just a few examples of services as organizational products. There are many SMEs providing services to various target niches in the British marketing environment. This is closely related to the ease of starting such service businesses, which require relatively little capital. For instance, Nwankwo and Gbadamosi (2009), in a study on Pentecostalism and entrepreneurial orientations among black ethnic minorities in London, report how these individuals are using the platform of their faith-based organizational affiliations to support their entrepreneurial ambitions. Some of these are lawyers, accountants, IT technicians and barbers. These entrepreneurs acknowledge the ease of market entry in these service businesses and how their personal contact networks (PCN) within these circles have contributed to their success.

Obviously, due to resource constraints associated with the running of their enterprises, SMEs have relative limitations on the extent of the range of products they can offer their customers via their marketing activities. Accordingly, it is difficult for them to compete directly with large-scale enterprises. However, customers remain ever demanding. Consumers make comparisons among alternative offerings for certain categories of product, and it is expected that SMEs that offer distinctive products apply their unique selling propositions (USP) in relation to quality and style to match the requirements of the target niches. For example, some SMEs target certain ethnic minority groups in the UK and are fully committed to providing them with required products or services. This approach often encourages repeat purchase and loyalty, and engenders a continuous good relationship between the two parties.

GROUP ACTIVITY

In a group of three, reflect on any recent news report of any economic importance. Discuss how this might translate into opportunities for you as a group of entrepreneurs. Identify the product type that could be uses to explore any potential opportunity.

LEVELS OF PRODUCTS: IMPLICATIONS FOR SME MARKETING

In product planning and management, three interrelated levels of product are commonly discussed. These are: (1) the core product, (2) the actual product, and (3) the augmented product.

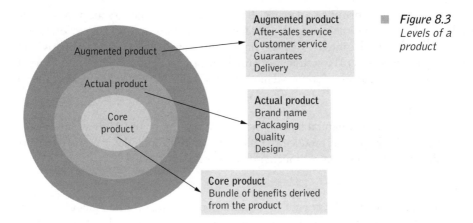

Figure 8.3
Levels of a product

The *core product* (see Figure 8.3) describes the benefit that a customer buys when he or she buys a product. It is what allows customers to solve problems and satisfy the basic needs that prompted them to purchase the product. The core product of a laptop computer bought by a customer is the ease of processing information and other things that the laptop facilitates. This area is one of the key challenges confronting most SMEs. While most SMEs are innovative, some do not really consider how their innovations satisfy the needs of the target market and the gap they are filling in the market. Consequently this leads to the sudden failure of such products.

The second level is the *actual product*, which encompasses elements like brand name, packaging, quality and design that function together to offer the buyer the core benefits desired for purchasing the product. For very creative and right-thinking entrepreneurs, this level of product is loaded with opportunities to transform their businesses. If well explored, it could actually be a way of gaining competitive advantage in the volatile marketing environment. This could involve ensuring that the desired level of quality expected by the customers is not compromised. For SMEs that are less endowed in major resources than larger corporations (Raymond and Croteau, 2006), ignoring the importance of quality is a gamble that can have very serious consequences. In fact, it has been shown that quality is an essential foundation for progressing to large-scale innovation for SMEs (McAdam and Armstrong, 2001). Similarly, despite the dominant role of large organizations, the merits of branding for SMEs are far-reaching. Wong and Merrilees (2005) argue that brand orientation might play a critical role in the growth of SMEs. If the quality meets the customers' expectations, such buyers would be willing to associate with the brand.

The third product level, the *augmented product*, offers additional benefits or services that distinguish the SME's offering from competitors'. Examples include after-sales services, customer service, guarantees and delivery. The size of SMEs, their flexibility and their closeness to their customers indicate that augmented product could be a powerful tool for them to achieve competitive advantage. They can fortify their relationship with their customers by building good customer services into their offerings. In this age, marketing is more about managing relationships than about the product in the transaction. An IT technician who calls his customers some days after the service to gauge their satisfaction level is more likely to get a repeat purchase and enjoy word-of-mouth communication from the customer than one who does not. The closeness of SMEs to their customers also means that they can easily identify problems related to their offerings and adopt service recovery as necessary.

Product line/product mix

A product line is the group of closely related product items offered for sale by the marketer that are considered to be a unit; a product mix is the collection of all products or services that an organization offers to its market. A product mix, therefore, consists of all the product lines of an organization. The number of product lines within the product mix is described as the *product width*, while the number of products within a product line is known as the *product line length*. Clearly, due to resource constraints, it is logical to acknowledge that, in comparison with large enterprises, SMEs could only manage less product width and product line length. Many SMEs rush their innovations into the market, some hurriedly engage in 'me-too' innovations and over-diversify, and this approach can considerably strain the performance of the existing products in the market. This is because such new investments might severely drain the available resources – finances and time – that could be better used on the existing products that are already performing well in the marketplace.

Branding

The American Marketing Association defines a brand as 'a name, term, design, symbol or any other feature that identifies one seller's good or service as distinct from those of other sellers' (AMA, 2010). This is a very useful definition as it clearly emphasizes the major role of branding – distinguishing offerings. A similar definition states that branding distinguishes a product or service from its unbranded counterpart through the sum total of consumers' perception and feelings about the attributes and the performances of the products (Jevons, 2005). The latter definition clearly brings in the relevance of consumers' perception. Both strongly support the explanation of Wilson and Gilligan (1997), that branding provides the basis for a consumer franchise and, if managed effectively, can allow for greater marketing flexibility and a higher degree of consumer loyalty. It is, therefore, not surprising that large corporations including Coca-Cola, PepsiCo, Nokia, Tesco, Wal-Mart and JC Penny ardently devote resources to managing their brands. Clearly, a discussion of managing product in the SME context will be incomplete without making due reference to branding. As SMEs relate to their customers in the course of their marketing transactions, branding can be a way of maintaining a strong bond between the two parties, if effectively used. Wong and Merrilees (2005) suggest that SMEs need to take a long-term investment approach to branding, and develop a strongly distinctive brand. They add that it is important for these businesses to develop an internal culture where all staff 'live the brand' on a daily basis; and to have a clear and consistent communication of their brand through marketing activities. All available official statistics indicate that SMEs constitute over 99 per cent of the enterprises in the UK business environment. With this number of SMEs, the possibility of consumers being inundated with numerous competing offerings cannot be ignored. This brings in the relevance of brands that not only distinguish the offering but also inspire loyalty if the branded products satisfy the target customers. Such brands offer the owner *brand equity* which is the positive return of the impact of the brand on the business. As a brand provides the owner with brand equity, the possibility of brand extension could be carefully explored for future inventions.

Packaging

One of the marketing stimuli closely related to managing product in SMEs is packaging. We have all received one product or another from our local stores in different boxes, delivered to

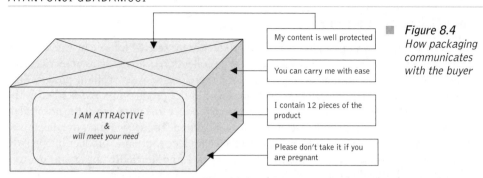

Figure 8.4
How packaging communicates with the buyer

us in bags, or supplied to people on our behalf wrapped in paper of different sizes and colours. These experiences often stay with us as consumers, inspiring different feelings and sometimes prompting our future behaviour in relation to these offerings. This shows that packaging plays different roles and can be perceived differently by different buyers. Accordingly, effective packaging might contribute to factors that provide SMEs the key to satisfying their customers more effectively than their competitors do.

Packaging plays several important roles in marketing transactions but these can be broadly categorized into *functional roles* and *commercial roles*. When packaging attracts customers, projecting the image of the product or that of the seller and communicating things about the seller, then it is deemed to be performing the commercial roles. When wondering why you have selected a brand of orange drink, chocolate, gum or detergent over another, the answer may well be effective packaging. Such packaging communicates quality to buyers and as many of consumers' purchases now take place in self-service commercial environments, the commercial role of packaging will maintain its relevance in marketing systems.

On the other hand, the functional roles of packaging cover product containment, user convenience and product preservation. Above all, an effective packaging strategy should make life easy for all the stakeholders – buyers, sellers, intermediaries and the public. This last point directs our attention to something significant. Today's consumers in the UK and European Union (EU) now crave for packaging that favours environmental friendliness. For instance, in 1994, the EU passed a packaging directive which is aimed at minimizing packaging waste by enabling reusing or recycling (Rundh, 2005). These additional considerations make it very challenging for SMEs to think of how best to improve their packaging. Ineffective and non-considerate packaging can be very frustrating, not only to the consumers but also to the stakeholders. Besides, consumers' attitudinal reactions to packaging also vary, indicating how essential it is for firms to be customer-driven in their choice of packaging designs for their products. For example, there is evidence which suggests that low-income consumers are not motivated to buy low-involvement grocery products by the attractiveness of the packaging but by its functional roles instead (Gbadamosi, 2009b). In fact, it is has been found that this consumer segment might think that manufacturers are ripping them off by using attractive packaging (Gbadamosi, 2009c). Now, the key issue for SMEs here is the increasing need for them to use their innovation to design effective packaging that will be a good fit for the purpose – it has to satisfy their customers, be cost-effective and portray the firm as a socially responsible establishment. This could give them competitive advantage when other strategies are failing.

NEW PRODUCT DEVELOPMENT IN SMES: INNOVATION, CREATIVITY AND PECULIARITIES

The marketing environment of SMEs is turbulent and dynamic. Consequently, the needs and wants of the consumers being served change as rapidly as the factors in the environment. Hence, firms are investing an increasing amount of resources and managerial attention in product innovation (Hyland *et al.*, 2001). Indeed, SMEs will need innovation to be able to stay in the game and survive the competition in their marketplace. So, what is innovation?

In a bid to answer this question, Deakins and Freel (2003) revisited Schumpeter's (1934) explanation of innovation. Five sources of innovation identified there are (1) introduction of new product or significant improvement of the existing ones, (2) introduction of new method of production, (3) opening of a new market, (4) discovering a new source of supply of raw materials or half-manufactured good, and (5) creation of a new type of industrial organization. After several decades, this explanation is still very useful and offers us a broad scope of innovation. Adding to this all-encompassing view, Deakins and Freel (2003) state that innovation is different from invention, as the former is holistic and involves the commercial application of the latter. This view is therefore in tune with the claim that innovation derives from the ability to see connections, to spot opportunities and to take advantage of them (Bessant and Tidd, 2007). Although resource constraints may impact SMEs' ability to explore innovation, evidence in the literature indicates that SMEs could be at an advantage with regard to innovation, due to their flexibility and ability to explore opportunities as they arise (Deakins and Freel, 2003). Now let us turn our attention to how SMEs develop new product.

The beginning of this chapter established from the literature (Carson and Cromie, 1990; Gilmore *et al.*, 2001) that there are differences in how SMEs and large corporations practise marketing. This argument can be extended to how these different enterprises develop new product.

Conventional marketing understanding sees the process of new product development (NPD) as depicted in Figure 8.5. This process starts with the generation of ideas and then acknowledges that not all of the ideas generated will be useful or feasible, meaning ideas are then screened. The product ideas that have survived the screening stage need to be changed into a form that is understandable to the consumers who will use them – this is the product concept. At the business analysis stage, costs, anticipated sales and the profitability prospects of the product are examined to gauge its overall economic viability. If the business analysis stage projects a very promising outcome, then the actual product is developed. Before launching the product fully, the firm is expected to offer the product to samples of the target market in selected geographical locations. This will give the firm the opportunity to assess the fitness of its marketing strategies.

The first major issue to consider here is that this process is systematic and assumes the importance of group decision making. With this in mind, we should ask whether this process will be a good fit for SMEs. One of the ways to address this is to revisit the characteristics of SMEs in order to gauge the appropriateness of this conventional NPD process in the SME context. The basic characteristics of SMEs identified by Carson *et al.* (1995) can be

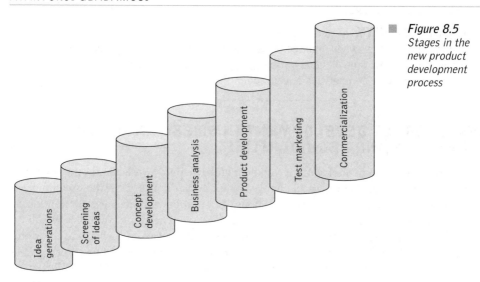

Figure 8.5
Stages in the new product development process

(Idea generations, Screening of ideas, Concept development, Business analysis, Product development, Test marketing, Commercialization)

summarized as follows: they operate predominantly at a local or regional market rather than national or international market, they tend to have limited market share and they are often owned by one person or a few individuals. The authors also add that SMEs are independent, in which case the owner-managers have ultimate authority to decide and manage the affairs of the enterprise. This means that SMEs are generally managed in a personalized fashion. A closer look at the NPD process and SME characteristics reveals that they are not perfectly compatible. However, this does not mean that SMEs do not develop new product; nor does it mean that they are not innovative – rather, it directs our attention to and justifies the need for a paradigm shift in SME marketing whereby NPD in SMEs can be robustly achieved.

NPD of course occurs in SMEs and entrepreneurs are certainly not short of ideas. Nevertheless, many new SME products fail prematurely. One of the common reasons for this is lack of finance to implement the concept. The significance of finance to NPD varies from one industry to another. As noted by Barringer and Ireland (2010), firms need to raise money to pay up-front costs associated with the lengthy product cycles in some industries. This can delay the implementation of new inventions or product ideas. In fact, in some instances, while the inventor is waiting for funds to develop the new product, the product idea may have been overtaken by newer inventions, and thereby rendered useless. From a different perspective, many owner-managers often venture into NPD but skip many essential phases in the process. Some are so passionate about the product idea that they forget that such ideas must meet the needs of the target customers. There have been some cases of inventors introducing products into the market without conducting a thorough business analysis, through which they will know whether they will be successful from a commercial standpoint or not. In other cases, one wonders what is really new about a new product if it does not really fill a gap in the marketplace or generate competitive advantage for the firm. The empirical study of Salavou and Avlonitis (2008) indicates that SMEs vary in relation to their product innovativeness. They identify three groups of SMEs on the basis of their product innovativeness: (1) the straight imitators (low level), (2) the product innovator (high level), and (3) the concept innovator (moderate level). In this classification, the product innovators are defined as those who develop more radical variations of their existing offerings and have a feel for what consumers like or dislike about their existing product. Consequently, consumers would more readily adopt their invention compared with the other two groups. This typology is really helpful as it shows that, while SMEs are noted to be adventurous about inventions, not all inventions would readily satisfy customers and be commercially successful.

Since the need to develop new product is intensifying due to changes in taste of customers, the onus is on SMEs to embrace effectiveness in their NPD activities. SMEs need to operate between two walls. One wall is their characteristics and limitations and the other is the integrity of their NPD. This is consistent with the view of Carson *et al.* (1995) that SME marketers should practise *marketing adaptation*, meaning that they need not be overly concerned about the rigour of their marketing techniques but still maintain the integrity of the process. This means they are still following the process, albeit loosely, as it involves giving due consideration to the peculiarities of SMEs.

GROUP ACTIVITY

In groups of three, each member should think of any two products that could be sold to specific groups of students in your university and identify those groups. In a group discussion with your colleagues, explain how you could make this into a commercial success and discuss the difficulties you might encounter in developing this product as an SME instead of a large-scale multinational firm.

PRODUCT LIFE CYCLE: IMPLICATIONS FOR MARKETING IN SMES

The term product life cycle (PLC) is very popular in the mainstream marketing literature. This popularity cannot be dismissed as a mere academic exercise. Rather, the unwavering interest in the topic stems from its being an invaluable tool for tracking the performance of products during their lifetime, in terms of their sales trends. Essentially, the PLC states that we can explain the life of a product by likening it to that of a human being. It holds that products, too, are born or introduced; they then grow, mature and reach the end of their life. The PLC consists of four stages – namely, (1) Introduction, (2) Growth, (3) Maturity and (4) Decline. The stages differ with respect to the degree of market knowledge of the product, market acceptance of the product and the prevailing competitive situation for the product. Hence, different marketing strategies are applicable in each of the stages. The stages are shown in Figure 8.6.

As Figure 8.6 indicates, at the Introduction stage, the product is still fresh in the market and requires all the entrepreneurial initiatives possible to be able to maintain its presence there. This stage is crucial – especially for products developed by SMEs – for a number of reasons. First, it requires heavy promotion investments to create awareness. There is a need for the organization or firm to create awareness of the new product through advertising. They need to encourage trial with sales promotion, and encourage intermediaries to help push the product through distribution channels. Second, in spite of all these efforts, the new product is unlikely to generate profit at this stage, which can be very discouraging for an owner-manager, who may have invested his or her life savings and secured a loan to see the investment through. For SMEs with limited funds, this could be the most challenging of all the stages. Most new products fail at this stage. It has been estimated that the failure rate of new products ranges from 60 to 90 per cent, depending on the industry and the particular definition of product failure (Dibb *et al.*, 2001). However, if NPD stages are handled carefully,

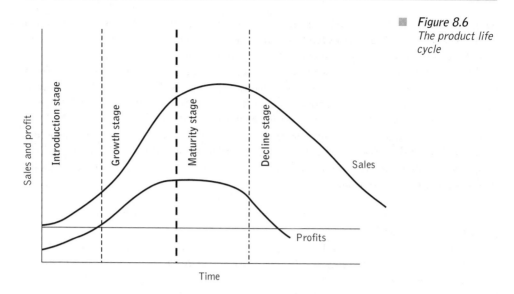

especially in a customer-oriented manner, the effort can be very rewarding as the product enters its second stage: Growth.

At the Growth stage, sales and profits grow, but so do competitors. SMEs, therefore, need to be very conscious of competition and encourage repeat purchase. An empirical study on determinants of new product performance in SMEs by O'Dwyer and Ledwith (2009) shows that competition orientation and product launch proficiency have strong links to new product performance. The closeness of the firm to their customers and the ability to be flexible in their marketing are very useful tools to ensure the product thrives at this stage and gains customer loyalty.

At the Maturity stage, sales growth levels off and profits start to fall. With many similar brands in the market at this stage, competition is a major threat; hence, effort should be directed at encouraging repeat purchase. This should also be the period where the owner-manger tries to think of other innovations such as modifying the product in some form.

The last of the stages of the PLC is the Decline stage. Due to many reasons, including change in consumer preferences, technological advancements and very stiff competition from domestic or international products, the sales of the product fall speedily. At this stage, SMEs might need to be more cost-conscious. They could reduce their spending on marketing communications and reduce the price of the product in order to be able to sell existing stock. Firms at this stage would be considering the options of whether to bring the product back to life with more investment or to just let go. The latter option could be a bitter pill for many SMEs to swallow but if the product does not look promising, especially from a commercial standpoint, it is logical to allow it to 'die' naturally and replace it with new inventions.

MANAGING DIFFUSION OF NEW PRODUCTS IN SMES

Evidence indicates that SMEs are not short of new product ideas and innovation, but some of the new products they introduce fail. One of the ways of managing new products and reducing the risk of their failure is to understand the process by which new inventions spread among members of a social system. This is known as the diffusion process (Rogers, 2003; Bessant and

Figure 8.7
Product
adopters
categories

Source: Rogers
(1962).

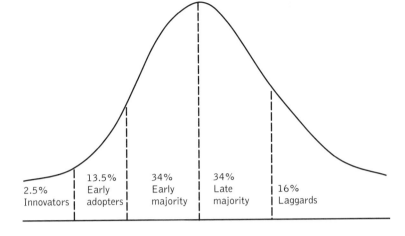

Tidd, 2007). Having this knowledge will help these firms on how they position their products in a customer-oriented manner.

Perhaps a good way to begin the discussion of product diffusion is to frankly acknowledge that the responses of people to new products vary. While some can be very enthusiastic and quickly receptive to new innovation, others tend to be very skeptical of these unfamiliar offerings. So, some individuals will adopt a new product early, while some will not until the very last days that the product is available for purchase. A widely referenced, seminal work on categorization of people in terms of their adoption of new product is that of Rogers (1962). According to Rogers, the pattern of adoption can be represented by the graph shown in Figure 8.7, with the percentages representing the proportion of the adopters of the new product as time progresses.

As shown in Figure 8.7, there are five categories based on the speed at which the new product is adopted: (1) Innovators, (2) Early adopters, (3) Early majority, (4) Late majority and (5) Laggards.

The Innovators are the first set of people who are interested in buying the product when it is newly launched on the market. They tend to be venturesome, young, well-educated, have high incomes and take pride in owning something new. They constitute a relatively small percentage (2.5 per cent) of the total of those who adopt the product. The Early adopters, who constitute 13.5 per cent of total adopters, buy the new product after the Innovators. They tend to be more community-oriented than the Innovators, very influential in the various

Figure 8.8
Factors
influencing the
rate of adoption
of new products

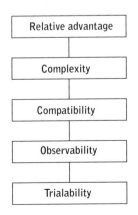

groups they interact with, are regarded as experts and are likely to be opinion leaders (Lamb *et al.*, 2010). Hence, they are often consulted by other groups who adopt the new product after them. The Early majority follows the Early adopters and are noted for adopting the new product before the average person. They represent 34 per cent of the total adopters of the product. Next are the Late majority – also 34 per cent of the total. They rarely assume a leadership role and are sceptical; they don't adopt the new product until after a majority of people have tried it. They are mainly prompted by word-of-mouth commutation to buy the product. The Laggards form the last 16 per cent of the total adopters of the product. They are typically very suspicious and cautious of new inventions and are only inclined to buy a product when it is about to be replaced by a newer model.

Figure 8.8 shows the five key factors that affect the rate of adoption of new products (Rogers, 2003). Apart from knowing the categories of adopters of new products, other useful information needed by SMEs are the factors that influence how consumers adopt new product. These have been identified as *relative advantage, complexity, compatibility, observability* and *trialability* (Rogers, 2003; Bessant and Tidd, 2007). If we consider each of these factors critically, it is noteworthy that they have inherent lessons and implications for how SMEs manage their new products in their highly competitive environment. Essentially, consumers will be interested to know whether the new product offers benefits they could not get from existing ones (Relative advantage). This is why it is important for SMEs to ensure that their inventions are filling gaps in the market. If the new product is too difficult to understand or use (Complexity), it might affect the rate at which it is adopted. The extent to which the new product conforms to the existing cultural values and knowledge (Compatibility) plays a key role in how quickly the product will diffuse. Being customer-oriented could help an SME to ensure that the product is consistent with existing values and knowledge. Also, if the benefits of using the product are easily observable, there is a high tendency for the adoption rate of the product to be fast. Trialability refers to the ease with which the new product can be tried in limited form or quantity.

There are a good number of useful implications for SME marketing from Rogers' work. Since SMEs typically target niches and rely on PCNs for their marketing, it is logical for them to identify and target the opinion leaders to get them involved in their offerings. As SMEs are resource-constrained and might not be able to invest in large-scale marketing communications, they could engage opinion leaders to generate very useful and effective word-of-mouth communications. SMEs could also incorporate the various characteristics of Rogers' adopters in the segmentation, targeting and positioning aspects of their marketing plan.

By considering the five key factors (Figure 8.8) that affect the rate of innovation and by ensuring that their products are managed accordingly, SMEs could avoid succumbing to the high rate of failure of new products. This is because these factors provide direction on how to be customer-focused, which is the route to success in marketing.

PRODUCT MANAGEMENT LESSONS FOR SMES

As consistently shown in the marketing literature, the characteristics of SMEs make mainstream marketing knowledge difficult to apply directly in the SME context. However, there are some key issues that could be addressed in relation to how SMEs manage their product. First, while innovations are good and could give SMEs competitive advantage, poor planning has the potential to affect the market suitability, sales and life cycle of new product. This is closely connected to the problem of poor knowledge of product portfolio management. Driven by the need to prove their creativity and innovation ability, some SMEs carry too many products, which consequently affects their financial stability. On the other hand, some ignore the signals to widen their operations and market too few products. Neither of these approaches would enable SMEs to realize their full potential. Another core and useful direction on product management is the need for SMEs to consciously establish very good links between the needs of their customers and the products they introduce.

SUMMARY

Product is a core element in marketing transactions for both large-scale enterprises and SMEs. As entrepreneurship is about opportunity recognition, having an understanding of how products are classified will be very useful in determining which offerings will best satisfy an SME's needs.

Although products could be broadly classified on the basis of their attributes and the type of buyers that buy them, they are usually conceptualized as having three levels – namely, the core product, the actual product and the augmented product. This knowledge could help SMEs to understand the elements that provide value to the customers and enable them to use their advantages of flexibility and closeness to their customers to satisfy them better than competitors. Owing to their resource constraints, the product line length SMEs can achieve will be relatively limited compared with large enterprises. However, SMEs can concentrate on niches with special identifiable needs and meet them more effectively and efficiently than competitors. As SMEs operate in a turbulent marketing environment, their adequate understanding and effective use of marketing stimuli like branding, packaging and quality may well see them obtain competitive advantage.

The process in the development of new products is systematic and generally involves group decision making. However, the characteristics of SMEs suggest there is a need for a paradigm shift in how SMEs develop their new products, involving maintaining the integrity of the NPD process and giving due consideration to the SME context, i.e. *marketing adaptation*. Having developed new products, it is important for SMEs to realize that such products often pass through stages, with each having implications for the success or failure of the product. The Introduction stage is very critical for SMEs because initial investments and commitments may not yield the expected profit immediately.

KEY TERMS
- Branding
- Innovation
- Marketing mix
- New product development (NPD)
- Opportunity recognition
- Organizational products/consumer products
- Packaging
- Product
- Product life cycle (PLC)
- Product line
- Product mix
- Resource constraints

REVIEW QUESTIONS

1. What is a product? Discuss the relevance of product to the marketing system. Justify your viewpoint with examples in the SME marketing context.

2. Discuss various types of products, classified on the basis of their attributes and explain the usefulness of such knowledge to small business owners.

3. Enumerate and discuss the major levels of products that must be considered by product planners. How can this knowledge help SMEs to gain competitive advantage?

4. To what extent might a SME which is involved in the marketing of cosmetic products and intends to operate in a European country use branding and packaging to their advantage?

5. Briefly discuss the stages in the NPD process and explain why this may not be strictly amenable to the SME context.

CASE STUDY 8: NEW PRODUCT DEVELOPMENT FOR ETHNIC MINORITY CUSTOMERS

Raymond Matthew (aka Mr Fred) was in his late 20s when he first arrived in the UK to join his family after living with his uncle in his home country for several years. Although he gained admission to a UK university for his postgraduate study when he arrived, he had to help the family run the convenience store which his father established when he arrived in the UK in November, 1985. This arrangement initially seemed a very good opportunity for the personal development of this young, energetic and ambitious individual who had determined at an early age that he would be self-employed.

However, after 7 years' helping run the family business, Mr Fred realized he might not be able to realize his entrepreneurial ambition as early as he had anticipated. The rivalry between him and his siblings grew considerably. Many times this became obvious to their customers. Then Raymond decided it was time to break out on his own and try to realize his ambition.

Given Mr Fred's background knowledge in engineering, the first idea that came to his mind was to be a supplier of industrial equipment to business organizations in the form of business-to-business transactions. After several weeks of deliberations, he realized that he was dabbling in sales of capital items and could not cope with the huge financial commitments required; he later dropped that idea. He also had the idea to venture into publishing women's weekly magazines. But when he realized the success of the existing ones like *OK!* magazine, *Hello, Heat, Complete Woman, Easy Living, Essentials, Teen Vogue* and *Grazia* and how they had effectively captured the market, he acknowledged that the market was already crowded and the chance of surviving in the sector would be extremely small. He therefore abandoned that idea as well.

Nevertheless, when all these ideas could not give him the quick and big success he dearly needed, Mr Fred finally came up with one that he thought could turn his fortunes around for good – body lotion. He developed a simple body lotion mainly targeting people of his ethnic minority. He then invested all his life savings and all his efforts in the development of the product. He stated, 'I am not struggling with the giants in the marketplace but only targeting my very small share of the cake'. But Mr Fred was shocked to find that, after the first few purchases by his friends, he had piles of unsold stock. The question in the mind of many of the target consumers was, 'Who would buy this new lotion, when we already have several good brands that we enjoy and are twice as cheap?'

As Mr Fred's worries increased every day, two of his friends lightly communicated to him that they believed not too many people were interested in the new lotion. His reply was, 'I have put all my life and money into this and cannot just stop now.' But one major question remains: How responsive was Mr Fred to customers' needs in his NPD effort?

CASE QUESTIONS AND TASKS

1. What do you think Mr Fred could have done differently concerning his efforts in developing new product?
2. Apply the concept of PLC to explain Mr Fred's predicament.
3. Explain how you can use your knowledge of product layers to improve on what this entrepreneur did.
4. What lessons have your learned from the approach of Mr Fred and how could this be of value to other SMEs contemplating investments in your locality?

BIBLIOGRAPHY

American Marketing Association (AMA) (2010), 'Marketing Power: Dictionary'. Online: http://www.marketingpower.com/_layouts/Dictionary.aspx?dLetter=B (accessed 25 February 2010).

Armstrong, G. and Kotler, P. (2009), *Marketing: An Introduction*, 9th edn, New Jersey: Pearson Education.

Barringer, B. R. and Ireland, R. D (2010), *Entrepreneurship: Successfully Launching New Ventures*, 3rd edn, New Jersey: Pearson Education.

Bessant, J. and Tidd, J. (2007), *Innovation and Entrepreneurship*, West Sussex: John Wiley & Sons.

Brassington, F. and Pettit, S. (2007), *Essentials of Marketing*, 2nd edn, Essex: Pearson Education.

Carson, D. and Cromie, S. (1990), 'Marketing Planning in Small Enterprises: A Model and Some Empirical Evidence', *Journal of Consumer Marketing*, Vol. 7, No. 3, pp. 5–18.

Carson, D., Cromie, S., McGowan, P. and Hill J. (1995), *Marketing and Entrepreneurship in SMEs: An Innovative Approach*, Essex: Pearson Education.

Deakins, D. and Freel, M. (2003), *Entrepreneurship and Small Firms*, Berkshire: McGraw-Hill Education.

Dibb, S., Simkin, L., William, M., Pride, W. M. and Ferrell, O. C. (2001), *Marketing: Concepts and Strategies*, Boston: Houghton Mifflin.

Gbadamosi, A. (2000a), 'Consumers' Redemption: Whose Responsibility?', *International Journal of Management Sciences and Information Technology*, Vol. 1, No. 1 (April), pp. 46–54.

Gbadamosi, A. (2009b), 'Low Income Consumers' Reactions to Low-involvement Products', *Marketing Intelligence and Planning*, Vol. 27, No. 7, pp. 882–899.

Gbadamosi, A. (2009c), 'Cognitive Dissonance: The Implicit Explication in Low-Income Consumers' Shopping Behaviour for "Low-Involvement" Grocery Products', *International Journal of Retail and Distribution Management*, Vol. 37, No. 12, pp. 1077–1095.

Gilmore, A., Carson, D. and Grant K. (2001), 'SME Marketing in Practice', *Marketing Intelligence and Planning*, Vol. 19, No. 1, pp. 6–11.

Hill, J. (2001), 'A Multidimensional Study of the Key Determinants of Effective SME Marketing

Activity: Part 2', *International Journal of Entrepreneurial Behaviour and Research*, Vol. 7, No. 6, pp. 211–235.

Hyland, P. W., Gieskes, J. F. B. and Sloan, T. R. (2001), 'Occupation Clusters as Determinants of Organisational Learning in the Product Innovation Process', *Journal of Workplace Learning*, Vol. 13, No. 5, pp. 198–208.

Jevons, C. (2005), 'Names, Brands, Branding: Beyond the Signs, Symbols, Products and Services', *Journal of Product and Brand Management*, Vol. 14, No. 2, pp. 117–118.

Kotler, P., Armstrong, G., Veronica, W. and Saunders, J. (2008), *Principles of Marketing*, 5th edn, Harlow: Pearson Education.

Lamb, C. W., Hair, J. F. and McDaniel, C. (2010), *MKTG*, 3rd edn, Mason: South-Western Cengage Learning.

McAdam, R. and Armstrong, G. (2001), 'A Symbiosis of Quality and Innovation SMEs: A Multiple Case Study Analysis', *Managerial Auditing Journal*, Vol. 16, No. 7, pp. 394–399.

Nwankwo, S. and Gbadamosi, A. (2009), 'Mediating the Effects of Black Pentecostalism in Entrepreneurial Orientations', *Institute for Small Business and Entrepreneurship Annual Conference*, Novas Centre, Liverpool, UK, 3–6 November.

O'Dwyer, M., Gilmore, A. and Carson, D. (2009), 'Innovative Marketing in SMEs: A Theoretical Approach', *European Business Review*, Vol. 21, No. 6, pp. 504–515.

O'Dwyer, M. and Ledwith, A. (2009), 'Determinants of New Product Performance in Small Firms', *International Journal of Entrepreneurial Behaviour and Research*, Vol. 15, No. 2, pp. 124–136.

Rae, D. (2007), *Entrepreneurship: From Opportunity to Action*, Basingstoke: Palgrave Macmillan.

Raymond, L. and Croteau, A. (2006), 'Enabling the Strategic Development of SMEs through Advanced Manufacturing Systems: A Configurational Perspective', *Industrial Management and Data Systems*, Vol. 106, No. 7, pp. 1012–1032.

Rogers, E. M. (1962), *Diffusion of Innovations*, New York: Free Press.

Rogers, E. M. (2003), *Diffusion of Innovations*, New York: Simon & Schuster.

Rundh, B. (2005), 'The Multi-Faceted Dimension of Packaging: Marketing Logistic or Marketing Tool?', *British Food Journal*, Vol. 107, No. 9, pp. 670–684.

Salavou, H. and Avlonitis, G. (2008), 'Product Innovativeness and Performance: A Focus on SMEs', *Management Decision*, Vol. 46, No. 7, pp. 969–989.

Schindehutte, M., Morris, M. H. and Leyland, F. P. (2009), *Rethinking Marketing: The Entrepreneurial Imperative*, New Jersey: Pearson Education.

Schumpeter, J. (1934), *The Theory of Economic Development*, Cambridge, MA: Harvard University Press.

Wilson, R. M. S. and Gilligan, C. (1997), *Strategic Marketing Management: Planning, Implementation and Control*, 2nd edn, Oxford: Butterworth-Heinemann.

Wong, H. Y. and Merrilees, B. (2005), 'A Brand Orientation Typology for SMEs: A Case Research Approach', *Journal of Product and Brand Management*, Vol. 14, No. 1, pp. 155–162.

Chapter 9

Pricing and pricing-related issues in SMEs

Paul Sergius Koku

LEARNING OBJECTIVES

After reading this chapter, you will be able to:
- develop appreciation for the interface between pricing decisions and law
- develop appreciation for the internal and external factors that affect pricing decisions
- be able to discuss pricing variables and the various pricing objectives
- understand the differences in the pricing process in SMEs and large organizations
- be able to do simple calculations involving markup and break-even volume.

INTRODUCTION

Regardless of firm size, pricing is one of the most critical activities that take place within the firm. The importance of the pricing process to a firm lies in the fact that pricing is the only means through which a firm can generate revenue. A mistake in the process could be costly to the firm. Pricing mistakes may not only make the firm less profitable but also they can result in a firm's bankruptcy and its eventual closure.

Because of its importance, pricing has attracted a significant research effort in many academic disciplines such as marketing, economics, and law. Because it can be easily mimicked by competition, firms do not rely solely on price for their competitive strategy. However, price's uniqueness as a strategic tool is reflected in the fact that it is about the only corporate activity that goes by several different names, depending on the context. For example, it is referred to as a "fare" in the transportation industry, a "fee" in education and its related business, "cover" in the entertainment industry, and "price" in many other situations.

Regardless of what it is called, the primary objective of price is to cover all the costs incurred in making a product/service and to produce profit while it still appeals to the intended target market. The issue of whether products or services must be priced to maximize profit is a seemingly simple but in fact rather vexing one and will not be discussed in detail here. However, suffice it to say that, while some economists believe that pricing must be used as a tool to maximize profit, behavioral economists take the view that profit maximization is not the object of the firm. Cyert and March (1963), for example, have argued that because of the interactions that take place within firms, the wide range of personal objectives that are held by the employees, as well as the constraints that exist, firms aim to achieve profits that would be satisfactory to their disparate stakeholders, instead of trying to maximize profits.

The concerns about pricing are not limited to large for-profit organizations alone. Small to medium-sized enterprises (SMEs) as well as non-profit organizations such as universities, municipalities, and public hospitals are also equally concerned about pricing strategy. Governments in many countries are interested in the pricing practices of firms because of either their political or economic philosophies. Governments that are interested in the free-market economic system also tend to be interested in the pricing policy of firms in pursuit of their economic policies. Other governments might be interested in price controls in the pursuit of their social policies. Governments' interest in the pricing policies of firms is expressed in the laws that are passed and enforced. For example, to ensure free markets, governments pass and enforce anti-collusion laws and other laws that prohibit pricing practices that seek to stifle competition (Stigler, 1987)

To attain certain social objectives, governments pass and enforce price controls or price ceilings. The existence of laws concerning pricing also suggests that firms must not be concerned by profit-maximizing objectives alone when they price; they must also be concerned about complying with existing laws on pricing. Firms that operate in several countries or different jurisdictions must be aware of the laws on pricing in the different countries/jurisdictions in which they operate, as there is no one universal law on pricing that is applied by every country (Koku, 2009).

The objective of pricing remains the same in both small and large organizations; however, those who set prices or play a key role in pricing differ. Prices of products and services are set in large organizations by product line managers in conjunction with marketing and sales departments or by a department that is solely responsible for pricing. On the other hand, prices are generally set by top management in SMEs. As such it is imperative for top management in SMEs to be thoroughly familiar with the issues associated with pricing of the products or services that they offer.

LAWS ON PRICING

It is consistent with economic theory of revenue maximization for a firm to charge different buyers different prices. This is true for both large and small firms as well as for-profit and non-profit organizations (Nagle, 1987). Let us take the case of universities and colleges, for example. These institutions charge consumers (students) different prices (tuition) based on where the students come from—such as in-state or out-of-state tuition, or national or international student tuition. They also do so by such other means as offering different scholarships and financial aid packages. Similarly, hospitals charge the insured and the uninsured different rates for the same treatment. Indeed, price discrimination is an ever-present phenomenon in business. However, because several states and countries have price discrimination laws that make certain types of price discrimination illegal, it is important that organizations know which types of price discrimination are permissible and where they are permissible.

Firms use different pricing strategies such as quantity discounts for retailers based on size and package and non-linear price schedules (where different segments exist), organizations have to be careful about the issue of price discrimination, which is defined variously by different authors. According to Kent Monroe, price discrimination is

> [w]henever there are price differences for the same product or service sold by a single seller that are not justified by cost or changes in the level of demand. Price discrimination

also occurs when two or more buyers of the same product or service are charged the same price despite differences in the cost of serving these buyers.

(Monroe, 2003, p. 250)

It is true that an organization may be willing to charge different consumers different prices for the same product/service based on the consumers' willingness to pay the different prices. This could be done in an effort to generate more revenue for the organization while selling the same number of units. Economists explain this phenomenon as an attempt by the organization to extract all the potential gains from trade and argue that this practice is possible because the different consumers or consumer groups have different elasticity of demand. Alternatively, it has been argued that different consumers may, based on their perceived benefits, assign different values to the same product, hence their willingness to pay different prices.

Even though price discrimination as defined above connotes charging different prices for the same product or service without cost justifications, the ambit of price discrimination could involve other business practices such as special promotions, rebates, and discounts (cash and quantity) that lead to price differences.

Price discrimination immediately evokes connotations of an illegal act, as discussed above. However, there are legally permissible or defensible price-discriminatory practices. How else could one explain the practice of students as a group being able to subscribe, through their universities, to newspapers such as the *Wall Street Journal* or magazines at prices below news-stand prices, or senior citizens being able to buy bus tickets at a discount?

The permissible price-discriminatory practices are generally regarded as exceptions to laws, such as the antitrust laws. The most well-known exception is cost-based pricing, i.e. a firm can charge different consumers different prices for the same product if the cost for serving these consumers is different. The practical application of this exemption is seen in instances where a firm charges a consumer who buys in larger quantities a lower price than a consumer who buys the same product in a smaller quantity. This prepares the ground for what economists call block pricing.

By using block pricing, a seller could extract additional profits from similar consumers who face a similar downward-sloping demand curve. Take, for instance, a situation where a seller is selling a roll of 36-millimeter film for $4.00 per roll, and a buyer values the first roll of the 36 millimeter film at $4.00, but the second at $2.00. Because the two rolls of film will cost the buyer $8.00 ($4.00 each) the buyer will buy only one roll of film. However, the seller can get the buyer to buy the two rolls if s/he puts them together and offers them for $6.00. Here, the consumer who buys a pack of two rolls of film pays less per roll of film than the consumer who buys only one roll of film.

One of the major motivations behind the antitrust laws is the prevention of a monopoly that could result from predatory pricing. Thus, the law makes an exemption for different prices to be charged for the same product if it is certain that the firm will not emerge as a monopoly, or the practice is not designed to injure competitors. Such a case could be said to exist when a company is going out of business. It also allows price changes for obsolescence of goods that are seasonal and perishable or closing-out-a-line sales, and court-sanctioned distress sales are also exempted.

THE ECONOMICS OF PRICING

Firms use their pricing strategy to serve several objectives. While generating revenue and profit are the obvious primary objectives, several secondary objectives exist. For example, the pricing strategy must not only complement the firm's distribution as well as its communication strategies but also the pricing policies should also be consistent with the nature of the product. A pricing strategy will not be complementary with the distribution strategy if a firm sells rare and expensive items, such as jewelry, using mass merchandisers. Similarly, the pricing strategy will not be complementary with the communication strategy if a seller advertises expensive jewelry using handbills (flyers) or tabloids. A pricing policy will be inconsistent with the product if a firm sells a high-quality product at a price at which consumers do not expect the product to sell.

These discussions suggest a number of issues. First, consumers often use price as an indicator of quality; thus, all things being equal, a high price is indicative of high quality. For this reason SMEs should be careful when they set price. A drastic reduction in price of a product that has been positioned as a high-quality product may only confuse buyers. They will think that the product's quality has also been drastically reduced.

Price, in addition to serving as a signal, also serves as an indicator of value (Zeithaml, 1988). However, value is defined differently by different authors. Some authors define value as

$$Value = \frac{Perceived\,Benefits}{Price}$$

However, others argue that consumers tend to define the value of a product in terms of its substitute, hence

$$Value = perceived\ benefits\ of\ a\ product/the\ price\ of\ its\ substitute$$

In either case, the role of price as an indicator of value is clear.

In spite of numerous studies on the subject, how consumers exactly use price in their purchasing decisions largely remains not well understood. It is, however, clear that, regardless of the definition of value, consumers use other non-price variables such as the *perceived value* of the product or service in their buying decisions. Perceived value-pricing strategy is therefore an appropriate strategy for not only large firms but also for SMEs. The firm that uses this strategy will rely on non-cost variables. It will try to determine the buyer's perception of the product or service's value and price accordingly. As discussed above, this type of pricing strategy is more appropriate when the pricing decision is made to be consistent with all the other marketing variables.

Regardless of how consumers use price information, it is clear that for some products consumers react to price changes by either purchasing more of the product or less of the product. This concept is known in economics as price elasticity of demand. It serves as one of the decision factors in changing price in many large organizations, and should be used by SMEs also.

PRICE ELASTICITY OF DEMAND

The price elasticity of demand is defined as the degree of responsiveness in quantity demanded given a unit change in price. Algebraically, it is expressed as

$$E = \frac{\%\,Change\,In\,Quality\,Demanded}{\%\,Change\,In\,Price}$$

There are a few points to note about E. Because it would be nonsensical to have dimensions, i.e. tons/price, the coefficient of elasticity does not have any dimensions. Furthermore, the absolute value of the coefficient is what is considered. Hence, in terms of the elasticity of demand, the effect of −2 is the same as the effect of 2 since |−2| is the same as 2. The demand is said to be elastic when the absolute value of E is greater than 1 (for example, 3, −4, 10, etc.), and is said to be inelastic when E is less than 1 (for example, .7, .65, .35, etc.).

The demand is generally elastic for goods and services that have substitutes. For example, one would expect the demand for products with close substitutes, such as for running shoes or laptop computers, to be price elastic. The same is true for services such as university education or retail stores that have several substitutes. For these goods, a unit change in price will result in more than a unit change in the quantity demanded. A percentage price change in tuition may result in a disproportionate change in the "demand" for education. The opposite is true for goods and services that do not have close substitutes. The demand for such products is price inelastic. The demand for quantity of common salt, for example, will not change significantly because of percentage price change—hence, such a demand is price inelastic.

Other factors that have been shown to affect the elasticity of demand include other uses of the product or service, and the ratio of the price of the product or service to the income of the consumer. Generally, the more uses for the product or service, the more elastic its demand. And the smaller the ratio of the price to the consumers' income, the less elastic its demand. On the other hand, the higher the ratio of the price to income, the more elastic its demand.

Some firms sell the same product or services at very different prices in different countries or geographic locations, not because of the additional costs incurred in making the products or services available, but because they price using the concept of the elasticity of demand. Prices are lower at locations where there are many substitutes and higher at locations where there are no close substitutes. However, a firm risks being accused of dumping if it sells below "fair market value" in foreign markets where there are close substitutes. Dumping could be a violation of the World Trade Organization's agreement between the signatory countries if it threatens material injury to an industry in the importing nation.

THE ISSUE OF CROSS-ELASTICITY

Cross-elasticity arises when the change in price of one product, let us say product A, affects the quantity of another product, let us say product B. Cross-elasticity plays an important role in a firm's pricing decisions, particularly if the firm sells several products that are used jointly, i.e. if some of the products are complementary. For example, razor blades and shaving sticks are complementary goods; therefore, an increase in the price of razor blades will more than likely affect the quantity of shaving sticks demanded. A firm that manufactures razor blades and shaving sticks will, therefore, have to take into consideration the effects of price change of one of the products on the other.

Similarly, the manufacturer of razor blades and shaving sticks will have to take into consideration the fact these products are used together into their initial pricing. A good strategy may be to sell the shaving stick at a much lower price, or even give it away free, and sell the razor blade at a premium, if the shaving sticks are designed in a way that the consumer has to buy the same manufacturer's razor blades. While complementary pricing strategy may be a common practice in large and multinational organizations, it is nonetheless germane to SMEs.

The availability and the price of close substitutes should also affect a firm's pricing decisions. As in the case of supplementary goods, a change in price of a product, let us say product C, affects the quantity demanded of its substitute, let us say product D, particularly if product D is a close substitute to product C. The concept of cross-elasticity is at work here again. The implication of cross-elasticity—not for SMEs only but for every firm—is that effective pricing decisions cannot be made by focusing only on margins; they also have to take into consideration the configuration of the entire market. This will include not only the other products that are made by SMEs and how they are used or demanded by the consumer, but also the availability of close substitutes.

PRICING STRATEGIES

Two basic pricing strategies, full-cost pricing and variable-cost pricing, form the principal foundation for other strategies. Because it is intuitive and rather simple to understand, most managers tend to apply what is commonly referred to as a full-cost pricing strategy. The objective of this strategy is to recoup the costs that go into making a product plus a markup. Full costs can be divided into three parts as follows:

- The direct costs incurred in making the product or service. These direct costs are generally direct labor and direct material.
- The product's or service's share of the production fixed costs (overheads).
- The producer's markup.

The markup can be lowered or increased, depending on the competitive environment.

The variable-cost pricing comprises only the direct costs, which are the direct costs of materials and direct labor costs. It is evident from the components of variable costs that a firm cannot survive using only variable-cost strategy. In practice, firms use variable-cost pricing for limited objectives and only for a short duration. They can, for example, be used to build traffic to the store, but manufacturers have to be ever so careful in using this strategy because they can be accused of predatory pricing, which is illegal in many jurisdictions. Firms use variable-cost pricing also for products that are being discontinued.

Products can, in some extreme cases, be priced below cost. This strategy is sometimes referred to as distress pricing and used when a product has become obsolete. Under distress pricing the product is simply priced at the cost of carrying it (that is, the cost of insuring the product and the space it occupies).

PRICING STRATEGIES FOR NEW PRODUCT INTRODUCTION

There are two primary new product introduction pricing strategies, which are known as skimming and penetration strategies. Skimming refers to new product introduction pricing strategy in which the initial price is high. This initial high price is lowered subsequently. There are several explanations for the use of skimming strategy. First, the innovating firm wants to recoup its investment in the new product as quickly as possible before competition sets in. Second, the innovating firm gets to enjoy economics of scale as the users of the new product grow in number. The firm then passes on to consumers, in the form of lower prices, the benefits (cost savings) of the economics of scale.

It is also reasonable to expect the innovating firm to develop cost-saving methods as it gets more experienced in making the new product. In order not to be under-priced by competition, the innovating firm also passes along these cost savings to the consumer. The skimming strategy is common in industries where new inventions require a substantial investment, such as the high technology industry and the pharmaceutical industry. Recent examples of new products in the high-technology industry where skimming strategy has been used include digital watches, calculators, cellular phones, and iPods. Examples of skimming in the pharmaceutical industry include penicillin, the entire class of cholesterol-lowering drugs, and patches for smoking cessation.

The penetration pricing strategy with new products is said to be used when the new product is introduced with an initially low price and increased over time. Most new products fall into this category when they are introduced with coupons which are later on eliminated. Introducing new products or services with coupons amounts to the use of price penetration strategy as the coupons serve as a price subsidy, and their elimination will result in the consumers having to pay the full price.

Even though we have emphasized the introductory phase of the product or service in skimming and penetration strategies, the entire *product life cycle* presents distinct opportunities for the firm to implement a different pricing strategy. Thus, a firm could use one type of strategy (for example, penetration strategy) in the product or service's introductory phase. It may use the full-cost pricing approach in the growth phase, promotional pricing strategy in the maturity phase, and a loss-leader approach in the declining phase.

PRICING OBJECTIVES

Irrespective of whether the firm uses full-cost pricing or variable-cost pricing strategy, the pricing objectives have to be first clearly delineated. There are three basic objectives—the firm must decide whether it wants to maximize revenue, maximize its pre-tax profits or maximize its market share. Even though maximizing revenue or maximizing pre-tax profits objectives could result in the same approach, they are not always the same. Many large firms could set their price to maximize their revenue by estimating their demand function. However, such practices are not widely used by SMEs because their pricing decisions are generally made by one or a few individuals as opposed to an elaborate pricing department in large organizations.

A firm may have to sell at prices lower than its competition in pursing maximization of market share as its objective.

PRICING WITH OTHER MARKETING VARIABLES

Even though pricing decisions are directed toward generating revenue, they cannot be made in isolation of other marketing variables such as the *product*, *place*, and *promotion*. Indeed, it is imperative that the pricing strategy be consistent with the firm's entire marketing strategy. The relationship between price and the *product* or *service* is the most obvious of the relationships between price and the other marketing variables. The firm will lose credibility if the price is not consistent with the quality of product or service that the firm is offering. Similarly, a firm cannot sell expensive and high-quality offerings using a mass-distribution strategy. The distribution strategy will undermine the product quality as consumers will assume that because mass-distribution strategy is being used, the offering (product or service) might not "truly" be a high-quality offering after all.

What about *promotion* and *place*? Just as an inappropriate distribution strategy will undermine the firm's credibility and the effectiveness of its overall marketing strategy, so too will inappropriate use of promotion and place. Media that are reflective of the quality or caliber of product or service being offered must be used. For example, one would expect advertisements of a high-quality watch that targets successful business people to be carried in such business-oriented newspapers as *The Times*, the *Wall Street Journal*, *Time*, *Newsweek*, etc., but not in newspapers or magazines that are considered tabloids.

In much the same way as advertising, one would expect the *place* where such high-quality watches are being sold to be reflective of their class. Certainly, one would not expect such watches to be sold by street vendors on the sidewalk because watches that are sold on sidewalks by street vendors are usually thought to be of low quality or shady origin.

THE ROLE OF THE THREE CS

The three Cs are *Cost*, *Customers*, and *Competition*. These three factors individually and collectively play a significant role in a firm's pricing decision. The role of cost in a firm's pricing decision is obvious as the firm must, at the very minimum, cover its production cost. The cost of production is directly traceable to the cost of the inputs—direct material and direct labor. If these costs are high the price of the product or service will also be high and vice versa. It is, however, important to note that the target customers will influence the quality of the input.

Given the importance of market segmentation in designing effective marketing strategies, it should be no surprise that an effective pricing strategy also calls for different prices for different consumer segments. For example, a newspaper publisher could sell to students at a price lower than the rack price. Similarly, senior citizens pay lower prices for certain services and products such as prescription drugs and public transportation. The elasticity of demand is the underlying economic argument behind charging different customer segments different prices. However, firms using this strategy have to be careful not to run afoul the strict price-discrimination laws that are enforced in many jurisdictions. Price segmentation using such variables as race or religion is not permissible, at least not in the United States.

The price of competitors' products, particularly close competitors, also matters. Because price-sensitive consumers do take the price of close substitutes into consideration, a firm will do well to pay attention to those prices. Some firms may not be satisfied knowing just the price of competitors; they may also want to know how competitors arrived at such prices. Since they cannot ask their competitors directly, they engage in what is called reversed engineering. In reversed engineering a firm takes apart the competitor's product, and prices each of the component parts. By so doing a firm may learn the actual cost of competitors' products and may also be able to estimate the markup on the product.

A firm that is armed with fairly accurate information on competitors' costs and markup will be in a better position to match competitors' prices. Hence, a common pricing strategy where products or services are similar is to match the price of the competition. Pricing to match competitors is, however, fraught with dangers. First, a firm can easily price below its cost or below its own required returns in an attempt to match competitors' prices. Second, matching competitors' prices can unintentionally lead to a price war in which every seller tries to under-price the competition.

RETURN ON INVESTMENT AND MARKUP PRICING

While pricing to match competitors is easy to implement, it does not take into consideration a firm's own cost of production or the required rates of return on its investments; it is, therefore, not a very useful strategy, at least in terms of realizing a firm's financial objectives. Markup pricing and return on investment pricing techniques incorporate the firm's financial objective in its pricing strategy.

Many firms in the services industry, such as law practices or accounting firms, practice markup pricing in which they add a standard markup on cost. How does the markup pricing work? Let us take a look at the following:

Direct labor cost/unit   = $10.00
Direct material/unit   = $5.00
Total fixed cost   = $100,000.00
Number of units produced   = 50,000.00

(For simplicity we can assume that all the units produced are sold.)

The direct cost per unit from the information above = $15.00 (i.e. $10 for direct labor per unit + $5.00 for direct material per unit). However, the total cost per unit will have to reflect each unit's share of the total fixed cost as well (this is one of the issues dealt with in cost allocation, which will not be discussed in this chapter). Since a total of 50,000 units have been produced, each unit's share of the total fixed cost is given as follows:

$$\text{Each unit's share of the total fixed cost} = \frac{\$100,000.00}{50,000.00}$$
$$= \$2.00$$

Therefore, the unit cost in producing the item = $17.00 (i.e. $15 + $2).

Now, let us assume that the firm applies a 20 percent markup on each unit produced. In that case the selling price will be as follows:

$$\text{Selling price of the product} = \frac{\text{UnitCost}}{(1 - \text{DesiredMarkup})}$$
$$= \frac{\$17.00}{(1 - 20\%)}$$
$$= \frac{\$17.00}{.80}$$
$$= \$21.25$$

The consumer may, however, pay more than $21.25 for the item if the firm does not sell directly to the final consumer, but instead sells through intermediaries. Because the intermediaries also have to add on their desired markup, the product might end up costing significantly more than $21.25. The final price will depend on the number of intermediaries through whom the product passes to get to the final consumer.

Pricing strategies that discuss the role of the intermediaries are discussed in detail in distribution channels issues which we do not cover in this chapter. However, it is important to know that a retailer, which many SMEs are, can apply markup as a percentage of its cost or its selling price. Take, for example, a retailer who buys an item for $20.00 and desires a 30 percent markup on cost—they will sell the item for $26.00 (i.e. $20 × 1.30). However, the same retailer who desires 30 percent markup on the basis of the selling price will sell the product for $28.57 (that is, $20/.7). It should be clear from this example that the price that the final consumers pay depends on whether the intermediaries apply their markup requirements using the cost price or the selling price as the basis.

In practice, particularly in small business settings, the owner or entrepreneur sets a profit goal and prices the product or service to achieve this goal. This type of pricing is referred to as target-return pricing. The attainment of the profit goal, however, involves the concept of break-even. In order for a firm to realize profit, the firm must first achieve a break-even volume, i.e. it must first sell enough to cover all the costs incurred in making the product. Therefore, the target-return price assumes having first attained a break-even volume. Let us assume here that the firm has invested $1 million in the project and desires 30 percent return on this investment. The break-even volume with the example given above is derived as follows:

$$\text{Break-even volume} = \frac{\text{FixedCost}}{\text{Contribution}}$$

where contribution = Selling Price – Variable Cost

which = $21.25 – $15.00

= $6.25

Using the figures above:

$$\text{The break-even volume} = \frac{\$100,000.00}{\$6.25}$$

= 16,000 units

The target-return price = unit cost + (desired return × investment)/unit sales. Here again, for the sake of simplicity, we dispense with the concept of the discounted streams of future income.

Using the figures in our example above:

$$\text{Target-return price} = \$17.00 + \frac{(30\% \times \$1,000,000.00)}{50,000}$$

= $17.00 + $6.00

= $23.00

VALUE PRICING

Even though value pricing may sound similar to perceived-value pricing, the two are not the same. The customer under the perceived-value pricing concept discussed earlier thinks the product or service is worth the price. However, under value pricing, the firm tries to set prices in a way that the price represents "an extraordinary bargain for the consumer." Thus, under value pricing, the firm not only charges price lower that its competitors but it also gives better services and guarantees than its competitors.

OTHER PRICING STRATEGIES

Other pricing strategies that firms use include product line pricing, psychological pricing, and transfer pricing. Product line pricing strategy is used by firms that produce more than one product or more than one product line. Under this pricing strategy, different product lines may carry distinctly different prices. The cross-elasticity between products in a line is relevant to product line pricing, and so are the product positioning and the interrelations between the offerings within the line. The lowest-priced product in a line might be positioned as the traffic builder, while the highest-priced product might be positioned as the premium item.

Taking the psychological pricing approach can lead sellers to price a product or service such that the price ends in a 9. For example, it is believed that a pair of shoes selling for $49.99 conveys a cheaper price than the pair selling for $50.00. Whether this is effective or not is debatable, but the fact is that we are constantly bombarded or surrounded by evidence of such practices. The psychological effects of pricing also lead sellers to set high prices, regardless of the cost, for conspicuous consumption items such as jewelry and fur coats, or items that involve consumers' ego, such as perfume.

Closely associated with psychological pricing is the concept of reference price. Sellers don't really use reference price because a reference price is simply the consumer's benchmark price that the consumer uses to make certain purchases. When using reference price in their pricing strategy, sellers generally display their products with the products that they wish to be associated with in the mind of the consumer.

Transfer pricing is practiced in situations where the firm makes one or several components of a final product that it assembles at the same or a different location. In this case the firm could set the price of the component parts that are made within the firm in different departments in order to arrive at a predetermined price of the final product.

The internet has revolutionized the way business is done and has opened global markets that may have been cost prohibitive to SMEs. Suddenly, an SME in the U.K. or the U.S.A. could, through a creative use of its website, receive orders from far away markets such as Singapore or Hong Kong, where it may not have actively participated previously. While these possibilities are exciting, they have also made pricing decisions for SMEs more complex. Because international markets involve other geographic locations that could be far away, SMEs now have to consider whether shipping charges, warehousing, insurance, and such associated costs should be reflected in their pricing decisions or dealt with separately.

Simply put, pricing decisions can be very involved and there is often a lot at stake whether the firm is a large multinational organization or an SME. Because an easy international presence can be achieved through the internet, pricing decision makers should be both knowledgeable on the economics of pricing and also familiar with the legal issues relating to pricing in the different jurisdictions in which they market their products and services.

REVIEW QUESTIONS

1. Which three Cs are relevant to pricing?

2. Why should an organization be familiar with the laws of the different states or countries in which it conducts business?

3. List the external factors that could affect an organization's pricing.

4. What is price elasticity of demand and how does it work?

5. Is price discrimination always illegal?

6. Jane sells Wow Chocolate Cookies, which she makes using a secret recipe, through retailers. She sells the cookies to the retailers at $20.00 per box. Calculate (a) the price the retailers should sell the cookies to final consumers for if the retailers' policy requires a 20 percent markup on cost and (b) what the price would be if the retailers required a 20 percent markup on the basis of the selling price?

7. Labor costs at Apple, Microsoft, and IBM have increased from $35.00 per hour at each of these firms to $50.00 per hour. At Toshiba's Japanese plants, however, labor costs have remained at approximately $30.00 per hour. The difference in these costs gives Toshiba an advantage in which of the following types of cost?
   a. Fixed cost
   b. Variable cost
   c. Semi-variable cost
   d. Marginal Cost
   e. Total fixed cost

CASE STUDY 9: DR. ZEE GOES SOLO

Dr. Zee has always been a social entrepreneur. As a high school student, he earned additional income by selling produce from an organic vegetable garden that he cultivated behind his parents' home. In college, while studying for a dual degree in mechanical and electrical engineering, young Siegfried Zee made extra money by selling shopping bags that were reusable and biodegradable.

After college, Siegfried got a job as an assistant engineer with a large multinational company where he worked on product development. He was well liked by his supervisor and colleagues. Commenting on his years with this firm, Siegfried later said that it was one of the most fascinating periods in his life. While he enjoyed his work and found working on new products stimulating, he still felt there was something missing in his life. After five years with Global Inc., Siegfried Zee decided to go back to graduate school and work on his doctorate in electro-mechanical engineering.

Siegfried traveled extensively around the world during his holidays while in graduate school and was for the first time exposed to people suffering from illnesses caused by waterborne diseases in many developing countries. He knew then what he wanted to do for the rest his life. He wanted to invent a simple water pump that could sell at a very low price. He surmised that he could sell them to governments in developing countries. Thus, while making a little money, he would also be helping to eradicate waterborne diseases.

Back at school, Siegfried spent his time away from studying on working on a design to manufacture a simple water pump that could be solar powered and powerful enough to pump water from several hundred feet underground. He was able to put a prototype together by buying the component parts from his savings. He tested the invention, which he called the "Magicmaker," in his parents' backyard, and the invention worked wonderfully. The pump could run for ten hours when the solar panels were fully charged from a five-hour exposure to the sun.

Siegfried successfully completed his Ph.D. in five years, at the age of 35, and was sought after by several academic institutions and multinational companies. However, Dr. Zee decided to form his own company, Zee Inc., and commercialize the Magicmaker. He and his parents invested $1 million in the project and Dr. Zee plans to launch in six months, selling through a network of dealers to whom he will sell the Magicmaker for $8,000.

From the various data assembled, the estimated annual maintenance cost of the Magicmaker is $100. Additional information on the Magicmaker is given below:

Material cost per pump	$5,000
Labor cost per pump	$1,000
Factory overhead	$200,000
Distribution (delivery) per pump	$500
Advertising	$20,000

Imagine that Dr. Zee has retained you as a consultant, and wants to meet with you next week for advice. Based on the above information, calculate the following:

1. Contribution per unit:
   a. $3,500
   b. $2,000
   c. $2,500
   d. $1,500
   e. $1,000.
2. Unit volume needed to achieve $20,000 profit:
   a. 120
   b. 200
   c. 160
   d. 108
   e. 100.
3. Break-even volume in units:
   a. 147
   b. 800
   c. 813
   d. 220
   e. 177.
4. Suppose Dr. Zee wants to realize 12 percent return on his investment at the end of the first year of operation. How much would that be?
   a. $120,000
   b. $26,400
   c. $28,800
   d. $146,000
   e. $10,000.

CORRECT ANSWERS

Review questions

6. (a) $24.00 (that is, $20 × 1.20)
   (b) $25.00 (that is, $20.00/.80)
7. b. Variable cost

Case study

1. d.
2. e.
3. a.
4. a.

BIBLIOGRAPHY

Brickley, James A., Smith, C. W., Zimmerman, J. L. (1997), *Managerial Economics and Organizational Architecture*, McGraw-Hill, Boston, MA.

Cyert, R. N. and March, J. G. (1963), *A Behavioral Theory of the Firm*, Prentice Hall, Englewood Cliffs, NJ.

Koku, P. S. (2009), "Which Laws Do Your Marketers Know? Some Legal Issues on Price Discrimination," *Conference Proceedings*, Academy of Marketing Science World Congress, pp. 409–419.

Kotler, P. (1994), *Marketing Management, Analysis, Planning, Implementation and Control*, 8th edn, Prentice Hall, Englewood Cliffs, NJ

Monroe, K. B. (2003), *Pricing: Making Profitable Decisions*, McGraw-Hill, New York, NY.

Montgomery, A. L. (1997), "Creating Micro-Marketing Price Strategies Using Supermarket Scanner Data," *Marketing Science*, 16, pp. 315–337.

Nagle, T. T. (1987), *The Strategy and Tactics of Pricing*, Prentice Hall, Englewood Cliffs, NJ.

Stigler, G. (1987), *The Theory of Price*, MacMillan, New York, NY.

Swan A. C. and Murphy, J. F. (1999), *Cases and Materials on the Regulation of International Business and Economic Relations*, 2nd edn, Mathew Bender, New York, NY.

Zeithaml, V. A. (1988), "Consumer Perceptions of Price, Quality, and Value," *Journal of Marketing*, 52, pp. 2–22.

Chapter 10

The reality of distribution faced by SMEs
A UK perspective

David Bamber

> ### LEARNING OBJECTIVES
>
> *After reading this chapter, you will be able to:*
> - understand the 'place' component of the marketing mix
> - gain insights into strategic and logistic distribution functions
> - review the main tasks of distribution
> - understand some of the complexities of distribution
> - analyse the interconnections distribution functions using the UK real market
> - analyse the case of an intermediary acting as a wholesaler to SME retail outlets.

INTRODUCTION

In this chapter we will look at the distribution channel situation faced by small- and medium-sized enterprises (SMEs), focusing in particular on the UK SME brewery trade and public houses (pubs) operated by sole traders. Attention will be paid to the close links between the supply chain, the distribution channels, the production of the product, the raw materials and the requirements of the consumers. There are independent partners that make either products or services available for the consumer or, indeed, other businesses. There may also be intermediaries – people in between the producer and the consumer – so there are different structures for distribution channels. The purpose of those channels is to add some value to the transaction processes and, indeed, the relationship processes between producer and, ultimately, the consumer. The gaps between suppliers, manufacturers and consumers are filled by the distribution channels. Using the distribution channels, the goods are made available to the consumer where and when they are needed. Those distribution channels add value to the marketing chain as they create space and time utility for businesses further down the chain. Clearly, the task of distribution is to add value in some way or other to the product or service so that there will be benefits for the producer, the consumer and intermediaries.

There are several tasks of distribution: promoting products, e.g. informing the market about new products; contacting, building up personal relationships; sorting goods for use in connection with each other and adapting these to the consumer's needs. Another function of distribution is to store the products so that they become available 'just in time', as needed by the consumer. In the microbrewery trade this can be satisfied by the brewery delivering the product. Additionally, there will be breaking down of the bulk so that the large quantities produced become manageable for the consumer and retailer. As already mentioned, there is also a transportation task. Hence, there are several functions connected with distribution and the flow of product between the two partners. Some flows are *forward flows* and others are *backward flows* and importantly still other flows concern exchange of information and knowledge. Physical distribution concerns shipment of products to the customer. This is the 'place' component of the marketing mix. There are many decisions to be made concerning distribution and these are likely to include decisions about the market coverage, channel distribution, warehousing, order processing, transportation and inventory management.

DISTRIBUTION OVERVIEW

The distribution function supports the marketing processes that focus on the fulfilment of customer demand. Successful distribution strategies allow the customer to access the product conveniently and provide pre- and post-purchase support for the business. There are two facets to distribution: the *logistical* and the *strategic*. The logistical distribution is called 'supply chain management' and this function sustains the strategic function. Logistics provide the regular transfer of goods, information and capital between different levels in the supply chain. It is the operation function that is informed by marketing intelligence. The strategic distribution function, on the other hand, provides a competitive advantage to the business within the distribution network. So, decisions about the strategic distribution function concern who, what, where, when and which business partners are to be involved in the fulfilment of customer demands. Generally, this will concern the selection of intermediaries between manufacturer and retailer and may also involve certain service functions.

There can be different types of intermediaries: those between the producer and the consumer, including wholesalers, agents, retailers, franchisees; the internet; overseas distributors; or alternatively there may be direct marketing from the producer straight to the consumer.

The wholesalers may split up the product into manageable sizes for resale by a retailer. Wholesalers generally purchase products, taking ownership and 'title' of those goods, from the manufacturers and resell to retailers. Wholesalers often store the products before selling on to the retailer. As a range of products may be available from one wholesaler, the wholesaler may assume some other marketing activities, producing brochures and promoting certain products. Agents, however, would generally be used in an international setting where it would be difficult or expensive for the producer to contact consumers directly.

The agent 'on the ground' secures an order for the producer or service provider and takes a percentage commission, or a flat fee, and would not usually take 'title' of any goods. Often agents are used by training institutes in the UK to recruit international students. A problem arises when agents are difficult to control, as they could serve several providers, playing one off against another and potentially having a stronger allegiance to a rival. Where the agents operate in state-of-the-art markets they would be expensive to train but could provide local knowledge and insights.

Retailers stand face-to-face with the consumer and are placed to have a strong relationship with the consumer. The consumer entering the typical retail outlet will be offered several brands and a series of goods, many of which will have been previously promoted by the retailer. The product's final selling price will most likely be determined by the retailer. Some retailers may offer services to the consumer as well as goods – for example, large retailers of electronic products offer credit facilities and repair service insurance. Incidentally, in 1856 Edward Clark, the business partner of Isaac Singer (inventor of the Singer sewing machine) developed a system for instalment selling and time payment purchasing that became the model for hire-purchase agreements. This provided people with low incomes an opportunity to own an expensive product that had the potential to help them earn money, through sewing, for themselves (Singer, 2007). Many large famous retail brands started life as SMEs, one such example is Marks & Spencer (M&S) which was founded by Michael Marks in 1884 when he opened a penny bazaar stall on Leeds' Kirkgate Market (M&S, 2010).

Internet technology may be used at any point in the distribution channel and provides a facility with low set-up costs. E-commerce uses systems such as shopping basket software and PayPal to transfer money from purchaser to seller around the world. The internet thus has the potential to reach a dispersed international market, providing a wide market with niche products. Isaac Singer also operated one of the first businesses that used a form of franchising, offering licenses to entrepreneurs to sell sewing machines across the United States of America and to train customers in their use (Singer, 2007). A franchise is a right granted, through a legal agreement, to an individual or group to offer another company's goods or services, usually at a certain location or in a particular geographical territory. This allows the franchisor to distribute products or services to a large marketplace. This benefits the individual franchisees who gain trust from the customers who are loyal to the established corporate image and brand. The franchisor is also likely to provide and support an up-and-running business model. The downside for the franchisee is that they are usually tied to buy certain products from the franchisor and they have to pay not only a one-off start-up fee but also regular ongoing royalties.

The distribution channel stretches from the producer of raw materials and the providers of utilities through to the consumer. A short supply channel may involve just the manufacturer selling directly to the consumer, whereas a long distribution channel may involve indirect selling from the manufacturer, the wholesaler, intermediary agents, the retailer and ultimately the consumer. The shortest indirect chain is from the manufacturer to retailer to consumer and this may be the manufacturer's preferred consumer marketing channel as it benefits from the close relationship of the consumer to the retailer. The main distribution tasks, all of which contribute to building a good relationship with the consumer and from which competitive advantage can arise, are summarized in Table 10.1. The distribution tasks are represented by the acronym 'RAINCAPP'.

Table 10.1 Tasks of distribution

Task	Description
Risk avoidance	The wholesaler assumes the risk of holding the stock.
Adjusting	The distributor adjusts the offering to match the customer needs. This may cover aspects such as sorting, assembling and packaging.
Information gathering	Intelligent information is selected, accumulated and distributed throughout the distribution channel.
Negotiation	Agreements on price and other offers are brokered.
Communication	The communication networks among manufacturer, distributors and consumer are facilitated.
Acquisition	Capital is acquired to meet distribution channel costs.
Promotion	Offerings are placed, promoted and distributed.
Physical distribution	Goods are transported and stored.

From the manufacturer's perspective, the main aim of the distribution strategy is to expose the product to the widest possible market. Hence, from the manufacturing SME's viewpoint, with relatively limited resources, the distribution decisions will extend from intense distribution through as many retail outlets as possible through to locally focused distribution through a limited number of niche outlets. The SME faces the daunting prospect of being just a small voice calling 'me too!' in the already overcrowded marketplace, where the big international companies dominate. So how can SMEs compete against such power? The SME must develop strong relationships with the customers at all levels of the supply chain, develop itself into a reliable brand and establish a credible reputation. Additionally, the distribution channel it selects will need to be supported by an efficient and effective infrastructure that can deliver products reliably.

A NICHE MARKET

Let us now think about modern times and the distribution of beer – in particular *real ale* – and the way it is distributed to outlets, pubs, supermarkets and off-licences. How is the beer moved around? It is usually moved around in containers and there are different kinds of containers, such as the barrel, which may be made out of metal or, more traditionally, of wood. There are tin cans and there are bottles. So the brewer needs these things to transport the beer and they need a mode of transport. Traditionally the beer barrels were transported from the brewery to the pubs using horse-drawn carts called 'drays', which have found much favour in local communities in the north of England and elsewhere, where shire horses, or dray horses, have come back into fashion and are displayed ceremoniously pulling perhaps six or eight large barrels of beer. These have been used as a status symbol for the re-emerging economy that is dedicated to quality and traditional, authentic values.

Almost every cereal has some kind of natural sugar in it and that can start fermenting because there is wild yeast in the air. Hence, people throughout history have found that while trying to store natural products – food, berries and grain – the storage has become alcoholic, due to fermentation. Indeed, in Africa the collection of the wild black plum and desert date have been used for millennia to produce low-alcoholic beverages, when mixed with sugar and water. Jars, used by ancient civilizations to distribute, store and transport the product, have been tested and shown to have contained beer as long ago as 4000 BC, and that is across the globe, in China and ancient Iraq. Beer was being produced as early at 7000 BC and there is evidence from 3000 BC of beer production in Iran (Hornsey, 2003). However, nowadays over 100 billion litres of beer is sold every year through retail outlets – mainly pubs, restaurants and supermarkets. Beer is a totally global product with revenues of over US$300 billion (Evans, 2004). It is big business, but it is also small business, and it is also medium-sized business. Although beer and cider were produced before the Industrial Revolution and sold on a small scale by farmer family brewers, they have also been produced and sold on a larger scale, since the seventh century, in the monasteries of Belgium and elsewhere. As Sumner (2005) notes, before canals and railways were built and used as the main network for transport in the UK, it was not profitable to transport beer more than a few miles inland. Each town or village would brew their own beer, with some pubs having a small brewhouse appended to the pub. In the late 1700s it was only in the larger cities like London and Manchester that breweries with larger production and distribution facilities developed.

In the UK right up to the 1970s the industry was dominated by a few key players producing low-quality products. There was a backlash against poor quality and consumers demanded better beer and a greater variety of products. In the 1970s beer was typically bland. The mass-producers had become complacent in the marketplace and were content on abandoning traditional brewing methods that had been passed down through generations; those brewing businesses having been originally small, medium-sized and often one-man businesses. The mass-producers had abandoned the quality that had been so insisted upon by the original founders. The backlash came from a small non-profit organization called Campaign for Real Ale (CAMRA). CAMRA is a UK-based consumer campaigning group that now has over 100,000 members (CAMRA, 2010). Unfortunately, the mass-market is still served by multi-national companies producing low-priced offerings typically labelled as 'Smooth Bitter'. It is 'nitro-keg beer': beer that has been chilled to ease the filtering off of any lingering yeast, making the beer sterile, before it is pasteurized to enable chemical stability and then pumped up with nitrogen and offered to the customer.

THE BUSINESS PROCESS

Koroneos *et al.* (2005) present a case study of beer production and conduct a life cycle analysis (LCA) to identify and quantify the environmental performance of the production and distribution of beer. The authors identify the raw material acquisition, industrial refining, packaging, transportation, consumption and waste management required in beer production. They also note that energy is used and there may be waste emissions, which include liquids and solids. Bottles and packaging are required and in the UK barrels or casks are needed to transport the beer from the brewery to the retail outlets.

Barrels made in the UK are often called 'casks' and hence there is much talk in the UK about 'cask ales' – beer in the barrel or 'cask'. Traditionally, the barrels have been made out of oak and produced by coopers, an ancient trade in England. The cooper makes wooden stave vessels in strips of wood to form the barrel shape, which is typically broader in the middle than at the top and bottom. The barrels are bound together with metal hoops. There are special kinds of barrels: hogsheads (large ones) and firkins (smaller ones). The casks are not only used for liquids such as beer but also can be used to store dry goods and to keep moisture out. Today, the wine and spirits industry usually uses barrels made by machines. However, barrels can be a sustainable product in themselves, for they can be remade and reused. So the larger barrels can be whittled down to make smaller new barrels. Or the old barrels that once stored wine can store a different product and the barrels can add to the flavour of the new products. Since the 1960s the wooden casks have gradually been replaced with aluminium casks (Parker, 2006).

Now, let us take a little walk into the traditional English pub (Jennings, 2007) – a real ale pub that is perhaps owned by the landlord or landlady (publican) and who has a small number of staff working for them. There is the publican and the other bar staff, who actually work the pumps, sometimes called *beer engines*, through which the beer is drawn from the cask in the cellar to be dispensed in the glass at the bar. Beer can also be poured straight from the cask, as often happens at beer festivals. The bar staff serve the customer with the beers and spirits and, indeed, soft drinks, crisps and other snacks. It is likely that the pub will also serve food. But, let's step back from the bar and think where the beer has come from. It has come ultimately from the brewer but it may have been through one of several distribution channels.

The brewer makes the product from the raw materials and then places the final product into the casks and the casks are sealed. Then they may be taken to a wholesaler where the proprietor of the pub may go and purchase that particular cask and, indeed, other casks from other brewers so that it is a one-stop shop for the proprietor of the pub. By using the wholesaler, rather than travelling around to independent brewers and collecting a number of barrels, the proprietor saves time. The brewers may be spread across the country, so that would take a lot of time and place heavy transportation costs on the business. However, if the brewers deliver to the wholesaler, then the proprietor can go directly to the wholesaler and get a variety of products to take back to the retail outlet and then create a range of interesting offerings to the consumer.

Let us return to the real ale pub. Typically, in a small business, the publican would place an order with the brewer and then go and collect the product or have the product delivered by the brewer themselves. It could be that the product is placed with an intermediary at the wholesalers. In this case, the wholesaler may deliver or the purchaser may collect from the wholesaler. The publican is charged for the service when they purchase stock from the wholesaler. That would increase the price of the beer above the price that it could be bought for directly at the point of production. Maybe the publican wants to go directly to the brewer. She will need her own transport, perhaps a transit van, and she will prearrange her visits to the brewer. The advantage of this is that the publican may get the latest products and beer varieties, which are often given special names. She may go to three or four breweries in the same vicinity and do a round trip, before bringing the beers back to the pub. This has the advantage that she may get first choice of the new beers and she also does not have to pay the extra cost to the wholesaler. That extra cost has arisen because the wholesaler has had to pay the brewer for delivery of the product and also needs to put their own markup on the product. So, although there are contractual efficiencies to be gained using the intermediary of the wholesaler, there alternatively may be other benefits that are of value to the publican in that products that are new reach the consumer quicker by direct contact with the producer – in this case, the brewers (Avis, 1995).

CONSUMER PREFERENCES

In the beer sector, real ale consumers are concerned about every single stage of the brewing and sales process. Hence, it is important to understand the production process. Beer starts life as barley and the brewing process starts there. Barley cannot initially be fermented into alcohol; it has first to be soaked in water and germinated. Then those soaked grains are heated and turned regularly and roasted to produce the malt. This process unlocks the natural sugars in the barley and it is these sugars which will eventually turn into alcohol so that the barley becomes malt. The higher the heat, the darker the malt. The malt converts to alcohol eventually and contributes to the colour and the flavour of the beer. Once we have the malt, it is crushed and mixed with hot water – water being a key ingredient – and becomes what is called mash (Hornsey, 1999). It is allowed to rest for several hours to let the sugar dissolve (see Zerodegrees, 2010, for an overview of the microbrewing process). The liquid absorbs the sugar and becomes the 'wort', which is later boiled. Flavours are added to the beer; traditionally, since the sixteenth century, this has included hops. At this stage, once the hops or other flavourings, ginger perhaps, have been added and filtered, yeast is added. Yeast is a fungus which feeds off the sugars in the wort, creating the by-products of alcohol and carbon dioxide. The yeast divides and grows, feeding on the sugars within the wort. Different varieties of yeast are used by brewers and they may go to great lengths to retain their own specific yeast variety because that adds to the distinct flavours; many brewers will keep their yeast under strict lock and key. After a number of days, when the remaining yeast turns sugar into alcohol, it becomes the ale. Hops (*Humulus lupulus*) were introduced into brewing in the fifteenth century from the Continent, but in 1524 Henry VIII had banned them. However, the ban was short-lived because Edward VI repealed it, so that in 1552 'ale' was legally classified as unhopped and 'beer' was an alcoholic beverage that was hopped (McVicar, 2004). Real ale drinkers consider there to be five important aspects to the taste of beer: its bitterness, its sweetness, its hoppiness, its maltiness and its flavour. The larger brewers and distributors required standardization of a sort with regard to beer descriptions, so the Cyclops system was developed by brewers and distributors in the UK (Cyclops, 2010). The problem was that different consumers in different locations described beer in their own, often local, dialect. The variation in descriptions could lead to confusion among customers and suppliers. The Cyclops system describes beer according to the three senses: sight, smell and taste. A beer's attributes are described using just three simple words for each of the senses. Flavour terms such as ginger, lemon or caramel can be used only if they can be indentified clearly in the beer. Additionally, scores up to a maximum of 5 are allocated for bitterness and sweetness, and the alcoholic strength of the beer is also presented. Exemplar information is shown below for Okells Eastern Spice Pale Ale.

Cyclops Information for Okells Eastern Spice Indian Pale Ale (IPA)

Beer Title:	Eastern Spice
Brewery:	Okells
Category:	Spiced IPA
Strength:	ABV % 4.5
See:	Light Gold
Smell:	Strong Citrus, Hop, Spice
Taste:	Spicy, Dry, Bitter
Bitter:	✓✓✓
Sweet:	✓✓

(Cyclops, 2010; Okells, 2010)

Some consumers are called *tickers* because they tick off in their own pristine notebook, or electronic notebook, the different kinds of beers that they have consumed. Tickers who have been ticking since the 1970s may well have a list of over 30,000 beers that they have tasted over three decades of consumption (Parking, 2010; James, 2010). It is of great value to them to see a new beer variety from a trusted brewer, which is often presented for the first time at one of the regional beer festivals. So the beer festivals act as a showcase for the brewers and as a means of delight for the consumer. At the recent winter ale festival in Manchester, there were over 300 beers available, served directly from the casks by gravity to the glass. Winter ales tend to be stronger and darker than summer ales. The competition here is not necessarily an economic one as such, although ultimately it will be. If the award-winning ale is from your brewery you will be delighted, as will the consumer. The competition here is to produce that award-winning ale and that is what craft-brewers pride themselves on: the ability to provide a distinct flavour that is awarded accolades by the consumer and the trade.

BREWERY LOCATION

A famous linear programming problem in mathematics is the transportation problem; typically, the objective is to minimize transportation costs. Here, the problem is where to locate a brewery and its various depots. Koksalan *et al.* (1995) considered the problem of selecting the best location for a new fourth brewery for a large beer company in Turkey. The authors noted that the main transportation costs arise when shipping malt from the two malt factories to the breweries and when shipping beer from the breweries to 300 different customer zones. Clearly, SMEs cannot afford the costs of employing high-powered mathematicians to solve their day-to-day problems, as the larger Turkish brewer could, but they have similar location problems. One such problem was faced by Richard Baker (Doggart, 2009). Richard had worked in the

Falklands on tourism and transport problems, but then decided to set up a brewery and first considered setting up on East Falkland. The problem was that the water quality was not right for the brewing process and the heavy cost of importation of raw materials would burden the potential brewery too much. On return to the UK, he set up a partnership and formed the Bowland Brewery. The location issue was resolved and the brewery would be located in the Forest of Bowland, which is designated as an 'Area of Outstanding Natural Beauty' in rural Lancashire (Bowland, 2010). The location was chosen not only for the excellent availability of high-quality water but also because of the large number of pubs in the area that are 'free houses' and able to sell any type of beer they want. The landlords of free houses also have the skills required to keep the beer in the tip-top condition that the consumer and producer demand. Hence, 90 per cent of the Bowland Brewery production is retailed within a 30-mile radius of the brewery, which keeps transportation costs to a minimum.

THE RETAIL SECTOR

The retailer in the beer sector may be in competition with the wholesaler. The wholesaler may collect together different varieties of beer from different brewers – the manufacturers – and offer these to the retailers: a one-stop shop. Indeed, the retailers in this case may well be offered a great variety of beers. However, the wholesaler perhaps will not have the enthusiasm to seek out the small microbrewers that may be scattered around the country. Therefore, the retailer may feel disenfranchised when using a wholesaler who does not have the bespoke new beer variety that the retailer and, indeed, his consumers are demanding. In this case, the retailer would necessarily need to approach the manufacturers in the microbreweries themselves. A classic text on wholesaling fruit and vegetables is Beckman and Engle (1951).

Alternatively, the retailer might decide from the very start that they will use their network of intelligence and, indeed, consumer network because in this sector the boundary between consumer, retailer and manufacturer is often blurred. Kent and Omar (2003) provide a strategic and operational overview of retailing across different sectors. The retailer is likely to be a consumer and the manufacturer is also likely to be a consumer and maybe, as is seen in the 'brewpubs', the manufacturer could be also a retailer. They have, in the microbrewery, done away with the vertical competition and combined the processes of manufacture and distribution and retail into the one outlet. The retailer may go straight to the brewer and purchase those bespoke products that their consumers are demanding. In this case, they may become the consumer and travel around, stay overnight and collect three or four different barrels of beer from different producers, perhaps one geographic area at a time. Supermarkets, such as E.H. Booth in the north of England, in recent years have been offering a wide variety of real ales in bottles. They offer over 200 bottled types, with 55 brewed locally in Lancashire, Yorkshire, Cheshire and Cumbria (Booths, 2010). E.H. Booth recognized that small SME off-licences that were offering bespoke beers in bottles to the real ale drinker were doing good business. It saw the potential to increase its market share by offering a large variety of real ales, and that potential has been realized. Other supermarkets have followed suit, such as Morrisons and Sainsbury's. Now they, too, offer real ale, often from local producers, from microbreweries as well as regional and macrobreweries.

THE WHOLESALER

One of the largest wholesalers of beer-related products in the UK is H.B. Clark & Co. (Successors) Ltd. Clark & Co. have a series of ten depots in the north of England, stretching from Stockport to Newcastle (Clark, 2010). They provide products and services for the beer trade, including beer festivals, tithed pubs and free houses. Their promotional material states that they are a one-stop shop: one call, one order, one invoice and one delivery. They have their own brewery but also take supplies of real ale from over 40 other breweries, many of which are SMEs. Typically Clark & Co. offer promotional discounts to bulk buyers – if several cases of one product are purchased then one case of another product could be free. Other supplies are on special offer. One division of the company, Fam Draught Minerals, offers a broad range of draught minerals through the provision of electric pumps and nozzle equipment to the bar top, saving the retailer time and effort in stocking and re-stocking fridges with bottles of Coke and lemonade, etc. They also provide year-round technical service for the equipment. As far as wine products are concerned, they also offer specialist advice from wine experts, and provide wine menus and glasses. They offer bar-top distribution points, such as the Jagermeister Machine (see Jagermeister, 2010) that dispenses the cooled herbal liqueur and the Guinness Surger that allows the lower-volume vendor to stock and provide the customer with cans of Irish stout manufactured by Guinness, rather than maintain large volumes of cask stout which would run the risk of spoiling if sales were not brisk enough. The Surger provides the consumer with the stout with its traditional creamy head and has low maintenance costs. Hence, this wholesaler not only imports and sources bespoke branded products, and distributes them to its depots, but also it provides back-up services, promotional materials and specialist bar-top point-of-sales equipment for SMEs and franchised retail outlets.

HORIZONTAL COMPETITION

Let us consider some kinds of horizontal competition within the beer sector. There are several outlets at the retail level. There are the supermarkets; there are the off-licences, specifically dedicated to selling mainly alcoholic products – beers, wines and spirits – as their main products; there are the pubs – there are tied pubs (tied to a particular brewery), tenanted pubs and managed pubs. There are various sports clubs and social and politically affiliated clubs. Then there are the breweries themselves and the microbreweries. Additionally, it is interesting to note that there are innovative solutions in the retail sector concerning beer retailing. In Southport, the Inn Beershop is run by Peter Bardsley, who has been granted a special licence to not just retail beer but also to use the retail shop as a café. Perhaps in this sector the laws of competition are broken and superseded by the laws of cooperation and collaboration, because Peter Bardsley's brother, Paul, runs the Southport Brewery and his other brother, John, runs Lancashire Heroes, an off-licence in the same town – each operating in a different way (Southport Brewery, 2010). Lancashire Heroes is a drink-in or take-out specialist ale shop that has over 300 different bottled beers, so the consumers' demands for variety and quality are satisfied (Siddle, 2010).

The microbreweries themselves also, to some extent, work in cooperation. One microbrewery might swap barrels with another microbrewery so that when the retailer comes to collect beer they can also offer a guest beer from another microbrewery that they have either a formal or informal agreement with, thereby giving the retailer increased choice. There is another type of retail outlet in this sector and it is the world-renowned beer festival. Typically in the UK now each town will have at least one beer festival, if not two or three. They may be run by charities or the local branch of CAMRA. They may be run by individuals for profit or not for profit. A famous beer festival is held in the vaults of Liverpool Anglican Cathedral. Again, this is a marketplace and a showcase for the brewers. The consumers benefit by having a wide range of beers available in one location.

Knowledge relationships

It is very important for SMEs to build up relationships and the sort of information that might be exchanged between the publican and the brewer is information about the product: whether in fact the customers liked the product, whether it sold well and quickly, or whether the customers did not like the product and have made some comments to enhance its presentation, flavour or quality. It may be that different customers have different tastes. Some would prefer golden-coloured beers and some would prefer darker-coloured beers. Some may prefer mild and others ruby beer. The publican will generally be experienced in taking into account different consumer preferences and will take note of these. Then the consumers themselves will be specialists on their particular preferred product, which could be products from a particular brewery. The consumer information about particular products can be passed to the manufacturer, the brewer. The brewer then can take appropriate action to adapt to the needs of the consumer. In fact most small independent brewers would have brewery visits, so not only can the consumers interact with the producer but also the producers can gain knowledge and information directly from the consumer.

In this sector, knowledge from the consumer and from the manufacturer, the brewer, is of paramount importance. To be on the cutting edge as a retailer in this sector one needs to know where the next new beer is coming from and its availability. The retailer may have what we call in marketing an agent; however, this could be a 'knowledge agent' who is not necessarily in it for the money but, rather, for the delight of the product. Here, knowledge could be transferred from agent to agent, consumer to consumer, manufacturer to manufacturer and manufacturer to consumer, and so on. Through the local branches of organizations such as CAMRA, which is split up into regions and districts branches, knowledge can be exchanged directly by mobile phone and the internet, and in person at events such as beer festivals. Knowledge would be quickly disseminated through the knowledge network, and this network is fairly closed – retailers can build strong links with manufacturers and over the years develop trusting relationships. Moreover, new manufacturers who display skill at producing quality products will come to trust reliable retailers. In this context the established reliable retailer has the power. Fast, quick and voluminous turnover would be of benefit to retailer and manufacturer and, indeed, to other manufacturers as well. So knowledge about where the next new product is going to be available would quickly reach the retailer via the knowledge agent who is part of the knowledge network (Warkentin et al., 2001).

SME RELATIONSHIPS WITH LARGER BREWERIES

It is interesting to note that even the world's largest breweries probably started as family businesses. Many family businesses have passed through the generations as they expanded. Like many microbreweries that survive the first few years of business, these now huge breweries often went from being a one-person business to family businesses as they expanded. Such a situation applied to the brewery founded by Charles Hall, who was born in 1751 and was a farmer's son. In those days many of the farmers brewed beer for the farm workers and Hall founded his own brewery in 1777. Maybe it was due to the entrepreneurial skills he learned in the farm business from his father that he was able to quickly build up his own brewery business. Early in the business he seized upon an opportunity to produce beer for the army and gained a contract to supply ale to the army camped near the coast of Weymouth during the Napoleonic Wars. A George Woodhouse then became his business partner and duly married Charles's granddaughter. The business took off from there and produced one of the traditional beers of England, based in the country's south-west: Badger Ale. Badger Ale is now brewed by Hall and Woodhouse Limited, who have been producing real ale since 1777. Although they are now a fairly large regional brewer, the brewing knowledge has been passed down through the generations of the Woodhouse family, with the top-quality ingredients always including Dorset spring water. Now Hall and Woodhouse have an estate of over 260 tenanted and managed pubs, mainly scattered along the south coast of England, in Devon and Kent. They have 180 tenanted pubs and 60 managed pubs, with 1,181 employees – putting them outside the scope of the SME category – but they are intimately connected with those lone traders and small businesses who are tied to them through the agreements of the tenancy (Hall and Woodhouse, 2010).

CONTRACTUAL COMPLICATIONS

The situation, however, in the pub trade is not as simple as that presented in many textbooks, which often present the classical picture for large businesses. As with most SMEs who find themselves in a position of intense rivalry, there is an additional problem that may arise in the pub trade in the UK: that the pub might actually be owned by the brewery and the publican may just rent the pub from the brewery. The publican could also be a sole trader who quite frequently is in a business partnership with a personal partner. In this case, the publican, as a sole trader, has a tenancy agreement with the brewery. The situation may be a little less clear if the brewery actually employs a manager to run the pub for the brewery, and this means that the pub is sometimes called a 'managed house'. In that case, it may be that the brewery itself is an SME and the manager is an employee of that SME. Sometimes, when the contract is between a self-employed publican and the brewery, the publican finances the pub with loans from the brewers themselves. However, all of these scenarios lead to the situation where the brewer demands, as part of the contractual agreement, that the publican/landlord purchases beer directly from them. The landlord is legally tied to purchase only from them and not from competitors. Such a contractual agreement gives the advantage to the brewer, so that the brewer receives a consistent demand for its products (Diallo, 2010). However, there may be problems for the consumer and, indeed, for the landlords themselves. In one region there may be a brewery which owns a majority of pubs in that area, so that it is very difficult within that small geographical area for the consumer to find other breweries' products. This is, in CAMRA's view, a form of monopoly, or cartel, which is actually illegal in the UK. There is no competition as such from different breweries because each individual tied pub is tied in to buying product from that one particular brewer or from the holding company's beer list. Clearly, across the country there will be different breweries, but for the local person there will be no competition, or a risk of poor competition. Indeed, in some contractual agreements between landlord and brewery, the brewery may tie in the supply of other things, such as soft drinks and spirits, and quite often these may be offered at inflated prices (Williams, 2009).

THREATS TO THE FREE ECONOMY

In contrast to the tied situation, the alternative situation does exist, albeit less commonly in the UK, where the pub is actually a 'free house': free to purchase products from wherever it chooses. That means it is not tied to any one particular brewery and it is free to purchase its product wherever it wants. So this kind of pub, the free house, can then purchase different kinds of beer from different breweries. From 1989 to 2003 there was partial freedom for tied pubs, which were legally permitted to stock at least one extra beer from another brewery. This gave consumers greater choice. The extra beer was often called the 'guest beer'. However, that particular law was repealed in 2003. This led to certain representations being made by CAMRA and others to the Office of Fair Trading (OFT) to investigate the potential monopoly, at least at the regional level if not at the national, caused by tying pubs into supply contracts with regional or national breweries.

CAMRA's members are generally consumers of real ale. The group campaigns for real ale, real pubs and consumer rights. In December 2009 CAMRA sent a complaint to the OFT that large companies were exploiting tie arrangements that prevent tied publicans from buying beer on the open market at fair market prices – this being, in their view, a direct contra-vention of the Monopolies Act. Then, after surveying pubs around the country, CAMRA pressed the OFT to investigate prices. Due to the lack of competition, the wholesale prices paid by the publicans that were in tied houses were over £20,000 per year larger than those in the prevailing competitive market. And that, in turn, means that consumers have to pay higher prices and often be content with poorer-quality beer and a restricted range of real ale. CAMRA invoked the Enterprise Act 2002 (OPSI, 2002) to challenge the legal standing of the OFT, who rejected CAMRA's 'super-complaint'. CAMRA then took its super-complaint to the Competition Appeals Tribunal. CAMRA believes that OFT had not seriously consid-ered whether the prevailing conditions permitted fair competition at the local level so that consumers can get better-quality beers and more choice and pub landlords can get a fair deal.

A FLEXIBLE BUT VOLATILE SECTOR

Microbreweries started in the late 1970s as a reaction to the larger brewers, spurred on by the formation of CAMRA. Consumers were demanding a greater variety of cask ale and a better-quality product. So from the beginning, the idea for microbreweries was that the business would be flexible. They would become agile and adaptable. They would experiment with their product to get better flavours and they would focus on customer service. A key innovation in the SME sector of brewing is that of the brewpub, pubs which also have a microbrewery, usually operated by one or two, or just a few more, people attached to the pub. One example is the Zerodegrees brewpub (based in Reading, England), which profits from being able to provide fresh beers brewed by the microbrewery on the premises (Zerodegrees, 2010). Consumers can be sure of product quality and fresh flavour. Zerodegrees, like many other pubs that brew their own beer, also offers additional consumer benefits. Zerodegrees combines its microbrewery with a trendy restaurant (Zerodegrees, 2010). Another brewpub is the Kirkstile Inn in the Lake District, in Loweswater. Like many brewpubs, it operate several businesses at once. So the Kirkstile will offer shelter to the local folk after church services, accommodation to fell-walkers, food in the restaurant and beer brewed in their own micro-brewery (Kirkstile, 2010). In the USA, a microbrewery is sometimes called a craft brewery, which also produces limited amounts of beer.

In was in the 1980s that microbreweries took off in the United States and it is now generally accepted that a microbrewery there produces fewer than 15,000 barrels of beer a year. These small microbreweries, run by a few people, adopt various marketing strategies that are different to large brewers'. They do not compete in the mass-market but on the basis of providing a unique product of high quality with a variety of flavours. They do not adopt a strategy that is focused on advertising and these small brewers have gained about 2 per cent market share in the UK. There are macrobreweries, of course, which have a larger number of employees. However, the market is far from being static and now the large brewers are introducing new brands to compete in the micro- and macrobrewery market. In some cases the microbreweries have been bought out by the larger mass-market breweries. This is because the mass-market breweries cannot focus on quality because their philosophy was built up on the mass-market and they cannot experiment in the same way that microbreweries can. Nor do they have the emotional attachment and energy that individual owners put into their business.

DIFFICULTIES CAUSED BY WAREHOUSING HOPS AND RISING OIL PRICES

There is huge advantage to the purchaser when a large variety of products are available at one location or warehouse, but when disaster hits, it hits the SME hard. A disaster could be caused by high concentrations of flammable product being stored in the warehouse. Supply cannot always be guaranteed, and shortages in supply can cause price rises, which must be passed on to the customer by the SME. It will be the larger firms that take up the remaining supply because they have the flexibility and the excess capital to absorb the price rises, so the SME is constantly under pressure from all sides.

Hops are used to flavour the beer. In 1996 the world acreage for hop cultivation was 215,000 acres. By 2006 this had decreased to 123,000 acres. Clearly hops were coming into short supply over this period. In England there were 17,000 acres of hop production in 1976, but by 2006 this had decreased to 2,400 acres. Prices obviously could not be maintained at their former low levels and had to rise. In 2006 there was a marked increase in the price of hops. However, the adverse fluctuations in supply and price were not the only problem for hops. There was also a fire in a warehouse. The fire at Yakima Valley in Washington incinerated 4 per cent of the US hops crop in 2006. Ten thousand bales, each weighing 200 pounds, were lost (Associated Press, 2006). Then, with bad weather in Europe and storms in the USA leading to poor crops, hop prices soared to 15 times their previous level – an unprecedented rise.

Other troubles are always on the horizon in the brewing industry. Remember the product has to be transported and in the UK this is usually via road, using the articulated lorries that use diesel as their fuel. In July 2008 oil peaked at around US$134 a barrel, having been less than US$30 a barrel at the start of 2004. The price dropped back to US$70 a barrel in 2010, but the years 2004–2008 saw price rise on price rise. Industrial action loomed from lorry drivers afraid of their businesses going bust. In the middle of the gloom it was not known if the price of oil would ever stop rising. After reaching $134 per barrel, would it pass $150? As it happened, oil dropped back to $70 a barrel (Oil Prices, 2010). So, first there was a hop crisis and then a fuel crisis; and both were followed by the global financial crisis of 2008. The world had been lending too much money and in 2008 was at risk of financial meltdown. Banks that had previously been eager to lend to anyone, including SMEs, now tightened their purse strings: the days of plenty were over. SMEs were facing an intensifying struggle. At the very time when money was required to survive in the brewery trade, it was being withdrawn.

An indication of the volatility of the sector is given by the number of openings and closures: from 1990 to 2009, 1,108 breweries opened in the UK and 542 breweries closed. This means that 566 new breweries were opened and remained open during that period. It is particularly interesting to note that in one year (1999) over 90 breweries closed. Most of all those breweries were microbreweries, employing a very small number of people, perhaps fewer than five. There were a small number of closures due to takeovers by larger breweries. The number of openings indicates the dynamic nature of business activity in the SME sector. It is a volatile business environment, but 566 UK microbrewery businesses have continued to succeed (Quaffale, 2010).

CONCLUSION

The variety of raw materials, brewers (manufacturers), distributors, retailers and consumers in the beer sector are indicated in Figure 10.1. The intricate flow of transactions and product between each can only be worked out through detailed business case analysis, as there are no standard business models in this marketplace. Here, the exchange interactions between producers and retailers are assisted by distribution channels. The channels create time and space for the partners. The channels may also provide additional services that add value to the interactions. The cost for the SMEs of assuming distribution themselves would be prohibitive if it were not for collaboration with potential rivals. The real ale trade relies on collaboration between brewers, rather than pure economic competition, so that high product-quality standards are maintained, as is the product variety demanded by the consumer, who are quality vetters and new-product seekers in this sector. The distribution is intimately connected with the supply of raw materials and is particularly susceptible to supply and price fluctuations. Systems such as the Direct Delivery System (DDS) can help ensure a constant demand for products from a large number of small brewers and can provide large franchise chains with an endless variety of products. Much trade, particularly between microbreweries and free houses run by sole traders, relies on strong interpersonal relationships and a knowledgeable support community. The franchise system that ties sole traders, as publicans, to large holding companies or breweries can be beneficial to both stakeholders, but the holding company may extract a high price for its expertise and tied products and that could effectively lead to brewery-owned monopolies at the local level. The consumer is far from being a silent partner in these transactions and demands not only quality products but also business sustainability based on traditional values and authentic production processes.

SUMMARY OF KEY POINTS

1. Distribution is 'place' in the marketing mix.
2. Distribution involves placing the offer with the consumer through intermediaries.
3. There are two entwined aspects to distribution: logistics and strategy.
4. There are complexities connected with distribution.
5. The real ale marketplace in the UK is driven by SMEs and the consumers' demands for authentic, quality products and variety.
6. The niche SME sector is volatile.
7. SMEs may be inextricably tied to larger companies in business.
8. Innovations in distribution are being driven by SMEs.

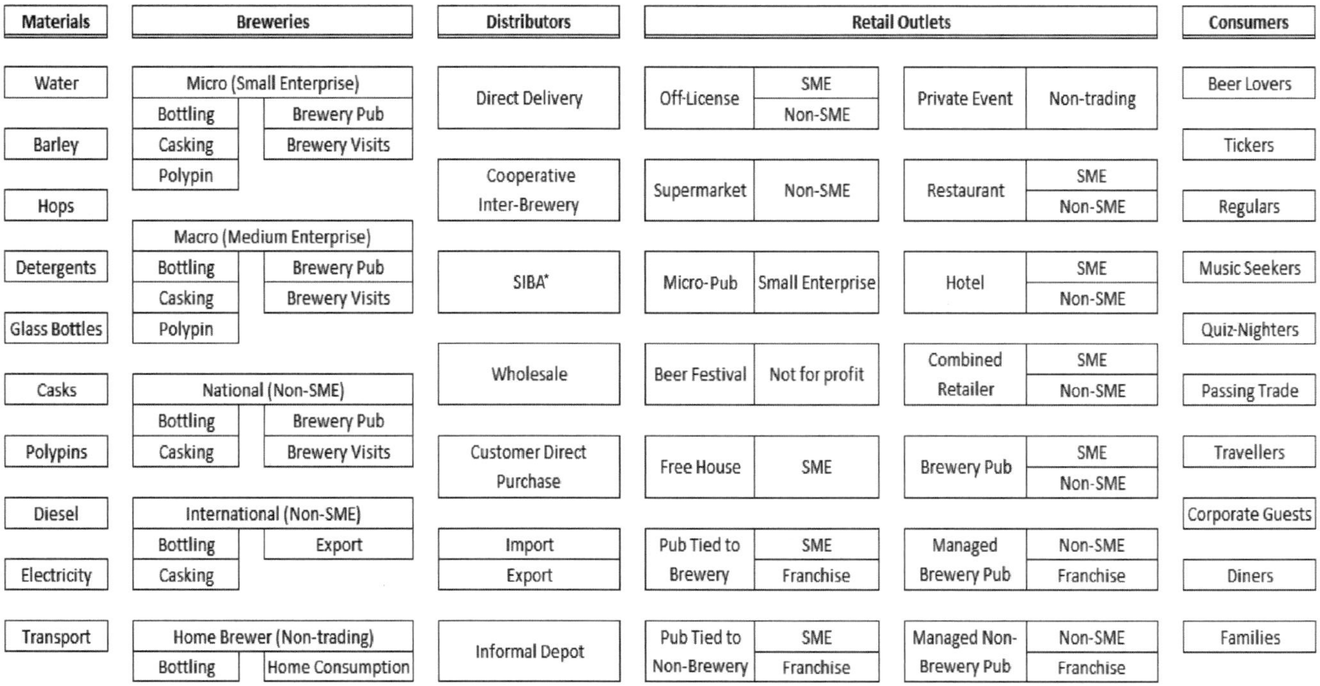

Figure 10.1 An overview of real ale distribution in the UK

Materials
- Water
- Barley
- Hops
- Detergents
- Glass Bottles
- Casks
- Polypins
- Diesel
- Electricity
- Transport

Breweries
- Micro (Small Enterprise): Bottling, Casking, Polypin | Brewery Pub, Brewery Visits
- Macro (Medium Enterprise): Bottling, Casking, Polypin | Brewery Pub, Brewery Visits
- National (Non-SME): Bottling, Casking | Brewery Pub, Brewery Visits
- International (Non-SME): Bottling, Casking | Export
- Home Brewer (Non-trading): Bottling | Home Consumption

Distributors
- Direct Delivery
- Cooperative Inter-Brewery
- SIBA*
- Wholesale
- Customer Direct Purchase
- Import | Export
- Informal Depot

Retail Outlets

Off-License	SME / Non-SME	Private Event	SME / Non-trading
Supermarket	Non-SME	Restaurant	SME / Non-SME
Micro-Pub	Small Enterprise	Hotel	SME / Non-SME
Beer Festival	Not for profit	Combined Retailer	SME / Non-SME
Free House	SME	Brewery Pub	SME / Non-SME
Pub Tied to Brewery	SME / Franchise	Managed Brewery Pub	Non-SME / Franchise
Pub Tied to Non-Brewery	SME / Franchise	Managed Non-Brewery Pub	Non-SME / Franchise

Consumers
- Beer Lovers
- Tickers
- Regulars
- Music Seekers
- Quiz-Nighters
- Passing Trade
- Travellers
- Corporate Guests
- Diners
- Families

Note: * Society of Independent Brewers

REVIEW QUESTIONS

1. Look up the lease agreements for Punch, Admiral and Enterprise on each company's website. Compare and contrast the leases and evaluate which might offer the best deal for (a) the leaser and (b) microbreweries. Resource websites: www.PunchTaverns.com, www.AdmiralTaverns.co.uk and www.EnterpriseInns.com.

2. Investigate how family brewery businesses, originally small businesses, have grown into large businesses. What key events, particularly in terms of distribution, were there in the histories of those particular businesses? Resource websites: www.Guinness.com and www.Moorhouses.co.uk.

3. Review standard texts on distribution and, taking into account the perspectives of different stakeholders, compare and contrast the real ale business with another sector of your choice.

CASE STUDY 10: SOCIETY OF INDEPENDENT BREWERS (SIBA)

The Direct Delivery System (DDS) was launched in December 2003 by the Society of Independent Brewers (SIBA) with the explicit aim of improving market access for participating breweries via the estates of major pub companies. Almost 600 micro-breweries are active in the British marketplaces and these small brewers have limited resources with tight economic considerations that demand a short supply line that is simple to operate. Generally, cask beer is unique to pubs and usually is consumed at the pub. Hence, cask ale enthusiasts, who are not all members of CAMRA, place themselves as market leaders who continually drive quality improvement, and consumer and producer responsibility, along with authentic cultural heritage.

Besides working with free houses the DDS has a portfolio of four substantial non-brewery-owned pub chains: Punch Taverns (Punch Taverns, 2010), Admiral Taverns (Admiral Taverns, 2010), Enterprise Inns (Enterprise Inns, 2010) and the Orchid Group (Orchid Group, 2010). Three of the four companies operate tied partnerships with self-employed leases. The Orchid Group is a large company that employs managers to run its business outlets.

Punch Taverns has a leased estate of 6,841 pubs. In those pubs the company has an agreement with the landlord who operates their own self-employed retail business as an SME, but leases the pub from the company and agrees to operate the pub in certain ways. Punch Taverns offers lease agreements with business partners. The company does not directly manage these pubs but provides detailed support as part of the lease agreement, which is usually ten years long. The SME partner usually pays an index-linked rent, which is periodically reviewed and based on a share of the pub profits. Clearly, this is a tied agreement as the SME partner is required to buy products – including all beers, cider and lagers – from the company (in some agreements there is the exception of one guest ale). There is also a section in the agreement that covers the management of gambling machines and quiz machines in the pubs. Punch Taverns state that 'the agreements provide a low cost entry into running a pub business with professional support'. Assistance is provided by the company for the business processes such as finance, purchasing, human resource management, order taking and credit management, and a business relationship manager and customer administration support are provided. Additional resources are provided for asset and personnel development.

Admiral Taverns was formed in 2003 and in 2010 boasted an estate of over 2,000 public houses, the majority of which are located across the UK in city centres and rural locations. It claims that each pub it lets is individual, 'just like our pub landlords, and we aim to make them focal points of their community'. The company encourages the licensees to 'run the business their way', while still providing the much-needed operational support. Although the group was only formed in 2006 it has grown to become the sixth-largest managed pub company and restaurant company in the UK. In 2010 they had 6,500 pub employees in the UK, which clearly places the business outside the SME designation. They have 8,590 outlets, restaurants and pubs outlets and the company is reportedly the 'best unbranded franchise in the world'. Eighteen per cent of the stock comprises restaurants, 38 per cent are pubs that serve bar meals, 25 per cent are pubs that serve light snacks and 19 per cent are pubs without catering facilities.

CASE QUESTIONS

1. Find out how the DDS operates and identify the services that it provides for a) free houses and b) the four large pub chains.
2. What advantages do small independent breweries gain by subscribing to the DDS?
3. Identify and undertake a review of one UK microbrewery using SIBA in its distribution strategy. Complete a Strengths, Weaknesses, Opportunities and Threats (SWOT) analysis for product distribution from the microbrewery.
4. There are other models of distribution, such as those organized by breweries themselves in collaboration with other breweries. Compared with the SIBA model, what advantages would such distribution systems have for a) pubs and b) breweries?

REFERENCES

Admiral Taverns (2010) 'Admiral Taverns', available at www.admiraltaverns.co.uk (accessed 1 March 2010).

Associated Press (2006) 'Fire destroys Yakima hop warehouse', 3 October, available at www.spokesman review.com (accessed 1 March 2010).

Avis, A. (1995) *The Brewer's Tale: History of Ale in Yorkshire*, Radcliffe Press, London.

Beckman, T.N. and Engle, N.H. (1951) *Wholesaling: Principles and Practice*, Roland Press, New York.

Booths (2010) 'Booths Super Market', available at www.booths-supermarkets.co.uk (accessed 1 March 2010).

Bowland (2010) 'Bowland Brewery', available at www.forestofbowland.com (accessed 1 March 2010).

CAMRA (2010) 'Campaign for real ale', available at www.camra.org.uk (accessed 1 March 2010).

Clark (2010) 'H.B. Clark Group of Companies', available at www.hbclark.co.uk (accessed 1 March 2010).

Cyclops (2010), 'Cyclops Trust', available at www.cyclopsbeer.co.uk (accessed 1 March 2010).

Diallo, U. (2010) 'Pub Companies "Pubcos" and tied tenants', FSB Policy Paper, Federation of Small Businesses, London, available at www.fsb.org.uk (accessed 1 March 2010).

Doggart, A. (2009) 'The beauty of Bowland', *Fylde Ale*, Issue 71 (Winter), 6–7.

Enterprise Inns (2010) 'Enterprise Inns', available at www.enterpriseinns.com (accessed 1 March 2010).

Evans, J. (2004) *The Book of Beer Knowledge*, CAMRA, St Albans.

Hall and Woodhouse (2010) 'The Hall and Woodhouse Business', available at www.hall-woodhouse.co.uk (accessed 1 March 2010).

Hornsey, I.S. (1999) *Brewing*, Royal Society of Chemistry, Cambridge.

Hornsey, I.S. (2003) *A History of Beer and Brewing*, Royal Society of Chemistry, Cambridge.

Jagermeister (2010) 'The herbal liqueur', available at www.jagermeister.com (accessed 1 March 2010).

James, M. (2010) 'Beer Ticking', personal communication from Michael James, real ale drinker.

Jennings, P. (2007) *The Local: A History of the English Pub*, History Press, Stroud.

Kent, T. and Omar, O. (2003) *Retailing*, Palgrave Macmillan, New York.

Kirkstile (2010) 'The Kirkstile Inn', available at www.kirkstile.com (accessed 1 March 2010).

Koksalan, M., Haldun, S. and Kirca, O. (1995) 'A location-distribution application for a beer company', *European Journal of Operational Research*, Volume 80, Issue 1, 16–24.

Koroneos, C., Roumbas, G., Gabari, Z., Papagiannidou, E. and Moussiopoulos, N. (2005) 'Life cycle assessment of beer production in Greece', *Journal of Cleaner Production*, Volume 13, Issue 4, 433–439.

M&S (2010) 'Marks and Spencer Ltd.', available at corporate.marksandspencer.com (accessed 1 March 2010).

McVicar, J. (2004) *New Book of Herbs*, Dorling Kindersley, London.

Oil Prices (2010) 'World oil prices', available at www.oilnergy.com (accessed 1 March 2010).

Okells (2010) 'Okells Brewery', available at www.okells.co.uk (accessed 1 March 2010).

OPSI (2002) 'The Enterprise Act, 2002', available at www.opsi.gov.uk (accessed 1 March 2010).

Orchid Group (2010) 'Orchid Group', available at www.orchidgroup.co.uk (accessed 1 March 2010).

Parker, P.M. (2006) *The World Market for Iron or Steel Tanks, Casks, Drums, Cans, and Similar Containers with Capacity of Less Than 300 Liters: A 2007 Global Trade Perspective*, ICON Group International, San Diego.

Parking, P. (2010) 'Beerticking: The Video', available at www.beertickersfilm.com (accessed 1 March 2010).

Punch Taverns (2010) 'Punch Taverns', available at www.punchtaverns.com/Punch (accessed 1 March 2010).

Quaffale (2010) 'Breweries opening and closing', available at www.quaffale.org.uk (accessed 1 March 2010).

SIBA (2010) 'Society of independent brewers', available at www.siba.co.uk (accessed 1 March 2010).

Siddle, J. (2010) 'Inn Beer Shop', *Southport Visiter*, available at www.southportvisiter.co.uk (accessed 1 March 2010).

Singer (2007) 'The history of the Singer® Sewing Machine', available at www.singerco.com (accessed 1 March 2010)

Southport Brewery (2010) 'Southport Brewery', available at www.southportbrewery.co.uk (accessed 1 March 2010).

Sumner, J. (2005) 'Powering the porter brewery', *Endeavour*, Volume 29, Issue 2, 72–77.

Warkentin, M., Bapna, R. and Sugumaran, V. (2001) 'E-knowledge networks for inter-organizational collaborative e-business', *Logistics Information Management*, Volume 14, Issue 1–2, 149–163.

Williams, S. (2009) 'Is the pub "tie" killing our locals?', *Norwich Evening News 24*, available at www.eveningnews24.co.uk (accessed 1 March 2010).

Zerodegrees (2010) 'A microbrewery', available at www.zerodegrees.co.uk (accessed 1 March 2010).

Chapter 11

Marketing communications for the SME

Teck-Yong Eng and Graham Spickett-Jones

LEARNING OBJECTIVES

After reading this chapter, you will be able to:
- understand differences in approach to marketing communications between large organizations and SMEs
- recognize the stages in promotional campaigns for SMEs in the wider context of marketing communication planning
- identify the main marketing communications tools used by typical SMEs
- be able to consider the wider context of human communication in relation to networks of relationships.

INTRODUCTION

Why do we need to study marketing communication for SMEs?

The task of marketing communication is to plan and apply marketing communications tools like advertising, sales promotion, personal selling and public relations. Marketing communication can cover practice across a wide range of marketing contexts, from large companies and political movements to small companies and individual traders. In the context of small- and medium-sized enterprises (SMEs), marketing communication deserves to be examined separately. Unlike large organizations, few SMEs have a dedicated in-house marketing communication specialist or the resources to outsource the role to specialist support agencies that deal with marketing communications like advertising, public relations and media buying. SMEs use marketing communication in ways more specific to their sector than do large organizations. This chapter examines the role of marketing communication for typical SMEs, including the communication tools, the communications mix and the strategic perspective of a network approach to developing marketing communication strategy.

Definitions and terms of marketing communication concepts

Marketing communications (plural) describes the methods and range of communications by which marketers may communicate, like television advertising or public relations. Marketing communication (singular) is a more encompassing and broad functional role that relates to the maintenance of social structure and associated relationships (van Riel, 1995). Both large and small companies use communications tools but larger organizations are more likely to focus on building the relationship customers have with a brand, while SMEs are more likely to focus on driving sales leads and providing access to product information.

Large companies are also more likely to coordinate a range of communications tools to manage their brands and to try to build customer relationships over time. This can be illustrated by the typical launch campaign for a major new brand (see Figure 11.1), when a campaign may move customers through campaign stages towards a deeper relationship:

- Stage 1 involves using advertising to build awareness with media messages.
- Stage 2 involves conversations, using direct channels of communication to capture data and build interest through involvement.
- Stage 3 is experiential, using opportunities for target customers to encounter brand information as part of their normal life.
- Stage 4 is personal, encouraging customers to take ownership of a brand and personalizing the relationship.

This is quite different from the typical way marketing communication is employed by SMEs. While there will be exceptions across a sector as broad as the SME one, taken as a whole marketing communications tools used by SMEs tend to have a coherent character relatively distinct from the communications mix favoured by large firms. SMEs tend to use the principal marketing communications tools (Fill, 2005) in specific ways (Spickett-Jones and Eng, 2006), such that:

- **personal selling** is a priority
- **PR** is mainly synonymous with publicity

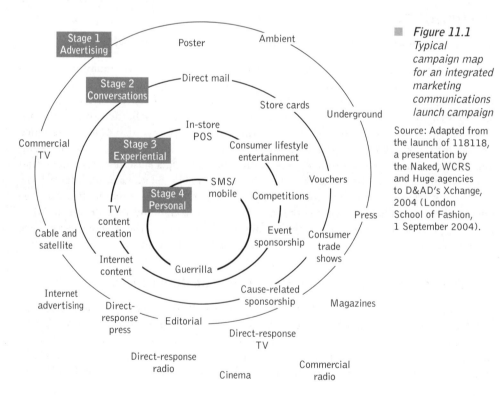

■ *Figure 11.1 Typical campaign map for an integrated marketing communications launch campaign*

Source: Adapted from the launch of 118118, a presentation by the Naked, WCRS and Huge agencies to D&AD's Xchange, 2004 (London School of Fashion, 1 September 2004).

- **sales promotion** has limited explicit use, reflecting that negotiated and incentive-based pricing is regarded less as a promotional tool than as a way of establishing trading terms
- **advertising** is given a low emphasis (e.g. display advertising), which reflects a perception of its limited usefulness
- **direct marketing** is largely syndicated catalogues, mail-shots and blanket email.

Looking for patterns in the uses of marketing communications tools by SMEs, research by Spickett-Jones and Eng (2006) suggests many SMEs focus on providing sales leads, establishing sales or maintaining existing relationships. When sponsorship is used by SMEs often it may have no clear relationships with the equity or public standing of an SME, or any clear association with its products. Testimonials and writing articles for trade magazines are used by some SMEs to help build profile and credence in the marketplace, but these are rare examples of an attempt to enhance the market perceptions and public standing of an SME by using more widely seen marketing communications activity.

Marketing communication agencies specialize in developing creative ideas and marketing communication campaigns. Large companies frequently outsource much of their marketing communications activity to professional communication service agencies which are often SMEs. While SMEs specializing in marketing communications may provide large clients with advice over marketing communication strategy, they tend to employ visible communication services for their own business in limited ways, such as classified advertising and PR (Dyer and Ross, 2003).

Characteristics of SME marketing communication

Staff in an SME may see the role of marketing communication from a different vantage point compared with a management team working for a large organization. For example, a large organization may be concerned with brand equity while an SME may be concerned with the

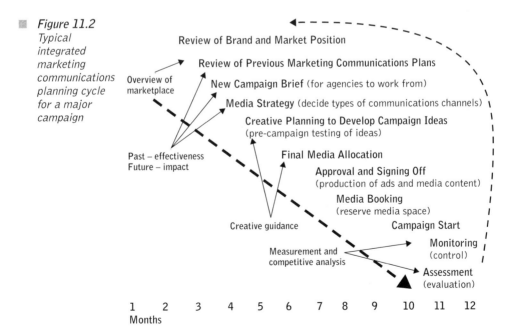

Figure 11.2
Typical integrated marketing communications planning cycle for a major campaign

Review of Brand and Market Position
Review of Previous Marketing Communications Plans
Overview of marketplace
New Campaign Brief (for agencies to work from)
Media Strategy (decide types of communications channels)
Creative Planning to Develop Campaign Ideas (pre-campaign testing of ideas)
Past – effectiveness
Future – impact
Final Media Allocation
Approval and Signing Off (production of ads and media content)
Media Booking (reserve media space)
Creative guidance
Campaign Start
Measurement and competitive analysis
Monitoring (control)
Assessment (evaluation)

1   2   3   4   5   6   7   8   9   10   11   12
Months

personal relationships of their most valuable customers. A multinational organization may seek to manage the equity of its brands across international markets by deploying forms of mass communication, including media advertising. This sort of activity may involve considerable resources and additional specialist skills found outside the company and acquired through delegating tasks to outsourced communication agencies. However, SMEs lack the capacity to support remote markets, and they may not have the resources for mass-media driven communications activity.

Although SMEs are confronted by limitations compared with large organizations, many SMEs operate successfully in carrying out marketing communication. A typical SME will tend to 'see' marketing communication as something they need to do occasionally to boost sales, i.e. marketing communications. Although largely invisible as part of an explicit marketing strategy, the role of marketing communication in typical SMEs can be outlined as below:

- SMEs tend to use marketing communication in an *ad hoc* way to support the network position of the organization, to maintain the infrastructure and relationships the SME needs to survive in its environment.
- Few SMEs will identify with a strategic and functional role for marketing communication which is similar to that found practised in larger organizations.

To understand SME marketing communication, it is necessary to consider how SMEs seek to support a successful position in the marketplace and what they do in communications terms to support market relationships that sustain their position.

Strategically, SMEs tend to manage key relationships within their supporting infrastructure by regular marketplace interventions using close personal relationships. This means they can sense marketplace trends and make regular adaptations rather than use longer-term planning frameworks. As a result, SMEs tend to have less need to devise conventional marketing strategies or to work with promotional campaigns where marketing communications activity has to show how it supports these strategies. Instead, the small size of SMEs encourages the sharing of roles and the fostering of relationships that develop into support networks because of key SME features:

- low bureaucracy
- highly motivated staff
- perceived shared-interest between staff and the enterprise
- staff willing to use their natural relationship skills to strengthen the business.

The use made of marketing communications tools by SMEs suggests these organizations tend to deploy communications tools for short-term tasks rather than to support any defined strategic marketing objectives, or to build distinctive and sustainable competitive positions in their markets. Nevertheless, many SMEs can be highly successful without this type of strategic planning behind their marketing communication. Since SME marketing communications activity is mostly sales driven and tactical (Spickett-Jones and Eng, 2006), it is appropriate to ask if marketing communication needs a strategic framework in an SME context. However, this partly assumes SMEs should behave like larger businesses and that they should be measured by similar approaches to strategic marketing and communication strategy. If perspectives on successful SMEs derived from conventional strategic marketing analysis fail to identify what sustains their success, it is appropriate to frame and examine SMEs' marketing

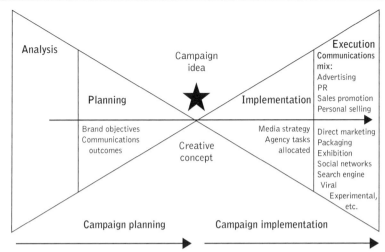

Figure 11.3
Typical cyclical marketing communication process for a large company campaign

communication differently. Thus, the following sections discuss how SMEs' marketing communication is practised through communication technology and a network perspective.

Communication technology and marketing communication

In the midst of rapid development in communication technology it is easy to be swept along by hype attached to possible implications for marketing communication. It is valuable, therefore, to see marketing communication in its context as part of human activity, to see how different types of communication impact on the way people operate in their social and physical environment. Neuroscientists suggest that an important part of human evolution can be attributed to the human brain's communication capacity. Unless there is a dramatic alteration to the way the human brain works, the usefulness of any development in communication technology is likely to be determined by the way the technology works with our existing brain capacity. Some neuroscientists (Kandel *et al.*, 2000) believe this capacity evolved because of two related adaptations in our human ancestors: the need to develop *technology* to help exploit the environment and the need to manage *cooperation* to create a cohesive social group. The same two forces are at work in the modern world when organizations seek to harness the power of marketing communication, via whatever technology, to build successful collaborations within the marketplace.

BOX 11.1: TECHNOLOGY AS AN ENABLER IN COMMUNICATION CONTEXTS

According to Alan Stevens, founder of Media Coach and a social media consultant, '[t]he key thing about social media is not just broadcasting but measuring the impact of what you do'. He recommends companies filter what other people are saying about their products and services, and provide immediate feedback (Moules, 2010). SMEs can take advantage of internet-based communication tools and software applications at a relatively low cost. For example, they can use the internet to recruit staff, respond to customer complaints, develop new business opportunities and monitor changes in the marketplace.

A communication technology's success will depend on the role it performs for human beings. How will a mode of communication help people achieve what they want to? The same will be true for an organization. When people have a high level of commitment to an enterprise and when they come into close contact with other people in their marketing environment, marketing communication and human communication can become inextricably linked. For marketing communication, the key marketing environment is represented by **people**. So identifying the roles of key people is a vital aspect of marketing communications in the SME context:

- **Who:** which people are most important and how to manage an appropriate relationship with different people will depend on the perceived importance of specific groups and individuals, and the scale of the market as well as the resources available.
- **What:** what type of relationship is feasible may depend on the available resources, **why** and **when** these relationships should be strengthened and the access to suitable communications technologies to manage these relationships.
- **Where:** key people in the marketing environment may be aligned to other organizations, perhaps in the supply chain, or they may work for suppliers of specialist services, like an advertising agency.
- **How:** in a networked economy every organization must have a supporting infrastructure and in essence that is what marketing communication is about. It enables an organization to relate to the most critical parts of the marketing environment and do this in meaningful and appropriate ways in order to win support.

Marketing communication opportunities for SME

As technology helps the communication landscape evolve, conveying the value in a marketing proposition offers an increasingly wide range of options. This can create new layers of complexity in the practice of marketing communication in terms of the following challenges:

- New channels of communication contend with older modes of communication but rarely displace completely the more traditional and established media.
- People's capacity for focal attention is likely to have remained largely unchanged but it is now spread across a wider range of communication channels.
- The greater availability of interactive technologies has created an evolving communication landscape that contains growing opportunities to exchange information, often driven by the proactive efforts of people in the marketplace who seek information. This has created new opportunities for SMEs to become more visible and accessible to a wider marketplace.

The changes in the communication landscape help to make this an exciting time to discuss marketing communication for SMEs. Once the communication roles and marketing objectives that support SMEs are better understood, there are possibilities for many SMEs to gain access to wider markets via new channels of communication. With expanding technology and communication infrastructure offering new opportunities for promotion and trade, SMEs can access new ways to support a wider marker presence and grow their business compared with expensive traditional media channels, like television.

However, new methods do not necessarily mean a low-cost strategy. For example, maintaining a social network site or entertaining customers with a 'Twitter' feed may give a company's followers rewarding information but maintaining a credible presence on such sites takes resources and dedicated effort. When those who work in an SME are enthusiastic and dedicated to what they do they may be keen to talk about their products and services, particularly to gain custom and support. However, to dedicate time and resources to do this online could distract from their main business – making the products and services that win the support of customers and perhaps give the staff a sense of achievement.

BOX 11.2: EXPLORING NETWORK OPPORTUNITIES

Social networking sites offer new opportunities through real-time interactive communication in networks. The company Divining Femininity is a case in point. The co-founder, Vena Ramphal, set up her company through a social media networking site, Twitter, with a co-founder. They launched their company with a tweet and were surprised to have more than 300 people view their posting in the first few hours (Moules, 2010).

As technologies mature, SME opportunities are likely to expand and become easier to access. Online channels are already starting to provide new entry points into different markets and new ways of communicating market value, even for very small SMEs. For example, independent artisan food producers (e.g. regional cheese makers, farmers raising rare breeds of livestock, brewers of traditional ales and speciality bakers) may carry the status of 'food heroes' in their local market. However good their products and however infectious their enthusiasm may be for these products, if a producer can reach only the markets their personal contacts can access then these markets will be strictly limited. Even though these producers may have limited personal skill and may lack the necessary resources to build a website or manage a presence on a social networking site, they can still access the services to do this by working in an alliance with those who do have such skills, and this can offer a model to make wider markets available to an SME at mutual benefit to all those in an alliance (see 'The Virtual Farmers Market' case study at the end of this chapter).

A network perspective to marketing communication

More recently, marketing has embraced a network theory model, where organizations are not seen as insular and distinct from their marketing environment. SMEs are part of a network in an interconnected model where what can be achieved depends on other organizations as well as the demand the network is capable of serving. In a network model, resources that create a distinctive and sustainable market capacity may not be owned by a particular organization but belong to the network, in the sense that it is the capacity to do things in an alliance of network capabilities that makes a particular strategy possible. This means that strategic resources may lie not *in* organizations but *between* organizations in the network.

In this network model, some relationships between organizations will not be about competing with each other or negotiating to win the best trading terms. Instead, success may depend on mutual interests that deal with resolving tensions and risks between organizations over levels of competition and points of cooperation. The concept of business networks implies a blurring of organizational boundaries. This is a theoretical challenge to conventional strategic analysis models that tended to treat each organization as a distinct entity. So, instead of industrial economic theory's sharply defined boundaries, some authors argue business relationships are characterized by competition and cooperation, or 'coopetition' (Bengtsson and Kock, 2000).

A network theory approach stresses the importance of both relationships and structural determinants on strategy. The notion of SMEs existing within a network of relationships shows how they are interdependent on the actions of other organizations within a value-chain concept. Thus, an SME plays critical roles in developing and managing networks of relationships in terms of how communication with the marketplace takes place. For SMEs marketing communication depends on:

- considering the resources an SME can access; some will be within the network and others in the relationships it is possible to develop
- leveraging the role of marketing communication to build a suitable network that gives access to key resources via interactive technologies and networking tools
- identifying where there may be scarce resources and unbalanced dependencies on key network partners, to reduce over-dependency or map strategic opportunities, e.g. access new markets.

BOX 11.3: GOING GLOBAL THROUGH CROSS-RELATIONAL NETWORKING

According to Mike Southon, many successful UK small businesses collapse under the pressure of geographical expansion. This is due to the difficulty of setting up networks of relationships and knowledge across national borders to deal with the complex legal, taxation, compliance and human resources issues (Southon, 2010). In the context of cross-relational networks, an SME's competitiveness can be affected by access and knowledge of certain critical resources, which may not be directly connected to the business but have implications for strategic decisions such as the legal system and supply chains.

From a network theory perspective, SMEs that view the potential for relationships to affect each other in cross-relational actions will develop a deeper understanding of their competitive position (Eng, 2005). A cross-relational view accounts for impacts not only between relationships but also across relationships which play some part in supporting the overall network. For example, a test of the levels of dependency between organizations as a measure of the relationships *within* networks and *between* participants would demonstrate variation of control and dependence on critical resources for an exchange relationship in networks. For SMEs, there are strategic implications for choice and development of relationships as regards different levels of relationship stability or rates of change in the marketing environment. For example, when there is rapid change in the environment an SME is likely to require strong relationships with network partners who can give access to the character of this change, or partners in the network who operate where the market is most dynamic. Thus, it is advantageous for SMEs to adopt a cross-relational view of networks in order to:

- identify critical relationships that support channels of marketing communication, which could include partners in networks of relationships not directly connected to an SME
- manage relationships that are critical but not directly connected by understanding the implications of their strategic actions at different levels of relationship

■ develop sources of core competence through development and investment of selective key relationships in networks with cross-relational impacts on control and dependency.

SUMMARY

For decades there has been a bias in marketing communication which, to a large extent, has overlooked SMEs. One reason for this neglect is because of a perceived bias in what marketing communication is thought to be about. This bias comes from the role and success of specialist marketing communications services, like advertising agencies.

Agencies try to manage arm's-length relationships with large markets for major clients, usually by trying to manage the sense of relationship people feel towards a brand. In a competitive world, clients want their promotional budgets to work as hard as possible, so agencies seek ever greater synergy by combining different promotional tools, often in complex and integrated marketing communications campaigns. Because agencies tend to work with large companies to produce some of the most publicly visible elements of marketing communications, like TV ads, these are often thought of as the pinnacle of good promotional practice. Being so public, many large-scale marketing communications campaigns give access to campaign materials for those who want to study marketing communication. This supports the idea that marketing communications 'is' what agencies do. This chapter has highlighted that the relatively large scale of marketing communications activity that agencies develop for large clients has tended to overshadow the deeper characteristics of SME marketing communication.

This chapter has focused on the basic communication tools employed by SMEs. In contrast to conventional marketing communication analysis, it can be seen that SMEs focus on communication strategies to enhance short-term survival rather than develop a grand marketing communication plan. SMEs utilize new technologies to combine their knowledge and skills with other partners and take advantage of new technologies. Apart from discussing the cost-benefit advantage of technology and alliance relationships with complementary resources, this chapter has presented a network perspective to identify and examine marketing communication opportunities and channels. From a network viewpoint, SMEs have the potential to overcome resource limitations, exploit network capabilities and identify and manage critical resources in the network. In particular, networks of relationships create interdependency, and SMEs that manage and develop not only direct relationships but also indirect and cross-relationships are more likely to develop and sustain their competitive position.

REVIEW QUESTIONS

1. Identify three major differences of marketing communication between large organizations and SMEs.

2. What are the main stages of a typical marketing communications campaign?

3. What are the marketing communications tools applicable to SMEs?

4. Which aspects of the new and digital communication environment are most significant for SMEs and why?

5. Interpersonal communications are often the most expensive and difficult to control but many SMEs rely heavily on forms of marketing communications that use such personal contacts. Why?

6. Why does an integrated marketing communication model not reflect SME marketing communications practice?

7. Suggest three practical examples of how information communication technology and media have been used in marketing communication for SMEs.

8. How does a network perspective of marketing communications help SMEs identify new opportunities?

9. Give examples of interdependencies between SMEs' marketing communication activities in networks of relationships.

10. Why is it important to examine cross-relational impacts of network relationships for developing competitive marketing communications strategy?

CASE STUDY 11: THE VIRTUAL FARMERS MARKET

In the UK the resurgence of interest in small-scale artisan food production has been accompanied by the growth in farmers' markets that are now common across the UK. Often, these markets take place on specific days of the month and in basic and improvised venues that provide a place where local producers can showcase their wares, i.e. a focal point where the opportunity to pool significant levels of product inventory brings local producers and local customers together.

Using gaming technology, this model has now been extended to the Virtual Famers Market (www.vfmuk.com), a website that showcases inventory from a much wider geographical area and broader product range than a local farmers' market can offer. The challenge is to reproduce online enough of the distinctive 'essence' that customers respond to when they are drawn to a local farmers' market. One barrier is the lack of opportunity to taste, touch and smell the food online.

Using technology from the gaming industry, the site is able to offer a supporting information architecture that blends product availability with marketing communication content. Doing this, the site resonates with customers' interests in food by providing topical information and newsworthy content about producers and their passion for food. It provides access to goods with accompanying video stories, offering customers access to a form of personable 'market patter', the sort of encounter that might be had at a real farmers' market. These are largely made by the 'food heroes' themselves, the people who are responsible for the artisan products on sale. Typically these videos are made with the sort of disarming and naïve production values that have become widely familiar and accepted in a 'YouTube world'. In this way the video content provides access to and insight into the character of the producer, and it does this with a sort of rustic and charmingly authentic mode of communication that suits the style of the goods these producers bring to the market. It conveys something of the experience to the customer, bringing the essence of the local farmers' market to their computer screen.

By clicking the 'Meet Your Producer' button next to different goods, customers have access to the provenance of a product, in the form of the artisan producer. Via the extended reach this technology offers, the sometimes quirky and enthusiastic personalities behind the goods can reach out to capture a wider market. This can be likened to the differentiation a major grocery brand might try to achieve with a TV advertising campaign, but in the Virtual Famers' Market customers who buy a small producer's chocolate sauce also 'buy' the people who make that chocolate sauce. Because the video stories are authentic and benefit from customers' perception of the 'authority' of the site, the goods on the site carry greater credence. In effect, this is not just a shopping site; by combining an opportunity to trade with a combination of promotional messages and marketing communication content, the site conveys information that can build a sense of trust to enhance the value of the goods on offer.

Virtual Farmers Market is effectively creating interest and potential loyalty among an already interested audience. This is using communication with the market to create interest, provoke trial and build reputation in the sort of engagement stages that management of brand equity via TV advertising has done for decades. But Virtual Farmers Market offers this to small retailers, SMEs who might never win a listing with a major grocery retail chain. A sense of access to the 'real' people behind the products conveys a heightened level of authenticity to customers, which lends the goods distinctive appeal.

A site like Virtual Farmers Market can combine a range of marketing functions in a converging platform, including commerce and marketing communication. Not only is it a potential media space for those who want to know more about artisan food but also it is a retail space making an inventory of attractive products more easily available, and a promotional space where different producers can communicate the passion and points of difference they offer in the hope the market will react favourably towards them. In an age of increasing convergence, the communication of marketing information and content via modern information technology is likely to be increasingly used by SMEs, even if the SMEs themselves do not host or manage the content directly. If the products and services are attractive enough, this presents a market for those who are willing to make such services more visible and accessible.

CASE QUESTIONS

1. Logan Dairy makes handmade and award-winning goat cheese in Yorkshire. The cheeses are sold from the farm mainly to local delicatessens and restaurants throughout East and West Yorkshire. One of their most successful cheeses is rolled in freshly milled black pepper to give a light spicy crust to the cheese before it is packaged. What are the advantages and disadvantages for Logan Dairy of promoting their products using the Virtual Farmers Markets?

2. Why would customers what to buy Logan Dairy cheeses from a local delicatessen? How would Virtual Farmers Market communicate the products' values and benefits in ways that mimic 'real' marketing communications?

3. What would you include in a communications mix to promote Logan Dairy cheeses and why?

4. Boursin is a cream cheese made in France by the multinational Unilever. One of the varieties comes prepared with cracked black peppercorns, like one of the

Logan Dairy's most popular cheeses. How would a company like Unilever differ in their approach to marketing communication from Logan Dairy, and why would this be different?

REFERENCES

Bengtsson, M. and Kock, S., 2000, 'Coopetition' in business networks – to cooperate and compete simultaneously, *Industrial Marketing Management* **29**, 411–426.

Dyer, L. M. and Ross, C. A., 2003, Consumer communication and the small ethnic firm, *Journal of Developmental Entrepreneurship* **8** (1), 19–31.

Eng, T.-Y., 2005, An empirical analysis of the influence of cross-relational impact of strategy analysis on relationship performance in a business network context, *Journal of Strategic Marketing* **13**, 219–237.

Fill, C., 2005, *Marketing Communications*, Prentice Hall: Harlow, UK.

Kandel, E. R., Schwarz, J. H. and Jessell, T. M., 2000, *Principles of Neural Science* (4th edn), McGraw Hill: New York.

Moules, J., 2010, To tweet or not to tweet is a business question, *FT Weekend, Money*, 16–17 January, 30–31.

Southon, M., 2010, My business, *FT Weekend, Money*, 27–28 February, 34.

Spickett-Jones, J. G. and Eng, T.-Y., 2006, SMEs and the strategic context for communication, *Journal of Marketing Communications* **12** (3), 225–243.

van Riel, C. B. M., 1995, *Principles of Corporate Communication*, Prentice Hall: London.

Chapter 12

Internet marketing

Jaya Akunuri

LEARNING OBJECTIVES

After reading this chapter, you will be able to:
- explain the concept of online marketing
- understand the various online tools available to small businesses that help them promote their products and build networks
- evaluate the benefits offered by internet marketing in comparison with traditional advertising tools in the context of SME marketing
- understand the need for entrepreneurs to employ an internet marketing strategy and how this has to be integrated with offline techniques.

BOX 12.1: HOW INTERNET MARKETING CAN BOOST BUSINESS

Kellie Allen left her full-time job in marketing to pursue her passion and hobby of making jewellery. She spent a great deal of time researching extensively on online websites to get an idea of what was being offered in the market. Apart from browsing through business websites of other jewellery makers, and online magazines like *Harper's Bazaar* and *Marie Claire*, she analysed online trends of jewellery being bought and sold by observing marketplace websites like Etsy, Ecrater and Ruby Lane. She decided that, despite the many websites selling jewellery, she too could get a piece of the web jewellery pie by setting up her own online business from her home in the Surrey countryside.

She took the plunge and launched her own website called 'Bejewelled' that would sell unique, high-quality jewellery specifically targeting computer-savvy working women who shun the bog-standard high-street range that everyone else has and prefer to shop around for exclusive designer jewellery that won't break the bank. The website was simple and clutter-free, with interesting content that described her passion and her jewellery. It had fast-uploading high-quality images and an easy way for customers to shop and pay securely. Being a marketer herself, she realized the importance of establishing her website with the help of the various e-marketing tools and a carefully designed e-marketing strategy.

Two years later, Kellie's business has grown and the website is bringing in a steady stream of customers. Kellie now employs an administrator who answers queries and processes orders; she also works with five other jewellery designers who sell their products through Bejewelled.

This morning, like any other day, Kellie wakes up and pours herself a hot cup of coffee. She then checks her email to see if there are any responses to her latest **email campaign** informing customers of a new design concept. She received three enquiries and she forwards these to her administrator. She then logs on to Bejewelled's **Facebook page**, which has over 800 fans comprised of friends, customers, jewellery suppliers, designers and other people from the industry. A customer who had recently purchased a pair of earrings for her mum posted a picture of her mum wearing the earrings on Kellie's wall. Kellie writes on the customer's wall asking her to keep the pictures coming and thanks her for the snap. She suddenly remembers that last night she had **tweeted** about an upcoming sale of her new jewellery range. She logs on to her **Twitter page** that has been customized with her logo and brand. She reads the tweets from her followers; most of them are from within the sector – professionals, designers, suppliers and other businesses. A good friend, also a jewellery designer, had sent her a link to a jewellery **e-blog** about a recent article on soldering silver. She continues to read it . . .

BUSINESS, BUT NOT AS USUAL!

The business world around the entrepreneur is changing at a very fast pace. The internet (a network that connects all computers the world over) and the World Wide Web (a medium that provides a platform for publishing information and delivering services) have overwhelmingly transformed the way people communicate and interact with each other. There is a whole new dynamic and seamless world of collaborations, communities and networks that is growing at a rapid pace in the online context, most of which is outside the direct control of the entrepreneur. In a marketing context, this change has had a profound impact on the way people scout for information and buy products and services. SMEs now have to adapt their marketing strategies to take advantage of the many opportunities provided by the omnipresent internet and the World Wide Web. Customers are everywhere, are connected at all times and demand to be dealt with promptly, politely and personally.

In this chapter we will define the term internet marketing and explore its role and relevance to today's entrepreneur. We will then analyse the various tools of online marketing and evaluate them against the more traditional approaches to marketing. The latter part of the chapter unravels the need for strategic thinking on behalf of the entrepreneur in developing an e-marketing strategy and explores some of the challenges posed by the internet.

WHAT IS INTERNET MARKETING?

A range of terms have been used by both academics and practitioners alike in describing the use of internet and other digital media for the purpose of marketing activities. The lines are blurred and the definitions overlap, but broadly speaking:

- Electronic marketing (e-marketing) or digital marketing refers to the use of internet-enabled *external* media such as web, email and wireless technology, and also includes management of digital customer data and electronic customer relationship management

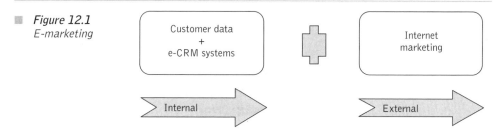

Figure 12.1
E-marketing

systems (e-CRM systems), which are *internal* to the organization. The term e-marketing has a broader context and scope (Smith and Chaffey, 2005).

■ Internet marketing or online marketing refers to using internet-powered applications to reach both existing and potential customers. It can be defined as identifying, anticipating and satisfying customers' needs using an *online* platform to foster exchange relationships between the organization and its customers.

The internet today has emerged as an attractive marketing channel for small businesses to explore and exploit by posting their content and building traffic to it effectively. A plethora of 'new media tools' have been added to the marketer's arsenal. These include websites, email, blogs, online articles, mobile phones, online PR and networking sites, search engine marketing (SEM), pop-ups – and the list goes on. But, why should small businesses bother with all these? What is in it for them? And is it worth their while to spend their energies on learning and engaging with these new tools?

THE GROWING IMPORTANCE OF THE INTERNET

It is expected that over the next three to five years, the volume of digital content will increase 10 to 100 times and that we are all on the verge of a 'big bang' in the communications industry that will provide the UK with enormous economic and industrial opportunities (DCMS & BIS, 2009).

A recent report published by OfCom (2009c) demonstrates the fact that the overall availability of various communications services across the UK is quite high. Most households in the UK now have access to the key broadcasting and telephony services. The report further states that the take-up of the internet at home has significantly increased from 65 per cent in 2008 to 73 per cent in 2009, led by the rise in PC and laptop ownership (from 70 per cent to 76 per cent) and people are now accessing the internet not only from home but also other environments.

The message is reinforced by data published in 2009 by the Internet World Stats demonstrating that nearly 47 million people in the UK use the internet on a regular basis – that's a 76 per cent penetration of the UK population.

Table 12.1 *Internet top 10 countries in Europe (September 2009) (figures in millions)*

	1	2	3	4	5	6	7	8	9	10
Countries	Germany	UK	Russia	France	Italy	Spain	Turkey	Poland	Netherlands	Ukraine
Internet users	54.2	46.7	45.3	43.1	30.0	29.1	26.5	20.0	14.3	10.4

Source: Adapted from Internet World Stats (2009).

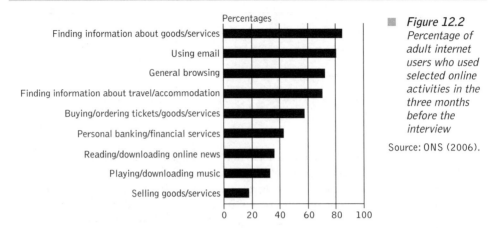

Figure 12.2
Percentage of adult internet users who used selected online activities in the three months before the interview

Source: ONS (2006).

The internet is the fastest-growing community in the world. According to data from the UK Online Measurement company (UKOM, 2009) and Nielsen, 35.5 million people were online in February 2009; this grew to 39.7 million in February 2010 (representing an astounding increase of over four million active internet users in just 12 months).

Furthermore, in a research survey conducted in 2006 by the UK Office for National Statistics, 85 per cent of the adult internet users said that they had gone online in the last three months *to find information about products and services.* Consumers these days spend a lot of time researching products and services online. Long gone are the days when the sales-person from a company could feed a buyer with asymmetric information. Nowadays people can find information about the industry, vendors, brands and products in just a few minutes, even without getting in touch with the company.

There is clear evidence that shoppers are abandoning the high street and are flocking online to take advantage of the empowering facilities offered by the net. Some 21.3 million people now shop online in the UK (BMRB, 2008), spending an average of £661 each. By 2011 this number is expected to increase to 32 million and the value of goods they buy online will add up to almost £52 billion (Forrester, 2007).

It is only natural for the marketers to follow consumers wherever they are going. The annual online adspend report of the UK Internet Advertising Bureau (IAB) gives a break-down of where the advertisers' money is going and suggests that internet marketing has flourished in recent years, becoming a multimillion pound industry that has increased from

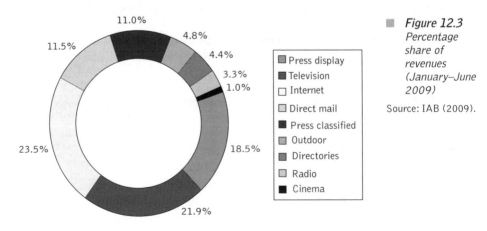

Figure 12.3
Percentage share of revenues (January–June 2009)

Source: IAB (2009).

£1 billion in 2005 to £3.54 billion in 2009. The first half of 2009 witnessed an important media milestone as online advertising became the UK's biggest media platform; with 23.5 per cent of the total UK adspend it surpassed TV advertising (21.9 per cent). In a span of six years the internet has gone from being the smallest ad medium to the biggest, representing a fundamental shift in consumer behaviour.

BOX 12.2: IS THE INTERNET REALLY A BIG DEAL?

- 75 per cent of UK households use the internet on a regular basis – representing a 200 per cent increase in the last 10 years (Ofcom, 2009b)
- UK internet users are spending an average of 23 hours a week online (YouGov, 2006)
- 90 per cent of consumers trust peer recommendations (Nielsen, 2009)
- Twitter is growing at 40 per cent per month – 80 per cent of Twitter usage is on mobile devices. People update anywhere, anytime . . . (Qualman, 2009)
- If Facebook were a country, it would be the third largest (China, India, the US, Facebook!) (Zuckerberg, 2010)
- 89 per cent of UK consumers own a mobile phone and mobile ad revenue totalled £28.6 million in the UK in 2008, up 99.2 per cent on 2007 (Ofcom, 2009a)
- There are over 200,000,000 blogs (China Internet Information Centre) and 34 per cent of these bloggers post opinions about products and brands (Universal McCann, 2008)

Is this a case of 'Lies, damn lies and statistics' or do these percentages mean something? In the light of these changes in the external technological environment, evaluate the implications for a small business.

INTERNET MARKETING AND SMES

The main constraints for SMEs from a marketing perspective have been identified by Carson (1985): limited resources, lack of specialist expertise and limited impact in the marketplace. The internet enables SMEs to engage with marketing by overcoming these constrains to a very large extent.

New technologies have improved interaction with consumers and enabled a level of consumer involvement and engagement with the brand, thus providing SMEs with opportunities that otherwise would perhaps not be available. Small businesses can use digital technology to revolutionize how they operate through online marketing and sales. This enables them to reach a global audience, thus extending their market scope beyond the confines of ther national borders. New media are relatively easy to create even for someone with very little technical inclination. It does not require a great deal of specialist knowledge to write professional emails, publish on blogs, set up networking sites, etc.

One could argue that, in some instances, the internet could disproportionately benefit small businesses. Most small businesses usually cater to niche audiences and sell niche products. Regardless of the physical location of the buyer and the seller, the internet enables these SMEs to position their products to people who are *looking for exactly those particular niche goods*. Therefore, it acts as a great leveller and enables any SME, however big or small, to compete with the more established players in the market, thus increasing market efficiency. SMEs can stamp their mark and have an impact on the marketplace because on the internet nobody knows how small you are!

Though it is widely accepted that the internet offers companies a wide range of opportunities, SMEs have been very slow in adopting these technologies. There is substantial research evidence (Gallagher and Gilmore, 2004; SBRT, 2005; Ofcom, 2006) that SMEs are failing to exploit the opportunities presented by e-commerce and not yet making effective use of it. British Telecommunication's Voice of Small Businesses survey (2009) revealed that the majority of SMEs in the UK are underestimating the importance of the web as an interactive platform, with just 13 per cent considering websites integral to marketing strategy and only 3 per cent using their site to communicate with consumers.

So, the question that begs to be answered is what can the internet really do for an SME? In research interviews conducted by Downie (2003), these were some of the perceptions of owner-managers about the potential benefits and drawbacks of an online presence to their company. Evaluate the pros and cons and contemplate whether a web presence can aid an SME or whether the risks outweigh the benefits.

GROUP ACTIVITY: BENEFITS AND DRAWBACKS OF WEB PRESENCE FOR AN SME

In research interviews conducted by Downie (2003), these were some of the perceptions of owner-managers about the potential benefits and drawbacks of an online presence to their company. Evaluate the pros and cons and contemplate whether a web presence can aid an SME or whether the risks outweigh the benefits.

Benefits	Drawbacks
Better competitive position compared with competition and wider market area	Can show weakness vis-à-vis competition
More customers accessible	Can be time-consuming to manage
Opportunities to cross market/network	Cost of establishment and maintenance
Better customer service	Difficult to know who is interested and who is browsing
Better communication with customers	Difficult to establish what and how much information to give
'Instant' promotion of product and company	Difficult to correct bad impression
Easier to identify customer contacts	If website inaccessible (e.g. being updated or host problem) customer unlikely to return
Better measurement of customer interest	Customers use your site to get information and then go elsewhere to buy
	If there is no website, potential customers will wonder why not
	Difficult to know just how cost-effective it is

THE INTERNET COMPARED WITH OTHER TRADITIONAL MARKETING MEDIA

You cannot approach people, you can be merely approached.

(Bickerton et al., 2000)

Traditional media can be referred to as the conventionally used marketing media like advertising (outdoor, print, TV, radio, cinema), PR, sponsorship, sales promotions, exhibitions, point of purchase, direct media and personal selling. Internet-enabled media are the newer marketing tools like brand websites, online advertising, email, SEM, mobile and interactive TV. The internet has drastically transformed the marketing landscape and is providing the marketer with countless opportunities to engage with the consumer. The last decade has witnessed a considerable shift in terms of marketing adspend from traditional media to internet-enabled tools. The internet was ushered in in the 1990s and by the mid 1990s, web adspend had reached a US$300 million mark and that number had almost tripled (Liodice, 2010) by the dawn of the new millennium. So why are marketers latching on to this trend?

Some of the differences that make new media far more exciting in comparison with traditional media are described below.

Interaction

The emerging philosophy of online marketing (and this is where it fundamentally differs from traditional marketing) is that people who consume the media are not *passive* in absorbing this information that is being hurled at them; rather, they are *active* initiators, creators and contributors (a *pull strategy*), who are customizing media for themselves as well as for those in their communities. The philosophy is one of true empowerment to the consumer.

Two-way communication

Non-interactive traditional media involves marketers *talking at* the customers. The advent of digital formats has facilitated a *dialogue* between the company and its consumers. As opposed to traditional media, new media is a two-way road. It's all about the conversations and it's important for the marketer to *listen* to what the consumers have to say and then to respond appropriately – this is the way forward in creating relationships with those who know you and like your brand. It has been well documented in academic literature that entrepreneurs rely hugely on both personal and social networking contacts. Online media further enables entrepreneurs to do what they are best at – interact with people, build relationships and *talk with their customers*.

It is non-intrusive

We have come a long way from the age of 'shouting from the roof' advertising (the *push strategy* of traditional media). Consumers are more sceptical than ever and do not believe everything they hear. They expect less interruption from the marketer and want marketing messages to be clear and meaningful. More importantly, they want to consume them whenever and wherever they please.

Wider access

Particularly from a small business point of view, the internet has opened the gateway for SMEs to communicate with and have access to a wider market that was previously unreachable. E-media increases the reach of small businesses and helps them stretch their wings more widely, even to global markets.

Time and cost savings

A small business is generally denied lavish marketing budgets and this means that the owner-manager has a limited choice of promotional tools. 'SMEs in general find it difficult to do the kind of marketing that is touted by academics and business advisors' (Carson *et al.*, 1995). Using traditional media has always been draining on the marketing budgets of SMEs, but with internet marketing a wider range of customers can be reached at no extra cost whatsoever. Small businesses can save in terms of time, cost and resources, which will most definitely improve their bottom line.

Web analytics

Now more than ever marketers can get a full view of the marketing landscape and measure the mood of the consumers and their perceptions about the brand by monitoring feedback. The internet enables small businesses to collect market research intelligence quickly and relatively cheaply. The online medium enables entrepreneurs to gain and build competitive advantage by providing a knowledge base and engraving their presence on the various networks. It provides an environment where marketers can test innovative ideas with very little risk, unlike traditional marketing where the effectiveness of a campaign can only be tested once it is rolled out. This aspect of new media is particularly advantageous to SMEs who need not shell out huge amounts of money on traditional marketing measurement tools. Web analytics can be used to discover who opened your mail shot and who they forwarded it to, to see the traffic volumes to your website and to find out exactly how long someone spent on your product pages, customer satisfaction surveys, and the like. These sophisticated online marketing tools are no longer the preserve of big businesses and with a simple click of a button SMEs can measure the effectiveness of the deployed e-marketing tools.

Individualized marketing

Traditional marketing is known for its reach to a mass-market. Internet marketing, on the other hand, enables a certain level of precision in target marketing. This process of tailor-made marketing can also be called *personalization* (Chaffey *et al.*, 2003). By collecting intelligence about customers, a marketer can then customize marketing messages for a specific target audience, thus ensuring that the advertising spend is being spent in the most effective way. Small businesses have been observed to do this already through the means of personal selling – the internet offers another platform for small businesses to reach their customers on that personal one-to-one level.

A 360° MARKETING APPROACH?

It is for the entrepreneur to juggle the offline and online tools and decide what is best for the business and the customers. All promotional tools, traditional and internet-based, should enable the marketer to establish and communicate the differential advantage. It is also essential that entrepreneurs do not look at these concepts as mutually exclusive; they should evaluate the need to adopt a transitional strategy that protects their investment in traditional marketing while also leveraging it to take full advantage of internet marketing.

The internet is pervasive and the scope of e-tools can be increased by integrating them with traditional media tools and by using them as supplements or substitutes. This allows

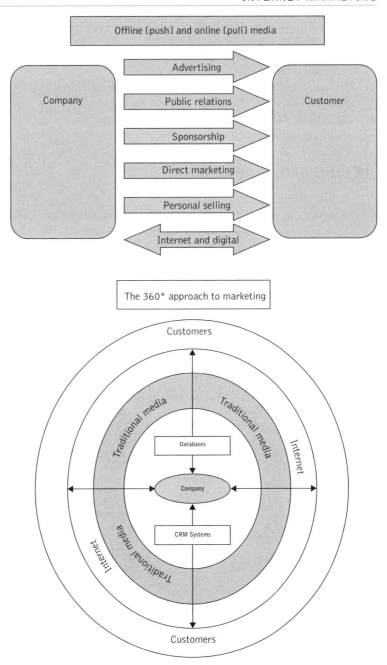

Figure 12.4
Offline and
online media

entrepreneurs to take account of the established marketing frameworks and adapt them to suit the context of his or her SME circumstance. In order to reduce the costs of the marketing programmes and improve their effectiveness, SMEs need to pursue a 360° multichannel approach to marketing.

This integration may be a result of the firm's active strategy or in some cases integration is primed by the consumers themselves. Examples include:

- Offers or promotions being published on product packaging which directs consumers to the company's website to claim them.
- Customer service calls, enquiries and complaints are often registered in a database and information retrieved accordingly.
- Most successful TV ads are watched online through sites like YouTube. Interactive TV and digital radio are classic examples of integration.
- The general shift of people going online to newspaper or magazine sites to read news, PR articles, magazine articles, etc.

ONLINE SME MARKETING TOOLS

In this section, we will focus on the many instruments that are at the entrepreneur's disposal for the purpose of communicating and transacting with various audiences. The main thrust and emphasis here, from an SME perspective, is that the internet not only offers a platform for the entrepreneur to delve into using the newer marketing tools (like emails, SEM) but also enables them to adapt and use some of the more formal marketing approaches in an online context (advertise though video uploads, build public relations through publishing blogs and articles, use promotions like e-coupons, etc.).

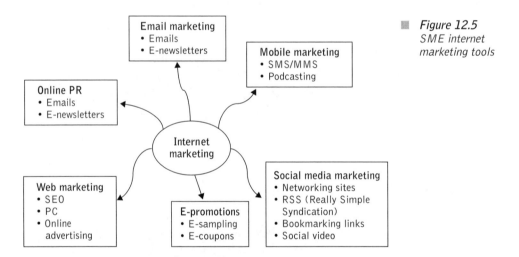

Figure 12.5
SME internet
marketing tools

Table 12.2 Comparison of traditional and online marketing

Traditional method	Online 'twin'
Print advertising Yellow pages	Display advertising Paid-search marketing Search engine marketing
Television, radio	Audio-visual uploads Webinars Interactive TV Podcasts
Public relations	Article marketing Blogging

Table 12.2 (continued)

Traditional method	Online 'twin'
Sales promotions	E-sampling E-coupons
Trade fairs/Conferences	Social networking sites Social bookmarking
Direct marketing	Email Mobile (SMS: short message service – service to send short messages from one phone to another, MMS: multimedia messaging service – service that allows harmonization of text messages enhanced by audio video clips)
Sponsorship	Banners Pay-per-click

Websites

Bickerton *et al.* (2000) compare a company's website to a 'billboard'. The task is to make it not only *informative* with the relevant information but also *attractive* enough that customers find their way to it. A website should convey accurate and compelling information about the products/services on offer as well as the systems, processes and expertise that the business is able to offer.

SMEs are usually in close contact with their customers and tend to know a great deal about them. This information should be used with the target audience in mind when building and designing the website. For websites to be effective they should:

- be clear, uncluttered, fast-uploading and easy to navigate
- reflect the personality of the brand while providing information about the products
- enable interactions with, or between, customers
- integrate other media tools where possible (for example, consumers should be able to subscribe to receive emails or newsletters, watch online videos, be able to download e-coupons or other goodies, etc.)
- have web-tracking software that provides you with vital information like number of visitors, location of visitors, most-viewed content/pages, clicks to sales, etc.).

British Telecommunication's Voice of Small Businesses survey (2009) revealed that, despite the rise in the number of small companies with their own websites (from 20 per cent in 2007 to 80 per cent in 2008), six out of ten small firms do not use their company website to sell their products and services. Most of these websites are not being exploited to their true potential in terms of acting as a dais for effective engagement with online consumers. So what can small firms do to generate continuous traffic on the website?

Search engine marketing (SEM)

Approximately 80 per cent of the web traffic tends to be generated from search engines like Google, Yahoo! and MSN Search so it is critical that the company's website is 'found' by these search engines' 'spiders' and is not lost among millions of others. With some effort and adequate research, small businesses can easily ensure that their website is visible and that it ranks highly in search engine results pages (SERPs). An important point for owner-managers to consider is to decide if they will venture into SEM themselves and do it *in-house* or whether they can afford to *outsource* the activity to an agency. The most commonly used methods of SEM are listed below.

Pay-per-click (PPC)

Pay-per-click search marketing refers to sponsored links that appear on the right-hand side and at the top of the results page. They are similar to conventional advertising and allow advertisers to create custom adverts by selecting keywords that best define their business. Advertisers do not pay when the ads are displayed but pay for *each click* on their ad, which results in a visit to their website.

Search engine optimization (SEO)

SEO involves providing the right clues and key words for the search engines so that the website appears in the 'natural' or 'organic' listings (the list on the left-hand side of the search results page with links that are not sponsored or paid for). In research conducted by MarketingSherpa (2005), 'heatmaps' of what online searchers read and click were generated. It was established that organic results are more valuable as they generate 75 per cent of clicks as opposed to PPC ads that generate only 25 per cent.

Email marketing

Email marketing simply means promoting products and services via electronic messages transmitted from and to internet host computers. It is a powerful, flexible and lucrative direct marketing tool that enables full individualization. Email marketing allows small businesses to communicate with their clients quickly and cheaply. SMEs must endeavour to generate a database of email addresses of current customers, prospects and other contacts. Depending on the target audience, messages can be customized so that they become relevant and interesting to the recipient. It is a good relationship management practice to ask permission and obtain consent before bombarding people with marketing messages. Consumers are picky about which email lists they subscribe to, so when they do give their consent, it is essential for businesses to safeguard their trust. This concept of offering people an 'opt-in' or 'opt-out' alternative is at the very heart of *permission marketing*, a term popularized by Seth Godin (1999). It refers to seeking the customers' permission to opt in, usually by offering them incentives, before sending any marketing information.

According to recent research published by the Direct Marketing Association (DMA, 2009), '51% of consumers stated that email is their favoured means of being contacted by companies'. This highlights the fact that consumers continue to rate email as their preferred channel for receiving marketing messages. Sending marketing messages via email is a potent way to communicate with potential customers. It is also one of the most effective, not only in terms of speed of delivery and response rates but also on return on investment – the DMA report also noted that 'commercial email returned a whopping $43.62 for every dollar spent on it in 2009'. When tapping into the benefits offered by email as a marketing tool SMEs should be wary of over-using it, which may spur consumers to unsubscribe from the mailing list.

E-newsletters

Owner-managers may also consider circulating or publishing online newsletters and/or magazines (e-zines) on a monthly or quarterly basis. These provide an opportunity to make genuine connections with consumers and help boost brand image and credibility.

E-promotions

Everyone loves a freebie! A simple trick for small businesses to use is to offer incentives to motivate potential consumers to try their products or to keep existing customers engaged with the brand. Free tools and services like free downloadable calculators, calendars, e-books, etc., can be offered when a consumer visits the website. Alternatively, consumers can opt in and choose to submit their details online in order to receive free e-samples and e-coupons.

Social media marketing

There are now hundreds of millions of consumers, prospects and other contacts worldwide using websites, social networks, blogs, micro-blogs, online forums and video-sharing sites and it is essential for marketers to engage with them.

▨ *Table 12.3 Online activities of UK internet users* by age (2009) (% of respondents in each group)*

	16–24	25–44	45–54	55–64	65+	Total
Sending/receiving email	94%	92%	88%	86%	82%	90%
Finding information about goods and services	64%	83%	80%	81%	75%	78%
Reading or downloading online news, newspapers, magazines	46%	58%	52%	47%	44%	52%
Playing or downloading games, images, films or music	70%	46%	35%	26%	16%	44%
Listening to web radio or watching web TV	53%	46%	35%	34%	25%	42%
Uploading self-created content	54%	44%	34%	29%	21%	40%
Posting messages to chat sites, blogs, newspaper groups, etc.	71%	45%	25%	19%	–	40%
Downloading software	46%	39%	31%	25%	25%	36%
Voice over internet protocol (VoIP)/video calls (via Webcam)	25%	23%	19%	19%	13%	21%
Selling goods or services over the internet	19%	23%	17%	13%	–	19%

Note: *Users who have accessed the internet in the past three months. Source: ONS (2009).

The internet is very much an integral part of the socio-cultural fabric of the society. During the last two years, while businesses have struggled to combat the global recession, a new phenomenon of social networking has boomed. Forty per cent of recent internet users in the UK stated that they posted messages to chat sites, blogs and newsgroups in 2009, up from 20 per cent in 2008. There was an increase from 24 per cent to 40 per cent of internet users who stated they uploaded self-created content online (ONS, 2009).

Customers are now engaging with brands on various levels. This shift in online behaviour facilitates a new platform for marketers to use social media tools to communicate with consumers and for customers to talk to companies and each other. This form of internet marketing is referred to as *social media marketing*.

Thomas Power, co-founder of one of the largest online business networks, Ecademy, says that '[o]rganisations over the next few years will move from being closed, selective and controlling to being open, random and supportive. This change will be driven by the Internet and social media.' Power calls this new approach to thinking about business 'network thinking' (Power, 2009). The various kinds of social media marketing are described below.

Article marketing

This is an online public relations technique that uses the internet to publish newsletters, articles and press releases. These can then be disseminated to interested agencies (consumers, journalists) by publishing them on the company website, by submitting them to online news feeds or by sending them via email to individuals on a subscription basis. Owner-managers who have something intelligent to say and who are well versed in the industry should engage with this form of marketing as it spreads the name of the company and the brand.

Blogs

Blogs are often described as online journals or diaries where individuals can publish company news and express opinions about concepts, issues, brands, etc. Blogs enable entrepreneurs to interact with consumers and other people in the industry at a very personal and informal level. They are an excellent and effective platform for small businesses to showcase their expertise and convey information about the products and services. They also provide a means for a two-way dialogue with consumers and are a good way to feel the pulse of the market and gather informal feedback from consumers.

Really Simple Syndication (RSS)

RSS is an extension of blogging. Automatic updates are sent to subscribers when any new content is posted. This enables the consumers to stay in touch as they are constantly informed of the new 'feeds' without having to visit the website or the blog.

Social networking

'It is widely known that marketing orientation in a small firm is characterised by the use of various contact networks, both formal and informal' (Hill and Wright, 2000). For entrepreneurs, building personal contact networks (PCNs) via networking has long been at the very heart of conducting business and building relationships. However, with the emergence of online social networking sites (BT Tradespace, YouTube, Facebook, Twitter, etc.), traditional physical networking events are being replaced by online platforms that foster close relationships with other entrepreneurs in the industry. 'Online networks can also help an enterprise to improve their business in other aspects such as recruitment, marketing, brand building, customer interaction, locating strategic partners and gathering business intelligence' (Business Link, 2007).

Social bookmarking

A relatively new generation of internet sites called social bookmarking/sharing sites have mushroomed in the forest of global online networks. Sites like www.stumbleupon.com, www.del.icio.us, www.digg.com and www.reddit.com allow you to bookmark websites, save the links, tag them with key words and also then share them with communities consisting of members who have similar interests. Entrepreneurs can use this simple technology and generate traffic to their website by making it easier for people to bookmark it. Another advantage is that through bookmarking sites an entrepreneur can look at who created a particular book-mark and also have access to that person's other bookmarked resources, thereby enabling the entrepreneur to build social connections and develop networks.

The buzz about buzz

Whether you like it or not your consumers are talking about you and your products! Social media marketing differs drastically from traditional advertising as it calls for connectivity, community and inclusiveness. Brands are being forced to let go of their one-way models of communication and engage with the consumer – it is evident that the consumer is now *in control*. Social media is here to stay and companies have to think about internet word-of-mouth strategies. Viral marketing is identifying and working with *key influencers* and developing *brand advocates* who deliver the messages organically to generate positive word-of-mouth. And, when word-of-mouth marketing works, it creates valuable buzz!!

There is no denying that by adopting social media tools small businesses can increase their new customer contacts and customer engagement. However, that is only the first step. Brands today require time and attention more than money and ads. Inspiring the networking community and using the social spaces effectively takes a lot of hard work, enthusiasm and loyalty. The other aspect that small businesses need to consider is that social media 'exposes' the brand and the workings of the organization. Companies that fall short on promises will be named and shamed in an instant. SMEs should, therefore, have a plan for dealing with 'negative buzz' in a way that consumers can see they are taking the feedback on board and are taking appropriate action. Entrepreneurs should acquaint themselves with 'network etiquette' and follow privacy and legal stipulations.

Mobile marketing

Mobile or wireless marketing occurs when marketers use mobile applications to communicate with consumers through the use of mobile phones or other wireless devices (data cards, netbooks, e-readers, gaming devices, etc.). Mobile marketing definitely ensures a wider and more personal reach in comparison with all other marketing tools. It can ensure greater

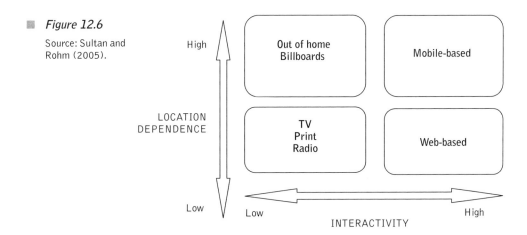

Figure 12.6

Source: Sultan and Rohm (2005).

attention from the recipient as the device usually accompanies the user and therefore ads could be more specific and targeted.

There is no doubt mobile marketing is gaining prominence in the advertisers' marketing mix. Mobile ad revenue totalled £28.6 million in the UK in 2008, up 99.2 per cent on 2007 (IAB, 2008). Mobile marketing is unique in comparison with other marketing tools in that 'it combines high levels of interactivity and degree of location specification' (Thome, 2009). Mobile phones can be used not only to deliver direct SMS and MMS messages to consumers but also various engagement-marketing campaigns like banners, coupons, video messages and advergames. This is only possible because the mobile function is shifting closer to the online experience as more and more consumers access the internet through their phones. Ofcom's (2009a) annual communication report states that 'more than 8 million people in the UK (16% of adults) accessed the internet on their mobile phone in the first quarter of 2009, up by 42% on a year previously'.

Similar to email marketing, small businesses who want to make use of this communication system will need to provide an opt-in option for consumers and then send targeted advertisements to the list of subscribers. It is essential for businesses to be creative in thinking up interesting ways to communicate with prospects or customers. By giving their consent, customers are inviting you into their personal space and marketers have to tread carefully and ensure that the recipient perceives the communication as 'adding value'. The disadvantage of using mobile marketing is that consumers consider their phones to be sacrosanct and personal and may find it intrusive to receive marketing messages.

Apart from the ones mentioned above, there is a plethora of other tools available in the online marketer's arsenal:

- **Online advertising:** advertising on paid-for spaces on websites of other companies. These could take the shape of banner adverts, small buttons, tall skyscrapers, pop-ups and the like.
- **Affiliate marketing:** partnering with other sites who display small banner adverts for your website for a negotiated fee.
- **Content sponsorship:** similar to sponsorship but in an online context; links the brand with related brands by highlighting the message such that it stands out from the other banner ads.
- **Photo and video sharing:** sharing personal photos and videos to engage with the consumers. Websites like Flickr and YouTube have grown tremendously in popularity over the last few years.
- **Chat rooms and forums:** similar to blogs; information is shared by people who are interested in similar issues, products, brands.
- **Connection and network building:** these sites allow you to cluster with like-minded people (mostly B2B – that is, business-to-business), e.g. LinkedIn, Ecademy.
- **Profile/market-building networks:** for building professional contacts and networks, e.g. BT Tradespace, Network 2012.
- **Online events and webinars:** similar to traditional exhibitions and trade fairs but on an online platform; enables broadcasting of online events and seminars, sometimes 'live' with audience participation and engagement.
- **Advergames:** online games accompanied by an email or viral marketing campaign using rich media games to deliver advertising messages.
- **Online contests:** e-contestants can be invited to participate in contests, thus generating interest and excitement and, thereby, brand awareness.

GENERATING AN E-MARKETING PLAN

Literature about marketing orientation of small firms (Quinton and Harridge-March, 2006) has highlighted the fact that entrepreneurial organizations frequently have difficulty in standing back from the customer interface in order to plan strategically. Quinton and Harridge-March emphasize that small firms are rarely 'strategists in the conventional sense' (p. 86). Entrepreneurs are characteristically preoccupied by the many 'everyday' tasks focusing on daily survival and lack long-term strategic planning.

Essentially, marketing online is not very different from marketing offline and requires the same planning metrics as the other media. It is still the same formula of understanding who your customers are, what do they want to buy, what augmented benefits can you offer over your competitors, how best do you communicate these to the target market and how do you build long-term relationships with your customers. Marketing through the internet should therefore be a *planned* process and a company's e-marketing strategy must be seen in the overall context of marketing planning and strategy.

It is crucial in the first instance to understand the external and internal environment within which the firm operates. External audit involves assessing competitor strategy, understanding consumer requirements and behaviour and evaluating intermediaries who can enable the business to deliver the e-objectives. The next logical step is to evaluate the strengths and weaknesses of the organization itself in terms of resource availability and limitation and assess existing e-strategies. Such in-depth analysis of the market and the business will provide the necessary context to set internet marketing goals that will direct future action plans. Developing an appropriate e-marketing strategy involves assessing the target consumers' needs and behaviour patterns and evaluating the firm's positioning strategy.

It is crucial at this point to stress that digital marketing cannot function in isolation and is most effective when used in conjunction with other marketing communication tools like the telephone, TV, direct mail or catalogues. In the coming years, the challenge for every marketer will be to 'cut through the clutter' of the overwhelming number of marketing messages that consumers are exposed to on a daily basis. The most effective way to achieve this is to place consistent and coherent brand experiences in the consumers' environment and let them choose when and how they consume those experiences. For example, an email campaign about a new product can be substantiated with 'adverbanners', mobile texts, online demonstrative videos, blog feeds and postal mail.

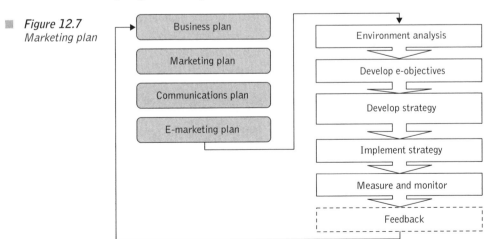

Figure 12.7
Marketing plan

The route for success for marketers is in being integrated across all marketing channels. Integration in this context should be a two-pronged approach:

- Vertical integration with the other 'promotional' elements. There needs to be a consistency acrosss all media plans and this will help consumers understand the commonality between different media channels.
- Horizontal integration with the 'place' aspects of the marketing strategy. SMEs may decide to sell products and services over the internet with very little consideration about the pre-sales and after-sales support that may be required, especially in B2B transactions where products could be more complex and/or of higher value.

As in any planning process, the *accountability* and *return on investment* of the activities need to be evaluated. It is essential to measure the performance of the online tools. Subsequently, activities generating positive results can be optimized and those generating negative results can be shelved.

E-MARKETING CHALLENGES

Despite the prevalence that the internet has gained in the last few years, one must not forget that it is still a relatively new technology (commercialized in 1993) and there are many hurdles to overcome, especially for owner-managers

Creating websites and other social media sites is simply not enough if they have static profiles and are being used merely as broadcast channels. The power of the online tools can only be leveraged if entrepreneurs regularly interact and communicate with their customers through meaningful content. It is all about generating leads, converting leads into customers and customers into brand loyalists and advocates.

Internet usage varies across countries and cultures in terms of the levels of access and usage. The use of the internet by SMEs opens doors and provides access to a wider market. Small firms are devoid of heavy market research budgets that enable them to investigate and understand local cultures in the global markets. This creates a great challenge for SMEs as they may have access to these markets but not an understanding of the factors that effect the business environment.

There is evidence that marketing in small firms is characterized by limited resources and lack of specialist expertise. Though using technology in the context of marketing is not heavy on the entrepreneurial pocket, it still calls for some level of financial resource allocation and competent personnel who have the expertise in 'understanding and using' the digital tools.

The internet's interactive nature means that applications, enquiries, orders, complaints and all other forms of communication are all generated in real time, 24 hours a day, 7 days a week. This poses a major challenge for small businesses as it calls for a major commitment on behalf of the owner-manager in terms of time and effort. There is a real cost in terms of the people-hours spent fostering and maintaining social conversations.

Communicating with customers on a regular basis has it own set of hazards because it exposes the business and owner-managers have to make sure that they are not saying something that is offensive, rude or incorrect. The other side of the coin is that entrepreneurs need to understand that the internet makes the business open and transparent and there will be times when consumers say things that could be damaging to the brand. At times like this, it will be important to take the feedback on board and, more importantly, to take appropriate and immediate action so that your customers see that you care.

BUZZ IN YOUR GROUP

Imagine you run your own online business and a customer has had a negative experience with one of your products and decides to blog about it online. Because the e-blog that they chose is very popular, the negative comments they posted get a higher ranking than your own website from a search for your company. That's surely unfair! How will you respond so that this negative posting does not ruin your brand image?

Small businesses often neglect an integrated approach to social media strategy because of the perception that social media is easy and cheap to use. There is also an inherent risk associated with small businesses and *scalability*. SMEs may be able to manage small-scale operations because of the small numbers involved but will they be able to sustain the expansion that the internet may bring in terms of large-scale operations? Like everything else, the buck stops with the owner-manager – the success of the online entrepreneurial marketing activity will depend on the entrepreneur's IT competence and entrepreneurial flair to proactively use the online platform in building extensive networks of wide and varied key contacts. It will also depend on his or her ability to steer the business in the right direction and manage growth with efficiency.

'While some entrepreneurs say that they have found early indicators that their social media efforts are paying off, there are others that are not so sure and believe that the hype right now exceeds the reality' (Needleman, 2010). If applied correctly, the use of technology in marketing can most definitely bring success to a small firm. It presents an entrepreneurial organization with the prospect of differentiation, thus enabling it to compete in the crowded marketplace.

AN INTERNET MARKETING CHECKLIST FOR ENTREPRENEURS
- Do not make consumers feel that they are receiving unsolicited communications from you. Provide consumers with an opt-in option where they grant permission to receive relevant marketing material.
- Content is crucial. Use the internet to create innovative and smarter marketing messages that are client-centric, thereby ensuring that the engagement with the consumer reaches far and deep.
- Build relationships that are based on trust and transparency. Once you have earned your consumers' trust, you need to make sure that you sustain it.
- Integrate e-marketing with other communication tools and operations systems.
- Have a strategic rather than *ad hoc* approach to internet marketing. In other words, do not engage with the e-tools for the sake of it but only if it is right for your business and your target consumers.

SUMMARY

Marketing in the context of SMEs has always been a contentious issue and a problematic area. It is documented in literature that the widely prevalent principles of marketing are based on large firms. Entrepreneurial marketing function differs from that of large firms in that it is considered to be more intuitive and *ad hoc*, revolving around networking, interaction and relationship building. Traditional marketing tools have always been beyond the access of a small firm's marketing budget. The last few years have witnessed the increasing use of the internet for e-commerce and a drastic change in the way people seek information and evaluate and purchase products and services. The advent of the internet has provided small businesses with an opportunity to augment their marketing function and access a wider population more quickly – with limited stress on finances. Internet marketing acts as a medium for entrepreneurs to transfer their skills of communication and networking onto an online platform and employ a range of e-tools that enable two-way communication and interaction between the SME and its consumers. It is, however, essential that owner-managers subscribe to these e-tools with caution and think strategically in terms of planning, enacting and analysing their e-marketing campaigns.

GROUP ACTIVITIES

Marketing debate

The internet enables a small business to advertise via banners, practise public relations by publishing articles and e-newsletters and sponsor live broadcasts and webinars. One could argue that traditional media have now become obsolete. On the other hand, some believe that for internet marketing to be successful there is still a need for it to be integrated with traditional media such as print, TV, radio, catalogues and direct mail. What do you think?

Marketing research

Form a small group and review the online promotional sites (brand webpages, Facebook pages, Twitter pages, blogs, etc.) of five small businesses of your choice. Analyse their promotional methods and make a list of the five best and most viable online methods for promoting and publicizing the SMEs. Justify your answers.

REVIEW QUESTIONS

1. How is internet market evolving and what are the implications to small businesses?

2. Discuss how online marketing tools vary from traditional media. Is one better than the other?

3. What do the terms 'viral marketing' and 'permission marketing' mean?

4. Discuss the various types of online tools available to owner-managers and evaluate them in terms of costs and performance.

5. Evaluate how search engine marketing may be beneficial to small businesses.

6. How can an entrepreneur leverage the use of mobile technology in his or her marketing plan?

7. What is social media marketing? How can entrepreneurs use social media to build and extend their personal contact networks?

8. Discuss some of challenges that the new media pose to the small business owner.

CASE STUDY 12: PLANET FRUGI – A PLANET FOR HAPPY CLOTHES, HAPPY CHILDREN AND HAPPY ADULTS

A long, long time ago on a planet far away there lived two concerned people called Lucy and Kurt Jewson. Being concerned for the planet, they decided to put their firstborn son in washable nappies for environmental reasons. They thought that they were taking another step along the long road called 'doing your bit'. And they were . . . but there was a snag. They were struggling to find clothing that would go over these cloth nappies. So, one day, being the entrepreneurial type, it occurred to Lucy that they could design their own range of baby clothes to fit over cloth nappies; the rest, as they say, was history!

Lucy says, 'We wouldn't have a company if it wasn't for the Internet.' The internet enabled her to do a lot of market research, from the comfort of her home, and she quickly discovered that there was no one making such specialized products and servicing this need. She realized this gap in the market to be a huge opportunity because cloth nappies are massively on the increase due to changing attitudes.

Cut4Cloth went 'live' on 1 June 2004 and the business thrived, selling beautiful baby clothes to fit over cloth nappies. As the business grew, they introduced newer product lines like baby essentials, baby accessories, clothing for 2- to 6-year-olds and maternity wear. The name Cut4Cloth became quite limiting considering the range of products on offer and that was how Planet Frugi came about – a planet where clothes are stylish but are also 100% organic, ethical and green!

Frugi's cotton comes from a certified fair trade supplier and the factory where the clothes are made is a certified fair trade factory as well. They give away 1 per cent of their turnover to charities and good causes through a scheme called '1% for the Planet'.

As an SME, Frugi has always relied extensively on the internet for spreading the word about their brand. Web 2.0 technology has massively helped improve Frugi's business in many ways. The attractive and colourful website (www.welovefrugi.com) provides a quick snapshot of what the core values of the company are. People can not only visit the website, click around to various pages and buy products but also they can find out about the ethics of the company, what the company is doing and where it hopes to go in the future.

Two-way communication with customers on the website has been crucial on many levels. It has allowed Frugi to express themselves to their customers and have a direct conversation with them. Customers thus feel part of the brand and as if they're helping to steer the brand, which they actually are.

Frugi pick 12 core customers, or Frugi Crusaders, to review their new designs and act as a sounding board for new ideas every season. Customers apply to be Crusaders, answering questions such as, 'What three words would best describe Frugi?', 'What is your favourite garment ever and why?' and 'Which should come first, jam or clotted cream on a scone in a cream tea?' These questions provide vital insights into their customers' lives, ethics, sense of humour and purchasing preferences. Frugi have a unique design process – when a new product is conceptualized, it is sent out to the Crusaders, who feed back and help Frugi to implement design changes.

The Frugi blog helps to generate a dialogue with Frugi's customers. Customers can put up both positive and negative responses. A Crusader posted a one-off negative comment on the blog recently, saying that she was unhappy with a particular product.

Lucy immediately responded to this by acknowledging the problem and assuring the cutomer that the design will be rectified. Anybody that looks at that particular sort of conversation on the blog will see the company as *honest* and *responsive*.

Crusaders also post reviews of products on the blog that are sent out by the design team – these are unedited as they understand that third-party reinforcement of their products is much more powerful than any other form of advertising. Mums trust other mums.

Frugi also blog about completely unrelated things – such as Fran and Lucy (employees) coming to work by tractor to Frugi when the snow struck, or Kurt's love of pasties. This increases the brand depth as consumers feel like they really 'know' the team and what is behind the company. It's almost akin to watching a soap opera! They also blog about other things they have found that they like, which can be very useful from a partnership marketing point of view. The key is that it has to be honest and not contrived. Customers would see through that very quickly!

Being a small company, finances are fairly limited in terms of marketing. Frugi have found that social networking sites like Facebook and Twitter create a buzz about the brand and the products. Customers review the clothes and then post what they think about them and that's really important. With the RSS feeds that come into the sites, there is a buzz growing outwards all the time, because people think, 'Oh, they've just joined the Frugi Facebook page. What's that?' Reviews and comments on social networking sites by real people have generated a lot of buzz and positive word-of-mouth for Frugi.

Customers who join the Frugi fan page on Facebook get to hear about promotions first and they even have their own special promotions that reward them just for being part of the Frugi fanbase. They also love putting their own photos of their children in Frugi clothing up on the Facebook page – which again works as third-party endorsement.

Frugi also use this forum to ask bigger questions like:

Do you think we should pay 1.9% of turnover to use a Fair Trade license mark when we already use Fair Trade cotton and thus pay the Fair Trade premium to the farmers? Our cotton comes with the FT mark, but if we want to use the logo on our clothing, we have to pay this huge fee that is purely a marketing charge. If we did this we would have to stop contributing directly to our 2 environmental charities we have supported for the last 5 years, through 1% for the planet.

Being a small company and barely profitable, this was a real conundrum for Frugi as they felt that it was a marketing charge versus real solid help to charities. (Bear in mind they also pay for organic certification too.) Frugi opened this issue up to its customers and let them decide via a Facebook debate. There was an overwhelming response from customers, who backed them with their decision to continue with the '1% for the Planet' scheme. For Frugi it was all about being transparent in its decisions, unlike a lot of other 'greenwash' companies.

Kurt tweets a lot about Frugi as well, and they have found that some really top-quality employees have been recruited because they have been watching out for Frugi's tweets. They have grown to like the brand and have become aware of vacancies via this channel.

From a business point of view, search engine optimization (SEO) has been really beneficial for Frugi. SEO allows them to get on the first page in the natural listings on a search engine. Before they rebranded to Frugi, the Cut4Cloth site had a fantastic ranking. It was No. 1 for organic baby clothes, so they linked the Cut4Cloth site with the Frugi site, thereby getting lots of connections to the Frugi site.

Web 2.0 technology is a really important part of Frugi's future as it allows them to transparently show all the workings of the company and promote brand values that are important to them. At the end of the day, that has a big effect on the bottom line.

Lucy was recently awarded the Entrepreneur of the Year award at the 2008 Cornwall and Devon Business Challenge Awards. Accepting the award, she said:

> We're pretty excited at being given this award as it reminds us how important it is to us to stay in touch with our customers – through Facebook, our blog, our e-newsletters and our crusaders, we're trying hard to keep in contact with you all and listen to all your feedback and ideas. It's all good stuff that helps us grow and improve. So, thanks to you all – we couldn't have got this award without you!

Sources: www.welovefrugi.com and www.businesslink.gov.uk

Reproduced with permission from Lucy Jewson, co-founder of Frugi.

CASE QUESTIONS

1. Identify who the target market is for Frugi. What is the company's segmentation, targeting and positioning strategy?
2. In comparison with 'traditional' advertising media, evaluate the opportunities that 'newer' media tools present to small businesses like Frugi.
3. Feedback on social networking sites by 'real' customers has generated a lot of buzz and positive word-of-mouth for Frugi. Evaluate the purpose of appointing Frugi Crusaders. What role do they play?
4. What kind of online relationships and networks are Lucy and Kurt building and how are these beneficial in the marketing context?
5. Is it OK for a company like Frugi to rely only on their online promotional methods or should they consider other forms of communication like advertising, exhibitions, sponsorship? What are the implications of adopting alternative methods of communication?

BIBLIOGRAPHY

BBC Online (2010). Social bookmarking links. [Online] Available at: http://news.bbc.co.uk/1/hi/business/8498163.stm (accessed 11 March 2010).

Bickerton, P., Bickerton, M. and Pardesi, U. (2000). *Cybermarketing: How to Use the Superhighway to Market Your Products and Services.* 2nd edn. Oxford: Butterworth-Heinemann.

British Market Research Bureau (BMRB) (2008). Consumer Confidence Monitor. [Online] Available at: www.bmrb.co.uk (accessed 18 March 2010).

British Telecommunications (2009). *The Voice of Small Business Report.* Available at: www.insight.bt.com/reports/The-Voice-of-small-business-2009 (accessed 14 January 2010).

Business Link (2007). Online networking. [Online] Available at: www.businesslink.gov.uk (accessed 19 March 2010).

Carson, D. (1985). The evolution of marketing in small firms. *European Journal of Marketing*. Vol. 19(5), pp. 7–16.

Carson, D., Cromie, S., McGowan, P. and Hill, J. (1995). *Marketing and Entrepreneurship in SMEs: An Innovative Approach*. Harlow: Prentice Hall.

Chaffey, D., Mayer, R., Johnston, K. and Ellis-Chadwick, F. (2003). *Internet Marketing: Strategy, Implementation and Practice*. Harlow: Financial Times/Prentice Hall.

Department for Culture, Media and Sport and Department for Business, Innovation and Skills (DCMS & BIS) (2009). *Digital Britain: Final Report*. [Online] Available at: http://image.guardian.co.uk/sys-files/Media/documents/2009/06/16/BERR-DigitalBritain.pdf (accessed 19 March 2010).

Direct Marketing Association (DMA) (2009). Marketing Gap Analysis. [Online] Available at: www.dma.org.uk

Downie, G. (2003). Internet marketing and SMEs. *Management Services*. Vol. 47 (7), pp. 8–11.

Forrester (2007). UK eCommerce forecast 2006–2011. [Online] Available at: www.forrester.com/rb/Research/uk_ecommerce_forecast_2006_to_2011/q/id/39977/t/2 (accessed 1 November 2010).

Gallagher, D. and Gilmore, A. (2004). The stages theory of SME internationalisation: A Northern Ireland case study. *International Journal of Management Cases*. Vol. 7(1), pp. 13–23.

Godin, S. (1999). *Turning Strangers into Friends and Friends into Customers*. New York: Simon & Schuster.

Hill, J. and Wright, L. T. (2000). Defining the scope of entrepreneurial marketing: A qualitative approach. *Journal of Enterprising Culture*. Vol. 8(1), pp. 23–46.

Hubspot (n.d.). *Internet Marketing Whitepaper: 5 Tips to Turn Your Website into a Marketing Machine*. [Online] Available at: www.hubspot.com

Internet Advertising Bureau (IAB) (2008). Online adspend fact sheets. [Online] Available at: www.iab.net (accessed 31 March 2010).

IAB (2009), Annual online adspend report. Available at www.iab.net (accessed 31 March 2010).

Internet World Stats (2009). Internet usage in Europe. [Online] Available at: www.internetworldstats.com

Liodice, B. (2010). 10 events that transformed marketing. *Advertising Age*, 18 January, Vol. 81(3).

MarketingSherpa (2005). *Google Eye Tracking Study: How Searchers See and Click on Google Search Results*. Enquiro Search Solutions.

Needleman, S. E. (2010). Entrepreneurs question value of social media: Marketing via Facebook, Twitter yields results for some, others say it's overrated; 'Hype right now exceeds the reality'. *Wall Street Journal*, 16 March. [Online] Available at: www.wallstreetjournal.com

Nielson (2009). Nielson online global consumer survey, July. [Online] Available at: http://blog.nielsen.com/nielsenwire/consumer/global-advertising-consumers-trust-real-friends-and-virtual-strangers-the-most (accessed 13 January 2010).

Ofcom (2006). SME engagement with digital communications services. September. [Online] Available at: www.ofcom.org.uk (accessed February 2010).

Ofcom (2009a). Communications market UK, October. [Online] Available at: www.ofcom.org.uk (accessed February 2010).

Ofcom (2009b). UK adults' media literacy, October. [Online] Available at: www.ofcom.org.uk (accessed February 2010).

Ofcom (2009c). The consumer experience. December. [Online] Available at: www.ofcom.org.uk (accessed February 2010).

Office for National Statistics (ONS) (2006). Use of the internet. Omnibus survey. [Online] Available at: www.statistics.gov.uk (accessed February 2010).

ONS (2009). Use of the internet. Omnibus survey. [Online] Available at: www.statistics.gov.uk

Power, T. (2009). *yourBusinessChannel*, 26 June. [Online] Available at: www.yourbusinesschannel.com/show/ideas/1005/is-your-business-culture-open-random-and-supportive-new-business-advice-from-thomas-power (accessed 8 April 2010).

Qualman, E. (2009). Statistics show social media is bigger than you think. [Online] Available at: http://socialnomics.net/2009/08/11/statistics-show-social-media-is-bigger-than-you-think (accessed 4 April 2010).

Quinton, S. and Harridge-March, S. (2006). The interaction of technology in entrepreneurial marketing: An illustrative case from a wine merchant. *Strategic Change*. Vol. 15(2), pp. 85–102.

Small Business Research Trust (SBRT) (2005). *Quarterly Survey of Small Business in the UK*. Small Business Research Trust.

Smith, P.R. and Chaffey, D. (2005). *E-Marketing Excellence: At the Heart of EBusiness*. 2nd edn. Oxford: Butterworth-Heinemann.

Sultan, F. and Rohm, A. (2005). The coming era of brand in hand marketing. *MIT Sloan Management Review*. Vol. 47(1), pp. 83–90.

Thome, V. (2009). How can mobile be employed most effectively in marketing? *Admap Magazine*. December. [Online] Available at: www.warc.com (accessed 17 March 2010).

UK Online Measurement (UKOM) (2009). The online media landscape. [Online] Available at: www. ukom.uk.net (accessed 3 February 2010).

Universal McCann (2008). *Universal McCann International Social Media Research*, March. [Online] Available at: www.universalmccann.com/global/knowledge (accessed 12 February 2010).

YouGov (2006). Internet Usage in the UK. [Online] Available at: www.today.yougov.co.uk (accessed 27 January 2010).

Zuckerberg, M. (2010). *The Facebook Blog*, July 2010. [Online] Available at: http://blog.facebook.com/ blog.php?poststart=10 (accessed 26 July 2010).

FURTHER READING

Chaffey, D. (2008). Effective digital marketing techniques for the SME: E-Business 2008 Conference. The National B2B Centre. 25 September. [Online] Available at: www.davechaffey.com/static/SME-Internet-Marketing.ppt (accessed 1 November 2010).

Chaffey, D., Mayer, R., Johnston, K. and Ellis-Chadwick, F. (2003). *Internet Marketing: Strategy, Implementation and Practice*. Harlow: Financial Times/Prentice Hall.

McDonald, M. and Wilson, H. (1999) *E-Marketing: Improving Marketing Effectiveness in a Digital World*. Harlow: Financial Times/Prentice Hall.

Pelsmacker, P. D., Geuens, M. and Bergh, J. V. (2010). *Marketing Communications: A European Perspective*. 4th edn. Harlow: Financial Times/Prentice Hall.

USEFUL LINKS

Business Link (www.businesslink.gov.uk)
eMarketer (www.emarketer.com)
Interactive Advertising Bureau (www.iab.net)
Small Business UK (www.smallbusiness.co.uk)
Department for Business, Innovation and Skills (www.bis.gov.uk)

Chapter 13

Growing market strengths
Management of innovations in high-growth SMEs

Michael Lewrick, Maktoba Omar and Robert Williams

> ### LEARNING OBJECTIVES
>
> *After reading this chapter, you will be able to:*
> - understand innovation in relation to SMEs
> - explore the methods of innovation in high-growth SMEs
> - understand the dynamics of innovation capabilities
> - understand the relationships among trigger, driver and supporter for innovation and business success
> - recognize stages of innovation development.

INTRODUCTION

The management of innovation in growing companies becomes essential to sustain business success and innovativeness. This contribution is a short excerpt of a study on the changes of innovation capabilities and provides a structured introduction to an innovation model to predict company success and potential. In addition, two innovation management audits (IMAs) are described, which are used to capture information needed to run the Innovativeness, Capabilities and Potential model (ICP). The underlying research focused on the review of the key theories in understanding the dynamics of innovation capabilities. Relationships among trigger, driver and supporter for innovation and business success have been analysed and applied in a validated innovation model. The ICP model has found application in measuring and developing regional innovation clusters as well as developing innovation strategy and initiatives in high-technology SMEs. The adoption and change of innovation capabilities has become of paramount importance for companies to survive, grow and succeed as a strong relationship exists between market performance and innovative products and services. Dramatic change and innovation dynamics are best observed in growing companies – especially in the transformation from a start-up phase to a more mature phase.

Small and large enterprises are affected by the increased turbulence in our business environment. Unexpected disruptive market changes or the appearances of new technologies require adaptation. Companies have to manage both continuous incremental changes and radical change. Some companies apply their innovation to large systems while others stick to incremental product and service improvements. When exploring the changes in managing innovations, various external and internal influencing factors and capabilities are of interest. Business literature offers numerous frameworks and models to manage mainly incremental product and service innovations. The discussion about dynamic capabilities was the first attempt to create holistic models, but there was still conceptual ambiguity and no consideration of operational practice. Hence, there is currently no single answer to the question of how to best manage innovation

As an introduction to the topic the history of innovation management is briefly reviewed and some of the common models and frameworks are outlined. The importance of the applied innovation management audit as a research instrument is emphasized and then the ICP model for analysing the success probability of start-ups is introduced. Finally, some outcomes will be described as examples of the ICP's potential contribution to theory and operational practice.

INNOVATION MANAGEMENT TODAY

Recent decades have been driven by globalization. We have witnessed the transformation from an industrial society to a service-, information- and knowledge-based society, and the development from central, hierarchial organizational structures towards decentralized and connected organizational structures (Hopfenbeck *et al.*, 2001). As a result enterprises have to respond dynamically and change their innovation style continually to survive in such an environment. As businesses grow in revenue, size and functional complexity it becomes essential to know which kind of innovation strategy and applied framework will lead to success. The question is not whether or not to innovate, but rather what are the influencing factors and capabilities needed during innovation change? Is it the customer, the social network, R&D, experience, organization learning or merely knowledge applied at the right time and place?

DEFINITION OF INNOVATION

The term innovation derives from the Latin term *innovare* (to make something new). Most definitions of innovation highlight the exploration and exploitation of new knowledge. The OECD (2005, p. 46) defines innovation 'as the implementation of a new or significantly improved product (good or service), or process, a new marketing method, or a new organisational method in business practices, workplace organisation or external relations'. Invention is the initial step in a long process of bringing a good idea to widespread and effective use.

Innovation is an important factor for the OECD countries to achieve higher innovative capacity and greater competitiveness. As many studies note, innovation is linked to technological development and drives structural change, which leads to high productivity and growth in GDP. Every enterprise has a critical role to play in this process, through introducing new innovations to the market, generating employment and spurring competition with existing firms. The indicators of economic success are firm entry and exit (turnover), and firm survival and growth.

INNOVATION MANAGEMENT MODELS

Innovation management models derive from technology-push and market-pull theories about the linkages among actors in the market, technology networks, knowledge management and social networks. Different models have evolved over time to represent the distinct causes or motivators of innovation. The linear or 'stage gate' models are set up in a step-wise manner and seem to be useful for incremental innovation. Such models are therefore deficient in coping with flexibility, rapid prototyping and top management support in the early stages. The stage-gate innovation process for products is described below:

Stage 0: Idea generation/collection
↓
Gate 1: Idea Screening (yes/no) Stage 1: Scoping
↓
Gate 2: Second Screening (yes/no) Stage 2: Build Business Case
↓
Gate 3: Go to Development (yes/no) Stage 3: Development
↓
Gate 4: Go to Testing (yes/no) Stage 4: Testing and Validation
↓
Gate 5: Go to Launch (yes/no) Stage 5: Launch

Other models depict innovation as an iterative process. 'Loop' models try to achieve their objectives mainly by trial and error. Dynamic models combine the stage-gate process with various loops and tangents to achieve the desired outcome. Figure 13.1 depicts an example of how innovation capabilities are interlinked, with the idea and innovation process following loops to transform ideas into innovations. The lowest level is the innovation strategy, which drives from the corporate and functional strategy of a company. The innovation capabilities function as trigger, driver or supporter to execute and implement the innovation strategy. These capabilties are essential to generate, develop and market ideas. The idea and innovation process provides a structured framework to bring ideas to market success. Successful

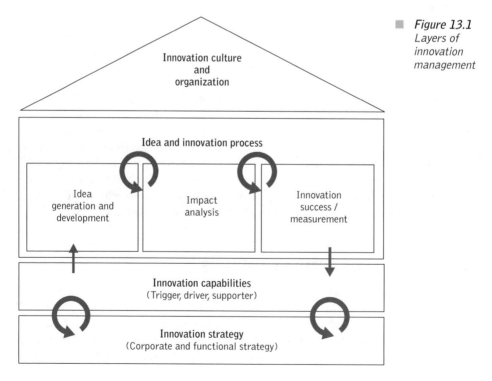

■ Figure 13.1
Layers of innovation management

companies apply the appropriate capabilities inside and outside of the company, develop structure in processes and procedures and create an innovation culture.

Some models integrate the prerequisite factors within the innovation process, while others merely list the external factors that must be present before innovation is able to take off. The more systematic models have the objective of integrating and building more flexibility into current product/service areas, and search for new opportunities. Social network theory by contrast realizes that organizational performance relates to knowledge sharing and the established trust relationships.

A review of the literature reveals various approaches towards innovation management. Research ranges from multidimensional to unidimensional typologies which result in the creation of multidimensional and unidimensional scales and validations. Generally speaking, the research attempts to answer the following questions:

a. **What is changed?** There is a focus on the types of innovation, namely product/service, process, organization, market innovation, administrative or technical.
b. **What is the degree of novelty?**[1] There are two kinds of change at opposite ends of the spectrum: incremental or continuous change and discontinuous or radical change.

Most research focuses on a single sector, an R&D project or merely one typology, e.g. product innovations. With regard to the organizational variables of innovation, outcomes are not so clear. A good example of this discrepancy is the correlation between the age of a company and its innovativeness – in some cases age is positively related to innovation (Sorensen and Stuart, 2000), while the opposite can also be found (Boeker, 1997). The same conflicting results can be seen in the influence of diversification (Ahuja and Lampert, 2001), centralization (Cardinal, 2001), size of the organization (Koberg *et al.*, 2003), and resource levels/resource-based views of innovation. The resource-based view is another good example of the lack of consistency in the literature as there is a debate about the relevance of this theory, which has been the basis for creating 'dynamic capabilities'. These are related to the influencing factors in the firm's environment (Eisenhardt and Martin, 2000). While some scholars see dynamic capabilities as the key success factor for competitive advantage, others argue that such capabilities do not exist (Winter, 2003). Others still focus on the tenure level of management without finding a clear correlation to innovativeness (Kimberly and Evanisko, 1981; Meyer and Goes, 1988; Rao and Drazin, 2002).

On the other hand, the research is in general agreement in some areas. For example, it is universally accepted that external factors, such as a dynamic environment, force companies to innovate and adapt (Meyer and Goes, 1988; Nohari and Gulati, 1996). In such a dynamic environment firms take more risks and innovate more (Kahneman and Tversky, 1979). The strong influence and correlation of individuals to the innovation process has been addressed by many scholars (Rao and Drazin, 2002; Keister, 2002; Sivadas and Dwyer, 2000). Other scholars have analysed the influence of the integrated product development process on innovation (Gerwin and Barrowman, 2002) or focused solely on the development of new products (Brown and Eisenhardt, 1995; Krishnan and Ulrich, 2001), or models investigating the relationships between factors involved in the adoption of high technology (Hamann *et al.*, 2007). The list could be expanded endlessly, comparing the different dimensions tested with the various outcomes. Most of the empirical studies on innovation are mainly focused on specific industries or on a specific project analysed over the time perspective. Holistic cross-sector analysis has not generally been adopted by researchers to identify changes in innovation styles. In addition, studies on the transition process from the start-up phase to a more mature phase of business cannot be found in this connection at all.

IMPORTANCE OF INNOVATION FOR SMES

Changing the innovation capabilities of an SME is vital for the business to survive, grow and succeed. We have observed and experienced many start-ups with enormous potential because of breakthrough services/products in an early stage but without the ability to come up with radical innovations a second or third time. However, some companies are able to walk the high wire of radical innovations over and over again, by keeping balance and achieving good performance. Others apply a different innovation strategy and framework by being innovative and selling the innovation to larger, more established companies, recognizing their lack of capabilities to market the invention by themselves. In contrast, some ventures continually tweak their 'standard programme' because of fear, lack of finance, wrong management, calm markets or other factors. The common innovation models are often too narrow for SMEs as most of them are designed for incremental product innovations.

INNOVATION MANAGEMENT SYSTEMS IN SMES

Analysis of the transition process in growing companies from a start-up to more mature status seeks to first explore the settings of the entrepreneur. Schumpeter (1934) defines the entrepreneur as an innovator, implementing change within markets by carrying out new combinations. The new combinations are seen in different ways, (1) the introduction of a new good or quality thereof, (2) the introduction of a new method of production, (3) the opening of a new market, (4) the conquest of a new source of supply of new materials or parts, (5) the carrying out of the new organization of any industry. Schumpeter associated entrepreneurship with innovation applied to a wide business context. As a result, the entrepreneur shifts the market away from equilibrium. His definition also highlights the combination of various resources. However, Schumpeter does not consider the managers of established entrepreneurial businesses. Penrose (1963, p. 7) agrees with Schumpeter and comments that 'managerial capacities are different from entrepreneurial capacities'. He characterizes entrepreneurial activity as the activity of identifying opportunities within the economic system. Consequently, innovation capabilities and innovation style change as businesses grow and a broader outlook becomes necessary. However, to come up with radical innovations, entrepreneurial characteristics – which mainly consist of behaviours, personal attributes and skills – must somehow exist in innovative mature companies. Gibb (2000, p. 24) summarizes such behaviour as:

(a) opportunity seeking and grasping;
(b) taking the initiatives to make things happen;
(c) solving problems creatively;
(d) managing autonomously;
(e) taking responsibility for, and ownership of, things;
(f) seeing things through;,
(g) networking effectively to manage interdependence;
(h) putting things together creatively; and
(i) using judgement to take calculated risks.

The decisive question is this: What causes radical innovation and growth? Many scholars favour the example in Verloop (2004, p. 69) which aims to provide a simple answer without outlining in detail what is essential to be successful:

innovation = invention + entrepreneurship
innovation culture = innovation infrastructure + good management

INDIVIDUALITIES

In addition to the individualities of the entrepreneur, he/she needs strength to influence growth and to undergo strategic decisions. The skills needed to start a business successfully are often not the same as the skills needed to manage a growing business (Di-Masi, 2006).

INNOVATION CAPABILITIES

The entrepreneur must change the innovation capabilities and innovation style of a business as it develops and grows. In many cases he/she is not able to make the transition. Possible causes for such ineffectiveness are lack of management tenure and experience, lack of managerial education or a lack in leadership capabilities. To manage the transition, time-honoured change management approaches (e.g. the three-stage change model of unfreezing–change–refreezing) are not adequate in turbulent, flexible and uncertain organizational and environmental conditions (Orlikowski and Hofman, 1997). Hence, the entrepreneur in transition is challenged to manage the *anticipated* changes (changes planned ahead of time and occur as intended) and *emergent* changes (changes that arise unexpectedly out of new opportunities, local innovations and which are originally not intended) (Mintzberg, 1987). The complexity of the system and influencing factors increases over the time perspective. Other factors might become the drivers for change, such as economic policies, social norms, ties and networks.

SOCIAL NETWORK THEORY

Another example to consider involves elements of the social network theory. A strong relationship might exist between the inter-organizational network and innovativeness. Some scholars state that start-ups particularly benefit from such networks (Baum *et al.*, 2000; Shan *et al.*, 1994; Stuart, 2000). A rich technical, productive and social relationship in an alliance network fosters experimentation and collective learning (Van Aken and Weggeman, 1998). Similarly, the organizational network utilizes a strong correlation and positive impact between collaborative activities and companies' capabilities to be innovative (Hagedoorn, 2002). However, increased functional complexity and a shift in risk aversion (e.g. establishment of a CFO) might cause the opposite and hamper radical innovations.

KNOWLEDGE

Knowledge is also a central element of innovativeness. Knowledge about customers, competitors, suppliers, processes and so forth provides the information and insight to manage uncertainty and risk. Diverse skills and continual learning are paramount for knowledge gathering and knowledge transfer. Davenport (1998, p. 7) condenses and describes knowledge as a 'fluid mix of framed experience, values, contextual information and insight'. Again, functional complexity and size of firm might be constraints on knowledge transfer and sharing. The two IMAs below have been structured around the influence of knowledge, social networks and other elements.

GROUP ACTIVITY

As mentioned earlier, the two IMAs developed from a broad literature exploration and were used to generate data to build a more meaningful and defensible pattern for changes in innovation styles. From this the following research questions have been formulated:

1. What are the influencing factors and capabilities that changes in innovation capabilities and styles produce?
2. How do firms change their innovations capabilities over the time perspective?
3. Is it possible to identify a general pattern of when and how changes in innovation capabilities occur?

Certainly many more sub-problems exist but it is more practicable to address these from the nucleus of the research via the research instruments (Start-up IMA and Mature IMA). In this stage it is necessary to provide an overview of the research methodology, including the selection of the research location and platform, research process and framework, experimental design, limitations and a summary of the hypotheses.

Innovation capabilities depend on various factors and antecedents – a defined pattern helps to understand how to manage innovation best.

CHANGE INNOVATION CAPABILITIES

To explore change innovation capabilities two major research criteria need to be satisfied. First, a location with a high number of technology-driven start-ups as well as numerous mature companies needs to be identified. Second, there needs to be a common platform on which all of the companies were founded.

These criteria are evident in the Munich region, which runs the Munich Business Plan Competition. The Munich region offers outstanding innovative companies who are active in the IT, biotech, aerospace, software, electronic components and other sectors. Moreover, Munich is one of the world's five most interesting high-tech locations alongside Silicon Valley, Boston, Tel Aviv and Austin. A unitary platform is enabled by utilizing the Munich Business Plan Competition. Since 1996, this competition has produced over 400 companies. It is derived from the MIT (Massachusetts Institute of Technology) idea of establishing a platform for universities, entrepreneurs and venture capitalists to set-up innovative companies to foster growth in the region. Only the combination of a common platform with the same formal prerequisites in a high-tech region allows such an exploration of changes in innovation styles.

RESEARCH PROCESS FRAMEWORK AND INSTRUMENT

The development of the two IMAs (Start-up IMA and Mature IMA) was based on a literature review to identify the critical factors and constraints with regard to innovativeness. Moreover, the relevant literature on knowledge management, entrepreneurship and social networks has been reviewed extensively. Additional elements such as context, content and organizational behaviour were incorporated in the IMAs to support the identification of the influencing factors for changes in innovation capabilities. Context is related to strategic decisions, performance objective and the ethical norms of innovations to generate a holistic understanding of risks, end-user context and the impact on society over time and space. Content is related to the technical, scientific and technological traits of innovations. It deals with the scope of work and the requirements of professional expertise and know-how to push innovations. Organizational behaviour is linked to the attitude of decision makers, power asymmetries and topics associated with corporate culture and the economic impacts of innovations.

The two IMAs were built on various capabilities and influencing factors, with over 52 questions each. To provide a rough overview of the context-dependent innovations which are influenced by antecedents, the elements of the IMA include the following: Basic Company Data and Characteristics, Product and Service Development (including Customer Orientation, Competitor Orientation, Market and Competitive Environment, and Diversification and Learning); Innovativeness (including the amount of incremental and radical innovations realized in the typologies: process, products, services administration, technical; incremental and radical innovation performance; resources for innovations); Innovation Capabilities (including Management and Knowledge); Social Networks (including organizational networks and inter-organizational networks) and Outcomes (e.g. utilization of measurement tools, management concepts, etc.).

Today's dynamic business environment makes it mandatory to combine different business resources to achieve innovation. It is usual to categorize business resources into Tangible (physical, financial), Intangible (technology, reputation, culture) and Human (skills/ know-how, capacity for communication and collaboration, motivation) (Gram, 2002). The IMAs explore incremental and radical innovations in processes, products, services, administrative and technical. Such an approach promises far-reaching insights to the entire spectrum of possible innovations. For each element the IMA asks for the number of innovations in a typical year to understand the effects of both incremental and radical innovation for each of the typologies.

At the end of each block of questions the Mature IMA asks about the past to understand how the company has changed the operational practice and affected their innovation style. In contrast, at the end of each block of questions the Start-up IMA asks about the future – how companies think they will be innovating in two years' time. Such an approach identifies various gaps between the present situation and the desired end, between the reality of mature companies and their original inspirations.

NEW ICP MODEL TO EVALUATE THE SUCCESS PROBABILITY OF START-UPS

The ICP model can be applied to evaluate start-up companies. The input data and knowledge is generated by utilizing the IMA as a central tool to obtain first-hand information from a new venture. Based on the outcomes, each question of the IMA is featured with importance factors leading to innovations and a performance level above average. In addition to a scorecard which shows the capabilities and potential (see Figure 13.2), the final result is a single diagram showing the success probability of the start-up.

The scorecard outlines some key capabilities for innovation and business succcess. The example in Figure 13.2 shows a company which is strong in utilizing the organizational

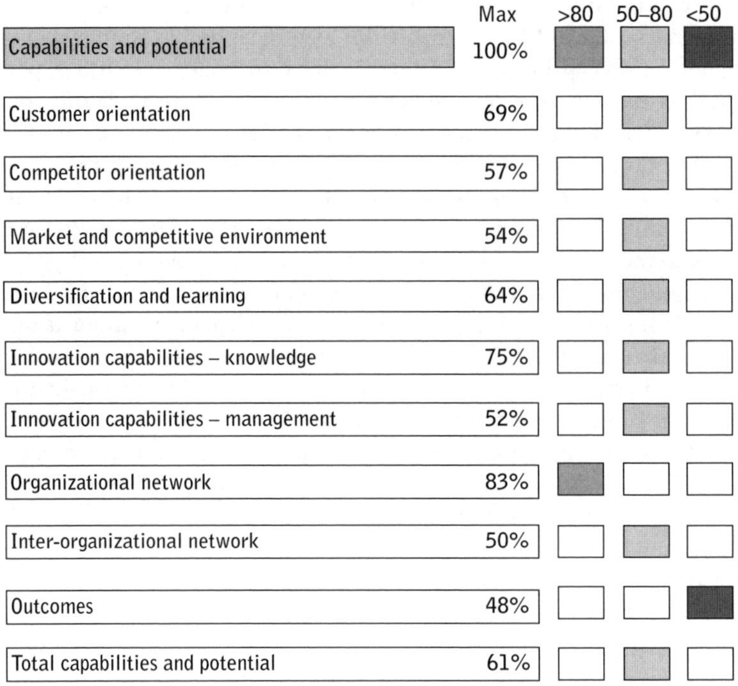

Capabilities and potential	Max 100%	>80	50–80	<50
Customer orientation	69%		▨	
Competitor orientation	57%		▨	
Market and competitive environment	54%		▨	
Diversification and learning	64%		▨	
Innovation capabilities – knowledge	75%		▨	
Innovation capabilities – management	52%		▨	
Organizational network	83%	▨		
Inter-organizational network	50%		▨	
Outcomes	48%			▨
Total capabilities and potential	61%		▨	

■ *Figure 13.2*
Scorecard
capabilities and
potential

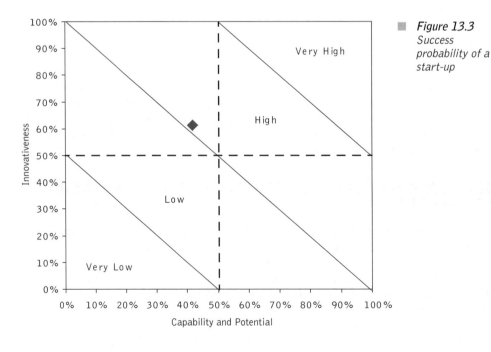

■ *Figure 13.3*
Success
probability of a
start-up

network. On the other hand, idea generation, impact analysis and innovation success are not strongly developed. Other capabilities seems to be average, with potential for improvement.

Figure 13.3 shows the success probability graph. Without outlining the complex calculations which lead to the success probability, the x-axis represents the Capabilities and Potential (explained above) and the y-axis represents the Innovativeness, which is derived from the total amount of innovations in all typologies and the innovation performance.

The statistical and qualitative validation of the operational model has proven the faithfulness of the ICP model. Model credibility is qualitatively validated by experts in the field, generating a faithful representation of the real world based on the perspective of the intended uses. The model finds application in both the evaluation of single companies and the analysis of companies within an innovation system or cluster. The model provides feedback to policy makers, entrepreneurs and venture capitalists to monitor initiatives, develop strong capabilities for innovation and business success, or benchmark against other companies.

The ICP model has been applied to improve innovation strategies and initiatives in various companies. It serves as a benchmark against companies in the same sector and provides support in assessing the maturity of different innovation capabilities leading to innovation success.

Economic benefits

Innovation and improvements in technology are generally recognized as the major underlying drivers of long-run economic growth. Aggregate growth is largely driven by dynamic changes in individual businesses. Every enterprise has a critical role to play in this process, through introducing new innovations to the market, generating employment and spurring competition with existing firms. The indicators of economic success are firm entry and exit (turnover) and firm survival and growth. Both elements are considered in the ICP model to evaluate the success probability and provide support to identify strengths and weaknesses in important capabilities. The holistic approach of the IMA includes important areas ranging from inter-organizational and organizational networks to management capabilities and skills, which have impact on growth and productivity through several mechanisms. Skills are critical to the effective use of physical capital (machinery and equipment) and can facilitate the absorption and generation of new ideas and innovations. In addition, networking and collaboration is recognized as a powerful driver for innovations. Commercially valuable innovations often do not arise in isolation, but develop out of collaboration between firms, universities, government research institutes and other players. The degrees to which such linkages exist influence the functioning of the innovation system in an entire economy.

Environmental benefits

In business, innovation is worthwhile only if it translates into new goods, services, or processes that enhance productivity and competitiveness. It is the dynamic process of innovation and productivity improvement at the firm level that drives aggregate productivity and economic growth. Innovative firms tend to exhibit the managerial and entrepreneurial skills that enhance productivity, are more profitable and have a greater propensity to export.

As mentioned earlier, aggregate productivity growth is ultimately driven by dynamic changes occurring at the level of firms. Entrepreneurial activity in the form of firm entry and exit plays an important role in this process. As well as contributing to aggregate productivity growth directly, the entry of new firms may increase competition and spur existing firms to innovate and invest in ways that raise their own productivity. Firm entry can also make an important contribution to job creation, thus raising aggregate labour utilization that is beneficial to the entire society. For firm entry and exit to have a noticeable impact on aggregate productivity, new firms need to not only enter the market but also survive and grow. The impact of firm dynamics on productivity is premised on new, more productive firms entering the market and taking market share away from less productive, exiting firms. Available resources from venture capitalists (VCs), business angels, investors and banks are allocated to the successful companies, leading to a more efficient allocation of resources and faster economic growth. The ICP model is designed as a powerful tool for the venture capital market. VCs provide an important source of funding for innovative ideas and are interested in start-ups with a high success probability. Providers of venture capital (usually specialized financial firms acting as intermediaries between primary sources of finance and firms) are willing to assume the higher risks inherent in such investments on account of the prospect of obtaining above average returns. Thus, venture capital has the potential to make an important contribution to nurturing the new firms that can make a significant contribution to job creation, productivity, international competitiveness and economic growth.

CONCLUSIONS

The concept of innovation has evolved significantly over the last few decades. This chapter has given a brief introduction to exciting new research investigating the change of innovation capabilities in growing companies.

A major contribution of this study is the pioneering of an extensive investigation of the transformation from start-up to a more mature phase of business to generate a more meaningful model for innovations. The results provide insights into the black box of innovation and how innovation occurs in different stages of company maturing. The analysis of cause-and-effect allows the exploration of the trigger, driver and supporter for innovation and business success. The two newly developed IMAs help to explore more profoundly *how* and *why* changes in innovation styles occur and what the outcomes are. The research succeeded in developing a new evaluation tool, the ICP model, to predict companies' success based on core capabilities and innovativeness in various typologies. The research design will assist other researchers to investigate the transformation of companies from a start-up phase to a more mature phase of business. Further research in this area is needed to understand more precisely how and why innovation happens, and the implications of changing the innovation style over time in order to sustain innovation.

Key points in developing innovation capabilities for SMEs are:

- Develop effective relationships with customers and suppliers to fully understand new technological developments that affect customers' needs (open innovation/customer centricity).
- Learn product development skills and processes (such as product design, prototyping new products, timing of new product introductions, and customizing products for local markets) entirely new to the industry (be a learning organization).
- Upgrade the companies' skills in the product development process in which the firm already possesses significant experience, strengthen the knowledge and skills for projects that improve efficiency of existing innovation activities, and share knowledge freely in the organization (knowledge management).
- Equip the company with staff from different industries and backgrounds (diversification).

■ Establish cooperative R&D agreements, joint design and manufacturing and introduce new products/services with other companies (open innovation/inter-organizational networks).

REVIEW QUESTIONS

1. How is innovation defined? What are the differences between innovation and invention?

2. What are the key layers of innovation that enable a company to set a culture of innovation?

3. What are the main models of innovation?

4. What kind of innovation capabilities exist?

5. How might the capabilities change over time for a high-growth SME?

CASE STUDY 13: GROWING A SOFTWARE COMPANY

Initial situation

You have been appointed as head of marketing for a company which was founded three years ago by two software developers. The venture was set up in the excitement generated by Web 2.0 and experienced strong growth in the first two years. The company is located in the Techno Park Zurich, an innovative environment with many high-tech start-up companies. There are now many other players offering similar services and it seems that the market environment is becoming increasingly dynamic. A recent economic crisis has decreased sales, and cash flow is steadily decreasing.

Over the last year the company has hired several employees with different backgrounds and skills. The total headcount is 32 employees. The founders have split responsibilities; one has taken the position of CEO and the other that of CFO. Both have no experience running a company and now they can't find time to do what they know best: developing innovative web services. The development of new services is now the responsibility of a highly motivated team of IT-oriented developers. The team is capable of designing and programming complex applications. A sales team has been formed to effectively sell what the developers have created.

Your challenge

You have agreed with the two founders that you will make a major contribution to the company within your first 100 days. The founders have hired you because you have experience in working with growing companies and you have promised to work cross-functionally, developing a strong concept to sustain growth and innovation success.

CASE QUESTIONS AND TASKS

1. Analyse which capabilities have been important for the company in a start-up phase and which capabilities might be needed in the future.

2. Which functions and newly formed divisions of the company should work more closely together and why?

3. What kind of marketing instruments would you apply to gather information, and to boost sales?
4. What capabilities should be considered when developing an innovation strategy? What kind of innovation (e.g. service, product, strategy, process innovation) could help the company to become more successful?

NOTE

1. The term 'novelty' does not only refer to technological innovation. Christensen (1997) uses the term 'sustaining innovation' to describe technological changes that improve performance of products and services that are perceived to be of added value to mainstream customers. In contrast, Christensen perceives 'disruptive innovations' as those technological changes whose introduction results in a creation of a whole new market. Further, he suggests that these disruptive innovations could initially be perceived by mainstream customers as being of worse value than the existing products or services.

BIBLIOGRAPHY

Ahuja, G., 2000, The duality of collaboration: inducements and opportunities in the formation of interfirm linkages, *Strategic Management Journal*, 21(3), pp. 317–343.

Ahuja, G. and Lampert, C., 2001, Entrepreneurship in the large corporation: a longitudinal study of how established firms create breakthrough inventions, *Strategic Management Journal*, 22, pp. 521–543.

Ancona, D. and Caldwell, D., 1992, Demography and design: predictors of new product team performance, *Organization Science*, 3(3), pp. 321–341.

Baum, J., Calabrese, T. and Silverman, B., 2000, Don't go it alone: alliance network composition and start-ups' performance in Canadian biotechnology, *Strategic Management Journal*, 21, pp. 267–294.

Blind, K. and Grupp, H., 1999, Interdependencies between the science and technology infrastructure and innovation activities in German regions: empirical findings and policy consequences, *Research Policy*, 28(5), pp. 451–468.

Boeker, W., 1997, Executive migration and strategic change: the effect of top manager movement on product-market entry, *Administrative Science Quarterly*, 42(June), pp. 213–236.

Brown, S. and Eisenhardt, K., 1995, New product development: past research, present findings and future directions, *Academy of Management Review*, 20(2), pp. 343–378.

Campbell, R. and Heffernan, J., 1981, Adult vocational behavior. In V. Walsh and Savickas, M. (eds), *Handbook of Vocational Psychology*, 1, Mahwah, NJ: Lawrence Erlbaum Associates, pp. 223–262.

Cardinal, L., 2001, Technological innovation in the pharmaceutical industry: the use of organizational control in managing research and development, *Organization Science*, 12, pp. 19–36.

Chandy, R. and Tellis, G., 1998, Organizing for radical product innovation: the overlooked role of willingness to cannibalize, *Journal of Marketing Research*, 35, pp. 474–485.

Christensen, C.M. (1997), *The Innovator's Dilemma*, Boston: Harvard Business School Press.

Coleman, J., 1988, Social capital in the creation of human capital, *American Journal of Sociology*, 94, pp. 95–120.

Davenport, T., 1998, *Working Knowledge: How Organizations Manage What They Know*, Boston: Havard Business School Press.

Day, G., 1994, The capabilities of market-driven organizations, *Journal of Marketing*, 58, 4, pp. 37–52.

Dewar, R. and Dutton, J., 1986, The adoption of radical and incremental innovations: an empirical analysis, *Management Science*, 32, pp. 1422–1433.

Di-Masi, P., 2006, *Defining Entrepreneurship*. Online: http://www.gdrc.org/icm/micro/define-micro.html (accessed 27 January 2006).

Eisenhardt, K. and Martin, J., 2000, Dynamic capabilities: what are they?, *Strategic Management Journal*, 21, pp. 1105–1121.

Faber, J. and Hesen, A., 2004, Innovation capabilities of European nations: cross-national analyses of patents and sales of product innovations, *Research Policy*, 33, pp. 193–207.

Finkelstein, S. and Hambrick, D., 1990, Top management team tenure and organizational outcomes: the moderating role of managerial discretion, *Administrative Science Quarterly*, 35, pp. 484–503.

Germain, R., 1996, The role of context and structure in radical and incremental logistics innovation adoption, *Journal of Business Research*, 35, pp. 117–127.

Gerwin, D. and Barrowman, N., 2002, An evaluation of research on integrated product development, *Management Science*, 48(June), pp. 938–953.

Gibb, A., 2000, Corporate restructuring and entrepreneurship: what can large organisations learn from small?, *Enterprise and Innovation Management Studies*, 1(1), pp. 19–35.

Gram, R., 2002. *Contemporary Strategy Analysis*. 4th edn. Oxford: Blackwell.

Grimm, C. and Smith, K., 1991, Management and organizational change: a note on the railroad industry, *Strategic Management Journal*, 12, pp. 557–562.

Hagedoorn, J., 2002, Interfirm R&D partnerships: an overview of major trends and patterns since 1960, *Research Policy*, 31, pp. 477–492.

Hamann, D., Williams, R. and Omar, M., 2007 Branding strategy and consumer high-technology product, *Journal of Product and Brand Management*, 16(2), pp. 98–111.

Hitt, M., Hoskisson, R., Johnson, R. and Moesel, D., 1996, The market for corporate control and firm innovation, *Academy of Management Journal*, 39(October), pp. 1048–1119.

Hopfenbeck, W., Müller, M. and Peisl, T., 2001, *Wissensbasiertes Management: Ansätze und Strategien zur Unter-nehmensführung in der Internet Ökonomie*, Landsberg/Lech: Moderne Industrie.

Hoskisson, R., Johnson, R., Yiu, D. and Wan, W., 2001, Restructuring strategies of diversified business groups: differences associated with country institutional environments. In M. Hitt, E. Freeman and J. Harrison (eds), *The Blackwell Handbook of Strategy*, Oxford: Blackwell, pp. 433–463.

Kahneman, D. and Tversky, A., 1979, Prospect theory: an analysis of decisions under risk, *Econometrica*, 47, pp. 263–291.

Katz, R., 1982, The effects of team longevity of project commitment and performance, *Administrative Science Quarterly*, 27, pp. 81–104.

Keister, L., 2002, Adapting to radical change: strategy and environment in piece rate adaption during China's transition, *Organisational Science*, 13(5), pp. 459–474.

Khan, A.M. and Manopichetwattana, V., 1989, Innovative and non innovative small firms: type and characteristics, *Management Science*, 35(5), pp. 597–606.

Kimberly, J. and Evanisko, M., 1981, Organizational innovation: the influence of individual, organizational, and contextual factors on hospital adoption of technological and administrative innovations, *Academy of Management Journal*, 24, pp. 437–713.

Koberg, C., Detienne, D. and Heppard, K., 2003, An empirical test of environmental, organizational, and process factors affecting incremental and radical innovation, *Journal of High Technology Management Research*, 14, pp. 21–45.

Krishnan, V. and Ulrich, K., 2001, Product development decisions: a review of the literature, *Management Science*, 47(1), pp. 1–21.

Landry, R., Amara, N. and Lamari, M., 2002, Does social capital determine innovation? To what extent?, *Technological Forecasting and Social Change*, 69, pp. 681–701.

Leonard, D., 1998, *Wellspring of Knowledge: Building and Sustaining the Sources of Innovation*, Boston: Harvard Business School Press.

McElroy, M.W., 2000, The new knowledge management, *Knowledge and Innovation: Journal of the KMCI*, 1(1), pp. 43–67.

Markham, S. and Griffin, A., 1998, The breakfast of champions: associations between champions and product development environments, practices and performance, *Journal of Product Innovation Management*, 15(5), pp. 436–454.

Meyer, A. and Goes J., 1988, Organizational assimilation of innovation: a multilevel contextual analysis, *Academy of Management Journal*, 31(December), pp. 897–923.

Mintzberg, H., 1987, Crafting strategy, *Harvard Business Review*, 65(July–August), pp. 66–75.

Nahapiet, J. and S. Ghoshal, 1998, Social capital, intellectual capital, and the organizational advantage, *Academy of Management Review*, 22,(2), pp. 242–266.

Nohari, K. and Gulati, S., 1996, Is slack good or bad for innovation? *Academy of Management Journal*, 39, pp. 799 – 825.

OECD, 2005, *Oslo Manual: Guidelines for Collecting and Interpreting Innovation Data*, Paris: OECD.

Orlikowski, W. and Hofman, D., 1997, An improvisational model of change management: the cases of groupware technologies, *Sloan Management Review*, Winter, pp. 1–15.

Penrose, E., 1963, *The Theory of the Growth of the Firm*, Oxford: Blackwell.

209

Rao, H. and Drazin, R., 2002, Overcoming resource constraints on product innovation by recruiting talent from rivals: a study of the mutual fund industry, *Academy of Management Journal*, 45(June), pp. 491–507.

Rothwell, R., 1992, Successful industrial innovation: critical success factors for the 1990s, *R&D Management*, 22(3), pp. 221–239.

Savage, C., 1990, *5th Generation Management: Integrating enterprises through human networking*, Bedford, MA: Digital Press.

Schumpeter, J. 1934, *The Theory of Economic Development*, Cambridge, MA: Harvard University Press.

Shan, W., Walker, G. and Kugut, B., 1994, Interfirm cooperation and startup innovation in the biotechnology industry, *Strategic Management Journal*, 15, pp. 387–394.

Sivadas, E. and Dwyer, F., 2000, An examination of organizational factors influencing new product success in internal and alliance-based processes, *Journal of Marketing*, 64, pp. 31–49.

Sorensen, J. and Stuart, T., 2000, Aging, obsolescence, and organizational innovation, *Administrative Science Quarterly*, 45(March), pp. 81–112.

Stevens, J., Huber, E. and Ray, L., 1999, The welfare state in hard times. In H. Kitschelt *et al.* (eds), *Continuity and Change in Contemporary Capitalism*, Cambridge: Cambridge University Press, pp. 164–194.

Stringer, R., 2000, How to manage radical innovation, *California Management Review*, 42(4), pp. 70–88.

Stuart, T., 2000, Interorganizational alliances and the performance of firms: a study of growth and innovation rates in a high-technology industry, *Strategic Management Journal*, 21, pp. 791–811.

Tether, B., 2002, Who co-operates for innovation, and why: an empirical analysis, *Research Policy*, 31, pp. 947–967.

Tsai, W., 2000, Social capital, strategic relatedness and the formation of intraorganizational linkages, *Strategic Management Journal*, 21(9), pp. 925–939.

Utterback, J., 1974, Innovation in industry and the diffusion of technology, *Science*, 183(February), pp. 620–626.

Van Aken, J. and Weggeman, M., 1998, Management of innovation networks as learning alliances: overcoming the Daphne-dilemma, *R&D Management*.

Verloop, J., 2004, *Insight in Innovation: Managing Innovation by Understanding the Laws of Innovation*, Amsterdam: Elsevier.

Wiersema, M. and Bantel, K., 1992, Top management team demography and corporate change, *Academy of Management Journal*, 35, pp. 91–121.

Winter, S., 2003, Understanding dynamic capabilities, *Strategic Management Journal*, 24(10), pp. 991–995.

Zahra, S., Ireland, R., Gutierrez, I., and Hitt, M. 2000a, Privatization and entrepreneurial transformation: emerging issues and a future research agenda, *Academy of Management Review*, 25, pp. 509–24.

Zahra, S., Ireland, R. and Hitt, M., 2000b, International expansion by new venture firms: international diversity, mode of market entry, technological learning, and performance, *Academy of Management Journal*, 43, pp. 925–50.

Chapter 14

SME retailing in the UK

Ogenyi Omar and Peter Fraser

LEARNING OBJECTIVES

After reading this chapter, you will be able to:
- understand the current issues and trends in SME retailing in the UK
- appreciate the key features and competitive position of SME retailing
- gain basic knowledge of the benefits and drawbacks of SME retailing
- recognize the challenges and opportunities facing owner-managers in competing with larger retailers.

INTRODUCTION

SME retail companies in cities and town across the UK tend to face many operational problems, including increased market competition from larger chains across the country, changing consumer shopping habits, insufficient levels of financial investment, low business and management skills, poor knowledge of current legislation, lack of sector-specific support systems and poor staff training in retail marketing. In spite of these numerous problems, SME retailers play an important role in providing cities and towns product, services and retail formats. The contribution made by SME retailers to the business landscape in the UK is often not recognized or given due regard by performance indicators, which fail to address their input into the socio-economic activities of the UK high streets. Being small tends to be a handicap in a business environment, and the problems faced by SME retailers in the UK are directly applicable to SME retailers in many other countries in Europe and North America.

In the UK, SME retailers have been largely ignored in the past and their contribution to the local community is only just beginning to be appreciated. Unfortunately, unlike the larger retail chains that have sophisticated public relations department with undisputed lobbying power, SMEs have little opportunity to influence government policy because they do not always have a common voice. Also, unlike the larger chains that have a clearly defined business and marketing strategy, many SME retailers have no strategic direction, which makes them even more vulnerable in such a fast-changing competitive environment.

The purpose of this chapter is to review the operational dimensions of SME retailers in the UK and highlight the difficult retailing issues faced by these retailers in the fast-changing and competitive UK retail environment. It documents the contribution made by the SME retail sector and identifies the critical success factors while taking their size disadvantage into consideration.

The chapter is structured in the following way. After this introduction an overview of the general retail environment is given; this is followed by a theoretical review, an SME retail sector examination, an analysis of the impact of competition on growth strategy, a discussion of contributions and critical success factors, and, finally, a prediction for the future.

DEFINITION OF SMES IN RETAILING

It is important to note that, in general, there is no single official and universal definition for a small firm (Mukhtar, 1998). However, the US Small Business Administration (SBA) has traditionally defined small businesses as having 'fewer than 500 employees' (SBA, 2001). While its size standards were recently revised and now vary by industry as defined by the North American Industrial Classification System (NAICS), with the exception of the wholesale trade, the maximum size for most sectors remains at 500 employees. Meanwhile, other studies have failed to detect and discriminate the differences and nuances between the 'larger' small firms (e.g. a firm with 450 employees and £15m in revenues) and truly small firms (e.g. a firm with seven employees and between £30,000 and £450,000 in sales) (Haksever, 1996; Ibrahim et al., 2004; Sawyer et al., 2003). Since there is no unanimous agreement as to the definition of a SME, it is important to always search the current literature for other definitions of small businesses.

According to Mukhtar (1996), a wide range of definitions are used in practice. The Wiltshire Committee's definition of SMEs is often used by researchers and states that an SME

> is a business in which one or two persons are required to make all the important management decisions such as finance, accounting, personnel, purchasing, processing or servicing, marketing, selling, etc., without the aid of internal specialists and with specific knowledge in only one or two functional areas.
>
> (see Berryman, 1983)

The European Commission offers a more exacting definition. First adopted in 1996, it specifies size gradations for micro, small- and medium-sized firms based on three factors: headcount, annual turnover and annual balance sheet total (see Mukhtar, 1998). Recently, this definition was revised to reflect economic changes since 1996 (Commission of the European Communities, 2003) as follows:

- Micro: 10 employees or fewer, with a turnover of £2 million and a balance sheet of £2 million.
- Small: up to 50 employees, with a turnover of £10 million and a balance sheet of £10 million.
- Medium: up to 250 employees, with a turnover of £50 million and a balance sheet of £43 million.

In specific retailing terms, there are three approaches to defining and classifying retail firm size in the UK. The first definition concerns fewer than 100 employees (officially small- and medium-sized enterprises, with small defined as fewer than 10 employees and medium defined as between 10 and 100 employees). The second definition typical for the retail sector takes the number of outlets as a measure, distinguishing single shops from chains (consisting of more than one outlet). The third definition takes sales volume as a measure for classification.

BOX 14.1: HARPO'S – A SINGLE RETAIL OUTLET

Harpo's, a single outlet retailer of second-hand records, CDs, DVDs and music books, has just won the award 'Coketown's Best Independent Retailer' for the second year in succession. At the start of the business there was only a basic website. It seemed workable enough but was not very exciting or informative. John, in his mid-fifties, married and with three grown-up daughters from his first marriage, makes it clear that he had no business background or training. In his youth he started a civil engineering degree but dropped out as he couldn't cope with the mathematics on the course. In order to earn a living, John says he began working on a market stall in another city, selling second-hand records. His father, a wealthy civil servant, had never really been reconciled to the way in which his son bought and sold second-hand records for a living. But ever since John can remember he'd loved records and he relished trading, moving on from the stall to run a record shop. Then he wanted to live in the country with his then girlfriend and they were offered a small cottage outside Coketown. John used all his savings as a deposit on the cottage and took out a mortgage.

Needing to earn a living in Coketown, in 1976 John set up Harpo's with a partner, Simon. Simon had previously run a similar business and so John felt confident going into business with him. To assist with start-up costs they obtained a bank loan of £500. Six years later, in 1983, he bought out his business partner for £10,000 – he had found that his partner liked to spend money, whereas John was more cautious and wanted to have more control over events. The current premises represents the third location for Harpo's. John is still operating as a sole trader, though he has occasionally considered whether or not to convert it into a company in order to take advantage of the protection afforded by limited liability. One of his friends, an experienced businessman, told him that this would be a wise move, especially for the future value of the business. The business has two main product areas, one being the sale of tickets to events (mainly local pub gigs, amounting to 50 per cent of sales) and the other being the sale of second-hand records, CDs, DVDs and music books.

The business has developed a lot since being founded in the late seventies. John says that, although it has changed, the business has evolved gradually over the years rather than making any sudden jumps. What changes has he seen? Technology apart, his audience tends to be made up of either those in their 40s or 50s or students. He gets a buzz when he sees students come in. After all these years he still enjoys pricing records. His staff have been with him long term and they all have different skills. For example, if you ask his manager, he can give the 'A side' to any given 'B side'. One of his staff keeps John's knowledge up to date, being a DJ. One of his daughters, the youngest (Bridget), also works in the shop, although John explains this is because she does not know what to do with her life rather than because she wants to be part of the business. Of course, staff occasionally leave. Apparently one of his employees left amicably and went to work in a similar shop in the capital. When they talked by phone his ex-employee explained his new boss just looks up the catalogue price and applies that to each item, although in all likelihood it will remain on the shelf. John explains that he never does this – this is not London and he needs to shift stock.

There are certain heuristics or rules of thumb that John has developed over his years in business. He summarizes these as follows: look after your staff; pay your bills on time; save for retirement immediately from when you start (he hadn't and says he would retire tomorrow if he could); work long hours; do anything you can do yourself, yourself; always be nice to people – you never know when you might need a favour – and don't ask any of your staff to do anything you wouldn't do yourself. He also says always do your own bookkeeping. This not only saves money but also, more importantly, it helps you keep your finger on the pulse of the business. In particular, says John, pay your tax and pay it on time – then the VAT man won't come knocking. The best thing he learned at school is perhaps a little surprising. After he obtained an O level in woodwork, he was able to do his own shop-fitting. Even better, in the early days he did shop-fitting jobs for cash – once for a bank manager. This meant that he was able to keep his cash flow positive. He's only ever had to fire one person and that was for poor timekeeping. As for the future, he wonders about downloading of music and how long it will be before it affects his business.

CHARACTERISTICS OF SME RETAILERS

Operating an SME may seem an attractive proposition to the person who 'wants to be his own boss'. In general, there are few people who do not feel that they could run a small business successfully. But in the public interest several European countries demand some form of qualification and/or experience before people can run a retail SME. However, there is no law preventing people without qualifications or experience from owning a small business. Some characteristics can be ascribed to many retail SMEs, including long hours of operation, legal restrictions, an enormous volume of bookkeeping and accounting involving the complications of value-added tax (VAT), National Insurance contributions and income tax. In practice, the experience of existing SME retailers is likely to deter many prospective retailers, especially those wanting to be self-employed, as Box 14.2 highlights.

BOX 14.2: THE BARBER SHOP

After years of experience working for others as a barber, Bill is determined to open a business of his own. He strikes a deal with a prominent Chicago hotel. He will open his business in their flagship property, a gigantic 2,000-bed hotel, where he will have exclusive barber rights. Even better, if he is successful in the larger premises he has there he will be offered the opportunity to develop smaller shops throughout the nationwide hotel chain.

Bill commits everything he has to his enterprise, but quickly discovers that his business is not performing to expectations. Hotel visitors rarely stay for more than 2–3 days and often have their hair cut before coming to town. Being inside a hotel, and unable to advertise his presence on the street, Bill attracts virtually no passing trade. Alongside his hairdressing business he offers a shoe-shining service, which seemed to be attractive. His chairs are nearly always full, but the contribution made to profit scarcely dents his heavy overheads.

Bill is worried about the future prospects for his business if things continue as they are, and has asked you, as his friend, what you think he should now do. Draw up an outline action plan and advise him.

The lack of know-how at the start and expertise in merchandising and stock control in succeeding years can cause a small retailer to feel isolated and uncompetitive. Although there are several sources of help from both official and non-government organizations (NGOs), only a few SME retailers are aware of them. For this reason, the UK government, through the Department of Industry, has set up a series of Small Firms Information Centres and issued a series of free guides for small firms.

Things are not all that bad for SMEs retailers, however, and there are some advantages to being self-employed. For example, Blankson and Omar (2003) found that 'an inherent advantage SME retailers usually possess is a rapport with their customers and the locality, which is difficult for large stores to achieve'. Similarly, the flexibility of service to suit parochial needs, and informality of retail service procedures can build up goodwill and attract the timid customer who is overawed by large sophisticated stores.

The SME retailer's convenience aspect of being close to the local community should not be overlooked. Many SMEs stay open late and serve the local community in such a way that they cannot be dismissed lightly as uneconomical or old-fashioned. They form a very necessary and useful part of social life in the communities they operate in.

The traditional wholesaler is one of the props of the average private shopkeeper. His or her representative will call regularly on the shop, take orders and show samples, give advice and credit and supply in small quantities from the ranges of many manufacturers. For example, some wholesale pharmacists make daily deliveries of prescriptions to their client retailers.

A fair proportion of SME retailers are affiliated to voluntary groups and chains, with whom they agree to buy the bulk of their supplies while retaining their independence. Through this loyalty to the group, SME retailers benefit from low prices, advertising, a supply of promotional aids, advice and often financial help in re-equipping the business. The grocery voluntary groups are known as 'symbol groups', incorporating a number of wholesalers under their brand and lately developing their own-branded merchandise. Another source of supply to the SME retailer is the cash-and-carry warehouse. These are usually situated where occupancy costs are low, and the costs of sales representatives, delivery and credit are completely eliminated. By passing on these savings a cash-and-carry warehouse can sell at near to wholesale cost, gaining net margins from bulk-buying discounts. The most important feature of the cash-and-carry warehouse is that it does not sell to the public.

STRUCTURAL OUTLINE

The Office for National Statistics (ONS) counts more than 81,000 enterprises in the UK retail sector, with only 200 of them not belonging to the SME category. About 95 per cent of these enterprises are classified as small and less than 5 per cent as medium. According to figures from the ONS, more than 75 per cent of the outlets in the UK retail sector are single-operating firms and less than 25 per cent are regarded as multiple chains (see Table 14.1). The market share (in terms of sales) of small business is less than 10 per cent and the market share of medium-sized business is about 15 per cent. The multiples and the cooperatives have the largest share of the market. This share of the UK retail market tends to vary significantly among different retail sectors; for example, the market share of small business in the food sector is only 11 per cent, whereas small business in books claims more than 50 per cent of the market.

The UK retail sector is one of the country's largest employers and more than a quarter of those involved are active owners and their family members, a typical characteristic of small firms. In that regard, the UK retail sector is definitely dominated by SME retailers.

Table 14.1 *Classification of British retailing*

Type		Features
1	Multiple chain retailing, e.g. Next, Asda, M&S	Defined as having more than 10 outlets and having: Standardized products Competitive prices Creating customer familiarity with the store's corporate image Own-brand ranges of products
2	Cooperative retailing, e.g. CWS, CRS	Nineteenth-century origins; stronger in the north than in the south Original philosophy of fairness and consumer control Lack of coordination between the different co-ops Process of distributing dividends has reduced amount available for investment in new stores and locations Conflict of interest between those who see them in original terms and those who see them as more commercial entities Poor market focus and market image
3	Department stores, e.g. Selfridges, House of Fraser	Emerged in the nineteeth century as a development of the drapery trade Purpose to sell a wide variety of products under one roof as much as possible to middle classes Currently groups attempt to standardize facilities as far as possible
4	Independent retailers	Fewer than 10 outlets Major decline in total shop numbers due to fall in independents Financially incapable of changing or too conservative Personal service counts for much of the surviving trade
5	Voluntary chains, e.g. SPAR, Londis	Small businesses create buying and marketing strengths through contractual relationships
6	Franchises, e.g. Benetton, The Body Shop, McDonald's	Agreements between retailers and franchisees offering local expertise and money in exchange for marketing system of the franchise
7	Mail order, e.g. Littlewoods, Next Directory, Lands' End	Traditionally a means of enabling poorer households to buy on credit Market for traditional catalogues declining Updating through telephone ordering, targeted product ranges
8	Door-to-door selling, e.g. Kleeneze, Betterware	A declining form of selling, created by urbanization and easy access to high densities of population. Household goods are successfully distributed in this way
9	Mobile shops, e.g. groceries, fruit and vegetables, fish and chips	Reach consumers distant from local shops, e.g. housing estates and rural areas, as independent stores on wheels
10	Informal selling, e.g. Dorling Kindersley, Ann Summers	Party-plan shopping based on a local agent organizing friends and neighbours to look at products in an informal home environment
11	Periodic markets, e.g. Camden Lock Market, Petticoat Lane	The oldest form of exchange Many street markets compete to find success in fresh products, low-price clothing and household goods. Some markets become established and trade daily in a specialized area

In addition to the existing ways of distributing goods and services, it is possible to note the emergence of new retail concepts, originating in the USA or Europe, including discount warehouses and 'category killers', which enjoy continued growth in less competitive sectors with wider ranges and lower prices. Examples include Toys R Us, Pet City and IKEA, and discount food retailers such as Netto and ALDI.

RETAIL INDUSTRY RESTRUCTURING

In recent years, UK retailing has been restructured by the trend towards larger store sizes, which has been accompanied by a decline in independent retailing. The UK has higher-than-average retail concentration in almost all sub-sectors: the ten largest retailers combined have 37–38 per cent of all retail sales. In food retailing, concentration is increasingly apparent as regional multiples such as Wm Low, and now weaker national chains, such as Summerfield, have been acquired by stronger competitors.

Table 14.2 *Percentage share of retail sales by top five multiples in sub-sectors*

Product sector	% share of sales
Grocers	66
DIY	63
Mixed goods	61
Chemists (excluding Boots)	58
Electrical goods	36
Clothing	33

Source: Compiled from Key Notes, 2008 (author's adaptation).

During the 1980s, relaxation of planning policy enabled property developers and retailers to create new shopping centres, retail parks and, largest of all, regional shopping centres. Lakeside and the Metro Centre in Gateshead are typical of these extensive facilities. Larger store sizes were made possible and this resulted in wider product assortments, the development of new products and spacious, customer-oriented shopping environments. As a result the traditional town centre shopping areas and suburban parades have declined. This may be partly due to local and central government policies on retailing.

ORGANIZATION OF SMALL RETAILERS

Small retailers generally use simple arrangements because they contain only two or three levels of personnel – for example, the owner-manager and employees. In most cases, the owner-manager personally runs the business and oversees workers (Berman and Evans, 2001, p. 368). The owner-managers of a single store may be the entire organization and, as such, when they go to lunch or go home the store closes. But as Levy and Weitz (2004, p. 282) have observed, 'as sales grow, the owner-managers employ others to work for them'. In a small business organization such as the type in Figure 14.1, coordinating and controlling employee activities is easier than in large chain stores. The owner-manager simply assigns tasks to each employee and watches to see that these tasks are performed properly. Since the number of employees is small, SME retailers have little specialization (Blankson and Omar, 2003). At the same time, Blankson and Omar (2003) have documented that each employee performs a wide range of activities, while the owner-manager is responsible for all management tasks of the firm.

As sales increase, specialization in management may occur when the owner-manager

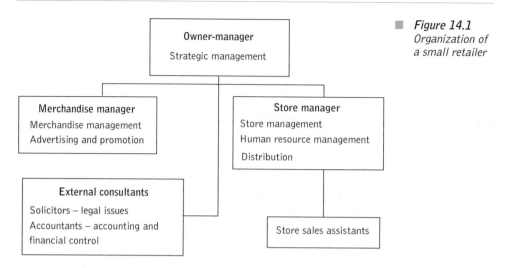

Figure 14.1
Organization of
a small retailer

employs additional staff or an external consulting team. Figure 14.1 illustrates the common division of management responsibilities into merchandise and store management. The owner-manager continues to perform strategic management tasks. The store manager may be responsible for administrative tasks associated with receiving and shipping merchandising and managing the employees (Levy and Weitz, 2004). The merchandise manager, who is sometimes referred to as the buyer, may handle the advertising and promotion tasks as well as the merchandising tasks. Often the owner-manager contracts an accountant to perform accounting and financial tasks while solicitors handle the store's legal issues. As the small retailer continues to grow, it may expand to become a medium-sized retailer, provided it operates within the government regulations.

Some SME retailers may only own one retail unit but others may own several units in several locations. In the UK, there are almost 2.2 million SME retailers accounting for nearly 35 per cent of total retail store sales. One half of SMEs are run entirely by the owners and/ or their families. These retailers generate just 3 per cent of total UK retail sales and many of them have no paid employees.

The high number of SME retailers in the UK is associated with the ease of entry into the retail marketplace (McGoldrick, 2002). As a result of low capital requirements and relatively simple licensing provisions, entry for many kinds of SME is easy. The investment per employee in retailing is usually much lower than for manufacturing firms. Retailer licensing, although somewhat more stringent in recent years, is still a matter of routine. Each year, tens of thousands of new retail businesses, most of them small independent retailers, open in the UK. This ease of entry into retailing coexists with the low market shares of many SME retailing firms in many goods/service categories. In the grocery retail category, for example, where large chains are quite strong, the four largest grocery retailers account for more than 65 per cent of sales.

Since a great deal of competition is due to the relative ease of entry into retailing, it is undoubtedly a strong factor in the high rate of retail business failures among new SME retail entrants. The ONS estimates that one-third of new UK retailers do not survive their first year and two-thirds do not continue beyond their third year. Most of these failures involve small independent retailers. On an annual basis, a large number of these SME retailers go bankrupt, in addition to the thousands of small retailers that just close down due to their inability to compete in a rapidly changing sector of the UK economy. In spite of this high rate of failure SME retailing has a variety of advantages, as well as some disadvantages. These advantages and disadvantages are listed in Table 14.3.

Table 14.3 Benefits and drawbacks of SME retailing

Advantages	Disadvantages
There is great deal of flexibility in choosing retail formats and locations, and in devising strategy. Because only one store location is involved, detailed specifications can be set for the best location and a thorough search undertaken. Uniform location standards are not needed as they are for chain stores. In setting strategy, small retailers do not have to worry about being too close to other company stores, and have great latitude in selecting target markets. Since many SMEs have modest goals, small customer segments may be selected rather than the mass-market. Product assortments, prices, store hours and other factors are then set consistent with the market.	In bargaining with suppliers, SMEs may not have much power because they often buy in small quantities. They may even be bypassed by suppliers or limited in the products made available to them. Reordering may also be tough if minimum order requirements are too high for them. In order to overcome this problem, a number of SMEs, such as DIY stores, have formed buying groups to increase their power in dealing with suppliers.
In so far as SME retailers run only one store, investment cost for leases, fixtures, workers and merchandise is very low. In addition, there is no duplication of stock or personnel functions. Responsibilities are clearly delineated within a store as identified earlier in this chapter.	Most SME retailers typically cannot gain economies of scale (low per-unit costs due to handling many units at one time) in buying and maintaining inventory. Due to financial constraints, small assortments are bought several times per year, rather than large orders once or twice per year. Thus, transportation, ordering and handling costs per unit are high.
SME retailers often act as specialists and acquire skills in a niche of a particular goods/ service category. They are then more efficient and can lure shoppers interested in specialized retailing.	Operations are often very labour intensive, sometimes with little knowledge of computer technology. Ordering, taking inventory, marking items, ringing up sales and bookkeeping may be done manually. This is less efficient than using computers (expensive for some small retailers in terms of the initial investment in hardware and software, although costs have fallen significantly). In many cases, owner-managers are unwilling or unable to spend time learning how to set up and apply computerized procedures.
SMEs exert strong control over their strategies and the owner-manager is typically on the premises. Decision making is usually centralized and layers of management personnel are minimized.	By virtue of the relatively high costs of television advertising and the large geographic coverage of magazines and some newspapers (too large for firms with one outlet), SMEs are limited in their access to advertising media and may pay higher fees for advertising compared with regular users. Yet, there are various promotion tools available for creative SME retailers.

(continued)

■ *Table 14.3* Benefits and drawbacks of SME retailing (continued)

Advantages	Disadvantages
There is a certain image attached to SME retailers, particularly small ones, that chains find difficult to capture. This is the image of a personable retailer with a comfortable atmosphere in which to shop.	A crucial problem for family-run retail business is an over-dependence on the owner's resources. Often, all decisions are made by this person, and there is no continuity of management when the owner-manager is ill, on vacation or retires. The leading worries for family-run retail business involve identifying successors, the role of non-family employees and management training for family members. Long-run success and employee morale can be affected by overdependence on the owner.
SME retailers are able to sustain consistency in their efforts since only one geographic market is usually served and just one strategy is carried out. For example, there cannot be problems due to two branch stores selling identical items at different prices.	There is a limited amount of time and resources allotted to long-run planning. Since the owner is intimately involved in daily operations of the firm, responsiveness to new legislation, new products and new competitors frequently suffers.
Almost all the SMEs have independence. Owner-managers tend to be in full charge and do not have to fret about stockholders, board-of-director meetings and labour unrest. They are often free from union work and seniority rules. This can enhance labour productivity.	
Owner-managers usually have a strong entrepreneurial drive. They have personal investments in their businesses – success or failure has huge implications – and there is a lot of ego involvement.	

THE UK GOVERNMENT POLICY AND RETAILING

The UK economy is characterized by many unique relations between retailers and their suppliers. The 'balance of power' in this relationship has changed significantly in the past four decades in favour of the largest retailers and this trend has been seen particularly in the grocery supermarket field. In reality, SME retailers have not benefitted much from such a shift in the power relationship. The largest supermarket operators have been able to take advantage of their structural market power, the use of information technology and generally increasingly sophisticated management to achieve considerable cost savings, not just in traditional merchandise purchases but also in newer areas such as fresh produce and petrol, as well as in the area of retailer-dominated physical distribution management. It is, however, debatable whether the development of such retailer–supplier relations is beneficial for consumers.

In one form or another, the government exerts considerable influence over a number of aspects of retailing in the UK. The best way to understand this is to put it in the context of consumer protection (see Omar, 1999). This can be interpreted as a vast range of government actions designed to ensure that the final consumer is best served and protected in the complete range of final consumption activities (see also Swann, 1979; Smith and Swann,

1979; Howe, 2003). One example of this is shop opening hours being regulated in ways that have implications for both retailing competition and consumer service (Davidson and Ervine, 1992). In this respect the UK retailing environment is particularly liberal, and since 1994 there have been few restrictions on shop opening hours. As Kent and Omar (2003) have noted, 'across the United Kingdom there is now an increasing incidence of 24-hour grocery supermarkets opening in addition to the widespread availability of smaller scale "convenience stores", and Sunday trading is also both widespread and popular with shoppers'. Beyond this, the two principal areas of government intervention in retailing in the United Kingdom are competition policy and land-use planning regulations. These are, however, only a few of the challenges that SME retailers may face in their daily operations.

CHALLENGES TO THE SME RETAIL SECTOR

SME retailing has long been a feature of the British economy, providing valuable local economic and social resources. However, the sector is facing the challenge of a continually changing retail environment. The sector is highly dependent on family financial resources, which greatly increases the potential negative economic and social impacts when small retailers fail to respond to these challenges adequately. Challenges to the SME retail sector in the British economy can be classified into external and internal challenges.

External factors

This sector plays an important role in the maintenance of strong economic and social resources in many towns and cities throughout Britain. Welsh *et al.* (2003) have commented on the challenge to convenience stores, remarking that

> these organizations are increasingly under threat from a number of external factors, including changing demographics, increased competition and changing consumer behaviour that combine to present an ongoing challenge to their survival and future development opportunities.

> (see also Baron *et al.*, 2001)

Economic and social change, competition from multiple retailers and location difficulties combine to create inadequacies in the SME retail environment. Economic development in the UK brings with it a higher standard of living for communities, and a greater share of resources devoted to retailing. This is true for all the developed countries of Europe and North America. Retail stores of various types are more numerous and large than elsewhere, and customer choice becomes more sophisticated. The major outcome of this development, however, is that retailing has become more sensitive to social, economic, fiscal and demographic changes. Examples of external factors that have the most influence on retailing include birth rate, lending rates, fashion, public opinion, employment levels, social behaviour and government legislation, among many others.

Table 14.4 Factors affecting SME retailing

External factors	Internal factors
• Changes in the UK economy	• Reasons for self-employment
• Changes in government policy	• Owner's business experience
• Changes in local authority policy	• Owner's education background
• Private-sector initiatives	• Owner's business training and skills
• Changes in the economies of scale	• Influence of role models in the family
• Changes in retail technology	• Influence of role models in the community
• Changes in demographic characteristics	• Influence of cultural or religious values
	• Family support and encouragement

Source: Welsh *et al.* (2003).

It is obvious that an increase in birth rate will normally result in population growth, with a consequent increase in demand. Specifically, the effect will be felt by SME retailers catering for children. In the same way, an increase in banks' lending rates will have several repercussions on the SME retail operation, including higher rates for hire purchases and bank overdrafts and less consumer spending power.

In terms of changes in public opinion, this effect can be drastic and drive away customers. Anti-smoking campaigns, for example, have a direct effect on pubs and their business – they also have a direct impact on the retailing of tobacco. This is related to changes in fashion, which extend beyond the mere design of clothes. For example, the miniskirt was responsible for the change to tights from stockings. Changes in social behaviour – for example, trends towards more foreign travel, more leisure and more DIY – result in new kinds of merchandise being demanded from SME retailers. Finally, transport systems and environmental regulations are additional problems that face the SME retailers.

Generally, the threats to the survival of SME retailers are related to operating costs, the availability of financial capital for reinvestment and bulk supply problems (*Baron et al.*, 2001). Many SME retailers are unable to price their goods and services at a competitive level because many of their customers are aware of supermarket prices. In addition, Smith and Sparks (2000) have highlighted the fact that changing the expectations of consumers and their needs may require the retailer to introduce new technology, which may cost them more financial resources to install.

BOX 14.3: A MULTIPLE BUTCHER SHOP

George is 42 and a butcher by trade. He inherited with his brother a small multiple founded by his grandfather. He and his brother are about to open a fourth butcher's shop in the high street to add to their long-established trio. It will open on 1 December in time for the Christmas and New Year peak. Despite all George's experience, this development feels like quite a gamble to him. When asked about the coming year, George shrugged. He hadn't been thinking of expansion but had been approached to find out what rent he would be interested in paying – the premises having stood empty for a while. He suggested a figure and an agreement was reached. He has warned his staff that the new shop will mean less-favourable conditions, as they will have to stay open into the evening and work split shifts. He has 70 staff across the three shops; several have retired lately and another, aged 70, is going to go in the new year. None have been replaced. He may have to consider redundancy at some stage, but he was not the first owner-manager to give me the impression that he puts paying his own staff first.

I raised this issue of local food, local shops. Would there be a move away from supermarket shopping as a result? He was sceptical, as he was about websites. His company has one but has never made much headway with it.

I asked about the apparent decline in cooking due to a rise in the use of prepared meals. Did he find his staff had to give more advice now? 'Well,' he said, 'certainly we do more preparation – chicken breasts with stuffing, a really good quick meal all pre-prepared. And we do a lot of barbecue portions – 'though this hasn't been a good year for barbecues . . .' George and his brother employ their own baker so prepare all their own pies and cooked foods. This part of the business was very profitable.

If the consumer market is a struggle, what about business-to-business sales? George was clearly very frustrated. The city council now has as its meat supplier a company based in another city 50 miles away. Public-sector bodies talk quality, local businesses and food miles, said George, but when it comes to the crunch all they care about is price. He more or less got an admission to this effect from a woman when he phoned up after the council's switch (later I thought privately that any council might be in legal trouble if they didn't take the lowest price). The same, we discussed, goes for the Natonal Health Service, universities and other contract purchasers. George commented that he knows all his suppliers, and he couldn't say that of the successful bidder.

Internal factors

Specific to small business retailing is the concern with respect to the age of owner-managers. Many owner-managers have an average age of 58 years, with almost 30 years in small retail businesses. This means that they are not likely to have sufficient knowledge in the area of retail technology and in current retail trends to compete. Welsh *et al.* (2003, p. 410) have remarked that

> the lack of knowledge of modern retail methods and small business management results in an inability to implement and interpret the controls necessary to facilitate sound management practice and prolonged business development.

Although owner-manager age may be a concern, it is not the only determining factor to SME retail success. Many other internal factors, such as the location of the business and its links with the local community, family participation and assistance, relevant skills of other store assistants plus the amount of funds available for reinvestment, will all contribute one way or another to small business success. Welsh *et al.* (2003) quote both Storey (1994) and Basu and Goswami (1999) as identifying that 'the willingness of the owner-manager to respond to the challenge of the changing retail environment may also be affected by age, reasons for business entry, and issues related to family and community influences, ethnic background and business succession' (Welsh *et al.*, 2003).

The size of small businesses cannot be ignored, as being small hinders effective competition. Being small in size is a disadvantage in that sufficient financial resources may be a problem; large or bulk merchandise purchases may be beyond a small enterprise and they may not, therefore, reap any economies of scale. Suppliers and retail banks may only agree to limited amounts of merchandise and funds respectively. SME retailers are also likely to face many operational restrictions, including the employment of staff and sources of supply. Although SME retailers face all these market challenges, they still are able to provide their customers with needed services and fill a niche or gap in the UK retail marketplace.

Impact of recession

The global economic downturn has affected SME retailers in the UK severely in recent years – much more than the large chains. The unorganized retail segment, comprising mainly SMEs, suffered a major setback as their financial resources and revenue declined in real terms. With customers shying away from bulk and expensive purchases, business volumes of retail stores have fallen drastically. This situation is, therefore, raising concern among SME retailers who usually operate on small margins.

As is usually the case when things are not going well, retailers are beginning to take the restructuring route to streamline their operations and drive down losses. An increasing number of SMEs are reviewing their strategies and evaluating various aspects of their administration, including financial options, risks, marketing strategy and resource management. In view of the current market dynamics, retailers are focusing on introducing value-retail and less capital-intensive formats that will help them nullify the adverse effects of the global economic deceleration. Some SME retailers are also adopting more effective business models such as speciality retail stores to draw consumers and revive sales.

BOX 14.4: SHOP-IN-SHOP FORMAT

The most favoured format among the UK SME retailers is the shop-in-shop format. Most SME retailers are opting for this business structure because it facilitates and enhances revenue generation and also allows optimum space utilization. In order to adopt this format, SMEs undertake shop refurbishment and at the same time reduce their shelf space for those products which do not sell well. By using this format small retailers are able to offer in a displayed space 'freebies' and discounts to augment their sales. In addition to offering discounts and restructuring their business operations, SME retailers are taking adequate measures to improve their supply chain management, using computer technology to improve the efficiency of their distribution and logistic networks and revamping their customer service provision to attract customers, in order to come out of economic recession.

As a result of the difficult times that SMEs are going through it has become important for SME retailers to restructure their businesses (Hogg et al., 2003). In particular, those SME retailers with less money to invest are reformatting their outlets and exploring alternative money-generation options to draw more customers. Many SMEs are shifting their stores to formats which require less financial and labour investment and have high business potential in order to boost their flagging sales.

RETAIL MARKET COMPETITION

Since the emergence of the discount retailing format in the 1970s and 1980s there has been a proliferation of discount chains, 'category killers' and other mass-merchandisers such as John Lewis, Marks & Spencer, Tesco, ASDA/Wal-Mart and Sainsbury's, which today dominate

British retailing with their national coverage and low-priced offerings achieved through economies of scale. Due to the high market concentration, SME retailers may often not be able to find any competitive space in the UK retail sector. Meanwhile, in spite of the high rate of business failure among SME retailers, many others are thriving and competing well in the British retail market (Kent and Omar, 2003, p. 80).

Both Miles and Snow (1978) and Porter (1985) consistently argue that 'firms with clearly defined strategies tend to outperform those without such clarity'. Based on Porter's view of the firm, larger retailers such as Marks & Spencer, John Lewis, etc., are more able to leverage internal and external resources through economies of scale in price reduction across product lines. They are also able to use sophisticated technologies to manage inventories. These larger retailers are able to use computer technology (e.g. the World Wide Web) and reach a wider customer segment by adopting cost leadership and/or product differentiation strategies. SME retailers can effectively compete with larger retailers by employing focus strategies to capture a segment of the target market not adequately served by the multiple retailers.

The adoption of such focus strategies may require the SME retailer to go beyond the traditional positioning strategy in order to meet the needs of various customer segments, and target the merchandise and retail practices to them appropriately (Bennison and Hines, 2003). This approach is a suitable strategy for an SME retailer with specialized retail marketing skills to compete in a niche retail market. It is possible for such an SME retailer to use its skill to establish strategic position and emphasize its superior product quality and customer service (Omar, 1995). In the UK, SME retailers who are successful within their communities are those that lay greater emphasis on market and/or product segmentation involving a focus strategy (Kent *et al.*, 2003). The competitiveness of SMEs in the UK retail sector is based, therefore, on a combination of a set of complementary resources and competencies, which converge in pursuit of a specific strategic position.

Continuous and successful existence in the UK retail sector is based on location advantages that enable ease of access to target customer segments. In that case, SME retailers who have no retail marketing skills but nevertheless have the following attributes are more likely to become better competitors. These attributes include the following:

- a keen understanding of the community marketplace
- being actively engaged in the day-to-day operations of the small retail business
- offering quality products at a competitive price
- providing superior customer service
- employing knowledgeable and motivated assistants
- receiving adequate support from suppliers
- adapting to relevant local retail culture
- having good community linkages
- having a positive business image.

All these attributes, when put together and deployed to pursue a focused differentiation strategy targeting relatively narrow customer segments, make an SME retailer highly competitive in the marketplace.

CONCLUSIONS

Retailing is a significant part of the total UK economic activity as it is in all the other European countries. SME retailers also represent a fair propotion of that econmic activity, as outlined in this chapter. In general, retailing is of importance to the government as well as consumers not only because of its economic contribution but also because of its size and the market power of individual retailers. The evidence suggests that retail markets do not necessarily work in perfect competition (Howe, 2003).

This chapter briefly discussed the operation of SME retailers, noting their economic and social contributions, their characteristics and some impediments to their operation. It has highlighted the lack of skills and know-how of many SME retailers at the start of their businesses, deficiencies which may bring an end to many of them within a year of start-up. A successful business calls for the development of a strategy to encompass all aspects of the business right from start-up in order to compete with other retailers and avoid closure. This will then place an enterprise in a position to respond proactively to changes in the external retail environment and maximize available opportunities.

This chapter has also discussed the limited availability of alternative resources in SMEs involving only the owner-managers and members of their family. This places increased focus on the skills and attitudes of the proprietor. One of the critical success factors in SME retailing is being aware of the changing external environment in order to develop suitable retail marketing strategies to meet the challenges.

Finally, and in summary, some of the specific issues relevant to all SME retailers therefore include:

- The lack of resources – primarily management's time and skills.
- The long opening hours – in order to compete with large retailers and meet the needs of shoppers who seem to take for granted increasing availability. For example, UK shops open noticeably longer hours than those, say, in France or Germany. These long opening hours usually result in owner-manager fatigue and lack of energy to maintain and develop strategic outcomes.
- Failure to delegate – this is a result of lack of staff to take on tasks, as well as an unwillingness to do this.
- Failure to monitor the competition and take ideas from them to maintain development.
- Lack of previous experience/training/education in the business sector.
- Failure to pay attention to basic promotion, in particular branding and the external appearance of the shop, including from shop and brand name to promotional signage to paintwork and signposting of opening hours.

The owner-manager needs to constantly question how the shop would be seen by a customer. Thus, the key advantages of SME retailing lie in the ability to be flexible, having the motivation for personal selling and developing a relationship with the customers. Related to this is the importance of focus, to differentiate the product range from that of a multiple retailer and develop an offering that does not emphasize price.

REVIEW QUESTIONS

1. SME retailing has been defined in a variety of ways. Using the knowledge gained from reading this chapter, define the term 'SME retailing' as you understand it.

2. What are the main differences between SME retailing and multiple retailing in terms of retail operation?

3. In your opinion, what do you consider to be the critical-success factors in SME retailing in the UK?

4. Discuss how you think a small enterprise operating from one store in a particular local community could attract customers to the store.

5. Describe the contributions made by SME retailing to the British economy.

6. Perhaps one of the key success factors in SME retailing is to identify a value-based strategy for responding to challenges in the retail environment. Explain briefly how SME retailers could respond to challenges in the UK retail environment.

7. Using the knowledge gained from reading this chapter, evaluate the advantages and disadvantages of SME retailing.

8. SME retailers are increasingly under threat from a number of external and internal factors. Discuss the effects of these factors and explain how threats could be minimized.

9. Evaluate how SME retailers could best cope with the impact of economic recession in the UK.

10. Explain how SME retailers could take advantage of their location proximity to their customers in the face of intense retail competition from the multiples.

CASE STUDY 14: BRITISH SHOPPERS HIT BY INFLATION SHOCK

Rapid rising prices and a weak pound have brought the shock return of inflation, according to official government sources. The government's official measure, the Consumer Price Index (CPI), jumped from 3 per cent to 3.2 per cent in November 2009. It stunned the city economists, who had predicted a fall to only 2.6 per cent. The increase was attributed to rising supermarket prices and the decision of many SME retailers to reverse the 2.5 per cent cut in VAT brought in by the government in an attempt to stimulate the economy. Gas prices went up by 33 per cent year on year. Another major contribution to the rise in the CPI came from fresh vegetables, which have gone up 23.8 per cent in a year, and almost 5 per cent in a month.

The Office for National Statistics (ONS) said carrots, cucumbers and courgettes are among those vegetables rising fastest in price. Other foods that have gone up dramatically include pizza and mayonnaise. A spokesperson for the British Retail Consortium said:

> The weak pound has increased the cost of imported food, such as fruits and vegetables, which aren't harvested in Britain at this time of year. The weak exchange rate has also made UK produce more attractive for overseas buyers, restricting supplies of beef and lamb at home and pushing prices up. Non-food goods such as clothing, footwear and some electrical goods are cheaper than they were this time last year.

A spokesperson for the ONS said, 'the inflation figure was much higher than expected, with the exchange rate probably to blame for now'. Transport prices also rose, reflecting an increase in the price of petrol of 3.2 per cent per litre between January and February 2009. ONS statisticians added that the cut in VAT from 17.5 per cent to 15 per cent, which was introduced in December 2009, was being reversed on the high street. 'It can be seen that many prices returned to the previous selling price in November 2009 or have even gone beyond that, and that is quite widespread.' The broader measure of inflation, the Retail Price Index (RPI), did fall slightly, from 0.1 per cent to 0.0 per cent, but this was also less than expected. Most forecasts predicted that the RPI, which includes the cost of housing, would go negative for the first time since March 1960, ushering in a period of deflation.

The RPI is widely used by employers as a benchmark for wage increases and its fall to zero means that most workers will get a pay freeze or only a nominal pay rise this year. The chief economist at the Chartered Institute of Personnel and Development said:

> For millions of workers, this will be a spring and summer of pay depression, as pay rises give way to widespread pay freezes or pay cuts. For the vast majority of workers, accustomed as most of us are to an annual boost to our pay packets, a pay freeze or pay cut will feel like a hardship, especially while the CPI measure of inflation continues to rise.

RPI inflation at below zero could lead to lower incomes for pensioners and reduced returns for savers. The unexpectedly high level of inflation forced the Bank of England's Governor to write a letter to the Chancellor explaining why it is still above the 2 per cent target.

Economists pointed to prices that are expected to fall over the coming months. Gas and electricity prices, though sharply higher than a year ago, are now starting to subside as the effect of cheaper oil starts to flow through. They also said that the latest rise in the CPI was unlikely to deter the Bank of England from continuing with quantitative easing or keeping interest rates at 0.5 per cent for an extended period.

CASE QUESTIONS AND TASKS

1. Explain the effects of inflation and how rising prices may negatively affect what consumers buy and consume.
2. The RPI is widely used by employers as a benchmark for wage increases. Discuss why the decrease in RPI may be a big worry for SME retailers and their employees.
3. The weak exchange rate has made UK produce more attractive for overseas buyers, restricting supplies of beef and lamb at home and pushing up prices. Explain what you understand by this statement.

Source: Compiled from various sources for the purpose of classroom teaching only (author's adaptation).

BIBLIOGRAPHY

Baron, S., Harris, K., Leaver, D. and Oldfield, B. (2001), 'Beyond convenience: the future for independent food and grocery retailers in the UK', *International Review of Retail, Distribution and Consumer Research*, Vol. 11, No. 4, pp. 395–414.

Basu, A. and Goswami, A. (1999), 'South Asian entrepreneurship in Great Britain: factors influencing growth', *International Journal of Entrepreneural Behaviour and Research*, Vol. 5, No. 5, pp. 251–275.

Bennison, D. and Hines, T. (2003), 'Retailing for communities: issues of inclusion and exclusion', *International Journal of Retail and Distribution Management*, Vol. 31, No. 8, pp. 385–388.

Bennison, D. and Jones, S. (2002), 'New strategies needed to reflect changing town centre activities', *Urban Environment Today*, Vol. 8 (August), pp. 6–7.

Berman, B. and Evans, J. R. (2001), *Retail Management: A Strategic Approach* (8th edn), New Jersey: Prentice Hall.

Berryman, J. (1983), 'Small business failure and bankruptcy: a survey of the literature', *European Small Business Journal*, Vol. 4, pp. 47–59.

Blankson, C. and Omar, O. E. (2003), 'Marketing practices of African and Caribbean small businesses in London, UK', *Qualitataive Marketing Research: An International Journal*, Vol. 5, No. 2, pp. 123–134.

Davidson, F. P. and Ervine, W. C. H. (1992), 'Legal issues in retailing', in Howe, W. S. (ed.), *Retailing Management*, London: Macmillan.

Haksever, C. (1996), 'Total quality management in the small business environment', *Business Horizon*, Vol. 39 Issue 2, pp. 33–40

Hogg, S., Medway, D. and Warnaby, G. (2003), 'Business improvement districts: an opportunity for SME retailing', *International Journal of Retailing and Distribution Management*, Vol. 31, No. 9, pp. 466–469.

Howe, S. (2003), *Retailing in the European Union: Structures, Competition and Performance*, London: Routledge.

Ibrahim, A. B., Soufani, K. and Lam, J. (2004), 'A study of succession in a family firm', *Family Business Review*, Vol. 14 Issue 3, pp. 245–258

Kent, A. E. and Omar, O. E. (2003), *Retailing*, Basingstoke: Palgrave Macmillan.

Kent, T., Dennis, C. and Tanton, S. (2003), 'An evaluation of mentoring for SME retailers', *International Journal of Retail and Distribution Management*, Vol. 31, No. 8, pp. 440–448.

Levy, M. and Weitz, B. A. (2004), *Retail Management* (5th edn), New York: McGraw Hill/Irwin.

McGoldrick, P. J. (2002), *Retail Marketing* (2nd edn), London: McGraw-Hill.

Miles, R.E. and Snow, C.C (1978), *Organizational strategy, structure and processes*, New York: McGraw-Hill

Mukhtar, S. M. (1996), 'A case for gender-based entrepreneurialism, business competence development model, and policy implications: a global perspective.' Paper presented at Forging Global Alliances.

Mukhtar, S. M. (1998), 'Business characteristics of male and female small and medium enterprises in the UK: implications for gender-based entrepreneurialism and business competence development', *British Journal of Management*, 9:1, pp. 41–51.

Nwankwo, S. (2005), 'Characteristics of Black African entrepreneurship in the UK: a pilot study', *Journal of Small Business and Enterprise Development*, Vol. 12, No. 1, pp. 120–136.

Omar O. E. (1995), 'Retail influence on food technology and innovation', *International Journal of Retail & Distribution Management*, Vol. 23, No. 3, pp. 11–16.

Omar, O. E. (1999), *Retail Marketing*, London: Financial Times/Pitman.

Porter, M. E. (1985), *Competitive Advantage*, New York: Free Press.

Roper, S. and Parker, C. (2006), 'Evaluation of brand theory and its relevance to the independent retail sector', *Marketing Review*, Vol. 6, No. 1, pp. 55–71.

Sawyer, O. O., Megee, J. E., and Peterson, M. (2003), 'Perceived uncertainty and firm performance in SMEs: The role of personal networking activities', *International Small Business Journal*, Vol. 21, pp. 269–290.

Smith, A. and Sparks, L. (2000), 'The role and function of the independent small shop: the situation in Scotland', *International Review of Retail, Distribution and Consumer Research*, Vol. 10, No. 2, pp. 205–206.

Smith, P. and Swann, D. (1979), *Protecting the Consumer: An Economic and Legal Analysis*, Oxford: Martin Robertson.

Storey, D. (1994), *Understanding the Small Business Sector*, London: Routledge.

Swann, D. (1979), *Competition and Consumer Protection*, Harmondsworth: Penguin.

Welsh, R., Bent, R., Seamon, C. and Ingram, A. (2003), 'The challenge to C-stores: Edinburgh South Asian responses', *International Journal of Retail and Distribution Management*, Vol. 31, No. 8, pp. 408–417.

Chapter 15

Relationship marketing and networks in entrepreneurship

Sue Halliday

LEARNING OBJECTIVES

After reading this chapter, you will be able to:

■ explain how a relational, networking perspective to marketing enables collaboration which, in turn, creates innovation, knowledge and, therefore, competitive advantage in entrepreneurship

■ discuss how relationships and networks combine as strategic resources in entrepreneurship to create the desired outcome of valued customer experience

■ demonstrate ability to apply this understanding to gain knowledge of the business world and test your own ideas for setting up in business

■ demonstrate your skills in entrepreneurial marketing using the contents of this chapter to apply solutions to the case study.

Please note and reflect on the following five key learning points that appear in the course of this chapter:

1. There is a huge range of possible relationships for the SME to focus on in their marketing strategy. As a small business, do not overlook the social context when thinking about marketing.
2. Relational competence and skills in creating contexts conducive to trust are essential for the SME.
3. Creating customer perceptions of high-quality relationships enables competitive advantage to be developed by the firm in the marketplace.
4. Consider how each of the ten foundational premises of the service-dominant logic to marketing fits relational, networking SMEs.
5. The successful SME is inherently customer-oriented and relational.

INTRODUCTION

Relationships and networks are vital to entrepreneurship and marketing. New businesses need to be entrepreneurial in their marketing as well as in their business ideas. Research indicates that greater profits lie in the direction of developing ongoing relationships with customers, despite the necessary costs of investing in both product and service quality, and in relationship-building competences (Chaston, 1997).

Indeed, relationships are at the heart of marketing. In the USA a new definition of marketing was produced in 2004, the first for decades, and it included the word 'relationships'. That definition was hotly contested and has now been adapted to the current definition:

> Marketing is the activity, conducted by organizations and individuals, that operates through a set of institutions and processes for creating, communicating, delivering, and exchanging market offerings that have value for customers, clients, marketers, and society at large.
>
> (American Marketing Academy, 2007)

So, in 2007 the word 'relationships' is no longer there, but a careful reading of this definition will reveal that the idea of building relationships is a prior assumption for this definition. More evidence of the centrality of relationships and networks is given by Evert Gummesson, a pioneer of relationship and network marketing, in his latest definition:

> Total relationship marketing is marketing based on relationships, networks, and interaction, recognizing that marketing is embedded in the total management of networks of the selling organization, the market and society. It is directed to long-term win-win relationships with individual customers, and value is jointly created between the parties involved. It transcends the boundaries between specialist functions and disciplines.
>
> (Gummesson, 1999, p. 24, cited in Gummesson, 2008)

Society is reorganizing around global communications facilitated by the internet, by the creation of virtual organizations and by 'click and brick' combinations of real estate and website customer contact points. This 'New Economy' is also one which increasingly welcomes, even demands, an entrepreneurial spirit. Value created in and by organizations is increasingly understood to be only potential value: it is realized, or made real, by the customer. In this way, the customer is the one who integrates a company's offerings. This demands greater flexibility from organizations and creates great opportunity for entrepreneurial marketing.

This chapter will focus on the topics of relationship marketing and networks at this interface of entrepreneurship and marketing. It covers:

- roots of relationship marketing (RM)
- the six-markets model of RM
- what a relationship is
- the two core concepts of RM – trust and commitment
- current context for entrepreneurial RM
- two fundamental propositions for entrepreneurial RM today
- networks for entrepreneurial RM
- future direction of RM and networks.

We conclude with a short case study on Dovetail – Workers in Wood Ltd, for you to apply all the content of this chapter to a real-life example of a small sustainable business. Questions are best answered as a team activity.

ROOTS OF RELATIONSHIP MARKETING (RM)

RM brings into question the assumptions inherent in traditional consumer goods marketing. It has long been stated that marketing cannot continue in a transactional and adversarial manner, but needs to build up relationships of many sorts (Webster, 1992). It is about seeing a relationship from the customer's perspective and understanding just what they seek in a relationship (Palmer, 1994). Relationships are often the result of past history and so an issue of checking on the political environment becomes important – asking what role government policy has in influencing marketing networks is always a worthwhile question. Relationships also lead to an emphasis on politics with a lower-case 'p' – on the informal, sometimes illicit power structures such as the influence of the old boy network/old school tie which has to be analysed in order for the entrepreneur to assess her market opportunities and develop relational strategies (Gummesson, 1987).

RM, historically, links three other concepts: services marketing, network/interactive industrial goods marketing and total quality management (see Christopher *et al.*, 1991, and Gummesson, 1991). One effect that certainly impacts upon the SME is that even in large firms all are involved in marketing. The term part-time marketer (PTM) was coined to emphasize this broader marketing function, which now includes internal PTMs such as top management, telephonists and external PTMs such as consultants, dealers, customers, media, investors. This change means that the smaller firm will find it easier to ensure that its employees are trained and expected to act as marketers, whatever their specialism. Gummesson links this to service production and consumption ('servuction'; see Langeard *et al.*, 1981):

> It means that the more marketing is built into the servuction process and the more the opportunities provided by the points-of-marketing are utilised, the less you have to worry about the marketing department – a major part of the marketing will occur as a result of natural customer contacts during the servuction process.
>
> (Gummesson, 1991, p. 68)

THE SIX-MARKETS MODEL OF RM

The six markets are the stakeholders where relationships can be built to grow the entrepreneurial business. These six markets are where relationships and networks take place and so we see this model in action in the case study at the end of this chapter. Read this carefully and you will be able to apply this model in practice (see Figure 15.1).

WHAT IS A RELATIONSHIP?

Once relationships rather than transactions are at the heart of marketing, understanding is needed into how customer relationships are formed, with models that focus on relationships, not transactions (Webster, 1992). Gummesson introduced the '30 Rs' for companies to work out their own specific relationship portfolio – as you can see this covers all of life:

Classic market relationships
1. Supplier and customer
2. The customer–supplier–competitor triangle
3. Network – distribution channels

■ *Figure 15.1*
*The six-markets
model*

Source: Christopher
et al. (1991).

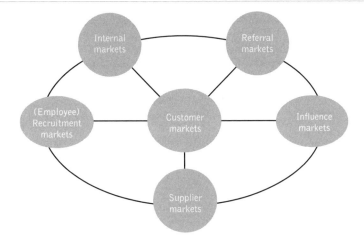

Special market relationships

4. Full-time marketers and part-time marketers
5. Customer and service provider
6. Many-headed customer and many-headed supplier
7. Relationship to the customer's customer
8. Close versus distant relationship
9. Dissatisfied customer
10. Monopoly relationship: customer or supplier as prisoner
11. Customer as 'member'
12. Electronic relationship
13. Parasocial relationships, with symbols and objects
14. Noncommercial relationship
15. The green relationship
16. The law-based relationship
17. The criminal network

Mega relationships

18. Personal and social networks
19. Mega marketing – the real 'customer' is not always found in the marketplace
20. Alliances change the market mechanism
21. The knowledge relationship
22. Mega alliances change the basic conditions for marketing
23. Mass-media relationship

Nano relationships

24. Market mechanisms are brought inside the company
25. Internal customer relationships
26. Quality providing a relationship between operations management and marketing
27. Internal marketing – relationships with the employee market
28. Two-dimensional matrix relationship
29. Relationship to external providers of marketing services
30. Owner and financier relationship

So you can see that there is a greater richness in relationship marketing which

> sees marketing activities as part of a larger context, inside as well as outside the company, which shall be beneficial to all parties in the long run, preferably also in the short run. Relationship marketing is a process, a chain of activities. It stresses flows and context. It represents a holistic attitude to marketing.
>
> (Gummesson, 1991, p. 64)

For further discussion on relational aspects of marketing, have a look at *Total Relationship Marketing* (Gummesson, 2008). For further implications for marketing as embedded in society see Chapter 23 on contemporary issues in entrepreneurship marketing.

KEY LEARNING POINT

There is a huge range of possible relationships for the SME to focus on in their marketing strategy. As a small business, do not overlook the social context when thinking about marketing.

When is a relationship a relationship?

It has been suggested that a relationship could only be said to exist when customers choose to use the language of interpersonal relationships – e.g. *my* builder/consultant/jeweller. Therefore, the richest approach is to focus on the customer's perspective in relationships and on any benefits they acquire from entering a relationship rather than undertaking a discrete set of transactions. It has been found that three primary types of benefits are appreciated (Gwinner *et al.*, 1998). Interestingly, confidence benefits were most highly prized, across the firms looked at, followed by social benefits and finally special treatment benefits. Confidence is defined as covering the sense of reduced anxiety, faith in the trustworthiness of the provider, reduced perceptions of anxiety and risk and knowing what to expect.

Confidence creation is a relatively straightforward tool for entrepreneurs to include in their relationship marketing plans. Relationships act to reduce risk, since what is not known or understood (such as the expertise of the builder or the marketing consultant or kitchen designer) is mitigated by personal knowledge of the builder, consultant or designer. This is one way in which trust is such an important element of RM – we will give further thought to this topic shortly.

Relationships are important to the SME. Research early on in the development of relationship marketing (Crosby *et al.*, 1990) found that effective relationship selling will be most critical when:

- the service is complex, customized and delivered over a continuous stream of transactions
- the environment is dynamic and uncertain in ways that affect future needs (demand) and offerings (supply).

This is where the entrepreneur is likely to be growing his/her business.

THE TWO CORE CONCEPTS FOR RM – TRUST AND COMMITMENT

The Morgan and Hunt model of RM (Figure 15.2) gives us two core concepts for RM – trust and commitment.

Trust

According to both buyers and sellers, trust is by far the most important factor characterizing a good relationship. It is relevant to SMEs to consider trust as part of societal norms, as part of the glue of social capital and contributing to the continuous web of business and social relations. Markets are part of society – they are what is called socially embedded, for far more than mere economic behaviours take place within the business arena. This is obvious when we reflect for a moment on how entrepreneurial behaviour varies across cultures. Singaporean Chinese are known for the persistence and work ethic that leads entrepreneurial businesses to thrive. Equally and connectedly, the family is supportive of this approach to business. In the UK corporate life is seen as far more 'natural' – and success is often understood as linked to the size of the company worked for. Again, from an era of greater social stability, many in their sixties and seventies in the UK are retiring on company pensions earned from long-term employment in one company. Younger generations in the UK have learned from the 'me' decades and from the 1980s and whole Thatcher period that to thrive it is possible and profitable to set up in business for oneself. So marketing is situated in the context of social norms – and the likelihood to trust is part of that social context. In a recent review of entrepreneurship and its links to marketing, social networking and relationships with customers and other stakeholders are seen as being at the foundation of entrepreneurial marketing (Hills *et al.*, 2008). Social networking is of course primarily a social norm.

Defining trust

'Trust' is a rich and complex concept. Trust, as distinct from naïveté, is rational, for it is not based on complete ignorance, but rather on a reasonable calculation made in the face of some ignorance. If there really was a setting with a perfect market where there was transparency of full information, then trust would be of no relevance for complete knowledge obviates the need for trust. Trust, therefore, functions in conditions of some ignorance. On the other

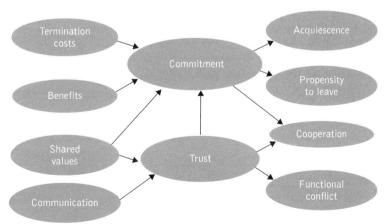

Figure 15.2
Model of relationship marketing (trust and commitment at core)

Source: Adapted from Morgan and Hunt Trust–Commitment model of relationship marketing.

hand, in a state of total ignorance there can be no reason to trust (and naïveté would then be exercised). Consequently, trust comes into play in conditions of ignorance of some aspect of the negotiation or interaction. In business this ignorance will often be caused by uncertain future outcomes. Hence the emphasis on management decision-taking processes – control is aimed for by making reasonable decisions based on acknowledged assumptions. SME owner-managers are often motivated by high levels of desire for control, and this, matched to skills in creating contexts conducive to trust, is at a premium in developing relational marketing for market growth.

KEY LEARNING POINT
Relational competence and skills in creating contexts conducive to trust are essential for the SME.

In the face of uncertainty, all writers on the topic of trust wrestle with where to place trust on a continuum with regulation at one end and opportunism at the other (see Figure 15.3). Opportunism calculates that nothing will create certainty and so takes action. Regulation ensures that optimal calculations are made, according to criteria of risk aversion, that information is fully shared and that vulnerability cannot be exploited. An option to reduce uncertainty between these two extremes is to trust, either initially ('placed trust') or increasingly during a process of relationship building ('trust as response'); another option is to take a risk (Halliday, 2004). Attitudes to risk vary, from risk aversion, through risk neutrality to risk seeking, and the entrepreneur's attitude to risk is a hotly contested issue. Are they risk takers? Or do they seek to reduce risk and to gain control by skills and knowledge which act to mitigate what might be risks if taken by others?

This is part of the broader realm of business life and is also part of social relationship building.

> Trust is the reliance by one person, group or firm upon a voluntarily accepted duty on the part of another person, group or firm to recognize and protect the rights and interests of all others engaged in a joint endeavour or economic exchange.
>
> (Hosmer, 1995, p. 392)

This definition embraces obligations and interests. In this way, trust is deeper than reliance on either promise or competence. Trust implies the personal characteristic of trustworthiness on the part of the trusted. Blanket trust rarely exists – rather, we trust someone in a constrained context and/or for a particular purpose (Blois, 1999).

opportunism_____ trust _____regulation

Figure 15.3
Responses to uncertainty according to perceptions of risk

How does trust work?

Placed trust

'Placed trust' is a trusting act which enables initial understanding for the service delivery, or alliance, or whatever dependence is involved. For the antecedents to 'placed trust' are out there, in society, in social norms, in communally understood competences, in scripts and roles and characters (Pavis, 1998). Relevant to SMEs is that 'placed trust' is an outcome of prior expertise and reputation building. Reputations depend on the 'embeddedness' of interactions in structures or networks of social relations (Raub and Weesie, 1990). This highlights the importance of another of the areas for networking in the six-markets model: influence markets. The social context for the entrepreneur is critical to her success.

In evaluating the successful functioning of 'placed trust', there is the interesting conundrum of how to evaluate the other's competence. Not to do so would open up the debate about trust to charges of irrationality once more and we have seen that not to have grounds for believing in this competence would be naïveté. If trustworthiness is to be assessed prior to entering a relationship, how then is the evaluation to be made? Would trusting an incompetent professional (or entrepreneur) be trusting or naïve? We can answer that it is trust, 'placed trust', because the context indicates that it is reasonable to assume competence. This gives a place for branding in entrepreneurial marketing, for within the act of trusting there is the expectation of a technically competent role performance, and branding can sum this up for the consumer in the form of an understood code in a symbol. This is an important message for entrepreneurs: entrepreneurs benefit from a good social reputation.

So, 'placed trust' depends on the trustworthiness of the other, and these societally embedded expectations are largely, by their very nature, met. When they are not (as in the English scandal of the murderous family doctor in Cheshire) there is outrage and horror. 'Placed trust' is robust, but is betrayed by such flouting of social norms. Researchers working on an MBA cohort found what they described as surprisingly high levels of initial trust. But let us consider this context. All students had successfully passed a selection process. All had very similar ambitions in joining the programme. For this context and purpose, as fellow MBA students, they could trust one another (i.e. place trust in one another). This is 'placed trust' and not the trust in response to the other's actions.

Commitment

Trust as response

Trust in response to the other's actions is the kind of trust most written about and it is understood in the literature to contribute to loyal purchasing by creating commitment (see the Morgan and Hunt model in Figure 15.2). It is the expectation of fairness that breeds commitment instead of the alternative over time, in conditions of dependency, of a desire to escape. Commitment in a mutually beneficial relationship is needed for profitability and for high levels of word-of-mouth recommendations; this is built upon 'trust as response' to behaviours on the service provider's part to create commitment to marketing relationships. Mutuality in relationships requires matching 'trust as response' with trustworthiness rather than reciprocal trustfulness. This trust can therefore be used in creating marketing relationships.

Entrepreneurs succeed when they build trust – this is often not articulated as a marketing strategy but as a result of interpersonal connections. Here we can see how central an element trust building is to the creation of a good entrepreneurial marketing strategy and plan. Trust as a response is most likely to create both repeat custom and new custom with friends of the customer – it creates commitment.

See the case study at the end of this chapter for a worked example of this informal relationship marketing strategy.

Spotlight on service quality

Customer perceptions of service quality are more important than any managerial or professional definition of quality internal to the organization (see Parasuraman *et al.*, 1985). Understanding the customer and the components of service quality in the mind of the customer can therefore give competitive edge to the service organization. From a focus on services marketing the spotlight is on service quality: expressed simply, companies providing high service quality, as perceived by their customers, tend to be the most profitable companies. Small businesses have the ability to grow and to be sustained by relatively fewer customers and so customer recommendation, as we demonstrate in the case study at the end of this chapter, is a key relational marketing strategy for the entrepreneur.

A major conceptual contribution from services marketing scholars has been to see that perceived service quality is the difference between expected service and perceived service. This gap can be a major hurdle in attempting to deliver a service which consumers would perceive as being of high quality. Ten determinants of service quality were tabulated as: access, communication*, competence, courtesy*, credibility, reliability*, responsiveness*, security, tangibles, understanding/knowing the customer*. Those denoted with an asterisk are clearly directly linked to the quality of the relationships, that, in our case, the entrepreneur or the SME itself has created. Those customers who seek a relationship in their business decisions will form profitable targets for the SME skilled in relationship development. In this way, segmentation of customers by relational and service quality expectations will often be useful in seeking competitive advantage.

> **KEY LEARNING POINT**
> Creating customer perceptions of high-quality relationships enables competitive advantage to be developed by the firm in the marketplace.

CURRENT CONTEXT FOR ENTREPRENEURIAL RELATIONSHIP MARKETING

A study of entrepreneurial marketing as a newly establishing discipline within marketing (see Morris *et al.*, 2002) emphasized that entrepreneurial marketing has a twin focus in interesting ways: a focus on innovation and creativity and a focus on relationship building to obtain a wider resource base. The former clearly takes from the entrepreneurship literature and practice, and the latter focus is developed from the RM approach discussed in this chapter.

Service-dominant logic to marketing

RM in SMEs now also needs to be understood as fitting in the latest theoretical context: the ten foundational premises of service-dominant logic (Vargo and Lusch, 2004). For the focus on relationships that has been described in this chapter has led to a re-evaluation of the marketing discipline. It has led to leaders of marketing thought in the United States proposing what they call a new logic to marketing – what they term a new dominant logic – the service-dominant logic (see Vargo and Lusch, 2004).

They charted developments in marketing (see Figure 15.4) as a move from marketing management as very much a function within the firm to a services marketing emphasis on process to the latest manifestation of this process focus, termed 'network management processes'.

KEY LEARNING POINT

Consider how each of the ten foundational premises of the service-dominant logic to marketing fits relational, networking SMEs.

Figure 15.4
Evolving to a
new dominant
logic for
marketing

Source: Vargo and
Lusch (2004, p. 4).

Pre-1900

Goods-centered
Model
of Exchange
(Concepts:
tangibles,
statics, discrete
transactions,
and operand
resources)

Thought leaders in marketing continually move away from tangible output with embedded value in which the focus was on activities directed at discrete or static transactions. In turn, they move toward dynamic exchange relationships that involve performing processes and exchanging skills and/or services in which value is co-created with the consumer. The worldview changes from a focus on resources on which an operation or act is performed (operand resources) to resources that produce effects (operant resources).

Twenty-first century

Service-centered
Model of Exchange
(Concepts: intangibles,
competences,
dynamics, exchange
processes and
relationships, and
operant resources)

Classical and Neoclassical Economics (1800–1920)

Formative Marketing Thought (Descriptive: 1900–1950)

- Commodities
- Marketing institutions
- Marketing functions

Marketing Management School of Thought (1950–2000)

- Customer orientation and marketing concept
- Value determined in marketplace
- Manage marketing functions to achieve optimal output
- Marketing science emerges and emphasizes use of optimization techniques

Marketing as a Social and Economic Process (Emerging paradigm: 1980–2000 and forward)

- Market orientation processes
- Services marketing processes
- Relationship marketing processes
- Quality management processes
- Value and supply management processes
- Resource management and competitive processes
- Network management processes

Table 15.1 *Service-dominant logic foundational premise modifications and additions*

	Original foundation premise	Modified foundation premise	Comment/Explanation
FP1	The application of specialized skills and knowledge is the fundamental unit of exchange	Service is the fundamental basis of exchange	The application of operant resources (knowledge and skills), 'service', as defined in S-D logic, is the basis for all exchange. Service is exchanged for service
FP2	Indirect exchange masks the fundamental unit of exchange	Indirect exchange masks the fundamental basis of exchange	Because service is provided through complex combinations of goods, money, and institutions, the service basis of exchange is not always apparent
FP3	Goods are a distribution mechanisms for service provision	Goods are a distribution mechanism for service provision	Goods (both durable and non-durable) derive their value with use – the service they provide
FP4	Knowledge is the fundamental source of competitive advantage	Operant resources are the fundamental source of competitive advantage	The comparative ability to cause desired change drives competition
FP5	All economies are services economies	All economies are service economies	Service (singular) is only becoming more apparent with increased specialization and outsourcing
FP6	The customer is always a co-producer	The customer is always a co-creator of value	Implies value creation is interactional
FP7	The enterprise can only make value propositions	The enterprise cannot deliver value, but only offer value propositions	Enterprises can offer their applied resources for value creation and collaboratively (interactively) create following acceptance of value propositions, but cannot create and deliver value independently
FP8	A service-centered view is customer-oriented and relational	A service-centered view is inherently customer-oriented and relational	Because service is defined in terms of customer-determined benefit and co-created it is inherently customer-oriented and relational
FP9	Organizations exist to integrate and transform microspecialized competences into complex services that are demanded in the marketplace	All social and economic actors are resource integrators	Implies the context of value creation is networks of networks (resource integrators)
FP10		Value is always uniquely and phenomenologically determined by the beneficiary	Value is idiosyncratic, experiential, contextual and meaning-laden

Source: Vargo and Lusch (2008).

These are still being formulated and tested out by academics but clearly these ten premises make interesting research questions for student dissertations at undergraduate or postgraduate levels. It is also interesting to note how closely these new foundational premises connect with the focus of this chapter: networks and relationships are seen as fundamental building blocks for marketing and co-creation of customer value. Here innovation is sourced from understanding how, variously, customers integrate resources to create a valued experience.

The core idea relevant to this chapter is encapsulated in:

FP8 A service-centred view is inherently customer-oriented and relational.

The latest additional premise is key for entrepreneurs tempted to focus on their new business proposition:

FP10 Value is always uniquely and phenomenologically determined by the beneficiary.

The two foundational premises of clear relevance to relationship marketing and networking in SMEs are:

FP4 Knowledge is the fundamental source of competitive advantage.

FP7 The enterprise can only make value propositions.

TWO FOUNDATIONAL PREMISES FOR ENTREPRENEURIAL RM TODAY

Knowledge is the fundamental source of competitive advantage

Innovation is the lifeblood of entrepreneurship. Innovation, as a construct linking novelty and creativity and the ability to learn, is the key differentiator between entrepreneurial marketing and mainstream marketing. How this mix can be enabled is a central question for entrepreneurial marketing as a discipline, or sub-discipline.

To learn there needs to be shared meaning and these meanings have to be shared within and across organizations and their customers. The flexibility required for success in start-up situations may be linked to the shared mindset required for successful learning.

In a recent report, 'Entrepreneurial and Small Business Marketing (ESBM)' is defined as 'managing resources and capabilities required to discover and develop new opportunities'. 'ESBM is contextual, is a process and content is situation specific and focused on creativity, opportunities, judgment and vision' (Carson, 2004). In fact, we can sum this up as learning from knowledge development. Knowledge itself is developed by co-creation of value with customers in networks.

We have seen that entrepreneurial marketing can gain from understanding marketers as actors playing evolving, dynamic roles in a process of adaptation. And how can parties adapt if they cannot learn? Learning is central: Day has noted that organizations continuously learn about their markets through the linked processes of market sensing and sense making (see Day, 2002). Our focus here is on the need to take this aspect of organizations when implementing a marketing programme. This is neatly modelled by Sinkula et al. (1997), who link together gathering market-based information for marketing programmes with organizational learning (see Figure 15.5).

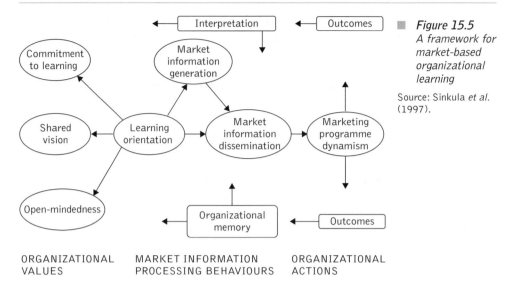

Figure 15.5
A framework for
market-based
organizational
learning

Source: Sinkula et al.
(1997).

Day has summarized the current position regarding the centrality of learning from information:

> To complete a continuous process of learning, the organization has to have a way to capture and retain the information and knowledge it has collected, and needs to be able to access this knowledge quickly and efficiently. Advances in information technology have made the process of designing and building these shared knowledge bases on a large scale much easier. The resulting knowledge base may be one of the firm's most valuable assets.
> (Day, 2002, p. 251)

The opportunity, the perception of a gap in the market, when accompanied by the important question 'Is there a market in the gap?' is the other key concept that unites these two disciplines. Information is the oxygen of marketing; marketers get market information in the form of feedback on customer service, on new ideas from customers, of research on why people are not or are no longer customers. For the entrepreneur this often comes from intuition, innovation and connectedness via the personal contact network (PCN – we will mention this in more detail later). What thinking has linked a focus on competences, on the entrepreneur and the marketer as individuals capable of creating personal networks and of having knowledge and intuition to share? RM links these ideas.

Researchers (see Kok et al., 2003) note that market-oriented product development may be regarded as an organization learning capability. It has been said that in the entrepreneurial, SME setting, marketing is learning.

The enterprise can only make value propositions

For the SME this means that, to a large extent, innovation is co-created with customers. Once we have identified as key issues relational management, learning and meaning creation and management we have the heart of the innovative process under scrutiny.

Value is created by so-called 'toolkits for user innovation and design' (see Franke and Piller, 2004), a method of integrating customers into new product development and design. These toolkits allow customers to create their own product, which in turn is produced by the manufacturer. Over the past few years many more firms have turned to the internet as a mechanism for communicating with their customers. Significantly, the internet enables manufacturers to communicate directly with their customers without the need for intermediaries such as retailers and wholesalers. It also provides the opportunity for firms to interact with customers, in particular with a collection of customers, and for customers to interact with customers. By interacting with potential customers on technology capabilities possessed by the firm opportunities for deploying and utilizing this technology may emerge. That is, genuine new product opportunities may be developed. So much so that Prahalad and Ramaswamy (2002, p. 36) write:

> The market has become a forum in which consumers play an active role in creating and competing for value. The distinguishing feature of this new marketplace is that consumers become a new source of *competence* for the corporation.

Somehow, the communications need to foster closeness – as Drucker writes, 'for communications to be effective, there has to be both information and meaning. And meaning requires communion' (Drucker, 2001, p. 341). This is all in fact easier for the entrepreneur and the small business, relying on interpersonal skills and networking.

To emphasize this important connection of the customer with value we can add in a model that overtly links cash flow to customer relevance. For 'relevance', read 'value'. Hills and Singh's (2000) *Research at the Marketing/Entrepreneurship Interface* provided a model of the small firm (see Figure 15.6). It is an important insight to link cash flow to the core business idea and, by this means, to value:

> The functional entity produces goods and services. Its relevance to customer's needs essentially determines how the firm's cashflow from operations changes. As customer relevance increases, cashflow from operations increases. As customer relevance decreases, cashflow from operations is reduced.

> (Hills and Singh, p. 198)

Entrepreneurial marketing continues to have retaining customers as its focus. Therefore, a key marketing process becomes the development of business relationships (see Gummesson, 1997).

KEY LEARNING POINT
The successful SME is inherently customer-oriented and relational.

NETWORKS FOR ENTREPRENEURIAL RM

We have seen and discussed how Vargo and Lusch, in 2004, charted developments in marketing as a move from marketing management as the real focus of the discipline, in which it is very much a function within the firm and a study of that function, to the perspective from the 1980s of marketing as a social and economic process. Services marketing emphasized processes

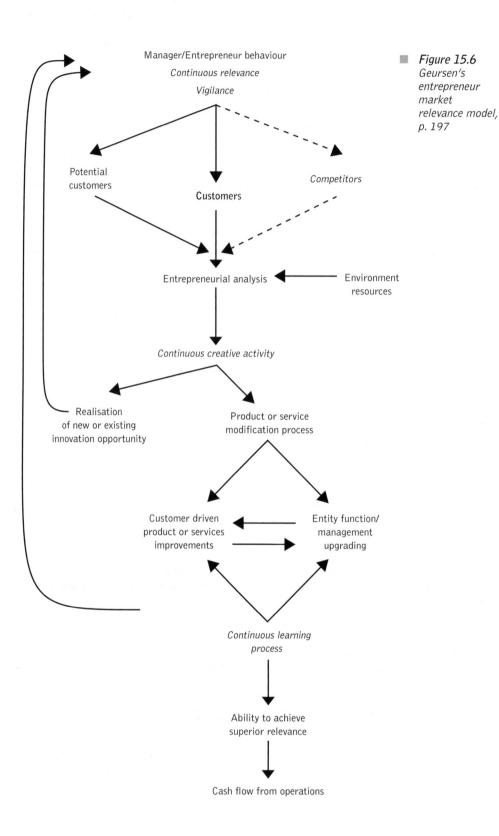

Manager/Entrepreneur behaviour
Continuous relevance
Vigilance

Potential
customers

Customers

Competitors

Entrepreneurial analysis ← Environment
resources

Continuous creative activity

Realisation
of new or existing
innovation opportunity

Product or service
modification process

Customer driven
product or services
improvements

Entity function/
management
upgrading

*Continuous learning
process*

Ability to achieve
superior relevance

Cash flow from operations

■ *Figure 15.6*
Geursen's
entrepreneur
market
relevance model,
p. 197

and those that focused on the customer led to the development of customer RM. Additional perspectives on value and quality, much as discussed in this chapter, followed and the latest manifestation of this process focus has been termed 'network management processes'.

Kay (1993) suggests that the *external linkages* that a company has developed over time and the investment in this network of relationships (generated from its past activities) form a distinctive competitive capability.

What is a network?

At some basic level, the first network into which human beings are, quite literally, born is the family. In classes on a masters programme on entrepreneurship not only does the UK attract a great many students from overseas but also those students are most often drawn from cultures where the family business predominates as a structure of size and ownership. Recent research reviewed the whole area of family businesses and found that they tend to outperform non-family firms (see Ibrahim *et al.*, 2008). Reasons given are various. They are found to be nimbler, more active in the community and both more quality- and more customer-oriented. Certainly the last three of these factors can be directly related to personal orientations in a family business. And so the actual network of the family is the basic network for the entrepreneurial firm. Non-family firms can emulate the focus on these areas without becoming a real blood-related family!

Personal contact networks (PCNs) have been focused upon by previous textbook writers (see Carson *et al.*, 1995, and Bjerke and Hultman, 2002). These can be seen as assets to the firm. They are not for sale. They are only realizable by the persons creating them. The feel is essentially personal and they will provide knowledge, market information and opportunities for learning that match the flexible unstructured approach to business development favoured by entrepreneurs. Although the scale is personal, it may be that new members of the PCN are sought for their ability to contribute a missing resource for the entrepreneur – be that resource finance, technical know-how or access to particular new markets. This is how networking fits into growing the entrepreneurial firm and finding the resources to feed this growth.

Another perspective on a network can be gained by looking at the network surrounding a patient who, once pictured as the centre of a complex network of service providers, can be re-imagined as effectively a network manager in a health-care setting (see Figure 15.7).

Networks can be small if they depend on real-time interpersonal knowledge – research on church size in the UK indicates that while the membership stays at 120–150 people feel they know each other, but once a church reaches 200 there are too many members for all of them to even know the names of every other member or to recognize them on sight. However, with the advent of the internet and Web 2.0 individuals can be part of much larger, complex, but virtual, networks. Social networking is still in its early days, but clearly there is potential for the SME in being part of this mostly social, but partly business, networking medium. Gummesson (2010) notes that network theory can tackle complex networks. He coins the term 'many-to-many marketing' and charts out a range of opportunities for the marketer who studies the 'Anna' network (Figure 15.7). In a 2006 journal article (see Gummesson, 2006, p. 349) he defines this version of marketing practice as the description, analysis and utilization of the network properties of marketing.

For the SME it is sufficient to note that they will be in a network and that a good marketing practice is to map that network and then plan how to develop the sets of relationships that it includes. Where does this small business fit into the 'many-to-many' setting? How many

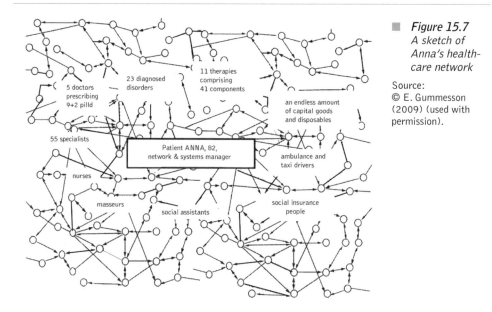

Figure 15.7
A sketch of Anna's health-care network

Source:
© E. Gummesson
(2009) (used with
permission).

networks is it part of? Marketing action involves prioritizing some actors in the network with whom maximum value can be co-created.

Developing marketing through the use of formal business networks

The key point of looking at networks is to develop the business by using them as a method of growth. Networks will be made up of people from across those six markets introduced earlier (see Figure 15.1). Rocks *et al.* (2005) noted a diverse range of members of networks used by SMEs in the grocery sector in Northern Ireland: 'other owner/managers within the channel, sales teams, channel intermediary, retailing and manufacturing firms, people within the food industry, distributors, agents, consumers, buying teams, UK multiples, symbol wholesales, consultancy firms, PR agencies, and trade associations' (p. 87). These networks were found to be flexible, but very stable and this was key to the value created within them. These were found to be formal, rather than informal, social networks.

Collaborative competence in networks

A useful framework for thinking about where the entrepreneur needs to collaborate to successfully grow the business is the six markets model (see Figure 15.1). The influence markets are those people who can make or break a small business's reputation. Many small firms can be strengthened by being recommended by mediators – perhaps professionals in their field such as accountants, lawyers and bankers. Small companies competing internationally might employ the local business club to recommend their work in global locations. Referral markets are even closer to the business in the sense that they can actually refer business to the small firm. Many industries have lists of approved suppliers – being part of the network is absolutely crucial. So is building a good relationship with customers, providing excellent after-sales care and so creating business through word-of-mouth (WOM) recommendation. (See the case study for an example of a business built on WOM.) Supplier markets, for the smaller business, will depend on interpersonal skills – the existence of finance at a competitive rate of interest or at the right time can be down to good relationships with bankers. The entrepreneurial business is in fact likely to be at the hub of a network of suppliers – see the case study for a fully worked example of this. Another textbook on entrepreneurial marketing (see Bjerke and Hultman, 2002) talks of the small firm becoming a virtual firm – or the hub of the network rather than one focused on the organization itself – a focal firm. This virtual firm is a series of linked members of a network, most probably connected electronically, where innovation is shared and learning fostered. In this way marketing for the SME is not just a smaller version of marketing in the large transnational firm.

We have seen, then, that collaboration is critical, and for the SME the outcome will not only be business contacts but also, less tangibly and no less importantly, learning. Hamel *et al.* (1995) lament that where 'the Japanese have generally learned more than their UK or US partners, this is not due to oriental deviousness, but to occidental indolence. The key to competing through collaboration is to have the mindset to learn' (p. 147).

Ongoing challenge

Creating positive, profitable relationships across networks, both informally and in structured ways, formally, in networks that are constellations of networks, is the constant challenge for the entrepreneurial business. Improving investor relations is hitting the headlines as an outstanding requirement for the SME seeking a listing (see Dawber, 2010). This competence presents a key challenge for you in understanding and, in due course, practising entrepreneurship marketing.

FUTURE DIRECTION OF RM AND NETWORKS

RM is perhaps no longer new; however, it is still of great relevance to the entrepreneur as it can be seen as that which links a business, its customers and the other stakeholders in the firm. For entrepreneurs, who may find it easy to focus on their innovative service or product, the key message is that interpersonal relationships, sometimes mediated electronically, are part of building a sustainable (and therefore, for serial entrepreneurs, a saleable) business.

RM has become established as an approach to marketing; a number of European professors set up a research project to assess RM's future as a way of doing business, to predict its likely strength in 2015 (see Bonnemaizon *et al.*, 2007). They found four themes current and likely to determine the future in RM:

1. *Increasingly RM will become a focus on a network of relationships connected to a business.* This perspective on the future is relevant to entrepreneurial companies because this is such a central feature of any successful entrepreneur's business. That this is to become more central essentially gives the SME competitive advantage. It also underlines that the wannabe entrepreneur needs to focus here when developing personal competences to set up in business.
2. *An element of this will be complex databases to hold customer-related data and using ICT to measure the value of relationships to the business.* This is of great relevance to the growth-minded entrepreneur/SME, as it is a reminder of the investment needed to turn a PCN into a foundation for significant development.
3. *Firms will have to involve customers less by selling to them, more by genuinely creating a two-way flow of information in order to play a role more in creating value with them rather than in delivering value to them.* This perspective on the future is relevant to entrepreneurial

companies because this, once again, is a central competence for the SME and so, once again, as this moves centre stage, so the SME gains competitive advantage.

4. *Consumer experience will be increasingly important. Yet this is less susceptible to management by the business.* This perspective on the future is relevant to entrepreneurial companies because the greater the personal contact and social embeddedness of the firm, the easier it is to influence the customer experience. 'Experiential marketing' (see Schmitt, 1999) views consumers less as rational decision makers who care about functional features and benefits, and more as emotional human beings who are concerned with achieving pleasurable experiences.

The personal, central role of the entrepreneur in the SME plays to a more emotional approach to marketing. This is increasingly important. A key idea to be found in Prahalad and Ramaswamy's (2004) *The Future of Competition: Co-Creating Unique Value with Customers* is that the power over the value chain will increasingly be in the consumer's head and hands and that winning firms will be able to co-create value with their customers. The good news is that the flexibility and customer-responsiveness that this implies on the part of the firm is well suited to the entrepreneurial SME. According to Bonnemaizon *et al.* (2007),

> [t]he future of relational marketing will depend on the ability to play with communities that can either destroy a firm or strengthen it. Between now and 2015, identifying consumer's experiences or those of a group of consumers, will create a marketing that is truly relational. This will be a wonderful challenge for any firm that understands the complexity of a relationship which will be increasingly facilitated by current and future modes of communication.

(p. 57)

REVIEW QUESTIONS

1. List out the benefits to customers of being in a relationship with an SME.

2. Why should an SME focus on relationship building in its marketing strategy?

3. Write out in one sentence your idea for setting up an entrepreneurial business.

4. List out the benefits to the customer of using your goods and/or services.

5. Give examples of businesses you can think of that would benefit from relational selling.

6. Are you a person who trusts easily? Are you trustworthy? List out why customers for your business idea should place their trust in you.

7. Now, write out your business idea in one sentence, making sure you include what potential value to them you are offering. Reflect on how this differs from your answer to Question 3.

8. What new understanding does a focus on relationships and networks give to the core entrepreneurship concept of innovation?

9. How do learning, knowledge and innovation connect?

10. Where is value to be found in the entrepreneurial business?

CASE STUDY 15: DOVETAIL – WORKERS IN WOOD LTD

John Kirby set up in business over 20 years ago just as the fitted kitchen was becoming an established requirement for the new homeowner. Large department stores all had fitted kitchen departments and John saw the opportunity to offer a more personal service to the top end of this market for those who could pay for this customization. Each kitchen is made by their skilled team of workers at their workshop in Hampshire; images can be viewed at the Dovetail website (www.dovetail.tc).

Background

Houses have always had kitchens – somewhere to prepare cooked food. For the elite in British society the kitchen was where servants produced food. After the First World War households became smaller, and by the 1950s space was at a premium in most middle-class houses. Efficiency led to the design of the fitted kitchen. In 2001 the UK fitted kitchens market was worth £3.2 billion annually. Modest growth was predicted for the 2002–2006 period; however, in 2006 sales of fitted kitchens grew by 16 per cent. In 2004 one SME in this area had invested in machinery and manufacturing space that produced one typical kitchen every 2 minutes! (see www.dovetail.tc). The market is dependent upon the economy; when the housing market is on the move it benefits from upgrades upon each sale cycle of the house.

The distribution chain is dominated by outlets such as MFI and IKEA and contains smaller DIY outlets and builders' merchants, as well as very many smaller, more customized options. At the most expensive end the chain stretches to the small team of craftsmen. Here we find, at this top end of the range, Dovetail – Workers in Wood Ltd., where the average price of a kitchen is £50,000. John and his team maintain exceptional standards of craftsmanship and service. These kitchens are built to last (the website includes a customer commenting that her eight-year-old kitchen remains great).

Dovetail design, project-manage, hand-craft and install their kitchens. They make a virtue of their small size to relate to their customers personally. Their website addresses issues in working in a small team: 'We play to our strengths and make up for each other's weaknesses.'

Customers

Customers are the lifeblood of this business, as they are of any business. The order book has steadily grown over 20 years and John has been able to move from having three or four months' work planned ahead to nearer a year of bookings. The firm has produced approximately one kitchen a month over the last decade.

In 2010 the UK recession began to bite and the order pipeline began to shorten to three to four months. This led John to advertise. His experience of this has been grim. He found himself competing with companies with much bigger advertising budgets, such as Smallbone of Devizes (www.smallbone.co.uk). John is finding that the potential customer is much more doubtful of his firm's capacity and, therefore, takes much more persuasion. The customer is also likely to be pursuing two or three companies at the same time, so that even if the kitchen is purchased, Dovetail's chance of success is reduced to one in three. Nevertheless, this sales channel now produces three or four kitchens a year, which is proving useful in the current recession, which has had a strongly negative impact on the housing market as a whole.

This experience has led John to value even more highly his past customer base. For they act as a vital referral market for the company. Ninety per cent of Dovetail's customers come to the firm via recommendation from friends. These friends have, albeit at second-hand, experienced the new Dovetail kitchen and, indeed, doubtless, heard the saga. Therefore, they are immediately confident that Dovetail can produce a great kitchen for them. They understand the prices charged, and will have a feel for the way that John involves his customers in the design as much as they wish.

In this way John's new customers have already learned what it is like to do business with Dovetail before they themselves commit to purchase. This is the value of the referral market. What does this cost Dovetail? Well, very little. While John has wondered about paying for these referrals, it really is a natural part of the process of producing delighted customers. So the real cost is to produce continually excellent service.

Customer comments are quoted on the website:

We simply love our new kitchen. John and his team were amazingly patient in working and re-working the design until we had something with which we were completely happy. They made many suggestions that we would never have thought of (such as built-in bins and crockery drawers instead of cupboards) and persuaded us to think boldly at times.

Dovetail was recommended to us by close friends and John Kirby and his team met the brief, they were alone in this. We enjoyed the relationship of working up the design, selecting materials and details with them.

There is a strong technical element to Dovetail's work, as another customer realized:

We were delighted with the kitchen that Dovetail built for us. It was a difficult space with some very strange angled walls but John Kirby came up with some creative solutions and managed to incorporate everything that we wanted.

Spotlight on service quality

For the business to flourish by obtaining referrals, the service quality has to be high. They get the basics right, as the following customer comments show:

The kitchen was also built on time and within budget.

You produced and installed a product of the very highest quality. The process was enjoyable and the result provides endless pleasure.

From the very start to the final fitting the service and quality was faultless.

The installation went very smoothly and, if any problems did crop up, they were overcome without us hearing about them.

In this market repeat custom has been rare. John's rural customers do not move house very often. Once they have bought their kitchen, they do not need another. He can count on the fingers of one hand those who have moved and so asked him to supply a second kitchen – and that includes a couple of customers who asked him to renew the kitchen in their second home! John does not admit to being influenced by fashion, claiming that he offers timeless classics. However, there are undoubtedly echoes of current fashion trends in his kitchens and he and his customers are undoubtedly attuned to what is being reported in the fashionable magazines.

Therefore, a key influence market is the glossy magazine selling dreams of the desirable country home interior. However, John has found that winning PR on his kitchens generates only very poor sales leads. These potential customers may share dreams of the aspirational kitchen with his clients on the website – they may not share their ability to pay. For a small company like Dovetail, with no one detailed to answer the phone all day, the volume of enquiries generated is also a headache. John now considers that this route to market is not profitable for him, as a small entrepreneur.

Networks

Suppliers are absolutely critical to his business success. And it is from them Dovetail effectively wins repeat business. Plumbers, electricians, architects and interior designers all recommend him to their customers again and again. John views this network of collaborators in the successful design and fitting of a kitchen as part of the team. He comments, 'You can never find the perfect supplier. I have learned to work with a good one and to bring them along during the process. I consider it my job to manage them: if they mess up, I mess up'.

Recruitment is an issue for Dovetail. It is a small team that depends on each member performing well for each customer. The work is a series of complicated tasks that is a learning experience for each project – John does not want to lose the skills and knowledge built up in the business. However, over the years he has employed new staff and has learned to go to the schools to catch them young. He asks the design teachers in local schools and colleges, with whom he carefully builds personal relationships, who of the youngsters has the essential, if elusive, spark. He uses their experience to drive his choice of new apprentices.

Once members of staff join the company John knows that he needs to create a climate that encourages them to perform to their potential and to stay. They celebrate the end of every project with an evening out – perhaps down at a local bowling alley. Over the years he has played host and even social worker, offering to arrange money management counselling for members of staff.

If there is one key to his success in terms of living his dream of setting up his own business he has found that it is all about relationships rather than all about his original profession: master carpenter. Relationships mean that customers and company can put up with a lot from each other. What is the key to his business success? 'If you are not perceived as trustworthy you have nothing to offer anybody.'

Source: www.jtcfurnituregroup.com, www.joneskitchens.co.uk

CASE QUESTIONS AND TASKS

1. Do you see evidence of customer value being co-created with customers? List this out.
2. Map out the stakeholders that might feature in a marketing plan for Dovetail using the six-markets model.
3. Do you think the six-markets model of RM is a good way to understand this small business?

4. What do you think are the three key success factors in this business? Why?

5. Why has John not grown his company over time? List out the issues in growing the entrepreneurial firm and how relationships and networks might act as both enablers and constraints.

6. Draw up a plan to double the size of the firm over the next three years.

7. Do you think this is a good idea? Justify your plans and/or your doubts.

REFERENCES

American Marketing Association (2007), Definition of Marketing. Available at: http://www.marketing power.com/aboutama/pages/definitionofmarketing.aspx

Bjerke, Björn and Hultman, Claes M. (2002), *Entrepreneurial Marketing: The Growth of Small Firms in the New Economic Era*, Edward Elgar Publishing, Cheltenham.

Blois, Keith J. (1999), Trust in business to business relationships: an evaluation of its status, *Journal of Management Studies*, 36(2), 197–217.

Bonnemaizon, Audrey, Cova, Bernard and Louyot, Marie-Claude (2007), Relationship marketing in 2005: a Delphi approach, *European Management Journal*, 25(1), 50–59.

Carson, David (2004), Towards a research agenda – a report to the SIG meeting, University of Stirling, January.

Carson, David, Cromie, Stanley, McGowan, Pauric and Hill, Jimmy (1995), *Marketing and Entrepreneurship in SMEs: An Innovative Approach*, Pearson Education, Harlow.

Chaston, Ian (1997), How interaction between relationship and entrepreneurial marketing may affect organizational competencies in small UK manufacturing firms, *Marketing Education Review*, 7(3), 55–65.

Christopher, M., Payne, A. and Ballantyne, D. (1991), *Relationship Marketing*, Butterworth Heinemann, Oxford.

Crosby, L. A., Evans, K. R. and Cowles, D. (1990), Relationship quality in services selling: an interpersonal influence perspective, *Journal of Marketing*, 54(3), 68–81.

Dawber, Alistair (2010), LSE looks to tackle problem of AIM investor relations, *Independent*, 15 March, p. 42.

Day, George S. (2002) Managing the market learning process, *Journal of Business and Industrial Marketing*, 17(4), 240–252.

Drucker, Peter (2001) *The Essential Drucker*, Harper Business, New York.

Franke, N. and Piller, F. (2004) Value creation by toolkits for user innovation and design: the case of the watch market, *Journal of Product Innovation Management*, 21(1), 401–416.

Geursen, G. M. (2000), Market orientation and the entrepreneur-led firm. Available at: http://smib.vuw.ac.nz:8081/WWW/ANZMAC2001/anzmac/AUTHORS/pdfs/Geursen.pdf

Gummesson, Evert (1987), The new marketing – developing long-term interactive relationships, *Long Range Planning*, 20(4), 10–20.

Gummesson, Evert (1991), Marketing-orientation revisited: the crucial role of the part-time marketer, *European Journal of Marketing*, 25(2), 60–75.

Gummesson, Evert (1997), Relationship marketing as a paradigm shift: some conclusions from the 30R approach, *Management Decision*, 35(4), 267–272.

Gummesson, Evert (1999), *Total Relationship Marketing*, Butterworth-Heinemann, Oxford, (2nd edition), cited in Gummesson, Evert (2002), Relationship marketing in the new economy, *Journal of Relationship Marketing*, 1(1), 37–57.

Gummesson, Evert (2006), Many-to-many marketing as grand theory: a Nordic School contribution. in lusch, Robert F. and Vargo, Stephen L. (eds.), *The Service-Dominant Logic of Marketing: Dialog, Debate and Directions*, M.E. Sharpe, London.

Gummesson, Evert (2008), *Total Relationship Marketing*, Butterworth-Heinemann, Oxford, 3rd edition.

Gummesson, Evert (2010), The new service marketing. In Baker, Michael and Saren, Michael (eds.) *Marketing Theory*, Sage Publications, London.

Gwinner, Kevin P., Gremler, Dwayne D. and Bitner, Mary Jo (1998), Relational benefits in services industries: the customer's perspective, *Journal of the Academy of Marketing Science*, 26(2), 101–114.

Halliday, Sue Vaux (2004), How 'placed trust' works in a service encounter, *Journal of Services Marketing*, 18(1), 45–59.

Hamel, Gary, Doz, Yves L. and Prahalad, C. K. (1995), Collaborate with your competitors – and win, in Ghauri, Pervez N. and Prasad, S. Benjamin (eds), *International Management: A Reader*, London: Dryden, 146–154.

Hills, Gerald E., Hultman, Claes M. and Miles, Morgan P. (2008), The evolution and development of entrepreneurial marketing, *Journal of Small Business Management*, 46(1), 99–112.

Hills, Gerald E. and Singh, Robert. P. (2000), *Research at the Marketing/Entrepreneurship Interface*, Institute for Entrepreneurial Studies, Chicago.

Hosmer, Larue Tone (1995), Trust: the connecting link between organizational theory and philosophical ethics, *Academy of Management Review*, 20(2), 379–403.

Ibrahim, Nabil A., Angelidis, John P. and Parsa, Faramarz (2008), Strategic management of family businesses: current findings and directions for future research, *International Journal of Management*, 25(1), 95–110.

Kay, J. (1993), *Foundations of Corporate Success*, Oxford University Press, Oxford.

Kok, Robert A. W., Hillebrand, Bas and Biemans, Wim G. (2003), What makes product development market oriented? Towards a conceptual framework, *International Journal of Innovation Management*, 7(2), 137–162.

Langeard, E., Bateson, J. E. G., Lovelock, C. H. and Eiglier, P. (1981), *Services Marketing: New Insights from Consumers and Managers*, Marketing Science Institute Working Paper, Cambridge, MA.

Morris, Michael H., Schindehutte, Minet and LaForge, Raymond W. (2002), Entrepreneurial marketing: a construct for integrating emerging entrepreneurship and marketing perspectives, *Journal of Marketing Theory and Practice*, 10(4), 1–19.

Palmer, Adrian (1994), Relationship marketing: back to basics?, *Journal of Marketing Management*, 10(7), 571–579.

Parasuraman, A., Zeithaml, V. and Berry, L. L. (1985), A conceptual model of service quality and its implications for future research, *Journal of Marketing*, 49(3), 41–50.

Pavis, Patrice (1998), *Dictionary of the Theatre: Terms, Concepts and Analysis*, University of Toronto Press, Toronto.

Prahalad, C.K. and Ramaswamy, Venkatram (2002), Co-opting customer competence, *Harvard Business Review*, 78(1), 34–39.

Prahalad, C. K. and Ramaswamy, Venkatram (2004), *The Future of Competition: Co-Creating Unique Value with Customers*, Harvard Business School Press, Cambridge, MA.

Raub, W. and Weesie, J. (1990), Reputation and efficiency in social interactions: an example of network effects, *American Journal of Sociology*, 96(3), 626–654.

Rocks, Steve, Gilmore, Audrey and Carson, David (2005), Developing strategic marketing through the use of marketing networks, *Journal of Strategic Marketing*, 13(2), 81–92.

Schmitt, B. (1999), Experiential marketing, *Journal of Marketing Management*, 15(1–3), 53–67.

Sinkula, James M., Baker, William E. and Noordewier, Thomas (1997), A framework for market-based organizational learning: linking values, knowledge and behavior, *Journal of the Academy of Marketing Science*, 25(4), 305–318.

Vargo, Stephen L. and Lusch, Robert F. (2004), Evolving to a new dominant logic for marketing, *Journal of Marketing*, 68(1), 1–17.

Vargo, S. L. and Lusch, R. F. (2008), Service-dominant logic: continuing the evolution, *Journal of the Academy of Marketing Science*, 36(1), 1–10.

Webster, F. E. (1992), The changing role of marketing in the corporation, *Journal of Marketing*, 56(4), 1–17.

Chapter 16

Internal marketing and service excellence in SMEs

Hina Khan

LEARNING OBJECTIVES

After reading this chapter, you will be able to:

- understand the influence and importance of internal customers on service excellence for SMEs
- understand the importance of internal marketing as an approach to achieve service excellence, particularly for SMEs
- investigate specific issues relating to the implementation of a service excellence approach in relation to internal marketing in SMEs
- explore to what extent service excellence can be implemented in practice in SMEs.

AIMS OF THE CHAPTER

The focal aim of this chapter is to provide a clear understanding of service excellence as a key differentiator in the service industry. The chapter also aims to explore the impact internal marketing has in terms of treating *employees as customers* and the effect this has on the implementation of service excellence within an organization.

Service excellence also plays an important role when implementing change, particularly when a company is repositioning its product or services and rebranding. Thus, this chapter will mainly focus on the importance of service excellence; how service excellence is implemented in small- and medium-sized enterprises (SMEs) with a particular force on how SMEs should treat their employees as customers in order to motivate them and, in turn, provide clients with outstanding service. It also identifies the practices that SMEs should be implementing in order to achieve this.

In addition, this chapter also explores how SMEs make changes within their organizational culture as well as how service excellence can be used to differentiate SMEs from their competitors. It also presents a simple comprehensive model of service excellence.

Finally, this chapter identifies that service excellence is seen as an ever-evolving journey – best practice in this area may become outdated due to the ever-changing nature of the competitive service industry. Therefore, it recommends that continuous benchmarking of internal activities takes place on a continuous basis (Khan and Hedley, 2009).

INTRODUCTION

In today's highly competitive business environment, satisfying customer needs in a way that enables an organization to achieve a sustainable advantage has become an extremely difficult task for any organization, and particularly for SMEs. Furthermore, this has become an even more difficult task for those SMEs that provide services that are intangible, inseparable, perishable and variable in nature.

Thus, service organizations constantly strive to achieve a competitive advantage through implementing different strategies that enable them to overcome the challenges associated with marketing a service. 'Service excellence' has been seen as one such strategic approach that can be adopted by any type of the organization, particularly by SMEs that have a flexible organizational structure. This enables them to obtain the required employee buy-in for the strategy more easily than large organizations with complex structures.

However, achieving service excellence does require lots of investment on a variety of resources such as personnel, money, materials, methods and time. Hence, for SMEs, the lack of sufficient capital required to invest in growing resources would act as a major barrier to maintaining service excellence on an ongoing basis. Furthermore, to implement service excellence in SMEs, excellent analysis, planning, implementation and controlling skills and inter-functional coordination within the organization are also essential. Hence, effective utilization of limited resources, expertise and assistance from external parties has become crucial for SMEs. However, the lack of expertise, the limited access to the latest technology and lack of sufficient funds to invest in processes and to make improvements in the physical environment where the service is delivered have made it extremely difficult for SMEs to achieve a competitive advantage.

Nevertheless, employees who deliver the service to the external customers, or who receive different kinds of service as an internal customer of the organization, seem to play a major role for SMEs. Hence, many SMEs strive to differentiate themselves on the basis of the *people factor* because it is the employees who represent the organization; the only live resource which interacts with customers and makes or breaks deals for a company. Hence, managing employees or the people factor effectively has become crucial, making an effective internal marketing strategy a critical success factor in achieving service excellence for SMEs. Often, SMEs lack resources, both financial and non-financial, and therefore implementing service excellence could be seen as a cost rather than a strategic resource. But internal marketing could be a cost-effective competitive strategy which SMEs could rely on to become successful. Thus, this chapter aims to provide an understanding on how a firm can achieve service excellence and the role that internal marketing plays in successfully implementing service excellence within an organization, with particular emphasis on SMEs.

SMES AND SERVICE MARKETING

Defining service

According to Kotler (2000), a service can be defined as 'any activity or benefit that one party can offer to another that is essentially intangible and does not result in ownership of anything'. Providing a similar view, Lovelock and Wirtz (2007, p. 10) describe service as a 'deed or performance', and that it is 'ephemeral – transitory and perishable'.

What makes services different from physical goods?

Even though many similarities can be found between product and service marketing practices, there are specific characteristics of a service that makes it different from that of physical goods. These include:

- intangibility
- inseparability
- perishability
- heterogeneity
- lack of ownership.

A brief description of each of these characteristics is provided in Table 16.1

Table 16.1 Characteristics of a service

Service characteristics	Description
Intangibility	Unlike physical goods, services do not possess any tangible aspect – they cannot be felt or tasted. Moreover, they do not possess any physical presence; therefore, the service receiver does not have an assurance of what they will receive or to what extent it will meet their needs.
Inseparability	Since the production and the consumption of the service occur simultaneously, it cannot be separated from the person providing it.
Heterogeneity	It is very difficult to provide a consistent service all the time due to the differences that occur when delivering the service (mainly due to human variables).
Perishability	Services cannot be stored as physical goods.
Lack of ownership	Unlike physical goods, services do not result in any transfer of property. Hence no ownership can be gained.

SERVICES MARKETING AND ITS IMPORTANCE

The 7Ps of services marketing

The marketing activities of any kind of organization are normally concentrated around the traditional 4Ps, or product, price, place and promotion. However, the distinctive characteristics possessed by services such as intangibility, inseparability, perishability and heterogeneity have made it essential for marketers to successfully market services to its customers. Thus, Gronroos (1978, p. 600) suggests that the 4Ps that make up the marketing mix be extended to the 7Ps to include physical environment, processes and people. This is in order to take account of the challenges posed by services marketing due to its being so different from physical goods marketing.

A brief description on each element of the 7Ps is provided in Table 16.2.

Table 16.2 The 7Ps of marketing

Marketing mix element	Description
Product	Product is the tangible good or intangible benefit offered to a customer in order to satisfy their needs.
Price	Price is the amount that a customer needs to pay in order to obtain the product or service.
Place	Place refers to the distribution method used to deliver the product to the customer.
Promotion	Promotion includes all forms of communication methods that a marketer may use to communicate with the target audience.
People	People refers to the service personnel who deliver the service. The appearance and the behaviour may have a greater impact on the quality of the service provided.
Process	This includes all sorts of procedures which are used to provide the service.
Physical evidence	This refers to the layout and appearance of the environment where the service is delivered. This also includes the brochures or any kind of equipment used to make tangible the intangibility of the service provided.

Despite the differences between services and tangible goods, the overriding need to identify and satisfy customer needs in a way that meets or exceeds their expectations has made it essential for service organizations to integrate specific service marketing tools in order to achieve and develop a service excellence–oriented organization.

The service sector continues to improve quality as 'competition heats up and organizations seek new competitive advantages' (Longnecker and Scazzero, 2000, p. 228). Many companies are now seeking new ways of developing and keeping a competitive advantage, and 'the latest attempts of improvement have largely been internally focused' (Tournois, 2004, p. 13). However, competitive advantage probably comes from 'outward efforts towards the consumers' presenting the case for both the 'inside-out' approach (i.e. internal marketing) and the 'outside-in' approach. Furthermore, instead of focusing on one of these approaches individually, the ideas should reinforce one another rather than oppose each other (Tournois, 2004).

In any organization, marketing activities are directed towards delivering on promises through external marketing campaigns. However, for a service provider, 'the scope and content of marketing becomes more complex', as there are three marketing sub-processes of service marketing: 'external marketing, interactive marketing and internal marketing' (Blois and Gronroos, 2000, p. 503). Moreover, employees act as part-time marketers and, therefore, it is highly critical to successful marketing in a service organization to include all employees who influence the customers when planning and designing processes to deliver service.

Service quality

'Customer satisfaction is the most efficient and at the same time, least expensive source of market communication, as a satisfied consumer will tell others of his satisfaction and recommend the product to potential customers' (Dubrovski, 2001, p. 924). Thus, for many service industries the quality of service delivered to customers is very closely related to the performance of employees (Lovelock and Wirtz, 2007).

Service quality comprises two fundamental components – 'technical quality (the core service or "what" is delivered) and the functional quality ("how" the service is delivered)' (Sharma and Patterson, 1999, p. 154). The 'simply better' companies don't worry whether they have a unique point of difference. Instead, 'they are obsessed about the one thing that matters: identifying what customers want and delivering it better than anyone else' (Mitchell, 2005, p. 28). However, in order to compete strategically, 'an organisation must make a commitment to provide the most efficient leadership, personnel practices and resources needed to address the number of people issues that drive the process of service quality' (Longnecker and Scazzero, 2000, p. 232). In addition and ultimately, service organizations who want to improve quality and overall performance must consider process issues as well people issues (Longnecker and Scazzero, 2000, p. 232).

INTERNAL MARKETING

What is internal marketing?

For most companies, the people are the company and help them gain competitive advantage. It is therefore 'obvious' that an organization must 'use and manage the most important resource in order to achieve customer satisfaction' (Kanji, 2007, p. 5). Employee satisfaction is necessary in order to support continuous improvement and satisfaction of external customers. Delighted employees, who feel proud of their work, deliver outstanding performance (Kanji, 2007, p. 5).

Internal marketing was first proposed as a solution to the problem of delivering consistently high service quality during the 1980s. An early definition from Berry (1981), as quoted by Ahmed and Rafiq (2003, p. 1179), was 'viewing employees as internal customers, viewing jobs as internal products that satisfy the needs and wants of these internal customers while addressing the objectives of the organisation'.

Internal marketing is a management philosophy and accordingly requires management to 'create, encourage and enhance understanding of and appreciate the roles of employees in the organisation' (Gronroos, 1978, p. 592). Parasuraman *et al.* (1991, p. 433) defines internal marketing as 'attracting, developing, motivating and retaining qualified employees through job products that satisfy their needs'. Ahmed and Rafiq (2003, p. 1184) agree and define internal marketing as 'a planned effort using a marketing-like approach, directed at motivating employees, for implementing and integrating organizational strategies towards customer orientation'. In order to create a service and customer oriented culture among employees, service organizations are increasingly trying to adopt the concept of internal marketing (Kang and Alexandris, 2002, p. 278).

KEY ELEMENTS OF INTERNAL MARKETING

According to Ahmad and Raffiq (2003), the five key elements of internal marketing are as follows:

- **Employee motivation and satisfaction**
  Internal marketing acts as a vehicle for staff acquisition, motivation and retention, which in turn leads to increased productivity and external service quality (see Figure 16.1).
- **Customer orientation and customer satisfaction**
  If internal marketing is to be successful, it should be customer-oriented or focused on

anticipating and satisfying customer needs. Hence, internal marketing can be considered as a tool that promotes customer-oriented behaviour among staff members.

■ **Inter-functional coordination and integration**
Internal marketing has a strong impact on each and every employee working within an organization, regardless of the division or function – whether they belong to marketing, human resource management or finance is of little consequence. Therefore, internal marketing requires an effective coordination and integration of all the functions within the organization

■ **Marketing-like approach**
Internal marketing seeks to identify and satisfy the needs of the internal customers/ employees. Internal marketing is integrated into marketing planning just like other marketing activities. Thus, internal marketing also adopts a marketing-like approach to satisfy internal customers by offering benefits and incentives to keep them loyal as well as to attract the best employees.

■ **Implementation of specific corporate and functional strategies**
In order to successfully implement internal marketing it is essential for an organization to integrate both corporate strategies related to internal growth and functional strategies for different functions within an organization.

However, despite the rapidly growing literature on internal marketing, not many organizations actually apply the concept in practice. The authors add that the number and range of activities and definitions available has led to difficulties in the implementation and adoption of the concept (Ahmed and Rafiq, 2003).

OBJECTIVES OF INTERNAL MARKETING

The objectives of internal marketing are to get the 'commitment of the employees to strategies and tactics of the firm and to create an environment where they feel motivated' (Blois and Gronroos, 2000, p. 506). It is the 'people factor in most cases that drives the customers away', and although firms believe in learning more about consumers' perceptions of their products and services, they 'invest very modestly in learning about what makes their employees act the way they do' (Wheeler, 2006, p. 97).

ADVANTAGES AND DISADVANTAGES OF INTERNAL MARKETING

There are numerous benefits that a firm can achieve through internal marketing (e.g. low employee turnover, greater service quality and a rise in service satisfaction). Furthermore, it is suggested that an effective internal marketing strategy also helps an organization to buy in employees to implement change within an organization. Thus, it can be seen that through establishing effective internal marketing strategy any organization, particularly SMEs, can benefit. While the associated high cost with initiating an internal marketing programme would have a negative impact for the SME in the short term, it will deliver an added value in the long run (Iacobucci and Nordhielm, 2000).

CONCEPTUAL DEBATES AROUND INTERNAL MARKETING

Despite demonstrations of the positive effects that internal marketing can have on organizations, the internal marketing approach has been challenged by many authors. 'The idea of internal customers might once have made sense, but it has become a dangerous illusion. Get rid of it before it detracts you from your real customer' (Steward, 1997, p. 119). In addition, Farner et al. (2001) and Harari (1991, p. 31) both debate whether internal customers are a valid idea and criticize the usefulness of the concept. They suggest that 'internal customer service' is simply good management with new terminology. It is just another method of attempting to bring the best out of employees in order to meet the increasingly demanding needs of the end customer (Farner et al., 2001, p. 353).

IMPLEMENTING SERVICE EXCELLENCE

Service excellence defined

Service excellence is all about the behaviour and attitudes of employees within an organization. It's as much about the people within the organization as the clients it is serving. Excellent, motivated people will have a 'can-do' attitude and be prepared to go that extra mile for clients. It is how to motivate employees through internal service excellence that is the concern of this chapter.

This subject is very interesting and highly relevant in today's competitive service industry. Services marketing and internal marketing are fascinating fields of academic study, which are firmly embedded in the real world. It is a very real topic for discussion because as consumers we 'consume' services as part of our everyday life and can relate to the feeling gained from receiving excellent customer service – and to that experienced when the service does not live up to our expectations.

While some research around service quality has focused only on the expectations of external customers, service marketing literature has generated the importance of internal marketing on service quality. Service excellence was defined by Gilthorpe (2006, p. 33) as 'the fundamental link between a happy and motivated workforce and a successful organisation'. She goes on to state that 'it's as much about changing hearts and minds as putting the correct processes in place'.

Significance of achieving service excellence for SMEs

In order to constantly deliver high quality products and services profitably, it requires 'an organisation to attain, sustain, and enhance the overall level of product and service excellence' (Swart and Duncan, 2005, p. 487). This is achieved by 'continually providing satisfaction of customer requirements and through utilizing the efforts of everybody in the company' (Swart and Duncan, 2005, p. 487). However, as customer expectations are increasing, 'service excellence is becoming a major competitive platform if only because current service is mostly so poor' (Quinn and Humble, 1993, p. 33). That said, the quality service movement is often accused of being 'merely slogans, fad and hot topics' (Farner et al., 2001, p. 350).

Furthermore, processes are the means 'by which a company harnesses and releases the talent of its people to provide high performance. Moreover the improvement in performance can be achieved only by improving the processes by involving people' (Oakland, 2001, p. 99). Figure 16.1 shows an alternative model for improved performance by involving all employees

Figure 16.1
Figure 16.1
The model
for improved
performance

within an organization and seeking to continually improve processes. Prabhu and Robson (2000, p. 312) also raise the issue of employee-related practices and suggest a significant association between those practices and operational performance.

The study by Khan and Hedley (2009) found that the overall consensus from both management and internal customers implied a collective, teamwork approach to business. The knowledge of exceeding expectations and working together for the benefit of one another was definitely apparent. Findings suggested that management's and employees' ideas associated with service excellence were interpreted on a similar level. Internal customers suggested that while external clients generally were seen as more important, they were beginning to understand the importance of internal customers. The client is king whether external or internal.

Service excellence encourages people to care for one another and work with the same goal in mind. It makes them feel valued and as a result they enjoy their job, which can only have a positive effect on external client service, as shown in Figure 16.1.

Service excellence is associated with the motivation and the value of team working and being able to differentiate between the levels of external and internal service. Thus, service excellence means being part of an environment where you are motivated, developed and valued and where you are happy to go that extra mile to deliver a better service to clients, both internally and externally (Khan and Hedley, 2009). Moreover, by 'consistently delivering high quality services in a profitable manner require an organisation to attain, sustain, and enhance the overall level of service excellence'. This is achieved by continually providing satisfaction of customer requirements and 'through utilising the efforts of everybody in the company' (Swart and Duncan, 2005, p. 487). This leads to delighted customers and, as a result, repurchases – as shown in Figure 16.1.

USE OF INTERNAL MARKETING AS A MEANS TO ACHIEVE SERVICE EXCELLENCE

The role of the people factor in implementing service excellence in SMEs

For most companies today, the people are the company, and it is therefore paramount that an organization 'use and manage [its] most important resource in order to achieve customer satisfaction' (Kanji, 2007, p. 5). An organization needs to get their training and development right so that frontline staff can infuse customers with their enthusiasm and commitment, which can then have a positive effect on overall business.

SMEs need to get the internal dynamics right and recognize that the needs of internal customers need to be satisfied in order to meet the needs of external customers. Everyone in the organization needs to 'deliver to others and more importantly to the clients'. Service excellence is about 'going beyond the client's expectations and leaving them with the feeling that they feel valued as a client'. However, service excellence starts with employees and in order to delight customers, organizations need to delight their employees too (Chaston, 1994, p. 45; Atkinson, 1990).

Thus, service excellence should not be referred to as an approach or programme but as a journey. The workforce should be aware that it's an ongoing journey. Hence, it should not be called a 'programme' as that would infer that it (service excellence) will come to an end. Service excellence should be a way of life for the organization. It should evolve but hopefully never end (Khan and Hedley, 2009).

The role of employees as brand ambassadors in implementing service excellence in SMEs

Companies must 'adapt their products and or services to remain competitive in the market-place' (Krell, 2006, p. 50). Companies need to keep updating their products and offerings in order to keep up with changes in the marketplace, trends, customers' demands and their competitors' offerings. If the changes are vast, 'a company's brand may no longer accurately reflect what it offers. Thus, requiring a brand overhaul' (Krell, 2006, p. 50). Many companies opt for rebranding in order to enhance the company's overall image. However, rebranding can present a risk to the company, which increases if the company wrongly begins the rebranding campaign with its customers before getting buy-in from employees on the new brand (Krell, 2006). The employees should be at the heart of implementing all these changes whether it is an introduction of a new product or service feature or rebranding of the current brand. It is the employees who actually make it happen, especially in the service sector, where employees *are* the brand.

In order to gain this buy-in from employees it is important that they feel 'their contribution is valued, their needs and personal priorities are recognised and that their participation makes a difference to them personally', as well as to the 'organisation as a whole' (Krell, 2006). Effective communication can 'strengthen both intellectual and emotional buy-in' (Krell, 2006). Particularly for SMEs, this process is even more crucial because of lack of resources and specialist expertise. The following model, REBRAND, illustrates the process of implementing rebranding or a change for the SMEs. The model demonstrates the importance of employees' participation in the process as well as highlighting the external and internal barriers faced by a company when going through a change.

As shown in Figure 16.2, the REBRAND process starts from recognizing internal and external brand barriers that would create a negative impact or hinder the effective rebranding process within an organization. This is particularly important for SMEs. These barriers could be both internal and external to the organization. Internal barriers could include barriers resistance to change, lack of employee motivation and top management commitment, lack of strong leadership, and the perception that money spent on developing the brand is a cost rather than an investment. This perception correlates with the reality of limited finance being available, especially for SMEs. The barriers external to the organization could be low brand awareness within target markets and low levels of brand equity, which need to be overcome in order to attract more customers. This is why the role of brand aiders is vital in helping to overcome the external barriers (Khan and Ede, 2009).

All the other elements, such as enhancing brand awareness and brand equity, building a positive organization culture, recruiting employees with specific skills and a positive attitude, seeking relevant aid from experts and external parties who can provide resources and expertise which are crucial for SMEs and developing strong relationships with employees and stakeholders could be regarded as the 'ways and means' through which an SME can achieve their ultimate goal of rebranding, which is providing an excellent internal and external service to both internal and external customers through empowering employees. The arrow in Figure 16.2 represents the ongoing nature of the process and the knock-on effect of each element.

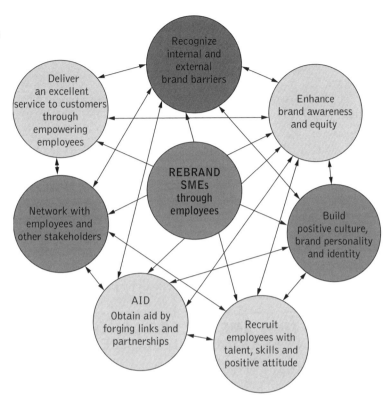

Figure 16.2
The REBRAND
framework for
SMEs

The REBRAND model provides a useful framework for SMEs to rebrand themselves through their employees. REBRAND stands for:

R = Recognize internal and external barriers to develop the brand.   Starting point
E = Enhance brand awareness and brand equity.
B = Build positive internal culture that promote internal marketing and develop a strong brand personality that provides a competitive advantage.
R = Recruit employees with the right skills and positive attitude who would ultimately act as brand ambassadors of the organizations.
A = Aid or seek help, emphasize the importance of seeking aid from other parties such as experts, of forging links and working in partnership in order to overcome brand barriers and to obtain skills and resources, which SMEs often lack due to limited capital availability.
N = Networking includes developing strong relationships with employees and all the other key stakeholders who influence and who are affected by the actions of the organization.
D = Deliver – this could be considered as the end result of rebranding, which is delivering an excellent service to both internal and external customers through empowering employees in a way that delights them.

Ways
and
means

End result

Furthermore, the above model suggests that a strong internal culture and effective internal communication can help drive the brand and company because employees feel empowered. The employees will therefore communicate consistent positive messages and work together towards common goals.

Forging links and working in partnerships is exceptionally valuable in helping organizations establish 'a name' and raise awareness of who they are and what they do. Working in partnership can be effective as it is mutually beneficial and encourages referral. Coupled with building relationships, these can really aid an SME's brand and help to overcome the external barriers of low awareness and a low level of brand equity (Khan and Ede, 2009).

Linked to brand aiders are the brand deliverers, who are the employees within the organization acting as 'ambassadors' of the brand. The employees represent the brand and it is their responsibility to build the mutually beneficial links and relationships necessary to aid the brand. Although the employees are internal to the organization, they communicate and deliver the brand externally to stakeholders (Khan and Ede, 2009). The most effective ways of communicating externally is found to place stories and case studies in the press and networking. These methods of communicating are linked to the brand aiders since they are often done in partnership and collaboration. Hence, SMEs should encourage the building of relationships and the forging of links (Khan and Ede, 2009).

BARRIERS THAT SMES NEED TO OVERCOME IN ORDER TO IMPLEMENT SERVICE EXCELLENCE

There are several factors and forces that may act as a barrier for an SME to successfully achieve service excellence within the organization. Some of the major barriers are explained below.

Lack of initial buy-in from employees

The major limitation to service excellence is the initial lack of buy-in from employees and the fact that many people tend to be cynical about the idea. People may take it seriously as a management technique as time goes on. When companies hire the right people and the right processes are in place, it leads to a change in the culture. Some critics say that service excellence is a term that is sometimes overused.

Lack of resources

Investing in both financial and non-financial resources are key to successfully implementing service excellence within an organization. SMEs, which are normally set up using the capital of individual owners, may lack the essential financial and non-financial resources required to develop structures and processes, and to provide training for employees. Hence, lack of resources is one of the major barriers to successfully implementing service excellence within SMEs.

Lack of top management commitment

Since most owners-managers are concerned about the short-term return on investment, obtaining the commitment of top management to implement service excellence, which is costly and time-consuming, in order to deliver return on investment can be difficult.

Lack of professional expertise

Many SMEs lack the professional expertise required to implement service excellence and associated processes such as managing change. Furthermore, they also lack the financial resources required to employ experts as external consultants to the organization. They may also lack the new managerial skills to manage such processes effectively. Hence, when implementing service excellence – which requires a range of expertise, knowledge and managerial skills – this lack of professional expertise may also act as a barrier to effective implementation for SMEs.

Resistance to change

Service excellence plays a crucial role when a company is introducing change. You can pin a lot of things on the service excellence process. It makes it easier to sell change. However, the danger is that it gets used for everything and goes too far. Things that are irrelevant can get the 'service excellence' tag (Khan and Hedley, 2009). This concurs with Farner *et al.* (2001, p. 354), who suggest that this new idea is just new terminology and disregard quality service movements as 'slogans' and a 'fad'. The concept of internal customers is criticized because it detracts an organization from the real customer. However, every organization will have a number of people who are cynical and see something like service excellence as a new management fad – this will pass with time.

Inability to retain high-calibre staff

The flat organization structure of SMEs often makes it difficult for employees to realize their career goals and potential to grow within the organization. This often contributes to a frustrating working environment which compels many experienced and skilled staff to move to another organization. Hence, when implementing an initiative such as service excellence, which is an ongoing process, this inability to retain high-calibre staff can hinder the effectiveness and efficiency of SMEs to implement it.

PRACTICAL IMPLICATIONS OF THE BARRIERS AND CHALLENGES FOR SMES

There are several practical implications for service sector organizations, particularly SMEs. First, the relationship between a motivated workforce and a successful organization that can be achieved by implementing service excellence is shown in Figure 16.3. Communication between teams throughout the organization is crucial. Recruiting the right people in the first instance is also vital in providing service excellence for clients. The attitude of employees plays a large role in contributing to the overall culture of a firm and it is therefore important to ensure that all employees buy into the culture of the organization and accept and live the values of the organization. Service excellence is also considered a continuous journey, ever-evolving but never ending. Hence, it helps organizations to create synergy.

ACTIONS THAT CAN BE TAKEN FOR SUCCESSFUL IMPLEMENTATION OF SERVICE EXCELLENCE IN SMES

This section presents the steps that can be taken by an SME to overcome the barriers when implementing service excellence. The individual steps form the acronym IMPLEMENT.

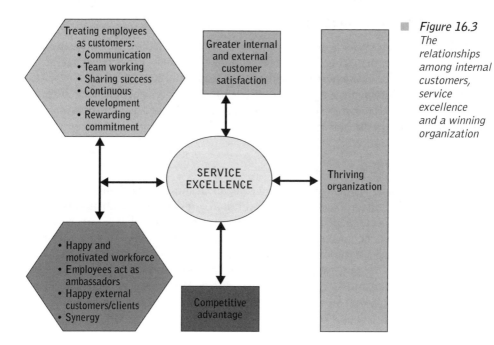

■ *Figure 16.3*
The
relationships
among internal
customers,
service
excellence
and a winning
organization

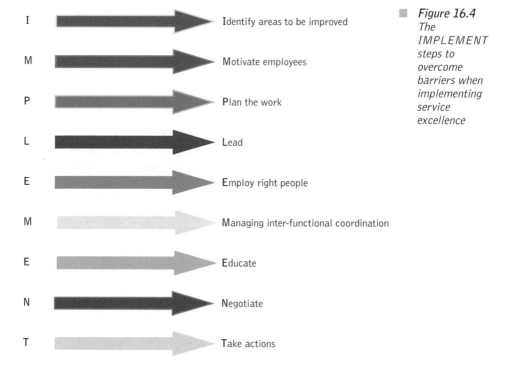

■ *Figure 16.4*
The
IMPLEMENT
steps to
overcome
barriers when
implementing
service
excellence

Identify areas to be improved

Identifying what prevents SMEs from achieving service excellence is crucial to successfully implementing service excellence. This could be achieved by identifying what kind of investments are required, what skills and knowledge need to be developed, and what processes and procedures need to be employed to achieve service excellence. Addressing these will enable SMEs to develop a service excellence–oriented culture which in turn will ensure effective implementation of service excellence within the company.

Motivate employees

Employee motivation and job satisfaction leads to service excellence which in turn has a positive effect on external customers. Basically, happy employees equal happy customers. This is apparent when an organization looks after the well-being of their workforce and trains them to ensure they are happy and committed. People, by their ability to provide excellent service both inside and outside the organization, aid organizational success. This is supported by a number of authors including Gilthorpe (2006), Pfeffer (1998) and Oakland (2001), who are of the general consensus that people-based strategies are highly effective in relation to organizational performance.

Plan the activities

Appropriate planning of how service excellence will be achieved in the organization – how the limited resources available for an SMEs will be utilized effectively and efficiently – is vital for a successful implementation of service excellence within an organization. Analysing the organization environment, identifying what kinds of changes and resources are required at the beginning of the planning stage will provide SMEs an opportunity to determine what strategies and tactics needs to be adapted if service excellence is to be achieved. Conducting a gap analysis of current levels of service satisfaction and required levels will also enable an SME to identify areas that need attention and plan appropriate strategies to close the gap in order to gain competitive advantage and achieve service excellence.

Lead

Leadership is crucial for the successful implementation of any kind of initiative within an organization. For SMEs limited by available expertise and financial resources, a task- and people-oriented leadership is essential to buy in employees to implement the changes that are essential to achieve service excellence. By providing task-oriented and people-oriented leadership, leaders will be able to ensure goals are achieved on time and issues that arise related to employee satisfaction are managed and addressed simultaneously.

Employ the right people

Recruiting the right people also aids service excellence. By selecting the right people who fit the culture of the organization, the organization will undoubtedly be highly successful. This can be achieved by 'attracting, developing, motivating, rewarding and retaining qualified employees through job prospects that satisfy their needs' (Parasuraman et al., 1991; Varey and Lewis, 2000, p. 176). This also implies the similarity between service excellence and internal marketing and how the two are interlinked and can overlap. While there is a degree of bias to be found in the research, there is enough evidence to support the claim. The research has proven that service excellence gives a clear indication of the importance of treating employees as customers and also the relevance of a service excellence approach for differentiating a service organization. This chapter has explored how a service excellence approach can help to differentiate an organization by focusing on motivating internal customers which leads to improved external service quality and which in turn creates customer loyalty and retention, and long-term financial success (Gilbert, 2000). Clearly, the task of developing and maintaining a service excellence approach and the application of internal marketing can be a long process and enthusiasm from management and employees alike can ensure that the approach is successful and ultimately differentiate a business.

Managing inter-functional coordination

Service excellence promotes interaction between all teams within the organization. Team working is essential and is seen by customers both internally and externally as a key differentiator between firms. With employees that genuinely care about each other, work for each other towards the same goal, service excellence can be achieved. Openly encouraging employees to seek to improve their processes and giving them an outlet to share their ideas helps to make them feel they can contribute to the organization (Khan and Hedley, 2009). It really makes a difference, giving them a sense of importance. People at all levels in the organization need to have input into the direction of the organization (Nixon, 1998). It is also recommended that sharing success and giving praise to employees who have done a great job, however insignificant, can give the workforce an incentive to work better and to go that extra mile to meet expectations, thus making them committed to the organization.

Educate

When implementing service excellence within an SME, educating internal customers about how the implementation will take place, what the organization expects from each and every individual employee and the team as whole, about the likely changes that would affect employees, about the short- and long-term benefits that employees will gain from service excellence and about how service excellence will contribute to the growth of organization will enable SMEs to reduce employee resistance and implement service excellence successfully.

Negotiate

Conducting effective negotiations between the management and employees is crucial to avoid the barriers to successful implementation of service excellence such as employee resistance and lack of commitment. This will also help SMEs to develop and maintain effective inter-functional coordination and positive relationship between the management and employees.

Take actions

Once service excellence is implemented within an SME, it is essential to carefully monitor all the people processes and physical evidence by taking appropriate actions to avoid failures and to ensure the success of strategy employed. Furthermore, as stated earlier, service excellence should be promoted as an ongoing journey and not just a programme as programmes come to an end.

Does service excellence really matter for SMEs?

Having weighed up the various arguments for and against internal marketing and service excellence, it is concluded that there is sufficient evidence to show that there is a link between a motivated workforce, service excellence and a successful organization. Although it is also noted that there is, as yet, no definitive measure of service excellence as such, repeat business from clients gives a good indication of it, together with the implementation of employee satisfaction surveys to understand the workforce as a whole and how their needs can be met (Khan and Hedley, 2009). There is an understanding that looking after your people is key to providing excellent service and that meeting their needs is as important as meeting those of the external clients. The objectives of internal marketing are to get the commitment from employees to create a motivated working environment. It is essential to note that internal customers are seen as just as important as the external customers (Blois and Gronroos, 2000).

SUMMARY

This chapter has defined services and identified that services differ from tangible goods due to their unique characteristics: intangibility, inseparability, heterogeneity and perishability. These make it particularly difficult for SMEs to differentiate themselves from the competition. The chapter therefore suggested that service excellence can be used as a strategic approach by SMEs to differentiate themselves from the competition. Furthermore, it also identified that effective management of people can enable SMEs to implement service excellence successfully.

The extent to which internal marketing can be used as a technique to implement service excellence within SMEs was then identified. Furthermore, service excellence and the importance of the role employees play can be seen as the link between a happy and motivated workforce and a successful organization. By understanding this relationship, it SMEs should be able to implement a management method in order to achieve synergy and further raise the bar in already highly competitive marketplaces.

Thereafter, the objectives, relative advantages and disadvantages associated with implementing service excellence for SMEs were identified. It was also identified that lack of initial buy-in from employees, lack of resources, lack of professional expertise and several other factors act as a barrier when trying to effectively implement service excellence within SMEs.

Finally, actions that can be adopted by SMEs to overcome these barriers were also identified. This can be achieved by integrating the IMPLEMENT framework presented in this chapter.

REVIEW QUESTIONS

1. Identify what is meant by a 'service' and how a service differs from tangible goods.

2. Discuss what is meant by internal marketing.

3. Explain what role internal marketing plays in implementing service excellence in SMEs.

4. Identify relative advantages and disadvantages that SMEs may encounter when implementing service excellence.

5. Identify what factors act as a barrier for effective implementation of service excellence within SMEs.

6. What possible actions can an SME undertake in order to successfully implement service excellence?

CASE STUDY 16: ALIZA RESTAURANT – FEELS LIKE HOME

Aliza is an Indian restaurant situated in an attractive riverside location. It was established by Mr Abhi Khan, who is a retired government officer, with his wife Aditi in 2004. The restaurant has grown significantly over the last three years. It employs ten full-time employees and six part-time employees. It has the ability to provide dining facilities for 20 people at a time.

The restaurant is extremely popular among locals. However, many customers are dissatisfied about the delivery of service. Even though the Aliza provides quality food, customers are very dissatisfied about the physical environment of the restaurant and they often tend to complain about the delay between the taking of their orders and the arrival of their meals. They are often left unattended.

In early 2010, Abhishek Khan, the son of Mr and Mrs Khan, joined the business as the managing director. He is a young and talented management graduate with sound business knowledge. As the new managing director, Abhishek is now conducting a review of the business. However, due to the flat organizational structure he realizes that the employees within the organization do not have a clear idea of the expectations of the business, and of what growth opportunities are available to them within the business. Moreover, during the last three years no employee has received any kind of training. When they are hired they are expected to hit the ground running. After having a couple of discussions with the key employees, he finds that many employees are demotivated and do not see themselves as part of the business. This was further confirmed by an employee who stated, 'No one cares about what is going on . . . we do our best and cannot wait to finish the work so that we can leave'. Furthermore, another employee stated, 'We have no say in the decision making or the development of the restaurant. We cannot do anything without the consent of Mr and Mrs Khan'.

The review of the financial accounts and marketing activities of the company indicated some interesting insights on the operations of the business. Even though the company has made profit, the numbers of new customers have declined and no records of particular customers were held within the business. Two highly experienced employees left the company last year and the employee turnover remains very high. However, Abhishek suspects that high workload and low pay could be the reason. All managerial decisions of the business are made on the basis of the personal judgement of Mr Khan and the restaurant maintains the same old menu. When Abhishek discussed this with one of his senior employees, he found that no employee other than the chef has the power to change or add anything to the menu. The restaurant still relies on the old recipes. There has been no research conducted to measure customer satisfaction and to understand the changing needs of the customers over time.

Given this negative environment, Abhishek is now planning to implement a change programme to drive his business to a better position through implementing service excellence. In order to assist this, he has hired you as a management consultant to obtain your views on what needs to be done in order to develop a sustainable and successful restaurant.

CASE QUESTIONS AND TASKS

1. Identify strategic and operational issues that the Aliza management should consider prior to implementing service excellence within the organization.
2. To what extent do you think implementing service excellence would benefit a SME like the Aliza restaurant?
3. Identify to what extent internal marketing can be used as a tool to implement service excellence in the Aliza restaurant.
4. Provide recommendations for the Aliza restaurant on how they should implement service excellence in a way that satisfies both internal (employee) needs and external (customer) needs.
5. To what extent do you believe service excellence can be used as a discipline to achieve a competitive advantage in the long run for an SME like the Aliza restaurant?

BIBLIOGRAPHY

Atkinson, P.E. (1990), *Creating Culture Change: The Key to Successful Total Quality Management*, IFS, Bedford.
Ahmed, P.K. and Rafiq, M., (2003), 'Internal marketing issues and challenges', *European Journal of Marketing*, Vol. 37, Issue 9, pp. 1177–1186.
Berry, L.L. (1981), 'The employee as customer', *Journal of Retail Banking*, Vol. 3. March, pp. 25–28.
Blois, K. and Gronroos, C. (2000) *The Marketing of Services*, Oxford University Press: Oxford.
Chaston, I. (1994), 'Internal customer management and service gaps within the UK manufacturing sector', *International Journal of Operations and Production Management*, Vol. 14, Issue 9, pp. 25–56.
Dubrovski, D. (2001), 'The role of customer satisfaction in achieving business excellence', *Journal of Total Quality Management*, Vol. 12, Issue 7–8, pp. 920–925.
Evans, J.R. and Lindsay, W.M. (2005), *The Management and Control of Quality: International Student Edition*, Thomson, South Western: Singapore.
Farner, S., Luthan, F. and Sommer, S.M. (2001), 'An empirical assessment of internal customer service: managing service quality', *Journal of Marketing*, Vol. 11, Issue 5, pp. 350–358.
Gilbert, G.R. (2000), 'Measuring internal customer satisfaction', *Journal of Managing Service Quality*, Vol. 10, Issue 3, pp. 178–186.
Gill, J. and Johnson, P. (2002), *Research Methods for Managers*, 3rd edition, Sage Publishers: London.
Gilthorpe, G. (2006), 'Lessons in service excellence', *Legal Marketing*, April/May, pp. 31–33.
Gronroos, C. (1978), 'A Service-Orientated Approach to Marketing of Services', *European Journal of Marketing*, Vol. 12, Issue 8, pp. 588–602.
Harari, O. (1991), 'Should internal customers exist?', *Management Review*, Vol. 82, Issue 6, pp. 31–333.
Iacobucci, D. and Nordhielm, C. (2000), 'Creative benchmarking', *Harvard Business Review*, Vol. 78, Issue 6, pp 24–25.
Kang, D.J. and Alexandris, K. (2002), 'Measurement of internal service quality: application of the SERVQUAL battery to internal service quality', *Journal of Managing Service Quality*, Vol. 12, Issue 5, pp. 278–291.
Kanji, G.K. (2007), *Measuring Business Excellence*, Routledge/Taylor and Francis Group: London.
Khan, H. and Ede, D. (2009), 'How do not-for-profit smes attempt to develop a strong brand in an

increasingly saturated market?', *Journal of Small Business and Enterprise Development*, Vol. 16, Issue 2, pp. 335–354.

Khan, H. and Hedley, K. (2009), 'Implementing service excellence to become a winning organisation', paper given at the Academy of Marketing Science Conference, Oslo, Norway, 22–25 July.

King, A.S. and Ehrhard, B.J. (1997), 'Empowering the workforce: a commitment to cohesion exercise', *Empowerment in Organizations*, Vol. 5, Issue 3, pp. 139–150.

Kotler, P. (2000), *Marketing Management: Millennium Edition*, Prentice Hall: New Jersey.

Krell, E. (2006), 'Branding together', *HR Magazine*, Vol. 51, Issue 10, pp. 48–54.

Longenecker, C.O. and Scazzero, J.A. (2000), 'Improving service quality: a tale of two operations', *Journal of Services Marketing*, Vol. 10, Issue 4, pp. 227–232.

Lovelock, C. and Wirtz, J. (2007) *Service Marketing: People, Technology, Strategy*, Pearson: Harlow, UK.

Mitchell, A. (2005), 'Differentiate all you want, but its back to the basics every time', *Marketing Week*, 11 August, pp. 28–29.

Nixon, B. (1998), 'Creating the future we desire – getting the whole system into the room', *Journal of Industrial and Commercial Training*, Vol. 30, Issue 1, pp. 4–11.

Oakland, J.S. (2001), *Total Organisation Excellence: Achieving World Class Performance*, Butterworth Heinmann: London.

Oviatt, B. M., and McDougall, P. (2005), 'Defining International Entrepreneurship and Modeling the Speed of Internationalization', *Entrepreneurship Theory and Practice*, vol. 29 (September), Is. 5, pp. 537–554.

Parasuraman, A, Berry, L.L and Zeithaml, V.A (1991), 'Refinement and reassessment of the SERVQUAL scale', *Journal of Retailing*, Vol. 67, Issue.4, pp. 420–50.

Pfeffer, J. (1998), *The Human Equation: Building Profits by Putting People First*, Harvard Business School Press: Boston, MA.

Prabhu, V. B. and Robson, A. (2000), 'Achieving service excellence – measuring the impact of leadership and senior management commitment', *Managing Service Quality*, Vol. 10, Issue 5, pp. 307–317.

Quinn, M. and Humble, J. (1993), 'Using service to gain a competitive edge: the PROMPT approach', *Long Range Planning*, Vol. 26, No. 2, pp. 31–40.

Reed, J. and Vakola, M. (2006), 'What role can a training needs analysis play in organizational change?', *Journal of Organizational Change Management*, Vol. 19, Issue 3, pp. 393–407.

Sharma, N. and Patterson, P.G. (1999) 'The impact of communication effectiveness and service quality on relationship commitment in consumer, professional services', *Journal of Services Marketing*, Vol. 13, Issue 2, pp. 151–170.

Steward, T. (1997) 'Another fad worth killing', *Fortune*, 3 February, pp. 119–120.

Swart, W., Duncan, S. (2005), 'A methodology for assuring the quality human performance', *International Journal of Computer Integrated Manufacturing*, Vol. 18, Issue 6, pp. 487–497.

Turnois, L. (2004), 'Creating customer value: bridging theory and practice', *Journal of Marketing Management*, Vol. 14, Issue 2, pp. 12–23.

Varey, R. J. and Lewis, B. R. (2000), *Internal Marketing: Directions for Management*. London: Routledge.

Wheeler, A.R. (2006), 'Retaining employees for service competency: the role of corporate brand identity', *Journal of Brand Management*, Vol. 14, Issue 1–2, pp. 96–113.

Wisner, J.D. and Stanley, L.L. (1999), 'Internal relationships and activities associated with high levels of purchasing service quality', *Journal of Supply Chain Management*, Vol. 35, Issue 3, pp. 25–35.

Chapter 17

International entrepreneurship and SMEs

Kevin Ibeh and Mathew Analogbei

LEARNING OBJECTIVES

After reading this chapter, you will be able to:
- explain the concepts of internationalization and SMEs
- discuss international entrepreneurship and clarify the synonymous sense in which it is used with SME internationalization in this chapter
- discuss the key facilitating factors for international entrepreneurship
- examine the major challenges and barriers to international entrepreneurship
- highlight appropriate managerial and policy approaches for promoting international entrepreneurship levels among SMEs.

INTRODUCTION

This chapter discusses 'international entrepreneurship' (IE) among small- and medium-sized enterprises (SMEs). It begins by outlining the relevant learning objectives and explaining key concepts, including internationalization and SMEs. Next, the emerging area of international entrepreneurship is explicated. This is followed by separate sections on the key facilitators and major barriers to international entrepreneurship. The final section summarizes the chapter and outlines managerial and policy implications.

INTERNATIONALIZATION AND SMES

The term 'internationalization' is widely employed to describe the process of increasing involvement in international operations (Welch and Luostarinen, 1993; Bell *et al.*, 2004). Not long ago, engagement in international activities was predominantly reserved for large, well-established organizations that were typically multinational enterprises (MNEs). This, however, changed with the significant advances made over the past few decades in transportation, information and communication technologies, and in global regulatory, financial and institutional environments. Smaller enterprises now increasingly operate outside their domestic markets under different arrangements, much like their larger counterparts (Ibeh, 2000; Fletcher, 2004). Some of these SMEs also appear to be creating new international ventures significantly earlier in their corporate history than their more traditional counterparts (Rennie, 1993; Knight and Cavusgil, 1996; Autio *et al.*, 2000; Oviatt and McDougall,

1994; Borchert and Ibeh, 2008). This phenomenon was a major impetus for the emergence of international entrepreneurship as a distinct research field (McDougall and Oviatt, 2000a; Coviello and Jones, 2005; Zahra, 2005).

Internationalization or IE can be undertaken through a variety of international market entry and development modes, including exporting (direct and indirect), licensing, franchising, management contracts, contract manufacturing, turn-key contracts, contractual joint ventures, strategic alliances, equity joint ventures, mergers and acquisitions and wholly owned subsidiaries (Ibeh, 2000). To these can be added inward internationalization approaches such as importing and licensing-in. These modes are associated with varying levels of strategic control and rewards, resource needs, costs and risks, and opportunities and threats (Westhead, 1993; Bell and Young, 1998; O'Farrell et al., 1998). Given SMEs' typically low resource base, they tend to serve international markets from their domestic bases, mainly via direct, indirect or internet-based exporting. This explains why much of the SME internationalization or international entrepreneurship literature pertains to exporting activity (Ibeh, 2006).

The repeated references to SMEs above highlight the need for a proper definition of the concept. This is undertaken in the following paragraphs.

Small enterprises have been variously defined (Carter and Jones-Evans, 2006). The Bolton Report (Bolton Committee, 1971), one of the earliest attempts in this regard, highlighted the following defining criteria:

- independent (not part of a large enterprise)
- managed in a personalized manner (simple management structure)
- relatively small share of the market.

This definition has, not surprisingly, been faulted on a number of grounds over the years. These include the relative nature of the concept of 'independence' (some firms may be legally independent but depend entirely on a larger enterprise for their economic activity) and the lack of clarity that often surrounds knowing when locus of control shifts from the owner-manager to a functional or hierarchical management structure in a growing business (Storey and Johnson, 1987; Woods et al., 1993; Storey, 1994).

A more robust definition was introduced by the European Union (EU) in 1994, and updated in 2004. This distinguishes between three types of smaller enterprises – micro, small- and medium-sized enterprises – associated with the employee, turnover and asset limits outlined in Figure 17.1.

These three size groups make up what is termed small- and medium-sized enterprises (SMEs). It is important to note that some EU countries have adopted their own interpretation of SMEs. Beyond Europe also, there is a wide variety of definitions. Hong Kong sees SMEs as manufacturing enterprises with fewer than 100 employees or non-manufacturing firms with

Enterprise category	Head count	Turnover	Balance sheet
Micro	< 10	€2m	€2m
Small	< 50	€10m	€10m
Medium-sized	< 250	€50m	€43m

■ Figure 17.1
SME categories

Source: Carter and Jones-Evans (2006, p. 10).

fewer than 50 employees. The USA defines an SME as a company employing fewer than 500 employees. All of these make it difficult to compare SMEs across countries (Carter and Jones-Evans, 2006).

INTERNATIONAL ENTREPRENEURSHIP (IE)

IE refers to a new research field that has recently emerged at the entrepreneurship–international business interface. It has been defined as a combination of innovative, risk-seeking behaviour that crosses national borders and is intended to create value in an organization (McDougall and Oviatt, 2000b). Also described as the discovery, enactment, evaluation and exploitation of opportunities across national borders to create future goods and services (Oviatt and McDougall, 2005), its essential contribution has been to illuminate the phenomenon of 'international new ventures' (INV), largely ignored by both entrepreneurship and international business theories. The former generally views new firm formation as a locally embedded process, while the latter does not really posit a role for smaller and inexperienced firms in the international markets (McNaughton, 2003).

The recent upsurge of interest in IE actually represents a return to Schumpeter's (1934) classic characterization of entrepreneurship as the creation of new markets. At the heart of entrepreneurial activity is innovation (Hitt et al., 2001). Schumpeter (1934) distinguished between invention and innovation, with invention being the discovery of an opportunity and innovation being the exploitation of this opportunity (Alvarez and Busenitz, 2001). IE success requires not just the discovery of a valuable innovation but also that the innovation be introduced successfully to world markets (Acs et al., 2001) or, in Schumpeter terms, the creation of new markets. This is the essence of IE.

What the IE research field has done, therefore, is to make INVs, born-globals and internationalizing SMEs the main focus of concerted scholarly attention. This, as McDougall and Oviatt (2000a) have noted, implies the search for more INVs and international entrepreneurs (see Quadrant II of Figure 17.2) and, more importantly, understanding the activities and key facilitating factors associated with this category of firms.

Factors facilitating IE

Oviatt and McDougall's (1994, 1995) early work on the international entrepreneurship research stream points to a number of key underpinning factors for successful IE. According to these authors, new ventures tend to possess certain valuable assets, use alliances and network structures to control a relatively large percentage of vital assets, as well as have a

Figure 17.2
Organizational
types and
contexts

Source: McDougall
and Oviatt (2000a).

		GEOGRAPHICAL SCOPE	
		Domestic	International
TYPE OF ORGANIZATION	Entrepreneurial	I	II
	Large, established	III	IV

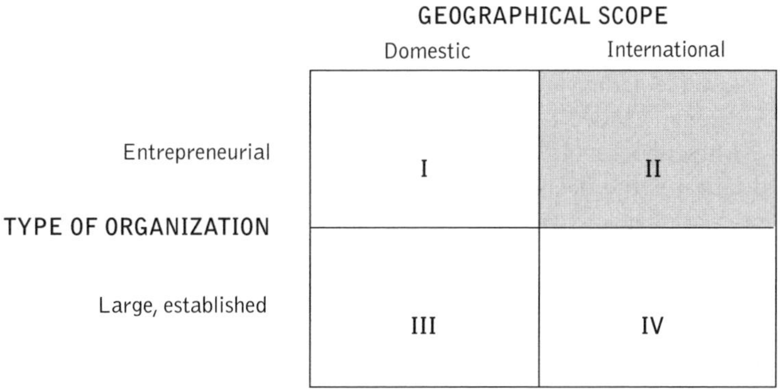

unique resource that provides a sustainable advantage that is transferable to a foreign location (Oviatt and McDougall, 1994, 1995). Scholars have developed the essential elements above into a set of key IE facilitating factors. These are discussed below under three broad categories, specifically decision-maker factors, firm-specific advantages and a firm's environmental factors (see Table 17.1).

Table 17.1 *Sample facilitating factors for IE*

Source	Characteristic	Indicative research
Decision maker	A global vision	Oviatt and McDougall (1995)
Decision maker	International experience	Reuber and Fischer (1997)
Decision maker	Internationally proactive	Knight (1997)
Decision maker	Highly networked	Coviello and Munro (1995)
Firm	Possesses knowledge-intensive assets	McDougall *et al.* (1994)
Firm	Possesses high-quality, differentiated products	Knight and Cavusgil (2004)
Firm	Provides a superior level of service	McDougall *et al.* (2003)
Firm	Pursues aggressive growth	Oviatt and McDougall (1994)
Firm	Pursues niche strategy	Andersson and Wictor (2003)
Firm's environment	Offers helpful support programmes	Alvarez (2004); Rodríguez-Cohard *et al.* (2008)
Firm's environment	Offers quality supporting infrastructure	Lado *et al.* (2004)

Source: Adapted from Borchert and Ibeh (2008).

Decision-maker factors

Most SME internationalization researchers are agreed on the central role of entrepreneurs, in their various manifestations as founders, decision makers or managers, in the internationalization process (Miesenbock, 1988; Ibeh and Young, 2001). Entrepreneurs, or individuals carrying out entrepreneurial actions (Andersson, 2000; Oviatt and McDougall, 1995), are the most important agents of change. They are typically associated with the capacity and willingness to take risks in realizing their judgements, to be innovative and to exploit business opportunities in a market environment (OECD, 2000). Their individual-specific attributes (knowledge, relationships, experience, training, skills, judgement and ability to coordinate resources) facilitate the recognition of new opportunities and assembling of socially complex, value-adding and advantage-creating resources (Schumpeter, 1950; Barney *et al.*, 2001; Alvarez and Busenitz, 2001; Gabrielsson and Kirpalani, 2004).

Miesenbock's (1988) early remark that the key variable in small business internationalization is the decision maker of the firm, who decides starting, ending and increasing international activities, powerfully captures the dominant view on this issue. In small firms, the decision power is often concentrated in the hands of one or a few persons and the CEO has a unique and influential role in the organization (Chandler and Janson, 1992). Bloodgood *et al.* (1996) found that more international work experience among top managers was strongly associated with greater internationalization of new high-potential firms in the USA. Also,

Westhead *et al.* (2001) found that older founders with more resources, denser information and contact networks and considerable management know-how were significantly more likely to become exporters, especially where industry-specific knowledge and experience were important. McDougall *et al.* (2003) suggested that managers of international new ventures had significantly greater international, industry and technical experience than their counterparts with domestic new ventures. Zucchella *et al.* (2007) found that founder-specific drivers were the most significant factors in SMEs' internationalization. Coviello and Jones (2005) evidently agreed, and called on researchers to incorporate entrepreneurial behaviour into models of internationalization.

International new-venture scholars have further highlighted the importance of the decision maker's commitment in facilitating IE, with more recent work reinforcing the relevance of both affective commitment and continuance commitment (Gabrielsson *et al.*, 2008). As these authors noted, affective commitment refers to the initial commitment stemming from the global orientation of the entrepreneur, while continuance commitment refers to the decision maker's continuing fidelity to the internationalization venture beyond initial take-off (Gabrielsson *et al.*, 2008). Related to this, evidence also suggests that decision makers with more positive attitudes towards exporting and more favourable perceptions of exporting risks, costs, profits and growth tend to exhibit greater IE behaviour (Ibeh, 2003).

Firm-specific advantages

Previous research has underlined the importance of a range of firm-specific factors in facilitating IE behaviour. One often investigated characteristic is firm size (variously measured by employee number, sales, ownership of capital equipment, financial capability or a combination of the above), which is sometimes viewed as a proxy for the firm's resource base. Although findings on the impact of firm size on IE behaviour have been mixed, the balance of evidence suggests its importance, particularly in initiating international activity (Dean *et al.*, 2000; Ibeh, 2006). Another characteristic that appears to influence international entrepreneurship is firm background, including previous experience of extra-regional expansion, inward internationalization (Andersson *et al.*, 2004; Ibeh, 2006), or international experience (Baldauf *et al.*, 2000; Lado *et al.*, 2004). The type of product/service marketed by a firm or the nature of its industry (e.g. extent of globalization) can also be a crucial facilitating factor (Tybejee, 1994; Ibeh, 2006).

There is an even stronger body of evidence that favourably links IE with firm capabilities and competencies (Francis and Collins-Dodd, 2004; Ibeh, 2005; Sapienza *et al.*, 2006). Among the most critically regarded of these capability factors is the firm's stock of knowledge assets, including technological and R&D know-how and market learning (Autio *et al.*, 2000; Knight and Cavusgil, 2004; Rialp *et al.*, 2005). This appears to have gained increased resonance in the recent IE literature, and is widely appreciated across different internationalization research traditions. Indeed, the Uppsala model (Johansson and Vahlne, 1977, 1990) actually suggests experiential market knowledge as the driving force of the firm's incremental evolution along the internationalization path. Relational capabilities are also highly valued, as established networks are considered vital for the early internationalization of new ventures (Coviello, 2006). The literature also suggests that relationships may provide a firm with access to key resources possessed by external parties, including knowledge, technology, social capital and market contacts, thus enabling it to bridge possible gaps to its internationalization (Håkansson and Snehota, 1992; Eriksson *et al.*, 1998; McLoughlin and Horan, 2000). Such network-based resource augmentation has been identified as an important trigger for rapid internationalization (Oviatt and McDougall, 1997; Autio *et al.*, 2000; Vissak *et al.*, 2007).

Other important firm-specific capabilities highlighted in the IE literature include research and product development; systematic market research; relational capabilities; distribution, delivery and service quality; and advertising and sales promotion. The possession of these capabilities and competencies enables a firm to identify the idiosyncrasies in foreign markets, develop the necessary marketing strategies and implement them effectively, thus achieving higher export performance (Cavusgil and Zou, 1994; Wheeler *et al.*, 2008).

Firm's environmental factors

Aspects of the SME's operating environments – industry, domestic market and foreign market environments – may affect IE behaviour positively or adversely (Carlos *et al.*, 2008; Wheeler *et al.*, 2008). Indeed, previous integrative reviews suggest that the so-called 'push' (e.g. adverse home market conditions, small domestic market) and 'pull' (e.g. and attractive market opportunities abroad) factors exert strong influence on initial IE behaviour (Leonidou, 1995). This is particularly significant given that SMEs tend to lack the necessary resources to control their operating environment (Ibeh, 2006). Taking domestic market factors, for instance, research evidence suggests that firms generally perform better when faced with a benign domestic environment (Robertson and Chetty, 2000). This could be indicated, for example, by the availability of helpful public- and private-sector internationalization support programmes (Alvarez, 2004), which typically act as an external resource bank from which firms can gain knowledge and experience, create or develop existing international networks and undertake more sophisticated foreign market analysis (Carlos *et al.*, 2008).

Foreign market factors usually influence firms' IE behaviour as well. For example, government restrictions or pressures in the target market have been known to affect firms' internationalization efforts by increasing or reducing their capacity and effectiveness (Beamish, 1993; Cavusgil and Zou, 1994; Baldauf *et al.*, 2000; Dean *et al.*, 2000; O'Cass and Julian, 2003). The levels of infrastructural development, cultural similarity and market competitiveness have also been identified as important factors. The evidence largely suggests that more IE activity is likely to occur if the foreign markets are culturally similar and have higher levels of infrastructural development (Lado *et al.*, 2004).

BARRIERS TO IE

SMEs are known to face several challenges and impediments as they attempt to initiate, develop or sustain IE activities. These constraints – resource-related, attitudinal, psychological, structural, strategic, operational – have been the focus of considerable research among internationalization and IE researchers (Leonidou, 1995; Hamill, 1997; Wright *et al.*, 2007; OECD, 2009). Leonidou offered a particularly useful four-category framework of internationalization barriers, thus:

- Internal-domestic: problems from within the firm such as lack of personnel with requisite knowledge and experience, negative perception of risk in selling abroad, etc.
- Internal-foreign: these are problems faced by SMEs in the foreign market environment as a result of their limited ability in, for example, modifying products or communicating with foreign customers.
- External-domestic: these barriers typically originate from the SME's domestic environment

and they include impediments such as complex documentations, inadequate infrastructure and lack of necessary government support.

■ External-foreign: the barriers in this category are experienced in the international markets and are not firm-specific. Examples include foreign government-imposed restrictions, language and cultural differences, and difficulties associated with establishing reliable overseas contacts.

A recent OECD report on this topic seems to highlight internationalization barriers of the mainly internal-domestic kind:

> Limited firm resources and international contacts as well as lack of requisite managerial knowledge about internationalisation have remained critical constraints to SME internationalisation. These resource limitations, especially of a financial kind, seem particularly prevalent among smaller, newly internationalising firms.
>
> (OECD, 2009)

The reference to the particular prevalence of financial constraints among smaller, newly internationalizing firms reinforces previous evidence that firms at different stages of the internationalization process typically encounter different sets of internationalization problems (Bell, 1997). Born-global firms investigated by Gabrielsson *et al.* (2008) deal with not only exporting risks but also limited finance and challenges associated with the global character of their operations. Another important finding to note is that decision-maker and firm characteristics often influence how well SMEs respond to perceived internationalization barriers (Ibeh, 2006).

SUMMARY AND IMPLICATIONS

This chapter has discussed IE among SMEs, identifying key facilitating factors and impediments to greater IE activities. Its focus on IE complements previous research on international business (which has focused on MNEs) and previous research on entrepreneurship (which has focused on SME venture creation and management within the domestic context) (Gabrielsson *et al.*, 2008). The chapter, thus, reinforces the reality that firm size and age are no longer prerequisites for international business (Autio *et al.*, 2000; Rialp *et al.*, 2005), as SMEs are now actively involved in international business like their larger counterparts.

In this new enterprise-keen world, born-globals, international new ventures, global start-ups and similar SME actors are known to internationalize at or near inception, facilitated by their key decision makers, firm-specific advantages and aspects of their operating environment. Their positive IE behaviour is also typically enabled by a robust capacity to neutralize and overcome varying forms of internationalization barriers/constraints.

The foregoing offers an outline of what needs to be done at managerial and policy levels to enhance the prospect of achieving the much needed boost in IE activities. For SME managers or decision makers, the emphasis, briefly stated, should be on capacity-upgrading initiatives aimed at replicating the kind of attributes and capabilities identified as critical facilitators of IE. Policy makers seeking to promote greater IE among SMEs might benefit from pulling at both of the major levers highlighted in the preceding paragraph. That is, designing and delivering support programmes to better equip SMEs with the abovementioned facilitating factors, while also taking practical steps to eradicate or minimize the prevalence of internationalization barriers and constraints.

REVIEW QUESTIONS

1. Comment on the view that successful international venturing is synonymous with excellent marketing.

2. Based on a brief desk research (preferably online), identify a born-global firm from any industry of your choice and discuss the key factors that seem to have facilitated this firm's early entry into international markets.

CASE STUDY 17: CMK'S INTERNATIONAL NEW VENTURES

CMK, a small, rapidly growing Canadian developer and manufacturer of quality, easy-to-use diagnostic kits, generates some 90 per cent of its revenues internationally, via exports to over 65 countries and joint-venture operations in the Netherlands. It was founded in the late 1990s by a physician owner-manager whose previous work in developing countries alerted him to significant levels of unmet demand. CMK's first markets were, thus, international rather than domestic, particularly as it had limited opportunities in the latter.

Partly owing to its limited experience and resources, CMK mainly served its international markets through distributors. It developed lasting relationships with these distributors, which facilitated the speedy introduction of its innovative products in international markets. The first set of markets entered, Turkey, Jordan and Iran, were those where the owner had worked and had contacts. CMK subsequently targeted other markets, namely Azerbaijan, Bulgaria, Cyprus, Greece, and later Saudi Arabia and Kuwait. By the end of its second year in business, CMK had successfully entered nine international markets. Later international expansion involved less reliance on CMK's owner's personal contacts. Rather, the company used a variety of channels in locating distributors and entering new markets in North and Latin America, South East Asia, Europe and the Middle East. By the end of its fourth year, CMK had successfully established its products in some 30 markets around the world.

In addition to a rapid internationalization drive, CMK also prioritized the development of its manufacturing operations. The enhanced reputation thus gained enabled it to joint-venture with its distributor in the Netherlands and facilitate local production of its diagnostic kits. This allowed it to better serve markets in Europe, the Middle East and Africa (the firm has entered a number of African markets in recent years), and to be more responsive to sudden changes in demand. For CMK, the ability to control manufacturing was of paramount importance since it wanted to ensure quality and also reduce cost. With the success of this Netherlands operation, CMK is considering similar international ventures in Turkey and other markets. This suggests a new phase in its international development – that of a direct foreign investor.

CASE QUESTIONS

1. Comment on the role of CMK's owner-manager in the establishment of this company's international ventures. Which particular decision-maker attributes helped CMK in its international opportunity recognition and exploitation?

2. Would you describe CMK as a born-global firm? Explain your answer, making

■ **280**

appropriate references to the literature. Which firm-specific factors would seem to have facilitated CMK's IE?

3. CMK essentially relied on foreign distributors to serve its international markets in its first few years of internationalization. Why? Which challenges or constraints should this company be mindful of as it seeks to progress its new phase of international development? What advice would you offer CMK?

Source: Adapted from Borchert and Ibeh (2008).

BIBLIOGRAPHY

Acs, Z.J., Morck, R.K. and Yeung, B. (2001), 'Entrepreneurship, globalisation, and public policy', *Journal of International Management*, 7, 235–251.

Alvarez, R. (2004), 'Sources of export success in small and medium-sized enterprises: the impact of public programs', *International Business Review*, 13, 383–400.

Alvarez, S.A. and Barney, J.B. (2001), 'How entrepreneurial firms can benefit from alliances with large partners', *Academy of Management Executive*, 15, 139–148.

Alvarez, S. and Busenitz, L. (2001), 'The entrepreneurship of resource-based theory', *Journal of Management*, 27(6), 755–775.

Andersson, S. (2000), 'Internationalisation of the firm from an entrepreneurial perspective', *International Studies of Management & Organisation*, 30(1), 63–92.

Andersson, S. and Wictor, I. (2003), ' Innovative Internationalization in new firms: born globals – the Swedish case', *Journal of International Entrepreneurship*, 1(3), 249–275.

Andersson, S., Gabrielsson, J. and Wictor, I. (2004), 'International activities in small firms: examining factors influencing the internationalization and export growth of small firms', *Canadian Journal of Administrative Sciences*, 21(1), 22–34.

Autio, E., Sapienza, H.J., and Almeida, J.G. (2000), 'Effects of age at entry, knowledge intensity, and imitability on international growth', *Academy of Management Journal*, 43(5), 909–924.

Baldauf, A., Cravens, D.W. and Wagner, U. (2000), 'Examining determinants of export performance in small open economies', *Journal of World Business*, 35, 61–79.

Barney, J., Wright, M. and Ketchen, D.J. Jr. (2001), 'The resource-based view of the firm: ten years after 1991', *Journal of Management*, 27(6), 625–641.

Beamish, P.W. (1993), 'The characteristics of joint ventures in the People's Republic of China', *Journal of International Marketing*, 1, 29–48.

Bell, J., Crick, D. and Young, S. (2004), 'Small firm internationalisation and business strategy: an exploratory study of knowledge-intensive and traditional manufacturing firms in the UK', *International Small Business Journal*, 22, 23–56.

Bell, J. and Young, S. (1998), 'Towards an integrative framework of the internationalisation of the firm', in Hooley, G., Loveridge, R. and Wilson, D. (eds), *Internationalisation: Process, Context and Markets*, London: Macmillan.

Bell, S. (1997), 'Globalisation, neoliberalism and the transformation of the Australian state', *Australian Journal of Political Science*, 32(3), 345–67.

Bloodgood, J., Sapienza, H.J. and Almeida, J.G. (1996), 'The internationalisation of new high-potential U.S. ventures: Antecedents and outcomes', *Entrepreneurship Theory and Practice*, 20, 61–76.

Bolton Committee (1971), *Report of the Committee of Enquiry on Small Firms*, Cmnd 4811, London: HMSO.

Borchert, O. and Ibeh, K.I.N. (2008), 'The quintessential born-global: case evidence from a rapidly internationalising canadian small firm', in Ndubisi, N. (ed.), *Internationalisation of Business*, Kuala Lumpur: Arah Pendidikan Books.

Carter, S. and Jones-Evans, D. (2006), *Enterprise and Small Business – Principles, Practice and Policy*, 2nd edn, Harlow: Prentice Hall.

Cavusgil, S.T. and Zou, S. (1994), 'Marketing strategy-performance relationship: an investigation of the empirical link in export market ventures', *Journal of Marketing*, 58 (1), 1–25.

Chandler, G.N. and Jansen, E. (1992), 'The founder's self-assessed competence and venture performance', *Journal of Business Venturing*, 7(3), 223–236.

Coviello, N.E. (2006), 'The network dynamics of international new ventures', *Journal of International Business Studies*, 37(5), 713–731.

Coviello, N.E. and Jones, M.V. (2005), 'Internationalization: conceptualizing an entrepreneurial process of behaviour in time', *Journal of International Business Studies*, 36(3), 284–303.

Coviello, N.E. and Munro, H.J. (1995), 'Growing the entrepreneurial firm: networking for international market development', *European Journal of Marketing*, 29(7), 49–61.

Dean, D.L., Menguc, B. and Myers, C.P. (2000), 'Revisiting firm characteristics, strategy, and export performance relationship: a survey of the literature and an investigation of New Zealand small manufacturing firms', *Industrial Marketing Management*, 29, 461–477.

Dunning, J.H. (1988), 'The eclectic paradigm of international production: A restatement and some possible extensions', *Journal of International Business Studies*, 19(1), 1–31.

Eriksson, K., Johanson, J., Maikgard, A. and Sharma, D.D. (1998), 'Experiential knowledge and cost in the internationalisation process', *Journal of International Business Studies*, 28(2), 337–360.

Fletcher, D. (2004), 'International entrepreneurship and the small business', *Entrepreneurship and Regional Development*, 16, 289–305.

Francis, J. and Collins-Dodd, C. (2004), 'Impact of export promotion programs on firm competencies, strategies, and performance: the case of Canadian high-technology SMEs', *International Marketing Review*, 21, 474–495.

Gabrielsson, M. and Kirpalani, V.H.M. (2004), 'Born globals: how to reach new business space rapidly', *International Business Review*, 13(5), 555–571.

Gabrielsson, M., Kirpalani, V.H.M., Dimitratos, P., Solberg, C.A. and Zucchella, A. (2008), 'Born globals: propositions to help advance the theory', *International Business Review*, 17, 385–401.

Håkansson, H. and Snehota, I. (1992), *Developing Relationships in Business Networks*, London: Routledge.

Hamill, J. (1997), 'The internet and international marketing', *International Marketing Review*, 14(5), 300–323.

Hitt, M.A., Ireland, R.D., Camp, S.M. and Sexton, L.D. (2001), 'Guest editors' introduction to the special issue strategic entrepreneurship: entrepreneurial strategies for wealth creation', *Strategic Management Journal*, 22(6/7), 479–491.

Ibeh, K. (2000), 'Internationalisation and the small firm', in Carter, S. and Jones-Evans, D. (eds.), *Enterprise and Small Business*, Harlow: FT Prentice Hall.

Ibeh, K.I.N. (2003), 'Toward a contingency framework of export entrepreneurship: conceptualisations and empirical evidence', *Small Business Economics*, 15(1), 49–68.

Ibeh, K.I.N. (2005), 'Toward greater firm-level international entrepreneurship within the UK agribusiness sector: resource levers and strategic options', *Management International Review*, 45(3) (Special Issue), 59–81.

Ibeh, K. (2006), 'Internationalisation and the smaller firm', in Carter, S. and Jones-Evans, D. (eds.), *Enterprise and Small Business*, Harlow, UK: FT/Prentice Hall.

Ibeh, K., Johnson, J., Dimitratos, P. and Slow, J. (2004), 'Micromultinationals: some preliminary evidence on an emergent "star" of the international entrepreneurship field', *Journal of International Entrepreneurship*, 2, 289–303.

Ibeh, K.I.N. and Young, S. (2001), 'Exporting as an entrepreneurial act: an empirical study of Nigerian firms', *European Journal of Marketing*, 35(5/6), 566–586.

Johansson, J. and Vahlne, J. (1977), 'The internationalisation process of the firm – a model of knowledge development and increasing foreign market commitments', *Journal of International Business Studies*, 8(1), 23–32.

Johansson, J. and Vahlne, J. (1990), 'The mechanism of internationalisation', *International Marketing Review*, 7(4), 11–23.

Juan Carlos, G., Levine, R. and Schmukler, S.L. (2008), 'Internationalisation and the evolution of corporate valuation', *Journal of Financial Economics*, 88, 607–632.

Knight, G.A. (1997), 'Emerging paradigm for international marketing: the born global firm', PhD thesis, Michigan State University.

Knight, G.A. and Cavusgil, S.T. (1996), 'The born global firm: a challenge to traditional internationalization theory', *Advances in International Marketing*, 8, 11–26.

Knight, G.A. and Cavusgil, S.T. (2004), 'Innovation, organizational capabilities, and the born-global firm', *Journal of International Business Studies*, 35(2), 124–141.

Lado, N., Martinez-Ros, E. and Valenzuela, A. (2004), 'Identifying successful marketing strategies by export regional destination', *International Marketing Review*, 21, 573–597.

Leonidou, L.C. (1995), 'Empirical research on export barriers: review, assessment and synthesis', *Journal of International Marketing*, 3(1), 29–43.

McDougall, P.P. and Oviatt, B.M. (2000a), 'International entrepreneurship: the intersection of two research paths', *Academy of Management Journal*, 43(5), 902–906.

McDougall, P.P. and Oviatt, B.M. (2000b), 'International entrepreneurship literature in the 1990s directions for future research', in Sexton, D.L. and Smillor, R.W. (eds), *Entrepreneurship 2000*, Chicago, IL: Upstart Publishing, 291–320.

McDougall, P.P., Oviatt, B.M., and Shrader, R.C. (2003). 'A comparison of international and domestic new ventures', *Journal of International Entrepreneurship*, 1, 59–82.

McDougall, P.P., Shane, S. and Oviatt, B.M. (1994), 'Explaining the formation of international new ventures', *Journal of Business Venturing*, 9, 469–87.

McLoughlin, D. and Horan, C. (2000), 'The production and distribution of knowledge in the markets-as-networks tradition', *Journal of Strategic Marketing*, 8, 89–103.

McNaughton, R. (2003), 'The number of export markets that a firm serves: process models versus born-global phenomenon', *Journal of International Entrepreneurship*, 1(3), 297–311.

Miesenbock, K.J. (1988), 'Small businesses and exporting: a literature review', *International Small Business Journal*, 6(2), 42–61.

O'Cass, A. and Julian, C. (2003), 'Examining firm and environmental influences on export marketing mix strategy and export performance of Australian exporters', *European Journal of Marketing*, 37, 366–384.

OECD (2000), *Is There a New Economy?*, First Report on the OECD Growth Project, OECD: Paris.

OECD (2009), *Top Barriers and Motivations for SME Internationalisation*, Report of the Working Party on SMEs and Entrepreneurship, OECD: Paris. Online: http://www.oecd.org/dataoecd/16/26/43357832.pdf (accessed 23 August 2010).

O'Farrell, P.N., Wood, P.A. and Zheng, J. (1998), 'Regional influences on foreign market development by business service companies: elements of a strategic context explanation', *Regional Studies*, 32, 31–48.

Oviatt, B.M. and McDougall, P.P. (1994), 'Toward a theory of international new ventures', *Journal of International Business Studies*, 25(1), 45–64.

Oviatt, B.M. and McDougall, P.P. (1995), 'Global start-ups: entrepreneurs on a worldwide stage', *Academy of Management Executive*, 9, 30–43.

Oviatt, B.M. and McDougall, P.P. (1997), 'Challenges for internationalization process theory: the case of international new ventures', *Management International Review*, 37(2), 85–99.

Oviatt, B.M. and McDougall, P.P. (2005), 'Defining international entrepreneurship and modeling the speed of internationalization', *Entrepreneurship Theory and Practice*, 29 (September), 537–553.

Rennie, M. W. (1993), 'Born global', *McKinsey Quarterly*, 4, 45–52.

Reuber, A.R. and Fischer, E. (1997), 'The influence of the management team's international experience on the internationalization behaviors of SMEs', *Journal of International Business Studies*, 28, 807–825.

Rialp, A., Rialp, J. and Knight, G.A. (2005), 'The phenomenon of early internationalizing firms: what do we know after a decade (1993–2003) of scientific inquiry?', *International Business Review*, 14(2), 147–166.

Robertson, C. and Chetty, S.K. (2000), 'A contingency-based approach to understanding export performance', *International Business Review*, 9, 211–235.

Rodríguez-Cohard, J.C., Liñán, F., and Guzmán, J. (2008), 'Temporal stability of entrepreneurial intentions: a longitudinal study', 4th European Summer University Conference on Entrepreneurship, Bodø Graduate School of Business and Nordland Research Institute, 22–26 August 2008, Bodø, Norway.

Sapienza, H.J., Autio, E., George, G. and Zahra, S.A. (2006), 'A capabilities perspective on the effects of early internationalization on firm survival and growth', *Academy of Management Review*, 31, 914–933.

Schumpeter, J. (1934), *The Theory of Economic Development*, Cambridge, MA: Harvard University Press.

Schumpeter, J. (1950), *Capitalism, Socialism and Democracy*, Harper & Brothers, New York, NY.

Storey, D.J. (1994), *Understanding the Small Business Sector*, London: International Thomson Business Press.

Storey, D.J. and Johnson, S. (1987), *Job Generation and Labour Market Change*, London: Macmillan.

Tyebjee, T.T. (1994), 'Internationalisation of high tech firms: initial vs. extended involvement', *Journal of Global Marketing* 7(4), 59–81.

Vissak, T., Ibeh, K.I.N. and Paliwoda, S. (2008), 'Internationalising from the European periphery: triggers, processes, and trajectories', *Journal of Euro Marketing*, 17(1), 35–48.

Vissak, T., Ibeh, K. and Paliwoda, S. (2007), 'Internationalising from the European periphery: triggers, processes and trajectories', *Journal of Euromarketing*, 17(1), 35–48.

Zahra, S.A. (2005), 'Toward a theory of international new ventures: reflections on a decade of research', Journal of International Business Studies, 36: 29–41.

Welch, L.S. and Luostarinen, R.K. (1993) 'Inward-outward connections in internationalization', *Journal of International Marketing*, 1(1), 44–56

Westhead, P. (1993), 'A matched pairs comparison of exporting and non-exporting small firms in GB', Working Paper No. 19, Small and Medium Enterprise Centre, Warwick Business School, Warwick.

Westhead, P., Wright, M. and Ucbasaran, D. (2001), 'The internationalisation of new and small firms: a resource-based view', *Journal of Business Venturing*, 16, 333–358.

Wheeler, C.N., Ibeh, K.I.N. and Dimitratos, P. (2008), 'UK export performance research 1990–2003: review and theoretical framework', *International Small Business Journal*, 26(2), 207–239.

Woods, A., Blackburn, R. and Curran, J. (1993), A *Longitudinal Study of Small Enterprises in the Service Sector*, Brunel University: Small Business Research Centre.

Wright, M., Westhead, P. and Ucbasaran, D. (2007), 'Internationalisation of small and medium-sized enterprises (SMEs) and international entrepreneurship: a critique and policy implication', *Regional Studies*, 41(7), 1013–1029.

Zahra, S. A. (2005), 'Toward a theory of international new ventures: Reflections on a decade of research', *Journal of International Business Studies*, 36: 29–41

Zucchella, A., Palamara, G. and Denicolai, S. (2007), 'The drivers of the early internationalisation of the firm', *Journal of World Business*, 42, 268–280.

Chapter 18

Cross-cultural marketing strategies
For SMEs

Robin Lowe, Isobel Doole and Felicity Mendoza

LEARNING OBJECTIVES

After reading this chapter, you will be able to:
- develop an appreciation of the challenges and opportunities facing small- and medium-sized enterprises (SMEs) in internationalizing across cross-cultural markets
- identify and compare the different strategic approaches to cross-cultural marketing adopted by SMEs
- understand the factors that drive SME internationalization
- contrast the alternative segmentation strategies of SMEs developing cross-cultural marketing strategies
- understand the role that relational strategies play in cross-cultural SME marketing.

INTRODUCTION

There is an apparent dichotomy in the development of SMEs. For a few of the most successful SMEs, growth rates seem to be accelerating as they pursue opportunities across the world at an ever-faster pace, driven and supported by the latest advances in information and communications technology. For many other SMEs, no matter where in the world they are situated, competition seems to increase. SMEs that have had a traditional and secure niche in the local business community are increasingly coming under attack from worldwide competition. It seems that no matter how small and specialized the local grocery or bookstore is, it has become part of the global market and has to compete with the global giants, such as Wal-Mart and Amazon.com.

SMEs have always been of great importance to the local or national economy because they create wealth and employment and frequently initiate innovation. The majority of smaller firms, however, are a less powerful force outside their home territory. Indeed, many SMEs, despite what may be competitive advantage in the product and service offering at home and their significant marketing capability, never move into international markets at all. However, the changes in the international trading environment, particularly information and communications technological developments, are increasing the opportunities for SMEs to become considerably more important in the future global economy, both in fast-growing business sectors, and in specific market niches, where innovation in mature industry sectors can lead to new opportunities for the smaller firm.

For many firms exporting is the first significant step in cross-cultural marketing. It is the stage in the internationalization process where firms recognize that cross-cultural markets provide the advantage of considerably expanded market potential with relatively little commitment and limited associated risk. Cross-cultural marketing, when defined as the marketing of goods and/or services across national and political boundaries, becomes the means by which SMEs can seek market expansion.

WHAT IS AN SME?

A number of definitions of the small- and medium-sized enterprise sector exist but the most commonly used terms relate to the number of employees in the company. The European Union, for example, defines a small firm as employing between 0 and 49 employees and a medium firm as employing between 50 and 249 employees.

According to UK government estimates there were 4.8 million private sector enterprises in the UK at the start of 2008, and of these 99.9 per cent of these were classed as SMEs. The number of people employed by SMEs was estimated at 13.7 million, and their combined turnover was £1,500 billion. However, because the SME classification includes sole operators (estimated at 24.4 per cent of total enterprises) as well as quite sophisticated businesses, it is not particularly useful for segmenting the smaller firms sector.

In this chapter, therefore, the review of smaller firm strategies is not restricted to firms with a specific number of employees but rather to those businesses in general which think and act like SMEs. Typically their strategies are closely linked to the owner's knowledge, capability and ambition. Indeed, they often become the very personification of their owner and are thus strongly influenced by the home country culture. This is something we will be discussing later in the chapter.

The reason for adopting this stance is that, for example, a garment-making firm with 250 employees has a very restricted capacity to internationalize, whereas a 250-employee financial services or computer software company could be a significant international player. Many quite large businesses have operated in the same way for decades, perhaps exporting to the same customers in the same countries for years. They are unwilling or unable to seek out new markets and stick to what and who they know. Such firms take business decisions within the 'inner' management group as they have done for years and in much the same way that family owners of small firms take decisions.

While family businesses share many of the problems of any business, the complexity of personal family relationships presents additional challenges. Often members of the extended family have a financial or emotional interest in the firm and feel that their often conflicting views about strategy should be taken into account. The loyalty and commitment of families to each other does offer stability, however, and where members of the extended family are located in different countries they can help with setting up a new arm of the business in a new market by providing financial support there, and help with the supply chain and finding customers. Asian family firms have been particularly successful with this.

Many of the fastest-growing international small firms very rapidly grow through the 250-employee ceiling without making significant changes to their international strategic approach. Typically the primary focus of small firms is on the short term and finding new customers and meeting their requirements. When the firm has a successful product or service, the managers are often reluctant to change it. However, without fully realizing it, the model and approach to their home and nearby markets is usually based around their detailed knowledge and an understanding of the needs of their customers. The danger is that, due to their lack of resources and expertise, these firms often do not take time to develop the same close relationships with customers in their new markets and instead may simply appoint an intermediary dealer or distributor to be the primary contact with customers. If they are unable to adapt their business mode and strategy quickly enough to take account of the different market conditions, social culture and ways of doing business, the firm might underperform.

Our discussion in this chapter, therefore, relates to issues such as these that do not significantly affect strategy development in the largest multinational firms that have real global power but are central to strategy development in smaller firms. Small firms are not small versions of larger firms but are driven by very different demands and a significantly different mindset.

THE IMPORTANCE OF SME ACTIVITY IN CROSS-CULTURAL MARKETING

Of the huge number of SMEs, only a small percentage, perhaps less than 5 per cent, have the ambition and capability to grow significantly. How many of them are likely to be involved in cross-cultural marketing is difficult to estimate.

The British Chamber of Commerce suggest that 25 per cent of SMEs export occasionally and 38 per cent frequently, but only 21 per cent export over half of their turnover (BCC, 2004). Recent research suggested that of the 100 fastest-growing firms in the UK, 50 per cent did not show evidence of any export activity and less than 15 per cent of the firms achieved more that 50 per cent of their turnover from exports (BIS, 2009).

The SME sector has also become more important as a creator of wealth and employment due to the downsizing in global firms. Large global firms are reducing their workforces across the world, and concentrating on increasingly outsourcing their non-core components, often to smaller firms. Employment in the public sector has been decreasing during this same period due to the extensive privatization of public-sector-owned utilities and agencies, such as gas, electricity, water and telephones. Further to this, an increased volume of public sector services, such as cleaning and catering, have been contracted out to private organizations. In many countries this has left the SME sector as the only significant growing source of wealth and employment.

The role and contribution of SMEs in the exports of an economy has, however, received increasing attention. The interest reflects both a national government concern with generating greater exports and the increasing focus on competitiveness in cross-cultural markets by SMEs themselves.

Despite this many SMEs ignore the potential of their products and services to be marketed across cultures and concentrate instead on their domestic markets. Even in the twenty-first century many SMEs regard exporting as an *add-on activity* and so withdraw from international markets when orders in the home market improve or conditions on international markets became unfavourable. By contrast, a small but significant minority succeed on international markets and show a strong commitment to further expansion in their international activities. Grimes *et al.* (2007) developed a profile of the internationalizing firms and it is possible to use this to characterize firms at each stage of internationalization.

BOX 18.1: THE AFRICAN CONTEXT

African cultural dynamics are evident not only in the management of SMEs and family-owned enterprises in sub-Saharan Africa but in larger and state-owned corporations (Darley and Blankson, 2008). Overseas companies seeking to do business with them would benefit, therefore, from an increased awareness of African cultural values and beliefs.

There are four main areas for consideration for overseas businesses wishing to make links with African companies: organizational behaviour, buyer–seller interaction, collaborative partnerships and negotiation.

1. Organizational behaviour
   The concept of *ubuntu* or reciprocity means that management policies respect elders, allow for fulfilment of social obligations, and recognize the role of symbolism and religion, as well as the authority of position and hierarchy.
2. Buyer–seller interaction
   Particular consideration should be given to non-verbal communications, context and notions of authority. As respect for elders is important it follows that authority increases with age. This has an impact on the choice of style for a sales presentation as well as the choice of representative making the pitch.
3. Collaborative partnerships
   In the African context networks and relationships are vital to the success of SMEs. African firms' attitudes to collaborative partnerships are characterized by extensive communication, consultation and interaction.
4. Negotiations
   The African negotiation strategy tends to take on a problem-solving approach in order to identify options suitable to both parties. The negotiated outcomes should promote the development of a long-term relationship and aim for long-term goals. Hierarchy is an ever-present influence in the negotiation process.

With these factors in mind, SMEs can be categorized as follows:

Domestic SMEs

The vast majority of SMEs provide lower income per hour than is possible from employment in larger organizations. Examples of this are the small convenience store where the whole family might be involved in the enterprise. Community enterprises are typically supported by public funds because they are seen as not simply providers of employment but also as change agents in achieving greater social inclusion, better health and improved education and housing. The challenge for them, as they achieve success in economic regeneration, is how to evolve from their initial 'social funding dependency' to become businesses within the mainstream business community.

The impact of this segment on the economy is limited because over the long term the number of births of new companies is often cancelled out by the number of deaths. Over shorter periods, however, the segment can be dramatically affected by changes in the national economy in general, and the local economy in particular (for example, if a major local employer closes down and has a knock-on effect on dependent businesses). New businesses in this sector can have a high displacement effect on the existing business base. For example, there are a relatively fixed number of hairdressers, local shops, car mechanics and market traders that are needed in the local economy and, in order to succeed, the new local businesses have to take customers from the existing firms, so putting them at risk.

Cross-cultural marketing, therefore, has little relevance to the majority of these businesses other than where it poses the threat of competition. In practice, however, a few lifestyle firms find a business formula, sometimes by accident, that is viable in cross-cultural markets, and so the firm becomes more ambitious as the opportunity for growth is realized.

BOX 18.2: KENNY'S BOOKSHOP

Family-run bookshop Kenny's branched out from the high street by offering its products online over 20 years ago. Exports now account for 70 per cent of their turnover and they have a warehouse of over 1 million titles in order to fulfil orders from all over the world. In the last few years they have been granted the lucrative status as official supplier to the National Library of China.

Conor Kenny, the owner of the Galway-based business, advises SMEs not to be put off exporting just because there are already large competitors in the global marketplace. He reminds SMEs that there may always be a niche for them that the big players have overlooked.

Kenny's USP (unique selling proposition) is specialist Irish-interest titles; however, another important tool in the fight to make a sale, according to their web sales manager Karen Golden, is price. They use price comparison technology to continually compare and re-price their products in order to keep one step ahead of the competition. This doesn't prevent them working collaboratively with the competition, however. Kenny's acts almost like a cooperative by carrying listings of booksellers on its website as a means of attracting buyers to the site.

Networked SMEs

For many SMEs the resources required to familiarize themselves with foreign markets are limited so the opportunity to gain this information through their current networks and relationships is vital. According to Agndal and Chetty (2007), there are two key types of relationships: business relationships at the level of the organization, for example with suppliers and distributors; and social relationships, which are reliant on the involvement of an individual.

Crick and Chaudhry (2010), in a study of UK-based Asian-owned businesses, conclude that Asian transnational entrepreneurs increase their competitiveness by maximizing their relationships with contacts in their country of origin. By having a strong trusted network which includes family and friends they were able to develop collaborative ventures, access resources and set up manufacturing operations in India to compete with cheaper imported goods from, for example, China.

Mangold and Foulds (2009) point out that consumers like to network with likeminded people. Social networking media is increasingly used by SMEs as a means of accessing consumer feedback as well as a cost-effective marketing communications tool. Advances in technology have enabled businesses to develop networking platforms and blog sites which encourage users to generate content and interact with other clients. Mulhern (2009) says that this usage of digital media promotes extended understanding of the consumer and encourages loyalty.

> ### BOX 18.3: MASALA MASALA
>
> Masala Masala was set up by London-based lawyer Priya Lakhani when she saw a gap in the market for fresh, healthy, authentic Indian sauces. To see how her sauces would fare in the mass-market, she tested them on her non-Indian friends, with positive results.
>
> This sense of community and sharing has been incorporated into the business model via a blog facility on their website which allows the general public to swap recipes. The company website and Facebook group also promotes the Masala Masala project, which offers a homeless person in India a hot meal for every pot of sauce sold. It pays charities, including Save the Children, to feed slum dwellers in Mumbai and Tamil Nadu in the south.

Supply-chain SMEs

The downsizing that has occurred in many global firms as a response to the global slowdown since 2009 has led firms to think about what is their core competence and answer the question, 'What business are we really in?' The response to this question has led a number of firms operating globally to identify those components and services which were parts of the overall product offer but which they regard as being peripheral to their business. As a result of this, many of these large corporations have decided to outsource more of their supplies.

In a study of Indian SMEs within the manufacturing sector, it was observed that developing their position in the supply chain was given strategic importance when considering competitive advantage. This is because most Indian SMEs supply components or parts to larger organizations and original equipment manufacturers (Singh et al., 2010).

Loane (2006) found that internet usage had become essential to supply-chain SMEs for them to upgrade their business processes and operations in order to collaborate effectively with their multinational clients.

SMEs with concentrated expansion into foreign markets

Whether as the result of an unsought opportunity or of necessity through saturation in the domestic market, many SMEs internationalize by targeting a limited number of overseas markets. Steve Smith, chairman of consultant Quest Worldwide, advises small businesses to identify emerging markets in fast-growing cities such as Shanghai and focus on them one at a time (Smith, 2008).

In a 2007 study of British SME retailers, it was found that organizations that traded in the luxury goods market chose to focus their internationalization strategy on fashionable cities around the world such as Paris and New York, as well as trade on their English style to increase their appeal to overseas markets (Hutchinson et al., 2007).

SMEs with dispersed expansion into foreign markets

Many SMEs internationalize by targeting customers rather than countries. This is typical in niche markets where the SME offers adapted products or services to meet the customer specification. The geographical location of these customers is less relevant and may result in the business trading all over the world.

Some SMEs view dispersed expansion as a way of minimizing the risk of dependency on concentrated foreign markets, overcoming the constraints of a small domestic market and maximizing on opportunities identified through marketing research activities. According to McNaughton (2003), these firms may set out to reach a number of markets at once or may add to their portfolio, learning from past experiences.

Born-global SMEs

Within this segment are hyper-growth firms that typically experience growth in turnover and employees in excess of 100 per cent over a three-year period. Typically they identify and exploit a unique and defendable niche in the market and develop products and services that are 'leading edge'. These are the firms that tend to make the news. In the last few years many technologically based businesses have found it necessary to be extremely ambitious in order to survive and grow and are 'born global'. These companies market their products and services around the world, and thus face the challenges of cross-cultural marketing from the first days of their existence. However, it is likely that the majority of new technology innovations will be relatively less culturally sensitive, and thus require a less locally adapted marketing approach than products and services that are competing in more traditional business sectors.

According to Andersson (2004), the attitude of the owner or director of a firm in the early stages of development is very important in high-growth industries. Firms led by entrepreneurs with a positive attitude to early internationalization tend to integrate this approach into their company culture.

THE INTERNATIONALIZATION PROCESS

Motivations and barriers

In many cases the SME will have overcome significant attitudinal barriers as they begin to look on cross-cultural marketing as akin to looking for new customers in the next town, next state or on another coast. According to Andersson (2004), cultural differences can vary from industry to industry as well as from region to region; therefore, analysis of these differences must be carried out at industry level.

Traditionally areas which firms have identified as barriers to internationalization centre on:

- fear of bureaucracy
- trade barriers in foreign markets
- transportation difficulties
- lack of trained personnel
- lack of incentive to move out of the domestic market
- lack of coordinated government assistance
- unfavourable conditions in international markets
- slow payment by buyers
- lack of competitive products
- payment defaults
- language barriers.

Thus for many SMEs their expansion into international markets can be a result of them overcoming such fears due to necessity when the environment in which they are operating becomes unfavourable and so the expansion into international markets becomes a matter of survival. Adverse environmental stimuli can include such things as:

- adverse domestic market conditions
- a downturn in their local economy
- increased competition from international suppliers
- the demands of their customers to supply them internationally
- the need to reduce unacceptable levels of inventories
- a downturn in the home market meaning they have excess capacity
- the need to spread the risk of business across several markets.

SMEs can develop internationally as a result of a deliberate proactive strategy to develop the business further, in which case the stimulus to do so could be due to such things as:

- the company identifying specific attractive profit and growth opportunities
- the company seeing competitive advantage in other markets through the repositioning of their product or service
- public policy programmes for export promotion
- the changing of foreign country regulations to provide opportunities
- the realization their company possesses a differential advantage in key export markets
- the presence of an internationally minded manager
- the opportunity to better utilize management talent and skills
- management beliefs about the value of cross-cultural marketing.

If a company sees only limited growth opportunities in the home market for a proven product it may well see market diversification as a means of expansion. This could mean new market segments within a domestic market but it may well mean geographic expansion in foreign markets. Thus companies try to spread risks and reduce their dependence on any one market. For example, BF Rail, a firm in the north of the UK, traditionally obtained 90 per cent of its sales from one customer – the company controlling the coal mines in the region in which it was located. When many of the coal mines began to close, BF Rail soon realized if they were to survive they needed to pursue a strategy of market diversification through international expansion.

Alternatively, the firm may identify market gaps. The proactive company with a well-managed marketing information system may identify foreign market opportunities through its research system. This could, of course, be by undertaking formal structured research or by identifying opportunities through a network of contacts scanning international markets for potential opportunities.

An economic recession can provide opportunities for internationalization for entrepreneurs and SMEs. In particular, during an economic downturn SMEs can exploit the favourable exchange rates to trade overseas and offset the weakness in the domestic market. On the other hand, however, difficulty accessing finance from risk averse lenders can make SMEs vulnerable.

The capability that that the World Wide Web has to bring together dispersed and fragmented markets has been a significant factor affecting SME internationalization. It has had the effect of enabling specialist suppliers to reach a global audience, niche suppliers to create a global niche business, and supply-chain members to more effectively contribute to the value chain of major internationals. Loane (2006) observes that small entrepreneurial organizations demonstrate significant internet usage to support their overseas activities. In particular, she notes that the internet and associated technologies are used not only for communications via email or social networks and marketing via websites but also as a knowledge-building tool, a distribution channel and a means of enhancing business processes.

CATEGORIES OF INTERNATIONAL DEVELOPMENT

According to a report by the British Chamber of Commerce, firms competing on cross-cultural markets can be categorized by examining their attitudes and behaviour towards competing internationally. They can be categorized into four segments:

- **Opportunists** make up 37 per cent of SME exporters and tend to be the smallest type of business in terms of employee numbers and turnover. They are reactive when it comes to export sales, do not research markets or develop written export strategies or rely on export sales. They sell directly to the customer rather than an agent or a distributor and do not tailor their services or products.
- **Developers** make up 17 per cent of SME exporters. They are also reactive and tend not to research markets although they may have some level of strategy in place. In contrast to opportunists, their export turnover is 50 per cent of their total annual turnover and there will be limited adaptation of products and services.
- **Adaptors** make up 26 per cent of SME exporters. Their export turnover is also around 50 per cent and they have a dispersed global presence. Although they may carry out some limited research they tend to learn as they go along and adapt accordingly. They are well positioned for export growth and demonstrate an awareness of missed opportunities.
- **Enablers** make up 20 per cent of SME exporters. They are proactive and make strategic choices about which markets to move into. They demonstrate an awareness of their customers' requirements and tailor their products and services to meet them (BCC, 2004).

MODES OF ENGAGEMENT

In the early stages of international development SMEs may treat cross-cultural markets as purely short-term economic opportunities to be pursued in order to maximize short-term profit. As firms become more involved in international markets they treat the resulting business opportunities as strategic to company development. Successful firms invariably build a distinctive competitive position across a range of cross-cultural markets. In examining cross-cultural marketing in SMEs, the type of mode of engagement employed and how firms build a competitive advantage across a range of markets are therefore important areas of consideration.

In exploiting cross-cultural market opportunities to generate revenue from international markets, SMEs have a number of modes of engagement to choose from. The main options we will consider in this section are as follows:

- indirect exporting
- direct exporting
- licensing.

In choosing an appropriate method of engagement there are a number of marketing and environmental factors, such as the nature and power of competition, the existing and anticipated tariff and non-tariff barriers and the nature of the product itself, and company factors, such its size and financial resources, skills, ambition and attitudes to international trade to take into account. However, firms consider three key strategic criteria too. The different methods of engagement require considerably different levels of investment. The methods offer very different levels of involvement in the market. For example, handing over many of the marketing activities in another country to an intermediary means the company may have little direct control over the marketing mix in that country, and therefore little direct control over its image, market positioning and reputation there. Finally, the methods pose different levels of risk to both finances and reputation if the new market venture underperforms or fails.

Indirect exporting

For firms that have little inclination or few resources for international marketing, the best option is to allow others to sell their products overseas. Indirect exporting allows them to benefit from opportunities that arise, such as selling excess capacity with the least possible convenience and expense. This method means that low levels of investment are needed and their involvement in the market will be low. While financial risk is normally low, problems can occur because of the firm's disconnection from the market. If the customer demand changes suddenly the indirect exporter may not become aware until it is too late to respond.

Direct exporting

Direct exporting is perhaps the most common form of international development and is typically more proactive, involving carefully selecting and managing an agent or distributor to handle the export sales. To be successful the exporter and intermediary must be both motivated and committed to the activity and be prepared to make the necessary investment in time and resources to understand the overseas market share, the marketing operations and decision making in order to reduce the potential risk.

Licensing

For innovative small firms with creative new products and services the challenge is to maximize the global sales potential before competitors find a way to exploit similar ideas and market opportunities. The investment required to do this alone is beyond the resources of most small firms and licensing provides an opportunity to achieve global sales and a significant income stream without the expense of production or hiring marketing, sales and operations staff. Licensing might include brands, products, characters, software, themes, and technology and process know-how.

STRATEGY DEVELOPMENT

The strategy development process

Having considered the various categories of SME modes of engagement in internationalization, we now turn to the factors which influence the strategic marketing development of SMEs.

There are an infinite number of strategies that an SME can adopt, but as they become more sophisticated they increasingly focus on meeting the needs of their chosen markets and differentiating their offer from that of their competitors.

The principal approach to cross-cultural strategy development follows three stages, normally referred to as **s**egmentation, **t**argeting and **p**ositioning (STP) markets:

1. Identification of the various consumer *segments* that exist within the business sector, using the various segmentation methods. It is important for SMEs to define cross-border segments with clearly identifiable requirements that it is able to serve.
2. The firm must then *target* the segments which appear to be most attractive in terms of their size, growth potential, the ease with which they can be reached and their likely purchasing power.
3. In seeking to defend and develop its business the firm needs to *position* its products or services in a way that will distinguish them from those of its local and international competitors and build up barriers which will prevent those competitors taking its business. Of course by specifically positioning to meet the requirements of its chosen segments (e.g. for a premium product), it may also be saying to other segments that it cannot meet their needs (e.g. for an inexpensive product).

INTERNATIONAL MARKETING SEGMENTATION

Market segmentation is the strategy by which a firm partitions a market into sub-markets or segments that are likely to manifest similar responses to marketing inputs. The aim is to identify the markets on which a company can concentrate its resources and efforts. In this way it can achieve maximum penetration of that market, rather than going for perhaps a market-spreading strategy where the company aims to achieve a presence, however small, in as many markets as possible. The two main bases for segmenting international markets are by geographical criteria (i.e. countries) and transnational criteria (i.e. individual decision makers.)

Country-based segmentation

The traditional practice is to use a country-based classification system as a basis for selecting international markets to enter. The Business Portfolio matrix, shown in Figure 18.1, encourages companies to classify potential target countries in three categories:

1. *Primary markets* are the best opportunities for long-term strategic development. Companies may want to establish a permanent presence in these countries and so conduct a thorough research programme. Firms expect to earn at least 30 per cent of export turnover in primary markets.
2. *Secondary markets* are where opportunities are identified but political or economic risk is perceived as being too high to make long-term irrevocable commitments. As a result these markets would be handled in a more pragmatic way due to the potential risks identified. A comprehensive marketing information system would be needed to continually monitor the situation. Usually secondary markets account for between 10 and 30 per cent of export turnover
3. *Tertiary markets* are the catch-what-you-can markets. These markets will be perceived as high risk and so the allocation of resources will be minimal. Objectives in such countries

would be short-term and opportunistic; companies would give no real commitment and would not carry out significant research.

Figure 18.1 illustrates the Business Portfolio matrix. The horizontal axis evaluates the attractiveness of each country on objective and measurable criteria (e.g. size, stability and wealth). The vertical axis evaluates the firm's compatibility with each country on a more subjective and judgmental basis. Primary markets would score high on both axes.

It has long been recognized that SMEs, when operating on cross-cultural markets, identify their primary markets as the ones where they feel most culturally at ease. Thus, the perception of the firm is that the psychological distance between the international market and their home market (known as the psychic distance) is relatively small. In cross-cultural marketing the psychic distance effect is usually a function of the firm's perception of risk and their knowledge of foreign market conditions. Firms will reduce the degree of commitment and risk exposure in markets where the gap is perceived to be much wider and these they would term tertiary markets.

This approach is a particularly useful device for a company operating in a portfolio of markets to prioritize market opportunity. Once the prime country markets have been identified, companies usually then use standard techniques to segment the markets within countries using such variables as demographic/economic factors, lifestyles, consumer motivations, geography, buyer behaviour, psychographics, etc.

The problem, however, is that, depending on the information base, it may be difficult to fully formulate secondary segmentation bases and achieve consistency across markets. The

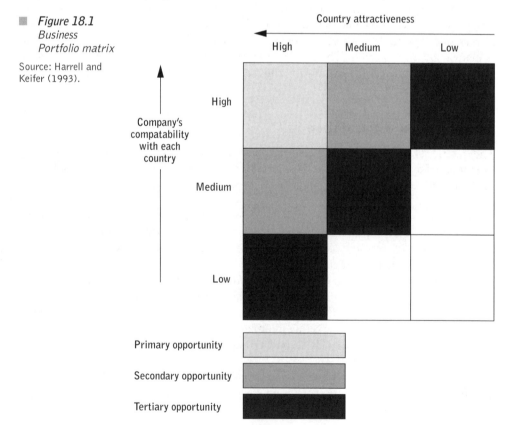

■ *Figure 18.1*
Business
Portfolio matrix

Source: Harrell and
Keifer (1993).

approach can run the risk of leading to a differentiated marketing approach which may leave the company with a very fragmented international strategy.

Transnational segmentation

If a company is to try to achieve a consistent and controlled marketing strategy across all its international markets, it needs a transnational approach to its segmentation strategy. To achieve a transnational segmentation approach, the country as a unit of analysis is too large to be of operational use. An alternative approach is to examine the individual decision maker using such variables as demographic, psychographic and behavioural criteria.

Demographic variables have obvious potential as cross-national segmentation criteria. The most commonly used variables include sex, age, income level, social class and educational achievement. Psychographic segmentation involves using lifestyle factors in the segmentation process. Appropriate criteria are usually of an inferred nature and concern consumer interests and perceptions of 'way of living' in regard to work and leisure habits, and include activities, interests and opinions. Objective criteria, normally of a demographic nature, may also be helpful when defining life segments. Research International, researching the transnational segments of young adults, globally divided them into four broad categories. 'Enthusiastic materialists' are optimistic and aspirational and to be found in developing countries and emerging markets like India and Latin America. 'Swimmers against the tide' on the other hand demonstrate a degree of underlying pessimism and tend to live for the moment and are likely to be found in southern Europe. In northern Europe, the US and Australasia are the 'new realists', looking for a balance between work and leisure with some underlying pessimism in outlook. Finally, the 'complacent materialists' are defined as passively optimistic and located in Japan (Research International, 2007).

Behavioural variables also have a lot of potential as a basis for global market segmentation. In particular, attention to patterns of consumption and loyalty in respect of product category and brand can be useful, along with a focus on the context for usage. Variables such as the benefit sought or the buying motivations may be used. Behaviourally defined segments may be identified in terms of a specific aspect of behaviour that is not broad enough to be defined as a lifestyle. An example of this is the extremely wealthy travellers who tend to buy the same fashion brands, stay at the same hotels and buy the same luxury products. This group not only includes the wealthy from traditionally wealthy nations but also those newly rich entrepreneurs from previously closed economies.

Despite the attractiveness of using individualistic characteristics, it is apparent that there is strong potential for significant differences in the patterns of consumer behaviour within global segments derived using this method. Also international similarities in lifestyle and behaviour do tend to be specific, and relevant primarily to specialist products and niche markets.

Parallels can be drawn for the business-to-business market, where the nature of the product or service and the overall market context might determine whether a country-based approach or a transnational approach is most appropriate. For example, a country-based segmentation approach might be most appropriate where there are many customers located in each country that frequently require high levels of local support from a service provider. A transnational approach might be the most appropriate in a situation where the exporter has a few potential customers located around the world with specialized requirements.

As more and more SMEs build up timely and robust customer information through web-enabled traffic either by email, web traffic or online purchasing, their ability to do this effectively has been greatly enhanced as a recent survey carried out by GetResponse, described in Box 18.4.

BOX 18.4: USING WEB TRAFFIC TO DEVELOP SEGMENTATION STRATEGIES

Email traffic now gives SMEs much more potential to be creative yet practical in the way they segment their customer base. According to GetResponse's 2010 Email Marketing Trends Study, over half (59.4 per cent) of SMEs segment their consumer lists and email leads according to their recipients' professed interests. Well over a third of SMEs also segment their customers by their click-rate activity. This of course gives SMEs the opportunity not to just segment customers by what they look like but also how they behave and, perhaps more important, how they seek their information. This gives small firms a unique insight into how best to talk and communicate with their customers, irrespective of what culture they sit in. Purchasing behaviour is also a useful segmentation criterion for companies who offer online purchasing. Nearly 30 per cent of SMEs segment customers by their customers' purchase history.

However, passive characteristics such as demographics are still seen as vital, with nearly a third of SMEs using demographics as a segmentation criterion.

Simon Grabowski, founder of GetResponse, said: 'Today's marketers are mindful of the importance of delivering relevant content and one-to-one messaging based on preferences and behaviours. It's all about putting the human element back into marketing.'

Source: www.marketscan.co.uk

Such approaches as these enable marketers to design strategies at a cross-cultural segment level and so take a more consumer-oriented approach to international marketing. In prioritizing markets, SMEs who may operate in a large number of geographical markets but with few customers may need to use existing customer data as their primary information base for segmenting existing and potential customers. Some writers argue that companies still need a secondary segmentation stage to identify the key countries where these transnational segments can be found, and that country environments (legal, political, social and economic) necessitate different marketing mix strategies, such as promotion and distribution.

Targeting approaches

For SMEs the key decision of targeting therefore will largely result from the methodology they have used to segment their international markets. If they have used a culturally or geographically based methodology the major targeting decision will relate to which country markets they are going to select and then how they should develop a market share within each country. Given the limited resources of SMEs and the narrow margin for failure, it is vital that their method of targeting country markets is effective.

Firms that establish a domestic base first before selecting further country market involvement develop either through an incremental process of country market diversification or by concentrating in a few countries following an initial expansion period. In this case the SMEs may concentrate their activities in a small number of markets in which a significant market share can be built. SMEs often select countries because of the close psychic distance, the network of contacts they have made there, or because they are able to piggyback on a larger organization in that market.

Following a market concentration strategy enables a firm to achieve market specialization, economies of scale, market knowledge and a high degree of control. For these reasons government support agencies often recommend that small firms follow a market concentration strategy in order to concentrate resources and achieve greater market share. However, this conflicts with the views of the SME following a niche marketing strategy where, with such a small potential market share in any one market, greater profitability is viewed as being best achieved by spreading across a number of markets.

Many SMEs successfully operating across a number of cross-cultural markets view themselves as international niche marketers, not necessarily as exporters to a particular foreign country market. Once they have exploited that particular niche, they look elsewhere in order to develop and for this reason they follow a market diversification strategy. Thus customer development in a number of cross-cultural markets is more important than market share acquisition in the country they had already entered. This is particularly important for born-global firms that are building a business around new technology. They must develop relationships with key customers in the markets that will be most influential in the diffusion of the new idea. Parrish *et al.* (2006) explain how niche marketing can be used in a mature sector, such as the global textile sector, to increase competitiveness despite the presence of strong rivals.

Firms can also become a strong force in a narrow specialized market of one or two segments across a number of country markets. An example of one such company is Macalloy, described in Box 18.5.

BOX 18.5: MACALLOY

Macalloy is a medium-sized company based in the UK that has grown very rapidly. It manufactures and supplies tensioning devices used in construction projects to support the roofs of large buildings and bridges, such as the Burj Al Arab Hotel, Dubai, the Korean World Trade Centre Pyramid, and the Millau Viaduct, illustrated on its website (www.macalloy.co.uk). It has a significant share of a niche market which it has exploited by targeting clients who develop and build such projects. The company uses it networks to scan the environment and ensure that it hears of any proposed project at an early stage. While the company builds its capability to deliver and support projects in particular regions or countries where it expects growth in major construction, its main focus is to target the major global companies that undertake these major capital projects.

Source: www.macalloy.co.uk

If a firm has used transnational approaches to segment their markets they may be well placed to develop a market diversification strategy and expand into a number of cross-cultural markets while only seeking to gain a superficial presence in each one. This market diversification approach reduces market risks, enables firms to exploit the economies of flexibility and to be more adaptable to different market needs.

Often firms following a market diversification strategy are more proactive than SMEs pursuing a market concentration approach and attach greater importance to the pursuit of minimizing market risk by operating in a number of different markets.

As said above, web-based marketing has made it easier for SMEs to operate across country borders and made it much easier for SMEs to view their international markets in terms of *customers* and not necessarily in terms of *countries*. This is leading many SMEs to seek the most profitable customers irrespective of the number of countries in which they are located. This is important as it gives them the means of focusing their strategies towards the needs of their customers and a much clearer view of how their products should be positioned in those markets. However, Servais *et al.* (2007) explain that even born-global SMEs use the internet only to a limited extent to sell their products and use it rather as a tool to support existing relationships.

Generic positioning strategies

Having identified the target segments, the SME must then develop its unique and distinct positioning by building upon its source of competitive advantage. In order to create competitive advantage, Porter (1985) suggests that firms should adopt one of three generic strategies: cost leadership, which requires the firm to establish a lower cost base than its local or international competitors; a focused strategy, where the firm concentrates on one or more narrow segments and thus builds a specialist knowledge of the target segment; or differentiation, where the firm emphasizes particular benefits in the product, service, or marketing mix that customers might perceive to be both important and a significant improvement over competitive offers.

It is very difficult in cross-cultural marketing for SMEs to follow a cost leadership strategy or even entertain aspirations of being the cheapest in their markets. Those SMEs that adopt a low-cost strategy to achieve cost leadership can be potentially vulnerable to price competition, either from local firms in the foreign country market or larger multinationals temporarily cutting prices to force the SME out of that market. Usually successful firms will choose to build competitive advantage by avoiding price competition and focusing on the achievement of margins through focus or differentiation. The problem for small firms pursuing a low-cost strategy is that it may lead them to put too much emphasis on internal matters in their efforts to simply contain costs rather than delivering superior value in the international market. To be successful on cross-cultural markets SMEs need to overcome the double hurdle of managing costs while at the same time competing on added value

Given the limited ability of small firms to pursue a low-cost strategy, superior performance is often viewed as being best achieved by delivering superior customer value through differentiated products/services for carefully selected market niches. Thus it is not the product/ service strength alone that is a critical factor in cross-cultural markets, but how the firm builds competitive advantage by creating superior value for its customers through its total product and service offer, supported by the effective use of the marketing mix.

Firms seek to differentiate their products from competitors in cross-cultural markets either by product innovation or by adding value through additional services, for example, by offering high levels of customer support and technical advice. SMEs competing in international markets do so with limited resources, and so any cross-cultural marketing strategy they pursue must be developed within that context. Successful firms will invest resources either in developing the capability to add value to their product offering to targeted customers worldwide or invest resources in ensuring they maintain superior product performance ahead of competitors worldwide in specific targeted cross-cultural niches.

Many SMEs base their cross-cultural marketing strategy on the generic strategy that has given them competitive advantage in domestic markets and then attempt to apply this same successful strategy in international markets. Again, however, their limited resources often force them to make a change to their strategy. They may have largely used a pull strategy in their domestic marketing and thus directed much of their promotional activity at their ultimate customers, whereas in international markets they frequently adopt a less costly push strategy. This means the firm promotes only to the intermediaries in the distribution channel and expects them to promote (or push) the products and services to the final customer.

Of fundamental importance to the development of an effective cross-cultural marketing strategy for some SMEs is having a very strong position in the home country. US firms have benefitted from having a huge potential domestic market. By contrast SMEs from emerging markets and from countries with smaller domestic markets often have to export merely to survive. There can be some dangers in entering sophisticated markets without a clear plan and robust business model. Crick and Spence (2005) found that internationalization strategy formation for high-performing SMEs is not always systematic and capable of being described by one single theory. Some firms take an opportunistic approach towards their internationalizing strategy and it is necessary to take a more holistic view of the organization and its context to explain its decisions.

Balabanis and Katsikea (2003) explain the further dimensions and suggest that there is some evidence to suggest that an entrepreneurial approach which involves risk taking, being proactive and innovative in developing strategies is useful in international marketing development.

A small number of dynamic SMEs challenge the assumptions on which markets are based and create uncontested markets (Kim and Mauborgne, 2005) where they are able to grow very rapidly. Cirque du Soleil and Dyson (see Box 18.6) are examples of companies that grew very quickly to become global players by meeting the common needs and interests of global customers. There is of course the danger that the most successful companies eventually get swallowed up by the multinationals. Two companies that adopted an ethical stance in business were taken over by global giants, The Body Shop by L'Oreal and Ben and Jerry's by Unilever.

BOX 18.6: FAST-GROWTH FIRMS

For SMEs the key to achieving fast growth and major international success is not just about being cheaper or offering slightly better value than their bigger, more powerful competitors but also about creating a new market that makes competitors irrelevant. Two organizations that have done this are Dyson and Cirque du Soleil.

Cirque du Soleil (www.cirquedusoleil.com) started off as a small group of French street performers. The company challenged the idea that a circus should have animals, which were expensive to keep. Moreover, many potential customers believed that it was no longer really acceptable to keep animals caged in circuses. Also circuses were largely targeted at children, but this meant a limit to ticket prices. Instead they created spectacular shows – without animals and for adults – that combined performance, art and music to become a worldwide phenomenon.

After many years of trying, inventor James Dyson invented a revolutionary vacuum cleaner onto the UK market that dispensed with the need for a bag and achieved better cleaning performance than its rivals. The cleaners were also a change from convention. They were brightly coloured, had a highly functional, chunky design and the dirt that had been collected was clearly visible. They were priced much higher than the competition, but because there was no direct competition the company grew rapidly to become a worldwide success. The company is continually innovating (see www.dyson.co.uk). For example, it had to produce a much smaller cleaner than normal for the Japanese market because of the small size of apartments. This, however, had a side benefit. At the same the company was trying to develop a new hand drier for public lavatories but was having trouble designing a small but sufficiently powerful motor. The development of the motor for the Japanese vacuum cleaners proved to be the solution for the hand drier problem.

NETWORK DEVELOPMENT

The primary focus in this chapter has been examining the cross-cultural marketing strategies of SMEs. So far we have examined the varying levels of involvement SMEs have in cross-cultural markets and discussed the need for an SME to select an appropriate segmentation approach to target priority customer groups across cultures. We have also looked at how SMEs establish a competitive positioning. However, the way an SME manages it organizational activities across international markets is central to the achievement of a viable long-term cross-cultural marketing strategy. SMEs have very limited resources to build any organizational structures and so rely heavily on developing a network of partners across markets in order to implement their cross-cultural strategies. Research has shown that successful SMEs appear to exhibit particular competence in their ability to build and utilize a series of relationships as a cost-effective (time and resources) way of identifying new market opportunities and reducing the risk of entering unknown markets.

The networking model can provide SMEs with the resources and the means to compete effectively in cross-cultural markets. Through a global network many smaller firms without the resources themselves can access the expertise, market knowledge and routes to market which they could not achieve alone. Hardman *et al.* (2005) suggest that to compete effectively with the largest competitors, small organizations have to achieve 'virtual scale' by working in alliances to achieve the necessary leverage. The internet can facilitate this and the success of the use of professional social networking sites has helped smaller firms access much wider business networks across cultures and markets. Previous to this SMEs often only had the resources to access business networks closest to where they were based.

Harris and Wheeler (2005) focus on the role of interpersonal relationships in the internationalization process and explain that strong, deep relationships are developed in wide social/personal and business situations that do not just provide information and access to networks but, more importantly, can be influential in directing strategy and can lead to the transformation of the firm. A number of studies of born-global firms have been made in different country contexts. Mort and Weerawardena (2006) have researched born-global firms and highlighted the importance of relationships and networking in enabling the identification and exploitation of market opportunities and facilitating the development of knowledge-intensive products.

A relational strategy is often central to the firm's long-term objective of maintaining their competitiveness in cross-cultural markets over time by giving the firm a number of strategic advantages:

- providing access to markets
- building barriers to entry by competitors

- improving the level of support to the end user
- tying-in customers to longer-term commitments to market development
- improving the speed of access to and accuracy of information on market changes
- building repeat business
- providing the connections to hold the cross-cultural marketing strategy together
- improving the effectiveness of communication links.

Firms build partnerships of varying degrees of intensity and use these relationships to enhance their capability to compete in different cultures. These relationships are valuable for a number of reasons. They help the SME to quickly gain the knowledge and information needed for cost-effective market entry, to build barriers to competition by establishing a locally responsive, adaptable and flexible distribution channel, as well as ensuring their customers in different markets around the world obtain effective service. The relationships can, therefore, be the firm's major communication link to their cross-cultural markets, both in relaying communications to the market to help build the firm's competitive advantage and in relaying information back from the market, which provides input into the decision-making processes of the firm. Relationships are the process by which the strategy is built, organized and implemented; it is the glue, a vital piece of the jigsaw.

Asian firms are typically most committed to relationship development as a central element of their cross-cultural marketing strategy. Indeed, it appears that some Asian firms develop their segmentation strategy around selecting target markets where there are strong cultural ties, as Box 18.7 shows.

BOX 18.7: CROSS-CULTURAL MARKETING CHINESE-STYLE

Chinese entrepreneurs are developing their cross-cultural marketing strategies by using existing networks of contacts. They operate through a network of family and 'clan' relationships in different geographical, political and economic systems. This approach reflects the Chinese culture and the Confucian tradition of hard work, thrift and respect for one's social network.

This provides the rationale for retaining a small business approach to cross-cultural marketing that is capable of a variety of business solutions at relatively low risk. However, Chinese management recognizes the need for innovation and growth, and to encourage greater openness to outsiders if they wish to compete effectively in cross-cultural markets.

Relationship development plays an important role in enabling firms to build the capability to achieve sustainable competitive advantage over the long term. Central to this is that through their relationships firms develop their knowledge base of the changes occurring in cross-cultural markets, thus enabling them to anticipate and deal with the challenges and changes in the marketplace. They use relationships to improve the quality of their decision making by seeking assurances that the decisions that they make are valid and appropriate for the culture of the market in which they are competing. As the managing director of a firm operating in many different international markets remarked:

Our information comes from customers around the world, but it's not just customers. Your contacts are in banking and in shipping, and they enable you to actually draw up a picture of what is really happening so you understand the culture of the country, not just what people want you to know.

Networks and relationships, therefore, can be critical to the success of SMEs all over the globe competing in across different cultural markets.

SUMMARY OF KEY IDEAS

Traditionally, explanations for the success of SMEs in cross-cultural markets have been sought in the marketing mix paradigm. This has meant the focus of research studies has been on explaining marketing transactions and exchanges rather than a long-term strategic focus on competitiveness. Thus, traditionally, the literature on cross-cultural marketing for smaller firms has generally viewed marketing as being treated as a tactical issue by the firms, and has neglected concern for such things as strategic positioning, the importance of developing a sustainable competitive advantage, quality issues, customer retention and building relationships.

In practice successful firms develop strategies based on delivering customer satisfaction to their target segments, thus ensuring high levels of customer retention by providing a high-quality total product and service offer. In this way they are able to establish clear positioning that is distinctive compared to local and other multinational competition. Central to the achievement of these objectives is the relational strategy developed by the SME and the success they have in developing an integrated network of partners across the cross-cultural markets in which they operate.

REVIEW QUESTIONS

1. How can the smaller business compensate for its lack of resources and expertise in cross-cultural marketing when trying to enter new markets?

2. How might a small specialist supplier of games software segment its international markets?

3. Many SMEs use their networks of relationships to research their markets. What advantages and pitfalls might there be in adopting this approach?

4. Competitive relationships are becoming increasingly important in achieving a global competitive advantage for SMEs. Why is this so? What are the implications for the making of strategic marketing decisions in a global market?

5. For a cross-cultural industry that has been affected significantly by internet marketing, explain how the drivers of internet marketing have affected the way SMEs compete on that market and how their cross-cultural marketing strategies have changed.

GROUP ACTIVITIES

Identify a particular SME that has successfully managed to compete across international markets that have seen substantial change. Examine the reasons why they have succeeded in achieving a competitive marketing advantage in such cross-cultural markets.

Identify the principle challenges that SMEs are likely to face over the next decade. What does your group think are the possible implications of these challenges for SMEs competing on cross-cultural markets?

What type of information should be collected by an SME trying to develop a cross-cultural marketing strategy?

Your group have changed from being in a marketing department in a large global business to being the marketing department of a small firm, selling to eight different countries. What differences in terms of strategy, resources and operations would your group expect to see and what might the implications be for the group when developing a marketing strategy for your new firm?

The biggest challenge for SMEs is growing internationally in a period of recession, in your groups discuss the problems SMEs face in such periods and identify ways in which entrepreneurial management can help to overcome such problems in developing internationally.

CASE STUDY 18: WILLIAMSON

Williamson is a UK medium-sized business that manufactures specialist kitchen knives. It has exported its products into a number of country markets within Europe and other countries in the world with which the UK has traditional ties. The company is seeking to develop its business in emerging markets that are growing more rapidly than its existing markets. The company markets its products in retail markets for consumers and also through trade channels into the hospitality and catering industry.

As Europe moves closer towards economic integration and retailers and distributors increase their internationalization, Williamson have found that retailers are increasingly buying on a region-wide basis. The diversity of the brand names and product lines that they have built up in order to meet the specific cultural needs of individual markets is becoming increasingly difficult to sustain as they aim to develop a more efficient and cohesive cross-cultural marketing strategy. They have decided they can no longer defend their competitive position in these markets using their existing strategy, and have had to refocus their thinking.

Typically, SMEs develop internationally by exporting to countries one after another, segmenting their markets principally on geographic but perhaps too on cultural criteria. As they develop their international markets further they also develop more sophisticated criteria for further segmenting their markets. Williamson have traditionally aimed to develop a strategy to satisfy the varying demands of each market and have segmented their markets on a country-by-country basis.

They have now started working towards reorienting their international strategy to develop a more integrated approach with a more cohesive and unified brand image. As Mark Darcy, the managing director said:

As the world becomes more and more integrated then whatever is happening in one market is vitally important to what is happening in another market. You can't consider, for example, Belgium as existing on an island and having nothing to do with what's happening, say. in Sweden. You have got to make sure that you're making a similar offering in your policies, they have got to be relevant to the country involved but you do need to be aware of what is happening in other markets.

The first building block of the change in orientation was to move to a customer-based segmentation approach across their international markets. Through this process, they have identified four clusters across their markets. At the same time, they have undertaken a rationalization exercise in the number of brands and product lines offered. The result has meant that for each market cluster identified they are competing on three price points for each product line:

> Broadly speaking we look for a good, better and best offering in whatever market in which we're operating. In the Iberian cluster, for example, there is a good, better and best offering appropriate to the needs of the market where the best offering is on par with the good offering in Northern Scandinavia.

The stimulus for the change to their strategy has come from the critical changes that they found that were taking place in international markets. It was crucial for Williamson that they built a knowledgeable understanding of those factors and assessed the implications of market changes on the way they developed their strategy, rather than simply accepting them in a passive way and relying on quickly reacting to any consequences. They recognized the need to reorient their strategic thinking and develop a potential solution.

The key element in this strategy reorientation process was gaining the insights from their multiple levels of customers. Williamson did not have the resources to carry out formal market research. Instead they have relied on their network of contacts, both their informal and their supply-chain partners, to help identify the changes in the environment in the various countries in which they are operating, particularly the relevant political, economic and legal changes. They have noted that the most important changes have occurred in the competitive landscape, with new and cheaper alternative suppliers offering competitive products. These new competitors appeared suddenly and unexpectedly and Williamson have often found it difficult to predict where the next challenge will come from as they have fought to retain and build relationships with their multinational retailer customers.

Finally, Williamson have noticed that their customers appear to be much more knowledgeable about their products and use social networking sites to discuss the merits of their product against their competitors. Williamson is rather frustrated that it is not easily able to use the positive communications and deal with the negative communications on such sites.

CASE QUESTIONS AND TASKS

1. Fully evaluate the advantages and disadvantages of Williamson using their networks and relationships in the markets in which they operate for building an information base to develop a cross-cultural marketing strategy.
2. What approach would you advise Williamson to take to develop a segmentation approach that could form the basis of a cross-cultural global strategy?

BIBLIOGRAPHY

Agndal, H. and Chetty, S. (2007), 'The impact of relationships on changes in internationalisation strategies of SME's'. *European Journal of Marketing*, Vol. 41, Issue 11/12, pp. 1449–1474.

Andersson, S. (2004), 'Internationalization in different industrial contexts'. *Journal of Business Venturing*, Vol. 19, Issue 6, pp. 851–875..

Balabanis, G. and Katsikea, E. S. (2003), 'Being an entrepreneurial exporter: does it pay?' *International Business Review*, Vol. 12, No. 2, pp. 233–252.

BCC – British Chambers of Commerce (2004), *BCC Language Survey: The Impact of Foreign Languages on British Business*, May, British Chambers of Commerce. Online: http://www.britishchambers.org.uk/policy/pdf/Language_Survey2.pdf (accessed 23 August 2010).

BIS (2009), 'SME Statistics for the UK and Regions 2008'. Press release, 14 October (corrected July 2010). Online: http://stats.bis.gov.uk/ed/sme/Stats%20Press%20release%202008%20edition%20-%20corrected%20version%20July%202010.pdf (accessed 23 August 2010).

Boyle, C. (2009), 'She saw a niche in the market and spiced up her sauces'. *The Times* (London), 21 December.

Crick, D. and Chaudhry, S. (2010), 'An investigation into UK-based Asian entrepreneurs' perceived competitiveness in overseas markets.' *Entrepreneurship and Regional Development*, Vol. 22, Issue 1, pp. 5–23.

Crick, D. and Spence, M. (2005), 'The internationalisation of "high performing" UK high tech SME's: a study of planned and unplanned strategies'. *International Marketing Review*, Vol. 14, Issue 2 (April), pp. 167–185.

Darley, W. K. and Blankson, C. (2008), 'African culture and business markets: implications for marketing practices'. *Journal of Business and Industrial Marketing*, Vol. 23, Issue 6, pp. 374–383.

Godfrey, R. (2009), 'Don't forget to do your homework'. *Export Guide Magazine*, 10 January. Online: http://www.britishchambers.org.uk/zones/media/articles-and-comments/don-t-forget-to-do-your-homework.html (accessed 23 August 2010).

Grimes A., Doole, I. and Kitchen, P. J. (2007), 'Profiling the capabilities of SMEs to compete internationally'. *Journal of Small Business and Enterprise Development*, Vol. 14, Issue 1, pp. 64–80.

Hardman, D., Messinger, D. and Bergson, S. (2005), *Virtual Scale: Alliances for Leverage: Booz, Allen, Hamilton Resilience Report*. Online: http://www.strategy-business.com/article/05315 (accessed 23 August 2010).

Harrel, G. D. and Keifer, R. O. (1993), 'Multinational market portfolios in global strategy development', *International Marketing Review*, Vol. 10, Issue 1, pp. 60–72

Harris, S. and Wheeler, C. (2005), 'Entrepreneurs' relationships for internationalisation: functions, origins and strategies'. *International Business Review*, Vol. 14, Issue 2 (April), pp. 187–207.

Hutchinson, K., Alexander, N., Quinn, B. and Doherty, A. M. (2007). 'Internationalization motives and facilitating factors: qualitative evidence from smaller specialist retailers'. *Journal of International Marketing*, Vol. 15, Issue 3, pp. 96–122.

Kim, W. C. and Mauborgne, R. (2005), *Blue Ocean Strategy: How to Create Uncontested Market Space and Make Competition Irrelevant*, Harvard Business Press, Boston.

Loane, S. (2006), 'The role of the internet in the internationalisation of small and medium companies', *Journal of International Entrepreneurship*, Vol. 3, pp, 263–277.

McNaughton, R. B. (2003), 'The number of export markets that a firm serves: process models versus the born-global phenomenon'. *Journal of international Entrepreneurship*, Vol. 1, Issue 3, pp. 297–311.

Mandelson, P. (Lord Mandelson Business Secretary) (2010) 'You can help Britain power a 21st century business boom'. *Daily Mail*, 13 January.

Mangold, W. G. and Faulds, D. J. (2009), 'Social Media: The new hybrid element of the promotion mix'. *Business Horizons*, Vol. 52, pp. 357–365.

Mort, G. S. and Weerawardena, J. (2006), 'Networking capability and international entrepreneurship'. *Journal of International Marketing Research*, Vol. 23, Issue 5, pp. 549–572.

Mulhern, F. (2009), 'Integrated marketing communications: From media channels to digital connectivity'. *Journal of Marketing Communications*, Vol. 15, Issue 2, pp. 85–101.

Observer (2009), 'Courvoisier: The Future 500: Where great minds think alike'. Sponsored supplement, 6 December.

O'Connell, S. (2004), 'Export door is wide open for small players'. *Sunday Times* (London), 18 April.

Parrish, E., Cassill, N. and Oxenham, W (2006), 'Niche marketing strategy for a mature marketplace'. *Marketing Intelligence and Planning*, Vol 24, Issue 7, pp. 694–707.

Porter, M. E. (1985), *Competitive Advantage: Creating And Sustaining Superior Performance*, Free Press, New York.

Research International (2007), 'Engaging the new consumer'. Online: http://www.tnsglobal.com/_assets/files/Engaging_the_new_consumer_Esoma07.pdf. Accessed 3 November 2008.

Servais, P., Madsen, T. K. and Rasmussen, E. S. (2007), 'Small manufacturing firms' involvement in international e-business activities'. *Advances in International Marketing*, Issue 17, pp. 297–317.

Singh, R. K., Garg, S. K. and Desmukh, S. G. (2010), 'The competitiveness of SMEs in a globalized economy: observations from China and India'. *Management Research Review*, Vol. 33, Issue 1, pp. 54–65.

Smith, S. (2008), 'Quest Worldwide'. *Sunday Times* (London), 19 October.

Walsh, A. (2009), 'Will bookshops be left on the shelf?' *Sunday Independent* (Ireland), 5 July.

FURTHER READING

Doole, I. and Lowe, R (2008), *International Marketing Strategy, Analysis, Development and Implementation*, 5th Edition, Cengage Learning.

Chapter 19

Franchising in entrepreneurship marketing

Kaushik V. Pandya

LEARNING OBJECTIVES

After reading this chapter, you will be able to:

- understand what franchising means and its importance in entrepreneurship marketing
- identify and distinguish franchising from other forms of business partnerships
- discuss the benefits of franchising to SMEs
- understand the steps needed for successful franchising
- discuss the implications of franchising.

Have you ever walked into a McDonald's, Burger King or any other fast-food restaurant and wondered who owns it? In some cases the individual restaurant would be a franchise and run by an entrepreneur. However, people often use the terms 'franchise' and 'franchisee' in everyday life without understanding their meaning or impact. Franchising is not a new word. Franchising it is not an industry, it is not production or manufacturing or even a product. It is a method of marketing goods and/or services of different business categories.

Franchising has proved to be very helpful, especially to SMEs, even during the recent economic recession. Looking into business history one can find many examples that resemble a franchised business – the guild system which was introduced in the City of London in the twelfth century is an example.

It is considered that modern franchising began in the 1950s when I. M. Singer & Co. created a dealership and service network to sell sewing machines to the public. This could be said to be an early development of a franchise network created with an intention to distribute and sell. And before that there was the example of automobile manufacturers and gasoline and the soft-drink companies who used franchising on a regular basis for the marketing of services and distribution of goods. As a principle of economics expounds, supply should follow demand. This phenomenon resulted in consumer demands uniformly emerging more and more, leading to the emergence of national chains. Franchising is the life and soul of many SMEs. Without franchising some SMEs would not exist. In strict legal terms, the word 'franchise' means a grant of rights from the crown. In other countries, such as the USA and Australia, 'franchise' means a grant by a governmental authority.

SO WHAT IS FRANCHISING?

Franchising is defined as

> the granting of a license by one party (the franchisor) to another (the franchisee) which entitles the latter to customize, manufacture, market, distribute and/or support goods and/or services, whereby the franchisor agrees to provide central commercial and technical support, and imposes the obligation to conduct a business in accordance with the franchisor's concept for the term of a written franchise agreement.
>
> (Hayfron *et al.*, 1998)

What this means is that enterprises can be arranged in various legal and business formats, of which the franchise is one of the most common. It is a method for distributing or expanding a company's goods, products or services through retail outlets owned by third-party independent operators. The third-party operator does business or trade in those products and services by adopting different marketing strategies and methods through the trademarked brand names and then, in exchange, the third-party operator pays royalties to the franchise owner.

The company that grants the independent operator the right to distribute its trademarks, products or techniques is known as the franchisor. The independent, third-party business person distributing the franchisor's products or services through retail or service outlets is called the franchisee. In a simple case, the franchisee and the franchisor work together as the franchisee owns the outlet they run and the franchisor looks after the marketing and other business ideas to be used for the products or services to be sold. In almost all cases the franchisor holds the intellectual property right of the product or the service.

The International Franchise Association has been in existence since 1960. It comprises franchisees, franchisors and suppliers.

There are different types of business relationships:

1. **Distributorship or dealership**. The dealer sells the products but trade does not take place under the name of the franchise. The dealer runs the business in his/her way, and there is more freedom to do your business or trade. One example of this is retail car sales where the dealer sells the brand names of the car manufacturers.
2. **Agency**. Here, there is sale of products or services on behalf of the supplier. The agent might be given a fixed fee for the number of products sold or services undertaken. One example is university agents in foreign countries. Some UK universities employ agents in different countries to 'recruit' students. The agent is paid a certain fee per student.
3. **Licence**. Here a licence is given to a licensee, awarding the right to sell the licensor's products with no restrictions on how the business is run. One example of this is the local public houses. The landlord sells the brand of the licensor but how he runs the business is up to him. He may, for example, have the right to hold a quiz night in the pub.

Other relationships such as joint venture, joint ownerships, etc., also exist.

GROUP ACTIVITY

1. Identify in your vicinity whether there are licensees, franchisees or other forms of partnership.

2. Name five franchising products or services within your vicinity.
3. What is the difference between a franchise and a joint-venture business?

BENEFITS OF FRANCHISING

The most important benefit of franchising is risk minimization. It is a well-known fact that starting a new business is very risky and 90 per cent of businesses fail in their first three years. The owners of the business have to go through a process of learning the specifics of the business. Depending upon the franchise agreement, the franchisor might provide the training if needed. The franchisor would 'soften' the blow of a steep learning curve. Thus, franchising is a way to reduce the risks of failure and improve sustainability.

Another important benefit of franchising is marketing. The franchisor helps and pays for the national and regional marketing. For example, McDonald's pays for all advertising in the national media. The individual franchisee in London or Southampton, for example, does not have to pay for this. All the franchisee does in this case is sell the cheeseburger to required specifications or offer the deals that have been advertised.

A further benefit is that a thorough study would have been done by the franchisor on the investments and trade before making any of the significant expenditures. A study on other existing franchisee businesses could be helpful for the newly starting franchisees to make sure they are a good fit for their business. The new franchisee can learn from the other existing franchisees.

A newly starting business or an untried business usually works on untried ideas or operation processes. Thus, there is a chance that the product or the service may not be successful. Franchisors usually sell a method of operation or a business format that has been tried and tested, so the franchisee is aware that the product or service is being sold successfully elsewhere.

A franchise also provides regularity in the system of operating a business. The consumer receives products of uniform quality efficiently and cost-effectively. Uniformity brings with it advantages such as mass purchasing power, brand identification, customer loyalty, etc.

As any new starter will know, starting a new business is a very difficult job, even for experienced managers and staff. The franchisors play a very important role in helping the franchisees to develop a business plan for their new franchise.

GROUP ACTIVITY
List the benefits of franchising. Use relevant examples to illustrate your answer.

ISSUES THAT CAN AFFECT THE SUCCESS OR FAILURE OF A FRANCHISE

In a paper by Hayfron *et al.* (1998), the authors raised issues that are specifically applicable to the manufacturing industry. However, those issues are equally applicable to the other industry sector franchises, and can be applied to SMEs. The main issues are identified below.

Franchisor and franchisee motivation

The main motivation for the franchisor would be to expand its business, not just being competitive. This would increase the business nationwide or internationally. The reason for franchisors such as McDonald's having franchises overseas may be to exploit untapped markets. For example, the fast-food market in India did not exist in the format that McDonald's introduced. In addition, if it is a manufacturing franchise, the franchisor would be able to respond quickly to market changes.

The financial rewards that come with this competitive advantage can also be a driving force. The franchisor is also motivated by the need to be closer to the market and customer needs. This is achieved by obtaining a good insight into the market from the knowledge that the potential franchisees may possess. In this case the franchisees could be highly motivated to work under an established name, for successful long-term self-employment, and the franchisor would be able to enter a new market. The franchisor will also be able to enter marginal, non-prime markets with relatively little capital investment and operating costs. The franchisor can also rely on highly motivated management (the franchisees) who may be working for themselves rather than for a salary. Thus, both the franchisee and franchisor would have motivation to develop a meaningful franchise.

Franchising feasibility

To embark on franchising, the prospective franchisor will have to carry out a feasibility study. While a wide variety of businesses can be franchised, Duckett (1998) identified key features that can ensure the success of a franchise. These include the following points.

Brand image
A brand image can easily be identified. Such a brand would enable the franchise to be competitive. Examples in the service industry are Prontaprint for photocopying, the letter 'M' for McDonalds, the Union Jack on the tail of British Airways aircraft, and the black horse on green background of Lloyds Bank. These are some of the most easily identifiable images to the public at large. Brands make it easy for franchisors to 'sell' the name and sometimes they may even be inundated with proposals from potential franchisees. This is because the franchisee may like to be part of a large network.

Duplication
A process or a service that can be duplicated is much easier to franchise. The easier it is to learn and duplicate the system, the easier it will be to franchise. The lessons learned from the original offering of a service can be useful in setting the same service elsewhere or even a network of same services. However, a restaurant that relies solely on the skills of one chef, or a product that relies on raw material that is only available locally, would be hard to franchise elsewhere.

Profitability and costs
The franchise has to make enough money for the franchisee and the franchisor to be interested. The income should cover all the franchisee's costs, management fees (to the franchisor) and make profit for the franchisee at the same time.

Pilot implementation
Pilot implementations are vital. This not only teaches the franchisee, especially the first-time

one, the basics and the tricks of the trade but also lets the franchisor have a look at the franchisee's potential. The pilot implementation will be on a proven format. This will also enable the franchisee and franchisor to understand and appreciate the cost involved and the potential benefit of the franchise to both.

Culture

When one sees or reads about an organization, one can 'feel' the type of organization it is. The feeling develops as to whether the organization is forward-looking or old and backward-thinking, responsive and trend-setting or reactionary. This feeling is referred to as culture. Culture refers to how the organization organizes and runs itself, its rules and procedures and beliefs and to how it conducts business with its suppliers and customers. There may be three cultures within a franchise: organizational culture, franchise culture and employee culture. Slack, Chambers and Johnson (2007) have identified various organizational cultures. These include: role culture, person culture, task culture, forward- and backward-looking culture and power culture. The role culture relies on the expertise of the individual who plays a specific role. Usually, this is best evidenced in large organizations. Task culture is used where individuals are organized in groups/teams to accomplish a specific task(s). Forward-thinking cultures embrace change and are risk-takers; backward-thinking cultures are the opposite. The person culture is mainly evident in NGOs and voluntary organizations.

The power culture is one that is appropriate for SMEs. In a power culture the key element is control. Decisions are centralized on one key individual or 2–3 individuals. As group work is not evident in a power culture and no consultation is involved, the organization reacts quickly to dangers around. This form of culture has disadvantages, e.g. lack of consultation can lead to staff feeling undervalued and demotivated, leading to high staff turnover.

The franchisor and franchisee need to have a good relationship and maintain good relationships with their respective staff. In an SME this would be paramount to ensuring the success of the franchise is not compromised. These different motivations and good working relationships are all part of the franchising culture.

Franchisors and franchisees are driven by different motivations. The former are driven by the need to expand their business and to make their brand name popular while the latter are driven by the desire to have and run a business and to be self-employed (to some extent).

Brand name and intellectual property rights (IPR)

We have identified that brand names and copyrights, together with goodwill, are the essential basis of franchising. An agreement on these has to be made before setting up the franchise. A franchisor should be careful of setting up the franchise in countries where there is poor IPR protection. This is because if the copyrights are infringed the franchisor will not have full recourse to litigation. It could also happen that a third party has already been using the trademarked brand of the franchisor and IPR are not enforced. Thus, the franchisor has to be careful to ensure that it would be able to enforce the IPR in the 'host' country.

Whether IPR are enforceable or not under the franchise agreement, the franchisor can impose two limitations on the franchisee:

1. That the franchisee works solely for the franchisor and its network, and not engage in business in location/territory where it would compete directly with another member of the franchised network, including the franchisor.
2. That the franchisee not disclose to third parties the know-how provided by the franchisor.

This would also require the franchisee to abide by this for a certain period of time after the franchise is terminated.

The franchisor may also be able to impose such terms on the franchisee (e.g. termination of agreement clauses) as may be predetermined. This is because it can stop the former franchisee from setting up a rival business with the experience and knowledge gained. In addition to the process of IPR there may be property involved. The property rights will not be the same as IPR. The ownership aspect is discussed below. The process of protecting property rights will be the same in the service industry as in manufacturing. However, the process may be easier to protect where the product involved is tangible. It follows that it may be easier to protect intellectual property in manufacturing franchising than in the service franchising. There are many complexities involved in this field and it is always recommended to consult a franchise lawyer where IPR are concerned.

Ownership of premises and/or equipment

The location of premises is of paramount importance. This would be investigated in assessing the feasibility of the franchise. The leasing or the ownership or premises and/or equipment can be used by the franchisor as a controlling device, or as insurance against the franchisee setting up a competitive operation on the same premises when the agreement comes to an end. If the premises are owned (not leased) then the landlord, i.e. the franchisor, will have control of any alteration to the premises. Through ownership the franchisor is also able to influence the general cleanliness of the premises that could affect the quality of the operations or the image of the franchise. Fast-food restaurants have to be clean, tidy and impressive. A single episode of bad publicity is not only bad for the franchisee but also for the whole franchise network and franchise image.

However, buying or leasing of the premises or equipment could be a disadvantage in terms of costs. The price of purchase of the premises or long-term leasing could dissuade the franchisor from accepting the franchise agreement. It could also be disadvantageous for the franchisee as the franchisor may insist on a particular use of premises or equipment that the franchisee may not prefer. However, the franchisee, if a small enterprise, may not have a choice as the cost could be high and therefore not affordable.

The ownership of equipment will be stipulated in the franchise agreement. The contract could require the franchisee to purchase the equipment from the franchisor or from an authorized supplier. The franchisor cannot insist on owning the equipment, unless the franchisor holds the rights to the equipment in question. Also, the franchisee cannot be forced to purchase goods or equipment from the franchisor if he/she can purchase the goods from alternative sources, provided it is of the same quality and specification. The franchisor may overcome this by ensuring that goods or components used in a particular process are brands owned by the franchisor or a specific supplier. The franchisee will then be required to buy the branded goods from the franchisor or the supplier. The reason for the franchisor to insist on the branded equipment or goods could be:

- the branded goods and equipment may be 'tried and tested' by the franchisor earlier in setting up other franchise
- the equipment or goods could be something that the franchisor might have negotiated and may, thus, procure more cheaply.

Risk management

Risks involved in this nature of enterprise need to be addressed. The main risk is the failure of the franchise. This could result from various spheres.

First, failure could stem from an unsuitable location and competition within the vicinity. In addition, there could also be failure due to poor working conditions between the franchisee and its employees on one side and the franchisor and its employees on the other side. This could ruin the future of the franchise and the long-term success of the franchise network. In such cases the franchisor would put in place measures such as induction (for franchisee and its employees), training (such as teamwork, communications, customer relationship, marketing, etc.) and communications (such as a regular newsletter, annual meetings, etc.). In this way the franchisor can build up initial relationships and also guard against disputes, present and in the future.

Even after having done a feasibility study and pilot implementation, there is still a small chance, even with a good product/service, that the arrangement could be a liability. This could be because the service/product was not what was advertised, not of the right quality, was over-priced, had design faults or was inappropriate, etc. In the culture of compensation it would be advisable to use the services of a lawyer who is well versed in franchise statutes and regulations. The lawyer would advise on legal issues such as advertising claims, appropriate warnings on labels (of products), quality of service/product and the taking out of insurance cover. In this way the chance of liability compensation and thus the risk of the franchise agreement collapsing are reduced.

Minimizing the risk would be a major requirement of any franchise. Thus, quality of service issues would need to be addressed.

Quality issues

Both the franchisee and franchisor should be aware of quality requirements. Slack *et al.* (2007) have identified some of the possible quality gaps which need to be addressed. Not only are they linked to the risks faced by the franchise but also they are linked to the operations and performance of the individual franchise. The franchise agreement puts the onus on the franchisee to undertake such operations and actions that are deemed necessary to fulfil his/her part of the franchise agreement. The franchisor must ensure the franchise agreement places a duty on the franchisee to exercise careful quality control over any products or components it sources. One franchisee failing to maintain quality levels can put the whole franchise network at risk of failure. Imagine a cockroach being found in a kitchen of a franchised restaurant, or a manufacturing franchise dropping its quality standards so that its product has poor after-sales service quality. This would have huge impacts on the whole franchise network.

This, in a way, implies that the franchisor has to regulate what the franchisee does. In manufacturing franchises the network could be small, so the franchise may not have too big a problem with regard to quality control. However, with the service industry, e.g. fast-food restaurants and international courier services, which might have hundreds if not thousands of franchisees, quality control may prove very difficult. This is where a comprehensive 'code of conduct' would be necessary, detailing, for example, the behaviour of the franchisee and employees (including the uniform to wear, behaviour towards customers and suppliers, training, etc.), the trademark and copyright requirements, the sponsorship and brand image requirements, the approved suppliers, the franchisee premises' appearance, etc. The franchisee would also be required to prepare regular and timely financial and other reports. All this will be stipulated in the franchise agreement.

Other issues

In addition, the franchise will need to be supported by appropriate information technology (IT). In service franchises, such as fast-food restaurants, reporting of business (which could be weekly, monthly or quarterly) would alert the head office to any problems or successes for a particular franchise. An expert system (an aspect of artificial intelligence for decision making) may also be in place to help individual franchises in decision making. This decision making would be standardized throughout the franchise network. This way the geographical position of the franchise would not be a problem when monitoring and controlling the franchise. In addition it would bring with it other benefits as well. Quick decisions can be made on the levels of customization of service/product, there will be no duplication of promotions, there will be fast roll-outs of new products/services and the whole franchise network can share the lessons of a single franchise. IT could also provide vital means of communication because sometimes the franchisee might feel isolated. As noted earlier, for a franchise to be successful a good working relationship between the franchisor and franchisee must exist. Thus, communication should not be neglected, and it will become paramount if the network grows on an international basis.

So now we know what franchising is and the benefits of it, how does one go about starting a franchise?

STEPS IN ESTABLISHING A FRANCHISE

Hayfron *et al.* (1998) have identified steps in establishing manufacturing franchising which can be extended to general franchising and apply to both franchisor and franchisee. The steps are:

- *Establish that there is a distinct exploitable business opportunity*. The franchisor should have at least some idea that there is a possibility of taking the business further. In most cases this would be a large organization, or maybe a multinational corporation (MNC), and the franchisee will be an SME. The franchisor would have done the 'ground work' and is looking for a franchisee or to develop some other kind of business partnership.
- *This is the time to do an individual SWOT* (strengths and weaknesses, opportunities and threats) *analysis*. From the SME perspective the franchisee should fully understand its own interests, background and business abilities, personal previous experience, jobs held, and capability to manage people.
- *Assess the feasibility of using franchising*. The franchisor may want to undertake a feasibility study. There are various factors to consider. One would be the physical location of the service or product. For example, a fast-food restaurant would be very profitable in, say, city centres, theme parks, out-of-town retail business parks, major railway stations or airports, etc. However, it would find it very difficult to be competitive or even to survive in a remote village, 50 miles from the nearest town. Setting up a new factory in a developing country where there is a lack of skilled workers would not be wise unless set-up costs include training of the local workforce. This would be balanced by cheap labour. The brand of the product would play an important role in the feasibility study.
- *Undertake research*. From the franchisee perspective it would be wise to be knowledgeable

about the competitiveness of the product or service. In fact, franchisees should undertake some research of their own. They should consider issues such as market growth rate, market structure and the level of market saturation. Part of this would include talking with the existing or former franchisees of the company, reading about the past history of the franchisor and about the market value of the franchise, etc. While the franchisor should undertake in-depth research, the potential franchisee should undertake some appropriate research themselves or commission consultants to do so.

■ *Develop a business plan.* Once both the franchisor and franchisee have undertaken feasibility studies, the franchisor may help the franchisee to develop a business plan, the SMART (specific, measurable, attainable, realistic and timed) way. This should include the franchisor having clear business aims and objectives, knowing the financial forecast, potential traps, etc.

■ *Establish a pilot operation.* The franchisor may consider that, rather than having a permanent franchise, s/he would prefer to 'test the water' before offering the franchisee a permanent or long-term contract. The pilot could be a one-year contract. This step would benefit both sides: the franchisor would be able to see the potential of the franchisee and vice versa. In addition, it might demonstrate a clear competitive advantage that the franchise would offer to both. It might always reveal how the franchise could be improved and how it could bring benefits to the wider community. It would also be an opportunity to foresee and iron out any potential problems in a long-term franchise. At this stage both parties need to have a clear idea about the supply chain. This would be paramount if the franchise is a manufacturing one.

■ *Develop the franchise package.* Following on from the pilot study, there could be issues both sides would like to cover. For example, if the franchise is a fast-food restaurant, who is responsible for the purchase of cookers, counters and other equipment and furnishings? Is this equipment on lease or purchased? If it is a service franchise, then who is paying for the office premises? Is it to be purchased or leased? Who is responsible for the contract with the end user? Unlike a chain system owned wholly by the company, the franchisor does not have to provide capital of any nature unless s/he wants to. These are some of the important questions that need to be asked as part of the franchise negotiations.

■ *Consider intellectual property right (IPR).* One of the important issues in franchising is the IPR. When purchasing the franchise, how many of the IPR are transferred from the franchisor to the franchisee?

■ *Develop the operations manual.* Once the franchise package has been developed, the franchisor will have specific ways that the product is made or the service is delivered. This will form part of the knowledge transfer between the franchisor and franchisee. In fact, this may form part of the whole franchise package. It may be so that in extreme cases failure by the franchisee to follow operations in the manual may be deemed a breach of the contract.

■ *Recruit the franchisee and finalize the franchise contract.* In some cases the franchisor would have a franchisee in mind when assessing the feasibility and undertaking pilot implementation. However, where this is not the case the franchisor may undertake to invite tenders. This is where an SME would need to make a competitive bid to win the franchise, taking into account the points raised above.

■ *Review the franchise operation.* Though the contract could be long-term – say, five plus years – there would be procedures in place as part of the operations manual or other sources where the franchisor would regularly undertake checks to ensure that the operations are followed according to the contract and other legal operational procedures. This step works both ways.

The steps discussed above have been used in many franchises to ensure that the franchise or franchising network achieves long-term success. The activity below will take you through many aspects of these steps.

> **GROUP ACTIVITY**
> In groups of three, take the scenario of a health-shop franchise and for each of the steps identified above give examples of the issues that will need to be discussed.

SUMMARY

In this chapter franchising has been discussed – what a franchise is, what the benefits of franchising are and the steps involved in developing a franchise. The discussion undertaken is applicable to a franchise in any industrial sector. In most cases the franchisor will be a large enterprise (and maybe an MNC) and the franchisee will be an SME. In some cases an SME could also be a franchisor, and could have a franchisee in a developing country.

REVIEW QUESTIONS

1. Define franchising. Name other types of business relationships that exist.
2. List the benefits of franchising.
3. One of the benefits of franchising is minimizing risk. Explain how this can be undertaken in a franchise.
4. What sort of marketing activities are undertaken in a franchise arrangement?
5. What motivates a franchisor to go into a franchise agreement?
6. Why is it easy to franchise a brand name?
7. How does culture play a role in franchising a brand name?
8. Who owns the premises in a manufacturing franchise?
9. What is risk management in the context of a franchise?
10. What are the quality issues that are likely to arise in a manufacturing franchise?
11. How can IT enhance the process of control and monitoring in a franchise?
12. List the steps in formalizing a franchise agreement.
13. Why is it necessary to undertake a pilot implementation prior to signing a franchise agreement?
14. Why should a franchisor undertake a feasibility agreement?

CASE STUDY 19: KAVIPA TAKEAWAYS

You are developing a franchise for a takeaway food restaurant called KAVIPA Takeaways. The restaurant is entirely internet-based. An order placed through the restaurant website is delivered within a vicinity of five miles. There is also a stipulation that if the food is NOT delivered within 60 minutes of the order then the customer gets a 25 per cent discount.

Discuss how you would go about developing this franchise and how you would ensure the franchisee meets with the required standards of the franchise. What potential benefits would be expected?

REFERENCES

Hayfron, L. E., Carrie, A. S., Bititci, U. S. and Pandya, K. V. (1998), 'Manufacturing franchising transferring the service experience', IEE Workshop on Responsiveness in Manufacturing, London.

Jobber, D. (2004), *Principle and Practice of Markeitng*, 4th edition, Macgraw-Hill International, UK.

Kotler, P. and Armstrong, G. (2004), *Principles of Marketing*, 10th edn., Upper Saddle River, NJ: Pearson Education.

Kotler, P. and Singh, R. (1981), 'Marketing warfare in the 1980s', *Journal of Business Strategy*, Winter, pp. 30–41

McAuley, A. (2001), *International Marketing: Consuming Globally, Thinking Locally*. Chichester: Wiley.

Slack, N., Chamber, S. and Johnston, R. (2007), *Operations Management*. Pearson, Harlow, UK.

Chapter 20

Competition and competitive advantage in SMEs

Maktoba Omar

LEARNING OBJECTIVES

After reading this chapter, you will be able to:

- specify the role of scale and scope of competitive advantage for internationalizing SMEs
- describe and explain how companies large or small are affected by competitive threats
- explain how companies gain competitive positions
- determine competitive motives and how to develop or confront them
- identify and discuss different ways of internationalizing the value chain
- critically evaluate how internationalizing SMEs compete in the global market.

INTRODUCTION

In the current economic climate, achieving profitable growth is a challenge for most companies, and more so for internationalizing SMEs. Until recently, most studies of entrepreneurship have concentrated on SMEs that compete in niche markets. But the reality is that a vast number of SMEs are now oriented outwards to the global marketplace and, accordingly, subjected to severe competitive pressures like large organizations. Indeed, SMEs are growing an international presence, although not always in the conventional sense. Realizing the potential opportunities for growth often requires gaining new insights into customers, employing technology in new ways to reach and communicate with customers and breaking down traditional barriers. All of these mean developing a stronger competitive orientation. Thus, the focus of this chapter is on exploring how to manage competitive threats. The chapter shows the difference between competition and hyper-competition, the latter coming as a result of the information age. It also examines competitive analysis strategies – how companies analyse their competitors as well as the process of identifying, assessing and selecting a competitive strategy

Competition was once thought of mostly in terms of price. It is now much more complex – the marketing map has been changed by many different forces. Small and large companies must now plan an effective marketing strategy. They have to identify their competitors, constantly compare prices and look at their promotions and distribution channels. They must also assess their competitors' objectives, strategies, strengths, weaknesses and reaction patterns and must select which competitors to attack and which to avoid. Identifying and assessing competitors is as important for internationalizing SMEs as it is for large international companies when gaining, building and sustaining competitive advantage.

WHAT IS COMPETITION?

Competition is rather like warfare: military terminology such as 'launching a campaign', 'achieving a breakthrough', 'company', 'division' and 'strategic unit' is common in business language (Jobber, 1995). A number of scholars (e.g. Jobber, Ries, Trout, Kotler and Singh) draw attention to the relationship between military competition and marketing strategy. Their work has stressed the need to develop strategies that are more than customer-based. They place emphasis on attack and defence against the competition and use military analogies to guide strategic thinking. Von Clausewitz states that military warfare is a clash between major interests that is resolved by bloodshed – that is the only way in which it differs from other conflict. It can with some accuracy be compared with commerce, which is also a conflict of human interests and activities.

Competition takes various forms. Through marketing extensions of a product line in market segments competitors emerge from their domestic markets to challenge firms in foreign markets. Firms may also diversify into new product markets to emerge as potent competitors. Existing competitors may also extend their product lines to enter new market segments. Competition can also develop from forward or backward integration by suppliers (Terpstra and Sarathy (2000, p. 172). Companies now face a much wider range of competitors. Even more broadly, competition may include any company that competes for the consumer's money.

There is, however, the myth that it is difficult for SMEs to evolve globally because of lack of knowledge and awareness of foreign markets. They also cannot achieve the same economy of scale and often lack financial and managerial resources. In fact, studies suggest that SMEs are more flexible in international trade than large firms (McAuley, 2001; Hollensen, 2001). Also, because product life cycles are shortening and consumer tastes are changing more often, smaller firms can adapt easily with more cost-effective market positioning than large firms (McAuley, 2001).

HYPER-COMPETITION

In the international market today there is a very quick reaction to competition. Speed is necessary to find out who is competing and to give an edge over the competition. Quick responses to competitive actions maintain competitive strength. A global competitor can immediately draw on resources, ideas or personnel (Terpstra and Sarathy, 2000), which will get a quick response from another strong competitor.

A second factor is the difficulty of defining a competitor. D'Aveni (1994) rather obviously points out that companies compete for a better position. But it is difficult to know how tomorrow's competitor will differ from today's. Will a company's competitor come from the same industry or from a different one? One example: Ricoh, a facsimile and copier maker, has now come up with a product that records moving images digitally, which is what a camcorder and a movie camera do, using different technologies. This development potentially puts Ricoh as a direct competitor with camcorder and movie-camera makers – something not possible 10 or 20 years ago (Kotabe and Helsen, 2001, p. 258). This kind of competition is known as hyper-competition.

Kotabe and Helsen (2001) state that hyper-competition is referred to as 'creative destruction that assumes continuous change', and that the basic form of such competition is aggressive. This type of competition can exist in the information and communications technology sector, which is populated by many high-growth technological SMEs, as well as, in the processed foods industry. In hyper-competition, companies compete on the basis of 'strongholds', timing, know-how, price and quality.

Strongholds refer to the strength of the company through the creation of barriers. A strong competitive position in some market segments provides the company with the capability to attack its competitor from a strong position (Porter, 1990).

Japanese firms have made the international market, especially Western and US competitors, aware that it is possible to achieve low cost and good quality. Previously, firms would have tended to become closer to one another in terms of prices and quality. Now all firms attempt to deliver higher quality for lower cost.

Timing and know-how is another base for competition, taking into account such things as technological leadership and being first to the market. When the market shifts to this type of competition all other assets such as technology and skills become weapons to gain advantages over competitors (Kotabe and Helsen, 2001).

COMPETITOR ANALYSIS

According to Terpstra and Sarathy (2000), global strategy must include a careful study of the competition and the likely reaction of each individual competitor. Such analysis usually starts with an assessment of the competitor's strengths and weaknesses, its mission, whether or not it is a leader in the market and how much competitive power it possesses (Terpstra and Sarathy, 2000). Internationalizing SMEs need to understand and monitor their competitors. Information about competitors can be obtained by market research and other forms of data collection. Kotler and Armstrong (2004) suggest managers of international marketing firms must be familiar with the following four factors:

- Competitor's objective: companies will need to know how important goals such as profitability, market-share growth, cash flow, technological leadership and service leadership are to the competitor. Knowing a competitor's current situation and objective will give the company an edge.
- Identifying the competitor's strategy: companies must look at all the dimensions that identify strategic groups within the industry, including factors such as product quality, customer services, pricing policy, distribution coverage, sales-force strategy, advertising and sales promotion and programme. They must also study the competitor's research and development, and manufacturing, purchasing, financial and other strategies.
- What can our competitors do? This question must be answered. Companies need to assess competitors' strengths and weaknesses by gathering data on the competitors' goals, strategies and performance over the last few years. The most common methods of collecting this data are through secondary data, personal experience and by conducting research with suppliers and dealers. Also, companies can benchmark themselves against other leading companies, comparing each company's products and processes to find ways of improving quality and performance. Benchmarking is becoming a powerful tool for increasing a company's competitiveness.
- Estimate competitors' reactions: knowing a competitor's objectives, strategy, strengths and weaknesses will help in estimating how it will react to a company's strategy. Some competitors will not react quickly or strongly; some might lack funds to react; some might

think their customers are loyal. Knowing the reactions of competitors will give a company a good chance to attack competition and defend the company's current position.

Jobber (1995) also points out that, because of the nature of a very competitive global market, it is important for an international company to define its competitors, scan its market and familiarize itself with the competitors' environment. Companies with similar core competence may pose the threat of entering with technically similar products. As emphasized previously, collecting data is important and will vary depending on the organizational culture and the type of products/services. Companies can also use customer value analysis which determines what benefits target customers value and how they rate the relative value of various competitors' offers (Kotler and Armstrong, 2004, p. 571). A competitor's strategies must be studied. This involves assessing the competitor's target market and differentiation strategy. This includes a study of the competitor's market, its product development and price strategy. Companies will need to work out the responses and reactions of their competitors to specific strategies, especially pricing strategies.

Based on the above the best internationalizing SMEs have an entrepreneurial management style, characterized by an informal approach to planning and heavily reliant on networks rather than bureaucratic planning procedures associated with larger organizations. Other factors which assist the SME to take best advantage of available opportunities are discussed by McAuley (2001).

MODES OF INTERNATIONAL COMPETITION

Are there standard approaches to global competition? It is possible for an internationalizing SME to lean on any of the approaches discussed by Terpstra and Sarathy (2000, p. 172):

- Competing as a low-cost producer: companies that can produce at lower cost than their competitors can achieve good quality at lower prices and good profits. A lower-cost production strategy is usually attached to high volume production. Economies of scale reduce costs, and learning and experience curve factors also lead to cost reduction. India is enjoying global economic resurgence today because of this sort of strategic positioning among its SMEs in the IT industry.

- Competing with differentiated products: companies will try to attract customers that their competitors do not have. The differentiated products may have superior design, be of good quality and be very reliable. Customers will pay for the company's product for good quality or for psychological reasons, or both. Firms that compete on this basis must monitor world markets to ensure that the features differentiating their products have not been copied by their competitors. The international competitor must constantly stay ahead of others and innovate and redesign the product constantly; otherwise it will lose its competitive advantage, because what is a differentiated product today will soon become a commodity. Once the product has become a commodity the lowest cost competitor will win. Laura Ashley, for example, gained global prominence as a result of being positioned as quintessentially English in its product development.

- Competing by seeking protected markets: companies may rely on government protection against foreign competition. This will pay in time by limiting the competitors' movements until the local company develops a differentiated product or lowers its prices. If it fails in these attempts, it can at least make profits until the foreign competitor figures out a way to evade the protection barrier, perhaps by setting up manufacturing and sales facilities within the protected sales market. Once that happens, of course, the inefficient, protected firm disappears (Terpstra and Sarathy, 2000, p. 172). This is not a robust strategy as forces of economic globalization tear down national frontiers in relation to production and consumption of goods.

DEVELOPING MARKETING COMPETITION STRATEGY

To develop a marketing strategy, companies need to be aware of their own strengths and weaknesses, customer needs and the competition. This approach, developed by Jobber (1995, pp. 555–556), is called 'the strategic triangle' (see Figure 20.1). This framework points out that to be successful it is no longer sufficient to be good at satisfying a customer's needs. Companies need to be better than the competition.

At this point, the five forms of competitive behaviour need to be mentioned.

1. Conflict: a type of aggressive competition where the aim is to push the competitor out of the market.
2. Competition: does not aim at pushing competitors out of the marketplace but aims to perform better than them. This could be through achieving faster sales and/or profit growth. At this stage monitoring the competitors' behaviour is very important.
3. Coexistence: occurs in three ways – firms coexist because they do not recognize their competitors, owing to the difficulty of defining marketing boundaries; a company may believe a competitor operates in different market segments; it may choose to recognize the territories of its competitors in order to avoid harmful head-to-head competition.
4. Cooperation: refers to two or more firms working together to overcome problems and to pool skills and resources. A growing trend is towards strategic alliances where firms cooperate in a joint venture or licensing agreement.
5. Collusion: firms come to an arrangement that inhibits competition in a market – price fixing, for example – to discourage customers from shopping around and looking for a cheaper deal.

WHO TO ATTACK AND WHO TO AVOID?

Internationalizing SMEs should not waste too much time attacking every competitor related to their business. Some should be left alone. Managers should build a strategy for selecting

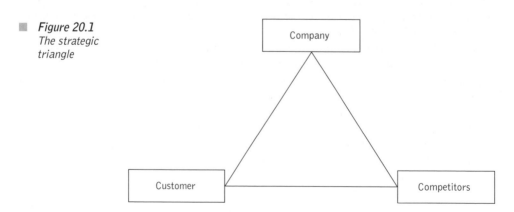

Figure 20.1
The strategic triangle

which competition to attack and which to avoid. Kotler and Armstrong (2004) suggest what to do with the following types of competitors:

- Strong or weak competitors: the idea is that companies should compete against a weak competitor because it takes less time and fewer resources. However, it is also important to consider competing with a strong competitor because it may sharpen the company's ability. Even strong competitors have their weaknesses and succeeding against them usually gives a great return.
- Close or distant competitors: most companies will compete with closer competitors rather than distant ones. That said, the existence of the internet has minimized the distance between businesses and, therefore, shrunk the distance between competitors.
- Good or bad competitors: it is important to know that there are several benefits gained from having competitors. They might help to increase total demand, share the cost of market and product development, serve a less attractive segment or lead to core product differentiation. Companies, however, have to be very careful in distinguishing between good and bad. Bad competitors are those who try to break the rules of an industry by buying a share rather than earning it. Good competitors play by the rules of the industry. They will try to shape the industry by good competition and attack the bad competitors.

Companies will try to avoid destroying weak competitors because they might create a stronger one. For example, in the late 1970s Bausch and Lomb moved aggressively against other soft lens manufacturers with great success. This move forced smaller, weaker companies to sell to larger ones such as Johnson & Johnson. Bausch & Lomb then faced a much larger competitor and suffered the consequences.

Companies should try to avoid what is known as marketing myopia. For example, Kodak held a comfortable lead position for many years; its closest competitor was Fuji. In recent years, however, Kodak's competitor has not been Fuji, but others such as Sony, Canon and other makers of the digital camera, which does not use film. Because of Kodak's myopic focus it was late entering the digital camera market.

GLOBALIZATION AND COMPETITION

A global competitor that is strong and unchallenged in its home market can undercut its competitors in their strong markets by deliberately channelling resources into those markets. Such a competitor can afford to gain market share using strategies such as price cutting, low profit or even losses for a while. These kinds of strategies will be met by another strong competitor and such an exchange of threats helps maintain the balance of power while firms have time to strengthen their competitive advantages. A global presence will help companies to plan for both offensive and defensive strategic responses, as circumstances warrant (Terpstra and Sarathy, 2000).

Competition has an influence upon the selection of the entry modes (Telesio, 1977); because of the increase in competition, managers are advised to enter the foreign market using a joint venture or license. It is risky for an international firm to share its resources and experience with another partner, unless it is difficult to imitate. Woodcock *et al.* (1994, p. 259) state 'a firm unnecessarily exposing critical resources to either imitation or transfer may provide its partnering firm with a competitive advantage in the future'. They also point out that a critical element is the perceived risk of either exposing or sharing the resources, and the results are the loss of the future competitive advantage. Bell's (1996) study indicates that, in the case of a highly competitive market, international firms prefer a wholly owned subsidiary to a joint venture, as a wholly owned subsidiary gives the firm a high degree of control over its resources. Gomes-Casseres (1990) shows that there is a significant relationship between competition and the mode of entry with regard to the preference for joint venture. Therefore, a stable competitive environment determines the entry mode selection (Knickerbocker, 1973). In a highly competitive market, international firms might select a high-involvement mode that means high a degree of control, or they might select a low degree of involvement, which means a low resources commitment.

A standardized product strategy dependent upon price positioning remains vulnerable to competition if product specifications exceed those necessary or understood in some foreign markets (Douglas and Wind, 1987). Therefore, the existence of global competition, according to Douglas and Wind, does not necessarily imply a need for global standardization. The competitive difference between two countries could lead the international firm to adopt the strategy of adaptation. However, to gain competitive advantages, firms may think of places close to cheap labour, raw materials (Wheelen and Hanger, 1995) or where they can gain an experience curve. An increase in profits and sales is the most encouraging motivation to become involved in a proactive international strategy (Samiee and Roth, 1992). Additionally, Douglas and Wind (1987) mention that the nature of competition that differentiates one country from another may lead the firm to the strategy of adaptation.

Competition and the selection of foreign markets

According to Terpstra and Sarathy (2000), three kinds of objectives are important for international companies to take into consideration to help them decide which market is attractive. These are:

- short-term and long-term return on investment
- market-share objectives, aimed at maintaining competitive balance and serving to provide credibility in exchanging threats with key global competitors
- involvement in lead markets, with learning objectives paramount, at least initially.

Profitable companies are interested in profits, seek high-growth markets where they encounter less competition, obtain higher margins and may consider early entry into protected markets.

Challenging companies that are aggressively challenging their competitors will get involved in a market based on growth characteristics and a market share held by key competitors. They enter markets that offer a chance of achieving a reasonable market share which could be used as a tool to exchange threats with the key competitors in the market.

Companies seeking to establish presence in a *leading market* will select a market based on growth prospects and the product life cycle, and give little attention to competitors and their market share or profit.

Companies deciding to be involved in a *protected market* will have to evaluate the likelihood of establishing a good relationship with the government. In less developed countries, that may happen through understanding the local environment.

In the SME context companies will have opportunities to go international and fight their place in the marketing among the competitors. McAuley (2001) suggests that much of the success of SMEs is based on attitude:

- believing that the world is your market

- believing the market is out there if you go to find/create it
- having an attack mentality
- understanding and cracking the foreign market; aiming to become a business insider in foreign markets; ensuring that bureaucracy is kept to minimum
- being led by entrepreneurial attitude
- desiring to create something new and international is new
- being flexible in their approaches
- being prepared to use multiple methods of market entry
- being prepared to buy in advice/expertise when needed, e.g. export houses or freight forwarders can supply the knowledge for shifting product.

COMPETITIVE ADVANTAGE

Competitive advantage is the advantage gained over competitors by offering customers greater value (Kotler and Armstrong, 2004). Douglas and Craig (1995, p. 106) define the company's competitive advantage in international markets as a process involving an examination of the underlying core competence to see whether the competitive advantage it has developed in its domestic market will extend to the host markets. Conditions in the domestic market may generate an advantage in competing internationally. On the other hand, the nature of competition and type of competitors in foreign markets differ and may impact on the relevance of its competitive advantages.

Porter's (1990) value chain analysis provides one clear, analytical approach for determining how efficiently value is added to the product. This dynamic approach encourages constant improvement or innovation. Basically, the value chain analysis suggests that those companies that add value more effectively than other firms are more successful in the marketplace. Porter (1990) further suggests that innovations may yield competitive advantage when such innovations anticipate market needs. Porter (1980) earlier argued within the context of business strategy that a generic strategy consists of two major choices. First is the choice regarding the type of competitive advantages pursued. The choice is between low cost and differentiation. Second is the choice related to the firm's competitive scope, which is reflected by the fullness of its target market segment. Porter's analysis of industry structure is economic, but its outcome is a theory describing marketing decisions. The competitive advantage strategy is divided into:

- Low-cost leadership: this can be maintained and margins preserved in the long term (Whitelock and Pimblett, 1997). Therefore, managerial attention to cost control is necessary to achieve cost leadership. A firm will try to reduce its production costs by accepting cheaper components, use standard production processes and seek a higher market share in order to reduce unit costs (Phillips *et al.*, 1983).
- Differentiation strategy: this is formed when the firm aims to differentiate within a small number of target market segments. This strategy requires providing the market with a product characterized by high cost as a result of using exceptional resources and high-quality material (Miller, 1986; Phillips *et al.*, 1983). The product design, brand image (Wheelen and Hunger, 1995; Porter, 1980), extensive research and complete consumer support are unique and valued by customers (Porter, 1985; Miller, 1986).
- Focus strategy: this is where a company seeks to focus on small numbers as segments. It is directed towards a 'particular buyers' segment of the product line or geographical market. Sharp (1991) states that low-cost firms aim for the entire market and exploit in every

segment. Porter (1985) points out that this strategy should be adopted only if a firm has the ability to gain the lowest cost of production within an industry. The focus strategy can be divided into two sub-strategies, one focusing on obtaining a cost advantage and the other based on developing a differentiation advantage (Porter, 1985).

Competitive advantage analysis

Understanding the competitive position of a firm will require the company to understand the competitive position of competitors, their objectives and resources. It needs to know if a competitor is strong or weak, local or international, old and established or new and fresh; does it go for long-term profit or strive for a rapid market share? Kotler and Armstrong (2004) point out that companies should also consider whether the competitor is a market leader (a company with the largest market share), a market challenger (a company that fights hard to increase its market share), a market follower (a company wanting to hold on to its share) or a market nicher (a company serving unattractive segments). However, positioning a company on the target market is not as easy as it seems, because some companies could be leaders in one market and nichers in another.

Careful analysis of the firm's competition position is very much required. One particularly useful technique in analysing a firm's competitive position is SWOT (strengths, weaknesses, opportunities and threats) analysis. A SWOT analysis divides information into two categories, internal and external; that is, strengths and weaknesses as internal factors and opportunities and threats as external factors. It must be noted that internal factors, seen as opportunities or threats to one firm, could be perceived differently in another firm, depending on their impact on the firm's position. Strengths and weaknesses include the marketing mix (price, product, promotion and place) as well as personnel and finance. Opportunities and threats include technological change, legislation, socio-cultural change and the change in the marketplace or competitive position.

SWOT helps international marketers identify a wide range of alternative strategies. For example, a strengths and opportunities strategy is used to maximize the company's strengths and market opportunities while the function of strength and threat maximizes the company's strength and minimizes its threat.

SWOT is not the only tool used to analyse competition – it is just one. The drawback of SWOT is that companies will merely compile lists rather than think about what is really important to their businesses. SWOT also presents the resulting list uncritically so that weak opportunities may appear to balance strong threats. Also, using the company's strength against the competitor's weakness might work once or twice but then it becomes predictable to your competitors (Kotabe and Helsen, 2001, p. 278).

SELECTING A COMPETITIVE STRATEGY

Terpstra and Sarathy (2000) state that international firms are advised to develop a map of all their major competitors and their interdependencies; then it is easier to adopt a 'game' that identifies all the players, their added value, their rules and the tactics that they follow. The game theory is useful in developing both competitive and cooperative strategies.

According to Jobber (1995), the core of success is to select a generic strategy and pursue it with enthusiasm, the reason being that below-average performance is associated with failure to achieve any of the generic strategies. The result leads to no competitive advantages,

		Strengths	Weaknesses
Internal Factors		Brand name, human resources, management know-how, technology, advertising, etc.	Price, lack of financial resources, long product development cycle, dependence on independent
External Factors			
Opportunities	Growth market favourable investment environment, deregulation, stable exchange rate, patent protection, etc.	S*O Strategy Develop a strategy to maximize strength and maximize opportunities	W*O Strategy Develop a strategy to minimize weakness and maximize opportunities
Threats	New entrants, change in consumer preference, new environmental protection laws, local content requirement, etc.	S*T Strategy Develop a strategy to maximize strength and minimize threats	W*T Strategy Develop a strategy to minimize weakness and minimize threat

Figure 20.2
SWOT analysis

Source: Kotabe *and Helsen* (2001, p. 277).

which leaves a company stuck in the middle position, resulting in lower performance than the cost leaders.

A firm needs to understand the generic basis for its success and resist the temptation to blur its strategy by making inconsistent moves. A focus strategy involves limiting sales volume.

Differentiation and cost-leadership strategies are incompatible. Differentiation is achieved through higher costs. However, there are some cases when both can be achieved simultaneously. For example, a differentiation strategy may lead to market-share domination, which lowers costs through economies of scale and learning effects.

CHOOSING THE RIGHT COMPETITIVE ADVANTAGES

According to Kotler and Armstrong (2004), if a company were fortunate to discover several potential competitive advantages, it must decide how many differences to promote and which ones as following:

- How many differences to promote? Companies should aggressively promote only one benefit to the target market. Crest toothpaste, for example, promotes protection; Volvo promotes safety. Companies that select one benefit and constantly deliver on it will probably become best known and remembered for it. There is also the fact that companies should position themselves on more than one differentiator. This may be important if more than one company looks at the same interest. At this stage companies will try to broaden their positioning strategies to appeal to more segments. In general, companies will need to avoid three major positioning errors:
  - *Under-positioning* – failing ever to really position the company at all. Some companies discover that the buyers do not know much about the company.

- *Over-positioning* – giving buyers too narrow a picture of the company. Thus, a consumer might think that the Steuben glass company makes only fine glass costing US$1,000 or more, when in fact it makes affordable fine glass starting around US$50.
- *Confused positioning* – leaves buyers with a confused image of a company. This implies that a company could have so many messages that it confuses customers so they forget the main purpose of the product.

- Which differences to promote? Kotler and Armstrong (2004, p. 262) also point out that companies must carefully select differences to distinguish themselves from competitors. The selected difference should satisfy the following criteria:
  - It delivers a highly valued benefit to the target market.
  - It is distinctive: competitors do not offer the difference, or the company can offer it in a more distinctive way than competitors.
  - It is superior to other ways that customers might obtain the same benefit.
  - It is communicable and visible to buyers.
  - It is pre-emptive: competitors cannot easily copy the difference.
  - It is affordable: buyers can afford to pay for the difference.
  - It is profitable: the company can introduce the difference profitably.

SOURCES OF COMPETITIVE ADVANTAGE

For an international company to create a differentiation or a lower cost position, it needs to understand the nature and location of the potential sources of competitive advantage. These sources are the superior skills and resources that contribute to competitive advantage. Their location can be aided by value chain analysis.

A company generally adopts sets of activities to service its products. These include designing, manufacturing, marketing, distributing and servicing. The value chain (see Figure 20.3) categorizes these into primary and support activities. This enables the sources of costs and differentiation to be understood and located. Primary activities include inbound physical distribution (e.g. materials handling, warehousing, inventory control), operations (e.g. manufacturing, packaging), outbound physical distribution (e.g. delivery, order processing), marketing (e.g. advertising, selling, channel management) and services (e.g. installation, repair, customer training). Support activities are built into the primary activities and these include firm infrastructure, human resource management and technology development. These activities support the primary activities and operate in all stages. Purchasing, for example, will take place within each primary activity, not just in the purchasing department. Technology, firm infrastructure and human resource management are relevant to all primary activities.

Figure 20.3
The value chain

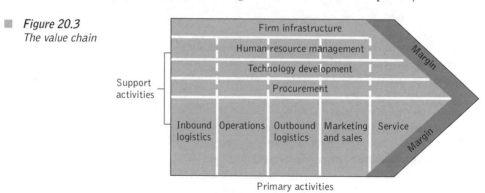

Primary activities

ANALYSIS OF COMPETITIVE INDUSTRY STRUCTURE

Competition is not limited to companies in the same industry, as companies may adopt different strategies for different competitive advantages. There is a possibility of changes in customers, as well as substitute products or services. A conceptual framework that portrays the multidimensional nature of a competitive industry structure is presented in Figure 20.4.

Michael Porter (1980) in his five-forces model states that, for industry competitors, the intensity of competition depends on the structure of competition, the structure of cost, the degree of differentiation, switching, strategic objectives and existing barriers. Porter's techniques for analysing industries and competitors show the following dimensions all making an impact on competition:

- Potential entrants pose the threat of entry. New entrants can make for high levels of competition in an industry, which reduces its attractiveness. The threat of a new entrant depends on the barriers to entry. Flexible entry barriers exist in some industries which are quite difficult to enter, such as the pharmaceuticals industry. Other industries are much easier to enter – the restaurant industry, for example. Key entry barriers include economies of scale, switching costs, capital requirements, access to distribution and expected retaliation.
- The bargaining power of suppliers is based on the cost of raw materials and components, which can have a major bearing on a firm's profitability. The higher the bargaining power, the higher the cost. Suppliers' bargaining power is high when there are many buyers and few dominant suppliers; when there are differentiated, highly valued products; when suppliers threaten to integrate backwards into supply and when the industry is not a key customer of the supplier.
- The bargaining power of buyers is critical when there are a few dominant buyers and many sellers, when products are standardized, when buyers threaten to integrate backwards into the industry, when suppliers do not threaten to integrate forwards into the buyers' industry, when the industry is not a key supplying group for buyers and when there are substitute products or the threat of substitutes. Porter (1980) defines substitute products as those that can perform the same function as the product of the industry. This can lower industry attractiveness because it constrains the freedom of existing firms to set prices. The substitute products threat includes the buyers' willingness to substitute, the relative price and performance of a substitute and the cost of switching to the substitute.

SUMMARY

This chapter has shown the difference between competition and hyper-competition, which comes as a result of very quick action and reaction in the market. It has reviewed and analysed the modes of global competition and the development of marketing competition strategy. Internationalizing SMEs must understand their competitors' objective, identify their competitors' strategy, assess the strengths and weaknesses of their competitors and estimate their competitors' reaction. Companies can adopt one of the three approaches to global competition: become a low-cost producer, adapt or differentiate the product or become involved in protected markets. Companies should analyse the competition and investigate its impact on the selection of a foreign market.

The chapter has also discussed the impact of competition upon the selection of the entry

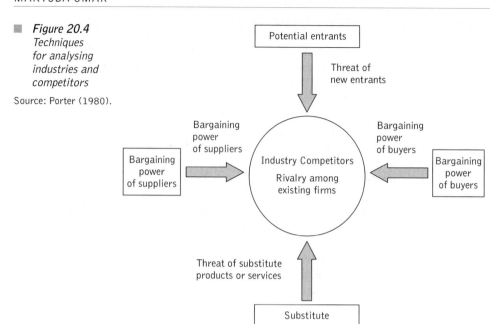

Figure 20.4
Techniques for analysing industries and competitors

Source: Porter (1980).

strategy, the methods of involvement overseas and whether to adopt a standardization or modification strategy.

In the present market, companies may be forced to adopt a global strategy to market their products or services as a consequence of the demand for their product and the threat of global competition. Therefore, internationalizing SMEs are advised to know their competitors, and their environment, their mission and their individual reaction to competition.

REVIEW QUESTIONS

1. How does the virtual value chain differ from the conventional value chain?

2. What is the difference between competition and hyper-competition?

3. Are there any disadvantages for an internationalizing SME attacking small, weak, close competitors?

4. Compare the modes of global competition in relation to low-cost producers competing with a differentiated product or by seeking protected markets.

5. How can a local SME compete against a global firm?

6. What are the main motivations for going global? Use any globalizing SME you know to illustrate your answer.

7. To what extent does the Asian market present a real challenge to the European companies?

CASE STUDY 20: HAIER

Haier Group is a 'white goods' manufacturer in China. Their full product line includes products such as refrigerators, freezers, wine cellars, air conditioners, beer dispensers, dishwashers, fans, water dispensers, small appliances and other electronic products. As a growing SME with most of its sales in its domestic market, Haier management realized that the traditional concept for exporting should be abandoned and believed that the purpose of exporting products was not only for revenue but also for brand recognition enhancement. Thus, they implemented a strategy to incorporate local resources of design, manufacture and distribution in foreign countries as part of their policy to exploit international markets. One-third of Haier products are manufactured and distributed in China, one-third manufactured in China and distributed overseas and one-third manufactured and distributed in foreign countries. Haier has established information centres and design institutes in foreign countries for development of competitive products on the basis of local consumers' demands. Haier CEO Zhang Ruimin summarized Haier's development policy as 'globalization plus localization': globalization means policy making with consideration of worldwide opportunities while localization means the process by which the Haier brand becomes recognized in local areas. The American division (Haier America) was founded in 1999, with headquarters in New York City and production facilities in South Carolina. 'We were the first Chinese company to open a factory in the U.S.', Shariff Kan, executive vice president of marketing for Haier America told CNET News in 2008 (Kanellos, 2008). Haier has given various reasons for the Camden, NC, factory, such as being able to respond quickly to orders from retailers while maintaining a low inventory, and cutting transportation costs from China, but arguably the main one is the strategic desire to establish the perception of Haier as an 'American company' (Zhao, 2003). The successful operation of the Haier America plant has helped Haier to reorganize its production structure, expand its market share in the United States, and effectively avoid the non-tariff barrier of international trade to operate a manufacturing plant in the United States.

Haier brand

In 1997 the state economic commission in Beijing had designated Haier one of six companies likely to become China's first global brands (Paine, 2007). By 2005 Haier was increasing its efforts to build a globally recognized brand, in part due to intense competition and price wars in the domestic (China) market (Palepu *et al.*, 2005). Evidence of its success includes ranking first in the 'Top Ten Chinese Brands in the Consumer Electronics Industry' (CES, 2007) and being ranked as the Most Valuable Chinese brand by the *Financial Times* in 2005. Haier has chosen sports as one focus of its global branding effort (Bonaglia *et al.*, 2006), in part by entering into a partnership with the US National Basketball Association, sponsoring soccer teams in Europe and becoming the official sponsor of the 2008 Beijing Olympic Games for white goods home appliances. Such partnerships with sports governing bodies confer upon them 'image transfer' and other benefits of association (Chadwick and Thwaites, 2005).

Globalization is being driven not just by the giant incumbent firms (Nolan *et al.*, 2002) but also by emerging firms internationalizing from the periphery. These firms capture competitive space from incumbents due to their ability to exploit the linkages

available through globalization and develop a culture of continual cross-border learning and value-addition (Bartlett and Ghoshal, 2000; Bognaglia and Goldstein, 2007).
Source: www.haier.com

CASE QUESTIONS AND TASKS
1. Which of the three stated modes of internationalization did Haier utilize? (low-cost (i.e. China production), differentiated or protected market first (China) followed by niche segments globally).
2. Explain Haier's strategy of internationalization in regard to wholly owned subsidiary versus joint venture (Bell, 1996) and cheap input factors (Wheelen and Hanger, 1995).
3. Discuss Haier's decision to enter the huge US market, in light of the market characteristics (Terpstra and Sarathy, 2000).
4. Regarding Terpstra and Sarathy (2000) and Jobber (1995), is Haier pursuing a differentiation strategy, a cost-leadership strategy, both or neither? Discuss.

BIBLIOGRAPHY

Bartlett, C.A. and S. Ghoshal (2000) 'Going global: lessons from late movers', *Harvard Business Review*, Vol. 78, pp. 133–142.
Bell, J. (1996) *Single or Joint Venturing? A Comprehensive Approach to Foreign Entry Mode Choice*, Ashgate Publishing, Avebury, UK.
Bonaglia, F. and Goldstein, A. (2007) 'Strengthening productive capacities in emerging economies through internationalization: evidence from the appliance industry', OECD Development Centre, Working Paper No. 262, July.
Bonaglia, F., Goldstein, A. and Mathews, J. (2006) 'Accelerated internationalisation by emerging multinationals: the case of white goods sector', MPRA Paper No. 1485.
Chadwick, S. and Thwaites, D. (2005) 'Managing sport sponsorship programmes: lessons from a critical assessment of English soccer', *Journal of Advertising Research*, Vol. 45, pp. 328–338.
D'Aveni, R. (1994) 'Hyper-competition: managing the dynamic of strategic maneuvering', Free Press, New York.
Delene, M., Meloche, S. and Hodskins, J.S. (1997) 'International product strategy: building the standardisation modification decision', *Irish Market Review*, Vol. 10 (1), pp. 47–54.
Doole, I. and Lowe, R. (2001) *International Marketing Strategy: Analysis, Development and Implementation*, Thomson Learning, Italy.
Douglas, S. and Craig, S. (1995) *Global Marketing Strategy*, McGraw Hill, New York.
Douglas, S.P. and Wind, Y. (1987) 'The myth of the globalisation', *Columbia Journal of World Business*, Vol. 21 (Winter), pp. 12–29.
Gomes-Casseres, B. (1990) 'Foreign ownership preference and host government restrictions: an integrated approach', *Journal of International Business Studies*, Vol. 21 (1), pp. 1–22.
Harp, B. (1991) 'Competitive marketing strategy: porter revisited', *Marketing Intelligence and Planning*, Vol. 9 (1), pp. 4–10.
Hollensen, S. (2001) *Global Marketing: A Marketing-Responsive Approach*, Prentice Hall, Harlow, UK.
Jobber, D. (1995) *Principle and Practice of Marketing*, McGraw Hill, New York.
Kanellos, M. (2008) 'China's Haier eyes U.S. living rooms', CNET News, 22 January. Online: http://news.cnet.com/Chinas-Haier-eyes-U.S.-living-rooms/2100-1041_3-6226826.html (accessed 23 August 2010).
Knickerbocker, F.T. (1973) *Oligopolistic Reaction and Multinational Enterprise*, Harvard University Press, Boston (Division of Research, Harvard Business School).
Kotabe, M. and Helsen, K. (2001) *Global Marketing Management*, Wiley, London.
Kotler, P., Brown, L. and Armstrong, G. (2001) *Marketing*, 5th edn, Prentice Hall, Sydney.

Miller, D. (1986) 'Configuration of strategy and structure: towards a synthesis', *Strategic Management Journal*, Vol. 7 (3), pp. 233–249.

Murray, A.I. (1988) 'A contingency view of porter's generic strategies', *Academy of Management Review*, Vol. 13, pp. 390–400.

Nolan, P., Sutherland, D. and Zhang, J. (2002) 'The challenge of the global business revolution', *Contributions to Political Economy*, Vol. 21, pp. 91–110.

Paine, L. (2007) 'The Haier Group', HBS No. 9–398–102.

Palepu, K., Khanna, T. and Vargas, I. (2005) 'Haier: taking a chinese company global', Harvard Business School, case 9–706–401, 17 October.

Phillips, L., Change, D. and Buzzell, R. (1983) 'Product quality, cost position and business performance: a test of some key hypotheses', *Journal of Marketing*, Vol. 47 (Spring), pp. 26–43.

Porter, M.E. (1980) *Competitive Strategy*, Free Press, New York.

Porter, M.E. (1985) *Competitive Advantage*, Free Press, New York.

Porter, M.E. (1990) *The Competitive Advantage of Nations*, Free Press, New York.

Samiee, S. and Roth, K. (1992) 'The influence of global marketing standardisation on performance', *Journal of Marketing*, Vol. 56 (2), pp. 1–17.

Sharp, B. (1991), 'Marketing orientation: more than just customer focus, *International Marketing Review*, Vol. 8, No. 4, pp. 20–25.

Telesio, P. (1977) 'Foreign licensing policy in multinational enterprises', DBA thesis, Harvard Business School.

Terpstra, V. and Sarathy, R. (2000) *International Marketing*, Dryden, Fort Worth, TX.

The Times 100 (n.d.) Online: http://blog.simonholdings.com/2009/02/2009-the-sunday-times-top-100-best-companies-to-work-for-awards-jenrick-achieves-6th

Wheelen, T.L. and Hanger, J.D. (1995) *Strategic Management and Business Policy*, 2nd edn, Addison-Wesley, Reading, MA.

Whitelock, J.M. and Pimblett, C. (1997) 'The Standardisation Debate of International Marketing', *Journal of Global Marketing*, Vol. 10 (3), pp. 45–66.

Woodcock, P.C., Beamish, P.W. and Makino, S. (1994) 'Ownership-based entry mode strategies and international performance', *Journal of International Business Studies*, Vol. 25 (2), pp. 253–273.

Zhao, Y. (2003) 'When jobs move overseas (to South Carolina)', *The New York Times*, 26 October. Online: http://www.nytimes.com/2003/10/26/business/business-when-jobs-move-overseas-to-south-carolina.html (accessed 23 August 2010).

Chapter 21

Entrepreneurship growth at risk

Hosein Piranfar

INTRODUCTION

No doubt massive global events such as the Asian Financial Crisis, the 9/11 attacks on the Twin Towers, the invasion of Iraq and Afghanistan, the global recession in 2009, the flu pandemics and climate change have created insecurity and risk awareness all over the world. Risk awareness is not just a matter for advanced economies and multinational companies; it is also relevant to smaller economies and smaller companies. Many people now have first-hand experience of how the volatility of oil prices and capricious environmental upheavals can affect lives and businesses. Most risk events used to be easily covered by insurance companies. But when the world began to shake under these calamitous events the insurance companies felt the strain, and the word got out that businesses should be able to look after themselves the same way as pensioners are increasingly expected to look after themselves. A few years ago, even before the outbreak of the flu pandemics and the global recession of 2008–2009, Gordon Brown (the then British prime minister) wrote in the *Financial Times* that companies should attempt to reduce or prevent their risks. Large businesses are expected to hedge their risks by means of portfolio management or outsourcing their production costs. Even small businesses are beginning to get pulled into the orbit by at least planning for business continuity. Despite the urgency to tackle risks, however, SMEs are still reluctant to prepare. They do take quality assurance more seriously, probably because suppliers and customers expect them to do so. Considering the close relationship between risk and quality assurance, one might hope that the SMEs will eventually realize that managing quality is akin to managing risk, at least in terms of preventing it. With quality, even the mitigation becomes simpler as quality may facilitate the transfer of risk and reduce conflict. Perhaps, knowing this relationship, ISO have now issued the ISO3000 standard to manage risk. It won't take long before local governments, business partners and customers will expect the SMEs to qualify for the ISO3000 if they want to continue to be in business. Essentially, in entrepreneurship contexts, planning for risk, crisis and probably failure is as important as planning for growth and success (Herbane, 2010).

DYNAMIC NATURE OF RISK MANAGEMENT

The hallmark of successful entrepreneurship marketing operation is growth/sustainability. Therefore, this chapter focuses on SME risk with particular attention to growth. At the moment, there is hardly any convincing application of risk management to small companies. The SMEs that we are inclined to look at here are smaller and more dynamic firms – such as the biotech or IT companies – that are generally much smaller than the maximum allowed by the European Union (EU) regulations. These dynamic firms have adapted some kind of quality management but rarely manage their risks and rely on insurance or the assistance of the larger companies that support them. It is only the larger companies that can afford to pay a risk manager. If SMEs have any money to spare they would rather go for a cheap quality manager to sort out their registration with ISO9000. Lewis Combstock, a quality assurance consultant, cites the case of a small-sized electronic company with multinational connections that seeks part-time assistance for running its quality management while keeping its risk management plans on hold until a better time. It was with this kind of problem in mind that Piranfar and Combstock (2008) suggested that quality managers should be trained to combine quality and risk management activities in their companies. It is argued in this chapter that there is a symbiosis between risk and quality. Although the company we studied had multinational links, in essence it was a small company of about 100 employees where the symbiosis could easily be felt. With the advent of the ISO3000 the concept of symbiosis is likely to take off, at least among dynamic SMEs.

In what follows the chapter focuses on dynamic innovative SMEs that are interested in growth who may find risk management of interest. Such companies are subject to risk in all aspects of their innovative production and marketing. Anything they do they do with speed. They grow fast or die quickly. If they survive they face a myriad of risks. Some of these risks relate to IS, quality, price, brand extension, borrowing, innovation, strategic alliances with other SMEs or large companies (*coopetition*) and, finally, to internationalization. These fields of activity are all laden with risks. The chapter looks at a few of these risks in detail and attempts some solutions in the hope that some SMEs will find risk management a doable thing.

It must be reminded that the scope of risks are a little wider than those covered here. For instance, important areas such as advertising, price and networking are deliberately excluded so that there is no duplication with other colleagues who are contributing in those areas. It was thought that any contribution to SME risk was worth the effort.

The intention in this chapter is to look at the ways small businesses grow and tackle the risks. It must be admitted that not all SMEs intend to grow bigger than they are. In very small firms where ownership and management are held by one or two people, growth may not always be desirable. It is hard for one or two people to run a large company. The tendency to grow is often dictated by the business environment, in particular the competitive environment. There are always some small firm managers who will resist the external forces in order to look after the family while keeping tabs on the business. Those who go for growth normally have a growth-oriented vision with clear objectives to achieve growth (Smallbone and North, 1995). In fact, most high-growth firms also have clear objectives aimed at growth, which means that growth is not coincidental for such companies. Clearly, risk would be an issue for growth companies who may ask:

- What if these objectives are not achievable?
- What if the failure of an objective affects the other objectives?
- What if the time to achieve is lapsed?
- What if the money to spend on objectives is insufficient?
- What if priority customers push for the achievement of some projects at the expense of the others?

Anticipation of these alternative events or risks is an attitude that will help the SMEs not only to grow but also to grow up. By growing up I mean learning as they travel down a hazardous road. Innovation and *organizational learning* feed on tackling risks and risky projects and are essential for building a healthy operations strategy that can facilitate *sensible growth*. Growth based on operations strategy is a less perilous route to take, but it needs people skilled in technology and skilled in the art of teamwork and communications.

DIMENSIONS OF RISK

The common perception of risk management is that it is a matter for banks and moneylenders. The financial-economic dimension of risk is a sure thing, but it would be wrong to assume that there are no other dimensions worth thinking about. It is true that in recent years the financial sectors in the West, in particular in Britain, have grown enormous, encouraging massive volumes of publications on financial risks. So much so that even textbooks titled *Operational Risks* turn out to be concerned with nothing but financial risks and the Basel II Accord (an international convention for calculating bank capital). Despite this obsession with financial risks, it is patently clear that there are risks everywhere. There are risks in production, distribution, selling, promoting, consuming, buying, journeying to work and in every aspect of our life in general. For example, the recent freeze in Britain saw many older people hospitalized, roads congested (leading to business disruptions), exams delayed due to illness and traffic jams, and so on. Even without the assistance of the infamous British weather, we face numerous risks that are not directly financial. To clarify this point a few non-financial dimensions of risk will be outlined below with a focus on growth SMEs.

The HR dimension and risk

High-growth SMEs also tend to employ high-skilled people. The ability to attract, develop and retain effective people goes with a growth strategy (Barringer and Jones, 2004). According to Robson and Bennett (2000), there is a positive association between employee skill level and the SME growth. However, plunging into fully blown HR management is quite risky, especially at the initial stages. What if the costs prove too much, or the employees get the training, learn and then run away with trade secrets? (Apparently Germans train new employees only in firm-specific tasks rather than generic transferable skills; see Sloman and Sutcliffe, 2004.) This is only one of the risks. Another big risk is what we nowadays term *organizational dementia* or *organizational memory loss*. Memory loss occurs when people are made redundant or simply retire. Much of the memory is kept in files or computers but there are particular types of valuable knowledge that cannot be encoded. This is called *tacit knowledge*. The senior employee who knows where things are or knows the man who knows who to talk to in time of crisis is a valuable carrier of tacit knowledge.

The inability to transfer tacit knowledge to other members of the organization before is regarded as memory loss for the organization. How do we deal with this risk? Should we stop making people redundant? Can we stop retirement or death? Alison Maitland (2001) has a sensible solution: encourage substantial social interaction among employees! This keeps the memory alive. This is a part of what is now referred to as *internal marketing*. Large firms are of course more susceptible to this type of risk than the SMEs. Why? It is simple: people in SMEs talk to each other more easily, thus helping with the flow of tacit knowledge from generation to generation. That is how some old small companies survive while giant organizations such as Lehman Brothers die! High-growth SMEs, however, shouldn't be complacent. In their hasty grab-and-grow spree, they are constantly unsettled. They have no time to learn. They have no memory to lose! Lack of slack (spare time) is the enemy of creativity and a source of risk. When people have no time to contemplate or have a chat with a customer or a colleague (the *internal customer* – in marketing parlance) they will fail to understand the market and will be puzzled why the demand is playing tricks with them.

A third dangerous HR risk is that of the cultural clash, which happens during the takeovers or mergers. When the growing SME acquires a smaller company or when a SME is acquired by a large company – for instance, a small biotech company being acquired by a large pharmaceutical company – the 'big brother' often refuses to understand the 'little brother'. The most disastrous situation is when the acquirer refuses to learn from the acquired how to tackle the market operated by the smaller company.

The economic dimensions of risk

Small businesses run out of cash very quickly. We can all visualize an angry entrepreneur gazing at a piece of paper, shaking his fist at any poor listener and asking 'How can they do this to me? I am expecting a positive balance, not this rubbish in red! [implying debt]'. Financing growth is a big issue for entrepreneurs. They can do it in a number of ways, such as using their own savings, profits and assets, borrowing or selling shares. The fundamental decision for many entrepreneurs is whether or not to accept external equity finance in return for part ownership of the business. By doing so small business owners risk their cherished control of the business they started. Many are opposed to this (Carter and Van Auken, 2005). Providers of finance aren't keen to open the purse either. The big uncertainty associated with SMEs is that it is difficult for lenders to assess the risk of an SME investment. Banks are not interested in the entrepreneurs' hopes and dreams and are not impressed by the negligible collateral held by these businesses (Harrison *et al.*, 2004). Banks are interested, instead, in perceived customer base and the size of market targeted by the SMEs. If they use their wits they can easily realize that a well-positioned SME may have the potential to expand the market or invade new markets. Unfortunately they tend to wait until a large company shows interest in the SME. By the time the lender finds out their potential merit, the SMEs are either dead or acquired. Faced by shortage of cash the SMEs are often unable to adequately fund operations and pursue market opportunities (Locke, 2004). Thus, it is understandable that firms with higher availability of external finance (high-leverage firms) grow much faster than low-leverage firms (Becchetti and Trovato, 2002).

339

Achieving lower growth than anticipated by the firm is of course a risk. It throws the firm into a vicious circle: no money, no growth, and nobody will lend you any money! Suppliers will avoid giving credit, and customers will avoid purchase partly because the SME has little money to invest in marketing. The risk of stagnation, however, is nothing compared with the risk of bankruptcy when all the investment in new people, premises and new product ideas fails to bear fruit. Considering the financial risk of growth, many SMEs resort to a no-growth policy which is itself a risk. Failure to grow may entail the risk of a hostile takeover. Sloman and Sutcliffe (2004) has shown that SMEs are always in danger of takeovers, sometimes because they are growing and other times because they are not growing. If they are growing the larger businesses will be keen to snatch them, and if they are falling behind, they will attract buyers who can see the potential. The poor chicken gets slaughtered whether it is a birthday or a funeral.

The market and product dimension

Unlike the vicious circle described above, successful product market development may on the other hand lead to a *virtuous circle* of growth and better income. Successfully growing small businesses often have to differentiate themselves. To compete in the market large companies create economies of scale, that is, they produce a lot while keeping the overhead costs down, so that the unit cost is down and profit margin is up. Lower unit costs and higher profits can of course lead to competitive edge. Small companies, on the other hand, are more likely to compete on the basis of innovation, exploring new markets or new segments in the old markets. Active engagement of small firms in the management of products and markets is therefore particularly important for achieving growth over an extended period. A constant awareness of new technologies, markets and competition, as well as the ability to carry out research and development (R&D) are vital to an organization's ability to successfully introduce new products into the market. In doing so, firms gain access to greater cash flow, enhance external visibility and legitimacy and improve market share – all necessary elements for their survival and growth (Barringer and Jones, 2004). Therefore, those businesses that are able to develop new products and services in existing markets, or enter new markets with existing products and generally broaden their customer base, are more likely to experience growth (Kelley and Nakosteen, 2005), and of course risk.

A basic framework for looking at growth is the Ansoff matrix. It is often presented as a number of options for growth. It is perhaps more beneficial if these options are explored in terms of the risks. The Ansoff matrix shows four growth options for business formed by matching up existing and new products and services with existing and new markets, as shown in Figure 21.1. The matrix essentially shows the risk exposure of a particular strategy for a company. Not only is each situation (quadrant) potentially at risk, but the level of risk will increase when the business moves into a new quadrant, whether horizontal or vertical. Market penetration (existing markets, existing products) is a bit like grabbing somebody else's lunch. If the SME decides to enter (penetrate) an existing market with current products it has to seduce the competitors' customers (grab their market share or 'lunch'). It is of course possible that by using some novel technique we manage to wake up some dormant customers who did not belong to anybody (think of a kebab van who tries to catch a vegetarian by emitting some appetizing scents: a burnt offering!). Understandably, staying with your existing product in your existing market is a low-risk option unless your competitors decide to hold on to their lunch and start a fight. Moving into a new market with an existing product, or developing a new product for an existing market, will expose the company to a whole new level of risk. The market may turn out to have radically different needs and dynamics than you may think,

	New markets	Market development	Diversification
	Existing markets	Market penetration	Product development
		Existing products	New products

Figure 21.1
The Ansoff matrix

or the new product may just not work or sell. Moving two quadrants and targeting a new market with a new product will increase the risk even more!

The risk of a grand adventure like jumping a quadrant is frequently failing to gain and retain customers. Outside the Ansoff matrix, however, lurks the risk of being gobbled up by a bigger or richer business if you are successful. Successful innovative SMEs are attractive to big business because they think that such companies know how to make new products and enter new markets. The fear of being acquired often leads to collaboration or internationalization.

Figure 21.2 shows how the special profit or *rent* was calculated for SMEs in a French survey (Groupe ESC Dijon Bourgogne, 2003). Rent in this context is similar to what economists call *economic rent*. The fact that an English version of the survey refers to David Ricardo makes it clear that the authors mean economic rent. The interesting feature of this survey is that it does not go for maximization of rent (profit). Rather, it clearly advocates optimization, especially for SMEs. Since the concept of *bounded rationality* was proposed by the Nobel Prize winner Herbert Simon in 1978 and then was popularized by textbook writers like Sloman and Sutcliffe we have come to terms with accepting optimization rather than maximization. Challenging maximization of profit, however, is a big hurdle for most young people especially those first-year students who may have never known anything different.

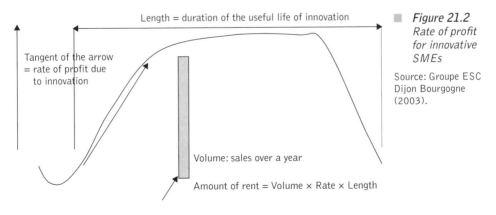

Length = duration of the useful life of innovation

Tangent of the arrow = rate of profit due to innovation

Volume: sales over a year

Amount of rent = Volume × Rate × Length

Figure 21.2
Rate of profit for innovative SMEs

Source: Groupe ESC Dijon Bourgogne (2003).

341

Profit maximization and SMEs

Basically, there are two scenarios: (a) that firms wish to maximize profits, but for some reason or another are unable to do so; or (b) that firms have aims other than profit maximization. Arguments for the first type are: information is insufficient; we do not know the true measure of profit (the accountants' measure or the economists' measure that includes opportunity costs). Working out the marginal revenue, essential for the calculation of maximization, is hard, especially for SMEs. Even if market research helps, it will be too late to capture the demand. Knowing the demand is one thing; guessing competitors' actions is another. Are they going to cut the price and grab your market share? The most difficulty to overcome when trying to maximize profit is the impact of the environment. The time period to maximize is another difficulty with risk implications: aiming at short-term profit may starve the firm of long-term investment and long-term profit.

The second scenario is where bounded rationality enters, and one may argue that managers aim at maximizing their own utilities and aim at a target level (profit *satisficing* as Simon believes; see Sloman, 2004) rather than maximum profit. They might go for sales maximization that leads to rewards with no questions asked. The strongest argument against maximization is that there are too many conflicting interests in an organization, such as those of the shareholders, workers, customers and creditors, that result in optimum profit rather than maximum profit. This is the essence of bounded rationality, which encourages growth.

It is in view of these arguments that one may find the French survey interesting. The additional merit of this survey is that it tailors its optimization not to economic theory but to the very nature of being small. In fact, the survey's chosen business units for research are a little on the low side of the EU definition of the SME limits. They consider six configurations based on the three components of the economic rent (see Figure 21.2). In their Oasis configuration of the three elements, volume is low, rate of profit is flexible from low to high and the duration or length is long. This is an appropriate combination for innovative small business aiming at growth and long-term profit.

For SMEs volume has to be low unless they are involved in a network; the length is long because of long-term investment and also because they are faced with many environmental elements that tend to erode the rent. They need to aim at a longer period so that after the effect of erosion and risks are taken into account, they should still be able to exploit the economic rent for a sufficient length of time.

METHODS OF SME GROWTH AND RISK

Collaboration

Establishing collaborative relations is a strong indication of growth intention, which can convince the bankers to loosen their purse. Since SMEs tend to join healthy partners, the bankers will be more willing to be relatively generous with credit. Collaboration often helps

Figure 21.3 'Oasis': optimal combination of volume, rate and length

Source: Groupe ESC Dijon Bourgogne (2003).

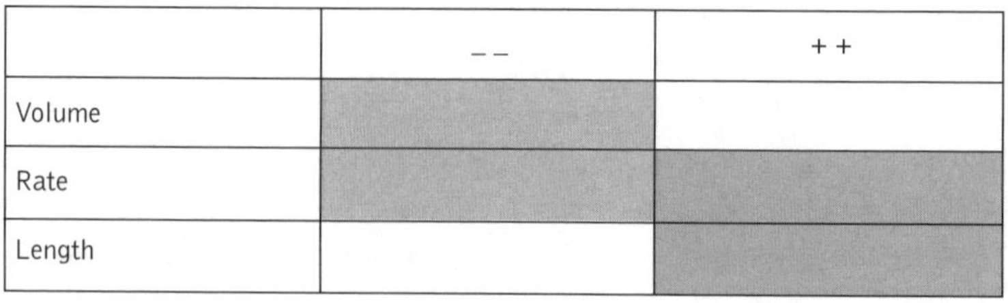

	– –	+ +
Volume	▓	
Rate	▓	▓
Length		▓

with reaching overseas markets too, which may serve as an additional leverage on creditors (mainly bankers). On their own, the SMEs do not have the reputation or the entry resources to access overseas markets. By networking and other forms of collaboration, however, they can penetrate these markets (Barringer and Jones, 2004). Collaborative relationships include joint ventures, networks, consortia, alliances and trade associations (Becchetti and Trovato, 2002).

Collaboration is a historical necessity and is often mutually beneficial. In nature, African ants cooperate with the acacia trees. They kill all the harmful insects, competing plants and sometimes even large herbivorous animals, and the tree in turn provides the accommodation rent-free (Figure 21.4). This collaboration will last forever unless storms, floods or other calamitous events separate them.

Business partners, however, are not always supportive. Some are like the Wudu bees who sting their partners to lay eggs inside them so that the hatchlings can be nourished on the victim's dead body. Business partnerships are full of opportunities and at the same time are full of risks. The Chinese word *wei-ji* (opportunity-danger) expresses this situation well. For the academics, business cooperation that contains risk and opportunities is known as *coopetition*.

The risks of collaboration

Firms can get into trouble due to new competitors entering the market, the company failing to achieve its own targets or when pioneering new technologies. Once a company is recognized as vulnerable potential partners shy away. This is especially critical when a firm's attractiveness to potential partners depends on the value that it can add to the partnership (Ahuja, 2000). When partners grow or change, the SME will be at risk or feel more vulnerable. To confront large dominant partners, or competitors in general, vulnerable SMEs may join hands and try to develop collective capability by pooling their resources and expertise. But the networked SMEs are not all equally vulnerable. A firm with a higher level of vulnerability will have weak bargaining power and will be at risk of being unequally appropriated by the partners. SMEs know that they are vulnerable to large competitors. They also know that the cooperation is based on complementary assets that cannot be easily transferred, thus making cooperation safer. Small biotech companies and big pharmaceuticals are a good example (see the section on supply chain risk below).

The worst type of vulnerability is psychological: an entrepreneur may partner out of insecurity with a company perceived to be stronger but that in fact turns out to be weaker, meaning there is nothing to gain. For instance, if a DIY shop collaborates with a builder assuming that he will buy a lot of building material, the shop will be disillusioned if they hear that the builder has lost his licence to operate in that area. This is like a game theory. Game theory experts love to drag readers into such psychological games (see Box 21.1). The agony

■ *Figure 21.4*
Collaboration between African ants and an acacia tree

Source: © Dan L. Perlma/EcoLibrary.org. Used with permission of being involved in a game forces many firms to invest in market research to identify their opponents' strength in the marketplace. They don't even spare themselves the ignominy of spying on others or passing on misleading signals.

BOX 21.1: THE PRISONERS' DILEMMA

This is a typical game applied to business. If two businesses collaborate on price they will both gain a reasonable profit. For example, if the maximum profit is £12,000 they will earn £6,000 each. But if they cheat to maximize their individual profit by reducing the agreed price in order to sell more they will run the risk of minimizing their profit. The one who reduces the price first earns the maximum profit.

These vulnerabilities lead to risks that can be outlined as follows. One is *technological risk*. If a firm is not careful, it could lose its secret and proprietary knowledge to the competitor-partner. If the SME is too weak or dependent on a large partner it can easily be acquired. Rothaermel and Deeds (2004) argue that, due to their initially weak bargaining position, new technology ventures tend to cede a disproportional amount of control rights to the financier of the R&D alliance. The larger partners have more power and control and can force smaller ones to take on proportionally bigger risk (Sulej *et al.*, 2001).

If the partner happens to be an opportunistic one, the SME might also confront legal issues. A dilemma SMEs face is that you need a capable partner who is at the same time demanded by others. Perhaps it is better to be safe with a less capable partner than be sorry? It is hard to tell: the rotten apple has a rotten customer.

The biggest risk of coopetition (competition combined with collaboration) is for the managers who have to walk the tightrope of acting in two fronts. The *risk of role conflict*, especially around the border lines, is all too real (Bengtsson and Kock, 2008). In addition, as time goes by, the incentive to invest more in cooperating or competing with a given firm will change. SMEs may be less adept at deciphering these changes, at estimating the evolving costs and benefits, and at making the necessary adjustment to the coopetition-based relationship (Morris *et al.*, 2007). SMEs might be able to mitigate the abovementioned risks by having multilateral relationships rather than bilateral ones (Lavie, 2007). Multilateral ties may be an effective way for SMEs to enhance their collective strength and reduce the risk of being controlled by large firms.

Supply chain risk

Supply chains or networks are a popular form of collaboration (see Box 21.3). Sometimes the big supplier or customer may decide to respect your independence just to load you with risks. Supply chain risk is gaining momentum as an important non-financial area for risk management. The number of studies in this field is rising exponentially. For a while scholars ignored the supply chains hoping that a dose of total quality management (TQM) combined with trust will remove the need for risk management. They assumed that if we shouted 'Trust, brother, trust!' loud enough businesses would begin to trust each other, thus reducing risks. Not all trust is idealistic. Trust based on objective necessity is fine. Such a trust would naturally prevent risk. Companies with complementary products need each other (abiding by necessity is freedom). Even if they were suspicious of each other they would still have to trust each other. But if there is no objective reason to collaborate preaching trust won't have much effect. The misconceived view of trust peddled by the 'trust merchants' in academia can indeed be very harmful to supply chains.

BOX 21.2: LIMITS OF TECHNOLOGY TRANSFER

One day a disturbed quality manager who was in charge of international customer relations of an electronics SME went to see a risk manager and said: 'Our customers in Sweden who buy most of our marine products are adamant that we should provide them with every bit of technical and financial information that they care to ask for'. The quality manager, in desperation, consulted his operations textbooks, the minutes of all the quality assurance meetings he had attended but found nothing to convince him that he should say no. They were all unanimous: trust the customer. He had the gut feeling that he should not give away every bit of information about their technology and finance. Eventually the risk manager came to his rescue with an article by Speckman and Davis (2004). It said: the transfer of technology should only be supply-chain specific, not universal. It gave him the right ammunition that he needed.

The information issue is a big dilemma for most SMEs who do not have sufficient knowledge about the risk of information concerning technology and finance (see Box 21.2 and the case study at the end of this chapter). Other areas of supply chain risks are demand fluctuations, different weighting of risks by the members of the supply chains, different focus on the stages of shared projects, sharing of the sales, etc. Supply chains also differ from industry to industry. For instance, passing on the weight of risks from client to contractor is a big problem in the construction industry, while large pharmaceuticals financing biotech SMEs and sharing the risks is an ongoing saga in drug business. Despite all the drawbacks, collaboration through supply chains seems to be a dominant form in SME networking (see Box 21.3).

BOX 21.3: THE MIRIAD PROJECT

MIRIAD, an EU-funded project studying SMEs in the Thrace region of Turkey has highlighted the supply chain-based nature of collaboration of SMEs in Turkey. It observes that the most important knowledge-based alliances are among the suppliers and customers irrespective of whether these are SMEs within Thrace or outside it. This implies that collaborative innovation is mainly rooted within the supply chains of these SMEs.

The MIRIAD project is funded by the Framework 6 Programme of the European Commission under the Regions of Knowledge 2 programme (FP6–2004-KNOW-REG-2) (project number: 029490).

Growth through internationalization and the risk

Many of the ideas on internationalization have been based on the experiences of multinational enterprises (MNEs). A few of these ideas apply equally to smaller firms (for instance, all enterprises have to consider and hedge for exchange rate risk, abide by rules and regulations of the host countries and be aware of their culture). The challenge for fast-growing SMEs is that they suffer both the risks of a vulnerable small firm as well as those of the larger firms when they grow.

Most small businesses do not export (Hamilton and Dana, 2003) but many do and that is the first step to grow internationally. Exporting to new geographic markets provides opportunities for firms to expand their customer base. An increase in sales volume may lead in turn to higher production capacity plus the possibilities of financial leverage to meet the market demands.

SMEs face certain disadvantages when compared with larger enterprises, which may inhibit their success in the local market as well as discourage them from pursuing international opportunities. Obviously, a major impediment to SME expansion, in comparison with large firms, is the lack of resources. Size has also been viewed as an obstacle to the internationalization of small firms, as well as the size of the host country. SMEs face some difficult problems early in the internationalization process. These are mainly (1) lack of economy of scale, (2) lack of financial and knowledge resources and (3) aversion to risk taking (Freeman *et al.*, 2006).

Traditionally, exporters as well as investors thought that selling abroad would depend on the number of incentives and risks. This idea is still correct but it does not tell us how a growing firm should avoid the hurdles and risks. One of the cleverest ideas came from Scandinavia (the Uppsala school). In the 1980s and 1990s when it was realized that exporting and investing overseas go hand in hand, people like Johanson and Vahlne (1977) began to observe that smart companies avoid risk by following, so to speak, the 'yellow brick road' (the magic route to reach the objective in *The Wizard of Oz*).

In a nutshell, as companies grow they begin to export to the more welcoming countries first, and then move to the more perilous ones later (the appeal of the market is measured as *psychic distance*). This is like picking up the low-hanging fruit first and then attempting to climb up the tree. So it is clear that exporters go through stages and may have to follow a line that is not always straight. Changing conditions overseas and the problems of updating commitments may turn the road into a more complex route. A successful SME would normally start in their home country, gather experience, learn and then move outwards. Learning from the market is never a linear process (Bell *et al.*, 2003). In order to reduce risk, firms generally start exporting to foreign markets that are close or have some cultural similarities with their domestic market. Following experience and learning curves, some firms may subsequently actively seek out more distant foreign opportunities. Scandinavians, for example, target other Scandinavian countries before they move to Europe or Africa. Lebanese fashion SMEs have recently been moving to Europe following their satisfactory experience in other Arab countries. The BBC World service recently (January 2010) reported that Turkish firms are similarly expanding a vibrant domestic soap opera market to neighbouring countries first. They are now present in Dubai, which is located at the southern edge of the Middle East. North Africa seems to be the next step.

Not all growing SMEs follow the road of minimum risk. It is understandable that technologically advanced SMEs will be impatient to follow the yellow brick road. In fact, if we look at the grand evolutionary ideas we will be able to see that companies do not always stick to the incremental route of gradual progress. Sometimes when gradual progress is slowed down they take the risk of innovation or *a big jump*. Many of these innovators die but some succeed. Those who succeed blaze the way for another round of gradual progress. According to Coeurderoy and Murray (2008), the young and dynamic small firms tend to internationalize rapidly despite frequently having limited market knowledge and negligible size advantages.

International adventures are potentially profitable but are at the same time likely to increase the vulnerability of young firms when they are competing in new foreign markets. The vulnerability is so high that the strategic error of entering the wrong foreign market is thought to be death – not just wasted investment. The chances of a young firm recovering from a major marketing blunder overseas are thought to be remote. Serious misjudgements are likely to carry the death sentence (Sapienza *et al.*, 2006).

Internationalization and country risk

A more convenient way to explain the risks to foreign entry is *country risk*. Some years ago people used to talk of *political risk* instead. It seems that nowadays political risk is being discussed as part of country risk, which includes economic risk, financial risk, cultural risk and a few other less-important categories. To calculate the country risk, experts work out the risks of each category and add them up within a regression model that of course includes multipliers and the error term. In marketing language these categories and their risks are often explained in the context of PEST analysis. In PEST we speak of *threats* rather than risks.

Whatever the term used, innovative SMEs are prepared to take risks in foreign markets because the demand in the home market is often insufficient and the competition is too powerful. It is also possible that internationalization will provide additional sales opportunities for products or services enjoying a comparative advantage (Sapienza *et al.*, 2006). Comparative advantage is actually simpler to understand than competitive advantage. If you have bananas in a hot country like Ghana you have a comparative advantage over freezing Russian markets. On the other hand, a small innovative company in Sweden may have a technological advantage over an Asian country like Vietnam. Innovative companies are often in the business of technology transfer which is costly and risky.

The risks or liabilities of a distant country are regarded as additional transaction costs when setting up international operations. These costs are made up of several components such as search costs (to find the right agents), negotiation costs with those agents, and compliance and enforcement costs. The transfer of novel technologies and intangibles adds to these risks in the case of more sophisticated high-tech SMEs (Knight and Cavusgil, 2004). Some people include the cost of mitigating these risks as part of ordinary accounting costs. Others think that this is not a very good idea because the risks for a young company are far more than a cost/benefit issue: it is a life-and-death risk! (Coeurderoy and Murray, 2008).

Political risk

This risk has an influential role on entry decisions by foreign firms. Political risks normally involve elements such as governmental stability, social classes, ethnic structure, religion, etc., but for technologically advanced SMEs the main political risk is the level of intellectual property protection given to these companies. The national origin of the companies entering the market is also important (the so-called country of origin effect). For instance, German firms appear more sensitive to intellectual property rights protection than the UK companies. However, the entry decision for the Germans does not depend on intellectual property alone; the similarity of the legal system of the market country to the German system will have a decisive role (Coeurderoy and Murray, 2008).

Financial risk

The financial risk indicator is based on quantitative as well as qualitative information. It has three components: repudiation of contracts by the government, expropriation of private investments and losses from exchange controls ('ICRG' in Perotti and van Oijen, 2001. ICRG stands for 'International Country Risk Guide', a source of data on country risk).

Cultural risk

The ICRG does not include this, but many researchers do. After all, the Scandinavians who started all this regard cultural affinity as a vital element in the decision to enter a foreign market. Small firms will naturally have to rely on cultural similarity more than multinationals. Large multinationals normally have sufficient means to deal with different cultures.

In large companies both the stage-by-stage approach and the factors of country risk are considered rationally with lots of experts in each field to guide. With SMEs all this information is filtered through the mental map of the founders or a few influential individuals. These maps are formed in the minds of these individuals by the following influences:

- individual experience, firm size and age
- market knowledge (of individuals and groups)
- foreign market selection criteria
- a variety of other factors such as ethical or personal considerations.

Employees with more exposure to other cultures tend to support internationalization. A study on fast-growing SMEs in the UK showed that individuals within the largely UK-based firms potentially lack international exposure and the geographic range of their mental maps is limited as a result. Firm experience is similar. If your company has never looked beyond the Dover rocks, your leaders will have a mental map of a little-Englander with no desire to enter foreign markets no matter what the risks and opportunities. Collinson and Houlden (2005) show that an existing UK-based relationship with a Dutch IT manufacturer led to their initial international investment in Holland. On the other hand, a failure to internationalize in Dallas, USA, by a British SME is blamed on lack of experience among senior managers, a failure to recruit locally and a mis-fit between the UK business model and the US market. The authors also mention examples of successful entry into German markets by British firms due to proximity and into the US due to a particular leaders' experience in the US.

Market knowledge complements the individual experience. This can be gained from studying the subject, or simply by learning from 'the man who knows'. Regarding size, the survey shows that British SMEs of a certain size and maturity are biased towards Europe and take risks for higher profit. Smaller SMEs go for the comfort zone, avoiding the risk of uncertainty. The exception of course is the innovative growth oriented companies who tend to take risk. The study, however, does not tell us how they make such decisions. They don't seem to be able to calculate the risks. The only thing they can do is base their decisions on what makes sense, at least in the earlier stages of internationalization. Although it is likely that at a later stage they might inject more reasoning or rationality in their decisions, we tend to believe that most SMEs' decisions to globalize will stay random or haphazard rather than well calculated. The same set of conditions that make sense to one SME leader before entering a foreign country may prove inadequate to another.

Growth through brand

We know that many companies survive on brands. Once the name of a product gets into people's heads they keep buying it until some bad news about it breaks out or their interest gradually dwindles. Brands are not just for survival. Companies also grow through brands, and in particular through brand extension. Growth happens when people buy more of the same product because of the brand name, or buy related products (line extensions). Creating new brands or achieving international status due to brand fame is among the additional benefits of branding. Brand extension is different from line extension: selling new types of ladies' bags is line extension while selling perfumes (a different category) by the same brand owner is brand extension. Brand extension is mostly for the big business but SMEs in growth sectors can sometimes latch onto big business to promote a brand. A small designer brand can co-brand with a big company's perfume products.

Brand extension is a cheap way to grow through branding, but it is risky. This risk does not belong to the field of unexpected risks. It is as certain as your local pub losing your custom if they keep adding more water to your favourite pint of beer. The erosion of brands through extension is the second-biggest risk brands run, the first being the sudden collapse of the brand, most often due to a health scare. As an example, if a good car company starts producing some lower-grade models the brand is eroded or diluted. Apart from the image erosion, there are other side effects such as distribution channel confusion that can annoy the main distributor. Another example is Vichy, which expanded into run-of-the-mill pharmacy products and lost its dermatology brand due to erosion. They also lost chemists as their main distribution channel. Risks of dilution are inevitable but sometimes, like many other risks, may lead to opportunity. It has been said that extension introduces new features that may temporarily dilute the brand but one day will become part of the kernel themselves. Virgin is a good example of a successful extension-based business model. They started as a small company, established a main brand around the owner's personality and then extended the brand into many businesses. The Virgin brand is the glue that holds all these diverse businesses together (Kapferer, 2007). This is in fact a strategic approach that small businesses are advised to follow. Generally, SMEs are thought to be unable to establish and sustain product brands. The handful of people who have looked at SME branding see it as corporate branding rather than product branding, as can be seen from the explanations below.

Abimbola (2001) is one of the very few people who looks at SME branding, emphasizing the owners' inventiveness, innovation and creative flair. She thinks branding is the same in principle irrespective of the size of a company, but suggests that SMEs, having fewer resources, require greater focus and effectiveness. For example, an SME should focus on the corporate brand or just one or two brands and run very tightly specified and targeted campaigns. Making use of the entrepreneur in public relations is also advocated by Abimbola. Doyle (2003) pays particular attention to how Dyson built a brand personality as part of its marketing. Wong and Merrilees (2005) studied branding in eight SMEs. They rank them on a ladder; at the bottom there is little branding and low-key marketing. In the middle, where the typical SMEs are positioned, the marketing improves but branding is still informal. At the top, the SMEs are strong in both marketing and branding (formal and informal). With them branding is integral to the business. They understand customer needs better. One firm added the letter 'A' to their name in order to appear on top of industry lists as a form of a free ad; another small firm posted a laminated description of its brand on the back of the office door to remind employees of its existence. Krake (2005), using ten case studies, offers a 'funnel' model of brand management in SMEs. The funnel demonstrates that SME brands are more personal in character. Company identity as a brand is another example of how writers refuse to limit SME branding to commodities (Rode and Vallaster, 2005).

The personality of charismatic leaders and the company's reputation (identity) as indicators of brand strength is further emphasized by Merrilees (2007). Using the histories of ten successful SMEs, he presents ten findings based on their recommendations. The following three rules seem to be more popular with these ex-SMEs: (1) the founder/owner has to take responsibility for getting stakeholder buy-in to the corporate brand, (2) branding sharpens the business model formulation (the example given is an up-market dry cleaning company that includes branding strategy in their business plan) and (3) the early communication of the SME's capabilities to the outside world will facilitate future branding.

An example of the third rule is Ozforex, an online foreign exchange service. They made an agreement with the Australian Gift and Homewares Association and became the preferred supplier of foreign exchange services to its 4,000 members, including importers and exporters.

Branding risk for SMEs

In addition to the generic branding risks outlined above, SMEs are subject to specific branding risks, which include:

- lack of ability to advertise regularly over a longer time period
- lack of speed in adapting to reputation enhancing behaviour (CSR, ethics)
- inability to involve the personnel in branding (e.g. software SMEs; see Ojasalo et al., 2008)
- overdependence on location branding, which involves the risk of being ignored outside the locality when the firm expands (e.g. hotels)
- umbrella branding with a large company that tends to assert total control, stifling the SME's independent brand
- the loss of quality suppliers or customers that may decimate brand value faster than a typical erosion
- falling behind in adapting to latest technology and, thus, dissipating the brand.

SUMMARY

The chapter has tried to make the point that risk management goes beyond financial risk and includes all lines and sizes of businesses in different sectors of the economy. Small businesses are likely to go for quality assurance if they can afford it, but it is increasingly evident that governments, local authorities and the economy in general are compelling SMEs to look after themselves by developing resilience in the face of risks and catastrophes. Although human resources are thought to be the best asset SMEs have, it is evident that growing SMEs will reach the stage when they will have to adopt a more formal HR system. Any increase in numbers is a cause for celebration but this is prone to increase the risks as well. Hence the need for a systematic risk management. Growing SMEs often have to make difficult decisions in other dimensions too. Deciding what route to take for growth will require a great deal of risk management. Do we want to stick with the existing markets and products or do we want to take the risk-and-reward route and venture into new products and new markets? The most difficult scenario is growth through internationalization, which may drag the SME into the hazardous territory of tackling country risk. SMEs that choose to develop through networking with fellow SMEs or a 'big brother' – for example, in the case of biotech companies and giant pharmaceuticals – face numerous risks of great complexity. It is often thought that sheltering with big business will reduce the risk of dependency on banks; but the reality is that SMEs have to face many risks *before* gaining support from big business. They have to complete substantial research before they are accepted for cooperation. Networking is not easy either. This may benefit the below-average firm but the high-flyers may suffer.

Finally, it was shown that branding, with its comforts and risks, can lead to growth. Generally, one may conclude that SMEs will need to learn to manage their risks, especially those concerning business continuity, so that they can survive and wrench some credit from creditors. The publication of ISO3000, the first-ever standard for risk management, is great news for SMEs who may use the standard to manage their own risk and make their partners in the supply chain do likewise.

REVIEW QUESTIONS

1. Some people argue that SMEs do not need to grow. Do you agree with this? If not, explain your reasons why they feel compelled to grow.

2. The concept of *sensible growth* is mentioned but not fully explained. Could you explain this for a small company that you can think of?

3. SMEs can 'grow up' through *organizational learning*, which is developed by tackling risks and risky projects and is essential for building a healthy operations strategy that may facilitate sensible growth. If you had a small company like Irfan's web-based little shoe shop introduced below, what sort of things might you learn that would direct you towards sensible growth?

4. Discuss organizational memory loss. How would you differentiate small, large and growth companies in terms of memory loss?

5. Discuss the various methods that SMEs can use to grow. Explain the advantages and disadvantages of each method.

6. One of the best ways SMEs can collaborate is with the members of the supply chains. Explain why the other forms of collaboration you have learned are more problematic.

7. What do you understand by *coopetition*? Use appropriate examples to illustrate your answer (students are required to develop a one-page case study to illustrate this method of cooperation).

8. Suppose you start a small family-run shoe shop in London importing fashionable shoes and selling them through the internet. You're overjoyed that the business is really starting to take off. You receive emails from some VIPs from Canada or the US informing you that they will be in London to act in a show or attend a football match and that they would like to visit you and have a good look at your range of shoes. This makes you think of expanding the premises so that you can properly entertain valuable customers. However, you delay expansion until you have 25 people working for you. What has changed in terms of HR management and risks?

9. In the pharaceutical business large pharmaceutical companies generally refuse to assist their small biotech partners until a late phase of their research when the risks have dwindled to nothing. Marketing experts believe that for the sake of fairness and better business cooperation the pharmaceutical companies should allow the biotech partners to have a share in the sale of the drugs produced. How would you compare this with urging the pharmaceutical companies to share the risks at earlier stages of the biotech research instead?

10. Explain why risks grow more if a firm jumps to the top right quadrant of the Ansoff matrix.

11. According to the Uppsala school, the decision concerning international entry has to involve *psychic distance*, which can be regarded as a measure of risk. Do you think this measure would apply the same way to small and large American companies investing in Thailand?

12. Most foreign entries start with exporting, then settle down to invest. Why do you think they do that?

13. ICRG, a large-rating organization, provides data on country risk consisting of economic, financial and political risks. They ignore cultural risks. Why do you think that is?

14. SMEs brand the company rather than a product. Why?

15. Risk management process normally consists of the following steps: identify risks (record them in your risk register); analyse them in terms of probability of occurrence; take action whether you want to ensure, transfer or retain risks; finally, monitor to see you have done it all right. Consider the shoe shop above with 25 employees. Suppose Irfan the owner-director invites you to work out the risks for him. Get into groups of 3–5 and apply the risk management process outlined in this question.

CASE STUDY 21: THE T-TRUCK COMPANY MANAGES ITS OWN RISKS

Vildan, who lives and studies risk management in London, used to travel to Turkey regularly in the hope of meeting up with the widely dispersed family. Her father and brother both lived in Paris driving industrial trucks and subcontracting. Her grandma was still living in Eastern Europe, and her mum was firmly located in Izmir (Turkey). Tarkhan Bei (Mr T) and son Mehmet moved to Izmir, borrowed heavily and bought a trucking company that boasted a Japanese brand name. The business supplies industrial trucks and associated equipment.

Owner-managed, the T-Truck company quickly grew to 40 employees, including some professional managers. Mr T attributed his success to his risk-taking nature, the good Turks working for him, and of course the brand. His mates used to joke about the brand: 'He borrows the Japanese industrial reputation the same way as he borrows his mate's pipe!' Mr T responded: 'My men are as good as Japanese technology. They service our products on-site over a 1,000 kilometers, from Izmir to Erzrum.' Despite good service, however, the variety of tasks and the cost to the customers nearly brought the company down. Mr T couldn't admit it to his mates but decided to discuss the risk with his family. Mrs T, who preferred shopping to 'accounts', dismissed risk as a matter for big companies. The son, Mehmet, said: 'Risk is risk, size doesn't matter.' Vildan giggled, pointing at Mehmet's nose. Mr T ignored the joke and grunted that his business was quite big, stretching from the East to the West. Vildan, noting that her dad was serious about risk, decided to settle the size issue by asking the following questions:

■ Is the ownership independent? Answer: 'Yes.'

- Are you alone in control? Answer: 'Yes, with the family of course.'
- Do you, as owner-manager, make all the decisions? Answer: 'Yes.'
- Is most of the risk on our shoulder? Answer: 'Yes.'
- Do you have less than 200 workers? Answer: 'Yes.'
- Are you a multi-task leader? Answer: 'Yes of course.'
- Can you increase the prices of your trucks? Answer: 'No, it is in God's hands.'
- Do you have a small share in the market? Answer: 'We cover the whole country but only a few!'

'Ok then,' said Vildan 'You are small, no matter what the size of your trucks or the family nose.' She added: 'If you follow the procedures properly, managing risk is easier for small businesses than for the big firms.' Realizing that she was talking sense and that she hadn't wasted his money in London, Mr T took heart and discussed the risk of delays and costs to the customers with her.

Vildan explained that the steps for risk management are the same for all firms except that it is easier for SMEs:

'These steps are: first establish a strategy for risk, for example you set the time to achieve targets such as profit, sales, etc. Then you identify risks. Look at the opportunities first, such as selling in the East where there are no competitors but where there are the risks of bad roads, bandits, etc. Normally, you identify a family of risks and then isolate them one by one. For small business this is simpler. Employees are the best source of information about risks. Beyond that you will need expert knowledge.

'Following identification, risk assessment is done by using a 3×3 grid to work out the probability of risk and its severity. Normally, risks at the top right end, shown in red, are critical needing attention, and the ones at the bottom left are negligible. After this, you set your risk appetite: This boils down to deciding the amount of risk you are prepared to stomach. Then you allocate resources to risks according to your appetite. If the risk is bigger than your appetite then you have to curb your exposure. Prioritization of risks according to their importance is a skilled job. You will have to pay some specialists! Otherwise you will be trapped in little risks and ignoring the big ones!'

Worried about paying for experts, Mr T started talking about central decisions, bureaucracy and cost of repairs. Vildan listened carefully and said:

'Your risk problem is simple and you don't need any of the formalities. Train the people and send them on their long journey but let them make on-site decisions. Dad, if you learn to trust them, they will make the right decisions. They will be happy and the customers will be satisfied.'

Mr T, who could only trust God and his purse, shook his head: 'Last year I put my trust in one of the biggest repair houses, telling them all about my Japanese suppliers and they decided to start their own truck company. So much for trust! Mehmet said philosophically: 'Trust in God but tie down your camel!'

Vildan had the right words to finally convince Mr T's suspicious mind: 'Dad, you should still trust good customers and suppliers, but within limits. You should only give supply chain-specific information away, not everything!'

After some prevarications Mr T decided to employ a number of capable technicians who would solve the customer problem as a first priority and then negotiate for the price. Mr T didn't like it first but was soon delighted with the results.

> ## CASE QUESTIONS
> 1. Do you agree with Vildan that risk management is easier for SMEs? Why?
> 2. Can we reduce risk appetite instead of reducing exposure to risk?
> 3. What is meant by supply chain-specific information?
> 4. How can you strike a balance between trusting skilled employees and preventing them from turning into competitors?

REFERENCES

Abimbola, T. (2001), 'Branding as a competitive strategy for demand management in SMEs', *Journal of Research in Marketing and Entrepreneurship*, Vol. 3, No. 2, pp. 97–106.

Ahuja, G. (2000), 'The duality of collaboration: Inducements and opportunities in the formation of interfirm linkages', *Strategic Management Journal*, Vol. 21, No. 3, pp. 317–343.

Barringer, B.R. and Jones, F.F. (2004), 'Achieving rapid growth – revisiting the managerial capacity problem', *Journal of Developmental Entrepreneurship*, Vol. 9, No. 1, pp. 73–87.

Becchetti, L. and Trovato, G. (2002), 'The determinants of growth for small and medium sized firms: The role of the availability of external finance', *Small Business Economics*, Vol. 19, No. 4, pp. 291–300.

Bell, J., McNaughton, R., Young, S. and Crick, D. (2003). 'Towards an integrative model of small firm internationalisation', *Journal of International Entrepreneurship*, Vol. 1, pp. 339–62.

Bengtsson, M., and Kock, S. (2008) 'Role conflicts in co-opetitive relationships', Working Paper, Umeå Business School, University of Umeå, Sweden.

Carter, R. and Van Auken, H. (2005), 'Bootstrap financing and owners' perceptions of their business constraints and opportunities', *Entrepreneurship and Regional Development*, Vol. 17, No. 2, pp. 129–144.

Collinson, S. and Houlden, J. (2005), 'Decision-making and market orientation in the internationalization process of small and medium-sized enterprises', *Management International Review*, Vol. 45, No. 4, pp. 413–437.

Coeurderoy, R and Murray, G. (2008), 'Regulatory environments and the location decision: Evidence from the early foreign market entries of new-technology-based firms', *Journal of International Business Studies*, Vol. 39, No. 4, pp. 670–688.

Doyle, E. (2003), 'A study of entrepreneurial brand building in the manufacturing sector in the UK', *Journal of Product and Brand Management*, Vol. 12, No. 2, pp. 79–93.

Freeman, S., Edwards, R. and Schroder, B. (2006), 'How smaller born-global firms use networks and alliances to overcome constraints to rapid internationalization', *Journal of International Marketing*, Vol. 14, No. 3, pp. 33–63.

Groupe ESC Dijon Bourgogne (2003) 'Risk assessment in SMEs, a proposed tool', *Cahiers du CEREN*, 4, pp. 31–40.

Hamilton, R.T. and Dana, L.P. (2003), 'An increasing role for small business in New Zealand', *Journal of Small Business Management*, Vol. 41, No. 4, pp. 402–408.

Harrison, R.T., Mason, C.M. and Girling, P. (2004), 'Financial bootstrapping and venture development in the software industry', *Entrepreneurship and Regional Development*, Vol. 16, No. 4, pp. 307–333.

Herbane, B. (2010), 'Small business research: Time for a crisis-based view', *International Small Business Journal*, Vol. 28, No. 1, pp. 43–64.

Johanson, J., Vahlne, J.-E. (1977), 'The internationalisation process of the firm: a model of knowledge development and increasing foreign market commitments', *Journal of International Business Studies*, Vol. 8, No. 1, pp. 23–32.

Kapferer, J-N. (2007), *The New Strategic Brand Management: Creating and Sustaining Brand Equity*, Kogan Page, London.

Kelley, D.J. and Nakosteen, R.A. (2005), 'Technology resources, alliances, and sustained growth in new, technology-based firms', *IEEE Transactions on Engineering Management*, Vol. 52, No. 3, pp. 292–300.

Knight, G. and Cavusgil, S. (2004), 'Innovation, organizational capabilities, and the born-global firm', *Journal of International Business Studies*, Vol. 35, No. 3, pp. 124–141.

Krake, F. (2005), 'Successful brand management in SMEs: A new theory and practical hints', *Journal of Product and Brand Management*, Vol. 14, No. 4, pp. 228–38.

Lavie, D. (2007), Alliance portfolios and firm performance: A study of value creation and appropriation in the US software industry', *Strategic Management Journal*, Vol. 28, No. 12, pp. 1187–1212.

Locke, S. (2004), 'ICT adoption and SME growth in New Zealand', *Journal of American Academy of Business*, Vol. 4, No. 1/2, pp. 93–102.

Maitland, A. (2001), 'Knowledge management: If downsizing, protect the corporate memory', *Financial Times*, 16 October, p. 9.

Merrilees, B. (2007), 'A theory of brand-led SME new venture development', *Qualitative Market Research*, Vol. 10, No. 4, pp. 403–415.

Morris, M.H., Kocak, A. and Özer, A. (2007), 'Coopetition as a small business strategy: Implications for performance', *Journal of Small Business Strategy*, Vol. 18, No. 1, pp. 35–55.

Ojasalo, J., Natti, S. and Olkkonen, R. (2008), 'Brand building in software SMEs: An empirical study', *Journal of Product and Brand Management*, Vol. 17, No. 2, pp. 92–107.

Perotti, E.C. and van Oijen, P. (2001), 'Privatization, political risk and stock market development in emerging economies', *Journal of International Money and Finance*, Vol. 20, No. 1, pp. 43–69.

Piranfar, H. and Combstock, L. (2008), 'Risk and quality management: The symbiosis', *i-manager's Journal on Management*, Vol. 2, No. 4, pp. 12–22.

Robson, P.J.A. and Bennett, R.J. (2000), 'SME growth: The relationship with business advice and external collaboration', *Small Business Economics*, Vol. 15, No. 3, pp. 193–205.

Rode, V. and Vallaster, C. (2005), 'Corporate branding for start-ups: The crucial role of entrepreneurs', *Corporate Reputation Review*, Vol. 8, No. 2, pp. 121–35.

Rothaermel, F.T., and Deeds, D.L. (2004), 'Exploration and exploitation alliances in biotechnology: A system of new product development', *Strategic Management Journal*, Vol. 25, No. 3, pp. 201–221.

Sapienza, H., Autio, E., George, G. and Zahra, S.A. (2006), 'A capabilities perspective on the effects of early internationalization on firm survival and growth', *Academy of Management Review*, Vol. 31, No. 4, pp. 914–933.

Sloman, J. and Sutcliffe, M. (2004), *Economics for Business*, 3rd edn, Prentice Hall, Harlow, UK.

Smallbone, D. and North, D. (1995), 'Targeting established SMEs: does their age matter?', *International Small Business Journal*, Vol. 13, No. 3, pp. 4–22.

Speckman, R.E. and Davis, E.W. (2004), 'Risky Business: Expanding the discussion on risk and the extended enterprise', *International Journal of Physical distribution and Logistics Management*, Vol. 34, No. 5, pp. 414–433.

Sulej, J.C., Stewart, V. and Keogh, W. (2001), 'Taking risk in joint ventures: Whose throw of the dice?', *Strategic Change*, Vol. 10, No. 5, pp. 285–295.

Wong, H.Y. and Merrilees, B. (2005), 'A brand orientation typology for SMEs: A case research approach', *Journal of Product and Brand Management*, Vol. 14, No. 3, pp. 155–162.

Chapter 22

Marketing planning in small businesses

Frances Ekwulugo

LEARNING OBJECTIVES

After reading this chapter, you will be able to:
- understand the implications of planning for SMEs
- understand the marketing planning process
- identify the major steps in the marketing planning process
- explain what a marketing plan should include
- develop the skill to carry out a marketing plan task.

INTRODUCTION

This chapter discusses the process and importance of marketing planning. It is often con-tended that the formal marketing approach is inappropriate for SMEs, largely on account of their relative small size and sometimes informal structure (Blankson and Omar, 2002). Although SMEs are more flexible than large businesses, they tend to apply a more flexible and informal approach to their management systems. It is believed that the embedded attributes of SMEs militate against conventional planning but the reality is that a formal approach to marketing planning affords SMEs a sense of direction and focus. We begin our discussion by trawling through some of the broader issues that might impact the planning process in SMEs and then focus on the structure of a marketing plan.

CONTRIBUTIONS OF SMES TO THE ECONOMY

In most countries, small businesses are seen as the growth engine of the economy (Stanworth and Purdy, 2003). SMEs represent at least 90 per cent of the employers, in numerical count, and they employ about 50 per cent of the workforce in the UK. Statistics across different parts of the world mirror these trends. The success of SMEs comes in part because they are more efficient in some ways than their larger corporate counterparts. Large firms have the ability to obtain economies of scale in some industries and can do things more efficiently because of their large operating size. However, it is argued that more than 50 per cent of small businesses fail during their first four years and this figure is even higher in some sectors.

There is a general consensus that the performance of SMEs is important for both the economic and social development of any country. From the economic perspective, SMEs provide a number of benefits which enable them to grow to form big businesses; hence, they are seen as the seeds of big businesses and sources of growth of the national economy (Kotey, 2005). SMEs are presumed to be more flexible than large businesses in decision making and responding to changes in the environment. The advantages they have over their large-scale competitors are due to their ability to adapt more easily to market conditions (Basu and Goswami, 1999). In many cases they are able to withstand adverse economic situations due to their flexibility. For example, they can quickly respond to increase in demand without any delay (Jamal, 2002). Some writers argue, however, that being small makes SMEs more vulnerable during economic turbulence (Stanworth and Purdy, 2003). Nevertheless, SMEs add value to the economic system. Additionally, SMEs induce improvements in the efficiency of domestic markets by intensifying competition and making productive use of scarce resources that facilitates long-term economic growth (LDA, 2004).

CONSTRAINTS ON SMES

Small businesses do experience various problems that constrain their activities, such as ownership and succession crises, lack of access to finance, lack of skills, regulatory issues and access to international markets, lack of support services from support agencies and inadequate equipment and technology. There are also indirect ownership impacts on a firm's activities, which tend to dictate the sources and amounts of funding available. It is reported that up to 50 per cent of new businesses cease trading within five years because of poor resources. Only the very few who are resilient enough survive, and even these achieve very little significant growth (Stanworth and Purdy, 2003). However, many studies have reported that not all SMEs want to grow. Some will prefer to keep their business as a family business. SMEs often lack specialist skills such as managerial skills which are needed for business development. There is an increasing need for start-ups to plan and develop a basic business plan, and also to conduct market research and financial planning, but many SMEs are lacking in these areas (Kraus et al., 2006).

MANAGEMENT STYLE

A vast number of SMEs are owner-managed and it has been identified that the culture of the owner-manager influences how the business is run (Fraser, 2004). In some cases, one person is directly involved in every important decision on day-to-day issues (e.g. customer enquiries, financial control, production, employee recruitment and rent reviews). Obviously there are bound to be a number of problems associated with this type of set-up. As the owner-manager does everything, naturally some of the required skills to deal with the complex issues in the businesses may not be in existence (Smallbone et al., 2005; Ram, 1999; Cook et al., 2003). However, there are now emerging some global dimensions to entrepreneurship and these have tended to challenge some of the assumptions about small businesses. Increasingly, many SMEs import goods from abroad and equally sell overseas. As a result they may require large sums of capital and knowledge to deal with international customers (Kotey, 2002). Against this background, the importance of the best proven managerial practices to embed entrepreneurial activities cannot be overestimated. Little wonder that companies are urged to be market-oriented in order to improve performance (Kohli and Jaworski, 1990).

Overall, studies on the management of SMEs show that their lack of management skills impedes their performance (Smallbone et al., 2005). The question, therefore, is: does the SME have adequate management skills to make the right decisions for an effective performance?

Small businesses typically develop and implement marketing strategies within several resource constraints and under the day-to-day pressures of business. For this reason, marketing may seem to be an unnecessary luxury (Blankson and Omar, 2002; Hogarth-Scott *et al.*, 1996). However, many authors have found that SMEs do practise marketing – but in rather idiosyncratic ways (Blankson and Omar, 2002; Pelham and Wilson, 1996).

THE FUNCTIONS AND PURPOSE OF MANAGEMENT – TOWARDS MARKETING PLANNING

Traditionally management consists of five functions: planning, organizing, communicating, coordinating and controlling. Planning is concerned with setting objectives, quantifying the targets of achievement for each objective, communicating these targets to other people in the organization and selecting the strategies, tactics, policies, programmes and procedures for achieving the objectives – the marketing plan is just one of these. A marketing plan is a document produced to guide the marketing of goods and services of a given organization. 'Marketing planning is simply a logical sequence and a series of activities leading to the setting of marketing objectives and the formulation of plans for achieving them' (McDonald, 2007, p. 27). Globally, change is occurring at an accelerating rate; there are uncertainties, challenges and opportunities affecting business operations. Therefore, making decisions requires knowledge to understand what the actual situation is and how the decision should be made. Planning therefore involves what to do in the future (objectives), how to do it (strategy), when to do it and who should do it (tactics). Marketing planning appears to be a simple step-by-step approach but in reality it is very complex. Consequently, there is a need for a formalized process to enable firms to achieve their stated objectives – relying only on sales forecasts and budgeting is not enough.

A marketing plan needs to answer the following questions:

Where are we now (current situation)? A marketing plan is produced within a context and this context should be taken into consideration. The SME context is unique to each sector. For example, the possible lack of finance and managerial skills may require that evaluation of marketing effectiveness, internal activities and external factors are properly analysed in relation to the specific context of the SME. An in-depth analysis of the context enables the owner-manager to understand where the business wants to be.

Where do we want to be (objectives)? Most businesses have mission statements and these are broad statements of what businesses exist for. Business objectives are formulated around the mission statement. Understanding where you are now helps point the business in its next direction.

How do we get there (strategy)? Strategy is normally developed to achieve the stated objectives. It is built around two key areas: the target market and the competitive advantage sought. The tactic is to identify the customers and analyse their characteristics, needs and wants. To gain a competitive advantage, the plan will examine the strategies of competitor companies' offerings.

How do we know we have arrived (evaluation and control)? In most SMEs, plans originate from within, e.g. ideas from staff or projects that help to achieve the ultimate objectives. SMEs sometimes work in teams and these often have close relationships with managers. This facilitates decision making and problem solving within the organization. Through planning, organizing and control, organizational tasks are coordinated to provide marketable products and services. Managers control these activities, resources and people to get desired results. The chosen method of control and evaluation will depend on the values of the manager and on certain organizational contingencies but the likely impact of managerial style on individuals and groups must be taken into account. The implementation of a successful plan will depend on these matters and on the skills and knowledge that the manager possesses.

THE IMPLICATIONS OF MARKETING PLANNING

Importance

Most SMEs are unaware of the importance of marketing planning; the usual complaint is that they don't have the time 'to waste on unnecessary routine tasks'. They may not be sure if the planning process is worth the time invested in it, even when they do not know what marketing is all about. Therefore, there is a need for SMEs to understand the external and internal factors. It is equally important for SMEs to understand their customers. Marketing planning will enable SMEs to exploit future opportunities (Blankson and Omar, 2002).

Planning problems

SMEs' response to the need to provide marketing planning could be influenced by the following:

- weak support from chief executive and top management
- lack of a plan for planning
- lack of line management support
- hostility
- lack of skills
- lack of information
- lack of resources
- inadequate organization structure
- confusion over planning terms
- numbers in lieu of written objectives and strategies
- too many details, too far ahead
- once-a-year ritual
- separation of operational planning from strategic planning
- lack of integration.

UNDERSTANDING THE ENVIRONMENT: EXTERNAL ENVIRONMENTAL INFLUENCES

Small businesses are struggling nationally and internationally in order to survive (Basu and Goswami, 1999). For an organization to survive and prosper there is a need to understand and adjust to the external environment (Drucker, 1954). Lack of response to the environment will result in the inability of businesses to meet the needs and wants of their stakeholders (Kotler, 2003). Responding to the environment means matching the capabilities of the organization with the changing environment. This scenario has meant that the success of SMEs depends in large part on the formulation and implementation of a viable strategy (Miles and Snow,

1978; Porter, 1980). Here, strategy means the way things are done in the organization, which is reflected in a firm's short- and long-term responses to the challenges and opportunities posed by the business environment. As previously stated, SMEs are more flexible than large businesses (Pelham and Wilson, 1996). All indications show that the external environment is generally assumed to be a given and outside the influence of the organization (Kotey, 2005).

COMPETITION

The growing number of SMEs has intensified competition among small businesses (Barrett *et al.*, 2002) on the one hand and large businesses on the other. For example, large supermarket chains in the UK such as Tesco and Sainsbury's are now competing with SMEs in some areas of activity. While some argue that this trend has increased supplier diversity and improved quality of goods provided (Ram and Smallbone, 1999), many are worried about the future of SMEs.

THE ANALYSIS STAGE

Market research

The first step in marketing planning is information gathering and analysis. This helps to identify the right market audience and how they could be targeted. It must be noted that the quality of the information gathered and the level of analysis will influence the decision made.

Internal analysis

The internal environment could be analysed under the following headings: production, market share, product management, distribution, price, promotion finance, sales, profitability, marketing mix variables, human resources, location and company image.

External analysis

The external environment could be analysed under the following headings: political, economic (all the economic forces), social (demography, culture and attitudes, consumer forces) and technological environment. Table 22.1 shows some examples of the external variables.

Table 22.1 PEST factors

Political	Legislation, human rights, regulatory constraints (e.g. labelling, product quality, packaging, trade practices, advertising, pricing)
Economic	Inflation, unemployment, energy, price, volatility, materials
Social	Education, immigration, emigration, religion, environment, population distribution and dynamics
Technology	Production technology, the internet, cost-saving, materials, components, equipment, machinery, methods and systems, availability of substitutes

The customer

According to McDonald (2003),

> Marketing planning is a process for: Defining markets, quantifying the needs of the customer groups (segments) within these markets; determining the value propositions

to all those people in the organisation responsible for delivering them and getting their buy-in to their role; playing an appropriate part in delivering these value propositions and monitoring the value actually delivered. For this process to be effective, organisations need to be consumer/customer driven.

It is important to establish why buyers would buy from the SME of interest and not from the competition. It is equally important to differentiate one's own business from the competition and be able to identify the USP (unique selling proposition). To keep customers, there is a need to develop relationships with customers, to educate, develop and be able to alter customers' understanding and attitude towards the organization's product. Developing relationships are particularly important, especially in business-to-business markets.

The market

To understand the market the following areas need to be analysed: the total market size, growth, trends; market characteristics, development and trends; prices, physical distribution channels; customers/consumers; industry practices. It is equally important to analyse competitors, examine demand and supply situations, as well as to identify who the customers are. Additionally, the analysis should include the identification of the competitive forces in the marketplace. Two concepts that could be used to achieve this are (a) Porter's five forces (entry barriers, buyer's power, supplier's power, availability of substitutes, extent of rivalry and switching costs) and (b) the industry concept of competition (number of sellers and degree of differentiation, entry barriers, exit barriers, cost structures, vertical integration, global reach). Some other variables to be covered include major competitors, size, market shares/coverage, market standing/reputation, production policies, marketing methods, extent of diversification, personnel issues, international links, profitability, key strengths and weaknesses.

CONTENTS OF A MARKETING PLAN

- SWOT (strengths, weaknesses, opportunities and threats) analysis
- assumptions
- marketing objectives
- marketing strategy
- contingency plan
- financial statements
- budget
- control and evaluation.

SWOT analysis

SMEs need to understand their current situation before they can create appropriate strategies, and this involves environmental scanning and analysis. They need to know where their products stand in the market and be able to set realistic objectives. SWOT analysis summarizes this audit under strengths, weakness, opportunities and threats and should be included in the plan. Strengths and weakness refer to the company's internal environment, while opportunities and threats refer to the external environment. Conducting a SWOT analysis enables organizations to be more focused. Most SMEs do not tap their core strengths and, therefore, miss future opportunities. SWOT analysis can be subjective but it does work when it is carefully conducted. It leads to the articulation of marketing objectives (see Table 22.2 for an example).

■ *Table 22.2* Examples of SWOT factors

Strengths	Weaknesses
Abundant financial resources	Lack of strategic direction
Well-known brand name	Limited financial resources
Raking in industry	Weak spending on R&D
Economies of scale	High cost of production
Superior product quality	Poor marketing skills
Committed employees	Undertrained employees
Opportunities	Threats
Rapid market growth	Entry of foreign competitors
Rival firms are complacent	Introduction of new substitute products
Changing customer needs/tastes	Product life cycle in decline
Opening of foreign markets	Changing customer needs/taste
New uses of product	Rival firms adopt new strategies
Government deregulation	Increased government regulation
Demographic shifts	Economic downturn
	New technology

Assumptions

Assumptions are based on real facts and estimates of what can be achieved in consideration of the past performance.

Marketing objectives

Objectives are clear statements of what the business intends to achieve. Objectives should be SMART – that is, specific, measurable, attainable, realistic and timed. To produce a SMART objective the marketing audit should examined to make sure it is based on realistic estimations.

> **GROUP ACTIVITY**
> Examine the objectives of any SME with which you are familiar (you can check out the internet, if it helps). How well do you think these objectives are being met?

Marketing strategy

To meet the objectives there is a need to establish strategies. Strategies describe how organizations can achieve stated marketing objectives, and are expressed in terms of the 4Ps (the marketing mix, see Table 22.3). It is the marketer's challenge to find or develop these 'Ps' in such a way that will meet customers' needs and wants relatively more efficiently than the competition. There are two models that may usefully impact the setting of strategies: product life cycle (PLC) and Boston Consulting Group Matrix (BCG matrix) (these are discussed elsewhere in this book). Also, the Ansoff matrix could provide a useful guide.

GROUP ACTIVITY

Assume you are the manager of a medium-sized cosmetic company. Sales for most of your product lines are down because the tastes of women are changing and there are more quality cosmetics in the market that are cheaper than yours.

Discuss the actions you would take to arrest the situation.

Most small businesses treat marketing strategy as a haphazard activity and make no effort to relate it to the main aim and objectives of the marketing plan. Small businesses should formulate strategies in their own way and not necessarily copy the strategy of big companies. Strategies could be set around the 4Ps (see Table 22.3).

Table 22.3 Marketing mix strategies

Product	Variety
	Performance
	Feature
	Design
	Packaging
	Brand name
Price	Discount
	Geographical pricing
	Payment terms
	Credit terms
Promotion	Advertising
	Public relations
	Trade promotion
	Direct marketing
	Digital marketing
	Sales promotion
Place (Distribution)	Pre-sale services
	Point-of-sale services
	Post-sale services
	Support staff
	Tasks and responsibilities

Contingency plan

A good plan will always have a back-up plan, or contingency plan, that will be put into operation if one or more of the assumptions of the original plan do not materialize.

Financial statements

The final part of the planning process is to show, in numeric and financial terms, what the outcome of the strategy will be in terms of revenues, costs and profit.

Budget

There is a need to develop a budget that projects the revenues, expenditures, profits and cash flows over the planning period. SME operators should evaluate the plan and expenditure to determine whether activities and cost are on track.

Control and evaluation

Considering the marketing audit, control is based on forecasts, budgets, schedules and metrics. A forecast is prepared based on the optimistic data on previous sales and predicted future sales and costs. Budgets are prepared based on past records and predicted figures. Metrics are used to measure outcomes and activities that helped to achieve the short-term objectives. Control and evaluation criteria can be established using a battery of ratios (e.g. profitability, activity, performance ratios). It is also possible to use the variables indicated in Table 22.4.

Table 22.4 Dimensions of feedback, standards and control actions

Feedback	Standards	Control/Actions
Sales figures	Against budget plus or minus	Stimulate/dampen down demand
Complaints	Number, frequency, seriousness	Corrective action
Competitors	Relative to us	Attack/defence strategies
Market size changes	Market share	Marketing mix manipulation
Costs/profitability	Ratios	Cost-cutting exercises
Corporate image	Attribute measures	Internal/external communications

SUMMARY

It is commonly said that many SMEs do not embark on marketing planning. This is because they are too busy to stop and get involved in what they often see as an unnecessary practice. They tend to concentrate on short-term production and financial priorities. SMEs think more in the short term rather than in the long term. Planning generates motivation and increased ambition. It enables managers to forecast events and explore the opportunities opened for the future. It informs managers and prepares them for future risk taking. Planning on its own does not establish success but a well-thought-through and carefully implemented plan is more likely to be successful. This chapter has discussed SMEs' marketing planning process. It followed a step-by-step process which can enable managers to think through their marketing planning process. The chapter also provided a basic framework for developing logical marketing plans.

CASE STUDY 22: CHILTERN SECURITIES

Chiltern Securities was founded in February 2006 by two friends. The company provides security services to local authorities and universities in the UK.

Chiltern does not have a mission statement and has never prepared a marketing plan for the business. According to the manager, 'We get by and we still make a profit without a marketing plan. We are very busy and it is a waste of time to start looking at all the bits'.

Currently, the company is focused on serving local authorities. The largest market share obtained to date is about 1 per cent for the security segment in the UK. Additionally, due to the niche positioning of the company, the company's growth is not moving as fast as they anticipated. They are currently planning to target the general market – namely, any company that is making more than £1 million turnover.

The company provides services to clients via temporary contracted staff, who have little experience and normally will leave for other companies if the jobs are not flowing quickly. The company's main business depends on the demand of local authorities. When the company is at full capacity they employ about 50 security officers, but in a quiet period the figure could be as low as ten. Chiltern has not considered training staff because they are temporary and causal; the company feels that training their security officers is a waste of resources as they will probably leave to join other companies.

Local authorities are complaining about the quality of staff that Chiltern sends to their premises. They have made several complaints but nothing has been done about this.

At the moment the councils are considering terminating the contract and engaging other security companies. However, the demand for Chiltern's services is increasing in the university sector, but this is not big enough to sustain the company and tends to demand fewer security officers when students are on holidays. Chiltern Securities is not aware of the councils' plans and are very complacent.

During the school holidays, Chiltern loses up to £10,000 per week. This is the scenario Chiltern wants to avoid but they do not know what to do in order to avoid the difficulties they are currently facing. The directors, on the other hand, feel that the results to date mean the company needs to reassess its management approach in order to ramp up higher growth levels.

CASE TASK

Working in teams, you are required to provide Chiltern Securities with an outline marketing plan applying the various tools and concepts covered in this chapter. Identify marketing strategy, planning, implementation and control.

REVIEW QUESTIONS

1. Why is a marketing plan considered to be important for SMEs?

2. What factors would you consider when scanning the external and internal environment?

3. Why is it important to understand the customer/consumer before embarking on marketing planning?

4. What measures can be used to monitor marketing outcomes?

BIBLIOGRAPHY

Barrett, G., Jones T., McEvoy, D, and McGoldrick, C. (2002), 'The economic embeddedness of immigrant enterprises in Britain', *International Journal of Entrepreneurial Behaviour and Research*, Vol. 8, No. 1/2, pp. 11–31.

Basu, A. and Goswami, A. (1999), 'South Asian entrepreneurship in Great Britain: Factors influencing growth', *International Journal of Entrepreneurial Behaviour and Research*, Vol. 5, No. 5, pp. 251–275.

Blankson, C. and Omar O. (2002), 'Marketing practices of African and Caribbean small businesses in London UK', *Qualitative Market Research: An International Journal*, Vol. 5, No. 2, pp. 123–134.

Cook, M., Ekwulugo, F. and Fallon, G. (2003), 'Start-up motivation factors in UK African Caribbean SMEs: An exploratory study', paper presented at the 4th International Academy of African Business and Development Conference, Westminster Business School, London, 9–12 April.

Curran, J. and Burrow, R. (1993), *Ethnic Enterprise and the High Street Bank*, ESRC Centre for Research on Small Service Sector Enterprises, Kingston Business School, Kingston University.

Drucker, O. (1954), *The Practice of Management*. New York: Harper and Row Publishers.

Eisenmann, T.R. (2002), 'The effect of CEOs equity ownership and firm diversification on risk taking', *Strategic Management Journal*, Vol. 23, No. 6, pp. 513–534.

Fraser, S. (2004), 'Finance for small and medium-sized enterprises', *A Report on the 2004 UK Survey of SME Finances*, Centre for Small and Medium Sized Enterprises, Warwick Business School, University of Warwick.

Hogarth-Scott, S, Watson, K. and Wilson, N. (1996), 'Do small businesses have to practice marketing to survive and grow?', *Marketing Intelligence and Planning*, Vol. 14, No. 1, pp. 6–18.

Jamal, A. (2002), 'Playing to win: A qualitative study of marketing mix practices of small ethnic retail entrepreneurs in the UK', Paper presented at the Academy of Marketing conference, University of Nottingham, UK.

Kohli, A. and Jaworski, B.J. (1990), 'Market orientation: the construct, research propositions and managerial implications', *Journal of Marketing*, Vol. 53 (October), pp. 40–50.

Kotey, B. (2005), 'Goals, management practices and performance of family SMEs, *International Journal of Entrepreneurial Behaviour and Research*, Vol. 11, No. 1, pp. 3–24

Kotey, B. and O'Donnel, C. (2002), 'Data envelopment analysis in SMEs: A study of the Australian food, beverage and tobacco manufacturing industry', *Small Enterprise Research*, Vol. 11, No. 2, pp. 107–120.

Kotler, P. (2003), *Marketing Management: Analysis, Planning, Implement and Control*, 11th edn, Englewood Cliffs, NJ, Prentice Hall.

Kraus, S., Harns, R., and Schwarz (2006), Strategic planning in smaller enterprises – new empirical findings, *Management Research News*, Vol. 29, No. 6, pp. 334–344.

London Development Agency (LDA) (2004), London BME Action Plan Business Support Advice.

McDonald, M. (2003), *Marketing Plans: How to Prepare Them, How to Use Them*, 5th edn, Elsevier Butterworth-Heinemann, Oxford.

McDonald, M. (2007), *Marketing Plans: How to Prepare Them, How to Use Them*, 6th edn, Elsevier Butterworth-Heinemann, Oxford.

Miles, R.E. and Snow, C.S. (1978), *Organizational Strategy, Structure, and Process*, McGraw-Hill, New York.

Pelham, A.M. and Wilson, D.T. (1996), 'A longitudinal study of the impact of market structure, firm structure, strategy, and market orientation culture on dimensions of small-firm performance', *Journal of the Academy of Marketing Science*, Vol. 24, No. 1, pp. 27–43.

Porter, M.E. (1980), *Competitive Strategy*, Free Press, New York.

Ram, M. (1999), 'Unraveling social networks in ethnic minority forms, *International Small Business Journal*, Vol. 12, No. 3, pp. 267–284.

Ram, M. and Smallbone, D. (1999), 'Ethnic minority enterprises in Birmingham', Paper presented at the 2nd Ethnic Minority Enterprise Seminar, London, November.

Smallbone D., Bertotti, M. and Ekanem, I. (2005), 'Diversity in ethnic minority business: The case of Asians in London's creative industries', *Journal of Small Business and Enterprise Development*, Vol. 12, No. 1, pp. 41–56.

Stanworth, J. and Purdy, D. (2003), *SME Facts and Issues: A Compilation of Current Data and Issues on UK Small and Medium Sized Firms*, London: Westminster Business School, University of Westminster.

Chapter 23

Contemporary issues in entrepreneurship marketing

Sustainability, ethics and social responsibility

Sonny Nwankwo and Darlington Richards

LEARNING OBJECTIVES

After reading this chapter, you will be able to:

■ develop an understanding of some of the potent contemporary issues (sustainability, ethics and social responsibility) confronting SMEs

■ understand how these might impact SMEs in their marketing operations

■ demonstrate an awareness of how these issues might be managed or integrated into marketing decision processes

■ understand that higher levels of sensitivity to sustainability, ethics and social responsibility values could contribute to marketing excellence and sustainable entrepreneurship.

INTRODUCTION

Today's operating market conditions, given their ever-growing level of turbulence and complexity, are likely to be profoundly impactive and strategically more demanding on SMEs than ever before. Acceptably, regardless of the taxonomical complications relating to how SMEs may be classified and defined or the tensions and contradictions arising from efforts to resolves these, there is no escaping the stark reality that many SMEs (especially high-growth SMEs) are increasingly exposed to meta-marketing pressures which large organizations have had to grapple with for a long time. Essentially, a recourse to 'smallness' is no longer a sufficient base to presume that SMEs are insulated from the demands, expectations and obligations that might arise from the wider macro-marketing system. Paradoxically, much of what had hitherto been explained away as extra-competition pressures (e.g. environmentalism) are increasingly finding their way into the mainstream strategic processes of companies and, accordingly, proving to be sources of competitive strengths. For example, Anita Roddick grew her The Body Shop chain from a *value-base* that was unconventional at the time – that is, an ethical stance of non-animal testing of her cosmetic products (see Box 23.1).

It may well be that navigating the contemporary marketplace, in all of its diverse pressure points, may turn out to be more testing for many SMEs than most entrepreneurs currently care to admit. Severe competition, industry capacity gluts, fragmented markets, economic globalization, rapid technological innovation and diffusion, depressed margins and rising costs, global crises that provoke images of the Great Depression and/or the biblical Armageddon are putting many companies between the proverbial rock and a hard place. To compound matters, businesses will be severely challenged to demonstrate higher levels of sensitivity to a much wider battery of renascent societal issues such as the impact of business on the environment, attitude towards promoting sustainable consumption, preserving the ecosystems, upholding the integrity of the marketplace and contributions to sustainable communities. For many SMEs, these are likely to pose 'new marketing challenges' to which they must not only respond but also are required, as a matter of good business practice, to proactively integrate into their strategic processes. More specifically, a growing number of companies will be looking to emphasize their commitment to social responsibility, ethics and sustainability values in an attempt to help differentiate themselves from their competitors and to enhance their brand and reputation (Jones *et al.*, 2008).

BOX 23.1: ENTREPRENEURS' HALL OF FAME: ANITA RODDICK

Love her or hate her, Anita Roddick was an incredibly influential entrepreneur who took a company from a single store to a major retailer and took on large-scale causes that impacted on so many lives. Her 'trade not aid' has invaluable consequences for nations and people around the world. But that is what entrepreneurs do. Entrepreneurs make change. When we look back in history many of the great achievers were thought of as 'nuts' until well after their deaths.

People scoff at things they don't know, can't understand or believe won't make a change. Roddick, founder of The Body Shop, was a true champion for corporate responsibility throughout the world. She viewed business in the greater context of a world that should respect nature, animals, people and employees. She believed business has a profound influence upon social and community economics and to a greater extent the balance of life. These ideals underpinned the strategic development of the company she founded.

Source: Adapted from www.ltbn.com for teaching purposes.

■ *Figure 23.1*
Anita Roddick, founder of The Body Shop

CHARACTERIZING THE MARKETPLACE

The premise of this chapter is that much of what occurs in the contemporary marketplace is governed by symbolic processes – that is, by a rich, ever-changing play of imagery about the relations between persons and things. According to Elliot (1999), the postmodern consumer no longer consumes products for their material utilities but consumes the symbolic meaning of those products as portrayed in their images. Products have become commodity signs and the real consumer has become a consumer of illusions – buying images, not things. Marketing is the active centre of these unfurling processes – in the degree to which it promotes what has been termed the *consumer society* and *hedonistic lifestyle*. O'Shaughnessy and O'Shaughnessy (2008) use the triple platform of marketing, the consumer society and hedonism to deal with some of the contestations around the 'dark side' of consumer marketing: accumulation and display of material possessions, satisfying transitory appetites and created wants, seeking positional goods for social status and social bonding, consumers taking their identity from their possessions, commodification of social life, the impact of fantasy and imagery in influencing buying and an image-saturated environment pressing consumers to buy. In the face of multiple pressure-points (and countervailing forces) which now seem to characterize the environment of marketing, some of the 'consumer society' questions long asked by Nwankwo *et al.* (1993) remain valid:

- How do consumers feel about the state of the marketplace and interrelationships with socio-economic systems in which it is embedded?
- What dominant values does business subscribe to? What drives these values?
- Do consumers trust business as an agency for sustainable development?
- What does the society expect of business (business being a societal institution)?
- Are consumers' views of the marketplace different from those of business?
- What is the nature of interaction among markets, marketing and society?
- What predictions can be made about the evolving marketplace?

In the beginning ...

In the early periods of industrial development, attention was largely focused on producing goods on an ever-increasing scale (the cliché *Fordism* is often applied to capture the mass-production mentality of the era, e.g. the Ford Model T). An ethereal model of rational choice, and concepts of fixed tastes and preferences, dominated economic thought (Leiss, 1983). The process of consumption was assumed to take care of itself. The marketplace was assumed to be the privileged locus for the *satisfaction of wants*. The situation is now changed dramatically, with emphasis shifting from consumer to conserver orientation. For example, the growing use of quality-of-life measures are pointers to attempts to gauge the 'subjective' impact of socio-economic circumstances on people's conception of wellbeing and the inter-subjective aspects of consumption – that is, the relation between the individual's taste and choices and the larger social setting.

Models of the marketplace

Each of us faces a set of moral dilemmas as individual consumers. Take, for example, consumers who care about the environment and are keen to conserve energy on the one hand, but on the other want to use air conditioners, heaters and other appliances that consume energy.

At the level of the individual, these everyday contradictions are difficult to resolve and are much more so in complex organizational settings. However, individuals as well as businesses endeavour to cope based on their respective cognitive models of the marketplace. Thus, how one views the way the interactions take place and are resolved reflects the one's *model of the marketplace*. Just as different people have different models of the marketplace and no single model applies to all situations, the same is true of businesses. However, from a marketing perspective, it has been suggested that a basic view will generally fit one of the following criteria (the schema was first presented by Greyer, 1997):

- Manipulative model: this model portrays marketing's role as basically that of persuading/seducing consumers to buy.
- Service model: marketing's role is to serve the consumer. This is encapsulated in the marketing concept (consumer sovereignty).
- Transactional model: this portrays marketing as a give-and-take operation which is mutually beneficial. Consumption is reflective of each individual's buying criteria (reasoned action).
- Relational model: marketing's role is not simply about satisfying the individual but about building a long-term partnership in which business and consumer are co-development agents.

These perspectives present marketplace interactions, particularly the consumer's situation in broad generality, as more significant than they were thought to be earlier. Many consumers are worried today about their deteriorating environment, the additives in their food, the side effects of the soap they use, the safety and reliability of the goods they buy, the pollution inherent in product usage, food mileage, carbon footprints, integrity of the marketplace (truthful consumer information, consumer education and consumer protection), etc. Increasingly, consumers are expressing a strong desire for a new value system in the marketplace and a higher quality of life in the community. Equally, there have been issues with the 'junk culture' that dominates modern society. Therefore, what is emerging is a growing trend towards re-evaluation of what we (as consumers) buy, how we buy and the purpose of what we buy. Essentially, the prime underpinning is presumably geared towards determining which aspects of consumption do or do not truly weigh up in the quality-of-life scale, with minimal injury to the environment and the community. All of these present serious challenges to business – more particularly the SMEs that may have limited absorptive capacity to engage but nevertheless are expected to respond proactively for their own long-term survival. To help unpack these issues, we lean towards three conceptual prisms: sustainability marketing, ethics and social responsibility.

SUSTAINABILITY MARKETING

Marketing, as a discipline, has continued to exhibit a remarkable capacity to reinvigorate itself and chart new directions in a manner that helps us to make sense of both the continuous and the discontinuous changes taking place in and around business. Theorists (e.g. Kotler *et al.*, 2009; Greyser, 1997) have chronicled the philosophical evolution of marketing to include the following epochal stages:

- product orientation
- production orientation

- sales orientation
- market orientation
- societal marketing orientation
- social marketing orientation.

Also evident in the contemporary chronicle is the *relationship marketing* concept and, more recently, *sustainability marketing*, reflecting the role of marketing in sustainable development. Sustainability marketing is used as a broad canvas to accommodate a range of concepts allied to sustainability such as ecological marketing, environmental marketing (which is sometimes used interchangeably with 'green marketing'), ethical marketing, consumerism and elements of social responsibility (Fuller, 1999; Belz and Peattie, 2009).

MARKING THE BOUNDARIES OF SUSTAINABILITY MARKETING

Although issues around sustainability are not altogether new (see Figure 23.2), the resurgence of interests in sustainability marketing is largely driven by the ideals embedded in the Brundtland Report on sustainable development – that is, development that meets the needs of the present generation but without compromising the ability of future generations to meet their own needs (WCED, 1987). As would be expected, there are serious contentions about what constitutes sustainable development and how it should be defined (this angle of inquiry is outside the scope of this chapter but for a bespoke treatment, see, for example, Nwankwo *et al.*, 2010). With this in mind, it is easy to appreciate the varying prisms from which marketing scholars have treated sustainability or sustainable marketing (Belz and Peattie, 2009; Jones *et al.*, 2008; van Dam and Apeldoorn, 2008; Fuller, 1999).

Sustainability marketing is defined as 'creating, producing and delivering sustainable solutions with higher net sustainable value whilst continuously satisfying customers and other stakeholders' (Charter *et al.*, cited by Jones *et al.*, 2008, p. 125). Fuller (1999, p. 4) explains the concept as

> a process of planning, implementing, and controlling the development, pricing, promotion and distribution of products in a way that satisfies the following three criteria: (i) customer needs are met, (ii) organisational goals are attained and (iii) the process is compatible with ecosystems.

We can, thus, conceptualize *sustainability marketing as the formulation and implementation of marketing strategies and activities (production, distribution and promotion decisions) in ways that are sensitive and respectful of both the natural and social environments.* This is a clarion call for marketing processes to be conscious of the need to use ecologically resilient resources (e.g. biodegradable packaging), reduce energy consumption and waste generation, support fair trade initiatives and promote healthier lifestyles and sustainable human ecology. These are by no means strange demands on entrepreneurs. Essentially, entrepreneurs are increasingly confronted with expectations to scale up their awareness of the impact of their operations on the quality of the natural environment, promote sustainable business practice and ultimately strike a balance between profitability and responsible environmental stewardship. For SMEs, sustainability marketing is analogous to the enactment of *multiple logics*, balancing sustainability and profitability in entrepreneurial practice (De Clercq and Voronov, 2009). This requires 'thinking outside the box', because 'companies should begin to prepare for a more sustainable millennium by re-examining the social and environmental impacts of their marketing strategies' (Charter *et al.*, cited by Jones *et al.*, 2008, p. 125). Obviously, companies (both small and large) effect and in turn are affected by a raft of millennium challenges such as those enumerated in the Millennium Project (see Figure 23.2 and also Belz and Peattie, 2009):

- How can ethical market economies be encouraged to help reduce the gap between the rich and poor? Despite the approbation of the Millennium Development Goals, the proportion of the world population living below the poverty threshold (less than US$2 a day) has not shown much significant decline. The literature indicates that SMEs are playing significant roles in poverty alleviation. The role of microfinance institutions in development, especially in Third World countries, is established in development discourses (see also Viswanathnan and Sridharan, 2009).
- How can growing energy demand be met safely and efficiently? How can shortages of life essentials (e.g. food, oil, water, pressures on energy supplies and other forms of life support infrastructure) be met?
- How can ethical consideration become more routinely incorporated into global decisions?
- How can sustainable development be achieved for all? The Millennium Ecosystem Assessment concluded that about 60 per cent of the ecosystem services that support life on earth are used unsustainably. Yet without sustainable growth, billions of people will be condemned to poverty, and much of civilization will collapse (State of the Future Report, 2005).
- How can population growth and resources be brought into balance? The global population has grown by 4 billion since 1950 and is now estimated to be in the region of around 6 billion; it is projected to reach 9 billion by 2050.
- Health: incidences of both curable and incurable diseases (malaria, HIV/AIDS, cancer, etc.) and the ease of transfer from livestock to humans of unfamiliar diseases have impacted quality of life in several regions of the world.
- Migration: massive movements in population groups from rural to urban areas, from developing to developed countries and displacements as a result of wars or natural disaster are key features of the modern age.

Figure 23.2
Fifteen global challenges facing humanity

Source: The Millennium Project: www.millenium-project.org. Used with permission.

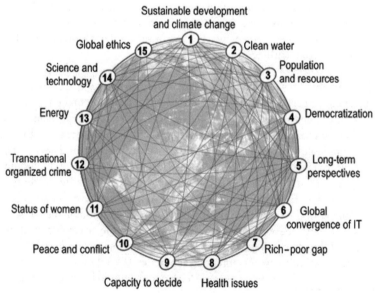

- Adverse climatic conditions: these are resulting in severe weather conditions, growing incidences of flooding, carbon emission and depletion of the ozone layer.

Towards a sustainability marketing orientation

Sustainability marketing embraces a wide array of activities that spans all areas of marketing functions, encompassing how products are produced, communicated and distributed; technology in use; purpose of production and end user/societal/sustainable concerns. The scope of activities is far-reaching, requiring full commitment and a value-driven approach to entrepreneurship. It is, in fact, a requisite philosophy and culture of sustainable entrepreneurship. An appropriate orientation will reflect the degree to which an SME integrates sustainability values within its entrepreneurial culture; a change in traditional marketing orientation (focused on widening marketing scope) to sustainability marketing orientation (SMO) (with added focus on protecting social stakeholders and the natural environment). A firm's SMO may be revealed along a continuum, at the opposite ends of which are located a reactive, low-profile stance and a proactive, high-profile stance (see Nwankwo, 1995, for an illustrative framework for diagnosing a customer orientation). Two issues (philosophical positioning and implementation readiness) are therefore important in this respect:

- *sustainability marketing orientation* (i.e. the degree of acceptance of sustainability ideals and how the values are embedded in the philosophy of entrepreneurship)
- *sustainability marketing strategy* (the extent to which sustainability values are integrated into marketing strategy processes and implementation decisions).

These two dimensions must gel together in any firm that wishes to be taken seriously on the sustainability marketing agenda. However, the 'acid test' lies in (a) how firms frame their understanding of sustainability marketing and (b) how they align their strategies to deliver the vision.

REDEFINING THE MUNDANE – HOW SMES CAN MAKE PROGRESS ON SUSTAINABILITY MARKETING

In one of the most recent and comprehensive expositions of sustainability marketing, Belz and Peattie (2009, pp. 271–272) argue that progress towards sustainability marketing requires the reframing and rethinking of many aspects of conventional marketing, including:

- an appreciation of social and ecological problems at macro level
- a basic understanding of the socio-ecological impacts of products on a micro level
- a change of emphasis from economic exchange to building and maintaining relationships with consumers
- a critical reflection on the basic assumptions of marketing, its norms and values
- moving beyond the consideration of products and services to see the delivery of benefits to consumers in terms of providing them with solutions
- an emphasis on the total economic and non-economic cost of consumption instead of simply price
- communication as a two-way dialogue that builds relationships with consumers rather than an emphasis on the unidirectional promotion of products to them
- the necessity of sustainability marketing transformations within and by the companies.

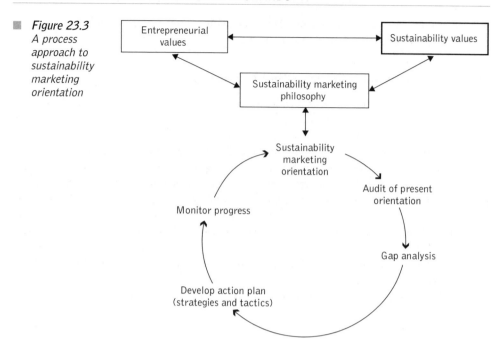

Figure 23.3
A process approach to sustainability marketing orientation

Figure 23.3 sets out the steps, rudimentarily, that SMEs may take to develop a SMO. In doing so, they will need to address the following questions:

- Purposefulness: *where* does the business want to be? Analyses at this level will lead to reconciling entrepreneurial values with sustainability ideals.
- Take a philosophical stance: *why* does the business want to be where it wants to be?
- Develop a sustainability market orientation mission. This must be futuristic and embedded within the ideals of sustainable development.
- Audit presentation orientation: *how* well balanced is the business now in terms of achieving its purpose?
- Develop action plan: *what* does the business need to do to get to where it wants to be?
- Monitor progress: is the business on course towards its stated mission?

ETHICS IN ENTREPRENEURSHIP MARKETING

What is ethics?

The concept of ethics refers to the moral principles and values that generally inform the conduct of individuals. Ethics refers to accepted principles of right and wrong that govern the conduct of a person, the members of a profession or the actions of an organization. It is the study of what constitutes right or wrong and good or bad conduct. Ethical behaviour, on the other hand, consists of the exhibition of those moral or ethical conducts that are considered appropriate within a society or an organization. Interestingly enough, the concept of ethics seems to be susceptible to all kinds of interpretations – that is, it is not only interchangeably used with morality but also it gets mixed up sometimes with law, etiquette and religion. And yet there are discernible differences.

Ethics is said to be something everyone likes to talk about, especially with the current spate of questionable behaviours within organizations, yet nobody knows exactly what it is. It has even been suggested that ethics has an individual value composition – that is, it is what the individual says it is. Because ethics, indeed moral standards, can mean different things to different people, who have many varied opinions or suggestions, it makes it absolutely necessary to articulate a perspective of ethics that is both relevant and comprehensible within a context, business, profession or society.

It is generally agreed that ethics is the study of what is 'right' and 'wrong'. One might immediately ask: "'Right" and "wrong" in relation to who or what?' The answers to this question becomes situational, environmental and circumstantial. This explains why reasonably ethical people may hold different and competing ethical positions on a number of issues, such as abortion, child labour, human rights, environmental preservation, unfair lending practices, etc. This also explains why, during the global meltdown of 2008, amidst contending widespread demands for economic and financial relief, many rational and even ethical people rationalized the moral hazard of bailing out some institutions.

Where do our moral/ethical standards come from? How is it the case that within the same society there could be overlappings in ethical and moral standards? It has been suggested that many things influence us in the moral principles we accept. These include early upbringing, education, the behaviour of those around us, the explicit and implicit standards of our culture, our experiences and our critical reflections of those experiences (Shaw and Barry, 2010).

In this myriad of value judgements, is the normative theoretical delineation of ethical concepts based on outcomes? These are the consequentialist and non-consequentialist theories of ethics. The consequentialist theorists are of the view that the moral rightness of an action is determined solely by its outcome. That is to say, if the consequences of an act are good, then that act is ethical; if the consequences of that action are bad, then that act is unethical. Actions are desirable if they lead to the best possible balance of good consequences over bad consequences. Problems with the consequentialist theory include measuring the benefits, costs and risks of an action, and the fact that the approach fails to consider justice.

The other question that arises is: 'Consequences for whom, the individual or the group?' It has been suggested that the two most important theories in this context are utilitarianism and egoism. Utilitarianism advocates taking into consideration everyone involved and producing the greatest proportion of 'good' for the greatest number of people. Egoism contends that individual self-interest is the primary objective. 'Enlightened self-interest' could not be better explained. Utilitarianism, on the other hand, explains the public and organizational ethical rationale for most decisions involving distributing social benefits much better.

Non-consequentialist (deontology) theories of ethics contend that the diminution of ethics to outcomes or consequences trivializes the meaning and essence of morality. Kantian ethics is based on the philosophy of Immanuel Kant, a leading non-consequentialist philosopher, who argued that people should be treated as ends and never purely as means to the ends of others. 'Right' and 'wrong' should retain their intrinsic value without reference to outcome. In the context of societal complexities and a constantly evolving business environment, one cannot but wonder about the practicality of deontology. Social and business decisions cannot be devoid of cost-benefit analysis in all decision making. For example, should a business make a decision to offer free health care to all of its employees without considering affordability, just because it is the right and moral thing to do, without taking into consideration the cost and its impact on the business's bottom line?

Ethical relativism is the other ethical concept justifiably based on the realization that because our ethics are, among other things, a function of our peculiar culture, environment, upbringing, society, etc., it is therefore conceivable that our ethics must necessarily be open to these variabilities. In his essay, 'Is business bluffing ethical?', Carr (1968) contends that business, as practised by individual and corporations, wears the impersonal character of a game – a game that demands special ethical standards. Essentially, business has its own norms and rules that differ from the rest of society, and a number of things that are normally thought of as wrong are actually permissible in a business context.

According to Shaw and Barry (2010), examples include conscious misstatement and concealment of pertinent facts in negotiation, lying about one's age on a curriculum vitae, deceptive packaging; automobile companies' neglect of safety (for example, Toyota's neglect of its breaking system in the USA in 2010) and utility companies' manipulation of regulators and overcharging of electricity users.

Carr's (1968) comparison of ethical relativism to poker is both instructive and illustrative, albeit misleadingly rationalizing:

> Poker's own brand of ethics is different from the ethical ideals of civilized human relationships. The game calls for distrust of the other fellow. It ignores the claim of friendship. Cunning deception and concealment of one's strength and intentions, not kindness and open-heartedness, are vital in poker. No one thinks any the worse of poker on that account. And no one should think any the worse of the game of business because its standards of right and wrong differ from the prevailing traditions of morality in our society.

The point though is that business must operate within a set of ethical rules of conduct that must take into consideration the established ideals, norms, rules and traditions of the larger society (see Box 23.2). What that means is that certain conducts for business are necessarily prohibited within a given society, and regarded as unethical.

BOX 23.2: VIEWS ON ETHICS

- *Mosaic Law*: do unto others as they do to you.
- *Pareto criterion*: choose actions that are likely to benefit one or more people at the expense of none.
- *Means-end ethics*: the accumulation of wealth is essential to ensure one's survival and growth.
- *Golden rule*: do to others what you would wish them to do to you.
- *Professional ethics*: no one in society is above the law, so everyone must comply with legislation regardless whether or not the law appears nonsensical.
- *Non-interventionist rule*: a free-for-all business practice can create benefits for everyone.
- *Organizational ethics*: there is one rule for business and another for private life.
- *Utilitarian principle*: taking the course of action which is likely to do the most good and the least harm.

There is no such thing as a universal or generally acceptable ethical conduct as ethics recognizes the relativity of moral conducts within nations, organizations and societies. What is acceptable behaviour in one nation may be considered unethical in another. Ethics becomes an issue across nations because of differing political systems, economic systems, legal systems and cultural values. Indeed, cultural relativism also argues that ethics are culturally determined and that firms should adopt the ethics of the cultures in which they operate. In other words, 'When in Rome, do as the Romans do.'

WILL WE WALK ON COMMON GROUND?

One day in the nineteenth century a British merchant ship docked in a Chinese port. It had been a long voyage. The crew members were given shore leave and took advantage of the opportunity to refresh themselves. In the course of the night, a British sailor got into a drunken brawl and killed a Chinese coolie.

The response of the local Chinese governor was immediate and exact. A posse of armed men trotted down to the quay, seized the first British sailor they met, chopped his head off, and trotted smartly back to barracks. The captain of the merchantman was outraged. He stormed into the governor's residence to make an angry protest.

The governor was surprised, and said: 'Why are you so angry? You English are so keen on justice. I have done justice. Have a cup of tea?'

'Justice?' replied the captain. 'What d'you mean "justice"? You executed the wrong man!'

'The wrong man?' asked the governor. 'I do not understand. You kill one of mine, so I kill one of yours. That's fair isn't it? After all, I could have killed 10.'

Questions

1. What ethical theory best describes the decision of the Chinese governor?
2. Summarize and evaluate other ethical issues raised in this case.

Source: 'Will We Walk on Common Ground', adapted from the *Financial Times*, 24 December 1999, for teaching purposes only.

Ethical behaviour in entrepreneurship marketing

Ethical behaviour in business is that premised on the generally accepted and permitted conduct in that line of business. These may also reflect the laws and regulations that affect social and economic behaviour in that society. For SMEs, this can be very challenging, given their organizational and resources constraints. And given the mushrooming of SMEs and their deadly competitive drive for market share and profit, the ethical compromises can be compelling. Because of the relative use of 'good' and 'bad' in the context of ethical behaviour in a particular business, how does one begin to rationalize the conduct of an estate agent who deliberately misrepresents the income of prospective homebuyers, and thus their capacity to make mortgage payments, just because he/she must meet a sales quota? Is it ethical to turn a blind eye to obvious falsehood? What should be the agent's ethical responsibilities? Again, is it ethical for a bank to package Credit Default Swaps (CDSs) and Collateralized Debt Obligations (CDOs), trade them to unsuspecting investors and brazenly go ahead to take out insurance protection for their eventual default, knowing full well that the underlying assets are worthless? In essence the bank is gleefully betting on the failure of a debt instrument it created. What is 'wrong' about insider trading? Where does the moral or ethical responsibility lie? Who is 'harmed' in these practices? There are no easy answers (see Figure 23.4 for possibilities).

Figure 23.4
Schema for evaluating ethical stances

	Legal	Illegal
Ethical	Ethical legal	Ethical illegal
Unethical	Unethical legal	Unethical illegal

Towards a strategic response

There is clearly no cut-and-dried answer to ethical questions or decision-making processes – they can be very situational. In SMEs the roots of unethical behaviour may be complex and generally reflect ethical dilemmas (situations where none of the available alternatives seem ethically acceptable) of small businesses; they nonetheless encompass familiar preoccupations like individual ethics, decision-making processes, leadership, performance expectations and organizational culture. It is also the case that some of the more common areas where ethical issues arise in SMEs are employment practices, human rights, environmental pollution, corruption and product and service quality and durability.

In order to assist SMEs to manage their ethical situations and sometimes dilemmas, it is necessary to articulate some ethical guidelines or code of conduct to help them and their employees navigate the myriad situational and environmental relativities and achieve a more acceptable utilitarian outcome. Because SMEs differ in their organizational focus and customer or stakeholder expectations, these guidelines should be dynamic and evolutionary. They will be different for every organization. This, indeed, makes it unrealistic to use a prescriptive model or form of dos and don'ts. However, helpful and useful ethical guidelines should contain some basics. According to Lamb *et al.* (2011), such guidelines have a number of advantages:

- the guidelines help employees identify what their firm recognizes as acceptable business practices
- a code of ethics can be an effective internal control on behaviour, which is more desirable than external controls like government regulation
- a written code helps employees avoid confusion when determining whether their decisions are ethical
- the process of formulating the code of ethics facilitates discussions among employees about what is right and wrong, and ultimately leads to better decisions.

SOCIAL RESPONSIBILITY

Social responsibility (SR) refers to the idea that businesses and business people should take the social consequences of economic actions into account when making business decisions, and that there should be a presumption in favour of decisions that have both good economic and good social consequences (Hills, 2011). It refers to a business and business people having healthy concerns about the society in which they operate. The newest theory in social responsibility, called *wholesome sustainability*, is best demonstrated by businesses taking into consideration both the long-range best interests of the company and the company's relationships to the larger stakeholder society in which it operates (Lamb *et al.*, 2011).

SR incorporates varied components that demand evolving obligations that are constantly changing with the dynamism of a rapidly evolving global environment. The concept of SR, in relative terms, may mean a set of different sensibilities and expectations in the UK, the USA, China, Brazil, South Africa or even India. It should be noted, therefore, that SR has a particular environmental and societal need correlation to it. A recent study that asked businesses whether they considered SR factors when making decisions found that in Brazil 62 per cent did, in Canada 54 per cent did, in Australia 52 per cent did, in the USA 47 per cent did, in India 38 per cent did, in China 35 per cent did and in Mexico 26 per cent did (One Planet Economy 2007).

SR has four seemingly interdependent components:

- economic (pursuit of profits)
- legal (obey the law)
- ethical (do what is right, fair and just)
- philanthropy (good corporate citizenship).

There are contentions as to the true ethical role of business, in terms of the SR of business. Do businesses have a primary and overriding purpose, as is stated in the memorandum and articles of incorporation setting up the business? This purpose is believed to be one of a duty of care and responsibility to the shareholders, for whom business assets are held in trust; the business cannot misapply these assets by 'giving back' and indulging general societal goodwill businesses unless such 'extra-curricula activities' are for the benefit and purposes of the business and in furtherance of generating profits/value to the shareholders. To the larger society, the business owes superior products and services, paying taxes and obeying the laws and regulations. The SR of business has, in recent times, been exaggerated to include all kinds of activities that hitherto belong to the government, including the provision of some social services like health care, educational services and food banks, to name a few. Governments collect taxes from businesses and other taxpayers for the purposes of providing such services; businesses ought not to have such added social responsibility beyond creating and delivering value to the customers.

Milton Friedman's doctrine (Friedman, 2002) is premised along these lines. He suggests that the only SR of business is to increase profits, so long as the company stays within the rules of law. He argues that when business executives spend more money than they need to to purchase delivery trucks with hybrid engines, pay higher wages in developing countries or even donate company funds to charity, they are spending company funds outside the company's overriding primary purposes. Better to pay dividends and allow shareholders the discretionary allocation of their social goodwill.

For SMEs, SR takes on a whole new meaning and significance. Should their level of SR be one of modified expectations or equal responsibility? Should they be subject to the same rules when it comes to child labour, human rights, environmental preservation, unfair lending practices, defective product liability, unfair trade practices, etc.? They should. To hold otherwise would not only be unfair but also would undermine the underlying premises of social ethical responsibility.

SR has different meaning and relevance to SMEs, depending on the kind of business, their particular focus or, indeed, emphasis. For example, a dry-cleaning business may have acute SR sensibilities when it comes to the chemicals it uses and its greenhouse impact on the environment. A small retail business may be ethically sensitive to its return policies, by ensuring that they are explicit and not incomprehensibly buried in the fine print of the

379 ■

receipt. Whatever their organizational focus it should indeed be the case that a business's SR recognizes its obligations to the larger stakeholder society in its product and service delivery.

Responding to SR

The absence of any agreement on what SR means implies that response strategies are likely to be varied, reflecting each player's philosophical positioning and sensitivity to social issues. Response models generally discernible from the extant literature include:

- Regulatory model: this model is encapsulated in the cliché *'the business of business is business'* – well, so long as regulations are adhered to.
- Defensive model: perhaps the best way to represent this model is *government of the society is not the business of business*. Therefore, business has a duty to put its interests first and protect them accordingly.
- Deceptive model: this response model is closely in line with the Machiavellian principle *the end justifies the means*. Many businesses are not really 'very open and truthful' about their social responsibility credentials.
- Accommodative model: proactively driving forward social agenda – business-driven social activism (e.g. The Body Shop).

SUMMARY

To use a theatrical analogy, today more than ever before SMEs perform on a stage where other actors (e.g. conscientious stakeholders, environmentalists, consumerists) and the sets (marketing environments) change frequently and there is no guarantee that the play will not be cancelled because of a lack of response from an unappreciative audience. Continuing with this analogy, SMEs should be certain that many of their performances will receive critical reviews from social observers, regulatory bodies, consumer interest groups, etc. Thomas Petit (1964), in his famous book *Freedom in American Economy*, reminded us that in every society there is more or less continuous interaction between social values and economic institutions. Values may be thought of as sustainability-derived normative standards which act as a filter in the articulation of ends or in pursuits of certain goals. Therefore, the concept of value will be a central tool in the analysis of how economic actors play their roles.

Indeed, sustainability, ethics and social responsibility (SESR) values bestride the modern entrepreneurial landscape like a colossus. In today's dynamic society, pressures to adapt and respond to renascent social and environmental values are proving enormous. For SMEs, it cannot be business as usual. The higher the level of commitment to the emerging values, the greater the chance of success in navigating the murky waters of entrepreneurship. SESR values are not transient values. They meet the criteria of acceptance of what constitutes dominant social values in sociological interpretations because they are:

- Extensive: the proportion of the population that hold and propagate SESR values has grown exponentially.
- Durable: SESR values are not a fad.
- Intense: SESR are not only receiving a surge of societal affirmation but also the severity of sanction connected with contra-behaviour is growing.
- Esteem – that is, prestige of value carrier: front runners in accepting and implementing

SESR values are held in high esteem and, accordingly, are more likely to achieve superior and sustainable market positioning.

KEY TERMS

- Environmentalism
- Ethical dilemma
- Marketplace integrity
- Social responsibility
- Sustainability marketing
- Sustainability values

REVIEW QUESTIONS

1. Distinguish between conventional marketing orientation and sustainability marketing orientation.

2. What obstacles do you anticipate that a typical SME might encounter in adopting a sustainability marketing orientation? How might such obstacles be overcome?

3. Should ethics matter to SMEs?

4. What do you understand by 'social responsibility'? Suggest how a named SME might develop a proactive SR stance through its marketing operations. Be sure to justify your suggestions.

GROUP ACTIVITY

Justify the logic of sustainability marketing. Using secondary sources of data, identify companies that achieved market growth as a result of adopting and implementing sustainability values.

Check out the following websites: (a) One Planet Economy Network (www.oneplanet economynetwork.org) and (b) One Percent Club (www.onepercentclub.org). Develop an argument, supported with real-life illustrations, to justify or debunk firms' commitments to sustainability. Should SMEs be encouraged to become members of such networks?

CASE STUDY 23: WHEN THERE IS NO LONGER HONOUR AMONG THIEVES

Opportunity recognition, speed and flexibility have become the holy grail of successful SME operations. In the present austere economic times, small-scale moneylenders, especially those operating in many inner cities, are becoming adept in their brand of 'entrepreneurial marketing'. With the recurrent company closures, job losses, tight formal employment markets, lack of growth in salaried employment and attendant family budgeting constraints, small-scale lenders are doing a brisk business and raising the bar in their entrepreneurialism. To compound matters, the banks (wising up after the near catastrophe brought about by the recession) have not responded proactively to entreaties to lend more to business and thereby ease the credit crunch – a situation that benefits 'loan sharks', as they are often called.

Recently, evidence of untoward practices started to surface in many parts of the UK as a result of the credit crunch. According to an official of the Trading Standards Institute, 'We are experiencing a considerable increase in the number of people who turn to loan sharks because it is becoming harder for consumers to obtain credit. If people are looking to borrow, they need to ask the lender to see their consumer credit license as this is proof the lender is legal'. Joining the campaign against loan sharks, the Citizens Advice Bureau and the Birmingham Illegal Money Lending Team, in association with the Office of Fair Trading in London, urged consumers during National Consumer Week 2010 to think carefully before dabbling in potentially life-threatening situations. 'We want to get the message out there that you are likely to get ripped off if you borrow from someone without a license and could end up costing a lot more than you are expecting.' The consumer minister, Gareth Thomas, had this to say: 'Let the unscrupulous and predatory lenders be warned – if they try to draw families into the murky world of illegal money lending, they will face investigation and prosecution by anti-loan shark teams working across the country.'

The fact is that some of the moneylenders operating in the country are not licensed. According to the Office of Fair Trading, anyone who borrows from an unlicensed moneylender is likely to get a loan on very bad terms, pay an extortionate rate of interest, be harassed if you get behind with your repayments and be pressured into borrowing more from them to repay one debt with another.

The banks have not come out unscathed either. They have been accused of bringing about the conditions that are leading more and more people into debt and now discriminating against the very people they have blacklisted as poor borrowers. Recently, the UK Chancellor of the Exchequer pointed out that 'the inability to access a bank account can prevent some of Britain's poorest people from joining mainstream society by making it more difficult for them to receive pay cheques and pay bills.' While this might be at the personal or consumer level, the same applies for small businesses who depend on the banks to be able to revitalize their operations.

Consequently, it is not surprising that small-scale moneylenders have recognized this opportunity and have been quick to respond to the growing need for quick loans. Furthermore, they have been flexible enough to make the cost of borrowing (at face value) less tedious. While this might have brought some form of respite for small businesses and individuals who can now secure finance more easily, there seems to be a catch, as the hidden costs of borrowing have given rise to questions. The ethical concerns range from (a) exorbitant interest charges – in one case an illegal loan shark charged one family an extortionate 1,200% interest (ITV News, 2010) to (b) use of violence rather than civil legal means to resolve credit default or repayment difficulties. Only recently, an ITV Wales investigation has found that while many families have struggled to bring home the bacon loan sharks have grown fat from their misery. Around a hundred are now thought to operate in Wales, dishing out quick cash but threatening violence when payments are missed.

The problem has now become so widespread that the UK government has set up a website to report loan shark activity, as well as to provide advice for potential borrowers. While all of these developments are happening, however, some questions need to be asked: Is there a need to regulate entry into financial services by SMEs? Should moneylender SMEs in the sector be made to advertise their ethical or corporate social responsibility ethos on their websites? Is it only a few of these small-scale lenders that are tarnishing the image of the sector? Are there any industry standards in this sector and who are the key leaders? What are the key ethical issues raised in this case?

QUESTIONS

1. What would be your suggestions for resolving the issues you have identified?
2. Assume that you have been hired by a group of 'industry players' to help develop an ethical statement. Give your presentation. You should be ready to outline what principles you considered and rationalized in finalizing your assignment.

Source: Compiled from Independent Television Network (ITN) news reports between 11 and 24 March 2010, and the Support Agency, Directgov, http://stoploansharks.direct.gov.uk/index.html (accessed 24 March 2010).

REFERENCES

Belz, F. and Peattie, K. (2009), *Sustainability Marketing*. Chichester: John Wiley.

Carr, A. (1968), Is business bluffing ethical? *Harvard Business Review*, Vol. 46, January–February, pp. 143–153.

De Clercq, D. and Voronov, M. (2010), Balancing sustainability and profitability in entrepreneurial practice: an institutional logics perspective. Paper presented at the ICSB 2009 World Conference, Seoul, 21–24 June.

Elliot, R. (1999), Symbolic meaning and postmodern consumer culture, in Brownlie, D., Saren, M., Wensley, R. and Whitington, R. (eds), *Rethinking marketing: towards critical marketing accounting*. London: Sage Publications.

Fraj-Andres, E., Martinez-Salinas, E. and Matute-Vallejo, J. (2008), A multidimensional approach to the influence of environmental marketing and orientation on the firm's organizational performance. *Journal of Business Ethics*, Vol. 88, pp. 263–286.

Friedman, M. (2002), *Capitalism and Freedom*. Homewood, IL: Richard D. Irwin.

Fuller, D. (1999), *Sustainable Marketing: Managerial-ecological Issues*. Thousand Oaks, CA: Sage.

Greyser, S. (1997), Janus and marketing: the past, present, and prospective future of marketing. In Lehman, D. and Jocz, K. (eds), *Reflections on the Futures of Marketing*. Cambridge, MA: Marketing Science Institute, pp. 3–35

Hills, C. (2011), *International Business: Competing in the Global Market Place*. 8th edn. New York: McGraw-Hill.

HR Magazine (2007), Global companies are giving back, 1 June, p. 30.

Jones, P., Clarke-Hill, C., Comfort, D. and Hillier, D. (2008), Marketing and sustainability. *Marketing Intelligence and Planning*, Vol. 26, No. 2, pp. 123–130.

Kotler, P., Keller, K., Brady, M., Goodman, M. and Hansen, T. (2009), *Marketing Management*. Hallow, Pearson Educational Ltd.

Lamb, C. W., Hair, J. F. and McDaniel, C. (2011), *MKTG 4*. 4th edn. Mason, OH: South-Western, pp. 32–34.

Leiss, W. (1983), The icons of the marketplace. *Theory, Culture and Society*, Vol. 1, No. 3, pp. 10–21.

Marc, G. (2005), Will social responsibility harm business? *Wall Street Journal*, 18 May, p. A2.

Nwankwo, S. (1995), Developing a customer orientation. *Journal of Consumer Marketing*, Vol. 12, No. 5, pp. 5–15.

Nwankwo, S, Chaharbaghi, K. and Boyd, D. (2010), Sustainable development in sub-Saharan Africa: issues of knowledge development and agenda setting. *International Journal of Development Issues*, Vol. 8, No. 2, pp. 119–133.

Nwankwo, S., Richardson, B. and Montanheiro, L. (1993), Consumer issues in the evolving environment:

characterisations of the UK marketplace. *Journal of Consumer Studies*, Vol. 17, pp. 313–323.

One Planet Economy (2009), Scenario Scoping Report. www.oneplaneteconomynetwork.org. Accessed 17 May 2010.

O'Shaughnessy, J. and O'Shaughnessy, N. (2008), Marketing, the consumer society and hedonism. In Tadajewski, M and Brownlie, G. (eds), *Critical Marketing: Issues in Contemporary Marketing*. Chichester: John Wiley, pp. 187–210.

Petit, T. (1964), *Freedom in American Economy*. Homewood, IL: Richard D. Irwin.

Shaw, W. and Barry, V. (2010), *Moral Issues in Business*. 11th edn. Belmont, CA: Thomson Wadsworth.

State of the Future Report (2005), 'Global challenges for humanity'. The Millennium Project. Available at: http://www.millennium-project.org/millennium/challenges.html. Accessed 14 June 2010.

van Dam, Y. and Apeldoorn, P. (2008), Sustainable marketing. In Tadajewski, M. and Brownlie, D. (eds.), *Critical Marketing: Issues in Contemporary Marketing*. Chichester: John Wiley, pp. 253–269.

Viswanathan, M. and Sridharan, S. (2009), From subsistence marketplaces to sustainable marketplaces: a bottom-up perspective on the role of business in poverty alleviation. *Ivey Business Journal*, Vol. 73, No. 2.

World Commission on Environment and Development (WCED) (1987), *Our Common Future*. Oxford: WCED.

Chapter 24

Religion and the SME

Andrew Lindridge

LEARNING OBJECTIVES

After reading the chapter, you will be able to:
- understand what religion is, what it constitutes and why religion should not be viewed as a homogenous entity
- recognize how religion affects behaviour and identity, and how this affects SMEs
- appreciate how religion affects SMEs at an operational level
- identify the marketing opportunities that religion offers SMEs
- appreciate how religion can be used by SMEs from a strategic perspective.

BOX 24.1: HALAL OR NON-HALAL?

Does Halal meat taste so different from non-Halal meat? Should we be bothered or, more importantly, should we even care? Depending upon your ethnic background, the size of your organization or the country you live in, the responses may vary from indifference to strongly emotional. (In case you do not know what Halal meat is, it is meat where the animal has been killed in such a way that the body is drained of its blood, as prescribed by Islamic law. At the same time prayers are said for the animal's soul as recognition for the loss of its life, which makes it in some ways more considerate than the way the West slaughters its animals.)

In fact the issue of Halal meat, in 2010, has become a hugely political issue in France where a franchised burger chain recently introduced Halal meat into its burger recipes. The restaurant, situated in a Paris suburb and operating as an SME, simply responded to its predominately Muslim community's needs and witnessed its sales increase rapidly over the following weeks. As far as business goes, this makes great commercial sense. After all, marketing gurus have spent years extolling the values of giving your customers what you want and reaping the profits in return.

The topical issue of religion is often inflamed by a biased media, personal ignorance or simply naïvety. Religion is often seen as a negative force that is the cause of all problems in a society – a perspective which brings us back to Halal burgers and France. The French government has now, rightly or wrongly, decided that the issue of Halal meat is a threat to secular France – a threat so great that the government is now considering making its sale illegal (along with Kosher (Jewish) meat – and any other religion's treatment of food that can be deemed non-secular).

Is Halal a threat to our Western secular societies? Should we even care, or, more importantly, what is religion and how does it affect SMEs? While the threat, real or not, of Halal to Western society is something we do not have the space to discuss here, we will be able to answer the other questions. By the end of this chapter you should be able to articulate what religion is and the problems and opportunities it poses for SMEs.

INTRODUCTION

The term 'religion' in the twenty-first century is likely to provoke feelings of tension and fear for some individuals and peace and tranquillity for others, but what exactly is religion? Before we explore this issue let us get one issue clear – the world may think it is getting more religious but it would appear that not all is what it seems.

Americans buy in excess of 20 million bibles every year, with each American home owning on average four bibles (*The Economist*, 2007). Yet according to a Gallup survey, half of Americans are unable to name the first book of the Bible (Genesis), two-thirds think the Sermon on the Mount was spoken by the evangelical preacher Billy Graham (it was in fact Jesus) and over 25 per cent do not realize what Easter is meant to celebrate (the Resurrection of Christ and the foundation of the Christian religion). The figures are not much better when it comes to reciting the Ten Commandments (only 60 per cent can do this), while 12 per cent of Americans thought Noah was married to Joan of Arc (a French knight who helped drive the English out of France in the fifteenth century).

Matters are not much better for Muslims either, with the general preference being to read the Quran in its first language – original, old, Arabic. In its original form, Arabic is difficult to understand for most Arabic speakers (who are use to a more modernized version), while only 20 per cent of Muslims actually speak Arabic.

What then can SMEs conclude about religion from this? First of all, religion should not be interpreted or understood from a strict perspective. Religion is often what individuals choose to believe. Second, and perhaps most importantly, religion should be viewed from an identity perspective. It is this perspective that offers the biggest opportunity for SMEs, as we shall discover.

TOWARDS AN UNDERSTANDING OF RELIGION

Religion has been described as one of the most important cultural forces and influences on human behaviour (Delener, 1990), reflecting an acceptance of another, superior, being over humanity (Durkheim, 1976). Such is the influence of religion over individuals that it is often considered to be the most important aspect of a group or society's cultural values, providing a *raison d'être* for that culture to exist. Religion covers a range of topics including beliefs, narrative, practices and symbolism that provide a sense of meaning to the individual's life. The world has six main religions: Buddhism, Christianity, Hinduism, Judaism, Islam and Sikhism. Although there are many other religions, these are the ones that most SMEs are likely to encounter.

When we consider religion and what it constitutes, it is important to recognize that religion is not a homogenous whole but rather a fragmented collection of sub-religions, all of which adhere to some shared, agreed-upon similarity. This fragmentation often arises from historical or cultural reinterpretations and, while important in understanding religion, they only need to be noted here. For example, within Christianity the following religions all share a common belief in Jesus but differ in how they expect followers to live their lives: Catholic, Orthodox and Protestant, the last of which can be subdivided further into Baptist, Church of England, Quaker and so on. While SMEs need not bother themselves with how these individual differences affect them, an awareness and consideration of these differences may be beneficial.

RELIGION, IDENTITY AND BEHAVIOUR

Having identified what religion is and the numerous sub-categories that exist within each religion, we now need to consider how religion affects an individual's identity and behaviour. This is important for SMEs to understand as this will have an effect on both their internal environments (such as staff) and external environments (such as marketing and strategy implications).

In understanding religion's effect on identity, and hence its relevance to SMEs, we need to consider social identity theory. Social identity theory states that an individual's self-concept, i.e. who they are, is derived from their membership of groups (Tajfel and Turner, 1986), such as religious groups. Group membership entails the roles and behaviours, which help the individual in determining their own sense of self-identity; for example, self-identifying yourself with your religion. This process may involve social role performance, where an individual adjusts their behaviour to satisfy the group's expectations – for example, adhering to religious teachings. By developing a particular social role performance, the individual is allowed to adapt their behaviours to suit the context and situation they encounter. Religion's role then in social identity is particularly important in meeting an individual's psychological needs, as religion impacts more comprehensively than other cultural meanings.

An individual's sense of self-identity, then, will not only provide a means of knowing who they are but also provide a means for determining their behaviour. After all, if religion includes a set of prescribed behaviours and provides a sense of identity, then it naturally follows that religion will affect an individual's behaviour. This effect may range from the need to pray through to observing religious rituals on prescribed dates – all important considerations for SMEs, as we shall soon see.

RELIGION AND ACCULTURATION

In discussing the role of religion in identity we also need to consider its importance from an ethnic minority perspective. Most developed economies have ethnic minority populations with differing religious orientations and, as I shall show, these groups can offer SMEs important marketing opportunities. To understand the importance of religion to these groups we need to understand how they relate not only to their religion but also to their own communities and the wider society they exist within. This involves a complex relationship called *acculturation*.

Acculturation describes a 'cultural change that is initiated by the conjunction of two or more autonomous cultural systems' (Social Science Research Council, 1954, p. 974). It represents a bi-directional process, with the individual's behaviours, identification and values relating to both their ethnic and their dominant culture. Therefore, an individual's ethnic and dominant cultural identities represent, to varying degrees, acceptance of both cultures. One of the most relevant models of acculturation groups ethnic minority individuals into differing levels of acculturation and is known as Berry's bi-directional acculturation model (Berry, 1990, 1992, 1997). Berry argued that an ethnic minority individual chooses between maintenance of their ethnic cultural values and the extent that they choose to engage with the dominant host group. This approach leads to four distinct acculturation outcomes: (1) integration (equal interest in engaging with both the dominant and ethnic culture), (2) separation (rejection of the dominant culture in favour of ethnic culture), (3) assimilation (acceptance of the dominant culture and rejection of their ethnic culture) and (4) marginalization (rejection of both cultures). The extent that an ethnic minority individual identifies with these categories will then determine not only their sense of identity but also their behaviours.

How then does religion manifest within these acculturation outcomes and why should SMEs be bothered? Research tells us that religion and its related activities are the most significant aspects of an ethnic minority's identity to be retained after language, leisure activities and dietary habits have changed. An adherence to religion then provides a means to maintain not only the individual's cultural values and identity but also their wider group's (Burghart, 1987; Mearns, 1995; Modood *et al.*, 1994; Vertovec, 1995; Williams, 1988).

The importance of religion, then, to SMEs is that ethnic minorities often demonstrate higher levels of religious adherence as a means of negotiating dissonance arising from cultural interactions. Religion provides individuals with a sense of their own ethnic self-identity in potentially difficult situations, such as dealing with experiences of racial discrimination (Dosanjh and Ghuman, 1997; Dreidger, 1975). Drawing upon religion as a tool for business may provide organizations with organizational, marketing and strategic opportunities, as we shall now explore.

RELIGION AT AN ORGANIZATIONAL LEVEL

The relevance and role of religion within SMEs is perhaps no different than that of larger organizations. Both organizational types exist in a multicultural world, where employees are often drawn from varying religious backgrounds, with each religious background often bringing with it different rituals, belief systems, etc., which often influence how an employee works.

Considering the role of religion within an SME presents the organization with a broad and often diverse range of legal requirements and stipulations that may be unique to one country or to a trading block of countries, such as the European Union. The purpose of this section, then, is not to laboriously list every legal act that may or may not affect SMEs but instead to explore the more generic implications of religion on the SME and its employees. However, as the British Chartered Management Institute argues, the emphasis on religion and the organization lies in the management understanding not only religious differences but also the wider legal implications. Religious issues may include rules and regulations regarding the wearing of the *hijab* (the headscarf worn by female Muslims), *yarmulkes* (the skull caps worn by Jewish males), crosses, turbans, etc., along with prayer and meditation breaks.

However, should an SME be expected to understand and accommodate all the religious needs of its employees? One perspective may argue that the approach required is one of empowering the SME's employees to request that their religious needs are met. This need should not be seen as being difficult to implement by the SME; instead, it should encourage employees to express how allowing this religious need to be met will benefit the SME. For example, if an SME has a large number of Sikh employees then these employees may argue that giving them time off work to celebrate Vaisakhi (the Sikh celebration marking the founding of the Khalsa – an event marking the first five people to be initiated into the now formalized Sikh religion) would respect their religious and cultural needs. The Sikh employees could promise that the time off would be made up and that having the time off would increase their work–life satisfaction and would indirectly lead to increased productivity.

How then should SMEs handle religious diversity among its employees? A general collection of guidelines was offered at the 2008 American Bar Association conference by employment lawyer Michael Homans of Falster/Greenberg PC (based in Philadelphia), Ingrid Johnson of Legal Services of Edison (in New Jersey) and Kevin Henry of the Coca-Cola Bottling Co. They suggested the following workplace practices regarding religion.

Do:
- encourage diversity
- promote tolerance
- promote non-denominational 'values' and ethics
- establish a mechanism to review and consider requests for accommodation
- encourage employees to report any discrimination or harassment
- train managers and HR professionals on religious discrimination, harassment and accommodation
- offer employees opportunities to promote voluntary participation in religious and non-religious activities outside work hours
- be wary of workplace proselytizing
- respect employee beliefs, privacy and dignity
- follow best practices to avoid religious bias, as you would with any equal employment opportunity category.

Don't:
- mandate attendance at religious services
- discriminate at work based on religion or non-religion
- base accommodation decisions on the religion at issue
- allow employees to condemn as 'evil' or 'damned' others who believe differently
- rely on literature of only one religion to promote values or company ethos
- give overly generous or solicitous accommodations to employees of one religion unless you are willing to do so for all
- accommodate individual conduct, speech or religious observances that create a harassing environment for others or otherwise impinge on other employees' rights.

Source: Grossman (2008).

RELIGION AND MARKETING IMPLICATIONS

Another aspect of religion and SMEs is how it affects what the individual consumes (after all, SMEs as we shall soon see can benefit from selling products that adhere to religious laws). To understand this we need to return to our previous discussion on social identity. If our social identity is constructed around a religion then as individuals our need to identify and reinforce that identity will encourage us to consume products that support our beliefs. We saw this earlier in the story of the French burger bar that sold Halal burgers to Muslims; French Muslims bought the burgers because they not only complemented their food tastes (representing their Western acculturated perspectives) but also their religious identities (as Muslims). This consumption act, although appearing to be simple – people eat burgers so why not French Muslims? – represents a much more complicated set of issues.

RELIGION AND MARKETING STRATEGY

For most SMEs marketing strategy will largely be dictated by financial limitations, so the following discussion assumes these limitations. In developing a marketing strategy various religious problems and opportunities will arise. While the following discussion cannot possibly cover all the ins and outs of developing a religious-friendly marketing strategy, it should provide some indication of some of the issues that should be considered.

Price

The traditional concerns that price confronts the SME with are still relevant here, such as how to price to maximize profitability or market share while maintaining competitiveness. However, religious considerations also need to be considered. For example, certain religions specifically state that acts of charity are not only desirable but should be freely offered (Islam and Sikhism, for instance). It is entirely feasible that a small aspect of the profit generated by selling a product be automatically attributed to a previously declared charity as a means of showing and affirming adherence to religious principles.

Product

Issues surrounding product and adherence to religious needs are complicated by different religions often having differing demands. While Christianity may not have any particular religious needs surrounding acts of consumption, other religions do. For example, from a strictly religious perspective SMEs selling products to the Hindu religious market should not include any aspect of animal-related ingredients (especially beef), while Judaism and Islam strictly prevent any consumption of any part of the pig, and the list goes on.

Promotion

Promotion can be particularly problematic for SMEs without the wider complications of religion being included. A good example of this was McDonald's (admittedly not an SME but a good example all the same) and the 1996 Atlanta Olympics. To celebrate the event, McDonald's printed paper bags for its takeaway meals with the various flags of competing countries. To ensure fairness and global coverage, McDonald's included the Saudi Arabian flag. The problem, and McDonald's foolishly did not recognize this, was that the Saudi Arabian flag contains a verse from the Muslim Quran. The Quran, which is central to the teaching of Islam, was now attached to a paper bag that was to be thrown away in a bin. Saudi Arabia protested that the paper bags were distasteful and offensive to Muslims around the world (owing to the Quran verse attached to the bag being thrown away). McDonald's apologized, withdrew the bag and learned a costly lesson.

How then should SMEs approach religion and its influence on promotion? If an SME is particularly targeting a religious group then some consideration of the religion's values and beliefs should be considered. This need not cost a lot of money; a quick chat with a local religious leader would offer valuable insights and offer powerful public relations for getting your message right – a point that McDonald's would have been wise to heed. Generally, though, a number of simple rules can be applied here:

- Don't use religious symbols, as these can be misconstrued by your target audience.

- Understand what religious symbols you can use. For example, in Islam the colour green is considered to be auspicious so using green in promotional materials would be deemed to be positive.
- Do not make jokes or ironic comments about religion in your promotional materials. As religion is embedded within culture, how one individual sees humour is not how another will perceive it.
- Sponsoring local religious events can often be a good means of raising your profile and showing your support for a religious community.
- If in doubt, talk to someone who would be able to offer you advice; inaction can often be more cost-effective than a crassly made wrong decision.

Place

Where the product is sold will largely depend upon what market segment the SME is targeting. In a country where the dominant religion is used as the segmenting variable then the normal rules of place will apply. However, if the SME is targeting a minority population then it is logical that the SME will ensure that their product is sold in the areas where that population dominates. However, this approach also introduces further complications, such as potentially smaller retail outlets unable to hold large amounts of stock, credit facilities for purchasing your products may be sought and, perhaps most importantly, a greater personal relationship between the SME and the local community may not only be sought but also be vital if the SME is to succeed in that market.

RELIGION AND CONSUMER BEHAVIOUR

If an SME is to consider targeting a religious group then it must also consider the wider social context and personal choices that influence the decision to consume a particular product (Cosgel and Minkler, 2004). For example, the social context refers not only to the laws and rules of a particular religion regarding what can be eaten (in the case of the French restaurant, Halal meat) but also the informal social norms that dictate appropriate behaviours. France's Muslim population is widely considered to be one of the most integrated, from an acculturation perspective, so eating a burger – a concept inherited from America – does not represent any particular religious-political issue. For other countries, where integration is not so evident or political opinions differ, this may not hold true. From a marketing perspective, any SME marketing a product that targets a religiously oriented group would need to consider the wider socio-political context that influences their potential market's consumer behaviours.

Personal choices also need to be considered, as the level of religious adherence will influence the extent to which a religious group will purchase a product. This refers to the extent that an individual is strictly religious in their identity and related behaviours.

Previous studies in how religion affects ethnic minority groups provide further insights into both the complications and the opportunities that religion offers SMEs. In particular, Lindridge (2010) studied the effect of religious difference in groups of second-generation British-born Indians who self-identified themselves as Hindu, Muslims or Sikhs. These differences, although reflective of these religious groups, offer some insight into the opportunities and problems that religion offers SMEs when considering how to market their products. In particular, Lindridge found:

- Religion directly affected their participants' consumption behaviours, with their level of brand orientation directly related to their level of religious adherence. While Hindus' and Sikhs' lack of brand orientation was directly influenced by their mother's socialization, Muslim participants felt branded products were un-Islamic – a response that was often in contradiction to their parents'.

- Hindu and Sikh participants were more likely to be influenced by their level of religion and consumption behaviours at a social level than Muslims. In particular, visits to religious institutions produced a need to demonstrate consumption of clothing, etc., that conformed to their community's social expectations – often traditional Indian clothing. Their Muslim participants were, instead, only concerned with meeting Islamic dress codes and often wore Western clothing to religious institutions.

- Wider family narratives around consumption inferred gender and religious differences, with fathers' and male siblings' narratives dominated by conspicuous consumption and to varying extents rejection of, or selective adoption of, aspects of their religion. For the male members of the participant families, religious adherence was not prevalent in their lives; instead, conspicuous consumption was used as a means to construct a social identity but also as a means to demonstrate self-worth and success to their wider community. This finding was not replicated among the female members of their families.

While this example illustrates the opportunities and complexities of religion for ethnic minorities it does illustrate the issues that SMEs face in marketing products to religious groups. How then should SMEs apply religion within a marketing context? Yankelovich and Meer (2006) called for markets to be segmented by non-demographic means to strengthen brand identity and create emotional connections with the organization's consumers. Yankelovich and Meer (2006, p. 124) note, 'Good segmentations identify the groups most worth pursuing – the underserved, the dissatisfied, and those likely to make a first-time purchase, for example'. This approach, then, supports SMEs using religion as a means of segmenting their markets on the basis of actual consumer behaviours that comply with religion's influence on consumption.

RELIGION FROM A STRATEGIC PERSPECTIVE

The final part of this chapter reviews how religion can be used by SMEs to establish a corporate strategy. Hopefully by the time you have read this you will have begun to appreciate that religion can be used by SMEs as an asset to further develop and support the organization. It is from this perspective that we now explore religion and corporate strategy.

In the previous section I suggested that religion could be used as a marketing tool to allow SMEs to target and develop specific market segments. Focusing SMEs' often limited resources on specific niche markets offers opportunities for market growth and profitability. This section continues this premise, using Michael E. Porter's (1980) work on organizational *competitive advantage* as a framework to illustrate how religion can be used from a strategic perspective to gain competitive advantage.

Competitive advantage, Porter (1980) argues, occurs when an organization is able to undertake one activity better than its competitors, and that activity is valued and sought by potential customers. To achieve competitive advantage an organization can undertake one of two strategies:

- *Cost-leadership*: all input costs are reduced to the lowest-possible level and the organization competes on being the cheapest in the market. This approach tends to be short-lived as often new lower cost competitors emerge.

■ *Differentiation*: the organization competes on one aspect of difference from its competitors, but a difference that the market and its customers are willing to pay for.

Reflecting on the needs of SMEs, Porter (1980) notes that within each of these strategies a niche strategy can be pursued, i.e. a cost-leadership niche or a differentiation niche. The emphasis on the niche here reflects that SMEs are unable to compete in larger markets against better-resourced and larger competitors. While it is unlikely that SMEs will be able to compete for long on a cost-leadership basis, the differentiation-niche strategy appears as more appropriate.

Religion has been identified with how individuals perceive themselves, how it affects employees and the potential benefits to SMEs and how it can be used within marketing strategy to increase market share and profitability. Each of these approaches has relied on using religion as a means of achieving a desired corporate objective. It follows, then, that SMEs could use religion as a means of achieving a niche-differentiation strategy and through this competitive advantage. How? Quite simply by focusing the organization's strategy onto a specific religious group and then ensuring that all aspects of the organization meet the above requirements, i.e. the organizational and marketing perspectives that have already been discussed.

Using religion as a means of achieving competitive advantage for SMEs is becoming increasingly common, and a growing number of organizations are specifically following this approach. Perhaps the best example is the emergence and growth of Mecca Cola, which is featured in the case study below.

SUMMARY

The purpose of this chapter has been to explore the business opportunities and problems that religion offers SMEs. The aim, then, has been to explore how religion affects not only the organization but also its marketing and strategic decisions.

From a problem perspective, religion may be perceived as a threat or an entity that is neither understood nor appreciated in its relevance to business. This chapter has suggested that the solution is not in avoiding the issues of religion but instead in embracing it by understanding what it can offer the SME.

Religion also represents opportunities for SMEs. From an employee perspective religion can be used as a means of engaging and motivating employees, representing a win-win situation for the SME and the employer. Marketing should also consider how religion can be used to target specific religious groups by offering products that reflect and support their religious needs. This approach lends itself to SMEs developing a niche-differentiation strategy and through this allowing the organization to achieve a competitive advantage.

> **KEY TERMS**
> - Acculturation
> - Competitive advantage
> - Consumer behaviour
> - Cost-leadership
> - Differentiation
> - Place
> - Price
> - Product
> - Promotion
> - Religion

REVIEW QUESTIONS

1. How important is religion in the contemporary environment of entrepreneurship marketing? Illustrate your answer with real-life examples.

2. Evaluate the connection, if any, between religious values and marketing values in an entrepreneurship context.

CASE STUDY 24: MECCA COLA

Mecca Cola is a cola drink that is sold in over 56 countries around the world and targeted specifically at the Muslim community. The origins of Mecca Cola lie in a combination of marketing opportunity and wider Muslim discomfort over America's policies towards the Middle East. The culmination of this discomfort manifested during the 2002 build-up to the American-led invasion of Saddam Hussein's Iraq, with many Muslims feeling that American policies were deliberately targeting Muslims. Anger towards American foreign policy was not limited to Muslims, with many non-Muslims in Europe also growing increasingly angry and despondent towards America as well. A report by the *Financial Times* at this time noted that within America 12 per cent of the population were boycotting American brands such as Coca-Cola, which they associated with American imperialism (Gapper, 2004). Being a brand associated with American culture suddenly appeared to be a commercial threat.

Mecca Cola, named after the Muslim holy city of Mecca, was launched in 2004. By tasting and looking like any other cola drink, and with its use of red and white labelling and packaging reaffirming its identity as a cola drink, Mecca Cola was able to compete against more-established competitors. However, closer inspection of the packaging reveals the political-social-religious origins of the brand. The labelling includes Arabic text that translates as 'Don't shake me, shake your conscience', with a picture of the Mosque in Jerusalem on the other side.

Owing to the relatively small size of the organization, hence its relevance as an SME example, Mecca Cola suffered from financial restraints, which affected its ability to market its product. These were resolved through relying upon the Islamic religious principles that supported the brand and, hence, appealed to its niche target market. For example, 20 per cent of Mecca Cola's profits were allocated for charity projects, with 10 per cent going to local charities and the remainder to support Palestinian children's charities. Cost restrictions prevented paid-for advertising so a dedicated website was developed (http://mecca-cola.com). The remainder of the publicity came from widespread press coverage interested in a new product that decisively and clearly aimed to be politically, religiously and commercially provocative.

CASE QUESTIONS

1. To what extent do you think Mecca Cola's success is simply down to opportunism?
2. Is the use of religion by Mecca Cola merely utilizing a fad that will eventually see Muslim customers returning to more popular brands such as Coca-Cola?
3. Mecca Cola is clearly using Porter's (1980) niche-differentiation strategy. What problems do you think other SMEs would experience using a similar approach to Mecca Cola?
4. Would the same use of religion work for other religious groups, such as a cola aimed at the Buddhist community?

REFERENCES

Berry, J. W. (1990), 'Psychology of acculturation'. In Berman, J. (ed.), *Nebraska Symposium on Motivation, 1989: Cross-cultural Perspectives. Current Theory and Research in Motivation*, Vol. 37, Lincoln, USA: University of Nebraska Press, pp. 201–234.

Berry, J. W. (1992), 'Acculturation and adaptation in a new society', *International Migration*, Vol. 30, pp. 69–85.

Berry, J. W. (1997), 'Immigration, acculturation, and adaptation', *Applied Psychology: An International Review*, Vol. 46, No. 1, pp. 5–34.

Burghart, R. (1987), 'The perpetuation of Hinduism in an alien cultural milieu'. In Burghart, R. (ed.), *Hinduism in Great Britain: The Perpetuation of Religion in an Alien Cultural Milieu*, London: Tavistock, pp. 224–251.

Cosgel, M. M. and Minkler, L. (2004), 'Religious identity and consumption', *Review of Social Economy*, Vol. 62, No. 3, pp. 339–350.

Delener, N. (1990), 'The effects of religious factors on perceived risk in durable goods purchase decision', *Journal of Consumer Marketing*, Vol. 7, No. 3, pp. 27–38.

Dosanjh, J. S. and Ghuman, P. A. S. (1997), 'Punjabi child-rearing in Britain: development of identity, religion and bilingualism', *Childhood: A Global Journal of Child Research*, Vol. 4, No. 3, pp. 285–303.

Dreidger, L., (1975), 'Search of cultural identity factors: a comparison of ethnic students', *Canadian Review of Sociology and Anthropology*, Vol. 12, pp. 150–162.

Durkheim, E. (1976), *The Elementary Forms of the Religious Life*, London: Allen & Unwin.

Economist, The (2007), 'The Bible v the Koran', 19 December. Online: http://www.economist.com/node/10311317?STORY_ID=10311317 (accessed 8 April 2010).

Gapper, J. (2004), 'Consumers prefer US brands despite foreign policy links', *Financial Times*, 23 February, p. 4.

Grossman, R. J. (2008), 'Religion at work', *HR Magazine*, December. Online: http://findarticles.com/p/articles/mi_m3495/is_12_53/ai_n31160711/pg_9/?tag=content;col1 (accessed 25 August 2010).

Lindridge, A. M. (2010), 'Are we fooling ourselves when we talk about ethnic homogeneity? The case of religion and ethnic sub-divisions amongst British Indians', *Journal of Marketing Management*, Vol. 26, No. 5–6, pp. 441–472.

Mearns, D. J. (1995), *Shiva's Other Children: Religion and Social Identity amongst Overseas Indians*, New Delhi: Sage.

Modood, T., Beishon, S. and Virdee, S. (1994), *Changing Ethnic Identities*, London: Policy Studies Institute.

Porter, M. E. (1980) *Competitive Strategy*, New York: Free Press.

Seul, J. R. (1999), '"Ours is the way of God": religion, identity and intergroup conflict', *Journal of Peace Research*, Vol. 36, No. 5, pp. 553–569.

Social Science Research Council (1954), 'Acculturation: an exploratory formulation', *American Anthropologist*, Vol. 56, No. 6, pp. 973–1002.

Tajfel, H. and Turner, J. C. (1986), 'The social identity theory of inter-group behavior'. In S. Worchel and L. W. Austin (eds), *Psychology of Intergroup Relations*, Chicago: Nelson-Hall.

Vertovec, S. (1995), 'Hindus in Trinidad and Britain: ethnic religion, reification and the politics of public space'. In P. Van der Veer (ed.), *National and Migration: The Politics of Space in the South Asian Diaspora*, Philadelphia: University of Philadelphia Press, pp. 132–156.

Williams, R. B. (1988), *Religions of Immigrants from Indian and Pakistan: New Threads in the American Tapestry*, Cambridge, UK: Cambridge University Press.

Yankelovich, D. and Meer, D. (2006), 'Rediscovering Market Segmentation', *Harvard Business Review*, Vol. 84, No. 2, pp. 122–131.

Chapter 25

Managing marketing resources
The consultant and the SME

Ian K. Bathgate

LEARNING OBJECTIVES

After reading this chapter, you will be able to:

- review entrepreneurial competencies and characteristics
- define the nature of consultancy
- review the need and role for consultants in the SME sector
- assess key issues in the management and relationship between SME resources and the marketing function.

INTRODUCTION

Previous chapters have focused on the differing aspects of SMEs. The aim of this chapter is to approach such aspects from a consultant's viewpoint, 'from the field' as it were. It situates consultancy within the repertoire of critical marketing (and, indeed, management) of resources for SMEs, which are frequently neglected. The effects of mismanagement are obvious: high failure rates.

Accepted knowledge is that up to 80 per cent of new businesses/SMEs fail in their first two years of existence. One of the reasons for this failure is that a large proportion of SME owners lack relevant management knowledge and skills. The typical entrepreneurial characteristics and skill sets of the typical SME owner-manager are that such skills are acquired over a longer time period than conveniently fits their time horizons. The quickest way of accessing those skills is to buy in the knowledge in the form of professional advisers and/ or consultants. The difference between the two is that the former can be rather short-term in nature and be delivered as part of a package of services, e.g. by a small business adviser from a bank. The latter can take place over a longer period of time and can be delivered by a professional consultancy firm (e.g. McKinsey) or by individual practitioners. Regardless of which is chosen the sector as a whole has experienced substantial growth and can be said to include accountants, bankers, business consultants, lawyers and educators.

Therefore, gaining access to and availability of consultancy advice has never been easier. Considering that over 90 per cent of all businesses are small then it can be seen that the market potential for consultancy/advice is great. However, despite contradictory research as to the effectiveness of that advice, it can be said in general that 'consultancy' can be a critical factor for the survival and growth of SMEs. Such services, instead of being seen as a 'bought-in cost', should rather be seen as a potential resource. The key word here is 'service'. The service that a consultant brings to the client is at best intangible and results in a reciprocal exchange between both parties. The exchange that takes place is a transfer of knowledge from one direction and fees and experience from the other.

The aim of this chapter then is to examine the context of the SME/consultant relationship from the perspective of:

- the sector as a whole
- the characteristics and competence skill sets of the SME
- the role of the consultant
- the differing perspectives of the service from an SME and consultant stance
- the nature of the service and the key resource issues.

THE CONTEXT OF CONSULTANCY – THE SME SECTOR

A useful starting point when considering the SME/consultancy interface is the SME sector as a whole. SMEs have been recognized as being fundamental to the economic growth and employment opportunities in Western economies especially since the 1980s. Valry (1999) estimated that 50 per cent of the USA's economic growth in the preceding decade came from SMEs, while Birch (1979) stated that 66 per cent of the increase in employment in the USA between 1979 and 1986 was attributable to SMEs with 20 or fewer employees. Encouragement and the nurture of enterprise and entrepreneurial behaviour among firms and individuals is currently a vital part of the UK government's policy. However, definitions of what constitutes a small firm vary and it is this fact that begins to complicate the sector and sets the context and nature in which consultancy/advice takes place.

Gore *et al.* (1992, p. 15) remarked that: 'Like the proverbial elephant the small firm is one of those things that is recognised when seen but difficult to define.' Storey (1994) notes the absence of a single uniform definition of a small firm, but we instinctively know what they are. The key to understanding this paradox is to understand the main difference between the large company (e.g. a multinational corporation (MNC)) and the SME. In terms of objective measures the MNC will have high levels of capitalization, sales, employees, debt, stakeholders and so on. The SME when compared against such measures would by simple observation be smaller. However, there is also another aspect: definition through sectoral analysis – used as a base for differentiation. For example, a small motor manufacturer such as the Morgan Motor Company would be very different to a small firm in the plumbing sector. Indeed, in terms of employees, sales, profitability, etc., if both Morgan and 'A Plumber' were identical then Morgan would be considered a niche player in its market while 'A Plumber' would be seen as being a large organization in its market. It is really a matter of perception, and context aids definition and differentiation.

As Storey (1994, p. 9) states, 'in some sectors all firms may be regarded as small, while in other sectors there are possibly no firms which are small'. The Bolton Committee (1971) provides us with some form of definition from an 'economic' and 'statistical' perspective. From an 'economic' viewpoint SMEs must meet the following criteria:

- they have a small market share
- they are managed by owners/part-owners in a 'personalized' way – that is, no management structure
- they are independent.

The current definition of SMEs is that published by the European Union (EU) in 1996 and updated in 2004. This was an effort to recognize the many differing perceptions of what constituted an SME across member states. It took into account the changing economic environment and calculated financial thresholds that ensured SMEs within larger organizations did not benefit from SME support schemes. Only genuine SMEs were to be supported. The new definitions thus considered the financial backing and economic strength of an SME. In redefining the typology of SMEs the EU considered three types, the micro, small- and medium-sized. To quote from the *Official Journal of the European Union*:

1. The category of micro, small- and medium-sized enterprises (SMEs) is made up of enterprises which employ fewer than 250 persons and which have an annual turnover not exceeding EUR 50 million, and/or an annual balance sheet total not exceeding EUR 43 million.
2. Within the SME category, a small enterprise is defined as an enterprise which employs fewer than 50 persons and whose annual turnover and/or annual balance sheet total does not exceed EUR 10 million.
3. Within the SME category, a microenterprise is defined as an enterprise which employs fewer than 10 persons and whose annual turnover and/or annual balance sheet total does not exceed EUR 2 million.

This information is summarized in Table 25.1.

Table 25.1 SME categories

Enterprise category	Headcount	Turnover	or	Balance sheet total
medium-sized	< 250	≤ €50 million		≤ €43 million
small	< 50	≤ €10 million		≤ €10 million
micro	< 10	≤ €2 million		≤ €2 million

Source: *Official Journal of the European Union* (2003).

However, it can be seen that this definition also has its drawbacks. The difficulty lies in where and when does the centre of power shift from the few (i.e. owner/part-owner) to the many (i.e. functional area/management structure)? When does the micro business become a small and then medium-sized business? Headcount, turnover and balance sheet may give us objective comparisons but a more subjective market-focused approach may be necessary. This is especially true for the consultant. In any given consultancy interface, while an appreciation of the definitions/nature of the organization and sector are useful, a more focused analysis of the context of the consultancy is probably more valuable. What all this really does is highlight the broad base of the SME sector and, therefore, the wide degree of differentiation in that sector. It is not a case of 'in what respects are SMEs similar'; rather it is the degree to which they differ. A useful starting point for analysis then is from a competency, structure and strategy perspective, as put forward by Storey (1994).

SME COMPETENCIES, STRUCTURE AND STRATEGY

Storey (1994) presents a view that there are in general three contributory factors to SME growth: the entrepreneur (competencies), the firm (structure) and strategy. These can be seen as the sides of a triangle with each side supporting the others. Structure allows for the exploitation of competencies which allows for strategic development and therefore growth; the three are interlinked. This can form a structure or base for analyses of the SME.

Competencies

Why are competencies important? The answer lies in the need for organizations regardless of size to gain a strategic marketing and competitive advantage in the marketplace. How firms gain this advantage has been the subject of vigorous debate between marketing scholars (e.g. Cravens, 1988; Day, 1988; Day and Wensley, 1990) who have emphasized that companies that grow and sustain superior market positions are those that possess unique competencies. This is an important lesson that is frequently lost in many SME contexts. It is often the case that many SMEs simply 'muddle through' in their marketing operations without regard to the need to develop the critical competencies that would sustain their long-term growth.

It is important to recognize though that SME competencies are not the same as MNC competencies. SMEs have unique characteristics and therefore competencies that differentiate them from MNCs. It can be regarded as a grouping of relevant skills relating to a specific activity – for example, unique skills in selling, customer relationships, servicing outlets, product innovation, etc.

The very nature of how these competencies are structured and managed in SMEs is very important. In MNCs, for example, these competencies are invariably clustered into departments or divisions. They become centres of expertise. In an SME these competencies are spread around the organization; the owner may not be a specialist nor possess specialist competencies, e.g. specialized market knowledge. These skills and capabilities are critical marketing resources and where lacking are gained through the use of specialist consultants which must be managed proactively and strategically.

A further consideration is that the competencies of the SME are not formally structured but invariably reside in one or few people, usually the entrepreneur/owner-manager who has therefore to display a range of competencies for different aspects of the business. The result is that the owner-manager or entrepreneur becomes a generalist rather than a specialist. This is probably the key issue that complicates the process of developing and growing SME competencies. It is from this position that a consultant's intervention may be instigated.

A useful approach in understanding this dynamic phenomenon is to divide competencies into two broad categories: technical competencies and decision-making competencies. For example, technical competencies would include marketing functions while decision-making competencies are broader in scope and are the skills developed by the entrepreneur to give strategic direction to the SME in terms of the technical areas. In reality both of these competencies need to be possessed by the SME owner but it is the balance of these two characteristics that is important to the future growth. But as we have seen previously, the SME is restricted in its capabilities which in turn affects the above two competence dimensions.

It is the lack of these skill sets/competencies that leads to failure. Pech and Alistair (1993) noted that the prime reasons for failure of SMEs can be stated as:

- lack of financial planning (*decision making*)
- absence of business records (*technical*)
- no understanding of use of business records (*decision making*)
- poor cash flow management (*technical*)
- poor debtor management (*technical/decision making*)
- poor inventory management (*decision making*)

400

- poor costing, pricing *(technical)*
- poor market research *(technical)*
- over-borrowing *(technical)*.

It could be stated that the constraints on SMEs in developing critical competencies are rooted in the lack of financial resources and the necessary skills to make the most of what limited resources they have. They lack expertise also in key functional areas of the business, such as marketing. The entrepreneur then, if not in possession of multiple skill sets, has to become a 'jack of all trades' but seriously runs the risk of becoming 'master of none'. The entrepreneur calls in a consultant when they realize that rather than being the embodiment of the business they should actually be managing it. This was well summarized in a study (Mughan *et al.*, 2004, p. 428) which indicates a need for 'strategic and soft management skills and knowledge which enable owner-managers to critique their own organisation, re-engineer it and build the competencies needed to succeed in competitive environments'.

Strategy

Why then do SMEs have particular problems with their competence bases and how does this affect strategy? The answer is that the paradigm of multiple skill sets can lead to a variable, unstructured and uncoordinated response to decision making. This is exacerbated by the fact that due to its size the SME has no control over its micro- and macro-environment. This means that from a strategic perspective they will always be reactive and vulnerable to environmental volatility, unless they occupy a niche market with few competitors.

If we regard the characteristics of typical entrepreneurs/owner-managers to include being change-focused, risk-taking, motivated, task-oriented, influenced by cultural background and appreciative of the influence that power has on the SME, then it can be deduced that technical competencies and most decision making, and therefore strategic response, is straight forward and opportunistic in nature and takes place within an unstructured internal environment. Strategy therefore becomes, where present, short-term. It should be noted though that lack of formal structure can also work in the SME's favour, because they can be flexible and the ideal vehicles to deliver innovation to the market whether that is in the technical dimensions of their offering (e.g. product or service design) or in their decision making (marketing strategy).

Structure

In terms of the third aspect of Storey's (1994) three-factor approach, research has shown that a structure facilitates competence development and strategic decision making. Structure also supports a marketing orientation that can contribute to growth; indeed, this is the basis of marketing theory. Debates exist, however, around whether such an orientation results from a specific set of organizational behaviours (Kohli and Jaworski, 1990) or a type of organizational culture (Slater and Narver, 1995).

Becherer *et al.* (2001) state that because SMEs are by definition smaller and therefore less bureaucratic they tend to reflect the owner's characteristics and leadership style. Internal characteristics then will reflect the ability of an SME to adopt a market orientation.

A useful addition to the debate is Hardy (1992), who suggests that every member of the management team in an SME is also a member of the marketing team and should possess marketing competencies. These competencies include identification and solution of perceived marketing issues. He also identifies a set of sub-skills such as identification and analysis of market opportunities, detailed competitor and market analysis, forecasting such things as market and channel behaviour, financial analysis and the management of market information. This represents a broad palette of competency, the lack of which could lead to consultancy recruitment.

In summary, an SME has the possibility because of its nature and structure to offer a unique approach to marketing. It can be said that this is based on:

- the dedication of owner/staff
- an opportunity-focused style based, however, in some instances on a sales orientation
- dynamic customer interface
- flexibility, speed of reaction/response due to lack of formal hierarchies
- easy access to market and management information.

There is though a discrepancy between theory and practice and this is rooted in the nature/competencies of the owner-manager in so far as:

- they are generalists and not specialists
- there is a short-term focus rather than long-term (symptomatic of a sales orientation)
- planning is lacking
- their decision-making style limits their ability to analyse and implement competencies and their ability to identify marketing opportunities, which in turn limits strategy, implementation, organization and control.

Taking the discrepancy between theory and practice as a guide, it is useful for the consultant to be appreciative of the links that exist between entrepreneur competencies, decision making and learning.

THE LINKS AMONG SME COMPETENCIES, DECISION MAKING AND LEARNING

As can be seen from the preceding section, most owner-managers are unlikely to see themselves as 'experts' in any field purely because they have sole responsibility for all aspects of decision making. Even in larger SMEs experience has shown that as the business has grown the owner can be reluctant to delegate responsibility. For example, in one case the owner, despite having recruited an experienced manager from a competitor, would still try to make decisions on minutiae rather than deal with the larger picture. The result was that the focus of organizational decisions was on firefighting rather than development of a growth strategy. The organization had reached a plateau of growth and could not see where the next phase of growth was to come from. In smaller SMEs, decisions made in one specialist area are unlikely to be taken as independent decisions because the defined area may not be distinct but part of another area. This overlap leads to confusion in both decision making and delegation.

A key approach here is that there should be, on behalf of the owner, a consideration of the fact that as the environment changes so does the decision-making competence within the SME. As noted by Boam and Sparrow (1992, cited in Carson and Gilmore, 2000), competencies have a life cycle too! Competencies should evolve and grow alongside the SME and these should be based on four core competencies identified by Carson and Hill (1992, cited in Carson and Gilmore, 2000): Knowledge, Experience, Judgement and Communication. These core competencies form the basis for both informed technical aspects of the business and decision making in functional areas, e.g. marketing. The four core competencies are needed to achieve Experiential Learning (K + E + J + C = EL), which contributes to the competency base for SME marketing decisions. Carson and Gilmore (2000) deal with these aspects in great detail. It is certainly true that without the development of a competency base SME survival is at risk. Engaging a consultant's services is one method of gaining expert competence in particular functional and decision-making areas.

However, looking merely at the SME from a competence, structure, decision-making and strategic perspective gives only a general idea of some of the contextual difficulties the SME/consultant interface presents. To give a more rounded analysis of the client/consultant relationship it is useful to look at the gap in the general contextual perception of the interface by both parties and then the nature of the service provided.

THE GENERAL CONTEXT OF THE CONSULTANT/SME INTERFACE

As discussed previously, a large number of SME failures are due to limited management knowledge and skills. As a result the consultancy sector has grown significantly at all levels. In 2002, 95 per cent of all UK SMEs had used an external adviser over the previous three years (Bennett and Robson, 1999). The literature and research around this area is confusing. Some, for example, Ramsden and Bennett (2005), have found that there is no reluctance on behalf of owner-managers in seeking advice. Others have found that, despite the fact that advice to SMEs has a positive impact on an SME's performance and survival and has a societal value in terms of economic regeneration, there is still a reluctance to seek advice (Christensen and Klyver, 2006). This can be for various reasons, some of which (cited by SMEs) are that consultants or advisers are:

- too expensive
- there is a non-performance gap
- there is a preference by owners to use informal networks such as family.

From a consultants perspective research has shown that SMEs:

- lack professionalism and therefore cannot participate fully in the consultancy process
- lack of strategic outlook
- have a propensity towards firefighting resulting from a focus on smaller issues.

Ramsden and Bennett (2005) differentiate between the 'hard' (e.g. profit, turnover, costs) and 'soft' (ability to manage/cope) outcomes of the consultancy process. With larger organizations these can be accommodated as separate entities. However, due to the nature of SMEs these outcomes are combined and could be seen as parts of the total package of services provided. Outcomes then become confused and interlinked. They go on to conclude that the 'widest effects of external advice seem to be intangible, such as reassurance or reducing uncertainty' (Ramsden and Bennett, 2005). This can lead to dissatisfaction.

In general the size of the SME has an impact in the type of advice sought and types of suppliers of that advice. This means in reality that despite the general increase in SME failures there is also an increase in seeking advice. Within that there are different types of advice and different levels of success and reasons for success. This presents a very diverse picture of consultancy within the SME market. Generalizations can give some help but each SME consultancy will be different and should be regarded as such.

If the issue is to be analysed in greater detail it should then be approached from the apparent gap in understanding of the context of each participant in the process. The next section looks at this from an SME and consultant/adviser contextual base.

THE RELATIONSHIP FROM AN SME PERSPECTIVE

For the SME there is a large choice when it comes to selecting a consultant. Consultants/advisers come in many guises and functional areas. Large accountancy firms offer such specialist services as do marketing agencies and other professional sector businesses. The government offers aid in the guise of agencies such as Business Link and there are a large number of individual consultants plying their trade. A relative newcomer to the area is from the university sector, where consultancy services are seen as a source of what is termed 'third-stream income'. Universities have traditionally sought external funding but this has been mainly for research purposes. With the EU now becoming more active in the recent past, especially in regional development areas, funding for SMEs linked to regeneration via University Knowledge Exchange has proven to be popular. Such activities provide not only revenue but provide the academic with up-to-date industry practice.

However, there is a divergence in opinion as to the effectiveness of consultants/advisers to SMEs cited by Dyer and Ross (2007). There are studies that show a positive effect (McLarty, 1998; Dyer and Ross, 2007) there are also those that show the opposite (e.g. Robson and Bennett, 2000). It is safe to state though those professional adviser–client relationships are not always smooth. Research into this area has indicated a number of reasons. From a client–adviser perspective the nature of the entrepreneur as an independent and risk-taking entrepreneur does not always fit with the need to seek advice, which could be construed as being symbolic of failure. An owner's inflated opinion as to their own competence set may also create barriers which are difficult to overcome. There is also the question of confidentiality and the possible circulation of confidential information, which translates into an issue of trust and a questioning of professional integrity. By far the biggest problem cited by Dyer and Ross (2007) is that there is a perception among SME owners of a deficiency in the services offered to SMEs or that the service is inappropriate. A common perception is that the adviser can offer little to the SME as the advice is expensive, impractical and displays a lack of understanding of the SME environment. The fact that an adviser has little or no experience of running a small business leads to a widening gap between beliefs on the one hand and values on the other.

The root of the problem could be one of culture. The culture of the SME owner is as previously discussed one of independence, risk taking or intuitive decision making characterized by trust and informality in communication within the SME team. In effect, a 'learning by doing' approach is adopted. In such an example experiential learning then takes precedence over theory. These then act as contextual filters through which a consultant interacts with the SME client and form the basis from which the SME evaluates the effectiveness of the activity. The result is that for a successful consultancy to take place the consultant should adapt to the context from which the SME is operating. A sensitivity or empathetic approach is needed from the consultant. Another consideration could be that from an SME perspective owner-managers do not have an adviser recruitment cycle, there is no specific routine to adhere to.

As such it might be stated that there is a lack of experience-based understanding of the context of their own role as owner in the consultant interface (Christensen and Klyver, 2006).

THE RELATIONSHIP FROM A CONSULTANT/ADVISER PERSPECTIVE

If we then approach the context of the relationship from a consultant/adviser's perspective an interesting dichotomy presents itself – almost a situation of opposites. Dyer and Ross (2007) have conducted an analysis of the world of the professional consultant in order to try to understand the context of the consultant. They state that most work either for large organizations, 'professional bureaucracies' or 'government-supported agencies', with a number in private practice. They invariably have a formal education and training in business which is based on a 'rational, analytic and quantitative approach'. The net result is that the professional adviser is an expert normally in a functional area of business whose decision-making process is based on rational analysis and conclusions about prescribed courses of action that can be easily defended.

From an organizational perspective most consultants begin their working life in large bureaucracies such as banks, accountants, law firms and other professional services. All of these are characterized by hierarchies and formal procedures, some of which are present in the form of professional bodies. Recruitment is invariably graduate-based and so a common mindset predominates. Indeed, there is evidence to suggest that organizations attract candidates who exhibit these characteristics/mindset (Maister *et al.*, 2000, cited in Dyer and Ross, 2007). In order to break this cycle HR policies within the professions may have to change to one of diversity. However, because of the demands of the professions and the need to maintain expert status in order to ensure career development it seems likely that the profile of professional recruitment will not change quickly.

It is quite easy then to see that in terms of communication, cultural roots and learning styles the adviser and the SME owner could be diametrically opposed to the professional adviser. On one side there is the SME owner whose decision-making process is rooted in emotions and on the other a professional adviser who is rooted in the world or rationality. It is little wonder then that such relationships can founder on the rocks of incompatibility.

This scenario is rather simplistic though as most SME owners have the aim of growing their business and developing strategic cohesion among the team. The basis of this is putting emotion aside and making sound, rational decisions in the functional and technical areas of their organization. This is very similar to the environment and decision-making imperative of professional advisers and their organizations. The two worlds may be closer than imagined at first glance. One aspect that has already been touched on is that of empathy between both parties. If an empathetic relationship can be established early on in initial contact then the possibility of a building of trust over the longer term is possible. As adviser–owner relationships mature then the commonalities of purpose and lowering of potential conflict barriers emerge. However, Dyer and Ross (2007) do state that problems do also exist in long-term relationships and that those encountered in this phase are different to those encountered in the early phase. The stage in the life cycle of the relationship then is important. One should also consider the stage in the life cycle at which advice is sought. Different stages of the SME life cycle throw up different problems, for example market expansion/penetration in the early stages and the phasing in/launch of newer products or services or expansion into new markets. Trust and relationship building then are the basics for a successful consultancy project through what Schein (2002, cited in Christensen and Klyver, 2006) calls 'levels of mutual acceptance'. To sum up using the words of Kierkegaard (cited by Christensen and Klyver, 2006):

> If you truly want to succeed in taking another human being to another place, you must first and foremost take care to find him where he is and depart from there. This is the secret of all art of helping. Anyone who cannot do that, he is himself in a state of unreality, when he finds he is able to help another man. I must understand more than he – but indeed first and foremost understand what he understands. When I do not do so, my better understanding is no use to him.

A further complication in the process is in the nature of the consultancy service.

THE NATURE OF THE CONSULTANCY SERVICE

The nature of consultancy should be seen from a traditional service perspective. That is, the characteristics of services are intangibility, inseparability, perishability and heterogeneity. A further perspective is that in a consultancy context these characteristics are based both on task interactivity and on personal interactivity and take place over a longer and more intense time period. This is brought about by the fact that the consultant is unsure as to the needs of the client and the client is unsure as to the type of service required (Bennett and Robson, 1999). As has been seen in the preceding section, the success or failure of this interaction should be based on a foundation of trust and relationship building. However, Bennett and Robson demonstrate there is a difference and commonality between business advice and consultancy. These differentiated but overlapping characteristics can be seen from the above base of intangibility, inseparability, perishability and heterogeneity.

Looking first at intangibility there is a recognized continuum in so far as some services are totally intangible, e.g. training, while some have tangible results, e.g. banking services. Most consultancy work ends and is signed off with the production of a written report, i.e. a tangible end to an intangible process.

Inseparability is a given as the client–adviser interface is of an interactive nature which is necessary to scope and refine the project. This takes place over a long period of time and in a phased manner. Heterogeneity is based on the fact that not all services can be the same at every delivery point. This is certainly true of consultancy as the needs and demands of individual SMEs will and do vary considerably. Consultancy services then become bespoke offerings to each client that draw on the broad experience of the service provider. There can be similarities but no two projects are ever the same. For both parties then there exists the problem of quality control which can be solved through an interactive process. Constant and structured management of the project by the consultant ensures a degree of quality checks.

Perishability means that services cannot be stored; they are destroyed at the point of consumption. In a consultancy context issues and advice, e.g. strategic, are given by the consultant. In effect intellectual property rights are transferred from consultant to client for use. Once given such advice is consumed and as such cannot be reproduced in any further situation as the circumstances under which such advice was given have changed. This can be seen as an episodic process; once advice is given and used the next episode in the process begins. For a new client such advice has to be re-tailored to the new environment. Therefore, each service interaction is unique and represents something of high cost and high relevance to the client but may not be viewed as such from the consultant's point of view as the SME is but one of a number of clients with differing problems. Again, an empathetic relationship is crucial here and the delivery of outcomes agreed in a brief is vital for SME satisfaction.

Business advice, although sharing most of the above features, is distinguished by the fact that it is delivered in a shorter time frame and may not be commissioned but offered as part of a package. This could be as a value-added service from a bank adviser or from a free web-based government advice service such as Business Link. The service of an adviser then may be regarded as low or zero cost and from that perspective may not be perceived as being as valuable as that of a consultant. The ritual of the commissioning process also reinforces this high cost/value perception as this acts as a cue to the degree of professionalism being bought. As Bennett and Robson (1999) state, the result is a high 'human asset specificness' of the business service supply process, which in turn depends on knowledge-based technical skills exchanged with the client.

A slightly different perspective is given by a study of the role of consultants in Spanish industry (Soriano *et al.*, 2002). The study states that the key question for SMEs is whether to retrain in-house staff or to hire external advice to supply missing skill sets. Retraining current staff is a lengthy and costly process and as the necessity for particular skill sets is of an immediate nature it is, in the long run, cheaper to hire consultants. Indeed, the authors' research shows that clients place more importance on the quality of the work commissioned than on the price. This, however, is dependent on the size of the organization. Smaller businesses are more affected by pricing issues. It is really a balance between price and quality that would drive repeat business.

Christensen and Klyver (2006) found that there were a number of different learning perspectives on behalf of both consultant and client. These were observed from the first contact where consultants concentrated on the key issue at hand while the clients were focused on the sense of occasion and attitudes of the consultant. This translated into a client focus on the task to be performed. As the process continued there appeared to be a change in emphasis. The client's focus went from empathetic behaviour to one of focus on action-oriented outcomes resulting in a request that the consultant spend more time in the firm. The consultants in general did not emphasize their expertise but their focus changed in trying to help the client help themselves which sometimes resulted in returning to the same questions because of lack of client commitment. Increasingly this appears to be the result of a mismatch of client/consultant perceived and expected outcomes. A further problem came with the termination of the contract. This further reinforced a communication problem that is very common. Consultants viewed the service complete as per the parameters of the brief and the time allocated to it. Clients though viewed completion on the basis of when the recommendations were implemented. Follow-up then becomes an important aspect of the service and should be built into the brief, with that brief explained and agreed before commencement of the project. This is common sense with larger organizations but is very typically neglected in SME consulting. Therefore, the process can be seen within the context of a number of paradigms.

The first is the expert paradigm, where the consultant is perceived to be at the forefront of knowledge and knowledge transfer in their respective field. The second is the process paradigm, where the process leads to a growth of consultant knowledge about the client and therefore how to customize the service. The adviser is a 'change agent' who listens, analyses and then recommends courses of action thus transforming the business. It is a paradigm in which the rational thought process of the consultant overcomes the socialization and value-creating aspects of the process.

In their 1995 study, Haakansson and Snehota (cited in Christensen and Klyver, 2007) developed a useful model that can be applied to the process of client–consultant service and interaction. This is called the Industrial Network model. The idea behind this model is to view interactive behaviour and the respective outcomes from a functional viewpoint that is focused on the micro rather than the macro. As such standard rules and routines of interaction are formed from the direct and indirect interaction of the key players. In this case these are the clients, the consultants and the resources they control. The client and consultant operate from their own paradigm context or network and interact with each other via their respective resources in a specific time frame.

A number of conclusions then can be reached when analysing the nature of the service within the context of client–consultant relationships:

- The service provided is intangible in nature because it is knowledge-based.
- The consultant's task is to add value through the supply of relevant expertise to the SME at different functional levels. This may or may not include that of other services.
- The advice given then becomes part of a process; it is not instantaneous. It can be seen as an example of the exchange process that is at the base of marketing theory.
- The service is based on the development of personal relationships and therefore trust in the longer term.
- Assessment of the service is based on both objective and subjective criteria. Objectivity is easier in the delivery of tangible products to mass or niche markets. This becomes difficult where services are concerned due to the factors discussed above.
- Satisfaction levels are difficult to measure without a relationship existing and a degree of empathy on behalf of the consultant.

The overall result of consultancy engagement, despite being affected by the sections already considered, is through the achievement of set goals and SME performance as identified in the client brief. In many instances this is ultimately influenced by how resources are managed by the SME. The next section looks at some issues in this area.

CONSULTANTS, SME PERFORMANCE AND RESOURCE MANAGEMENT

A useful starting point in assessing the performance of an SME is by looking at its ability to manage its resources via the marketing function. If it is agreed that marketing is the interface between an organization and its internal and external stakeholders then the management and allocation of scarce organizational resources can be seen to lie at the heart of a marketing orientation. An alternative view put forward by the American Marketing Association (2007) is that marketing is 'the management process of planning and executing the conception, pricing, promotion and distribution of ideas goods and services to create exchanges that satisfy individual and organizational objectives' – this would also involve the collection and dissemination of market intelligence. This suggests an approach that is both strategic and functional/operational, which most commonly exists in larger organizations. This may not apply to many SMEs because of their nature. As Simpson *et al.* (2006) state, 'no definition of marketing for SMEs can readily be found in the literature and those attempts at definition or discussion often link marketing with entrepreneurial behaviour'. This would indicate an entrepreneurial approach to the management of resources.

From an SME/consultancy perspective it can be stated that most SMEs approach marketing from a sales orientation and have no real understanding of the broader perspectives of what constitutes a marketing orientation and, therefore, the marketing concept. Romano and Ratnatunga (1995) categorized marketing in SME culture as an understanding and analysis of customer wants and needs. They also categorize it as a strategy, i.e. as related to the performance and positioning of the SME. Lastly marketing is seen as tactics, via the implementation of the 4Ps to influence performance and growth. Their conclusion was that marketing in SMEs was rather arbitrary.

This raises a significant point. If it is recognized that SME owners are lacking in the competence base of marketing, i.e. they are generalists not specialists, then complex marketing solutions may not be relevant to the SME and a more functional overlapping approach/solution from the consultant may be necessary. This does not mean though that the owner-manager does not think strategically – it merely indicates that the strategic approach of larger organizations does not fit comfortably within the SME situation and that an adaptable approach is necessary. Thus, a marketing orientation that involves putting the customer at the heart of the activities of the SME will depend on how the marketing concept is adapted and/or implemented and how those marketing resources are managed. It is to be remembered that the implementation of the marketing concept is an expression of how deeply rooted a marketing orientation is in an organization.

To look at the basis of resource management, a useful starting point is the resource-based view (RBV) of it as a foundation for strategy. There is a proven link between strategy and performance at both firm and functional level. The RBV paradigm is the result of an idiosyncratic use of a firm's resources as a basis of strategy. It recognizes that there is a broad base of strategically relevant resources that affect a firm's performance. These represent an organization's unique set of assets and include:

- the degree of experience, competencies/capabilities and skills, etc., that reside in the organization's workforce
- an organization's systems and processes that underpin an organization's marketing and operational strategies
- the physical assets of the organization such as plant and machinery, location vis-à-vis markets and materials
- an organization's patents/intellectual property rights and brand equity/reputation,

Marketing expertise or orientation could, therefore, be regarded here as a contributory factor in the creation of those unique assets. Spillan and Parnell (2006) took the RBV paradigm and looked at the relationship between seven variables that were associated with firm performance and the marketing function. Their analysis shows the key problem areas in resource management that a consultant encounters. The seven variables are:

1. Customer orientation: this is a philosophical stance discussed previously that enables a consultant to assess the degree to which decisions and activities are consumer-centric.
2. Coordination: this is a measure of the degree the different parts of the organization work together in response to customer needs.
3. Capabilities: a measure of the speed of organizational response to customer needs.
4. Customer interaction: the degree to which customers are involved in the process.
5. Customer data: the timely collection and analysis of relevant intelligence.
6. Customer orientation in action: the organization/customer interface.
7. Speed of action and performance measurement against objective measures such as sales, profit, retention, etc.

The authors concluded that the two key resources that most affect an SME's performance are a customer-orientation philosophy and a structure that supports flexibility and coordination among departments. These two aspects are at the core of the development and delivery of an SME's marketing strategy. From a consultant's point of view, in analysing how an SME creates market driven strategies they will need to assess the degree to which the company is market-oriented. From this position they will then be able to discover how the SME finds/ could find superior customer value and then position that value in the market on the basis of utilization of unique capabilities/assets and establishing strategic relationships. In terms of implementation a market-oriented strategy requires a relevant cultural paradigm to be present in the SME and a solid market intelligence delivery system. This may or may not require organizational change and a degree of training or organizational learning.

SUMMARY

To summarize, the role of consultancy in SMEs is vital and can contribute to the long-term growth of a company. The engagement of a consultant/adviser is, in reality, akin to buying in the expertise the SME may not possess and can prove a cheaper option than recruiting staff in the longer term. Key issues to consider, however, are:

1. There is no concise definition of SMEs. The EU has attempted to refine its definition by recognizing the broad scope of the sector.
2. The breadth of the sector brings a breadth of different and unique issues for the consultant to address.
3. SMEs have different competencies from MNCs which results in a generalist approach to decision making.
4. SME competencies can be divided into technical and decision-making sets and they should seek to achieve a balance between the two.
5. SMEs are hampered in the longer term by lack of financial resources and limited resources and expertise in key functional areas such as marketing.
6. The result is a need for multiple and overlapping skill sets which leads to an unstructured and uncoordinated response to decision making.
7. An SME can achieve growth by addressing issues in the three areas of competencies, structure and strategy. Competencies are based and developed according to environmental change and the experiential learning of the owner-manager.
8. There is a recognition of the need for a consultant's services but a general reluctance to appoint.
9. In any consultancy there is cultural gap between the characteristics of both parties. An empathetic approach is needed by the consultant to close the gap.
10. Consultancy by nature is a service and can therefore be analysed on the basis of intangibility, inseparability, heterogeneity and perishability.
11. The consultant acts as a change agent.
12. The key points of analysis fall within the remit of the management of resources which directly affect the performance of the SME. The RBV paradigm is an aid here as marketing can be considered a 'unique asset'.
13. The application of this unique asset in the form of the marketing concept is based on the marketing orientation of the firm and is centred on seven key variables. The most important of which are customer orientation and flexibility and coordination among departments.

REVIEW QUESTIONS

1. Discuss the relevance of consultants to SMEs. Use appropriate examples to support your argument.

2. Discuss the differences in approach to marketing by SMEs and MNCs.

3. What is the nature and role of competencies in SMEs?

4. Discuss the possible points of conflict in the relationship between a consultant and SME. How would you overcome them?

5. Discuss the nature of consultancy from a services perspective.

6. How can the RBV paradigm help in managing resource allocation in SMEs?

CASE STUDY 25: ACE CLEANING SERVICES

The following is based on a real-life consultancy client. Names and figures have been changed for issues of confidentiality.

Ace Cleaning Services is an SME operating in the contract cleaning sector. The company was started in March 1990 by John Smith, managing director. John's goal along with many other SMEs was to compete on the basis of providing a quality service and to grow the business from word-of-mouth referrals. Ace began as an 'off-vehicle service' to private individuals and corporate clients. This was literally a 'one-man show' and relied only on John cleaning vehicles and carpets with his van and equipment. The business was successful; John provided a good service and as a consequence the business steadily grew and won regular commercial contracts. This growth was organic with very little debt coverage. John's entrepreneurial character drove the business forward. He gradually took on more staff, predominantly part-time, and then established a management team operating from a head office on an inner-city industrial estate.

The period following the year 2000 saw the company diversify its offerings across a broad range of ancillary services including domestic cleaning, contract cleaning, vehicle cleaning and collection, window cleaning, environmental cleaning including horticultural waste, clearing of clinical waste, facilities management and security.

Ace now employ over 200 staff (including both full-time and part-time). They are still based in their original HQ but have regional centres in Bristol, Hull and Manchester, where they have a significant client base. They are a national company and are willing to establish themselves where the contacts are won. The team at HQ are all full-time and comprised of John and a management team of four people which includes finance, sales, account and operations management. There is a sub-level of 15 administrative support staff and the rest of the staff are part-time. Turnover has grown to £3 million and it is the intention of the management team to increase this to £9 million in the next ten years. This will be based predominantly on the acquisition of new business. The company has identified the public sector as an opportunity to expand but at the moment 90 per cent of clients reside in the private sector.

John is a very proactive entrepreneur and is constantly seeking new markets to exploit. He appreciates the need for marketing and has employed consultants before to produce a marketing plan. This, however, has not been implemented.

From an operational perspective Ace are operating an inefficient paper-based system with minimal computerization such as the current use of Sage software to facilitate CRM. The system relies on shared responsibility without the necessary training and staff expertise to exploit market opportunities. New clients are won through telemarketing and direct sales via the 'sales office'. This is manned by three members of staff whose strategy is to win a new client in a particular area and then try to win further business in that area in order to utilize the service team fully and bring down costs. There is a commission-based system based on new business won. The team do target larger national clients and send relevant managers to establish client requirements and then recruit team leaders. John also maintains contact with an e-list of public-sector contracts which are pitched for by competitive tendering. So far no business has been won on that basis. Customer satisfaction is stated as being a priority and surveys are conducted via face-to-face liaisons and by A4 questionnaires.

The business environment is especially competitive due to the recession. A survey of the industry has revealed that the past two years has proven to be one of the most difficult trading environments since 1945. The strong growth experienced up until 2004 and forecast to continue into 2009 (AMA Research/Trade Estimates) has not been experienced (see below).

Viewed from a macro perspective key trends that will affect the workplace have been identified in a recent CMI trend analysis (March 2008) as follows:

- The economic forecasts suggest that the UK will slowly emerge from recession this year but with large debt.
- For the SME sector almost 1 in 3 owners estimate the value of their market has decreased significantly in the past 12 months (NatWest 'Business Intelligence', 2009).
- For most SMEs (43 per cent) economic impact on the level of demand has been an issue but there have also been issues around finance, cash flow, costs, exchange rate and staffing (see above). The result has been severe market turbulence.
- The UK workplace is undergoing severe transformation with key drivers being new technology and global competition. As such employment patterns, work activities and corporate structures are being affected.
- The structure of the workforce is becoming more individualistic, older, more mobile, more international and ethnically diverse.

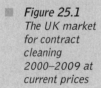
Figure 25.1
The UK market for contract cleaning 2000–2009 at current prices
Source: AMA Research/Trade Estimates.

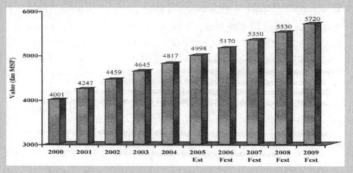

- The workforce is ageing; since 2000 the number of young people of working age has fallen by 60,000 each year. The number of workers over the age of 65 currently stands at 1 million (AON estimates) but could treble by 2018.
- The demands of the skilled workforce are placing greater demands on the employer in terms of training, flexibility, work–life balance, etc. Such issues are forcing their way onto the political agenda.
- As the economy becomes more service, and knowledge-based the demand for high value-added services increases.
- The key trend among organizations is for them to develop the capacity for knowledge management through the 'upskilling' of the labour market. There is an increasing trend towards 'flatter' organizations.
- It is a necessity to enhance innovation and innovative practice as a means of developing a competitive advantage in the market.

From a micro perspective the cleaning industry as defined above employs *c.*900,000 people in the UK (CSSA) and encompasses a broad range of cleaning services. The great majority (86 per cent) of cleaning firms have ten or fewer employees (Asset Skills). The industry has long suffered from an image problem because it is a cost that is not immediately seen to be relevant to clients' profits or budgets. It is no longer regarded as a single service but in many instances has been incorporated into a range of services under the 'Facilities Management' portfolio. It can therefore be seen as a single service or part of a product package incorporating security, cleaning, disposal, etc., for multi-site or single-site corporations. Indications are that it is a bespoke approach that gives a competitive edge.

The cleaning services sector has traditionally been seen as 'recession-proof' as all organizations need a cleaning service and it is seen as essential. However, recent surveys have shown that the recession has had an impact on the sector. Due to differing definitions of the market there is a discrepancy on market value. Asset Skills estimates the contract cleaning market to be worth £5.6 billion (2007). This excludes public and private organizations that employ their own staff. However, research has indicated a contraction in the market over 2009 to £4.9 billion; this effectively puts the market back to 2004 levels. According to CSSA (a professional body), the sector has mirrored changes to GDP which fell by 0.6 per cent in the second quarter of 2009. The outcome of this squeeze is that traditional price competition in the market will intensify with some companies willing to take a negative profit margin to win or retain business. Structurally, the contract cleaning industry, although highly fragmented, is continuing a process of consolidation, mostly through the acquisition of contract cleaning companies by facilities management companies – 91 per cent of the market is now controlled by 125 companies (1.25 per cent of all companies).

There is optimism though that the sector will experience some modest recovery in mid to late 2010, with a growth of 7 per cent projected between 2007 and 2013. At the moment though the sector is still experiencing price competition, rising labour costs, the burden of new immigration legislation, declining volume demand and various micro issues that negatively impacted upon the market in 2009 such as decreasing customer loyalty. The recession led to the sector attempting to shore up profits through a focus on cost-cutting.

The market can be segmented into three key areas:

- contract cleaning
- domestic cleaning
- specialist cleaning, including carpet/upholstery, wheelie/refuse bin and waste disposal, highway and land, vehicle washing and valeting (a large market).

Using demographic segmentation the market for cleaning services can be segmented into several key groups:

- Domestic – of no strategic interest to CASS. There is potential though for domestic cleaning for older people via local authorities with the ageing demographic profile of the UK.
- Office/facilities management – competitive tendering process.
- Accommodation businesses, including hotels/chains, holiday parks/chains, B&Bs, guest houses, are key markets for cleaning. Holiday villages such as Pontins, Butlins and Haven experienced a 12 per cent increase in demand during Easter 2009 with similar growth forecast for 2010. Hotels, however, experienced a steep decline in market demand in 2009 due to drops in leisure and corporate travel. Researchers indicate a 200 per cent increase in insolvency rates for the year. However, budget chains such as Travelodge bucked the trend, reporting a year-on-year sales growth of 20 per cent. Budget chains represent a significant market segment for cleaning services.
- Food and catering – having legal requirements to maintain standards of hygiene and cleanliness generates a significant customer base. Restaurants, fast-food outlets, takeaways, pubs and clubs make up this sector, which also includes subsidized canteen facilities for local authorities/schools/colleges/universities/ health/institutions.
- Letting agencies – with the rise of rental accommodation this could prove to be a potential market.
- Retail outlets.
- Nursing and residential homes. There are 18,570 residential homes in the UK with multiple chains developing.
- Public sector – 35 per cent of cleaning contracts are outsourced but as indicated budget cuts may affect this market. In the National Health Service (NHS) unions state that outsourced cleaning services are 4 per cent cheaper than those in-house but they are considered poor quality by NHS managers. Such opposition to outsourcing and the campaign to bring in-house will impact upon the tenders offered in this segment.
- Manufacturing – significant cutbacks due to falling orders in 2009 with recovery predicted 2010.

Research has shown the approximate sectoral percentages to be as follows:

- business services: *c.*30 per cent
- public sector including health and education: *c.*18 per cent
- banking and finance: *c.*15 per cent
- distribution sector: *c.*10 per cent
- manufacturing: *c.*10 per cent
- the rest: *c.*17 per cent.

In a recent survey of the cleaning industry the majority of owners stated the key challenges were:

- The recession, which has resulted in:
  - cash flow problems
  - competition forcing cost reduction
  - difficulty in maintaining efficiency
  - weak pound/dollar making product buying expensive.

Accordingly some organizations have moved their cleaning back in-house or cut back cleaning budgets. This has led to severe price competition for new business including challenges from new franchise operations.

- Recruitment and retention:
  - There is slowing of staff turnover and while there are vacancies in some firms there are higher staff levels in others.
  - National Minimum Wage (NMW). As wages make up 75 per cent of all costs these have to be absorbed by companies. Due to the competitive environment they cannot always be passed on, especially in long-term contractual negotiations. In some situations where contracts have been put up for tender clients have asked for shorter working hours/less work so they do not have to absorb higher NMW costs. The government has indicated rises in NMW 2009–2014.
  - The 'informal economy' and employment of illegal employment of migrant labour pose a significant threat to the professionalism and image of the industry.
  - For some companies retention of senior staff is an issue.
  - Changes that are taking place in local government resulting in restructuring due to budget cuts are impacting on the sector.
- The adoption of 'environmentally friendly' work practices, e.g. daytime cleaning and chemical-free cleaning products invoke a cost on the sector.
- The increasing need for accreditation to enable qualification for tender bids e.g. ISO 9001, ISO 14001 (green credentials), OHSAS 18001 (H&S).
- Increasing government legislation.

John and his team are now at a crossroads and have recruited you as consultant to assist.

CASE TASK

Your task as consultant to the business is to:

- conduct an analysis of the business
- identify critical success factors for the business
- identify key impacting variables for the business.

Once this has been completed you are to come up with a viable marketing plan to take the company forward.

BIBLIOGRAPHY

American Marketing Association (2007), 'Definition of Marketing'. Available at: http://www.marketing power.com/aboutama/pages/definitionofmarketing.aspx. Accessed 21 January 2010.

Becherer, R.C., Halstead, D. and Haynes, P. (2001), 'Marketing Orientation in SMEs: Effects of the Internal Environment', *Journal of Research in Marketing and Entrepreneurship*, Vol. 3, No. 1, pp. 1–17.

Bennett, R.J. and Robson, P. (1999), 'Intensity of Interaction in Supply of Business Advice and Client Impact: A Comparison of Consultancy, Business Associations and Government Support Initiatives for SMEs', CBR Research Programme on SMEs, Working Paper No.142.

Bennett, R.J. and Robson, P. (1999), 'The Use of External Business Advice by SMEs in Britain', *Entrepreneurship and Regional Development*, Vol. 11, pp. 155–180.

Bennett, R.J. and Robson, P.J.A. (2003), 'The Advisor–SME Client Relationship: Impact, Satisfaction and Commitment, *Small Business Economics*, Vol. 25, pp. 255–271.

Bennett, R.J. and Smith, C. (2004), 'The Selection and Control of Management Consultants by Small Business Clients', *International Small Business Journal*, Vol. 22, No. 5, pp. 435–462.

Birch, D. (1979), *The Job Generation Process*, MIT Programme on Neighbourhood and Regional Change, Cambridge, MA.

Blankson, C. and Stokes, D. (2002), 'Marketing Practices in the UK Small Business Sector', *Marketing Intelligence and Planning*, Vol. 20, No. 1, pp. 49–61.

The Bolton Committee (1970), 'Report of the inquiry on small forms'. Cmnd 4811, London: HMSO.

Carson, D. and Gilmore, A. (2000), 'SME Marketing Management Marketing Competencies', *International Business Review*, Vol. 9, No. 4, pp. 363–382.

Christensen, P.R. and Klyver, K. (2006), 'Management Consultancy in Small Firms: How Does Interaction Work?' *Journal of Small Business and Enterprise Development*, Vol. 13, No. 3, pp. 299–313.

Cravens, D. (1988), 'Gaining Strategic Marketing Advantage', *Business Horizons*, September–October, pp. 44–54.

Day, G. (1988), *Market Driven Strategy: Processes for Creating Value*, Free Press, New York.

Day, G. and Wensley, R. (1990), 'Assessing Advantage: A Framework for Diagnosing Competitive Superiority', *Journal of Marketing*, Vol. 52, April, pp. 1–20.

Dyer, L.M. and Ross, C.A. (2007), 'Advising the Small Business Client', *International Small Business Journal*, Vol. 25, No. 2, pp. 130–151.

Freeman, S. (2000), 'Partnerships between Small and Medium Enterprises and Universities That Add Value', *Education + Training*, Vol. 42, No. 6, pp. 272–77.

Gore, C., Murray, K. and Richardson, B. (1992), *Strategic Decision Making*, Cassell, London.

Haakansson, H. and Snehota, I. (1995), *Developing Business Relationships*, London: Routledge.

Hardy, K.G. (1992), 'Marketing Competences for Every Manager', *Business Quarterly*, pp. 51–53.

Hill, J. (2001a), 'A Multi-Dimensional Study of the Key Determinants of Effective SME Marketing Activity: Part 1', *International Journal of Entrepreneurial Behaviour and Research*, Vol. 7, No. 5, pp. 171–204.

Hill, J. (2001b), 'A Multi-Dimensional Study of the Key Determinants of Effective SME Marketing Activity: Part 2', *International Journal of Entrepreneurial Behaviour and Research*, Vol. 7, No. 6. pp. 211–235.

Kohli, A. K. and Jaworski, B. L. (1990), 'Market orientation: the construct, research propositions and management implications', *Journal of Marketing*, Vol. 54, pp. 1–18

Lauder, D., Boocock, G. and Presley, J. (1994), 'The System Support for SMEs in the UK and Germany', *European Business Review*, Vol. 94, No. 1, pp. 9–16.

McLarty, R. (1998), 'Case Study: Evidence of a Strategic Marketing Paradigm in a Growing SME', *Journal of Marketing Practice: Applied Marketing Science*, Vol. 4, No. 4, pp. 105–117.

Mughan, T., Lloyd-Reason, L. and Zimmerman, C. (2004), 'Management Consulting and International Business Support', *Education + Training*, Vol. 46, No. 8/9, pp. 424–432.

Official Journal of the European Union (2003), online at: http://eurlex.europa.eu/JOMonth. do?year=2003&month=5. Accessed 11 December 2009.

Pech, R. and Alister, M. (1993), 'Critical Factors for Consulting to Small Businesses', *Journal of Management Consulting*, Vol. 7, pp. 61–63.

Pech, R.J. and Mathew, A. (1993), 'Critical Factors for Consulting to Small Business', *Journal of Management Consulting*, Vol. 7, No. 3, pp. 61–63.

Poolton, J., Ismail, H.S., Reid, I.R., Arokiam, I.C. (2006), 'Agile Marketing for the Manufacturing-base SME', *Marketing Intelligence and Planning*, Vol. 24, No. 7, pp. 681–693.

Ramsden, M. and Bennett, R.J. (2005), 'The Benefits of External Support for SMEs: "Hard" Versus "Soft" Outcomes and Satisfaction Levels', *Journal of Small Business and Enterprise Development*, Vol. 12, No. 2, pp. 227–243.

Romano, C. and Ratnatunga, J. (1995), 'The Role of Marketing', *European Journal of Marketing*, Vol. 29, No. 7, pp. 9–30.

Robson, P.J.A. and Bennett, R.J. (2000), 'SME Growth: The Relationship with Business Advice and External Collaboration', *Small Business Economics*, Vol. 15, No. 3, pp. 193–208.

Simpson, M., Padmore, J., Taylor, N. and Frechnell-Hughes, J. (2006), 'Marketing in Small and Medium Enterprises', *International Journal of Entrepreneurial Behaviour and Research*, Vol.12, No. 6, pp. 361–387.

Slater, S.F. and Narver, J.C. (1994), 'Does Competitive Environment Moderate the Marketing Orientation-Performance Relationship?', *Journal Of Marketing*, Vol. 58, No. 1, pp. 46–55.

Slater, S. and Narver, J. (1995), 'Market orientation and the learning organization', *Journal of Marketing*, Vol. 59, No. 3, pp. 63–74.

Soriano, D.R., Roig, S., Sanchis, J.R. and Torcal, R. (2002), 'The Role of Consultants in SMEs: The Use of Services by Spanish Industry', *International Small Business Journal*, Vol. 20, No. 1, pp. 95–103.

Spillan, J. and Parnell, J. (2006), 'Marketing Resources and Firm Performance among SMEs', *European Management Journal*, Vol. 24, No. 2/3, pp. 236–245.

Storey, D.J. (1994), *Understanding the Small Business Sector*, Routledge, London.

Tunwall, C.A. and Busbin, J.W. (1991), 'Consulting Effectiveness in Smaller Companies: Guidelines for the Consultant and User', *Journal of Organisational Change Management*, Vol. 4, No. 4, pp. 15–23.

Valry, N. (1999), 'Innovation in Industry', *The Economist*, Survey Insert.

Chapter 26

Entrepreneurship marketing in informal economies

Anayo D. Nkamnebe and Nnamdi O. Madichie

INTRODUCTION

The informal economy refers to the paid production and sale of goods and services which are unregistered by, or hidden from, the state for tax and/or benefit purposes but which may still be legal in all other respects (European Commission, 1998; Portes, 1994; Thomas, 1992; Williams and Windebank, 1998). As such, the informal economy includes only paid work that is illegal because of its non-declaration to the state for tax and/or social security purposes. Paid work in which the good and/or service itself is illegal (e.g. drug trafficking) is thus considered unpaid work (Williams, 2007).

Before you start wondering why we are talking about the informal sector in a textbook dedicated to SME marketing, it should be pointed out that for a long time now discussion on SME marketing seems to have focused majorly on the *formal economy*, with a concomitant neglect of SME marketing in the *informal economy*. Paradoxically, the bulk of small business activities in developing countries (especially micro enterprises in which a significant proportion of the population is engaged – up to 60 per cent in some African economies) is hugely accounted for through the informal economy (see Cisse, 2001).

Furthermore, the numerous independent and unregistered businesses across the globe that account for as much as 60 per cent of global economic output have been part of the informal economic system. With the globalization of markets, the prevalence of informal economy has persisted and, indeed, expanded due to the ease with which it can be imported through migratory pipelines (e.g. ethnic minority businesses spread across different parts of London; job displacement and strict enforcement of regulations force many consumers and producers into the informal economy). Arguably, businesses in the informal economy play major socio-economic roles in the exchange process. In the Third World, however, it has been recognized for several decades that the undeclared sector acts as 'an incubator for business potential and . . . transitional base for accessibility and graduation to the formal economy', and that many undeclared workers show 'real business acumen, creativity, dynamism and innovation' (ILO, 2002, p. 54). During the past few years, a similar view of undeclared work has started to emerge in Europe (Renooy *et al.*, 2004; Small Business Council, 2004; Williams, 2004, 2006). But what exactly is undeclared work and how does it relate to the topic on the informal sector? The next section provides the multifarious definitions of the sector, which is primarily informal economy driven.

THE INFORMAL ECONOMY – IN SEARCH OF A DEFINITION

The phrase *informal sector* has proved difficult to define universally. As a result, different meanings and measurements have been proposed. In most cases these definitions and measurements vary widely and tend to militate against reasonable conclusions and generalizations. Most often, the informal sector has been confused with deleterious activities such as smuggling, black-marketeering, illegal transactions, the underground sector and unofficial transactions (see Williams, 2004, 2005a, 2007).

Despite the unpopular labels of the informal sector, from 'cash-in-hand work' through the 'shadow economy' or 'underground sector', it remains a construct that has been in constant flux – both theoreticallly and practically. This constantly evolving pattern thus makes it difficult to observe, study, define and measure.

Despite this fluidity, attempts have been made by economists and social scientists to define and – even more laboriously – measure it. As expected, the result of such efforts has yielded as many definitions as there are authors. One of the popular definitions of the informal economy conceptualizes it as the paid production and sale of goods and services which are unregistered by, or hidden from, the state for tax and/or benefit purposes but which are legal in all other respects (European Commission, 1998; Williams and Round, 2009). Taking this as a working definition, the sector remains informal by falling outside the regulatory framework of most governments for tax purposes.

The regulatory framework

Evident from the definition above is the fact that small business marketers, who are the predominant operators in the informal economies, can be distinguished from their mainstream counterparts on the basis of business registration. An unregistered business (typical of an informal economic activity) is most unlikely to pay taxes even though it might not necessarily be engaged in unlawful activities. On this basis, SME marketers should not be confused with those other operators that engage in criminal activities such as arms dealers, child traffickers and brothel operators (especially in the UK, where the practice is illegal).

To illustrate this point, two theoretical perspectives have been used to explain the emergence of the informal economy. The first is the argument that the increasing informalization is a direct consequence of government over-regulation of the economy, which leaves these small players little room for survival. Under such circumstances, the informal economy tends to provide a strategic choice for survival. Harney (2006 p. 374), for instance, captured this reality in his description of a typical informal Neapolitan neighbourhood of La Pignasecca:

> [B]y the early afternoon the municipal police are gone so the street vendors set up their cardboard tables, lay their tarpaulin and sheets and arrange their goods – inexpensive children's electronic toys, kitchenware, linen, lingerie, binoculars, calculators, perfume, posters of pop stars, and football players – on the main thoroughfare without fear of fines.

The second perspective sees the informal economy as

> an unavoidable expression of the uneven development inherent in late capitalism . . .[thus] evasion of regulation is simply part and parcel of a cost-cutting imperative on the part of small entrepreneurs struggling for survival in the marginal and diminishing market space left over by the expansion of corporate capital.
>
> (Jones *et al.*, 2006, p. 358)

Following this orthodoxy, it is argued that capitalism was a key driver of the informal economy because those displaced from the formal sector by corporate capitalists take solace in the informal economy. Again, with the globalized market system, Nkamnebe (2006) argued that most sub-Saharan African economies may find it difficult to catch up with the dominant economies and would, therefore, resort to the informal economy for survival. This somewhat explains the increasing expansion of the informal economy in developing economies.

Arguably, using these two perspectives to explain a rather complex informality phenomenon may amount to triviality. In reality, the emergence and growth of the informal economy is predicated upon myriad economic, political, cultural and migratory influences (see Williams, 2004, 2005a; Jones *et al.*, 2006). While the difficulty of defining an informal economy due to the shifts in the nature of the construct has been recognized, the framework in Table 26.1 suggested by Schneider (2002) may be helpful for developing a middle-ground definition of the concept.

Table 26.1 A taxonomy of types of underground economic activities

Type of activity	Monetary transactions		Non-monetary transactions	
Illegal activities	Trade with stolen goods: drug dealing and manufacturing; prostitution, gambling, smuggling and fraud.		Barter of drugs, stolen goods, smuggling, etc. Production or growing drugs for personal use. Theft for own use.	
	Tax evasion	Tax avoidance	Tax evasion	Tax avoidance
Legal activities	Unreported income from self-employment: wages, salaries and assets from unreported work related to legal services and goods.	Employee discounts, fringe benefits	Barter of legal services and goods	All do-it-yourself work and neighbour help

Source: Adapted from Schneider (2002).

KEY FEATURES OF THE INFORMAL ECONOMY

Essentially, most operators in the informal economy are largely the poor and middle-income earners in developing or emerging economies and/or ethnic minorities and immigrants in the more advanced economies. Arguably, they are mainly occupants of the so-called bottom of the pyramid (BOP) that have been recognized as constituting a substantial portion of the economic activities of modern economies. For instance, Humphreys (2004) estimated the total purchasing power of all ethnic minorities in the US for 2009 amounted to about US$1.5 trillion. Anderson and Billou (2007, p. 14) captured the potential of this market thus:

> Consumers at the very bottom of the economic pyramid – those with per capita incomes of less than $1,500 – number more than 4 billion. For more than a billion people – roughly one-sixth of the world's population – per capita income is less than $1 per day.

The 20 largest emerging economies include more than 700 million such households, with a total annual income estimated at some US$1.7 trillion. This spending power was approximately equal to Germany's annual gross domestic product about a decade ago (Prahalad and Hart, 2002). The spending power of Brazil's poorest 25 million households, for example, amounts to US$73 billion per annum, while China's poor residents account for 286 million households with a combined annual income of US$691 billion. India has 171 million low-income households with a combined US$378 billion in income. Given this picture, it is obvious that SME marketing in the context of informal economies would tend towards BOP marketing strategies. This chapter, therefore, examines the nature, size and dynamics of informal economy and discusses marketing strategies that are applicable in such settings.

MEASURING THE INFORMAL ECONOMY

The informal economy is by definition unregistered by and/or hidden from the state. As such, estimating its prevalence is a difficult task. Until now, measurement methods have ranged from techniques that indirectly measure its magnitude by using proxy indicators to methods that attempt to directly measure its prevalence (for reviews, see Bajada, 2002; Thomas, 1992; OECD, 2002; Renooy et al., 2004; Williams, 2004; Williams and Windebank, 1998).

So far as indirect methods are concerned, proxy indicators used to assess the prevalence of the informal economy include non-monetary indicators such as the prevalence of very small enterprises and electricity demand, monetary proxies such as the number of large denomination notes in circulation, the cash-deposit ratio or level of cash transactions and income/expenditure discrepancies either at the household and/or national level. Over time, however, there has been a waning interest in these indirect proxy measurement methods (for reviews, see Thomas, 1992; OECD, 2002; Williams, 2004, 2006). The strong consensus that has emerged is that indirect methods are not only relatively inaccurate as measures of size but also limited in their usefulness for understanding the distribution and nature of such work. This is the conclusion of both OECD experts in their handbook on measurement methods (OECD, 2002) and the most recent European Commission report on undeclared work (Renooy et al., 2004), as well as a host of academic evaluations of direct and indirect methods (Thomas, 1992; Williams, 2004, 2006; Williams and Windebank, 1998).

Recently, therefore, much greater emphasis has been placed on more direct survey methods to measure the magnitude of such work (OECD, 2002; Renooy et al., 2004; Williams, 2006).

Reflecting this, the European Commission recently evaluated the feasibility of conducting a direct survey of undeclared work across the European Union (European Commission, 2005).

In the UK Her Majesty's Revenue and Customs (HMRC) commissioned consultants to develop methodologies for conducting direct surveys of the informal economy (HMRC, 2005). The major impetus for these direct surveys is the current poverty of knowledge on its size and distribution. Until now, most direct surveys have tended to be small-scale, usually conducted on specific localities which take the household as the unit of analysis (e.g. Barthe, 1985; Fortin *et al.*, 1996; Lemieux *et al.*, 1994; McCrohan *et al.*, 1991) and focus on off-the-books transactions in the domestic services sector (e.g. Howe, 1988; Leonard, 1994; Pahl, 1984; Warde, 1990; Williams, 2004, 2005a, 2006; Williams and Windebank, 2001). Few extensive nationally representative sample surveys (for an exception, see Pedersen, 2003) have been conducted and surveys of businesses (rather than households) are notable by their absence.

This current shift towards using direct surveys rather than relying on indirect proxy indicators, of course, has its critics. The major criticism, usually from the users of indirect methods, is that direct surveys naïvely assume that respondents will reveal to them, or even know, the prevalence of informal work. Yet the evidence appears to be that direct surveys produce fairly reliable and valid data. For example, Pahl (1984) found that when the results from individuals as suppliers and purchasers were compared, the same level of informal work was discovered. Similar conclusions have been identified in previous studies (e.g. Leonard, 1994; MacDonald, 1994; Williams, 2004, 2006; Williams and Windebank, 2001). The implication, therefore, is that respondents are not secretive about their informal work. Just because it is activity hidden from or unregistered for tax and/or social security purposes does not mean that respondents are unwilling to discuss it with researchers.

Having stated this, however, it is important to recognize that the direct (household) surveys so far conducted have been carefully and delicately designed, with data on informal work being gathered usually within the context of a broader study of 'household work practices' (Leonard, 1994; Pahl, 1984; Warde, 1990; Williams, 2004, 2006). That is to say, they have tended to investigate the practices households use to get a variety of domestic tasks completed and whether household members undertake tasks for other households (either on a paid or unpaid basis) in order to identify the prevalence and nature of informal work.

Even if honesty of response (and, thus, reliability of the data) does not appear to be a valid critique of most well-designed direct survey methods, two salient criticisms of direct methods remain:

- On the one hand, direct approaches have so far largely investigated only informal work used in relation to service provision in particular (especially domestic services) and final demand (spending by consumers on goods and services) more generally, rather than intermediate demand (spending by businesses). Final demand, however, accounts for just two-thirds of total spending. There exists a strong case for extending direct investigations to include business surveys rather than solely household surveys.
- On the other hand, most direct surveys have so far tended to be confined to small-scale, often qualitative, studies of particular localities, groups or sectors. The result is that it has been difficult to gain any representative picture at the national level of the overall prevalence, nature and distribution of informal work.

In sum, there has been a gradual shift away from indirect towards direct survey methods when measuring the prevalence of informal work. Small-scale, mostly locality-specific, studies have been conducted and there has been a heavy emphasis on using the household as the unit of analysis as well as on only examining domestic service provision rather than taking business as the unit of analysis and examining the full range of goods and services provision. In late 2004 the UK's Small Business Service (SBS) took the decision to include a series of questions on informal work in a nationally representative survey of small businesses so as to provide the first national business survey of the prevalence and impacts of such work.

The SBS Annual Small Business Survey

The aim of the 2004–2005 Small Business Service (SBS) Annual Small Business Survey was to gauge the needs of small businesses, assess their main concerns, and identify the barriers that prevent them from fulfilling their potential. The survey was based on telephone interviews with a large sample of 7,505 UK small businesses. The telephone interviews for this survey were conducted in the fourth quarter of 2004 and the first quarter of 2005 (SBS, 2006; Williams, 2007).

When constructing the sampling frame, the intention was not to reflect the distribution of firms in the UK by size or by their geographical distribution. Instead, more micro (1–9 employees), small business (10–49 employees) and medium-sized businesses (50–249 employees) were sampled than would be required to match their proportion in the UK economy (and fewer sole traders and partnerships without employees), and more firms in Wales and Scotland were sampled so that these countries' businesses could be analysed in detail.

The decision by the SBS to include questions on the prevalence and impact of the informal economy in this 2004–2005 survey arose directly out of a Small Business Council (2004) report that sought to evaluate the extent and nature of the informal economy and propose ways of tackling small businesses working on an off-the-books basis. In that national report, a lack of evidence was identified concerning not only the overall magnitude of this 'hidden enterprise culture' but also the economic sectors, businesses and geographical areas in which such work took place. Both the Small Business Council (2004) report and the government response to its recommendations (SBS, 2005a) agreed that improving the evidence base was a necessary precursor to concerted and targeted public policy action.

In his forward to the government response to the SBC report (Small Business Council, 2004), the UK Minister of State for Industry and the Regions states: 'We do not have as clear a picture as we would like of the scale and nature of the informal economy' (SBS, 2005a, p. 1). While the full report, in summing up the government's perception of its knowledge on the informal economy, stated that 'the size and composition of the informal economy is uncertain' (SBS, 2005a, p. 5), the report concluded in the final paragraph that 'more research is required both into the size and character of the informal economy' (SBS, 2005a, p. 19). This explicit recognition of the lack of an evidence base was further reinforced later that year by an Office of National Statistics (ONS) report on data sources on the informal economy. This concluded that there is currently little or no extensive data available of the magnitude and distribution of the informal economy (ONS, 2005).

Reflecting the wider emerging consensus that indirect methods which measure the informal economy using proxy indicators are both unreliable and invalid (OECD, 2002; Renooy et al., 2004), these reports were thus highlighting the lack of any direct national survey of the extent and distribution of such work.

Until 2007, most direct surveys of the informal economy took the household as the unit of analysis and focused upon provision in the domestic services sector (e.g. Leonard, 1994; Pahl, 1984; Warde, 1990; Williams, 2005b). The few studies that have taken businesses as the unit of analysis have been small-scale ethnographic studies based on face-to-face qualitative interviews conducted by academics and focusing on a small number of firms in particular localities working in a specific sector (e.g. Jones *et al.*, 2004; Ram *et al.*, 2001, 2002a, 2002b, 2003). This SBS survey was, thus, the first study in an advanced economy to conduct an extensive survey of businesses with regard to the prevalence and impacts of informal work. Indeed, given that small businesses employing fewer than 250 comprise 99.9 per cent of all enterprises in the UK economy (SBS, 2005b), this survey comprises a relatively comprehensive portrait of UK business opinion.

Extending the discussion beyond the confines of the UK economy, another separate study by Guesalaga and Marshall (2008) used the buying power index (BPI) methodology to evaluate the size of the BOP informal economy. This approach was used in order to estimate the business opportunities as measured by the purchasing power of these economies. According to these authors, the justification for using the BPI in the context of low-income consumers is twofold. On the one hand, this approach has been successful in measuring the relative buying power of people in specific geographic areas, in many different contexts – thus making the instrument valid and generally acceptable. On the other, most of the literature on the BOP assesses the opportunities in the low-income sector based on a purchasing power driven by population, income or both, without considering the 'expenditure' dimension (see Box 26.1 for a brief summary of the major conclusions about the various regions).

BOX 26.1: CONSUMPTION PATTERNS ACROSS REGIONS BASED ON BPI

Relative to the total market, the BOP sector accounts for, on average, more than 50 per cent of the purchasing power in developing countries, with Africa being the most prevalent BOP region. Asia is, by far, the region with the highest purchasing power, relative to Africa, Eastern Europe and Latin America and the Caribbean. In addition, the results show that, in terms of income tiers within the BOP segment, the greatest buying power resides in the lowest tier (annual income of US$1,000 or less) in the case of Africa and Asia, but in the second tier (annual income between US$1,001 and US$2,000) in the case of eastern Europe and Latin America and the Caribbean. As income level rises, the various regions show different characteristics:

- *Africa:* as the income level rises, people in Africa spend more in household goods, health, transportation, and information technologies and communication, and less in food and energy.
- *Asia:* as the income level rises, people in Asia spend more in housing, transportation, and information technologies and communication and education, and less in food.
- *Eastern Europe:* with an increase in the income level, people at the BOP from Eastern Europe spend more in housing, household goods, information technologies and communication and education, and less in food.
- *Latin America and the Caribbean:* as income increases, people spend more in housing, health, transportation, information technologies and communication and education, and less in food, energy and household goods.

RELATIONSHIP BETWEEN THE INFORMAL AND FORMAL ECONOMY

Despite the conflicting conclusions over the nature and size of the informal economy, the general impression is that the size of the global informal market is robust enough to warrant coordinated strategies to harness it. Going by the recent global economic crisis, it has become clear that no economy in the world is immune from failure, such that even the largest economies and Fortune 500 companies are considering investing in sectors hitherto considered unprofitable. Indeed, at the height of the recent global financial crisis, the organized private sector (OPS) in an emerging market context such as Nigeria alluded to the fact that the informal economy was the 'backbone' of that economy. The same holds true in most economies of the world where the informal sector is a dominant player (see Table 26.2 for some of the statistics from 1999 to 2000). Accordingly, the infomal economies of the developing countries and other underserved markets deserve increasing corporate attention. Guesalaga and Marshall (2008, p. 413) captured this emerging trend thus:

> [W]ith markets in the developed economies experiencing slow growth . . . private companies should look for business opportunities in emerging markets with low-income consumers; that is, at the bottom of the pyramid (BOP). There is an untapped potential for marketing to this sector, which is composed of approximately four billion people worldwide.

The main argument for targeting the BOP market is that there is significant purchasing power in this segment. Prahalad and Hammond (2002) once stated that 'tier 4 represents a multitrillion-dollar market', and argue that multinational corporations should see an attractive opportunity in the BOP. Likewise, Hammond *et al.* (2007) estimated that people at the base of the pyramid – with annual incomes below US$3,000 – constituted a US$5 trillion global consumer market annually. In both cases, the argument is that, based on income level and population at the BOP, purchasing power of low-income consumers exists (Guesalaga and Marshall, 2008). Though it is difficult, if not impossible, to calculate the exact size of the informal economy, the work of Schneider (2002) provides a reasonable guide.

Table 26.2 Selected sizes of informal economies in the world

Region	% of GDP	Highest	Middle	Lower
Africa	42% for the years 1999/2000.	Zimbabwe (59.4%), Tanzania (58.3%) and Nigeria (57.9%).	Mozambique (40.3%), Cote d'Ivoire (39.9%) and Madagascar (39.6%).	Botswana (33.4%), Cameroon (32.8%) and South Africa (28.4%).
Asia	26% of official GDP for the years 1999/2000.	Thailand (52.6%), Sri Lanka (44.6%) and Philippines (43.4%).	India (23.1%), Israel (21.9%) and Taiwan and China (19.6%).	Singapore (13.1%) and Japan (11.3%).
South and Latin America	41%.	Bolivia (67.1%), Panama (64.1%) and Peru (59.9%).	N/A	Chile (19.8%) and Argentina (25.4%).

(continued)

■ *Table 26.2* *Selected sizes of informal economies in the world (continued)*

Region	% of GDP	Highest	Middle	Lower
Transition economies	38% for the year 1999/2000.	Georgia (67.3%), Azerbaijan (60.6%) and Ukraine (52.2%).	Bulgaria (36.9%) and Romania (34.4%).	Hungary (25.1%), Czech Republic (19.1%) and Slovak Republic (18.9%).
West European OECD	18% for the year 1999/2000.	Greece (28.6%) and Italy (27.0%).	Denmark (18.2%) and Germany (16.3%).	Austria (10.2%) and Switzerland (8.8%).
North America and Pacific OECD countries	13.5%	Canada (16.3%), Australia (15.3%), New Zealand (12.7%) and the United States (8.8%).		

Sources: Cisse (2001) and the Bureau of African Affairs (2003).

MARKETING IN THE INFORMAL ECONOMY

Early thinking was that the informal economy only existed in the 'underground' or 'black' markets that are prevalent in the developing economies of the world (see Box 26.2). However, recent evidence conceptualizes market informality as a global phenomenon.[1] Initial predictions of the modernization theory of the 1950s and 1960s suggested that informality was a consequence of underdevelopment that would disappear as soon as the undeveloped economies became more advanced. Indeed, Schneider (2002) used the estimation of informal economy sizes of 110 developing, transition and OECD countries to illustrate the global dimension of informal marketing dynamics. With the increasing size and pervasive nature of the informal economy across the globe, and the prevalence of micro, small- and medium-sized enterprises (MSMEs) in this sector, a focus on SME marketing in the informal sector has emerged (see the seminal paper by Carson, 1990). Such focus affords twenty-first-century marketing practitioners the robust knowledge base for hybridizing formal and informal markets.

As McGregor (2005) once argued – from the perspective of a Canadian study – there is a collection of marketplace imperfections around which consumer movement issues are conventionally organized: product choice and safety, package and labelling, pricing strategies, information and advertising, selling, promotion and distribution, complaints and redress, repairs and warranties, consumer education and protection of comsumers' interests. She went on to assert that patronizing SMEs exposed consumers to many challenges and potential market failures (see McGregor, 2005, p. 12), which include questionable selling practices, handling complaints and redress, as well as repairs and warranties. Some key pointers that emerged in the context examined by McGregor include the following problems:

- inability to be a repeat customer or to return a product to a store
- potential of dealing with untrained staff
- likelihood of shopping in stores that cannot meet service expectations
- probability of encountering staff with very limited knowledge of consumers' needs and buying patterns.

To highlight some of the dark sides of the informal market, two special issues of the *International Journal of Social Economics* (Vol. 35, Nos 9–10, 2008) were dedicated to the informal economy and organized crime. In one of the papers from the former, Walle (2008) highlighted some very instructive insights into the growing blur the boundaries between the formal and informal economy. Starting with a restatement of the informal economy as 'those income generating activities occuring outside the state's regulatory framework', the author argues that 'the scope and character of the informal economy are defined by the very regulatory framework it evades' (Walle, 2008, p. 657).

In other words, informal economic activities are untaxed, unlicensed and largely unregulated economic activities usually characterized by their small scale of operation. Tripp (2001) suggested that although these activities may be defined as illicit (such as some of the marketing practices of Lebanese in West Africa – see Box 26.2) depending on the country in question, they nevertheless account for the majority of new jobs created in African economies.

BOX 26.2: THE INFORMAL ECONOMY'S DARK SIDE – LEBANESE IN WEST AFRICA

The Lebanese community across West Africa is thought to be between 80,000 and 250,000 strong.

Although many Africans openly state how much they hate the Lebanese in their respective countries, the latter's seeds seem to have been sown into the fabric of West African economics, politics and culture. The Lebanese tenacity, aptitude for business and drive to succeed means they have not only continued to do business but also thrived in both the formal and the informal economies.

It is likely that the Lebanese chose to go to West Africa around the time America tightened its entry requirements, after high levels of immigration during the previous century. The French government also ran a recruiting campaign in Beirut looking for middlemen to work during the boom in West African groundnut farming at the same time as there was an agricultural crisis in Lebanon.

The Lebanese in West Africa have always been merchants, using their connections abroad to source goods for import, and – like other migrant groups – using their family networks to keep their costs down. As a result they have built a strong economic presence across the region.

Lebanese businesses have become the backbone of most markets in West Africa, spanning numerous sectors from car importing, mining, oil services and defence contracts to the more shadowy worlds of gunrunning, diamond smuggling and crude-oil theft.

Doing business in politically volatile West Africa is not easy. With a poorly functioning legal system, contracts and other business agreements can be virtually worthless. The Lebanese have discovered that the best way of surviving where the regime you're doing business with could be overthrown tomorrow is to court the powerful – whoever they are. Any aspiring West African 'big man' knows he has to do business with the Lebanese if he has any hope of getting rich.

Source: Walker (2010).

However, there could be three identifiable categories of markets: a legal market for goods and services, a market of illegal goods and services (i.e. organized crime) and an informal market for legal goods and services. These markets have begun to exhibit blurred boundaries in a variety of ways and often merge. Citing the case of Brussels, Walle (2008, p. 658) highlights how in most cases formal and informal markets share a mutual sort of significance. The location of numerous official European institutions in Brussels has attracted non-governmental organizations and other lobby groups whose demands for services such as couriers, catering, cleaning and even babysitting have also risen. Services in these sectors have been provided for by the informal sector – often due to the rather lax attitude towards formal regulation because they are hard to monitor.

SUMMARY OF KEY POINTS

1. The informal economy refers to the paid production and sale of goods and services which are unregistered by, or hidden from, the state for tax and/or benefit purposes but which may still be legal in all other respects.
2. As such, the informal economy includes only paid work that is illegal because of its non-declaration to the state for tax and/or social security purposes.
3. Two theoretical perspectives have been used to explain the emergence of the informal economy. The first is the argument that the increasing informalization is a direct consequence of government over-regulation of the economy.
4. The second perspective sees informal economy as 'an unavoidable expression of the uneven development inherent in late capitalism' which made 'the evasion of regulation is simply part and parcel of a cost-cutting imperative on the part of small entrepreneurs struggling for survival in the marginal and diminishing market space' (Jones *et al.*, 2006, p. 358).
5. Essentially, most operators in the informal economy are largely the poor and middle-income earners in developing or emerging economies and/or ethnic minorities and immigrants in the more advanced economies.
6. Consumers at the very bottom of the economic pyramid – those with per capita incomes of less than US$1,500 – number more than 4 billion.
7. For more than a billion people – roughly one-sixth of the world's population – per capita income is less than US$1 per day.
8. The 20 biggest emerging economies include more than 700 million such households, with a total annual income estimated at some $1.7 trillion.
9. The informal economy is by definition unregistered by and/or hidden from the state. As such, estimating its prevalence is a difficult task. Until now, measurement methods have ranged from techniques that indirectly measure its magnitude by using proxy indicators to methods that attempt to directly measure its prevalence.
10. Recently, therefore, much greater emphasis has been placed on more direct survey methods to measure the magnitude of such work. Reflecting this, the European Commission recently evaluated the feasibility of conducting a direct survey of undeclared work in the EU.
11. The current shift towards using direct surveys rather than relying on indirect proxy indicators, of course, has its critics. The major criticism, usually from the users of indirect methods, is that direct surveys naïvely assume that respondents will reveal to them, or even know, the prevalence of informal work.
12. The aim of the Small Business Service (SBS) Annual Small Business Survey is to gauge the needs of small businesses, assess their main concerns, and to identify the barriers that prevent them from fulfilling their potential.

13. The decision by the SBS to include questions on the prevalence and impact of the informal economy in the 2004–2005 survey arose directly out of a Small Business Council (2004) report that sought to evaluate the extent and nature of the informal economy and propose ways of tackling small businesses working on an off-the-books basis.

REVIEW QUESTIONS

1. Compare and contrast the marketing practices adopted in the informal economy of two countries – Ukraine and Russia – with the United Kingdom.

2. What sectors, largely as a result of the marketing practices adopted, are more prone to be characterized as informal in the UK? Compare with any other country you have either lived in or visited in the last 3 years.

3. Can you provide an explanation as to why these sectors identified as predominantly informal tend to be so?

4. Is it fair to portray the informal marketing sector as an 'underground' or 'hidden' economy? Why or why not?

5. What is the best approach to mainstreaming the marketing practices in the informal economy?

GROUP ACTIVITY

Visit Robert Peston's blog at BBC.co.uk and read the article 'A legal right to a bank account', published on 23 March 2010. Online at: http://www.bbc.co.uk/blogs/thereporters/robertpeston/2010/03/a_legal_right_to_a_bank_accoun.html (accessed 26 August 2010).

Your Task:

In groups of three or four discuss the implications of the UK government punishing cash-in-hand jobs. You are expected to base your discussions around the proposals for nationwide bank accounts 'eligibility' for all UK employees. The following BBC.co.uk stories will assist you in your task:

- 'New 50% tax rate comes into force for top earners', BBC News, 6 April 2010. Online: http://news.bbc.co.uk/2/hi/business/8604215.stm (accessed 26 August 2010).
- 'Budget 2010: Darling aims to help UK business', BBC News, 24 March 2010. Online: http://news.bbc.co.uk/2/hi/business/8585144.stm (accessed 26 August 2010).
- 'Budget 2010: Plans to provide bank accounts for all', BBC News, 23 March 2010. Online: http://news.bbc.co.uk/2/hi/business/8582234.stm (accessed 26 August 2010).

CASE STUDY 26: UNDECLARED WORK

Until recently, undeclared work in advanced capitalist societies has largely been viewed in negative terms as contributing little if anything to economic and social development. The conventional public policy approach has, thus, been to eradicate such work. Most European governments have sought to deter such work with increasingly punitive measures, increasing the penalties and coordinating strategy and action to improve detection rates. Such an approach has been supported by supranational agencies such as the European Commission and the International Labour Organization, as well as by academic commentators such as Castells and Portes (1989). In the UK, for example, the Chancellor of the Exchequer commissioned a report in 1999 which concluded that deterrence was the most appropriate way forward:

> [A]s long as people can profit by not declaring their work, it will be impossible entirely to eradicate the informal economy. Therefore, the most effective way of tackling the problem is significantly to improve the likelihood of detecting and penalizing offenders. What is needed is a strong environment of deterrence.
>
> (Grabiner, 2000, p. 19)

The outcome was a series of tougher penalties and improved detection methods. In recent years in Europe, this representation of undeclared work as a site of entrepreneurship has also been taken up by a strand of social democratic thought, which views undeclared enterprise as an asset, but only if this endeavour can be harnessed and moved into the formal economy. If formalized, this would contribute to the development of an enterprise culture and the achievement of fuller employment. This emergent discourse finds a clear expression in the EU Employment Guideline 9 on undeclared work, first adopted in 2001. As the then commissioner Anna Diamantopoulou put it:

> Member states must increase efforts to quantify undeclared work, to cut it down *and to transform it into regular employment.* This is vital because of the direct link between combating undeclared work and hitting the Lisbon target of full employment by 2010 within a sound macroeconomic environment.
>
> (European Commission, 2002, p. 1, emphasis added)

In order to transfer such work into the formal economy, deterrents are seen as necessary but are insufficient by themselves – they need to be combined with 'enabling' initiatives. As the 2003 version of the Guideline insisted, there is a need for both push initiatives ('sticks') in the form of 'improved law enforcement and the application of sanctions' and a range of pull initiatives ('carrots'), namely a 'simplification of the business environment' and the provision of 'appropriate incentives in the tax and benefits system' (European Commission, 2003). Similarly, in Ukraine, although the emphasis is on deterrents such as stricter sanctions, there is also a growing focus on a limited range of incentives including the simplification of reporting systems and the registration process as well as the provision of incentives for labour to leave the undeclared sphere.

Whether such 'enabling' policy initiatives actually differ from the neoliberal advocacy of deregulation is questionable. Though the call is for undeclared work to be brought into the legitimate realm rather than for the formal economy to be deregulated, the initiatives advocated seem to amount to little more than a 'low road' approach that seeks to strip away formal regulations and eliminate taxes. There is a need to explore a 'high road' approach to legitimizing undeclared work, in the context of an appreciation of the complex character of undeclared work.

Sources: Renooy *et al.* (2004); Williams (2004, 2006); and Novoseletsky (2000).

CASE QUESTIONS

1. To what extent would you agree or disagree that deterrents are necessary but insufficient in tackling the problem of undeclared work in the informal market?
2. Should there be any punitive measures put in place against informal sector marketers? If so, to what extent and what sort of measures may be most appropriate?
3. In 2003, a cross-national survey showed that 43 per cent of all informal work is found to be concentrated in the home repair and maintenance sector. What entrepreneurship marketing implications do these figures have for the formal sector?

NOTE

1. Examples exist across the developed world, from the consumer transactions with SMEs in Canada (McGregor, 2005) to the case of rural England (Williams, 2007) and the matrix approach to informal markets adopted for the European Union (Walle, 2008).

REFERENCES

Anderson, J. and Billou, N. (2007), 'Serving the world's poor: innovation at the base of the economic pyramid', *Journal of Business Strategy*, Vol. 28, No. 2, pp. 14–21.

Bajada, C. (2002), *Australia's Cash Economy: A Troubling Issue for Policymakers*, Aldershot: Ashgate.

Barthe, M.A. (1985), 'Chômage, travail au noir et entraide familial', *Consommation*, Vol. 3, No. 1, pp. 23–42.

Bureau of African Affairs (2003), www.stat-usa.gov

Carson, D. (1990), 'Some models for assessing small firms marketing effectiveness: a qualitative approach', *European Journal of Marketing* (special issue), Vol. 24, No.11, p. 60.

Castells, M. and Portes, A. (1989), 'World underneath: the origins, dynamics and effects of the informal economy', in A. Portes, M. Castells and L.A. Benton (eds), *The Informal Economy: Studies in Advanced and Less Developing Countries*, pp. 11–37. Baltimore, MD: Johns Hopkins University Press.

Cisse, M. (2001), 'Needs and wants of the informal sector and of small firms in terms of vocational skills and knowledge as seen in a developing country in Africa', paper presented at the International Conference Linking Work, Skills and Knowledge, Interlaken, Switzerland, September.

European Commission (2005), *Feasibility Study of a Direct Survey of Undeclared Work in Europe*, Brussels: European Commission.

European Commission (2003), 'Council resolution on transforming undeclared work into regular employment', *Official Journal of the European Union*, 29 October, C260. Online at: http://europa.eu.int/eur-lex/en/archive/index.html

European Commission (2002), 'Commission calls on governments to do more to fight the shadow economy', press release IP/02/339, Brussels: European Commission.

European Commission (1998), *Communication of the Commission on Undeclared Work*. COM (98)-219, Brussels.

Fortin, B., Garneau, G., Lacroix, G., Lemieux, T. and Montmarquette, C. (1996), *L'Economie Souterraine au Quebec: Mythes et Realités*, Quebec: Presses de l'Université Laval.

Grabiner, Lord (2000), *The Informal Economy*, London: HM Treasury.

Guesalaga, R. and Marshall, P. (2008), 'Purchasing power at the bottom of the pyramid: differences across geographic regions and income tiers', *Journal of Consumer Marketing*, Vol. 25, No. 7, pp. 413–427.

Hammond, A.L., Krammer, W.J., Katz, R.S., Tran, J.T. and Walker, C. (2007), *The Next 4 Billion: Market Size and Business Strategy at the Base of the Pyramid*, Washington, DC: World Resource Institute, International Finance Corporation.

Harney, N. (2006), 'Rumour, migrants, and the informal economies of Naples, Italy', *International Journal of Sociology and Social Policy*, Vol. 26, No. 9/10, pp. 374–384.

HMRC (Her Majesty's Revenue and Customs) (2005), *The Informal Economy: Developing a Methodology*, London: Her Majesty's Revenue and Customs.

Howe, L. (1988), 'Unemployment, doing the double and local labour markets in Belfast', in C. Cartin and T. Wilson (eds), *Ireland from Below: Social Change and Local Communities in Modern Ireland*, Dublin: Gill & Macmillan.

Humphreys, J. (2004), 'The multicultural economy 2004: America's minority buying power', *Georgia Business and Economic Conditions*, Vol. 64, No. 3. Athens, GA: Selig Center for Economic Growth, University of Georgia.

ILO (International Labour Office) (2002), *Decent Work and the Informal Economy*, Geneva: International Labour Office.

Jones, T., Ram, M. and Edwards, P. (2006), 'Shades of grey in the informal economy', *International Journal of Sociology and Social Policy*, Vol. 26, No. 9/10, pp. 357–373.

Jones, T., Ram, M. and Edwards, P. (2004), 'Illegal immigrants and the informal economy: worker and employer experiences in the Asian underground economy', *International Journal of Economic Development*, Vol. 6, pp. 92–106.

Lemieux, T., Fortin, B. and Frechette, P. (1994), 'The effect of taxes on labor supply in the underground economy', *American Economic Review*, Vol. 84, pp. 231–254

Leonard, M. (1994), *Informal Economic Activity in Belfast*, Aldershot: Avebury.

McCrohan, K., Smith, J.D. and Adams, T.K. (1991), 'Consumer purchases in informal markets: estimates for the 1980s, prospects for the 1990s', *Journal of Retailing*, Vol. 67, No. 1, pp. 22–50.

MacDonald, R. (1994), 'Fiddly jobs, undeclared working and the something for nothing society', *Work, Employment and Society*, Vol. 8, pp. 507–530.

McGregor, S. (2005), 'Consumer transactions with SMEs: implications for consumer scholars', *International Journal of Consumer Studies*, Vol. 29, No. 1, pp. 2–16.

Nkamnebe, A.D. (2006), 'Globalised marketing and the question of development in the Sub-Saharan Africa (SSA)', *Critical Perspectives on International Business*, Vol. 2, No. 4, pp. 321–338.

Novoseletsky, E. (2000), 'The program to bring activities out of the shadow economy is on the agenda', in J.M. Szyrmer and D. Snelbecker (eds), *Reforms for Ukraine: Ideas and Actions*, pp. 32–59, Kiev: Centre for Social and Economic Research.

ONS (Office of National Statistics) (2005), *Data Sources on the Informal Economy and Entrepreneurship*, Office of National Statistics, London.

OECD (Organisation for Economic Co-operation and Development) (2002), *Measuring the Non-Observed Economy, Organisation for Economic Co-operation and Development*, Paris: OECD.

Pahl, R.E. (1984), *Divisions of Labour*, Oxford: Blackwell.

Pedersen, S. (2003), *The Shadow Economy in Germany, Great Britain and Scandinavia: A Measurement Based on Questionnaire Surveys*, Copenhagen: Rockwool Foundation Research Unit.

Portes, A. (1994), 'The informal economy and its paradoxes', in N.J. Smelser, and R. Swedberg (eds), *The Handbook of Economic Sociology*, Princeton, NJ: Princeton University Press.

Prahalad, C.K. (2004), *The Fortune at the Bottom of the Pyramid: Eradicating Poverty through Profits*, Upper Saddle River, NJ: Wharton School Publishing.

Prahalad, C.K. and Hammond, A. (2002), 'Serving the world's poor profitably', *Harvard Business Review*, Vol. 80, No. 9, pp. 48–57.

Prahalad, C.K. and Hart, S.L. (2002), 'The fortune at the bottom of the pyramid', *Strategy and Business*, Vol. 26, pp. 54–67.

Ram, M., Edwards, P., Gilman, M. and Arrowsmith, J. (2001), 'The dynamics of informality: employment relations in small firms and the effects of regulatory change', *Work, Employment and Society*, Vol. 15, No. 4, pp. 845–861.

Ram, M., Edwards, P. and Jones, T. (2002a), 'Employers and illegal migrant workers in the clothing and restaurant sectors', London: DTI Central Unit Research.

Ram, M., Jones, T., Abbas, T. and Sanghera, B. (2002b), 'Ethnic minority enterprise in its urban context: South Asian restaurants in Birmingham', *International Journal of Urban and Regional Research*, Vol. 26, No. 1, pp. 24–40.

Ram, M., Gilman, M., Arrowsmith, J. and Edwards, P. (2003), 'Once more into the sunset? Asian clothing firms after the National Minimum Wage', *Environment and Planning C: Government and Policy*, Vol. 71, No. 3, pp. 238–261.

Renooy, P., Ivarsson, S., van der Wusten-Gritsai, O. and Meijer, R. (2004), *Undeclared Work in an Enlarged Union: An Analysis of Shadow Work – An In-Depth Study of Specific Items*, Brussels: European Commission.

Schneider, F. (2002), 'Size and measurement of the informal economy in 110 countries around the world', paper presented at a Workshop of Australian National Tax Centre, ANU, Canberra, Australia, 17 July.

SBC (Small Business Council) (2005), *Government Response to the SBC Report on the Informal Economy*, London: Small Business Council.

SBC (2004), *Small Business in the Informal Economy: Making the Transition to the Formal Economy*, London: Small Business Council.

Small Business Service (2005a), 'Government Response to the Small Business Council Report on the Informal Economy', Department of Trade and Industry, London.

Small Business Service (2005b), 'Statistical press release URN05/92', Small Business Service, Sheffield.

Small Business Service (2006), *2004/05 Annual Small Business Survey*, Sheffield: Small Business Service.

Thomas, J.J. (1992), *Informal Economic Activity*, Hemel Hempstead: Harvester Wheatsheaf.

Tripp, A. (2001), 'Non-formal institutions, informal economies, and the politics of inclusion' (Discussion Paper No. 2001/108), Washington, DC: The World Bank.

Walker, A. (2010), 'Tenacity and risk – the Lebanese in West Africa', BBC News, 25 January. Online at: http://news.bbc.co.uk/2/hi/8479134.stm (accessed 9 April 2010).

Walle, G. (2008), 'A matrix approach to informal markets: towards a dynamic conceptualisation', *International Journal of Social Economics*, Vol. 35, No. 9, pp. 651–665.

Warde, A. (1990), 'Household work strategies and forms of labour: conceptual and empirical issues', *Work, Employment and Society*, Vol. 4. No. 4, pp. 495–515.

Williams, C.C. (2007), 'Tackling undeclared work in Europe: Lessons from a study of Ukraine', *European Journal of Industrial Relations*, Vol. 13, No. 2, pp. 219–236.

Williams, C.C. (2006), *The Hidden Enterprise Culture: Entrepreneurship in the Underground Economy*, Cheltenham: Edward Elgar.

Williams, C.C. (2005a), 'The undeclared sector, self-employment and public policy', *International Journal of Entrepreneurial Behaviour and Research*, Vol. 11, No. 4, pp. 244–257.

Williams, C. (2005b), 'Tackling the informal economy: towards a co-ordinated public policy approach', *Public Policy and Administration*, Vol. 20. pp. 38–53.

Williams, C. (2004), *Literature Review: Small Businesses in the Informal Economy: Making the Transition*, Preliminary Draft Report for Small Business Service and Small Business Council.

Williams, C.C. and Round, J. (2009), 'Evaluating informal entrepreneurs' motives: evidence from Moscow', *International Entrepreneurial Behaviour and Research*, Vol. 15, No. 1, pp. 1355–2554.

Williams, C.C. and Windebank, J. (2001), 'Reconceptualising paid informal exchange: some lessons from English cities', *Environment and Planning A*, Vol. 33, No. 1, pp. 121–140.

Williams, C.C and Windebank, J. (1998), *Informal Employment in the Advanced Economies: Implications for Work and Welfare*, London: Routledge.

Chapter 27

Organizational environment and SME marketing practices in an emerging economy

Robert Hinson and Kofi Dadzie

LEARNING OBJECTIVES

After reading this chapter, you will be able to:
- appreciate the influence of the organizational environment on marketing practice
- understand transaction marketing from a developing country SME context
- understand database marketing from a developing country SME context
- understand interaction marketing from a developing country SME context
- understand network marketing from a developing country SME context.

INTRODUCTION

Wilson and Stokes (2004) citing Coviello *et al.* (1997) argue that SME marketing practice can be distinguished into four types:

- transaction
- database
- interaction
- network Marketing.

Stokes (2000) then goes on to argue that interaction and network marketing in particular rely on informality and marketing communications, thereby providing a direct bridge to the entrepreneurship literature. In this chapter we showcase all four of the aforementioned types of marketing and examine their practice among small firms in the developing economy context of Ghana, West Africa.

Research has shown that differences in the marketing environment between developing economies – especially African countries – and that industrialized countries like the US and western Europe have significant impact on the nature of managerial marketing practices (Dadzie *et al.*, 1988; Dadzie, 1989; Kaynak, 1982; Samli and Kaynak, 1984). However, because much of this research has focused on various aspects of traditional transactional marketing practices, especially market orientation, little is understood about how environmental conditions impact other aspects of contemporary marketing practices (CMP) – especially relationship marketing – in emerging markets. Moreover, recent research has challenged the accepted normative view that CMP is primarily relationship marketing (e.g. Berry, 1995; Gronroos, 1991; Webster, 1992), suggesting that under some market conditions firms emphasize transactional marketing with different aspects of relationship marketing activities. Consequently, it is unclear how environmental conditions impact variations in CMP in emerging market conditions. This issue is critical because some aspects of relationship marketing may be unnecessary for some markets (Day, 2000). We seek to contribute to a clarification of this issue by investigating the nature of managerial marketing practice in the emerging market economy of Ghana.

The purpose of this chapter is to examine the relevance of both the Miles and Snow strategic typology and the CMP framework as useful tools for understanding the nature of managerial marketing practices under typical environmental conditions in Ghana. The environmental management literature contains several frameworks for diagnosing the impact of environmental conditions on organizational actions such as the CMP. One of the most widely used of such frameworks is the Miles and Snow strategic typology (1978). However, the robustness of the Miles and Snow strategic typology for crafting contemporary marketing strategy is yet to be verified, much less in an emerging market context (i.e. in Ghana), which is what we seek to examine. We will investigate the extent to which firms with different organizational strategies differ in their CMP in Ghana. The chapter begins with a review of the typology and its relevance for crafting CMP in general. Next, we present the study methods and analysis. The chapter concludes with a discussion of our findings.

THE MILES AND SNOW STRATEGIC TYPOLOGY: AN OVERVIEW

Miles and Snow's strategic typology is a useful theoretical framework for categorizing as well as understanding the processes undertaken in adopting organizational strategies (McDaniel and Kolari, 1987, p. 19). In their typology of organization strategies, firms can be said to exhibit one of these behavioural patterns: defenders, prospectors, analysers or reactors. According to McDaniel and Kolari (1987, p. 20), Miles and Snow describe the first behavioural type – defenders – as those who have narrow product and market domains and tend not to search outside their domains for new opportunities. On the other hand, prospectors continually search for marketing opportunities and tend to be creators of change in the industry. Analysers are a blend of defenders and prospectors and, as such, operate in relatively stable and unchanging product and marketing domains. Finally, reactors are said to lack a consistent strategy and simply respond to environmental pressures when forced to do so.

Similar to Miles and Snow's four strategic behavioural patterns, Thomas and Ramaswamy (1996) delineate a set of three variable strategic behaviour types (developed from Miles and Snow's typology) in explaining their tripartite alignment theory. Adopting this framework, they highlight prospectors as managers or organizations that emphasize innovation as the cornerstone of competitive advantage.

In contrast, defenders stress cost efficiency as the basis of competition. Accordingly, they focus on creating narrow stable domains through a limited mix of product and customers and aggressive efforts to protect the domain from competitors (Miles and Snow, 1978, p. 39). Analysers, on the other hand, pursue hybrid strategies that exhibit some features of the prospector and defender types. In rapidly evolving domains, they operate like prospectors, while in stable segments they adopt a defender approach (Miles and Snow, 1978). In keeping with this posture, they adopt dual core technologies that have both stable and flexible components (Thomas and Ramaswamy, 1996).

Adapting Miles and Snow's typology even further, Panell and Wright (1993) have also explored the use of the typology in the context of a dynamic, growing and highly volatile service industry. This contrasts with most previous research which has considered the strategy-performance relationship in relatively low degrees of dynamism and volatility.

Mckee *et al.* (1983) have additionally adopted the Miles and Snow typology, with a focus on strategic adaptability and firm performance. The Miles and Snow typology is, therefore, stretched to the extent to which firms in the (reactor-defender-analyser-prospector) categories develop adaptive capability to respond to the market (Mckee *et al.* 1983).

According to Miles and Snow (1978), the reactor is assumed to lack adaptive capability because, in the absence of a strategic orientation, it fails to develop the mechanisms needed to sense and respond to changes in the market. This could be as a result of a lack of clearly articulated strategies, or a poor link between strategy and the organization's structure and processes, or maintaining the organizational status quo despite environmental changes. The defender deliberately reduces adaptive capability by selecting a stable and narrowly defined market domain. In such a deliberate act, it is unlikely to notice market change or to be unable to adapt to change if it is noticed (Miles and Snow, 1978). The analyser maintains a stable domain, wherein it can operate with relative efficiency, but also attempts to identify emerging opportunities. Since it is not first to enter the new product market, it has the advantage of observing and learning from the new product problems of other firms and as such is able to achieve an above-average new product success rate (Miles and Snow, 1978). The prospector focuses on identifying and capitalizing on emerging market opportunities and, thus, places its primary emphasis on researching and communicating with the market and consequently bearing the associated inherent costs.

In brief, the Miles and Snow (1978) strategic typology captures the business-level strategic trade-off between external and internal orientation and its resulting strategy formulation (McDaniel and Kolari, 1987). The typology has been extended to capture the tripartite alignment between managerial characteristics and strategic orientation and its resulting per-formance implications (Thomas and Ramaswamy, 1996). Finally, Mckee *et al.* (1983) extend the typology even further to test the proposition that the effectiveness of a particular strategic orientation is contingent upon the dynamics of the market. In this study, we extend the Miles and Snow strategic typology to a developing transitional economy to try to understand the nature of CMP in selected industrial sectors.

GHANA AS AN EMERGING MARKET ECONOMY AND THE INCIDENCE OF ORGANIZATIONAL STRATEGY

Ghana is a typical emerging African economy with macro-economic conditions similar to other emerging African economies such as Nigeria, Bostwana and the Ivory Coast (see Table 27.1). Ghana has a population of over 23 million and an economy supported by the export of cocoa and natural mineral resources. The country has, since the mid 1980s, under-taken programmes and policies geared at harnessing the full potential of its economy. This has resulted in growth in the economy at a rate of 6.3 per cent per annum in recent years. Although market conditions in emerging sub-Saharan economies are different, with some countries seemingly doing better in certain areas, Ghana has been selected as a basis for this study due to the relative stability in its political and economic environment. Ghana's economy since 2000 has experienced growth rates averaging 5.5 per cent per annum, compared with less than 5 per cent for the half-decade before (ISSER, 2008). A recent World Bank survey of the nature of business sectors indicates that Ghana has moved into the top 100 countries in rankings with respect to ease in doing business (World Bank, 2007). It also takes, relatively, a shorter time (42 days) to start a business in Ghana (World Development Indicators, 2008). The business environment has also enjoyed tremendous support from the government of Ghana.

This pattern of high growth rate suggests Ghanaian managers will have less incentive to practise core relationship marketing activities and, perhaps, emphasize traditional transactional marketing activities. However, like most emerging African economies, the Ghanaian business environment has been characterized by persistent uncertainty. For example, rising energy costs throughout the last two years have had adverse effects on most sectors of the economy. Historically, such shortages have led to the persistence of a sellers' marketing environment and an emphasis on de-marketing (Dadzie, 1989). This variety of environmental conditions suggests managers in Ghana are likely to pursue different organizational strategies in part because of environmental differences and in part because of internal organization differences (size, mission, capabilities, etc.). Hence, we propose that Ghanaian managers' perception of the prevailing business environment will influence their perception of how their organizations interact with their environment, as proposed under the Miles and Snow strategic typology.

Table 27.1 Micro-economic indicators of business environment

Indicator (2007)	Ghana	Nigeria	Ivory Coast	Botswana
Population (in millions)	23.46	147.98	19.27	1.88
Gross domestic product (in US$ billions)	15.25	165.69	19.57	11.78
GDP growth (annual %)	6.3	6.3	1.8	3.8
GNI per capita Atlas method (US$)	590	930	910	5,840
Industry (%)	25	39	26	55
Services (%)	38	28	51	43
Agriculture (%)	36	33	23	2
Time required to start a business (days)	42	34	40	108
Market capitalization of listed companies (% of GDP)	15.6	52.1	42.7	50.0
Number of internet users (per 100)	2.8	6.8	–	4.3

Source: World Development Indicators database, September 2008.

Based on the above profile of the Ghanaian economy, we predict that managers will emphasize modern transactional marketing over the more costly relationship marketing until the economic conditions in Ghana make it profitable to engage in relationship marketing practices alone. We therefore hypothesize as follows:

Hypothesis 1: Organizations in Ghana differ in their strategy orientation as a function of environmental conditions.

THE INFLUENCE OF ORGANIZATIONAL STRATEGY ON CMP

Implicit in the preceding discussion is the assumption that different organizations emphasize different aspects of CMP as a rational response to the nature of their environmental conditions. We propose that these differences are less pronounced for transactional marketing and more pronounced for core relationship marketing practices, especially interaction marketing and network marketing for reasons related to the environmental conditions in Ghana.

Transactional marketing (TM) emphasis

TM is broadly defined as managing the traditional marketing mix elements (product, price, promotion and place) to attract and satisfy current and potential customers. Miles and Snow (1978) examine the link between organizational strategy and individual elements of the marketing mix. They propose that organizational types emphasize different aspects of various marketing mix activities because of the different perception of environmental demands. In the product domain, for example, Miles and Snow argue that '[p]roduct development in a defender is usually a simple extension into clearly related areas' (1978, p. 37), while for a prospector, 'maintaining a reputation as an innovator in product and market development may be as important, perhaps, even more important, than high profitability' (p. 56). Analysers are like prospectors in that they pursue 'the well-conceived addition of new products development' (p. 77) and at the same time pursue 'steady growth through market penetration and product development' (p. 79). With respect to pricing practices, the authors suggest that all organizational types share similar emphasis on pricing for different reasons. Differentiated pricing strategies do not seem to be the preoccupation of any of the organizational types. Defender firms can focus on reducing manufacturing and distribution costs and remain competitive on a price or product quality basis because of their emphasis on a stable environment. Similarly, by the prospector focusing on 'finding and exploiting new product and marketing opportunities' (p. 55), we could infer that price may not always be as important as compared with other marketing mix elements. These views, overall, suggest that all strategy types share more similarities than differences in TM practices. Accordingly, we hypothesize that:

> Hypothesis 2: When Ghanaian managers evaluate their organization as a prospector, analyser or defender they place a similar emphasis on transactional marketing practices.

Database marketing (DM) emphasis

DM refers to marketing practices with a transactional focus through information technology to enhance one-to-one exchanges (Peppers and Rogers, 1995). Miles and Snow (1978) argue that a defender seeks to minimize manufacturing and distribution costs in order to be competitive. Accordingly, we propose that defenders practise DM as a critical cost reduction and competitive weapon. DM practice will also be critical for prospector firms as it facilitates 'finding and exploiting new product and market opportunities' (Miles and Snow, 1978, p. 55), as it will for analysers who can be characterized as 'avid followers of change' (p. 71). Based on this argument, we hypothesize that:

> Hypothesis 3: When Ghanaian managers evaluate their organization as a defender, prospector or analyser they practise DM with a similar degree of emphasis.

Interaction marketing (IM) emphasis

IM involves managing face-to-face relationships (Berry, 1983) and complex interpersonal interactions (Dwyer *et al.*, 1987). Miles and Snow propose that in a defender firm, marketing 'normally does not include activities such as research and promotion' and 'ranks well below the controller and production manager in terms of influences' (Miles and Snow, 1978, p. 42). We deduce from this argument that defenders practise little IM because they will not invest in the training of sales force necessary to interact with customers. Prospectors, on the other hand, can be expected to practise face-to-face interaction with customers because a prospector tends to be keen on 'finding and exploiting new product and market opportunities' (p. 55). Analysers, similarly, will practise IM because they tend to imitate prospectors' successful marketing practices (Snow and Hrebiniak, 1980). Hence, we hypothesize that:

> Hypothesis 4: When Ghanaian managers evaluate their organization as being a prospector or analyser they practise IM with greater emphasis than when they view their organization as a defender.

Network marketing (NM) emphasis

NM involves the development of inter-firm relationships through coordination of activities among multiple parties in the entire value chain (Anderson *et al.*, 1994; Coviello *et al.*, 2002). Compared with other relationship marketing practices, it requires the largest amount of investment resources justifiable in an extreme competitive environment. Deducing from Miles and Snow's proposition that defenders tend to follow a niche strategy in a relatively stable environment and with a narrow product line, we propose that defenders will find it, relatively, easier to coordinate activities among their multiple parties and provide higher value in the value chain than will prospectors, who tend to have a broad product market domain. Since analysers tend to imitate successful practices of prospectors, they will place minimum emphasis on NM. Accordingly, we hypothesize that:

> Hypothesis 5: When Ghanaian managers evaluate their organization as a defender they place greater emphasis on NM practice than when they view their organization as a prospector or analyser.

DATA COLLECTION AND SAMPLE

The data used in this study was collected by and based on standard questionnaire and data collection procedures used in previous CMP research in advanced economies (Coviello *et al.*, 2002), Russia (Wagner, 2005) and Argentina (Pels *et al.*, 2004). This approach involved the use of executive and working MBA students of a local university. Although this data collection approach used a convenient sampling design, it has been found to be an effective way to collect data about company practices (Neelankavil *et al.*, 2000). To minimize potential bias from the use of a single-informant approach, we engaged students currently working with a company. In a few cases, students were assigned to companies they had previously worked for. In addition, informants were instructed to talk to other managers in their companies before completing the questionnaire. The data for this study was collected in 2008. These steps helped to reduce single-source bias.

The 2000 survey consisted of 180 managers in Ghanaian-based firms located in Accra, and the 2008 survey consisted of 120 Ghanaian managers also based in Accra. The typical manager was aged between 27 and 50 years (70 per cent) and had spent over three years with their current employer. A little over 25 per cent of the respondents' firms were consumer firms, 35 per cent were business firms and the remaining 40 per cent were both consumer and business firms. The breakdown of the firms by type of market offer was 45 per cent goods firms, 25 per cent service firms and the remaining 30 per cent were hybrid goods and service firms. The typical managers held positions of marketing/sales manager (35 per cent), administrative manager (20 per cent), customer manager (20 per cent) or other positions, including logistics and planning (15 per cent).

MEASUREMENT AND VALIDATION OF STUDY CONSTRUCTS

CMP

Following (Brodie *et al.*, 2007), we measured CMP as a formative construct, using the 36 indexes created from the classification scheme outlined in Coviello *et al.* (2002). Since e-marketing is more of a marketing tool than a marketing practice, we did not include it in this study. Thus, 36 individual indexes were derived by dividing the means of each of the nine dimensions of the four CMP constructs by 5 (a five-point scale). The indexes ranged from 0.0 to 1.0, with high indexes indicating stronger agreement with each of the four CMP constructs (TM, DM, IM and NM). Given that the constructs were originally developed in the US and other Western industrialized nations, we took steps to validate them in Ghana before administering them in the study. These steps included conventional procedures for validating formative constructs (Diamantopoulos and Siguaw, 2006; Diamantopoulos and Winklhofer, 2001; Jarvis *et al.*, 2003).

A convenient sample of working MBA students from a local university examined the questionnaire for (1) content specification and (2) indicator specification. Content specification requires that the measures capture 'the scope of the latent construct or the domain of content that the index is intended to capture' (Diamantopoulos and Winklhofer, 2001, p. 271). Indicator specifications, on the other hand, require that the measures be comprehensive enough to represent the scope of marketing. In both cases, our local collaborating faculty and MBA students were satisfied that the questionnaire represented the scope of the construct domain and the measures were comprehensive enough to capture CMP in Ghana. We verified indicator collinearity by examining the variance-inflation factors and all our regression results yielded variance-inflation factors that were well below the 10.0 benchmark (Hair *et al.*, 2006).

Respondents were given Miles and Snow's three strategic orientation types (prospector, analyser and defender) and asked to identify which type most described their firm's organization. To verify convergent validity of the strategy types, respondents were further asked to rate their firms on three specific strategies (low-cost provider, differentiation and niche strategies). An examination of the construct means across the three strategic types revealed significant differences on differentiation strategies consistent with the orientation of the three strategy types towards their environment.

Common method bias

As in any study involving a single respondent, for both the dependent measures (TM, DM, IM and NM) and predictor measures (strategic type and control variables) potential common method bias could be a problem. Accordingly, we took steps to minimize such bias in several ways. First, to ensure that respondents were knowledgeable about the subject and therefore minimize single-source bias (Mitchell, 1994), we restricted the study to respondents who worked in their respective organizations and also asked them to research their firm's marketing practices before answering the questionnaire. Second, we placed the predictor variable (strategy type) and criterion variable (CMP) at different parts of the questionnaire and assured participants of anonymity in order to minimize potential for context effects (Lindell and Whitney, 2001) and method bias.

An examination of all the inter-correlations among pairs of constructs revealed none to be over 0.70, thus suggesting that the constructs had less than half of their variance in common (MacKenzie *et al.*, 2005). Also, a factor analysis on the study variables indicated that the first factor accounted for less than 30 per cent of the common variance. Overall, the results of these tests suggested that common method bias was not a serious problem.

DATA ANALYSIS APPROACH

Examination of the study hypotheses involved three major types of analyses. The first type of analysis relates to testing the relevance of the major assumption underlying the Miles and Snow (1978) strategic typology for the Ghanaian context. This step entailed partitioning the data into environmental strategy clusters to determine the fit between strategic orientation and the business environment in Ghana. The results of the cluster analysis are summarized in Table 27.2. The second type of analysis relates to variation in CMP across the three Miles and Snow strategic types, using MANOVA/ANOVA. This type of analysis enabled us to control for the effects of market served and market offer. The results for both the univariate and multivariate analyses are presented in Table 27.3. In the third type of analysis, we examined the pluralistic hypothesis in detail by comparing how firms combine various aspects of CMP under (1) different strategic orientation (or organization strategy-level of analysis), and (2) without considering organizational strategy (or firm-level analysis). Both types of data were partitioned into two types of CMP clusters, using the 2008 data and the 2003 data. The results of all three types of cluster analysis are presented in Tables 27.4–27.6.

FINDINGS

Environmental fit of the Miles and Snow strategic orientations in Ghana

For managers and scholars interested in understanding the impact of emerging market environment on CMP, a critical first issue is whether or not organization strategy fits with demands of the Ghanaian business environment overall. The distribution of the data across organizational strategy type in Table 27.2 provides answers to this question. Looking at the results we see that the analysis yielded three clusters of environmental-strategy orientations, which correspond fairly well but not perfectly with the three types of strategy orientation proposed by Miles and Snow. The first cluster (35 per cent of the sample) corresponds to managers who were unsure about their firm's strategy orientation and did not select one of the three Miles and Snow strategy types (prospector, analyser and defender). However, an examination of the environmental profile of this first cluster indicates that the managers characterized their environment as being the lowest on market dynamism (M = .70), technological dynamism (M = 1.07), and government control (M = .70). Thus, this cluster corresponds to firms operating in the most stable environment. Accordingly, we labelled it as the 'Defender/Unsure' strategy orientation type. Subsequent analysis of the strategy practices (not reported) confirms this conclusion.

The second cluster, comprising the largest proportion (46 per cent) of the sample, corresponds to analyser orientation because it has the highest proportion of managers who evaluated their organization orientation as being the analyser type (M = .90). This cluster also is characterized by the second-highest level of perceived market dynamism (M = 3.20) and technological dynamism (M = 3.06), and the highest level of perceived government control (M = 3.68) of business activities. The third cluster was identified as prospector orientation by virtue of its high proportion of managers who described their orientation as being a prospector type (M = 1.00), and operating under the most dynamic, free-market environment of high market dynamism (M = 3.92), high technological dynamism (M = 3.99) and minimal state control (M = 1.98).

An examination of the multivariate F-values suggested that the clusters means were significantly different for prospector [F = 9.17, p<.001] and defender [F = 4.75, p<.05] firms but not for analyser firms, suggesting that the Miles and Snow typology is most effective in identifying firms at the polar ends of the strategic orientation continuum (i.e. prospector and defender). We note that other scholars and, indeed, Miles and Snow (1978) themselves have argued that analyser firms are not too different from prospector firms, an argument that may partially be reflected in our results. Nevertheless, the results suggest that Ghanaian managers were more able to categorize their strategy orientation along extreme ends of the Miles and Snow framework (i.e. prospector and defender types). Thus, verification of the environmental profiles is necessary in order to confirm the relevance of the analyser orientation. Our results suggest that analyser firms are similar to prospector orientation in that the former operate in a moderately dynamic free-market and government-controlled environment, while prospector firms operate in a more dynamic free-market but moderately government-controlled environment in Ghana.

These results are, therefore, consistent with our first hypothesis, which posits that Ghanaian firms differ in their strategy orientation as a function of differences in their perceptions of environmental conditions.

VARIATION IN CMP ACROSS STRATEGY ORIENTATIONS

On the focal issue of how environment-strategy differences impact variation in CMP, the results of MANOVA/ANOVA in Table 27.3 provide significant insight. The table indicates that the MANOVA effects were significant for IM [F = 2.47, p<.05] and NM [F=2.40, p<.5], suggesting that there are overall differences in core relationship marketing practices, IM, and NM as a result of differences in strategic orientation of the firms in our sample. These differences, however, are not significant for DM and TM. Thus, H2 and H3, which posit TM and DM are practised with a similar level of emphasis across all strategy types, are supported.

Looking at the univariate results for the two significant MANOVA effects (IM and NM) we see that the construct mean for IM is higher for prospector firms (M = .77, p<.05) and analyser firms (M =.78, p<.05) than for defender firms (M = .64, p<.10). Thus, our hypothesis that prospector and analyser firms practice more relationship marketing (H4) is supported for IM practices. Similarly, the mean for NM is higher for prospector firms (M = .73, p<.01) and analyser firms (M = .68, p<.05) than for defender firms (M = .60, p<.10). Thus H5, which posits that prospector and analyser firms are more relationship-marketing oriented is also supported for NM. These findings, overall, support Miles and Snow's assertion that perceptual differences in the organization's environment account for systematic differences in managerial practices, including marketing (McDaniel and Kolari, 1987). The similarities between prospector and analyser are however restricted to core relationship marketing practices, especially interaction marketing – not transactional and data base marketing practices.

COMPARATIVE ANALYSIS OF CMP IN GHANAIAN ORGANIZATIONS: DOES ORGANIZATIONAL ORIENTATION MATTER?

Although the analysis so far suggests that firms practise more relationship marketing in response to dynamic strategy orientation (prospector or analyser), it is still uncertain how much such variations differ without considering the strategy context or firm-level analysis only. To address this third and last issue, we examine the results of several cluster analyses aimed at exploring how firms combine various aspects of CMP or the pluralistic hypotheses (Coveillo et al., 2002) in Tables 27.4–27.6.

The cluster analysis results for the strategy-orientation level of analysis in Table 27.4 suggest that under the strategy context there are no pluralistic marketing practices in Ghana, unlike in the US (Coviello et al., 2002) and Argentina (Pels et al., 2004). Rather, Ghanaian managers in prospector firms emphasize IM while those in analyser firms combine TM/IM. Defender firms practise predominantly low marketing. By contrast, the firm-level analysis (i.e. without considering organizational context) yielded three clusters with pluralistic marketing emphasis among the largest cluster (49 per cent) and IM emphasis among the second-largest cluster (51 per cent), while the smallest cluster (9 per cent) performs no marketing at any appreciable level (12 per cent). The low scores for the low marketing cluster suggest that the firm-level analysis may be less interpretable.

The second way in which the information from the strategy-orientation level analysis provides greater insight than the firm-level analysis relates to consistency with the MANOVA results. The information in the strategy-level analysis (Table 27.4) indicates that CMP among Ghanaian firms in our sample differ primarily with respect to core relationship marketing practices, namely IM and NM. This is consistent with the findings in the MANOVA results. In addition, Table 27.4 suggests that DM practice, and to some extent TM practice, do not vary across firms with different strategic orientation. This finding is also consistent with the findings of the MANOVA results. By contrast, the firm-level analysis indicates that CMP differ across all four aspects (TM, DM, IM and NM), implying a lack of confirmation of the MANOVA results.

The third way in which the information from the strategy-orientation level analysis provides greater insight than the results of the firm-level analysis relates to the link between pluralistic marketing practices and external environmental/market conditions. In the strategy-orientation level analysis, all CMP clusters are significantly different on the three external environmental conditions of market dynamism, technological dynamism and government control in the 2008 data. By contrast, in the firm-level analysis, none of the CMP clusters is significantly different on the type of market served (consumer versus business) and type of market offer (goods versus services) variables commonly used in firm-level analysis by previous CMP scholars (e.g. Coviello et al., 2002; Pels et al., 2004). Thus, it appears that in Ghanaian context, the link between CMP and environmental conditions is stronger when the external context is included than when only market conditions are included in the firm-level analysis only. Collectively, these findings suggest that variations in CMP in Ghana are better explained by the contingent effects of organizational strategies for interacting with the external environment than a firm-level analysis focusing on market conditions.

SUMMARY

Empirical implications

Given the debate in the academic literature about the relevance of various aspects of CMP, understanding the nature of actual practices is critical for scholars and managers interested in developing and improving marketing practices in emerging market economies such as Ghana. Moreover, in actual practice, firms are likely to develop marketing capabilities that are consistent with the demands of their business environment, a constraint that is reflected in their operating organization strategy. Thus, a critical question is the relevance of such marketing frameworks as Miles and Snow and the CMP framework which were developed in advanced market economies of US and other Western industrialized nations for the African context. Our empirical results affirm the relevance of both frameworks for Ghanaian managers in two ways. First, most mangers are able to identify the focus of their strategy orientation within the Miles and Snow typology. Even though some managers could not identify their organizational orientation on the three strategy types, environmental profiles provided by the managers were still very useful in further identifying their strategy orientation. Second, strategy orientation appears to explain variation in CMP in Ghana more intuitively than firm-level analysis based on market conditions alone.

Theoretical implications

From a theoretical perspective, our results provide insight into Coviello *et al.*'s (2002) conceptual framework and proposition that CMP are pluralistic. First, our results suggest that the organizational environmental contexts vary; so does their impact on the role of various aspects of CMP in the organization of the marketing function. However, such variations only apply to the more core relationship marketing activities such as IM and NM. This means that DM and TM still play a fundamental role in all firms while for firms in more dynamic environment, interaction marketing and network marketing are increasingly the norm.

Second, theoretically, the pluralistic hypothesis of CMP appears to hold at the firm-level of analysis only but not at the strategy-orientation level of analysis. This finding may be a reflection of the need to focus on actual versus academic research. Managerially, managers formulate marketing strategies by considering a host of other managerial issues including their mission, resources, environmental demands and market selection. Therefore, consideration of the strategy context is more relevant for actual managerial marketing practice, while a focus on firm- level analysis may be convenient for academic analysis. Hence, CMP scholars should integrate the strategy context into their research and dialogue if they are to bridge the gap between CMP theory and practice.

Managerial implications

Under the current macro-economic environment in Ghana and other emerging market economies, managers are under pressure to improve managerial marketing practices by developing CMP capabilities in the relationship marketing domain. At the same time, cost constraints warrant that such investments be timed strategically in areas of marketing capabilities that are most relevant to the changing competitive environment. Our study offers several guidelines as to how such a dilemma should be resolved. First, it suggests that managers can use the Miles and Snow strategic typology as a diagnostic tool to determine the unique needs of their environments and organizational strategies. Such applications can be accomplished by following the steps outlined in this study.

Another implication pertains to the relative roles of various marketing activities in a given organization. It appears that regardless of the environmental context, all firms need to integrate DM into traditional TM activities. This form of modernization can be less costly than the development of core relationship marketing activities such as NM. Moreover, full-scale pluralistic marketing practices common in the US and other Western industrialized market economies were not found in the Ghanaian study. This may be in recognition of the belief that not all relationship marketing activities may be necessary or affordable, especially in emerging market context.

Thus, managers can determine optimal combinations of various CMP to cut cost by more actively defining their CMP on the basis of how much change occurs in their business context within the limitations of their organizational strategy. For firms in highly dynamic emerging free-market environment and already pursuing a prospector organizational strategy, our study suggests an integration of TM with IM practices may be helpful. For firms facing similar environment conditions but slightly more stringent government-controlled environment and operating under analyser strategy an emphasis on TM and DM may be strategically useful.

Finally, for firms operating under a less dynamic and government-controlled environment and following the defender strategy, minimal investment in TM and DM seems to be the norm. However, such an approach is short-term and would have to be transitioned to some combination of relationship marketing and TM in the very near future. For these firms, the dominant approach used by analyser firms (TM/IM) may be desirable because it would be less costly than any large-scale investment in NM.

REVIEW QUESTIONS

1. How important is the organizational environment to entrepreneurs for planning marketing strategy?

2. Under what conditions should SMEs consider transactional marketing practices?

3. Under what conditions should SMEs consider database marketing practices?

4. Under what conditions should SMEs consider an interaction marketing strategy?

5. Under what conditions should SMEs consider a network marketing strategy?

6. When should SMEs consider a hybrid CMP approach?

Table 27.2 Environmental profiles of strategy orientations of Ghanaian firms

Cluster label	Defender/Unsure	Analyser	Prospector	F-value
Strategic type				
PROSP	.00	.0	.95	9.17[‡]
ANALYS	.00	1.00	.00	1.20
DEFEND	.17	.00	.00	4.75[†]
NORESP	1.00	.00	.00	2.00
Proportion (%)	35	46	32	9.95[§]

(continued)

Table 27.2 *Environmental profiles of strategy orientations of Ghanaian firms (continued)*

Cluster label	Defender/Unsure	Analyser	Prospector	F-value
Environmental characteristics				
MKTDYN	.70	3.20	3.92	
TECHDYN	1.07	3.06	3.99	54.00[§]
GOVTC	.70	3.68	1.98	80.9[§]

Notes: †   p<.05
     ‡   p<0.01
     §   p<0.001

PROSP = Prospector orientation, ANALYS = Analyser orientation, DEFEND = Defender orientation, MKTDYN = Market dynamism, TECHDYN = Technological dynamism, GOVTC = Government control.

Table 27.3 *Construct means across strategic types (2008 data)*

	Prospector	Analyser	Defender	Sample mean	F-value
Marketing practices†					
TM index	.71[†]	69b	.6bc	.66	1.74
DM index	.65a	.66a	.59b	.63	.88
IM index	.77a	.78a	.64b	.73	2.47*
NM index	.73a	.68b	.60c	.67	2.40*
Model summary (multivariate test)					
Wilks' criterion				3.90*	
Pillai's trace				2.90	
Hotelling-Lawley trace				2.95*	

Notes: †Measured on a 5-point scale with 1 = weakest and 5 = strongest. Index derived by dividing mean ratings by 5. Values with the same letters are not significantly different at p<.05 level.

*By international benchmarks (Coviello *et al.*, 2002) scores higher than .81 are considered to be higher than average; scores from .61 to .80 are moderate; and scores below .61 are low average index of CMP.

Table 27.4 *Clusters of CMP: strategy-orientation level of analysis (2008 data)*

Cluster label	Low (Defender) marketing	IM (Prospector)	TM/IM (Analyser)	F-value	P<
Marketing practices					
Transactional	.61	.72	.76	3.08	.056
Database	.59	.71	.68	1.76	.18
Interaction	.64	.82	.77	5.05	.008
Network	.60	.78	.73	3.60	.031
Prospector	.14	.70	.00	1.20	.120
Analyser	.00	.00	.90	15.65	.000
Defender	1.00	.00	.00	2.00	.200

Table 27.4 Clusters of CMP: strategy-orientation level of analysis (2008 data) (continued)

Cluster label	Low (Defender) marketing	IM (Prospector)	TM/IM (Analyser)	F-value	P<
Environmental profile					
Market dynamism	.94	2.63	4.10	47.46	.000
Techn. dynamism	1.39	3.76	4.20	92.78	.000
Govt. control	.49	3.21	2.90	85.72	.000
Proportion (%)	21	34	45		

Table 27.5 Clusters of CMP in Ghana: firm-level analysis (2008 data)

Cluster label	Extremely low marketing	Practise IM	Pluralistic	F-value	P<
Marketing practices					
Transactional	.23	.65	.81	14.08	.000
Database	.14	.60	.82	8.63	.000
Interaction	.24	.78	.87	11.19	.000
Network	21	.62	.85	18.29	.000
Environmental profile					
Market dynamism	1.62	3.52	3.82	66.48	.000
Techn. dynamism	1.75	3.42	3.84	61.67	.000
Govt. control	1.21	3.83	1.78	78.04	.000
Proportion (%)	09	39	52		

Table 27.6 Clusters of CMP in Ghana: firm-level analysis (2003 data)

Cluster label	Pluralistic marketing	Practise NM	Mod Pluralistic	F-value	P<
Marketing practices					
Transactional	.72	.72	.73	1.81	.000
Database	.82	.74	.74	6.05	.000
Interaction	.82	.75	.72	4.88	.000
Network	.86	.80	.73	9.55	.000
Environmental profile					
Market dynamism	3.56	2.88	2.38	43.12	.000
Techn. dynamism	3.38	2.67	2.78	17.90	.000
Consumer services	.08	.04	.02	.790	.463
Business services	.10	.05	.09	1.20	.120
Proportion (%)	51	10	39		

REFERENCES

Anderson, J. C., Hakansson, H. and Johnanson, J. (1994), 'Dyadic business relationships within a business network context', *Journal of Marketing*, Vol. 58, No. 4, pp. 1–15.

Berry, L. L. (1983), 'Relationship Marketing', in Berry, L. L., Shostack, G. L. and Upah, G. D. (eds), *Emerging Perspective of Service Marketing*, American Marketing Association: Chicago, IL.

Berry, L. L. (1995), 'Relationship marketing of service – growing interest, emerging perspective', *Journal of the Academy of Marketing Science*, Vol. 23, No. 4, pp. 236–245.

Brodie, R., Winklhofer, H., Coviello, N. and Johnston, W. (2007), 'Assessing e-marketing adoption: The role of IT and firm performance', *Journal of Interactive Marketing*, Vol. 21, No. 1, pp. 2–21.

Coviello, N. E., Brodie, R. J., Danaher, P. and Johnston, W. (2002), 'How firms relate to their market: an empirical examination of contemporary marketing practices', *Journal of Marketing*, Vol. 66, No. 3, pp. 33–46.

Coviello, N. E., Brodie, R. J. and Munro, H. J. (1997), 'Understanding contemporary marketing: development of a classification scheme', *Journal of Marketing Management*, Vol. 13, No. 6, pp. 501–522.

Dadzie, K. Q. (1989), 'De-marketing strategies in shortage market environments', *Journal of the Academy of Marketing Science*, Vol. 17, No. 2, pp. 157–65.

Dadzie, K. Q., Akaah, I. P. and Riordan, E. (1988), 'Incidence of market typologies and pattern of marketing activity performance in selected African countries', *Journal of Global Marketing*, Vol. 1, No. 3, pp. 87–107.

Day, G. (2000), 'Managing market relationships', *Journal of the Academy of Marketing Science*, Vol. 28, No.1, pp. 24–30.

Diamantopoulos, A. and Siguaw, J. (2006), 'Formative vs. reflective indicators in measure development: does the choice of indicators matter?', *British Journal of Management*, Vol. 17, No. 4, pp. 263–282.

Diamantopoulos, A. and Winklhofer, H. (2001), 'Index construction with formative indicators: an alternative to scale development', *Journal of Marketing Research*, Vol. 38, No. 2, pp. 269–277.

Dwyer, F. R., Schurr, P. J. and Oh, S. (1987), 'Developing buyer–seller relationships', *Journal of Marketing*, Vol. 51, No. 2, pp. 11–27.

Gronroos, C. (1991), 'The marketing strategy continuum: towards a marketing concept for the 1990s', *Management Decision*, Vol. 29, No. 1, pp. 7–13.

Hair, J., Black, B., Babin, B., Anderson, R. and Tatham, R. (2006), *Multivariate Data Analysis*, 6th edn, Prentice Hall: Upper Saddle River, NJ.

ISSER – Institute of Statistical, Social and Economic Research (2008), *The State of The Ghanaian Economy in 2007*, Institute of Statistical, Social and Economic Research, Ghana: University of Ghana.

Jarvis, C., MacKenzie, S. and Podsakoff, P. (2003), 'A critical review of construct indicators and measurement model misspecification in marketing and consumer research', *Journal of Consumer Research*, Vol. 30, No. 2, pp. 199–218.

Kaynak, E. (1982), *Marketing in the Third World*, Praeger: New York.

Lindell, M. K. and Whitney, D. J. (2001), 'Accounting for common method variance in cross-sectional research designs', *Journal of Applied Psychology*, Vol. 86, No. 1, pp. 114–121.

McDaniel, S. W. and Kolari (1987), 'Marketing strategy implications of the miles and snow strategic typology', *Journal of Marketing*, Vol. 51, No. 4, pp. 19–30.

MacKenzie, S., Podsakoff, P. and Jarvis, C. (2005), 'The problem of measurement model misspecification in behavioral and organizational research and some recommended solutions', *Journal of Applied Psychology*, Vol. 90, No. 4, pp. 710–730.

Mckee, D. O., Varadarajan, R. and Pride, W. (1983), 'Strategic adaptability and firm performance: a market-contingent perspective', *Journal of Marketing*, Vol. 53 (July), pp. 21–35.

Miles, R. and Snow, C. (1978), *Organizational Strategy, Structure, and Process*, McGraw-Hill: New York.

Mitchell, V. (1994), 'Using industrial key informants: some guidelines', *Journal of the Market Research Society*, Vol. 36, No. 2, pp. 139–144.

Neelankavil, J. P., Mathur, A. and Zhang, Y. (2000), 'Determinants of managerial performance: a cross cultural comparison of the perceptions of middle level managers in four countries', *Journal of International Business Studies*, Vol. 31, No. 1, pp. 121–140.

Panell, J. A. and Wright, P. (1993), 'Generic strategy and performance: an empirical test of the miles and snow typology', *British Journal of Management*, Vol. 4, pp. 29–36.

Pels, J., Brodie, R. J. and Johnston, W. J. (2004), 'Benchmarking business-to-business practices in emerging and developing economies: Argentina compared to USA and New Zealand', *Journal of*

Business and Industrial Marketing, Vol. 19, No. 6, pp. 386–396.

Peppers, D. and Rogers, M. (1995), 'A new marketing paradigm: share of customer, not market share', *Managing Service Quality*, Vol. 5, No. 3, pp. 48–51.

Samli, A. and Kaynak, E. (1984), 'Marketing practices in less developed countries', *Journal of Business Research*, Vol. 12, No. 1, pp. 5–18.

Snow, C. C. and Hrebiniak, L. (1980), 'Strategy, distinctive competence, and organizational performance', *Administrative Science Quarterly*, Vol. 25, No. 2, pp. 317–335.

Stokes, D. (2000), 'Marketing and the small firm', in Carter, S. and Jones-Evans, D. (eds), *Enterprise and Small Business*, Pearson Education: Harlow, UK.

Thomas, A. and Ramaswamy, K. (1996), 'Matching managers to strategy: further tests of the miles and snow typology', *British Journal of Management*, Vol. 7, pp. 247–261.

Wagner, R. (2005) 'Contemporary marketing practices in Russia', *European Journal of Marketing*, Vol. 39, No. 1/2, pp. 199–215.

Webster, F. E. (1992), 'The changing role of marketing in the corporation', *Journal of Marketing*, Vol. 56, No. 10, pp. 1–17.

Wilson C. and Stokes, D. (2004), 'Laments and serenades: relationship marketing and legitimation strategies for the cultural entrepreneur', *Qualitative Market Research: An International Journal*, Vol. 7, No. 3, pp. 218–227.

World Bank (2007), 'Doing business report 2007'. Available online at: http://web.worldbank.org/

World Development Indicators (2008) 'Key development data and statistics'. Available online at: http://data.worldbank.org/data-catalog/world-development-indicators. Accessed 9 March 2009.

Index

Note: page numbers in **bold** refer to figures and tables.